Food

IN THE

Food

IN THE

A READER

EDITED BY

CAROLE M. COUNIHAN

ROUTLEDGE
NEW YORK LONDON

Published in 2002 by
Routledge
29 West 35th Street
New York, NY 10001

Published in Great Britain by
Routledge
11 New Fetter Lane
London EC4P 4EE

Routledge is an imprint of the Taylor & Francis Group.
Copyright © 2002 by Routledge

Printed in the United States of America on acid-free paper.

10 9 8 7 6 5 4 3 2 1

Library of Congress Cataloging-in-Publication Data
Food in the USA : a reader / [edited] by Carole Counihan
      p. c.m.
   Includes bibliographical references and index.
   ISBN 0-415-93291-9 — ISBN 0-415-93232-7 (pbk.)
    1. Food habits—United States. 2. United States—Social life and customs. 3. United States—
Social conditions. 4. Food supply. I. Counihan, Carol, 1948–

GT2853.u5 F663 2002
394.1'2'0973—dc21
                                         2002017785

THIS BOOK IS DEDICATED TO MY PARENTS

LOUISE WATSON COUNIHAN (1917—1992)

AND

EDWARD AUGUSTINE COUNIHAN, III (1914—1979)

CONTENTS

★★★

PART IV ★ FOOD SIGNIFYING IDENTITIES

PART V ★ FOOD AND THE EMERGING WORLD

ACKNOWLEDGMENTS

★★

I feel lucky to be working in the field of food and culture studies because over the past two decades so much interesting work has appeared. In addition to those represented in this volume, several contemporary scholars have stimulated my thinking about food and culture, including Carol Adams, Arlene Avakian, Anne Becker, Amy Becker-Chambless, Susan Bordo, Anne Bower, Martin Bruegel, Kim Chernin, Darra Goldstein, Barbara Haber, Lynn Hunt, Sherrie Inness, Miriam Kahn, Steven Kaplan, Anna Meigs, Ellen Messer, Mimi Nichter, Jeffery Sobal, Penny Van Esterik, M. J. Weismantel, and Doris Witt. I was fortunate that there were so many wonderful articles to choose from, and I regret that I could not include several excellent articles because they exceeded my page limits.

I must give thanks to many people who have contributed to this work. First, I want to thank the three outside reviewers of the book proposal who offered encouragement and advice: Warren Belasco, Sidney Mintz, and especially Amy Bentley who made several suggestions that have vastly improved this volume. Naturally, I absolve reviewers of any remaining faults. I thank my editor at Routledge, Ilene Kalish, for her unflagging energy, intellect, and support, and the contributors to this volume for their cooperation and enthusiasm.

I thank my student assistant, Rebecca Gray, editorial manager of this project, without whose work it would never have reached completion, and the other Millersville University students who have worked for me over the years: Justin Garcia, Kimberly Graham, Karen Lindenberg, Nicole Keiper, Paula Miller, Becky Newman, Angela Reisinger, Angela Rhodes, Kris Trozzo, and Tricia Wolfe. I thank my many supportive colleagues at Millersville University, especially Marlene Arnold, Rosario Caminero, Sam Casselberry, Aida Ceara, Ruth Davis, Barb Dills, Bill Donner, Hank Fischer, Pat Gibble, Mary Glazier, Ximena Hearn, Kim Mahaffy, Rita Marinho, Carol Phillips, Carla Ritter, Norma Rivera-Hernandez, Scott Schaffer, Rika Schmitt, Beverly Skinner, Derek Shanahan, Nancy Smith, Rita Smith Wade-El, Barb Stengel, George Stine, Diane Umble, Tracey Weis, and Darla Williams. I thank my parents, Louise and Edward Counihan; my stalwart siblings, Susan, Ted, Chris, and Steve; and my stepdaughter, Marisela and her family. I thank my husband, anthropologist Jim Taggart, for his continual partnership in scholarship and in the raising of our sons, Ben and Willie Counihan Taggart. I thank Ben and Willie for their deep thoughts and twinkling eyes.

Lastly, out of gratitude to the Millersville University Women's Studies Program for years of intellectual and personal support, and the people of Antonito, Colorado for welcoming my family into their community, I am donating the royalties from this book to the Millersville University Women's Studies Endowment and the Adams State College Antonito Scholarship.

FOOD AND THE NATION  1

INTRODUCTION:

FOOD AND THE NATION

CAROLE M. COUNIHAN

1

★ OVERVIEW

The goal of this book is to bring together a representative selection of recent scholarly articles that highlight the contributions of food and culture studies to understanding the contemporary United States. It asks five main questions: (1) What is U.S. food and is there a national cuisine? (2) How have U.S. food and cuisine been made and at what cost? (3) How have people used eating, fasting, and commensality to cope with power, exploitation, connection, and identity? (4) How do foodways signify identity and keep cultural traditions and personal stories alive, even under conditions of oppression? (5) How is the spread of the capitalist, profit-making food economy around the globe affecting food quality and access, and what alternatives to corporate food production and distribution exist?

Articles in this book examine what U.S. food tells us about who we are. They give a picture of how foodways—beliefs and behaviors surrounding the production, distribution, and consumption of food—reveal race-ethnic, class, gender, and national identity and power. The articles are as multistranded as the ways food unfolds in our lives. Taken together they suggest that human well-being depends not only on having sufficient food but also on establishing meaningful and affirming relationships surrounding food.

But many people in the United States and the world do not have adequate food nor do they have positive commensal experiences. At least 800 million people eat less than 2000 calories a day and suffer chronic hunger and malnutrition (Conway 1999a:352). This is in violation of the United Nations International Covenant on Economic, Social, and Cultural Rights, which, however, has not been ratified by the United States (*Economist* 2001). In fact, "at the World Food Summit in November 1996, the United States issued a written declaration that the right to adequate food is 'a goal or aspiration' but not an international obligation of governments" (*Canada and the World Backgrounder* 1997). Hunger is a frightfully extensive problem with severe human consequences. Yet even when people have enough food, they still must struggle to control their foodways to ensure a healthy diet, to keep alive cultural traditions, and to affirm their self-worth—issues that the articles in this book approach from diverse disciplinary perspectives.

All articles included in this volume were originally published between 1988 and 2001 and they represent a cross section of the rich scholarship on food that has erupted over the past two decades. Hundreds of websites and several interdisciplinary food journals sprouted during this period, including *Food and Foodways*, *Journal of Gastronomy*, *Ecology of Food and Nutrition*, *Culture and Agriculture*, *Nutritional Anthropology*, *The Digest*, *The Association for the Study of Food and Society Journal*, *Gastronomica*, and *Slow*.[1] Foodways scholarship has burgeoned with major work appearing across many humanities and social sciences disciplines, including anthropology, folklore, geography, history, literary criticism, psychology, and sociology.[2] In selecting articles for this volume, I was animated by three main concerns. First, I wanted to give as rich a sense of the diversity of U.S. foodways and people as possible. Second, I wanted original scholarship demonstrating an array of disciplinary approaches and methodologies. Third, I wanted articles addressing pressing social concerns centered around food, identity, and power.

This book includes articles that deal directly with race-ethnic, class, gender, and national identity. African-Americans, Asian-Americans, European-Americans, Latinas/os, and Native Americans are represented. The literature on the melting pot is more abundant on European American than on other groups, for whom ethnographic and historical studies of foodways are sparse but increasing.[3] In the extant literature, it is clear that food has played a major part of cultural survival and affirmation; the demise of foodways often signifies cultural extinction.

Approximately two-thirds of the articles in this book are authored by cultural anthropologists and American studies scholars. Anthropologists have been influential pioneers in food and culture studies as well as significant contemporary contributors (Counihan 2001). American studies has included historical and literary analysis and been a fertile arena for ethnic studies foodways research. One-third of the articles come from a wide array of fields, including African-American studies, communications, community nutrition, ecology, folklore, history, literary criticism, sociology, and women's studies. Together, the articles show the broad reach of food as a research topic and analytical tool. Several are based on ethnographic fieldwork in diverse communities. Others conduct symbolic analyses of food in literature, cookbooks, television advertising, and corporation trade journals. Still others look at food in historical documents. Through disciplinary depth and breadth, this volume hopes to introduce readers to diverse perspectives, methods, and literatures in foodways research and to define the field of food and culture studies in the United States.

U.S. food and culture studies is the interdisciplinary field crossing the social sciences and the humanities that explores foodways, food work, and food meanings. It examines relationships and processes surrounding making, cooking, and eating food. This volume brings together articles from U.S. food and culture studies to address five main questions about food and U.S. national identity.

★ PART I: FOOD AND THE NATION

The first section, "Food and the Nation," addresses the question What is U.S. food? It asks whether we have a national cuisine and how regional, immigrant, ethnic, and corporate cuisines have contributed to it. John Hess and Karen Hess start the collection with the new introduction to the 2000 edition of their bold 1972 classic, *The Taste of America*, a witty invective on the decline of U.S. food quality and the rise of a cuisine based on the ubiquitous tastes of sugar and salt. In "The Taste of Y2K," the Hesses bring us up to date on the state of the nation's cuisine, noting good news and bad. They celebrate farmers' markets, organic produce, bakeries, and good coffee, but lament the excesses of microwave cooking, chemical processing, toxic pollution, genetic engineering, agribusiness, and economic inequality. They poke fun at the ways glamour and pretentiousness have replaced taste as the salient attributes of food. But in spite of the glum trends, they conclude, "Here and there, good people are feeding the hungry, defending nature, rediscovering real cooking. There is hope."

In "Eating American," a chapter from his book *Tasting Food, Tasting Freedom* (1997), Sidney Mintz argues that there is no American cuisine and asks, "Why...is having a cuisine important?...Could it be good not to have a cuisine? If you don't have one, can you get one?" Mintz describes how U.S. foodways sprung from Europeans' conquest of North America and how today they act as assimilation pressure on immigrants. Profit-making imperatives dominate the definition of cuisine, and fast and processed foods prevail in the national diet and culinary culture.

Donna Gabaccia draws out a different dimension of U.S. cuisine in the introduction to her book *We Are What We Eat: Ethnic Foods and the Making of Americans* (1998). She argues that ethnic food is truly American food because immigrants have continually contributed diverse traditions, tastes, and hybrids to the melting pot. She asserts U.S. cuisine is defined by the fact that immigration has been continuous and people "have eagerly sought new foods and new taste....As eaters, all Americans mingle the culinary traditions of many regions and cultures within ourselves. We are multi-ethnic eaters." Gabaccia, Mintz, and the Hesses all take a sweeping approach to U.S. foodways, and draw attention to important characteristics of U.S. cuisine that subsequent articles consider in detail: its profit-making imperative, its multiethnicity, and its nutritional and gustatory deficiencies.

The last two articles in part one approach the question of what is U.S. food by looking at two very different icons of our foodways: Thanksgiving and the "meal-in-a-pill." Janet Siskind asks what meanings about nation and family are reproduced in Thanksgiving, our most important commensal ritual. She claims that Thanksgiving is a widely practiced family-centered ritual, which expresses "being American" and reproduces cultural ideologies about white privilege while integrating diverse ethnic traditions into a national consensus.[4] Warren Belasco interrogates futuristic food technologies by analyzing the history and lore surrounding the "meal-in-a-pill," an enduring food symbol. The idea of a meal contained in a tiny pill expresses central middle-class Anglo-American values on mobility, efficiency, and science. But the meal-in-a-pill never materialized because, Belasco suggests, it was ultimately incompatible with the social, aesthetic, and political-economic contexts of food production and consumption in the United States.

★ PART II: MAKING U.S. FOOD

The second section, "Making U.S. Food," includes case studies about the processes and costs involved in the production of U.S. food and cuisine. Articles on Italian American, Native American, and African-American food consider how the U.S. diet has emerged through the amalgamation, hybridization, and erasure of diverse ethnic cuisines. Articles examine the decline of agriculture, the rise of industrial food, and the role of the military and corporations in creating food markets and gustatory desires.

Three articles address how and why so-called ethnic foods of some of the diverse groups peopling North America have survived, changed, or died. The case of Italian food in the United States is interesting because it readily became integrated into the national cuisine, in contrast to many other immigrant foodways. Harvey Levenstein argues that Italians clung to their foods in the New World because of their traditional centrality to family life and women's identity. Several political factors favored the integration of Italian cuisine such as Italy's alliance with the United States in World War I. The number of nutritious and inexpensive Italian dishes made without meat raised their popularity during the two World Wars and the Great Depression. The increasing integration of Italian Americans into "white" culture fostered the spread of their foodways.

African-American cuisine underwent a different development process due to the historical conditions of racism, segregation, and the northern migration of thousands of African-Americans. Tracey Poe examines the emergence of soul food out of "Black urban identity." When African-Americans migrated to Chicago and other northern cities in the first half of the twentieth century, they created an urban, black culture by cooking and eating their traditional southern foods, marketing them in restaurants and grocery stores, and practicing commensality.

Anthropologist Christiana E. Miewald examines a different dimension of ethnic foodways by looking at the impact of European colonization and capitalist agriculture on Native American foods and cultures. She finds loss of land and decline in subsistence farming, hunting, and gathering resulting in deterioration of diet and health, but also a continuing use of native foods and an awareness of their cultural and nutritional importance. Both Poe and Miewald suggest that foodways can be a form of resistance to erasure, a theme taken up further later in the book.

Mark Weiner's article provides a case study of food industry development by focusing on Coca-Cola. He examines how World War II became a vehicle for the global economic penetration of Coke and its emergence as the most popular fizzy, caffeine-laden bottle of water and sugar in the world (Pendergrast 1993). He shows how Coca-Cola became a symbol of U.S. national identity during World War II through close ties between the U.S. military and the Coca-Cola company, the messages in Coke's advertising, and the emotional ties overseas GIs felt with Coke as revealed through their letters.

Anthropologist Deborah Fink's "Farm Boys Don't Believe in Radicals" provides another case study on the food industry, focusing on the labor process in meat packing (Fink 1998). After conducting participant-observation and interviews in a meat-packing plant in Perry, Iowa, she describes the grueling work of slaughtering animals and packing meat, compounded by pressure to work 60-hour weeks due to low wages and threats of firing. Workers are physically and emotionally exhausted and never have enough time to care for self and family, much less any time to recreate or do union work.

While Fink's piece indicates the workings of class in the meat-packing industry from the point of view of the laborers, the late anthropologist William Roseberry looks at the opposite end of corporate food production through close analysis of two major trade magazines of the coffee growers' association. He shows their purposeful efforts to manipulate taste and shape purchasing decisions. Consumption patterns continually reenact class relations locally and globally, and class exploitation underlies much commodity consumption, especially of coffee. ˙

★ PART III: COMPLEXITIES OF CONSUMPTION

Articles in this section examine diverse aspects of consumption. They investigate how people have used eating, desiring food, self-denial of food, and commensality to cope with issues of power, exploitation, connection, and identity. The first article, by Amy Bentley, is part of her investigation of the social and symbolic aspects of food in wartime United States (see Bentley 1996, 1998). She begins with Norman Rockwell's famous 1943 image *Freedom from Want* and argues that this depiction of the widely celebrated Thanksgiving ritual was one of many wartime images that supported social order, abundance, and the status quo. But these images of familial tranquility and bounty contrasted with people's wartime experiences of family rupture, death, anxiety about the future, and rationing. While workers, women, and people of color made real advances during the war, images of white or black women serving meals to families reinforced race, class, and gender hierarchies. Bentley's article shows how the emotionally laden meal is a key terrain for the reproduction of cultural values.

The annual Jewish Seder, an important religious ritual centered around a meal, reflects in intense manner the role of all commensality in affirming social connections, defining cultural values, and remembering history. Sharon Sherman applies the perspective of folklore and the methods of ethnography and history to unveil the practices and meanings of the highly symbolic Jewish Seder. She uses her own memories of family Seders throughout the years as well as interviews with eight relatives to describe the ritual's evolving practice and ongoing affirmation of Jewish family, identity, and culture.

Historian Joan Jacobs Brumberg and psychologist Ruth Striegel-Moore look not at commensality but its negation, anorexia nervosa. In "Continuity and Change in Symptom Choice: Anorexia," they demonstrate the fruitfulness of cross-disciplinary collaboration in understanding culturally embedded psychopathologies. They examine changes in the constellation of symptoms associated with anorexia in the nineteenth and twentieth centuries with particular emphasis on the girls' language, family dynamics, attitudes toward food and body, and increase in hyperactive exercise and bulimia. They contribute to the vast literature on anorexia nervosa by linking historical depth to psychological interpretation.[5]

Sociologist Becky Thompson's article looks at a different kind of consumption problem, compulsive eating, through a qualitative study of heterosexual and lesbian African-American, Latina, and white women (see Thomson 1994). She argues that compulsive eating is a survival strategy to combat physical, emotional, and sexual abuse resulting from the scourges of racism, sexism, and homophobia. She contests claims that compulsive eaters are weak-willed and out of control; rather she argues that compulsive eating and obesity can protect women from abuse and provide solace, although they can also create problems associated with being fat in an obesophobic society.

Ecologist Gary Paul Nabhan's article explores why the O'odham Indians of the Sonora Desert have the highest diabetes rates in the world. Combining scientific and ethnographic approaches, he investigates traditional foods and their nutritional value. For thousands of years, the O'odham were adapted to a desert diet of acorns, mesquite pods, tepary, and lima beans, which had a slow and steady rate of sugar absorption and protected them from diabetes. After World War II, wage labor displaced the hunting-gathering-farming subsistence economy resulting in poverty, unemployment, and rising consumption of government commodities, canned food, and refined sugar. This has resulted in a radical increase in diabetes and obesity, which are growing national consumption concerns (Sobal and Maurer 1997, 1999).

Anthropologist Irene Glasser looks at another complexity of consumption by examining public commensality in a soup kitchen in a central Connecticut city, where she conducted ethnographic research in the mid-1980s. Glasser found that the soup kitchen's overriding ethos of commensality where all are welcome to eat and no questions or payments are asked provides a positive environment fostering dignity and empowerment for people in need. Soup kitchens are a refreshing alternative to the punitive and mean-spirited nature of much government assistance, although they and similar volunteer efforts alone are unlikely to solve the problems of U.S. or world hunger (Poppendieck 1998). The soup kitchen article and the others in this section address diverse ways in which eating, fasting, and commensality can express disorder, stability, and identity for individuals, families, and communities.

★ PART IV: FOOD SIGNIFYING IDENTITIES

Part four, "Signifying Identities," examines how narrating food stories, passing on recipes, remembering meals, doing kitchen work, and advertising food have served as explicit enactments of U.S. identities. All articles address gender and describe how people struggle to use food to claim positive identities against ideologies that oppress them.

Rafia Zafar addresses how remembering, writing about, and passing on recipes keep African-American cultural traditions and personal stories alive (see also Bower 1997). Writing cookbooks is problematic for black women because of all the ways cooking signifies "slavery, servitude, and oppression." But she argues that they can also be redemptive by examining two famous cookbooks, Verta Mae Smart-Grosvenor's (1992) *Vibration Cooking: Or the Travel Notes of a Geechee Girl* and Carole and Norma Jean Darden's (1978) *Spoonbread and Strawberry Wine: Recipes and Reminiscences of a Family*. Zafar demonstrates the power of cookbook analysis in determining cultural identity, and concludes that recipes along with contextual information help keep African-American history and culture alive.

In fiction and film, food can be a powerful multivocal symbol.[6] Eileen Chia-Ching Fung examines food, masculinity, and Chinese American identity in Frank Chin's novel *Donald Duk*, "a *Bildungsroman* of a Chinese American boy learning about his ethnicity through his father's participation in food preparation, festivity, and story-telling in San Francisco's Chinatown." Her analysis points to the many ways that food symbols in literature powerfully demonstrate ethnic, class, and gender dissension and solidarity.

Sociologist Josephine Beoku-Betts uses ethnographic interviews and observations to demonstrate how food keeps cultural traditions alive through daily practice among the Gullah people of the Georgia and South Carolina Sea Islands. Also known as the Geechee, these people are the subjects of Smart-Grosvenor's *Vibration Cooking*, Julie Dash's beautiful Afrocentric feminist film *Daughters of the Dust*, and her article "Rice Culture" (Dash 1997). Gullah women interviewed by Beoku-Betts describe how their foods connect them to the natural environment, affirm West African roots, and reproduce contemporary Gullah culture. Through cooking, exchanging recipes, and sharing food, women affirm African-derived values of motherhood, female relationships, family, and community.

Carole Counihan's ethnographic narrative of a Latina from southern Colorado explores how women can use food as voice to assert a counterhegemonic worldview. Feminist ethnography suggests that food-centered life history interviews can unlock the tongues of many muted women and provide them a way to describe the world in affirming ways. A middle-aged Latina from the San Luis Valley of Colorado named Bernadette told many food stories that displayed not only class, ethnic, and gender oppression but also solidarity enacted through commensality. While Counihan presents a Latina's way of using food as voice, James Taggart constructs a Latino man's food-centered narrative from the same community from interviews with his longtime collaborator José Inez (Joe) Taylor. The narrative uses Taylor's food stories to express his subjective experience of becoming and being a man.

The last essay in this section focuses on fast food.[7] Kate Kane's "Who Deserves a Break Today? Fast Food, Cultural Rituals, and Women's Place" looks at how McDonald's advertisements use meal images to signify and propagandize gender hierarchy. She does a Marxist feminist textual analysis of a McDonald's television commercial frame by frame to argue that it normalizes women serving men food and performs visual slight-of-hand by depicting as "fun!" the repetitive drudgery of fast-food labor. She argues that McDonald's tries to appropriate the powerful imagery of "Mother" and simultaneously fosters women's alienation from food.

★ PART V: FOOD AND THE EMERGING WORLD

Part five, "Food and the Emerging World," asks what our foods will be like in the future and how they will define the United States in the context of global culture and economy. How is the spread of the capitalist, profit-making food system on a worldwide basis affecting food quality and equitable access, and what alternatives to corporate food production and distribution exist? Harriet Friedmann's "The International Political Economy of Food: A Global Crisis" gives an overview of the United States within the world food system in the second half of the twentieth century.[8] This period was characterized in the West by national agricultural regulation, protectionist trade restrictions, the export of a U.S. agro-industrial food model, and chronic food surpluses, while Third World countries experienced increasing imports of basic foods and declining prices for export crops. Friedmann asks whether the future of agro-food politics will be dominated by the "accumulation imperatives" of transnational corporations or by "movements for livelihood and democracy."

In "China's Big Mac Attack," anthropologist James Watson uses a case study of McDonald's in Beijing and Hong Kong to address a related question, "Is globalism—and its cultural variant McDonaldization—the face of the future?" Certainly, McDonald's outlets (and myriad other U.S. fast-food restaurants) are proliferating globally, totaling 25,000 in 119 countries and serving billions of hamburgers and fries. McDonald's has become an international symbol of the United States and threatens to homogenize global cultures and cuisines. Watson, however, argues that McDonald's has to some extent become "localized." The corporation hires enterprising native workers as managers, provides locally relevant foods like spicy wings in Beijing, and fits into, rather than causes, cultural changes favoring eating out. Watson's perspective differs from that of Eric Schlosser (2001, 239) who accuses McDonald's of creating "an empire of fat" concomitant with its global expansion.

Anthropologist James McDonald explores food globalization by examining how NAFTA has affected farmers and food production in both the United States and Mexico. He argues that NAFTA has exacerbated Mexico's decline in basic food production and increase in export crop production, worsening human misery and social dislocation in Mexico. In the United States NAFTA has benefited large agribusiness dairy producers but contributed to the decline of small producers and rural farming communities in the midwestern United States. He concludes that when final Mexican tariff barriers for most agricultural products fall in 2003 as mandated by NAFTA, "Small-scale dairy farmers on both sides of the US–Mexico border will find little reason to rejoice."

Similarly, biotechnology development leaves little to rejoice. Gerard Middendorf et al.'s "New Agricultural Biotechnologies: The Struggle for Democratic Choice" examines the potential far-reaching consequences of agricultural biotechnologies on farming, the environment, and the global agrofood system. These biotechnologies permit the exchange of genetic material among all living organisms and transform them into commodities largely under the control of private, profit-making corporations. The authors argue for the democratizing of science and technology to allow public discussion of their human consequences, and they offer models of how this can be done.

In "Hunger in the United States: Policy Implications," Marion Nestle examines inequalities and inadequacies in food access in the United States and the history and current status of policies designed to remedy them. She demonstrates that the United States produces more than enough food to feed its population and that overproduction and waste are serious problems. Yet she also finds that hunger and malnutrition are severe and that minimum wage incomes, federal programs, and private charity have been insufficient to redress them. She argues that a comprehensive political program to raise the minimum wage, subsidize housing, and provide child care, job training, and universal health insurance is the best way to reduce poverty and hunger.

The book ends with Betty Wells et al.'s "Growing Food, Growing Community" about Community Supported Agriculture (CSA) in rural Iowa. CSA is an alternative to agribusiness and transnational corporate control of food. CSA benefits small farmers and citizen-consumers by providing local markets for fresh vegetables, fruit, meat, milk, eggs, and wool. It also becomes a "potential comprehensive strategy of local action" uniting people into more empowered communities and offering hope for the kind of democratic control of farming and food security that are essential to full human rights.

In addition to CSAs, there are other bright spots in the future of food: organic farming, sustainable agriculture, farmers' markets, food cooperatives, international fair trade organizations, and unionization of farm workers locally and globally.[9] One effective program is Participatory Rural Appraisal (PRA), which empowers knowledgeable local farmers in agricultural planning and leads to improved crop production and democratized distribution (Conway 1999a). Another encouraging sign is the Slow Food movement, which arose in Italy in 1986 "in direct response to the opening of a McDonald's restaurant in Rome's famous Piazza di Spagna" (Stille 2001:11). Slow Food hopes to turn globalization into a positive force through "eco-gastronomy" centered on maintaining traditional foods and biodiverse environments and circumventing agribusiness. With 65,000 members in 42 countries, Slow Food has increasing political clout but is only a tiny force when compared with the world's almost one billion hungry people (Cohen and Pinstrup-Anderson 1999).

As I write this introduction four weeks after the World Trade Center, Pentagon, and Pennsylvania attacks of September 11, 2001, U.S. fighter planes are dropping bombs and U.S. C-17 cargo planes are air-dropping food packets over Afghanistan, one of the poorest countries in the world. The U.S. airdrop of food to the Afghani people is one glimmer of hope in these terrible times, but it is largely symbolic given the extent of hunger in Afghanistan and the smallness of the gesture.[10] But it is a tiny step in the right direction toward sharing food and wealth on the global scene. Charity, however, is not the solution. To end hunger and to secure global peace we must ensure equitable sharing and control of resources and jobs around the world.

11

NOTES

1. *Slow* is the publication of the Slow Food movement (Stille 2001).
2. There is so much good recent scholarship on foodways that it would be impossible to cite it all. Some important anthologies are Avakian 1997; Counihan and Van Esterik 1997; Curtin and Heldke 1992; Flandrin and Montanari 1999; Goodman, Dufour, and Pelto 2000; Humphrey and Humphrey 1988; Inness 2001; Long 1998; Mack 1999; Pillsbury 1998; Scapp and Seitz 1998; Shortridge and Shortridge 1998. Some important recent works on U.S. foodways not cited elsewhere in this volume are Adams 1990, Belasco 1986, Bell and Valentine 1997, Blum 1999, DeVault 1991, Gussow 2001, Levenstein 1988, 1992, Mintz 1996, Nichter 2000, and Sobal and Maurer 1997, 1999.
3. I found widely divergent coverage in the social sciences and humanities on U.S. ethnic foodways. On African Americans and food, see Deck 2001, Hughes 1997, Joyner 1971, 1984, Parker 1998, Parker et al. 1995, Smart-Grosvenor 1992, Spivey 1999, Whitehead 1992, Witt 1999. On Native Americans see Gladwell 1998 and Powers and Powers 1984. On Asian Americans, see Cobb 1988, Wang 1998, and Wu-Tso et al. 1995. On food and lesbian and gay identity, see Carrington 1999.
4. On Thanksgiving, see also Appelbaum 1984, Deetz and Anderson 1972, and Pleck 1999.
5. There is a vast literature on eating disorders; see Counihan 1999. Some important interdisciplinary titles are Bordo 1993, Bruch 1973, and Brumberg 1988, 1997.
6. Two good collections on food and literature are Schofield 1989 and Hinz 1991. See also Cobb 1988, Parker 1998, and Wang 1998. On food and film, see Kides and Fuller 1993, and LeBlanc 1989.
7. On fast food, see Leidner 1993, Newman 1999, Reiter 1991, and Schlosser 2001.
8. Some recent sources on food globalization are Bonanno et al. 1994, Barndt 1999, Conway 1999a, 1999b, Griffith 2000, Leopold 1985, Magdoff et al. 2000, Messer et al. 1998, Watson 1997, and Witt 2001.
9. In addition to the sources cited in note 8, see Altieri 1995, Buck et al. 1997, and Mooney and Majika 1995.
10. The Lancaster, Pennsylvania, *Intelligencer Journal* (10/8/01) described the 37,500 food packets dropped by two C-17 cargo planes over Afghanistan: "The airdrops are delivering 'humanitarian daily rations,' plastic pouches enriched with vitamins and minerals.... The food, wrapped so that one packet has enough for one person for one day, does not contain any animal products so as not to violate any religious or cultural practices. Muslims, for example, do not eat pork.... The yellow plastic packets are about the size and weight of a hardcover book. They have a picture of a smiling person eating from a pouch, a stencil of an American flag, a notation that they were made by Rightaway Foods of McAllen Texas, and this greeting in English: 'This food is a gift from the United States of America.' Inside are several smaller packets with food such as peanut butter, strawberry jam, crackers, a fruit pastry, and entrees such as beans with tomato sauce and bean and potato vinaigrette. The packets provide at least 2,200 calories per day. The packets are also designed to flutter to the ground rather than drop straight down to minimize the possibility that they could hit and injure someone."

REFERENCES

Adams, Carol. 1990. *The Sexual Politics of Meat: A Feminist-Vegetarian Critical Theory*. New York: Continuum.

Altieri, Miguel. 1995. *Agroecology: The Science of Sustainable Agriculture*. Boulder: Westview.

Appelbaum, Diana Karter. 1984. *Thanksgiving: An American Holiday, An American History*. New York: Facts on File.

Avakian, Arlene Voski, ed. 1997. *Through the Kitchen Window: Women Explore the Intimate Meanings of Food and Cooking*. Boston: Beacon Press.

Barndt, Deborah, ed. 1999. *Women Working the NAFTA Food Chain: Women, Food and Globalization*. Toronto: Second Story Press.

Belasco, Warren J. 1986. *Appetite for Change: How the Counterculture Took on the Food Industry, 1966–1988*. New York: Pantheon.

Bell, David and Gill Valentine. 1997. *Consuming Geographies: We Are Where We Eat*. New York: Routledge.

Bentley, Amy, ed. 1996. "American Foodways and World War II," special issue of *Food and Foodways* 6, 2.

———. 1998. *Eating for Victory: Food Rationing and the Politics of Domesticity*. Urbana: University of Illinois Press.

Blum, Linda. 1999. *At the Breast: Ideologies of Breastfeeding and Motherhood in the Contemporary United States*. Boston: Beacon.

Bonanno, Alessandro, Lawrence Busch, and Enzo Mingione, eds. 1994. *From Columbus to ConAgra*. Kansas City: University Press of Kansas.

Bordo, Susan. 1993. *Unbearable Weight: Feminism, Western Culture, and the Body*. Berkeley: University of California Press.

Bower, Anne L., ed. 1997. *Recipes for Reading: Community Cookbooks, Stories, Histories*. Amherst, MA: University of Massachusetts Press.

Bruch, Hilde. 1973. *Eating Disorders: Obesity, Anorexia Nervosa, and the Person Within*. New York: Basic Books.

Brumberg, Joan Jacobs. 1988. *Fasting Girls: The Emergence of Anorexia Nervosa as a Modern Disease*. Cambridge: Harvard University Press.

———. 1997. *The Body Project: An Intimate History of America Girls*. New York: Random House.

Buck, Daniel, Christina Getz and Julie Guthman. 1997. From Farm to Table: The Organic Vegetable Commodity Chain of Northern California. *Sociologia Ruralis* 37, 1:3–20.

Canada and the World Backgrounder. 1997. "Struggle for Power." May 1997, 62, 6:6–9.

Carrington, Christopher. 1999. *No Place Like Home: Relationships and Family Life among Lesbians and Gay Men*. Chicago: University of Chicago Press.

Cobb, Nora. Food as an Expression of Cultural Identity in Jade Snow Wong and Songs for Jadina. *Hawaii Review* 12, 1:12–16.

Cohen, Marc J. and Per Pinstrup-Anderson. 1999. "Food Security and Conflict." In *Food: Nature and Culture*, special issue of *Social Research*, ed. Arien Mack, 66, 1:375–416.

Conway, Gordon. 1999a. "Food for All in the Twenty-First Century." In *Food: Nature and Culture*, special issue of *Social Research*, ed. Arien Mack, 66, 1:351–373.

———. 1999b. *The Doubly Green Revolution: Food for All in the Twentieth-First Century*. Ithaca, NY: Cornell University Press.

Counihan, Carole M. 1999. *The Anthropology of Food and Body: Gender, Meaning and Power*. New York: Routledge.

———. 2001. Food in Anthropology. *International Encyclopedia of Social and Behavioral Sciences*. Oxford: Elsevier Science Publishers, 8: 5715–5719.

——— and Penny Van Esterik, eds. 1997. *Food and Culture: A Reader*. New York: Routledge.

Curtin, Deane W. and Lisa M. Heldke. 1992. *Cooking, Eating, Thinking: Transformative Philosophies of Food*. Bloomington: Indiana University Press.

Darden, Carole and Norma Jean Darden. 1978. *Spoonbread and Strawberry Wine*. New York: Doubleday.

Deck, Alice A. 2001. "Now Then—Who Said Biscuits?" The Black Woman Cook as Fetish in American Advertising, 1905–1953. In *Kitchen Culture*, ed. Sherrie A. Inness. Philadelphia: University of Pennsylvania Press, pp. 69–93.

Deetz, James and Jay Anderson. 1972. The Ethnogastronomy of Thanksgiving. *Saturday Review* 55, 48: 29–38.

DeVault, Marjorie L. 1991. *Feeding the Family: The Social Organization of Caring as Gendered Work*. Chicago: University of Chicago Press.

Douglas, Mary, ed. 1984. *Food in the Social Order: Studies of Food and Festivities in Three American Communities*. New York: Russell Sage.

Economist. 2001. "Righting Wrongs." 360, 8235: 18–21.

Fink, Deborah. 1998. *Cutting into the Meatpacking Line: Workers and Change in the Rural Midwest*. Chapel Hill: University of North Carolina Press.

Flandrin, Jean Louis and Massimo Montanari, eds. 1999. *Food: A Culinary History*. English edition edited by Albert Sonnenfeld. New York: Penguin.

Gabaccia, Donna. 1998. *We Are What We Eat: Ethnic Foods and the Making of Americans*. Cambridge: Harvard University Press.

Gladwell, Malcolm. 1998. The Pima Paradox. *The New Yorker*, February 2, 1998, 44–57.

Goodman, Alan, Darna Dufour, and Gretel Pelto. 2000. *Nutritional Anthropology: Biocultural Perspectives on Food and Nutrition*. Mountain View, CA: Mayfield.

Griffith, David. 2000. Work and Immigration: Winter Vegetable Production in South Florida. In *Poverty or Development: Global Restructuring and Regional Transformations in the U.S. South and the Mexican South*, eds. R. Tardanico and M. Rosenberg. New York: Routledge.

Gussow, Joan Dye. 2001. *This Organic Life: Confessions of a Suburban Homesteader*. New York: Chelsea Green.

Hess, John L. and Karen Hess. 1972. *The Taste of America*. New York: Penguin.

———. 2000. *The Taste of America*. With a new introduction by the authors. Urbana: University of Illinois Press.

Hinz, Evelyn, ed. 1991. *Diet and Discourse: Eating, Drinking and Literature*, special issue of *Mosaic*. Winnipeg: University of Manitoba.

Hughes, Marvalene. 1997. Soul, Black Women, and Food. In *Food and Culture: A Reader*, eds. Carole Counihan and Penny Van Esterik. New York: Routledge, pp. 272–280.

Humphrey, Theodore C. and Lin T. Humphrey, eds. 1988. "*We Gather Together*": Food and Festival in American Life. Ann Arbor: UMI Press.

Inness, Sherrie A., ed. 2001. *Kitchen Culture in America: Popular Representations of Food Gender, and Race.* Philadelphia: University of Pennsylvania Press.

Joyner, Charles W. 1971. Soul Food and the Sambo Stereotype: Folklore from the Slave Narrative Collection. *Keystone Folklore* 16:171–178.

———. 1984. *Down by the Riverside: A South Carolina Slave Community.* Urbana: University of Illinois Press.

Kides, Paul Lou and Linda K. Fuller, eds. 1993. *Beyond the Stars: Studies in American Popular Film. The Material World in American Popular Film.* Vol. 3. Bowling Green: Bowling Green State University Popular Press.

LeBlanc, Roland D. 1989. *Love and Death* and Food: Woody Allen's Comic Use of Gastronomy. *Literature and Film Quarterly* 17, 1:18–26.

Leidner, Robin. 1993. *Fast Food, Fast Talk: Service Work and the Routinization of Everyday Life.* Berkeley: University of California Press.

Leopold, Marion. 1985. The Transnational Food Companies and Their Global Strategies. *International Social Science Journal* 37, 3:315–330.

Levenstein, Harvey. 1988. *Revolution at the Table : The Transformation of the American Diet.* New York: Oxford University Press.

———. 1992. *Paradox of Plenty. A Social History of Eating in Modern America.* New York: Oxford University Press.

Long, Lucy M., ed. 1998. Special Issue: Culinary Tourism. *Southern Folklore* 55, 3.

Mack, Arien, ed. 1999. *Food: Nature and Culture.* A Special Issue of *Social Research,* 66, 1.

Magdoff, Fred, John Bellamy Foster, and Frederick H. Buttel, eds. 2000. *Hungry for Profit: The Agribusiness Threat to Farmers, Food, and the Environment.* New York: Monthly Review Press.

Messer, Ellen, Marc J. Cohen, and J. D'Costa. 1998. *Food from Peace: Breaking the Links between Conflict and Hunger.* Washington: International Food Policy Research Institute.

Mintz, Sidney. 1996. *Tasting Food, Tasting Freedom: Excursions into Eating, Culture, and the Past.* Boston: Beacon.

Mooney, Patrick H. and Theo J. Majika. 1995. *Farmers' and Farm Workers' Movements: Social Protest in American Agriculture.* New York: Twayne Publishers.

Newman, Katherine. 1999. *No Shame in My Game.* New York: Vintage and Russell Sage Foundation.

Nichter, Mimi. 2000. *Fat Talk: What Girls and Their Parents Say about Dieting.* Cambridge: Harvard University Press.

Parker, Emma. 1998. "Apple Pie" Ideology and the Politics of Appetite in the Novels of Toni Morrison. *Contemporary Literature* 39, 4:614–643.

Parker, Sheila, M. Nichter, M. Nichter, N. Vuckovic, C. Sims, and C. Rittenbaugh. 1995. Body Image and Weight Concerns among African American and White Adolescent Females: Differences That Make a Difference. *Human Organization* 54, 2:103–114.

Pendergrast, Mark. 1993. *For God, Country and Coca-Cola: The Unauthorized History of the Great American Soft Drink and the Company That Made It.* New York: Scribners.

Pillsbury, Richard. 1998. *No Foreign Food: The American Diet in Time and Place.* Boulder, CO: Westview.

Pleck, Elizabeth. 1999. The Making of the Domestic Occasion: The History of Thanksgiving in the United States. *Journal of Social History* 32, 4:773–789.

Poppendieck, Janet. 1998. *Sweet Charity? Emergency Food and the End of Entitlement.* New York: Penguin.

Powers, William K. and Marla M. N. Powers. 1984. Metaphysical Aspects of an Oglala Food System. In *Food in the Social Order: Studies of Food and Festivities in Three American Communities,* ed. Mary Douglas. New York: Russell Sage Foundation, pp. 40–96.

Reiter, Ester. 1991. *Making Fast Food: From the Frying Pan into the Fryer.* Montreal: McGill-Queen's University Press.

Scapp, Ron and Brian Seitz, eds. 1998. *Eating Culture.* Albany: SUNY Press.

Schlosser, Eric. 2001. *Fast Food Nation: The Dark Side of the All-American Meal.* Boston: Houghton Mifflin.

Schofield, Mary A., ed. 1989. *Cooking by the Book: Food in Literature and Culture.* Bowling Green, OH: Bowling Green State University Popular Press.

Shortridge, Barbara G. and James R. Shortridge, eds. 1998. *The Taste of American Place: A Reader on Regional and Ethnic Foods.* Lanham: Rowman and Littlefield.

Smart-Grosvenor, Verta Mae. 1992. *Vibration Cooking: Or the Travel Notes of a Geechee Girl.* New York: Ballantine.

Sobal, Jeffery and Donna Maurer, eds. 1997. *Weighty Issues: Fatness and Thinness as Social Problems.* Hawthorne, NY: Aldine de Gruyter.

———. 1999. *Interpreting Weight: The Social Management of Fatness and Thinness.* Hawthorne, NY: Aldine de Gruyter.

Spivey, Diane M. 1999. *The Peppers, Cracklings, and Knots of Wool Cookbook: The Global Migration of African Cuisine.* Albany: SUNY Press.

Stille, Alexander. 2001. Slow Food: An Italian Answer to Globalization. *The Nation* 273, 6:11–16.

Thompson, Becky. 1994. *A Hunger So Wide and So Deep: American Women Speak Out on Eating Problems.* Minneapolis: University of Minnesota Press.

Wang, David Der-wei. 1998. Three Hungry Women. *Boundary 2,* 25, 3:47–76.

Watson, James L., ed. 1997. *Golden Arches East: McDonald's in East Asia.* Stanford: Stanford University Press.

Whitehead, Tony L. 1992. In Search of Soul Food and Meaning: Culture, Food, and Health. From *African Americans in the South: Issues of Race, Class and Gender,* eds. Hans A. Baer and Yvonne Jones. Athens: University of Georgia Press, pp. 94–110.

Witt, Doris. 1999. *Black Hunger: Food and the Politics of U.S. Identity.* New York: Oxford University Press.

———. 2001. Global Feminisms and Food: A Review Essay. *Meridians,* 1, 2: 73–93.

Wu-Tso, Pamela, I-Li Yeh, and Chick F. Tam. 1995. Comparisons of Dietary Intake in Young and Old Asian Americans: A Two-Generation Study. *Nutrition Research* 15, 10:1445–1462.

13

THE TASTE OF Y2K

JOHN L. HESS AND KAREN HESS

"[The Taste of America] moved me in a very significant way," says Michael London, an upstate New York baker and a guru in the nation's bread movement. "I always appreciated [Karen Hess's] scholarly perspective and the depth with which she considered bread." He liked the volume so much that he went out and bought 15 copies and gave them to his employees.

Atlanta Journal-Constitution, *March 15, 1998*

We composed The Taste of America a quarter of a century ago on a glitch-free typewriter built half a century before; we are tiptapping this update into a "word processor" assembled in 1999 and already obsolete. In the interim, "Kool-Aid like Mother used to make" became Kool-Aid like Grandmother used to make, and most Americans are now one more generation removed from the memory of real food. So how did the taste of America survive that explosion of creation and destruction, of progress and regression, of ceaseless change and limitless absurdity that was called the American Century? Well, first the good news. We Hesses are eating better than in 1975, when we had to bake our own bread and roast our own coffee. In 1999, real bread is to be found again, here and there. Good coffee arrived with Starbucks (though at steep prices, accompanied by trendy folderol and mediocre pastry, and already showing signs of the same corporate decay that sapped the quality of Chock Full o'Nuts and Pepperidge Farm a generation earlier). We deplored, and James Beard defended, the ubiquitous iceberg lettuce; today, we are offered a range of salads and greens that were unknown to most Americans in 1975, though they were familiar to our forebears.

Our assault on the malignant stupidity of New York's permanent government in driving out farmers' markets caught the eye of a young architect-urbanist named Barry Benepe. On the spot, he set out to bring the farmers back. Fighting every foot of the way against bureaucratic obfuscation and hostile wirepulling, he steadily built up what is now a thriving string of more than 20 Greenmarkets. Many farmers credit Greenmarket for their survival. Chefs and consumers love it for its fresh seasonal produce and its heirloom varieties. Officials commend Greenmarket to tourists and pretend to be its sponsors. (But victories do not stay won. In the spring of 1999, we had to fight off a mysterious attack on the permit for our neighborhood Greenmarket. And developers once again were casting eyes on the Fulton Fish Market.) There are of course more venerable farmers' markets around the country, but Benepe's rich experience has been helpful to many people concerned with saving them and organizing new ones.

Another victory: We excoriated the plague of pop history and appealed for serious study of culinary history. Though still young, it has become a respectable discipline. A number of publishers have responded to our call for the reedition of historic manuscripts and books. Several of them have been widely credited with awakening a large public to the enormous contribution of Africans to the American diet. *What Mrs. Fisher Knows about Old Southern Cooking*, for example, is a facsimile edition of what appears to be the first cookbook written by an African-American woman, an ex-slave. And a lovely cookbook it is.

Pop history did not go away, however, nor did any of the other high crimes and misdemeanors we impeached. (We could hardly foresee that the comestible event of the century would be a delivery of pizza to the Oval Office.) Our text stands unchanged; by and large, what has happened to our foodways has followed paths clearly described therein. For example, admirers of Julia Child boasted then how bad a cook *she* had been when she discovered cuisine; today, our most prestigious guides boast how bad their *mothers* were. (Ruth Reichl, recently lured by *Gourmet* from *The New York Times* by a reported bonus of a million dollars, calls her mother the Queen of Mold. Does that make her the Princess of Mold?)

For another generational shift, consider that in the closing year of the twentieth century, a noble Meals on Wheels program sponsored by New York chefs and foodies appealed for help with the slogan, "If you can boil water, you can cook." Twenty-five years ago, if you could mimic Julia Child's gestures, you were a French chef; today, if you can boil water, you're a cook. Actually, the latter definition is closer to reality, for the reheating of prepared food has become the dominant form of cooking in many homes and indeed at most public feeding stations.

Apropos, our book made fun of the microwave oven, whose only useful function is precisely to reheat. It was not, and is not, indispensable for that, but its triumph has proved superbly Thorsten Veblen's dictum that invention is the mother of necessity. In the 1970s, the industry enlisted the food media to persuade consumers that a microwave could do nearly anything a stove could do, faster and better (never mind the risk). A favorite recipe of ours, by the most successful microwave hustler, called for making a lemon meringue pie in no fewer than 20 incredibly adept steps, timed to the microsecond. A syndicated column titled "Micro Ways" proposed a recipe for *saltimbocca alla Romana* that called for browning the veal on the stove, then microwaving it on HIGH 6 to 7 minutes and on MEDIUM 6 to 7 minutes more. (The classic recipe calls for a maximum cooking time of 5 minutes, on a stove of course.) Or, microwave scallops for 23 murderous minutes in 8 steps, ending with one minute on the stove. That first step for the veal and the last one for the scallops were meant to brown out a grave shortcoming of the machine. A food chemist from Minneapolis told us a fortune was awaiting the company that found "a way to put a crust on something in a microwave."

We met that chemist in New Orleans in 1980 at the convention of the Institute of Food Technologists, whose program bore an ad headlined "Eat your heart out, Mother Nature." Research papers explored the effect of PHMB on the shelf life of fish, why cottonseed flour turns brown in biscuits, the flowability of mozzarella cheese, and the characteristics of comminuted fish and meat. New products to be sampled included "real" fruit juices (which then had to have 10 percent fruit, later reduced to 5 percent), an artificial sweetener, synthetic cheeses, soy-based ice cream, ham made of viscoelastic gluten, imitation bacon, extended crab paste, and veal-flavored rabbitburgers. It was the flavor, not the rabbit, that was on sale. A chemist who had helped fabricate it said it tasted like beef. Asked why not sell rabbit flavor, a salesman chimed in that rabbit was too gamy, and the chemist agreed that it was too bland, which he explained was what the public understood as gamy. (Trust us, we couldn't make that up. And who would know better? At the time, gourmet writers were pushing turkey breast as tasting like veal.)

We shared a cab with a researcher for General Foods (now a subsidiary of something else). "In five years," she said, "we'll have wonderful things. Everything will be balanced nutritionally, like pet food. All we need is to educate the public." After she debarked, the driver said, "I don't want no Alpo diet." But his was a view not to be heard inside the Superdome, where another vision of the future was a line of breadings to give "convenience" foods crisp coatings designed to conceal their lack of flavor. The line was called Newlywed Foods...

Eat your heart out, Mother Nature. Soon after our book appeared, the Hudson River was found to be poisoned with PCBs and the public was advised to eat its fish no more than once a week. Then Lake Erie was found to be toxic, and the same advice was issued. We broadcast a suggestion that we locate five more poisoned bodies of water, so that we might eat fish seven days a week. No problem; it would be hard today to be confident that any body of water is untainted. But, yes, there has been change. Concern about the safety of our food, air, and water has become the conventional wisdom. Our largest polluters award themselves medals for conservation. Both major candidates for the presidency in Y2K, it is safe to predict, will be sworn defenders of the environment. Both will also have been enthusiastic in promoting NAFTA and GATT, which gravely undermined U.S. and foreign controls on the export and import of toxic chemicals. (At this writing, our government is fighting to force Europe and Canada to accept our hormone-spiked beef, while objectors to it in this country have been muzzled by food-libel laws in 13 states. Oprah Winfrey proved in Texas that those laws were unconstitutional, but media less willing to pay for litigation have been censoring scripts.) Lobbyists and politicians and tame media became skilled at environmental newspeak. Thus, every raid on our natural resources is now headlined as the rescue of what remains. Thus, a clause tucked into a bill purporting to protect the food supply, passed by Congress and signed by President Clinton, quietly repealed the Delaney Clause, a landmark ban on carcinogens that industry had been lobbying against for 30 years.

When we were writing about the petrochemical-driven Green Revolution, we could not foresee the exploits of genetic engineering. We could not imagine that patents would be granted on plants redesigned not to improve quality but to withstand increased use of herbicides and pesticides. Chemicals are cheaper than labor, so Monsanto found a ready market for a new variety of cotton that could stand up to its herbicide; TV news acclaimed it with pictures of the stooping children it would replace. Monsanto's weedkiller worked fine; unfortunately, the first crop of the new

17

cotton failed. It went back to the gene shop. Another wrinkle: the new patented grains have profit insurance in their chromosomes; their offspring are sterile, so growers can no longer set aside part of the crop for replanting. *O tempora, O mores.*

Expanding production, low market prices, and high interest rates have squeezed farmers harder than anybody could foretell. They surely contributed to the financial storms that have devastated the Third World. For all Americans, the early 1970s, when we were writing, marked a turning point. Until then, the rising tide did lift nearly all boats, at least somewhat. Since then, the poor have become literally poorer, and the rich incredibly richer. The gap bothered us when we were writing in 1975; by now it has become obscene. While a substantial number of Americans continued to prosper, a majority have seen their earnings stagnate or decline. The slide has been masked by easy (though costly) credit, fewer childbirths, and an increase in households holding down two or more jobs. Already in 1975, as we noted, such households had no time for cooking, except as a weekend hobby, or to be enjoyed vicariously. We remarked also that, as with sex, dissatisfaction with what people were getting appeared to spur talking about it. But who could have imagined food channels on TV? Some foreign guests have been fine; other shows we've glimpsed have ranged from passable to awful. One, sponsored by the Food Network, *Gourmet* magazine, and Cap'n Crunch, a sweet breakfast cereal, promoted using the product as breading for lamb chops. A chef exclaimed at the "junk" visiting performers were required to use: "canned chili, airfoam whipped cream, not a speck of good olive oil and not even one good vinegar." As a teaching guide, the new medium is not much better than the recipes on the package. Producers, desperate to keep channel surfers from surfing on, feature cooking races, clowns, and, as one producer confided, "cute" performers. Who pays the piper calls the tune.

Our final "De Gustibus" column in the *Times* concluded, "As long as fashion editors tell us what to eat, we shall eat badly." The line disappeared on the copy desk. Thereafter, fashion triumphed, totally. In a favorable report on an expensive restaurant (the only kind she reviewed), Ruth Reichl remarked that the chef's creations "did not always work," but they were "never boring." What could better express the ethos of fashion? In a Reichl review, the first question posed is what sort of people dine there. At one place, Ruth, the daughter of the Queen of Mold, swooned upon spying the Queen of Mean, the ex-convict Leona Helmsley, in romantic congress with an attractive younger male; unfortunately, they were out of earshot. We're talking glamour.

We attended the birth of nouvelle cuisine in France and knew its creators well. Theirs was a brilliant effort to lighten the classic cuisine, featuring a fanatic pursuit of the dwindling sources of artisanal produce. Soon, however, it was taken up by the fashion world and its meaning transformed into novelty for its own sake. Food had to be new, it had to be now, it had to be different. It became not good but glamorous. Thousands of bright young people abandoned other callings to toil over the hot stove, which French professionals ironically call the piano. A seemingly unlimited supply of venture capital financed a proliferation of tax-sheltered dining places, which won feverish coverage by a proliferation of food critics. (Since the restaurant mortality rate is staggeringly high, critics need to move quickly; a review of a "hot new hero" by Gael Greene in *New York* magazine appeared a day after his restaurant closed.) As, to repeat Sacha Guitry's immortal words, nothing is so out of fashion as fashion, fad followed fad with bewildering speed. Kiwi fruit speckled the national table (and dentists drilled for gold in kiwi plantations until that bubble burst); vegetables shrank in size like Alice in Wonderland; the jalapeño pepper burned every yuppie palate; blackened fish, the invention of a cagey Cajun, darkened menus across the land. The gazetteer was mined for new ethnic fashions, seldom authentic and almost never pure. (At the moment, "Pan-Asian" and "Fusion" are rife.) Even American food is occasionally reported to be coming back, but who knows anymore what that means? A decade ago, the *Times* raved about a "patrician" restaurant that had dropped its French menu in favor of American cuisine. The star-spangled menu: raw tuna seared black, smoked quail vinaigrette, vegetable terrine, crab ravioli, foie gras on fava beans, baby corn, and shredded confit. American, *quoi*. Dig the foie gras; it has become a staple in fashion feeding, along with truffles, caviar, and other pricey ingredients. A fad as we write slathers fish with foie gras, and Italian truffles if the chef is shooting the works. In fashion, price is of course the essential ingredi-ent; how else would the clientele judge quality? Extravagance is not pointless; it is the point, and it always has been. Long ago, we enjoyed Craig Claiborne's advice on "What to Do with Leftover Caviar" (you take a one-pound tin and . . .); the other day, the *Times* told readers to marinate a tuna steak in a quart of olive oil, and then dis-card the oil. If you have to ask what it cost, you can't afford it. (We leave the prices in our text unchanged for the amusement of readers at our quaint notion of what was costly in 1975. For what it may be worth to readers in the distant future, we note that by 1999 the $100 menu and the $100 wine raised no critical eyebrows.)

19

We dwell on the *Times* because it is the bellwether. Others follow its quirks slav-ishly, for example, by purporting to try everything on the menu and to return sev-eral times. That may seem scrupulously fair (should the drama desk adopt it?) but for the critic it turns dining into Russian roulette. A *Times* critic was happy to report that on a second visit "those spoiled mussels were transformed." Journalism has its heroes, but until now, who would eat tainted shellfish and return to it a second time? Unless—*honi soit qui mal y pense*—the critic tried it out on her guests. Anyhow, they all emulate the *Times*. When our neighborhood weekly reported in 1982 that service in a new restaurant was "polite but could be more attentive," that the scallops were "good, but overcooked," and that the pastry was "good, but too doughy," it was following the example of the *Times's* then reigning Oxymoronic Critic. She had found one high-toned restaurant "glowing and plush, if undistin-guished"; another also "undistinguished" but "bright and felicitous"; a third, "color-ful and refreshing but headsplittingly noisy"; and a fourth, "pleasant, comfortable and unprepossessing." In a fifth the beef was "fine if served rare but dull if over-cooked," while in a sixth it was the pasta that was fine, "provided it's not under-cooked or overcooked." That last restaurant received a lot more praise and abuse, and a rating of three stars ("Excellent"). In other words, readers were invited to spend a lot of money there, and however it turned out, they couldn't say they had-n't been warned. They had also received this sophisticated advice: "Drinks are large, so wine is superfluous, which is just as well because the selection is mun-dane." No, we've no idea what a mundane wine list would look like, but we salute class when we meet it.

We listed the junk-food favorites of our gourmet mentors as reported in 1974; the *Times* in 1986 found the then current gastronomic stars staving off hunger with Doritos-and-guacamole, Snickers, pretzels, M&M's, Oreos, fortune cookies, franks and beans, and, in the case of the impresario Joe Baum, "anything from any street corner that has fried onions." Baum, incidentally, was credited with the invention (reinvention, actually) of the theme restaurant and of the refrain "Hello, I'm Bruce and I'll be your waiter this evening," followed by a long recitation of dishes that are not on the printed menu. Another veteran restaurateur, George Lang, derided these pretensions at a conference of foodies, as they were then calling themselves. He satirized "Bruce" as recommending "the breast of guinea hen marinated in lavender vinegar, wrapped in cherrywood-smoked salmon, stuffed with goat cheese, and topped with a dandelion beurre blanc." Lang was dismayed when several of the foodies asked for the recipe. More recently, the humorist Bill Bryson imagined his waiter proposing "a crêpe galette of sea chortle and kelp in a rich *mal de mer sauce*, seasoned with disheveled herbs grown in our own herbarium." But it is high impossible, really, to satirize the willful complexity and pretension of cuisine in pricey restaurants and on food fashion pages today.

A cheerier note: We were gratified to learn in the *Times*, in 1999, about a "New Look at Dieting: Fat Can Be a Friend." The writer said we had been getting the wrong message for three decades now. And who had been the most influential purveyor of that message? None other than the *Times*. When we voiced our skepticism about the cholesterol phobia in that paper in 1973, it was over that writer's objection. In the years that followed, she and her colleagues valiantly fought to get salt and fat and eggs and cheese and butter off our tables. They had to reverse field now and then to report their discoveries that there was good cholesterol as well as bad, that babies need salt, that a lot of people need more Vitamin C, that olive oil was harmless, and that margarine could be harmful. But they carried on. Just as Fannie Farmer listed comparative nutritive values of different varieties of fish, the *Times* a century later began reporting the chemical composition of every recipe, to the milligram. After we hooted that the precision was a put-on and that the values given each ingredient were in fact guesswork, the *Times* first rounded the numbers and added the word "approximate," and then quietly gave up.

We were enchanted recently when the food section's health maven exclaimed: "Some people were never fooled. Butter is, in fact, better. Its silken, rich qualities could never be duplicated by the most ingenious food chemist whipping up the latest alternative. And beyond that, as science now confirms, the hardened and greasy colored vegetable oil known as margarine is even worse for your heart. Trying not to be smug is difficult." It should have been easy. No journalist had campaigned more persuasively against butterfat and egg yolks, those deadly carriers of cholesterol, although as the lean years rolled by, she began to meet dissents worthy of reporting. Now, since there is no believer like a convert, she offered a recipe for large appetizers calling for 3 tablespoons of butter and 3 of heavy cream. Per serving.

The rehabilitation of butter and cream did wonders for fashionable cookery—or would have done, were it not for the addiction to complexity. Reichl, for example, offered a chef's recipe for "The Most Voluptuous Cauliflower," calling for 1¼ cups heavy cream, 1½ cups grated Gruyère cheese, ¼ cup mascarpone cheese, ½ cup grated Parmesan cheese, and 2 tablespoons butter, all for the florets of a single cauliflower. "Voluptuous glop," we call it. Also in the *Times*, Thomas Keller, one of California's priciest chefs, offers "Fillet of Sole Véronique" to demonstrate how Escoffier's recipe "can be transformed into something that feels both modern and regional." Aside from the silly characterizing garnish of peeled grapes, Escoffier's recipe is a classic example of the elegance of simplicity: fillets of sole poached in a *fumet* of white wine and appropriate aromatics, which is separately reduced to a glaze, given body by beating in a little butter, this spooned over the fillets and the whole given a quick swipe under the broiler. Keller "transforms" it into something "modern and regional" by stuffing the hapless fillets with "2½ cups diced brioche

(⅛ inch by ⅛ inch) or Pepperidge Farm thin-sliced bread," both sultana and black raisins, as well as melted butter, the glazing calls for adding hollandaise sauce and an entire cup of heavy cream to a separately made *fumet*. And the garnish of peeled grapes. All for four fillets of gray sole, which have been antiseptically poached in body bags of "plastic wrap." "Time: 1 hour 30 minutes, plus 1 to 2 hours for soaking fish bones." We do the Escoffier original, minus the grapes, in 15 to 20 minutes, and it is more flavorful.

Now, despite all the relentless nagging about dieting, Americans are said to be more obese than ever—or is it in part because of the nagging, the incoherent advice, and the dedication of fashion art to the anorexic figure? In addition, of course, to the Clintonian-affirmed basic American diet of pizza, hamburgers, and popcorn. In any case, the exploitation of neurosis about diet is as profitable as ever. In a modest effort in 1999, the drug company Hoffmann–La Roche engaged some of New York's costliest and most caloric restaurants to offer low-fat menus designed to be taken with its new antiobesity pills. The program was labeled "The Taste for Healthy Living."

We said above that we the authors were eating better than we did in 1975, but many Americans are eating worse. Wages and welfare benefits never did catch up with inflation, and the guarantee of subsistence to families with dependent children was repealed in 1996. We remarked that Americans had forgotten how to cope with hard times; that surely hasn't changed. And by and large, our observation is that most of those Americans who can afford to eat well still don't know how. It is indeed so evident that the other day the manager of an expensive Chinese restaurant in Manhattan coolly told a reporter that he served factory chicken to Americans and real chicken to Asians, and both were satisfied. Ah, well, lots of people try to learn, and some do. The conscience lives, intelligence lives, the palate lives. Here and there, good people are feeding the hungry, defending nature, rediscovering real cooking. There is hope.

EATING AMERICAN

SIDNEY MINTZ

A year or so ago, a colleague who was teaching a course in science writing asked me to offer a lecture on food to her class. I chose as my subject aspects of the history of domestication. I regard domestication as one of the most important technical achievements in the history of our species. The lecture was well received, I thought. But in the discussion that followed, someone asked a question that had to do in part with American eating habits. When I responded, I mentioned in passing that I did not think that there is such a thing as an American cuisine. I thought nothing about it as I said it; though I had never discussed the subject with a class before, it wasn't a new idea. But in the next five minutes of the dialogue, I came to realize I had said something that some members of the class found at the least hurtful, if not downright insulting. My gaffe (if that is what it was) became clear almost immediately. I was asked by one student whether, since I believed we had no cuisine, I also believed we had no culture. I responded with amazement. I talked momentarily about (North) America's[1] highly regarded art, literature, drama, and poetry, claiming as I said it that our music was gradually achieving a stature equal to that we had won in these other fields. Even as I spoke I realized that the questioner was really wondering whether she had come across one of those awful persons who cannot resist running down his own country and, with her question, was just looking for proof. (I recall thinking that I had better mention some names—such as Ives, Gershwin, Bernstein, Joplin, Menotti, and Copland—in my answer, or I might be in even more hot water.) Another student took a different tack. He talked happily about "eating Thai" one night, and "eating Chinese" the next, and asked rather plaintively whether *that* couldn't be "our cuisine." He plainly felt that having access to a lot of different "cuisines" was a wonderful idea—and certainly better than meat loaf. It was all amiable enough; but I knew I'd said something a lot of people did not like to hear, nor want to believe. Before the class ended, the instructor invited students to write papers about my lecture; after a week she sent me copies of two of them, written by class members. Reading those papers made it additionally clear that I had touched a nerve. Neither paper included any comments on domestication; both talked about cuisine. If America didn't have a cuisine, these folks implied that it should; and they were certainly not prepared to accept my view of things. Though neither said it outright, I could infer that both wondered about my motives. As a consequence, I was left as interested in their sensitivity as I had been in the topic. Why, I asked myself, is having a cuisine important—is it because other people have one? Do people really think having a cuisine is like having a music, or a literature? *Is* having a cuisine like having a literature? Could it be good *not* to have a cuisine? If you don't have a cuisine, can you get one?

One reason I want to write about American eating is my eagerness to explain more clearly what I meant then. Whatever the case, it seems important to make clear that not having a cuisine is *not* like not having a literature; indeed, not having a cuisine—assuming I can make any case at all—might be a price we should be happily prepared to pay for "what's great about America."

Anyway, "eating American" is too large and too complex a subject to be tackled in this chapter, and I have to acknowledge that right away. There are a score of highly appropriate subjects I ought to raise here. But covering all those would fill another book. Still, I want to try once more to explain myself in regard to cuisine—this time, I hope, more convincingly.

When it comes to food, grasping our particularity as a nation requires us to get some sense of where our history differs from that of other countries, especially European countries.[2] The United States is extremely large in area and population, when compared to any European country but Russia. Even in this hemisphere, only Brazil and Canada are about as big, and neither is as populous. These are two obvious ways in which we differ from most places. We are predominantly European in origin, and mostly Protestant in religion. Of course we are also a young country by European historical standards—about two centuries (or seven generations) old.

The whole New World stands apart from the Old, especially from Europe, because its vast areas, as well as the aboriginal peoples who occupied them, came to be dominated by relatively small populations, and in the recent past. The conquerors mostly came from a confined but important area of the Old World: Western Europe. In terms of numbers, during the first two centuries or so, it seems likely that more Africans entered the New World than did Europeans; but their population did not grow in place as fast as did that of the Europeans; and they were almost entirely powerless, as were the indigenous peoples of the hemisphere. Hence, though Africans certainly figured importantly in the conquest and its aftermaths, though they were later joined by substantial migrant Asian populations, and though some native peoples of the hemisphere survived the impact, the Europeans were the powerholders. Their overlordship was achieved in the course of less than two centuries. Spanish and Portuguese domination, from what is the Southwest of the United States today to Tierra del Fuego, was largely in place by 1700. The insular, Caribbean region was divided up among five powers, all warring upon Spanish hegemony. That other New World areas farther north took longer to become colonial was as much a function of European wars as it was of any serious indigenous resistance.

In effect, seven nations—and to a large extent, people from those seven nations only—predominated in the conquest: Spain, Portugal, Britain, France, the Netherlands, Denmark, and Sweden. Norway, Germany, and Italy were not yet countries; but in the eighteenth century, German migration to the hemisphere was substantial, and in the nineteenth, so was Scandinavian, Italian, and East European migration. By the end of the eighteenth century, the United States had become a sovereign state, the hemisphere's first. Most Americans at the start of the nineteenth century were white and North European in origin. What the United States fully shares with many of its New World neighbors is its newness as a nation, and its being composed almost entirely of the descendants of migrants, coming from elsewhere. We share with Canada, Chile, Argentina, Uruguay, and perhaps Costa Rica the background fact that the vast majority of today's inhabitants are descended from migrants who came from Europe.

A particularly cruel consequence of conquest was the runaway depopulation of immense areas, due to the combined effects of disease, war, enslavement, and inhuman labor practices. The early movements of Europeans and Africans to the hemisphere were soon followed by others; and that movement of new peoples, especially to the United States, has literally never ceased. Except, of course, for the descendants of Native Americans—anciently descended themselves, in turn, from migrants from Asia—all North Americans are originally from somewhere else, particularly from Europe.

25

In the United States immigration continued apace during the nineteenth and twentieth centuries. While its volume relative to the settled population has declined, the absolute numbers have remained high; and in the last half century, the origins of the newcomers have become much more diverse. Immigration laws in the nineteenth century had been aimed at maintaining the ethnic structure of United States society as it was then constituted, largely North European; only since World War II was that bias modified legislatively. The pace of continued immigration, while shared with some other hemispheric nations, is another relevant marker of North American distinctiveness.

At the same time that immigration has continued, national history has been marked by steady territorial expansion. The Louisiana and Gadsden purchases, the purchase of Alaska, the Spanish American War, the acquisition of Hawaii, Puerto Rico, the Virgin Islands, American Samoa, for example, and the North American imperialist policies these military conquests and purchases represented, all played a part. But while Europeans were migrating to colonial areas such as Canada, South Africa, and Australia, in our case migrant Europeans were coming to what was already a sovereign and democratic country—becoming citizens as well as inhabitants. In each instance of additional expansion, there followed further settlement, as in Hawaii and Alaska, Puerto Rico, and the (U.S.) Virgin Islands. This expansion and incorporation is another distinctive feature of United States society worthy of mention here. In most of the Americas, people who came from elsewhere had their future quite firmly charted for them by their class status on arrival; in the United States, that was not so much the case. Public education, expanding economic opportunities, and the openness of the political system produced unexpected and dynamic results.

Since its establishment as a nation, the United States has been marked by a high degree of mobility, above all geographical. Expansion westward meant a spreading out and filling up of the country as it grew. Such expansion involved military, then cultural, aggression against Native Americans, a part of our history which has come to be acknowledged publicly, more and more. Less noticed has been the enormous long-term benefit of seemingly infinite land resources for farming and, even more, ranching—a steadily dwindling treasure upon which the nation has fattened for centuries, and the presence and availability of which have profoundly affected the way our eating habits (and other habits) have taken shape.

From early on, this was a highly mobile country, not only occupationally but also economically. Perhaps upward mobility is particularly noticeable when the rising group includes newcomers. Today, the bankers, generals, CEOs, and members of Congress in this country who have recent foreign forebears are legion. This makes us different, and, in the eyes of, say, Englishmen or Germans, it may also make us seem rather undiscriminating. Imagine the German army with its top general a child of Turkish immigrants! Or the British army led by a child of Pakistani immigrants!

From the end of the eighteenth century onward, different regions of the new land called the United States gave rise to somewhat different diets. One reason for these differences was the wide variation in natural environments—the Southwest versus the Gulf Coast versus New England versus the Northwest Pacific, for example. Another was the differing food habits of various migrant groups. Broad differences between, say, New England cooking and Southern cooking can certainly still be sketched in. On a narrower canvas, we can speak of "Cajun" cooking, say, or "Pennsylvania Dutch" cooking, and still have it mean something. In the Midwest, some Scandinavian culinary traditions were established; in large Eastern cities, Italian and East European cooking habits took hold. To these older patterns have been added numerous others since World War II, of which Asian foods and cooking methods, only poorly represented in this country before, are the most visible, though not the only ones.

Yet such variety does not equal a cuisine, and is not the same as a cuisine. There are at least two reasons why such an assertion may seem unwarranted. On the one hand, there do appear to be *regional* cuisines, which I described as the only "real" cuisines, anyway. On the other, I have contended that national cuisines are not cuisines in the same sense. So I must explain myself.

Since our beginnings as a nation, Americans have sought ways to integrate and assimilate newcomer populations within some generalized American culture. Though prejudice against both African Americans and American Indians (and in its more recent forms, toward other nonwhite populations as well) has militated against that process, most newcomers have been encouraged to forgo their traditional cultures in order to "become American." What this means is not always so clear. But the public educational system, above all, and the tremendous power of peer pressure, working on both children and adults, has helped to reshape the behavior and outlook of successive generations of new arrivals.

Several different things are happening at once. More people coming from different places continue to arrive. They are subject to pressures to change their ways, including their foodways, by an Americanization process that goes on in the schools, in the media, and in the course of daily life. The demands of new jobs and new lifestyles, and the desires and claims of the children of migrants, put great negative pressure, great pressure to change, upon older, imported standards. Geographical and socioeconomic mobility accompanies these new pressures. We are not surprised to find Hmong tribespeople in Montana, Vietnamese fishermen in Texas, Sikh and Korean storekeepers in California. In many different ways, some subtle and some obvious, these people are changing their behavior and, unbeknownst even to themselves, some of their values as well, as they "become American." How these migrants may identify themselves culturally is not in dispute, particularly if they continue to use their native language; but the cultural identity of their children is a different issue and likely to be changing rapidly.

That there are powerful pressures toward sameness, working particularly upon children, may be thought to increase the homogeneity of American food habits.

Such foods as hot dogs, hamburgers, ice cream, and pizza are integral to acceptable adolescent behavior, regardless of origins; young people are intensely aware of it. In a certain way, then, these pressures do push toward homogeneity. But while learning to eat ice cream, and at fast food and ethnic restaurants, has the effect of increasing homogeneity of a kind, this experience is not the same as learning, or creating, a cuisine. Strictly speaking, by learning such behavior people are becoming sociologically more alike, but it is not really clear that they are becoming culturally more alike.

Americans eat out at ever-higher levels of frequency, and barring serious economic contractions, that trend will continue. At this point, nearly one-half of the money spent on food is spent on eating out. But we have little data on how eating-out patterns vary by class. It seems to me that eating out could only be cuisine-related if it means Japanese-Americans were going to Japanese restaurants, and Italian-Americans to Italian restaurants. But in such a case, we wouldn't be speaking about an American cuisine, but about the "national" cuisines of other nations, being eaten by persons historically descended from immigrants from those nations. Sociologically, that doesn't seem important at all, especially because the people doing it would probably not think of it that way. At the same time, I don't think that there is a reliable manner in which to speak of unhyphenated Americans going to unhyphenated American restaurants to eat American cuisine, because I believe that what they eat cannot be convincingly described as cuisine.

Of course we can describe what is eaten in culinary terms, and that may be adequate for some readers. What would the category include? Certainly hamburgers, and probably Southern fried chicken, and clam chowders and baked beans, steak, ribs, and perhaps chili, and hot dogs, and, now, pizza, and baked potatoes with "the works." We would have a dessert list beginning with apple pie, and we could have many dishes based on maize. But there is no need to enumerate here all of the dishes that might be on the list because there are so many good American cookbooks that do the job, and no end of irrepressible enthusiasts.[3] Despite those things, however, the list of ten favorite lunch and dinner "entrées" for 1994, collected by the NPD market research group, starts off with pizza and ham sandwiches and hot dogs, and ends with cheese sandwiches, hamburger sandwiches, and spaghetti. I don't think anyone wants to call that array a cuisine.

Of the items on any more serious list, nearly all of the dishes would be assignable to regional cuisines, which is as it should be: all so-called national cuisines take from regional cuisines. The maize dishes, lobsters and terrapins, the steaks and pork roasts, the Boston baked beans, soft shell crabs and Manhattan clam chowders would all deserve to be here. But regional cuisines in the United States have undergone great change in the last half century, most of it diluting or modifying the cuisines themselves. The destruction of native stocks of such foods as salmon, shad, striped bass, terrapin, and crabs has seriously undermined regional cuisines, for instance. But even more has been done to change them by commercialization, a major debilitating influence.

Local variation in cuisine is under continuous pressure from commercial enterprise aimed at profiting by turning into a national fad every localized taste opportunity. Any natural product that is available in a place or a season, and any distinctive cooking or flavoring method, excites merchants, packers, and processors intent on broadening their market. Of course not all of the products travel, and many do not travel well. In the view of food businessmen it makes good sense to alter the nature of such goods in order to make them available elsewhere, even if they no longer are (or taste like) what they were at home. In the course of the "development" of these new goods, their character is altered, and the manner in which they had been prepared is likely to be modified—more commonly, simplified or abandoned. In many cases the new product is no longer the same as the old product, and is prepared in new ways, which are reduced and cheapened versions of the old ways. What happened in recent years with "blackened redfish" is a fair example: swift vulgarization of its preparation, substitution of other fish for redfish, cheapening of the recipe, and another fad soon forgotten. The regional foods most likely to remain more authentic are exactly the ones that cannot be shipped, or do not travel well, or are either difficult or impossible to copy. But not surprisingly, that they are difficult or impossible to copy has never discouraged a North American food salesman. Hence certain foods that are regionally distinctive become known to people elsewhere who have never eaten them except in the form of substitutes lacking any resemblance at all to the original.

Such bowdlerization of food is still less frequent in Europe and elsewhere. While restaurants in northern Germany may vaunt their Bavarian dishes, retail food markets are not likely to sell modified variants of Bavarian food. The same is true for France, and indeed for all of Europe. While one can eat *bouillabaisse* in a Paris restaurant that resembles *bouillabaisse* in Marseille, the retail food stores of Paris do not yet offer Parisians a *bouillabaisse* "exactly like the one you ate in Nice, that you can now make at home—and in just minutes!" To be sure, perhaps they soon will, so strong are the pressures to "modernize." But I suspect that commercialization of this sort has been especially effective in the United States because we lack a standard cuisine against which to test the sales pitch. Given our heterogeneous origins, with what do we compare a new food, when deciding whether to try it (or, for that matter, whether we like it)?

It is easy to romanticize the food of other cultures, and to underemphasize worldwide trends toward westernized food patterns. We Americans are probably not so exceptional as I may seem to make us out to be. But in much of the world the food repertory is still more closely tied to seasonal availability. There are still large populations subsisting on foods drawn from a relatively narrow geographical region. In many vast areas elsewhere there are peoples who still cook in more and eat out less than we, and whose diet contains one or several staple foods eaten every day, perhaps even at every meal. Such people are differently equipped from most of us to judge any new food.

By "most of us" I mean here literate Americans of the middle class, probably with some college education, travel experience, and familiarity with ethnic restaurants. We are not given to judge each food novelty against a background of commonly recognized foods that we all eat frequently. We tend to try new foods, seeking novelty in eating, as we do in so many aspects of life. We are inclined to identify that novelty with knowingness, with sophistication; and certainly being open to new experience is a good value, most of the time. Because of our openness and the dynamism of the food vendors, in the United States in recent years consumers have learned about hummus, falafel, bagels, "designer" coffees, coriander, basil, arugula and radicchio, Jerusalem artichokes, jicama, quinoa, buckwheat groats, new rice varieties (jasmine, arborio, basmati), lactose-free milk, scones and other sweet breads (not sweetbreads!), breads baked with ingredients such as tomatoes or olives, a staggering variety of capsicums, soy milk, tofu and dried soy products, previously neglected seafoods such as monkfish, "artificial" crabmeat (surimi), and many subtropical fruits, such as mangoes, soursops, red bananas, and star apples, and a dizzying number of packaged foods designed to relieve our worries, especially about fiber and fats.

We may each individually decide which items in this cornucopia we like, and which we do not like. Some of us may even take up cooking or using one or another of them in our meals at home. If so, such foods will not be jostling with our cuisine; they will be jostling with our quiche, our pasta, our chicken breasts, our hamburgers, our peanut butter-and-jelly sandwiches, our barbecues, our steaks, our ham sandwiches, and our yogurt. These are among the things we eat the most. We can, if we wish, call them our cuisine.

As suggested earlier in this book, I do not see how a cuisine can exist unless there is a community of people who eat it, cook it, have opinions about it, and engage in dialogue involving those opinions. This is not to say that people cannot debate the merits of various restaurant renderings of *quesadillas* or *chao dze*; but that is not the same as having a cuisine. On the one hand, then, the regional cuisines of which we may speak have tended to lose some of their distinctiveness in the dilution and "nationalizing" of regional specialities. On the other, I do not believe that any genuine national cuisine has emerged as yet from this process. We do have a list of favorite foods, which we eat all of the time, and that list is broadly representative nationally; I have already enumerated most of it.

29

What, then, does typify American eating habits? It is clear that class, regional, and ethnic differences profoundly affect differences in eating behavior. A noticeable number of Americans now seek organically grown fruits and vegetables. About 7 percent of the nation is said to be vegetarian. Many people eat along lines prescribed by religious identity; others—but nowhere near so many as we may think—take considerations of health very seriously in the way they eat. There are also differences at the group level which betray class origins or class prejudices. In alcoholic choices, the attention paid to bread, the label-reading habit, the intense concern about weight, the sympathy toward vegetarianism, and the respect given "foreign" foods, some segments of the American middle class exhibit difference. But for the majority of the American people (including many in the above list), the following features are probably correct: eating out frequently, often choosing fast foods, as well as ordering take-out food to eat at home; eating much prepared and packaged foods, which require only intense heat or nothing at all to be "cooked"; continuing to eat diets high in animal protein, salt, fats, and processed sugars, low in fresh fruits and vegetables; drinking more soda than tap water; and consuming substantial quantities of labeled (low fat no cholesterol fat free lots of fiber no palm oil good for you) foods, packaged to encourage the consumer to feel less guilty about what he is really choosing to eat.

This list is discouraging and negativistic; of course not everyone eats this way, or all of the time. But it is worth pondering the fact that food labeling, and considerable publicity about healthier eating, have not significantly affected food habits nationally, at least not yet. The ten major sources of calories in the United States diet, according to the Department of Agriculture, are whole and low-fat milk; white bread, white flour, rolls, and buns; soft drinks, margarine, and sugar; and ground beef and American cheese. Such a list is worrisome, at the very least on health grounds, especially because of the fats and sugars. But if you are a reader who reacts by saying to herself, "But I never eat *any* of that stuff!"—then ask yourself who does.

The importance of sugar and fats in the American diet is striking, particularly in view of the educational efforts to warn people of the need for moderation in these regards. During the twentieth century in this country, increases in fats and sugar consumption have accompanied a progressive decline in the consumption of complex carbohydrates (Cantor and Cantor 1977; Page and Friend 1974). Carbohydrate consumption in the years 1910 to 1913 was two-thirds potatoes, wheat products, and other such "starchy" foods, and one-third sugar, the so-called simple carbohydrate. By the nineties, however, the share of complex carbohydrates was down to half, that of sugars up to half. Over time, more and more of what was left of complex carbohydrate consumption took the form of deep-fried, salted, and sweetened particles, so much so as to produce a special name, "munchies," for such foods. Though there are annual variations in fat and sugar consumption, both average figures have remained high since the end of rationing after World War II. In 1991, Americans consumed 164.9 pounds per person of sweeteners, and of those, 140.6 pounds were calorie-carrying (as opposed to noncaloric) sweets. If the Institute of Shortening and Edible Oils is right in its estimate that fats consumption (in meat and dairy, and in bottles and packages—that is, both "visible" and "invisible" fats) for 1993 was 137 to 138 pounds, then when combined with caloric sugars the total fats and sugars figure is 277.6 pounds per person per year. While this figure is based on disappearance statistics (thus probably overestimating actual consumption), it is nonetheless astonishingly high. The secular shift toward fats and sugars has been accompanied in turn by significant increases in the average weights of both men and women. Many authorities now estimate one in three Americans to be twenty or more pounds—that is, clinically—overweight. The implications for health and health costs of these statistics are now so well known that there is no need to review them here.

Americans also continue to increase the frequency with which they eat out, and the frequency with which they eat in fast-food restaurants. The numbers are interesting: in 1993, 6 percent of total per capita income was spent by Americans in restaurants; only 7.2 percent—1.2 percent more—was spent on food eaten at home. (Incidentally, spending only 13.2 percent of total income on food is an astonishingly low figure, when compared worldwide.) Eating out, Americans had 793,000 "eating places" (including here not only hot dog stands but also army mess halls) to choose from; and in them they spent 276 billion dollars.

While individual customers choose freely what they eat, they must do so in terms of what the food service offers. Eating out reduces the individual's ability to choose the *ingredients* in her food, even though it may increase the length of the menu from which she can choose. The tendency to snack remains important in American eating habits; indeed, some weakening of the luncheon pattern may be attributable to the strengthening of the morning and afternoon "breaks" (Mintz 1982), with the effect of making fast food at noon a more attractive option. In 1993 snack food sales reached a gross of nearly fifteen billion dollars. Drink patterns in 1994 were consistent: 49.6 gallons of soft drinks, followed by 31.3 gallons of tap water, 26 gallons of coffee, 22.5 gallons of beer, and 19.1 gallons of milk.

The Department of Agriculture predicted a rise in per capita beef consumption in 1995, following 1994's 67.3 pounds. Beef consumption dipped in the years 1991 to

1993, but it is now rising again. Pork consumption is also expected to rise, as is chicken. Pork consumption had dipped slightly in 1990 to 1991, but it rose again in 1992 and has stayed up; chicken consumption has simply continued to rise steadily. Increases in meat consumption are paralleled by increases in the consumption of low-fat products—*any* low-fat products. Nabisco's Snackwells, with sales of 400 million dollars in 1994, are a glowing illustration. This seemingly contradictory behavior tends to substantiate an earlier assertion: people are both eating what they feel they want and buying other foods in order to feel less guilty. They're eating *them*, too.

The dizzying overdifferentiation of food actually increases sales enormously and, as I have pointed out elsewhere, is rationalized as giving the consumer what she wants:

> Making the product "right" for the consumer requires continuous redefinition and division of the groups in which he, as an individual consumer, defines himself. The deliberate postulation of new groups—often divisions between already familiar categories, as "pre-teens" were created between "teenagers" and younger children— helps to impart reality to what are supposedly new needs. "New" foods, as in the sequence skim milk:half and half:light (table) cream:heavy (whipping) cream split differences in order to create new needs. New medicines, as in the treatment of daytime headaches and nighttime headaches or daytime colds and nighttime colds, do the same. (Mintz 1982, 158)

31

In all of the processes connected with American eating, the element of *time* is extremely relevant, yet barely noticed. When Americans speak of "convenience" in regard to food, they also mean time. It is simply assumed by most of us that we have too little time. I have argued elsewhere that the insistence upon the shortness of time and the pressures of busyness in American life is in one sense completely spurious. Americans are repeatedly told that they do not have enough time, I think because it serves to increase their aggregate consumption. Doing several things at once is touted as evidence of leadership; but what it does for the economy is to increase consumption. People are supposed to be able to drink coffee and talk on the telephone while they drive, smoke while they read, and listen to music while they exercise. Vaunting such skill makes good corporate advertising sense; people use up more stuff that way. No one seems impressed by the fact that Mozart didn't chew gum or watch TV while he was writing piano concertos.

As with anything else, not having the time to eat is a function of how much time is thought to be needed for other things. To take the easiest example, Americans would have more time to cook and to eat if they spent less time watching television. The shortness of time is in many ways, then, a coefficient of a view that our time is in short supply, but also already appropriately distributed. Most "convenience food" is successful because of prior conceptions about time. But much such food would not succeed if Americans cared more about how and what they ate. That they do not is a fact of great importance; it implies not only that they lack a cuisine, but also that they probably will never have one. What does the American future hold, so far as eating is concerned?

In a series of brilliant recent papers, Cornell University scientist David Pimentel and his colleagues have predicted sweeping changes in American agriculture, and hence in American eating patterns over the next half century.[4] Indeed, the changes that these scientists forecast, if they do occur, will be more radical in their effects on American eating than even those of the last half century—which is to say a very great deal. Demographic, agricultural, and other factors enter in. Pimentel and his colleagues, working from present trends, predict a doubling of the national population by 2064; a reduction in arable land (through both erosion and urbanization) in the neighborhood of 180,000,000 acres, or 38 percent, in the same period of time; and a total exhaustion of national fossil fuel resources in not more than two decades. The figures on rapidly diminishing water supply are similarly worrisome.

This is an unbelievably grim scenario. If it eventuates, food exports (now calculated at an average of about $155 per person per year, given our present population) would be reduced to zero. For Americans, food costs would increase by a factor of between three and five—at worst, up to more than half of total income. Should these calculations prove correct, however, the *composition* of the American diet would also have to change substantially. While nearly two-thirds of the national grain product of the United States, grown on over 100 million acres, is now used as livestock feed, by 2060 all of it would have become food for us, not for our cattle and pigs and poultry. In effect, Pimentel sees North Americans coming to eat as most of the rest of the world eats, with meat representing a much reduced fraction of our total caloric and protein intake. Since India's nearly one billion people and the People's Republic of China's even larger population get 70 to 80 percent of their calories and nearly all of their protein from grains and legumes, such a change in the United States would be in the direction of aligning North American consumption with that of the rest of the world. It would also contribute to a vast improvement in American health. Substantial farmland could be returned to agriculture; the number of bypass and cancer operations would certainly decline.

But will it happen? As I write, McDonald's looks ahead to a rapid expansion of its enterprises in such places as the People's Republic of China, where it aims to add 600 retail establishments in the next decade, and Japan, where it now boasts more than a thousand. Whatever the scenario for the United States, many companies are working hard to spread our way of eating worldwide. Nor is there evidence that many Americans are much concerned, either about our fossil fuel consumption or our diet. Driving cars and eating meat are highly valued acts; though both involve the expenditure of unimaginably large quantities of water, soil, cereals, and fossil fuel, there is no collective indication that anyone is deeply concerned. Only sudden shortages reveal, as if in lightning flashes, how deeply held such consumption values are; Operation Desert Storm was a case in point. Indeed, one "solution" to the Pimentel prophecies is war. Successful aggression could keep meat and gas available and affordable, at least for a good while longer. Its effects on American moral integrity would be utterly disastrous. But the enormity of the decisions involved in such trade-offs would not be clearly grasped until *after* the decisions were made. There is a real trap in our not separating what we are free to do, but need not do, if it is a bad idea—from what we cannot help doing, *even though* it is a bad idea, because we think someone is trying to stop us from doing it.

No one can look down the road and predict how the American people will behave, fifty years from now. One sinister prophecy is embodied in the words of Josef Joffe, the editorial page editor of *Süddeutsche Zeitung*, who writes: "It is profligacy—being hooked on the sweet poison of consumption—that might yet lay low the American economy and thus American might."[5] But the worry is not that we will let our consumption gluttony destroy our economy; it is, rather, that we might let our obsessive notions of individual freedom destroy our democracy. The long-term lessons of our economic and agricultural policies are there to be learned now. But we have to be willing to learn them.

NOTES

1. We Americans—we people of the United States—need to be reminded all of the time that the term "American," which we unconsciously claim as our own, is used by everybody else in this hemisphere. Our neighbors to the south feel with justice that they have an equal claim upon it. Hispanic Americans use the term "North American" to refer to us North Americans, as well as to Canadians. Most Canadians are prepared to call us Americans because they consider themselves Canadians. From here on I will use "American" to mean "North American."
2. The historical literature on North American food and eating is substantial and impressive. A charming place to begin is with Arthur M. Schlesinger's "Food in the Making of America" (1964).
3. A genuine difficulty with my own line of argument is how discouraging—and probably elitist—it may seem to those who truly want to see an American cuisine take shape. It would be easy to conclude that I object to the *idea* of an American cuisine, when in fact I only think it is impossible now to create one. The people who believe we can create a cuisine also believe, and with more reason, that American *cuisines* (in the plural) once existed. No reader of Betty Fussell's *I Hear America Cooking* (1986) can deny the still-visible roots of regional culinary distinction she uncovers. Such works as Damon Lee Fowler's *Classical Southern Cooking* (1995) and Edna Lewis's wonderful *In Pursuit of Flavor* (1988) are eloquent defenses of Southern cuisine. But I do not believe that an American cuisine either preexisted, or has arisen from, regional American cooking. Christopher Kendall, the eloquent publisher and editor of *Cook's Illustrated*, discusses these issues thoughtfully. But I think that his conclusions end up making my point. "It is my belief," he writes:

   > that at six o'clock in the evening most adult Americans are standing on common ground. We need to get a good dinner on the table, and it makes little difference where we live or who our ancestors were. For better or for worse, we share a modern lifestyle and therefore share the need for a modern American cuisine. Let's stop running helter-skelter down the road to diversity, a path that leads to culinary anarchy. Culinary elitism offers no answers to our culinary dilemma.
   >
   > Anyone who doubts the value of a melting-pot cuisine should consider Thanksgiving, the one holiday most Americans cherish. In the simplest terms, Thanksgiving is about 240 million people eating the same menu on the same day. We compare notes on how the turkey was cooked, on the flakiness of the pumpkin pie crust, and on the components of the stuffing. It feels good to share the menu with our neighbors. Despite the abundance on the table, it's also a meal that has echoes of our ancestral frugality; the leftovers are eagerly consumed over the long weekend.
   >
   > As a culture, we gain much from a shared cuisine. It helps to bind us together in a time when we are constantly being pulled apart by expressing our individuality. We should heed the lessons of Thanksgiving. Let's give thanks for our own foods, reflect on the practical legacy of our culinary past, and then set out to retool American cooking for the next century. But let's do it together. We are in desperate need of common ground. [Kendall 1995, I]

   Kendall roots for what we haven't got yet, while telling us we can get it because we've already got it. I wish I could be convinced that he is right.
4. See Pimentel and Giampietro 1994a; Giampietro and Pimentel n.d.; Pimentel, Harman, Pacenza, Pecarsky, and Pimentel 1994; Kendall and Pimentel 1994; Pimentel and Giampietro 1994b.
5. *New York Times*, April 25, 1995, A23.

REFERENCES

Cantor, Sidney and Michael Cantor. 1997. Socioeconomic factors in fat and sugar consumption. In *The Chemical Senses and Nutrition*, ed. M. Kate and O. Maller. New York: Academic Press.

Giampietro, Mario and David Pimentel. n.d. The Tightening Conflict: Population, Energy Use, and the Ecoology of Agriculture. *NPG Forum.*

Kendall, Christopher. 1995. Common Ground. *Cooks Magazine* 13:1.

Kendall, Henry W. and David Pimentel. 1994. Constraints on the Expansion of the Global Food Supply. *Ambio* 23, 3:198–205.

Mintz, Sidney W. 1982. Choice and occasion: Sweet moments. In *The Psychobiology of Human Food Selection*, ed. Lewis M. Barker. Westport, Conn: Avi Publishing Co.

Page, Louise and Berta Friend. 1974. Level of use of sugars in the United States. In *Sugars in Nutrition*, ed. H. L. Sipple and K. W. McNutt. New York: Academic Press, pp. 93–107.

Pimentel, David and Mario Giampietro. 1994a. U.S. Population Growth Threatens Irreplaceable Farmland. *Clearinghouse Bulletin* 4, 11.

Pimentel, David and Mario Giampietro. 1994b. Food, Land, Population and the U. S. Economy. Washington, DC: Carrying Capacity Network.

Pimentel, David, Rebecca Harman, Matthew Pacenza, Jason Pecarsky, and Marcia Pimentel. 1994. Natural Resources and an Optimum Human Population. *Population and Environment* 15, 5:347–69.

Schlesinger, Arthur M. 1964. Food in the Making of America. Pp. 220–40, in his *Paths to the Present*. Cambridge: Houghton Mifflin.

WHAT DO WE EAT?

DONNA GABACCIA

In 1989, hungry Houstonians learned they could buy "New York deli" without leaving town—at the newly opened Guggenheim's Delicatessen. The restaurateur offering bagels, rugelach, herring, corned beef, and cheese cake at Guggenheim's was Ghulam Bombaywala, an immigrant from Pakistan. Bombaywala had already worked for years in a Houston steakhouse and a local Italian restaurant and had also operated a small chain of Mexican restaurants. Before opening Guggenheim's, Bombaywala went to New York to do his own research, eating in different delis three meals a day for five days. Back in Houston, Bombaywala sought partners, and he borrowed the recipes for Guggenheim's from one of them, a Mrs. Katz.[1] Bombaywala did not seem to know that Germans, not Eastern European Jews, had opened New York's first delicatessens. And needless to say, most Houstonians devouring Guggenheim's New York deli were neither Germans, Eastern Europeans, Jews, nor New Yorkers. But then neither was Bombaywala.

The same year, three transplanted easterners with suspiciously Italian-sounding names—Paul Sorrentino, Rob Geresi, and Vince Vrana—opened their own New York Bagel Shop and Delicatessen in Oklahoma. Bagels packaged by Lender's had been available for years in local frozen food compartments, as were advertisements offering recipes for "pizzles," made of frozen bagels topped with canned tomato sauce. As businessmen looking for a market niche, Sorrentino, Geresi, and Vrana wagered that the most knowledgeable and sophisticated of Oklahoman consumers would enjoy freshly baked "New York–style" bagels, which were chewier than their frozen counterparts. Like many retailers in the South and West, however, their New York Bagel Shop and Delicatessen offered bagels with sandwich fillings—everything from cream cheese to "California-style" avocado and sprouts.[2]

Meanwhile, in far-off Jerusalem, a New Yorker, Gary Heller, concluded that Israelis too could appreciate bagels, given an opportunity. Importing frozen dough from Manhattan's Upper West Side H & H Bagels (begun in 1972 by the brothers-in-law Helmer Toro and Hector Hernandez), Heller did the final baking of his bagels in Israel. He quickly acquired orders from a national supermarket chain and from Dunkin' Donuts, which was about to open its first Tel Aviv franchise. After a long journey from Eastern European bakeries through the multiethnic delis of New York and the factories of a modern food industry, the bagel had arrived in the new Jewish homeland.

Heller knew that Americans transplanted to Israel would buy his bagels, but to make a profit, he had to sell 160,000 of them to native consumers, in competition with a local brand under license from Lender's Bagels. As Heller noted, Jews born in Israel (sabras) "think bagels are American, not Jewish." Israelis knew "bagele"—the closest local products—only as hard, salt-covered rounds, unlike Heller's product, or as soft sesame ellipses. And these, ironically, were baked and sold by Arabs.[3]

A grumpy cultural observer pauses at this point, well-armed for a diatribe on the annoying confusions of postmodern identities in the 1990s. It is easy to harrumph, as Octavio Paz once did, that "the melting pot is a social ideal that, when applied to culinary art, produces abominations"—bagel pizzas and bagels topped with avocado and sprouts surely qualify.[4] Paz would find a typical American's eating day an equally abominable multiethnic smorgasbord. The menu might include a bagel, cream cheese, and cappuccino at breakfast; a soft drink with hamburger and corn chips, or pizza and Greek salad, at lunch; and meat loaf, stir-fried "vegetables orientale" (from the frozen foods section of the supermarket), and apple pie for dinner. Wasn't eating better when delicatessens served sausages to Germans, when Bubbie purchased bagels at a kosher bakery, and when only her Jewish children and grandchildren ate them, uncorrupted by Philadelphia cream cheese? When Houston savored chili from "Tex-Mex" vendors? When only Oklahomans ate their beef and barbecue? And when neither pizza, tacos, nor bagels came from corporate "huts" or "bells," let alone a Dunkin' Donuts in Tel Aviv?

As a historian of American eating habits, I must quickly answer any potentially grumpy critics with a resounding no. The American penchant to experiment with foods, to combine and mix the foods of many cultural traditions into blended gumbos or stews, and to create "smorgasbords" is scarcely new but is rather a recurring theme in our history as eaters.

Consider, for example, the earlier history of the bagel. It is true that in the 1890s in the United States only Jews from Eastern Europe ate bagels. In thousands of nondescript bakeries—including the one founded in New Haven around 1926 by Harry Lender from Lublin, Poland—Jewish bakers sold bagels to Jewish consumers. The bagel was not a central culinary icon for Jewish immigrants; even before Polish and Russian Jews left their ethnic enclaves or ghettoes, their memories exalted gefilte fish and chicken soup prepared by their mothers, but not the humble, hard rolls purchased from the immigrant baker. As eaters, Jewish immigrants were initially far more concerned with the purity of their kosher meat, their challah, and their matzos, and with the satisfactions of their sabbath and holiday meals, than with their morning hard roll. They and their children seemed more interested in learning to use Crisco or eat egg rolls and chicken chow mein than in affirming the bagel as a symbol of Jewish life or as a contribution to American cuisine.

Still, the bagel did become an icon of urban, northeastern eating, a key ingredient of the multiethnic mix that in this century became known as "New York deli." The immigrant neighbors of Eastern European Jewish bakers were among the first to discover the bagel and to begin its transformation from a Jewish specialty into an American food. Unconvinced by the turn-of-the-century arguments of home economists that Americanization required them to adopt recipes for codfish and other

New England–inspired delicacies, consumers from many backgrounds began instead to sample culinary treats, like the bagel, for sale in their own multiethnic home cities. In New Haven, by the mid-1940s, for example, the Lenders' bakery employed six family workers, including Harry's sons Murray and Markin, who still lived at home behind the store. Hand-rolling bagels and boiling them before baking, two workers could produce about 120 bagels an hour, enough to allow the Lenders to meet expanding demand from their curious Italian, Irish, and Russian neighbors. The Lenders soon produced 200 dozen bagels daily.

No one knows who first slathered bagels with cream cheese—a product introduced and developed by English Quakers in their settlements in the Delaware Valley and Philadelphia in the eighteenth century. The blend of old and new, however, proved popular with a wide range of American consumers. With a firm grasp on regional marketing, Harry Lender's sons reorganized the family business in 1962 and decided to seek a national market. They purchased new machines that could produce 400 bagels an hour. The machines eliminated hand-rolling and substituted steaming for boiling. Flash-freezing and packaging in plastic bags for distribution to supermarkets around the country soon followed.

When union bagel bakers protested the introduction of the new machines, bagel manufacturers responded by moving production outside the Northeast. Along with the manufacturers of "Jewish" rye bread and other products common to deli display cases, the Lenders had learned "You don't have to be Jewish" to purchase and enjoy Jewish foods. With mass production for a mass market, they learned "You don't have to be Jewish" to produce them, either. In the late 1970s, Lender's was still family-owned and managed, but it employed 300 nonunionized and mainly non-Jewish workers.

In 1984 Kraft purchased Lender's as a corporate companion for its Philadelphia brand cream cheese. All over the country, consumers could now buy a totally standardized, mass-produced bagel under the Lender's label. A bagel, complained Nach Waxman, owner of a New York cookbook store, with "no crust, no character, no nothing."[5] This was a softer bagel, and—like most American breads—sweetened with sugar. Following in the tradition of the long-popular breakfast muffin, bagels emerged from factories in a variety of flavors associated with desserts and breakfast cereals—honey, raisin, blueberry, cinnamon.[6] Sun-dried tomato bagels followed in the 1990s, along with other popular flavors inspired by Mediterranean cuisines. Broney Gadman, a Long Island manufacturer of bagel-steaming equipment, believed that American consumers wanted a bland bagel. They were "used to hamburger rolls, hot-dog buns and white bread," he explained. "They prefer a less crusty, less chewy, less tough product—You needed good teeth" to eat hand-rolled and boiled bagels.[7]

Waxman and Gadman made a sharp distinction between mass-produced factory bagels (or cinnamon and sun-dried-tomato bagels) and "the real thing." They preferred authenticity, as defined by their memories of bagels in the Jewish ghettoes of the past. As millions of Americans with no bagel eaters in their family trees snapped up Kraft's Lender's brand, and as sabras came to appreciate American bagels at Dunkin' Donuts in Tel Aviv, Bubbie's descendants, along with a multiethnic crowd of well-educated Americans fascinated with traditional ethnic foods, searched elsewhere for their culinary roots and a chewier bagel.

Some of them found authenticity with Bombaywala's renditions of Mrs. Katz's recipes. Others discovered they could buy "real" bagels again from the Lenders. For Murray and Markin Lender chose not to follow their family brand into employment with corporate Kraft. Instead, they opened a suburban restaurant that offered, among other things, a bagel of crust and character, ideal for Nach Waxman. A host of

37

small businessmen like Bombaywala and the Lender brothers revived hand-rolling and boiling, sometimes in full view of their customers.

The history of the bagel suggests that Americans' shifting, blended, multiethnic eating habits are signs neither of postmodern decadence, ethnic fragmentation, nor corporate hegemony. If we do not understand how a bagel could sometimes be Jewish, sometimes be "New York," and sometimes be American, or why it is that Pakistanis now sell bagels to both Anglos and Tejanos in Houston, it is in part because we have too hastily assumed that our tendency to cross cultural boundaries in order to eat ethnic foods is a recent development—and a culinary symptom of all that has gone wrong with contemporary culture.

It is not. The bagel tells a different kind of American tale. It highlights ways that the production, exchange, marketing, and consumption of food have generated new identities—for foods and eaters alike. Looking at bagels in this light, we see that they became firmly identified as "Jewish" only as Jewish bakers began selling them to their multiethnic urban neighbors. When bagels emerged from ghetto stores as a Jewish novelty, bagels with cream cheese quickly became a staple of the cuisine known as "New York deli," and was marketed and mass-produced throughout the country under this new regional identity. When international trade brought bagels to Israel, they acquired a third identity as "American." And finally, coming full circle, so to speak, the bagel's Americanization sent purists off in search of bagels that seemed more authentically "New York Jewish."

If the identity of bagels emerged from an evolving marketplace, can we say the same of bagel eaters' identities? What, after all, does "what we eat" tell us about "who we are"? Again, too easily, we assume a recent, sharp departure into culinary eclecticism or consumerist individualism from the natural, conservative, and ethnically rigid eating habits of the past. In fact, eating habits changed and evolved long before the rise of a modern consumer market for food. Human eating habits originate in a paradoxical, and perhaps universal, tension between a preference for the culinarily familiar and the equally human pursuit of pleasure in the forms of culinary novelty, creativity, and variety.

Neither the anthropologist nor the man on the street doubts that humans can be picky eaters, or that humans can exhibit considerable conservatism in their food choices. If you doubt popular wisdom, imagine serving a plate of tripe, corn fungus, or caterpillars at a diner in Garrison Keillor's Lake Woebegone. Psychologists tell us that food and language are the cultural traits humans learn first, and the ones that they change with the greatest reluctance. Humans cannot easily lose their accents when they learn new languages after the age of about twelve; similarly, the food they ate as children forever defines familiarity and comfort.

But cultural conservatism, while it cannot be ignored, cannot explain the history of the bagel, where instead we see evidence of human adaptability and curiosity. Cooks know this combination well: they substitute ingredients when necessary, even in well-loved recipes; they "play with their food" on occasion, just for the pleasure of finding new tastes. When people of differing foodways come together, whether cooks or merely eaters, they will almost invariably peek into one another's kitchens. They will not like all they find, but they are usually curious and excited to try some of it.

Two closely related histories—of recurring human migrations and of changes in the production and marketing of food—help us to understand why and how

American eating habits, and identities, have evolved over time. The migrations sparked by the European empires of the sixteenth and seventeenth centuries mixed the foodways of Spanish and indigenous Americans in today's Southwest and Florida; English, French, Dutch, or German culinary traditions were combined with Indian practices in the Northeast; and African, English, Scotch-Irish, French, and Native American eating habits influenced the cuisine of the Southeast. During the long nineteenth century, successive waves of Irish, British, German, Scandinavians, Slavs, Italians, Jews, Chinese, Japanese, and Mexicans changed the face, and the eating patterns, of American farmlands and cities. In the early decades of this century, though restrictive laws lessened immigration from Europe and Asia, internal migrations of southern white and black sharecroppers to Detroit and New York, and of foreclosed "Okies" and "Arkies" to the West, transferred eating habits from one American region to another. And in today's world, again, new immigrants from Asia, the Caribbean, and Latin America bring the smells and tastes of their homeland cuisines to Miami, New York, Minneapolis, and Los Angeles.

39

Four hundred years ago climate and terrain placed harsh restraints on local eaters, reinforcing regional identities, and even today we do not expect Iowans to fish for cod, or eat much of it. The United States remains a nation of many regional environments, and its culinary and ethnic history has been shaped by regionalism, reinforced by territorial expansion from the Atlantic to the Pacific, and then beyond to Alaska and Hawaii. Already in 1550, however, sugar traveled the world because merchants could make huge profits by offering it for sale in nontropical climes. Today, changing technology, the use of fertilizer, and plant and animal breeding have vastly altered any local environment's impact on farming and consuming. Although regional eating habits persist in the United States, they are no longer straightforward reflections of a seaside location or a prairie continental climate.

If our eating is more homogeneous today than in the past, we can thank (or blame) a national marketplace through which the standardized foods of modern food industries have circulated. As farms gave way to "factories in the field," as huge canneries replaced women's domestic labor, and as the corner grocery store gradually gave way to supermarkets, the most ambitious businessmen, regardless of cultural origin, dreamed of capturing regional, and then national, markets by producing a few food items in massive quantities. Corporate food business fostered standardized foods and national connections, while migrations repeatedly introduced new sources of culinary diversity. Migrations also produced new "communities of consumption," which generated small businesses to serve their taste for distinctive foods.[8] Today, food corporations position themselves to compete in a wide variety of market segments defined by ethnicity, gender, age, and income. Yet their most successful competitors are small businessmen like Ghulam Bombaywala and the Lenders, whom many consumers trust to deliver "the real thing."

Commercial food exchanges neither created nor eliminated the fundamental tension between our longing for both familiar and novel foods. While mass production delivered huge quantities of a few standardized, processed foods, expanding markets also linked producers and consumers of diverse backgrounds and tastes, opening opportunities for new blends, new juxtapositions, new borrowing. Food businesses large and small have lured adventurous consumers with novelties while soothing others with traditional foods. American eaters' search for the familiar and the novel became matters of consumer choice, just as producers' and retailers' experiments with both innovation and traditional techniques became marketing strategies.

It is easiest to see how food choices reflect the eater's identity when we focus on culinary conservatism. Humans cling tenaciously to familiar foods because they become associated with nearly every dimension of human social and cultural life. Whether in New Guinea or New Bedford, humans share particular foods with families and friends; they pursue good health through unique diets; they pass on food lore, and create stories and myths about food's meaning and taste; they celebrate rites of passage and religious beliefs with distinctive dishes. Food thus entwines intimately with much that makes a culture unique, binding taste and satiety to group loyalties. Eating habits both symbolize and mark the boundaries of cultures. Scholars and ordinary people alike have long seen food habits, both positively and negatively, as concrete symbols of human culture and identity. When we want to celebrate, or elevate, our own group, we usually praise its superior cuisine. And when we want to demean one another, often we turn to eating habits; in the United States we have labeled Germans as "krauts," Italians as "spaghetti-benders," Frenchmen as "frogs," and British as "limeys."

40

To understand changing American identities, we must explore also the symbolic power of food to reflect cultural or social affinities in moments of change or transformation. Today, as in the days of the Columbian exchanges, Americans eat what students of linguistics call a "creole," or what cooks describe as a gumbo or a stew. We quite willingly "eat the other"—or at least some parts of some others, some of the time. Eating habits like these suggest tolerance and curiosity, and a willingness to digest, and to make part of one's individual identity, the multiethnic dishes Paz deplored. As food consumers, Americans seem as interested in idiosyncratic and individualistic affiliations to the foodways of their neighbors as they are in their own ethnic and regional roots. Ultimately, then, as students of American eating we must not only understand what we eat, and celebrate the many ethnic reflections of who we are, but we must also understand the roots of our multiethnic creole foodways, and ask of them, too, "If we are what we eat, who are we?"

NOTES

1. Lisa Belkin, "A Slice of New York (On Rye) in Texas," *New York Times*, September 6, 1989.
2. Terri L. Darrow, "Cowboys and Bagels," *Restaurant Hospitality* 73, 5 (May 1989): 30.
3. David B. Green, "Betting That Lots of Israelis Will Take to American Bagels," *New York Times*, July 31, 1996.
4. Octavio Paz, "At Table and in Bed," in *Convergences: Essays on Art and Literature* (Orlando: Harcourt, Brace, and Jovanovich, 1987), pp. 68–99.
5. Molly O'Neill, "Bagels Are Now Fast Food, and Purists Do a Slow Boil," *New York Times*, April 25, 1993.
6. See foreword by Murray Lender in Nao Hauser and Sue Spitler, *Bagels! Bagels! and More Bagels!* (Chicago: Rand McNally, 1979).
7. Daniel Young, "The Bagel's New York Accent Is Fading," *New York Times*, September 6, 1989.
8. Here I borrow from Daniel Boorstin, *The Democratic Experience* (New York: Random House, 1973), pp. 89–114, 145–148.

THE INVENTION OF THANKSGIVING:

A RITUAL OF AMERICAN NATIONALITY

JANET SISKIND

5

Though traditions are invented and nations imagined, Thanksgiving is a day on which all persons who consider themselves Americans celebrate or avoid a ritual family feast, centered around a stuffed turkey. For many it is a four-day holiday, a precious long weekend. Football games are scheduled and televised throughout the nation; an elaborately constructed, now-traditional Macy's parade may be viewed. There are special services, which some attend, and turkeys and other foods are given by churches and other charitable organizations to the poor. Servicemen overseas are fed the traditional Thanksgiving dinner at great public expense. There are those who counterculturally contest the mythic representations of this day; there are those who firmly decide *not* to go home or *not* to eat turkey, but it is impossible to be an American and be unaware of Thanksgiving. If "American culture is whatever one cannot escape in the United States" (Varenne, 1986: 6), then Thanksgiving is inescapably part of American culture.

Thanksgiving and July 4th are the two most important, purely American, holidays, celebrated only and by all those who consider themselves American citizens. July 4th is an occasion for politicians, backyard barbecues and marching bands. It usually provides a welcome three-day summer weekend, but it is no longer, as it was once, a serious ritual event. Thanksgiving far more subtly expresses and reaffirms values and assumptions about cultural and social unity, about identity and history, about inclusion and exclusion. Thanksgiving is highly structured and emotion laden, with its celebration of family, home and nation. Though for some people Thanksgiving is a secular celebration, for most it is also religious (in the common anthropological sense of making reference to the supernatural), as a prayer is said before the meal and/or people attend a church service, which includes a special Thanksgiving sermon.

"Modern celebration of Thanksgiving Day is a ritual affirmation of what Americans believe was the Pilgrim experience, the particularly American experience of confronting, settling, adapting to, and civilizing the New World" (Robertson, 1980: 15). For the great majority of Americans, of course, their relation to these Pilgrims is neither biological nor cultural, neither ethnic nor religious. Thanksgiving is a time to establish, affirm and believe that this is their culture history. In Anthony Wallace's sense that the goal of ritual is a transformation of state to some desired end (Wallace, 1966), participation in this ritual transforms a collection of immigrants into Americans by connecting them to a cultural history stretching back to the "founding" of the country. The tradition of America, that immigrants will be incorporated—or, at least, their children will be—as true members of the society is accomplished, and the belief that we are "a nation of immigrants" is confirmed and validated.

In every household that considers itself American or desires to be considered American, Thanksgiving brings family members back home, physically and emotionally, ritually transforming attenuated ties of kinship into a strong bond. The Thanksgiving feast charges the set of meanings incorporated in being or becoming an American with the emotional intensity and significance of family. At the same time, Thanksgiving invests the value of family ties with an aura of religion and patriotism.

Turkey is the central symbol of Thanksgiving. In schools throughout the country children make pictures of live turkeys, with brilliant feathers; pictures of turkeys appear on magazines, in store windows. On Thanksgiving Day, the turkey makes a gala entrance, served on a platter, roasted, stuffed, quite dead. Robertson suggests that "Turkey is consumed at Thanksgiving feasts because it was native to America, and because it is a symbol of the bounteous richness of the wilderness...." (Robertson, 1980: 15). It symbolizes precisely what Robertson suggests and even more. The stuffed turkey represents the Native Americans, sacrificed and consumed in order to bring civilization to the New World.[1] It is a model of and a model for the "other", and in this national communion its ingestion connects proper Americans to their spiritual ancestors, the Pilgrims.

The myth that validates the Thanksgiving ritual is taught in schools throughout November. Robertson tells the story as follows:

> The Pilgrims, persecuted in England and unhappy in Holland, took the ship *Mayflower* and sailed ultimately to a place they called Plymouth, near Cape Cod. They met with harsh times and starvation through the winter, while they struggled to build log cabins to live in and hunted to get food. In the spring, the Indians taught them how to plant corn (maize) and fertilize it with fish, and how to plant other Indian foods. When the harvest was in, the Pilgrims had a feast of thanksgiving to which the Indians came. At the feast they ate the corn, beans, squash, and pumpkins which they had learned to grow from the Indians, and they ate wild turkeys and other game the Indians had taught them to hunt. And they gave thanks to God for the new land, for their new life in it, and for all the bountiful things He had given to them. (1980: 15)

This myth, known to all Americans, resonates against the other deeply held cultural images of violence between Whites and Indians: pioneers and Indians, cowboys and Indians.

At Thanksgiving, everyone knows that across the nation members of every other household are simultaneously feasting on stuffed turkey, sweet potatoes, pumpkin pie and cranberry sauce.[2] The experience is part of feeling oneself a member of the nation, of the imagined community, taking part in a 400-year tradition. However, in its present form, Thanksgiving dates back only to the end of the 19th century. In Hobsbawm's phrase, it is an "invented tradition", one "which seeks to inculcate certain values and norms of behaviour by repetition, which automatically implies continuity with the past" (1983a: 1).

The purpose of this article is to look more closely at the elements that are currently brought together in a ritual and myth of origins—giving thanks, family feast, the symbolism of the turkey and the meaning of the Pilgrims—to empower a nationalist identity. The sources and historic moments that are considered here are only partial (a total deconstruction would involve a library of history, literature, art and social science) and are those that most closely relate to Thanksgiving Day itself.

★ NO, VIRGINIA, THERE WAS NO FIRST THANKSGIVING

The Pilgrims of Plymouth, like the Puritans in other Massachusetts and Connecticut settlements, religiously observed only the Sabbath, days of fasting or humiliation, and days of thanksgiving. These days of fasting or thanksgiving, like the Sabbath, were serious occasions for long sermons, prayer and abstinence from work and play. They were announced, originally, by the leader of the congregation. When events were seen to signify the displeasure of the deity, a day of fasting would be announced; or, if events signified his beneficence, a day of thanksgiving would be proclaimed (Baker, 1989;[3] Love, 1895). Such days were observed frequently throughout the year. On days of thanksgiving, a meal may have been taken the evening before or between or after sermons, but the preparation and consumption of a meal was not an important ritual activity.

The celebrated historic feast in Plymouth clearly does not fit as a day of thanksgiving. It has been construed as a harvest festival, descended from an English custom of the Harvest Home (Hatch, 1978: 1053), a politically motivated feast to maintain the colony's alliance with the Wampanoag Indians (Humins, 1987: 61), but it also closely resembles the Algonkians' feasts,[4] at which people from many places came to take part in ceremonies related to the yearly cycle of corn. They danced, hunted for venison, and played games (Butler, 1948: 26). These ceremonies were "performed usually but once or twice a year... their usual time is about *Michaelmass*, when their corn is first ripe..." (Denton, 1670, quoted by Butler, 1948: 25). Michaelmass occurs at the end of September and the date of the Plymouth feast has been placed between 23 September and 11 November (Love, 1895: 75 footnote).

The connection between these three days of feasting in Plymouth in the fall of 1621 and our celebration of Thanksgiving is purely, but significantly, mythological. There are other contenders for the honor of holding the "First Thanksgiving", such as 9 August 1607, by colonists traveling to Popham Colony in Maine, and 4 December 1619, by settlers of a small plantation, the Berkeley Hundred, Virginia (Hatch, 1978: 1053–4). But the search for the site of the very first Thanksgiving is part of the origin myth itself. Why, between 1880 and 1900, the Pilgrims became the authentic American ancestors, Plymouth became the chosen site of our national origin myth, and Thanksgiving its expression and celebration is one of the questions explored below.

★ A CHOSEN PEOPLE

While there is no direct continuity between the feast at Plymouth in 1621 and our November Thanksgiving feast, there are rhetorical and ideological continuities to Puritan beliefs of their destiny and mission as a chosen people. An extensive literature documents the Puritan identification of themselves with the biblical Israelites, and, as Leach has pointed out, the Israelites themselves needed mythical justification that they were indeed "the divinely ordained owners of the whole promised land..." when in empirical fact "the land in question has a very mixed population..." from which they religiously excluded themselves (Leach, 1969: 53–4). In a similar fashion the New England settlers sought help from the Native Americans, took their land and fields, but regarded *them* as heathen savages or devils. "And the thanks were, of course, given to God..." (Robertson, 1980: 16). Puritan belief interpreted the plague and epidemics that killed off "90% to 96% of the inhabitants [Native Americans] of southern New England" as proof of God's good intentions (Loewen, 1991: 13).

Roger Williams's is one of the few alternate texts to survive. He argued against Puritans' belief and effort to identify themselves as a chosen group of Saints, England as Babylon, and America as the New Canaan (Bercovitch, 1978: 43). Williams had also proposed that Native Americans were people who could be dealt with, not devils, not merely pawns in the hands of the Puritan's deity. He was, of course, exiled.

"Through...rhetorical ambiguities the clergy explained the meaning of the American wilderness. What seemed merely another worldly enterprise, financed by English entrepreneurs, was in reality a mission for 'the Generall Restoration of Mankind from the Curse of the Fall....'" (Bercovitch, 1978: 43). The calling of a congregation to fast or thanksgiving was part of this world view, which perceived all events as due to the intervention of the Lord on the part of his chosen people.

The major source for studying when, where, by whom and on what occasions days of thanksgiving were announced is a carefully documented work, *Fast and Thanksgiving Days of New England*, written by the Reverend William De Loss Love, Jr of Hartford, Connecticut, and published in 1895.[5] Love constructed a "Calendar", which records every documented announcement of a fast or thanksgiving in the New England and Middle Colonies (later states) from 1620 to 1815 by town, colony, state or nation. A recent source, *Thanksgiving: An American Holiday, An American History* by Diane Appelbaum, less scholarly but nonetheless informative, takes the story up to the present.

The leaders of Puritan congregations in the New England colonies found frequent occasions to call for days of fasts to placate the Lord, who had sent droughts, starvation or Indian attacks, and days of thanksgivings to give proper thanks for a lucky harvest, the defeat of an enemy, a critical rainfall.

The authority to announce days of fast or thanksgiving was originally a church leader's prerogative, but at Plymouth Colony civil authority exercised this power as early as 1623 (Love, 1895: 85). In 1636 a law was passed "concerning the appointment of fasts and thanksgivings" which stated "That it be in the power of the Governor & Assit to comand solemn dates of humiliacon by fasting &c, and also for thanksgiving as occasion shall be offered" (Plymouth Colony Records, xi.18, quoted by Love, 1895: 87). This authority, however, was contested. Despite the 1636 law, the first documented day of thanksgiving to be celebrated throughout the New England colonies was announced in 1637 by the entire church leadership of the New England colonies to celebrate the defeat of the Pequot Indians. According to Trumbull: "This happy event gave joy to the colonies. A day of public thanksgiving was appointed, and in all the churches of New England devout and animated praises were addressed to Him who giveth his people the victory" (Trumbull, 1797: i.93, quoted by Love, 1895: 135).

In 1676, the ministers were in disagreement with the secular leadership, the governor and magistrates of Massachusetts. There had been encouraging progress in the war against King Philip, leader of the Wampaneog people and their allies, who were making a last desperate attempt to save their lands and their people from the genocidal forces of the settlers. The secular leadership of Massachusetts wanted to declare a day of thanksgiving; the religious leadership wanted a day of fasting. The secular council of Massachusetts won, and a colony-wide day of celebration was announced (1895: 200).

The contest between religious and secular leaderships concerned many issues—control over people, taxes and tithes—and in addition it was a struggle for the control of the "dominant culture" (Bercovitch, 1978: xiii), the Puritan "rhetoric and vision [which] facilitated the process of colonial growth. And...effectually formed a powerful vehicle of middle-class ideology: a ritual of progress through consensus, a system of sacred-secular symbols for a laissez-faire creed..." (27–8). This is the true continuity of American culture with its Puritan ancestry. The transfer from religious leader to secular of the authority to announce fasts and thanksgivings included a transfer and transformation of Puritan rhetoric to the scarcely more secular rhetoric of American political discourse and American civil religion (Bercovitch, 1978). In appropriating the power to call the people to give thanks or pray for forgiveness the secular government appropriated the Puritan rhetoric for its own.

45

It is possible to see from Love's Calendar that at Plymouth Colony the actual announcements alternated between church and secular authority well into the 18th century. By 1735, however, with the exception of Massachusetts Bay where the clergy was powerful, all proclamations of fasts and thanksgivings were made by the civil authorities. By 1775, the secular authorities had won even in Massachusetts. After this date, notwithstanding an occasional proclamation by a cleric in Pennsylvania, New York or New Jersey, overwhelmingly this power was exercised by the secular authorities.

At the time of the Revolution, the authority to appoint days of fasting and thanksgiving became an issue in the debate over the powers of the Federal Government and the States. In the autumn of 1777 "came the surrender of Burgoyne, in consequence of which the first Continental thanksgiving day was appointed, December 18, 1777" (1895: 400). In 1778 Congress appointed "a spring fast, April 22, and an autumn Thanksgiving, December 30", and though several states anticipated these dates, they kept the national date too (1895: 344). Under Washington, the Congress continued to proclaim fast and thanksgiving days for the nation, but state governments also continued independently to set a day aside each year for celebrating a thanksgiving connected to harvest time.

Fears of continuing social or economic revolution, resentment of unequal wealth and power, these fueled the arguments after the Revolution over Federalism and anti-Federalism, separation of Church and State, and from John Adams's time until 1815, no days of thanksgiving were set. President James Madison set a day of thanksgiving for 13 April 1815, to celebrate the peace with Britain, but claimed in a letter written several years later that it had only been a recommendation (in Stokes, 1950: 491).

From the post-revolutionary period to the Civil War the rhetoric of chosenness and national mission appears to have been expressed in July 4th oratory celebrating the Revolution and the triumph of the Republic as furthering God's plan (Bercovitch, 1978: 140–52). The states celebrated Thanksgiving during this period, and it developed into an autumn family celebration, as discussed below. The struggle and trauma of the Civil War again brought an appeal to the deity for direct guidance and support of the nation, and Lincoln proclaimed several days of thanksgiving for Northern victories during the Civil War period.

These proclamations followed the tradition of religiously giving thanks to the deity (Sandburg, 1939, vol. 2: 359, 446; vol. 3: 46, 229), and fully exploited sacred rhetoric, combining the mission of the nation with the uniqueness of its relation to God. He set 6 August 1863 "as a day of national thanksgiving", inviting "the people of the United States to assemble on that occasion in their customary place of worship, and, in the forms approved by their own consciences, render the homage due to the Divine Majesty for the wonderful things he has done in the nation's behalf . . ." (15 July 1863, quoted in Sandburg, 1939, vol. 2: 359). In both 1863 and 1864 (along with other days) a day of thanksgiving was proclaimed for the last Thursday in November. President Johnson and succeeding presidents followed Lincoln's precedent and continued to set the last Thursday in November as an annual Thanksgiving, thus fully appropriating the ritual for the nation over the individual states and laying the groundwork for its further development as a political-religious ritual of nationality.

As Steinberg pointed out in an article published on Thanksgiving Day, 1981: when the Union is troubled or questioned, announcements of Thanksgiving are a political response. In addition to Washington's and Lincoln's proclamations, Steinberg cites Herbert Hoover's during the Great Depression of the 1930s and Ronald Reagan's in the 1980s (Steinberg, 1981).

★ FEASTS AND HOMECOMINGS—EARLY AND MID-19TH CENTURY

By the time of Lincoln's announcements, a late autumn thanksgiving, complete with feast, had become customary, though reference to neither Pilgrims nor origin myth was in evidence. Although originally both fasts and thanksgivings were occasions for long sermons and abstinence from work and play, as early as 22 December 1636, in Scituate, Massachusetts, part of the Plymouth Colony, there was a celebration which combined a day of thanksgiving with a congregation-wide feast. "This is the earliest example in the Plymouth Colony of feasting in connection with a thanksgiving day . . ." (Love, 1895: 88). There may, of course, have been earlier occasions, but they are not documented. This combination of feasting with an announcement of a thanksgiving (still not *the* Thanksgiving) was repeated at Scituate on 12 October 1637 and again on 11 December 1639. As Love makes clear, "This does not prove that the day had assumed an annual character, but it shows an important feature of the development towards that, namely, the thanksgiving feast" (p. 89). Even in Boston, part of the strict Puritan Massachusetts Bay Colony, there is evidence of a feast after the religious services for thanksgiving at the time of the pan-colony thanksgiving of 1636 (p. 135).

Feasting as a form of celebration had been part of an earlier English tradition associated both with harvest festivals and thanksgiving days (Love, 1895: 50, 76–7), suppressed but apparently not exterminated by the Puritan strictures.[6] The re-emergence of a feasting tradition may have been eased by the fact that, while strict avoidance of holy days and other Anglican idolatry had sharply set apart Puritan reformers in England, the early colony faced no competition to its faith, and rules could be relaxed. The announcements of thanksgivings, therefore, became calls to feast as well as to prayer, and as thanksgiving tended to be limited to a single occasion in the fall the feast was ritualized.

The household became the site of ritual performance in contrast to the earliest thanksgivings which were community-wide or congregational in character. The gradually emerging tradition in New England was one which emphasized the family household rather than the community. Reverend Love, the champion of Thanksgiving, approved this change and demonstrates its significance:

> As the household became the self-sustaining unit of their life, it was better that the family should feast together, rather than that the richer should invite the poorer, or that they should divide into three companies as Lothrop's church did. (1895: 421)

While charity to the poor has remained a concern of churches, the community model of shared obligations, relations of dependency and respect was replaced by a model of separate, equivalent family units. A homogeneous imaginary community was constructed out of these household building blocks in place of the real village and congregation, with its known divisions of class and wealth. Colony, state or nation became the site of social identity as secular authorities created a moment during which each household knew that all other households were celebrating in the same way at the same time. Thanksgiving celebrates and obfuscates the destruction of community, constructing the family and nation as the only bastions against a Hobbesian world, and making the appearance of proper family relations, as demonstrated by full observance of the feast, the requirement and proof of national identity.

Love's Calendar shows a progression of increasing simultaneity of decision as to fast or thanksgiving. In the early years each town or church appeared to decide quite independently whether to fast or give thanks. By the 1770s, the announcements were made primarily colony-wide, and by looking at which kind of day was announced by each colony within a two-week period, it is possible to see that there was an increasing tendency for the still separate colonies to announce the same kind of observance, fast or thanksgiving. These observances were sometimes on the same date, sometimes within the same week or two (pp. 464–514). As the colonies, and later the states, continued to announce fasts and thanksgivings, increasingly there was a single fast in the spring and a single thanksgiving in the late fall.[7] By 1863, most of the states had been announcing an autumn thanksgiving celebration each year, although it was not necessarily the same day each year (Love, 1895: 407).

By the mid–19th century, Thanksgiving had become associated with homecoming (Baker, 1989). The simple virtues of the past were merged with the return home to the rural family farm and the rural extended family. Returning home for Thanksgiving was both a metaphor and a ritual performance of solidarity, renewing or validating family ties. In 1858, "it was reliably estimated that upwards of 10,000 people left New York City to spend the holiday in New England" (Appelbaum, 1984: 76).

Based on the study of more than a thousand of the most popular textbooks used in the 19th century, Ruth Elson noted that in the first half of the century "side by side with unstinted praise of industrial progress", there was an "idealization of an American society which was still predominantly rural" (Elson, 1964: 25). In the second half of the century "the cultivator of the soil is at the same time a cultivator of virtue...", and there was "a strong element of nostalgia, of looking back to a simpler, more rural, and more virtuous America" (1964: 27). These textbooks are filled with stories telling endless memories of childhood on the farm and equating the simpler past of the individual with the "simpler past of the society" (1964: 29).

Elson concludes that the world created in 19th-century schoolbooks was essentially a world of fantasy, and considering the thoroughgoing transformations of American life in the first half of the 19th century it is difficult not to agree. This was a period in which the rapid development and expansion of industrial capitalism was changing the environment, the laws, the relations of production, the population, etc. Factories and cities, capitalists and workers were replacing family farms and artisanal production. Slave resistance and the growing power of the northern manufacturing class was threatening the South. Abolitionist ministers preached sermons against slavery on the state-held Thanksgiving Day.

But for most Americans, Thanksgivings were a time for sentimental pilgrimages as tens of thousands of people returned to their rural homes within the period of a week or two. With the establishment of a national, annual day of Thanksgiving everyone knew that all over the country others were also traveling homeward, that in every decent home throughout the nation preparations were under way, and that on that special Thursday we were all sitting down to a large turkey feast. The annual national holiday appropriated for the State these apprehensions of community, familial solidarity and Christian prayer which had already entered the developing sense of nationality.

★ NATIVE AMERICANS BECOME INDIANS/TURKEYS

Served up on the Thanksgiving table, roasted well and nicely stuffed, the turkey became the focus of the feast in the early 19th century (Appelbaum, 1984: 267). As Robertson and others have suggested, this American bird symbolizes the bounty, the conquered wilderness, the imposition of civilization on the American continent. Yet before the 19th century, all these had been symbolized by a multitude of different foods; "the presence of three or four kinds of meat emphasized the status of this meal as a major feast, but a chicken pie signified that the feast was Thanksgiving dinner" (Appelbaum, 1984: 268).

Practical reasons undoubtedly can be found for turkeys becoming less expensive and more available at this time, but no such approach can explain the elaboration of attention to live turkeys destined for the table. Like the Aztec custom of decorating and feasting their human offerings to the gods before the day of sacrifice, the turkey in the farmyard was fed and admired. In the mid-19th century as today, pictures of live Tom Turkeys in full feather appeared at Thanksgiving time in magazines and decorations (Baker, 1989), prefiguring their ritual presentation as the Thanksgiving offering.

More than just a part of the wilderness that has been civilized, the Thanksgiving turkey powerfully symbolizes the Indians. It is a symbol of a symbol, since the concept of "Indian" is already a reduction of all the varied individuals and nations of Native America into a homogeneous "other". The term reduces and conceals all those who lived in the past as well as those who live in the US now, defining them only in terms of the dominant culture.

There are several recent studies that have analyzed literature, philosophy, popular culture and government policy to trace how Native Americans were conceptualized, perceived and treated as "Indians"—the differences among them expunged, the differences between them and Whites misperceived, exaggerated and distorted (see, for example: Berkhofer, 1978; Matz, 1988; Neuwirth, 1982; Stedman, 1982). The duality of the images constructed of the Indians is noted by each study, and there is a rough agreement on how these images shifted over time as the dominant culture succeeded in expropriating more of their lands and controlling more of their lives. In the 17th and 18th centuries the predominant imagery portrays Native Americans as savage heathens or noble savages. In the early and mid–19th century they are portrayed as either treacherous, therefore, bad or dead and, thereby, good. From the late 19th century through most of this century the contrast has been between degraded (bad) and vanished (good). The categories certainly overlap in time and meaning and history. In the East, where the Native Americans had been cleared from their lands by the mid–19th century, the possibility of nostalgically romanticizing the vanished or disappearing Indians was available earlier than in the West.

It is this construction of Indian that is stated symbolically in the Thanksgiving images of live and stuffed turkeys. An early example of this Indian imagery is particularly interesting as it gives some hints of how the meanings of Indian and turkey might have come to merge.

Two of the early thanksgivings celebrated victories over Native Americans. The first, in 1637, was the defeat of the Pequots; the second, in 1676, hailed success in the war against the Wampaneogs and their allies. As on the first occasion, the Indians were viewed as a trial sent by God to test his chosen people, and the victory was proof of his continuing covenant with his chosen people. In the 17th-century description of this event, the representation of Native Americans as heathen/noble savage is clearly stated and elaborated.

According to the records of Plymouth church, shortly after the proclamation of a day of thanksgiving for the defeat of the Wampaneog, their leader, King Philip, was captured and killed in Rhode Island. "Captain Church and his company went the next day...to Rhode Island, and on Tuesday started through the woods for Plymouth" (Love, 1895: 202). On that Thursday, as the congregation at Plymouth finished their thanksgiving, Captain Church's company arrived carrying the head of King Philip (1895: 203). As the historian Increase Mather described it in 1676, thus "did God break the head of that Leviathan, and gave it to be meat to the people inhabiting the wilderness" (Mather, 1862 [1676]: 197).

Mather's cannabalistic reference first transforms the Indian leader into the biblical monster sent to try Job, a non-human in contrast to "people", and next into a serviceable foodstuff. The environs of Plymouth are referred to as "a wilderness", a wilderness that the "people" are struggling to transform into a garden or civilization. On the other hand, the Indian leader was referred to as a King, in that sense a respected enemy, whose defeat demonstrates God's favoring of his chosen people.

The broadside, which carried the announcement by the Massachusetts council of this Thanksgiving, begins:

> The Holy God having by a long and Continued Series of his Afflictive despensations in and by the present Warr with the Heathen Natives of this Land, written and brought to pass bitter things against his own Covenant people in this wilderness, yet so that we evidently discern that in the midst of his judgements he hath remembered mercy.... (in Love, 1895: 200)

This broadside was decorated at the top with a woodcut of the seal of the Massachusetts Bay Colony. The seal shows an Indian of uncertain gender, apparently male, since "he" holds a bow in one hand and an arrow in the other, yet s/he is depicted with a suggestion of breasts. This androgynous Indian stands in a cleared landscape with three trees and is saying—the sentence is written on a streamer emerging from the Indian's mouth like a balloon in a comic strip—"Come and help us". The Indian's "Macedonian cry" is a call to be saved, taken from the biblical account of St Paul's missionary works: "And a vision appeared to Paul in the night: there stood a man of Macedonia, beseeching him, and saying, 'Come over into Macedonia, and help us'" (Acts 16:9).[8] The communication is one in which the vanquished become one with their conquerers, asking for help in becoming Christians and being civilized.

This broadside also combines two images of the Indian: On one hand, the Indian was constructed as an innocent, living in a garden-like environment, inviting conversion and civilizing; on the other, a dangerous 'Heathen Native'. There are suggestive parallels between these images of the wild beast to be eaten and the androgynous (domesticated?) native in the garden, with the wild and domesticated native turkey of North America.

Originally domesticated by the Aztecs, the turkey was brought to Europe and first described as part of a Christmas dinner in 1585 (Zeuner, 1963: 459). The early settlers found wild turkeys and, following the Indians' example, shot them for the table. The culinary expert Brillat-Savarin hunted wild turkeys near Hartford, Connecticut, in the late 17th century, noting that: "The flesh of the wild turkey is darker and with a stronger flavor than that of the domestic bird" (1949/1971, footnote 85). In the 17th century, town-dwellers unable to shoot them paid a shilling for them, and turkeys were still plentiful in 1889 (Root and de Rochemont, 1976: 70). Domesticated turkeys were gelded for docility and to increase the production of meat (Baker, 1989).

The co-occurrence of wild and domesticated birds makes a perfect metaphor for Native Americans. Like the turkey, Indians were either wild or domesticated. Although feared, wild Indians were more admirable in a sense, or flavorful, more "game", an enemy to be respected, if also to be killed. A Native American converted to Christianity and "civilization" was a domesticated Indian, like the supplicating, androgynous Indian on the seal of the Massachusetts Bay Colony, a validation of the Pilgrims' mission.[9] As a true "native of America" the turkey, wild and domesticated, could easily become a symbol for those other natives, constructed not as Americans but as Indians—others.

The Stuffed Turkey

By the mid–19th century, when the stuffed turkey began to take its place on annual Thanksgiving tables, the meaning of "the Indian" had changed considerably. Throughout the East and South, Native Americans had been cleared from the land, and there was no question as to the future fate of those still holding on in the West. Coexistence was unthinkable. Native Americans would vanish, either by massacre or by removal to some wasteland no one, at the time, wanted. In dime novels, billboards and museums (Matz, 1988), Indians are portrayed as treacherous and savage. This is the period of "the only good Indian is a dead Indian," and all the better when stuffed.

This period coincides with the time of the great home-comings, of dramatizing the rural farm. It is a time when harvest still had meaning if, for some, only nostalgically. Roger Abrahams (1982) provides some interesting insights into the meaning of seasonal festivals and into some of the symbolic statement of the stuffed turkey.

He points out that in contrast to rituals which celebrate life transitions, in which the energies of the participants are already raised by the situations that call them forth, seasonal rituals must provide that energy. They must emphasize and express a dramatic contrast between everyday life and the festival. Ordinary objects are made festive by "stylizing them, blowing them up, distending or miniaturizing them" (1982: 168). He lists all the symbolic images "in which the power of the most typical kinds of things may be condensed and then exploded" (1982: 175) and points out that it is the "lowly firecracker, the balloon, the wrapped present, the cornucopia, the piñata, the stuffed turkey, and Santa's stuffed bag [which are] the most powerful and pervasive images of our holidays" (1982: 175–6). For Abrahams, "these embody the essence of holiday wholeness on the one hand, then the breaking, cutting, exploding that allow everyone to share the now-freed energies and resources" (p. 176).

Considering the stuffed turkey itself, he states, "Thus, we witness the continuing importance of 'the Bird', the stuffed turkey at Thanksgiving or Christmas, a symbolic object which is capable of being presented whole and then cut to pieces, then shared and consumed by the family..." (1982: 176). This coupling of Thanksgiving and Christmas underlines the tremendous importance of the turkey at Thanksgiving, as a symbol not only of all that Abrahams suggests, but of its additional meanings as well. Turkeys are the central symbol of Thanksgiving, at Christmas they are merely part of the feast.

★ A NATIONAL THANKSGIVING

The southern states in the years following the Civil War did not accept a Thanksgiving Day which celebrated the reunification of the nation. This was partly due to the fact that northern ministers had used Thanksgiving as an occasion to preach abolition from their pulpits, but more significantly, the South was not ready to accept a national or northern cultural domination which not only abolished slavery but, under Reconstruction, gave full rights of citizenship to the freed slaves.

Reconstruction was shortlived, and its destruction involved a great deal of political and economic dealing between the politicians and the elites of North and South. This was a turning-point in national history, when the re-establishment of national unity was based on the exclusion of African Americans from full membership in it. Northern support and investment, for example, re-established southern cotton plantations, and northern agreement allowed the freed slaves to be segregated back into the cotton fields to supply northern textile mills and thus maintain its industries.[10] Northern factories refused to hire the freed slaves and looked instead to Europe for an immigrant workforce. The apparent cultural hegemony of the North[11] cloaked a collusion that restored power to the South, a power bickered over, but shared between the new industrial and the old plantation-owning elites.

Thanksgiving Day had become a firmly established and extremely significant annual national holiday, and the South joined the feast when Reconstruction ended.

51

In Alabama, Governor Houston proclaimed 23 December 1875 Thanksgiving "to honor the replacement of a reconstruction constitution by a new document that restricted black participation in state government" (Appelbaum, 1984: 164). Louisiana announced a special thanksgiving in 1877, when an all-white government was restored, and Georgia also celebrated thanksgiving upon the return of white supremacy (Appelbaum, 1984: 164). The stage was set for the development of the full-blown national ritual, combining the religious overtones of the Puritan rhetoric with the family-centered autumn feast.

★ ENTER THE PILGRIMS

Towards the end of the 19th century, the Pilgrims and the story of the "First Thanksgiving" become integral parts of the myth surrounding the observance of the Thanksgiving ritual (Baker, 1989; Loewen, 1991: 15). This picture of harmony between Pilgrims and Indians was not possible until the Indians had been completely vanquished, their lands appropriated, their futures thought to be annihilated. In the period immediately following the Civil War, the pictures of Indians and Pilgrims were violent images—a wounded Pilgrim or an armed sneaking Indian (Baker, 1989). When the Indian Wars began to fade from memory, everyone knew that it was only a matter of time before Indians vanished as a culture or a people and they could safely be incorporated as a symbol not only of sacrifice, but as part of the image of that lost Eden, in which Pilgrim and Indian, like lion and lamb, harmoniously joined together.

Before the 1850s, the only attention paid to the Pilgrims had been in the period leading up to the Revolutionary war. The old English symbols were to be discarded and new ones were needed. The Mayflower Compact was vested with great importance, and a large rock was taken from Plymouth harbor, which, breaking in half upon removal, was taken to signify to all the "breaking away" from the mother country (Myers, 1972: 298; Baker, 1989). A Pilgrim holiday, Forefathers' Day, was celebrated by an elite group of New England men. As New Englanders migrated West in the pre-Civil War period, they formed New England societies and continued an annual celebration of Forefathers' Day until 1812 (Myers, 1972: 295–301).[12] It had a brief resurgence in the 1830s, again in the 1880s and 1890s, and is still celebrated in Plymouth itself (Baker, 1989), but in general it is little known and of little significance.

Until the late 19th century, the Pilgrims had been seen as austere, distant figures, but fictionalized versions of their lives and times humanized them (Baker, 1989), and "books about life in colonial times enjoyed tremendous popularity" (Appelbaum, 1984: 218). "Plimouth Plantation", completed in 1650, had been printed in 1856. It was reprinted three times between 1895 and 1912 (Adams et al., 1968). With the addition of the Pilgrims and the First Thanksgiving, the holiday became a full-fledged ritual re-enactment of an origin myth of the nation.

Hobsbawm has pointed out that after the Civil War the United States faced a somewhat unique set of problems in establishing a sense of national identity.

> The basic political problem of the U.S.A., once secession had been eliminated, was how to assimilate a heterogeneous mass—towards the end of our period, an almost unmanageable influx—of people who were Americans not by birth but by immigration. Americans had to be made. (1983b: 279)

Hobsbawm continues this passage with the statement that Americans were produced by means of rituals, which were designed for this purpose.[13]

> The invented traditions of the U.S.A. in this period were primarily designed to achieve this object...the immigrants were encouraged to accept rituals commemorating the history of the nation—the Revolution and its founding fathers (the 4th of July) and the Protestant Anglo-Saxon tradition (Thanksgiving Day)—as indeed they did, since these now became...holidays and occasions for public and private festivity. (1983b: 279–80)

Other national rituals, Columbus Day and the pledge of allegiance in the schools, were also invented in this period to teach and control these immigrants, so threatening to American values, so essential to American industries. The explosion of interest in colonial history at this time was due to the "fear of immigrants and the cultural changes they might foment" (Appelbaum, 1984: 218). The Pilgrims provided a model of the good immigrant, imbued with religious conviction, a member of a Chosen People, striving to make a life in a new world. The inside spread of an 1887 *Life* magazine, showed a picture of the pilgrims superimposed over a picture of immigrants entering the country (Baker, 1989).

The success of these symbolic statements is dramatically stated in a piece of autobiographical fiction about a Russian immigrant girl in the early 1900s. It was written in 1903 by a Russian immigrant who had entered this country in 1892. She describes coming to America from Russia, full of hope and eagerness, being treated badly, feeling empty and lonely, distant from other Americans. She begins to read American history:

> I found from the first pages that America started with a band of Courageous Pilgrims. They had left their native country as I had left mine....I saw how the Pilgrim Fathers came to a rocky desert country, surrounded by Indian savages on all sides. But undaunted, they pressed on—through danger—through famine, pestilence, and want—they pressed on. They did not ask the Indians for sympathy, for understanding [like she does]. I, when I encountered a few savage Indians scalpers, like the old witch of the sweat-shop, etc....I lost heart and said: "There is no America!" Then came a light—a great revelation! I saw America—a big idea—a deathless hope—a world still in the making. I saw that it was the glory of America that it was not yet finished. And I, the last comer, had her share to give, small or great, to the making of America, like those Pilgrims who came in the *Mayflower*. (Yezierska, 1923/1989: 216–17)[14]

In other words, ask not what your country can do for you, but what you can do for your country.

The story describes the enormous need and the trick of myth that seems to satisfy it, using an imagined past as a promise to the future, changing perceptions instead of the world. Like all myth, the power of the story of the Pilgrims and the First Thanksgiving is shown by its capacity to refute experience; it is validated not by lived experience, but by the recitation of the code—in schools, in speeches, in the "common sense" of the culture, and in the self-fulfilling enactment of ritual. Incorporating the myth by taking part in the ritual celebration made of each immigrant's journey a reliving of this dreamtime.

The United States was not the only country faced with large immigration, but it was outstanding in the numbers and diversity of immigrants. For many immigrants, the old community remained the locus of loyalty, and some fulfilled their dream and returned there to buy a house or land. For many, it remained only a dream, and their children learned English, were taught the national mythology, to worship the flag and to learn the story of the "First Thanksgiving."

The process described by Hobsbawm in which the sentiments of attachment (not necessarily all positive, but usually intense) to a *real* face-to-face community, village, neighborhood, are transferred to the imagined community of the nation, took place throughout much of the world at about this same period, 1890–1914.

> The "homeland" was the locus of a *real* community of human beings with real social relations with each other, not the imaginary community which creates some sort of bond between members of a population of tens—today even of hundreds—of millions. (Hobsbawm, 1987: 148)

In the United States, Thanksgiving was and is part of the process by which for the immigrant real social relations of village, neighborhood or extended kin-group were broken apart and reformed. A study of French-Canadian, working-class immigrants in Rhode Island comments that in their celebration of Thanksgiving in November 1939, the important factor was the "affirmation of family togetherness" and that:

> This affirmation of family, in fact, may have accounted for the rapidity with which Catholic and Jewish ethnic households in twentieth-century America absorbed into their social calendar a holiday honoring a strange group of seventeenth-century Protestant zealots. (Gerstle, 1989: 191)

While the Pilgrims were among the early settlers of North America, they were neither the earliest nor the most typical. Jamestown, with its clear-cut commercial interests, is as early and as valid an ancestor as Plymouth. The Plymouth Colony itself lasted only two generations as an autonomous colony before becoming part of Massachusetts Bay Colony. As a site of mythic origins, Plymouth carries meanings precisely because it is unlike any other past or present American settlement. It was, and is, represented as a small homogeneous, egalitarian Christian community in which class differences were minimal, in which religion was central; a face-to-face community as a model of the national imagined community. It is a model which denies class domination, exploitation, racial and ethnic conflict and covers imperialism with the Pilgrims' cloak.

★ CONCLUSION

Thanksgiving powerfully shapes a sense of nationality to the emotions of homecoming. The joys and tensions, pleasures and pains of family life are activated in the preparations and joined participation of the feast. The preparation of the Thanksgiving feast is a traditional responsibility of women, the carving of the turkey usually the prerogative of the man of the house. Women wash the dishes after the feast while men watch violent games on television. Gender roles and family hierarchy are reaffirmed. The media and all the schools emphasize the importance at Thanksgiving time of the need to be with the family, and it is this need that is projected onto the wider screen of nationality.

The meanings of this national identity are part of every schoolchild's education, and to children the cycle of the year and their curriculum, in which year after year the October celebration and discussion of Columbus and his "discovery" is followed by November and the Pilgrims, lends an aura of naturalness and inevitability—the essence of mythic experience—to the invasion and colonization of North America. At Halloween, pumpkins are a mysterious note, but the chaotic disorder of the Halloween ritual is followed and put into order as the pumpkins become symbols of harvest and simplicity and Native America domesticated by the Pilgrim Thanksgiving.

In relegating the learning of the mythic elements of Thanksgiving symbols and their story to children, there is a particularly American synthesis of innocence and cynicism. At one level, everyone believes in equality, justice, including racial justice, harmony—including racial harmony—friendly Indians and trusting Pilgrims. At another level, these are beliefs for children. An adult knows that the real world is harsh, each for oneself, dog eat dog, except for moments in the life of the family, except for interactions with people like ourselves.

55

Inclusion and exclusion are essential elements of national identities. For the United States, the fact that the nation was built on the land of prior occupants has always been a contradictory empowerment to the sense of moral righteousness. Only God's mysterious plan clears the conscience of a chosen people, assuring them that those whom they conquer and have conquered were destined by their unrighteousness, their savagery, to be sacrificed. In the odd contradictions of mythic thought, recent immigrants may ritually become Americans, and their children will eventually be considered "native-born Americans", but Native Americans, the earliest immigrants to the continent, are excluded from this imagined community. As America has continued its imperialistic civilizing mission within and beyond the borders of the United States, the construct of "natives" as non-humans has incorporated many others. People such as the Mexicans suddenly became "natives" after losing their territory. The people of the Philippines, Cuba, the Dominican Republic and, perhaps Iraq, have also in turn been transformed into "native others" to be consumed if they rebuffed the civilizing mission.

The Pilgrim image is foregrounded when refugees are granted or denied asylum, allegedly on the basis of whether they search for freedom or merely economic survival. Russians, therefore, may be feasted, while Haitians are sacrificed. The color line plays a part, though it is not absolute, but people of color—Filipinos, Mexicans, Haitians, Guatemalans—are more likely to share the symbolic and actual fate of Native Americans.

African Americans seem to be defined as a different other. In the 1870s and 1880s, popular magazines included a number of images of African Americans in their Thanksgiving illustrations. These pictures showed them serving dinner to a white family, eating a sparse dinner or stealing turkeys (Baker, 1989). They are not full guests at the dinner table, but neither are they the main course.

As the quincentenary approached, debates over the meanings of Thanksgiving were assigned to the current division between multiculturalist and hegemonic conservative,[15] and now, as in the past, the conflict over meanings is inseparable from conflicts over power, political and economic as well as symbolic. Ruth Elson concluded her study of 19th-century textbooks with the statement that in presenting a unified society "only the social ideals of the more conservative members of the society were offered the Nineteenth-century child" (1964: 341). James Loewen, who is studying current American history textbooks, finds little improvement in this century and makes a plea, quoting an early Massachusetts colonist, who argued that, "our forefathers, though wise, pious, and sincere, were nevertheless, in respect to Christian charity, under a cloud; and, in history, truth should be held sacred, at whatever cost" (1991: 14).

Education is on the front lines today, and it is, indeed, difficult for a teacher, reasonably well read in current revisionist histories, to recite the conventional, traditional story.[16] There is more awareness today that Native Americans have not vanished, and there is disillusionment with the concept of the melting-pot or assimilation. The tremendous number of recent non-white immigrants challenges the national identity as Christian, white, Pilgrim. The future of Thanksgiving is hard to predict, contrive or control, but, like the Australian's dreamtime, if the present is transformed, there will be changes in the past, and a new form of the "First Thanksgiving" will emerge.

NOTES

I am grateful to James Baker, Director of Museum Operations at Plimouth Plantation, for his generosity in sharing his knowledge and library. For comments and suggestions I thank Anne-Marie Cantwell, Francoise Dussart, Brian Ferguson, Zoë Graves, Russell Handsman and Thomas Patterson.

1. Although I have found no other author who suggests this symbolism, there is a cartoonist who graphically showed a Pilgrim family grouped around a table, poised to eat an American Indian, served on a platter with an apple in his mouth, and already missing several body parts. The caption says: "For history let's say it was a turkey". This cartoon was drawn to my attention by Eric Wolf when I presented a version of this paper at the American Ethnological Society annual meeting, Spring 1991. It was created by Shawn Kepri and published in the late 1970s in *Velvet*.
2. There is, of course, variation around this menu. For some onions, for others turnips are traditional, and for newly arrived immigrants frequently some of their original dishes join the American national feast.
3. James Baker is Director of Museum Operations at Plimouth Plantation. He is an expert on Plymouth, Pilgrims and Thanksgiving, and "publishes" his findings by teaching them to the actors who portray the Pilgrims at the Plantation. He is engaged in continuing research for his book *The Image of the Pilgrim*.
4. I am indebted to Russell Handsman of the American Indian Archaeological Institute for pointing out the likelihood that our Thanksgiving can be traced back to the Pilgrims' appropriation of an Algonkian ceremony.
5. This was clearly a work of years of perusing documents in the Connecticut Historical Society, and Reverend Love received an honorary PhD the following year from his alma mater, Hamilton College. When I first consulted this book in 1989 in the Rutgers University Library, many of its pages were still uncut.
6. New Amsterdam followed the Dutch custom of combining fasting, prayer and thanksgiving on specially appointed days, fasting in the morning and feasting in the evening (Love, 1895: 168). There was less of a tendency towards a harvest-time celebration since, as Love suggests, it was a town more involved with trade than with agriculture (1895: 163). Yet, as he points out, the similar expectation of fast and thanksgiving led easily to a recognition of shared customs.
7. Sara Hale, editor of the Godey's *Lady's Book*, a best-selling magazine of the 19th century, is credited by several sources (see, for example: Appelbaum, 1984; Hatch, 1978; Steinberg, 1981) with influencing state governors in the 1850s, and even President Lincoln in 1863, to set the last Thursday in November as Thanksgiving. The tendency for this day to be chosen was clearly already present.
8. Thanks to Carolyn Freeman Travers, Plimouth Plantation, for recognizing this quotation.
9. The turkey may be contrasted to another bird symbol, the bald eagle—sky-born vs earth-bound, high-flying predator rather than ground-dwelling vegetarian, as hawk stands to dove. This contrast was expressed by Benjamin Franklin, who favored the turkey over the bald eagle for our national symbol:

   > For my part, I wish the bald eagle had not been chosen representative of our country; he is a bird of bad moral character.... The turkey is a much more respectable bird, and withal a true original native of America. (Franklin, 1784)

10. A particularly clear analysis of these relations in this period can be found in Steinberg (1989: 173–200).
11. The Reverend William De Loss Love's study of Thanksgiving provides an example of New England's bid for cultural hegemony. He was born in 1851 in New Haven, attended Hamilton College and Andover Theological Seminary. He was ordained as a Congregational minister in 1878, was involved in commercial and railroad enterprises in Boston, and served as pastor of Hartford's Congregational church from 1885 to 1910. He wrote two other books on the colonial period and was a member of the Sons of the American Revolution and the Connecticut Historical Society. His father, also a Congregational minister, had been a well-known abolition-

ist, who entered Atlanta with General Grant and preached a sermon there. While Love clearly documents the fact that there was no first Thanksgiving, the major message of his book was to demonstrate the moral and historical primacy of New England. Certainly his book was never popular, but it was part of the effort to spread the hegemonic myth in which Plymouth stands as the birthplace of the nation.

12. A menu of the first Forefathers' Day dinner is extant. It was held in December of 1769 and it was meant to emphasize simplicity, "all appearance of luxury & extravagance being avoided, in imitation of our worthy ancestors whose memory we shall ever respect" (Myers, 1972: 297). Neither pumpkins nor turkeys were served.
13. Hobsbawm regards schools as the second important means of making Americans, noting that "the educational system was transformed into a machine for political socialization by such devices as the worship of the American flag..." (1983b: 280).
14. Again, I am grateful to Russell Handsman for pointing out this remarkable piece of writing.
15. See, for example, a historian, David Hackett Fischer, in an Op-Ed *New York Times* article, dated 28 November (Thanksgiving Day) 1991. Writing from, appropriately, Massachusetts, in defense against unnamed and unknown enemies:

   Thanksgiving is under attack again. Multiculturalists have demanded that Pilgrim pageants be banished from elementary school. Apostles of political correctness grimly insist that Thanksgiving be declared a Day of National Mourning for Native Americans. (p. A27)

16. In November 1989, I visited two schools in New Jersey the week before Thanksgiving to see how it was taught. One was a parochial school and the other was a public school for gifted children. In each I was sent to the classroom of the most progressive teacher—the first, a native of Cape Cod, has researched the actual food that was eaten at the "First Thanksgiving" but, in teaching spelling, taught the words: turkey, sweet potatoes, squash, pumpkin pie, etc. She had taught the children about the Indians helping the Pilgrims, and the later battles as being due to the resistance of Indians to their lands being seized. The school was decorated with turkeys, each feather bearing a prayer. The second school was not decorated. The teacher played Native American music and knew a great deal about Eastern groups. In an impromptu assembly, she showed slides of living Native Americans and asked the children to remember their "Indian forefathers". Clearly, in some places, traditions are changing!

REFERENCES

Abrahams, Roger (1982). "The Language of Festivals: Celebrating the Economy", in V. Turner (ed.) *Celebration: Studies in Festivity and Ritual*, pp. 161–77. Washington, DC: Smithsonian Institution Press.
Adams, Charles et al. (1912). "Note", in Bradford (1912/1968), pp. xv–xvi.
Appelbaum, Diane (1984). *Thanksgiving: An American Holiday, An American History.* New York: Facts on File.
Baker, James (1989). Personal communication.
Bercovitch, Sacvan (1978). *The American Jeremiad*, Madison: University of Wisconsin Press.
Berkhofer, Robert, Jr (1978). *The White Man's Indian: Images of the American Indian from Columbus to the Present.* New York: Alfred A. Knopf.
Bradford, William (1912). *History of Plymouth Plantation 1620–1647.* New York: Russell & Russell, 1968.
Brillat-Savarin, Anthelme (1949/1971). *The Physiology of Taste* (translated by Mary Fisher), New York: Alfred A. Knopf [orig. pub. 1825].
Butler, Eva (1948). "Algonkian Culture and Use of Maize in Southern New England", *Bulletin of the Archeological Society of Connecticut* 22: 3–39.
Elson, Ruth (1964). *Guardians of Tradition: American Schoolbooks of the Nineteenth Century.* Lincoln: University of Nebraska Press.
Fischer, David (1991). "Multicultural Fowl", *New York Times*, 28 November, A27.
Franklin, Benjamin (1784). Letter to Sarah Bache.
Gerstle, Gary (1989). *Working Class Americanism.* Cambridge: Cambridge University Press.
Hatch, Jane, ed. (1978). *The American Book of Days* (3rd ed. based on the earlier editions by G. W. Douglas). New York: Wilson.
Hobsbawm, Eric (1987). *The Age of Empire, 1875–1914.* New York: Pantheon.
Hobsbawm, Eric (1983a). "Introduction: Inventing Traditions", in E. Hobsbawm and T. Ranger (eds) *Inventing Traditions*, pp. 1–14. Cambridge: Cambridge University Press.
Hobsbawm, Eric (1983b). "Mass-producing Traditions: Europe 1870–1914", in E. Hobsbawm and T. Ranger (eds) *Inventing Traditions*, pp. 263–307. Cambridge: Cambridge University Press.
Humins, John (1987). "Squanto and Massasolt: A Struggle for Power", *New England Quarterly* 60: 54–70.
Leach, Edmund (1969). "The Legitimacy of Solomon", in *Genesis as Myth and Other Essays*, pp. 25–83. London: Jonathan Cape.
Loewen, James (1991). "History Textbooks and the First Thanksgiving", *Radical Historians Newsletter*, no. 65.
Love, William De Loss (1895). *The Fast and Thanksgiving Days of New England.* Boston: Houghton Mifflin.
Mather, Increase (1676). *The History of King Philip's War.* Boston: Samuel Drake, 1862.
Matz, Duane (1988). *Images of Indians in American Popular Culture since 1865*, Illinois State University, dissertation.
Myers, Robert (1972). *Celebrations: The Complete Book of American Holidays.* Garden City, NY: Doubleday.
Neuwirth, Steven (1982). *The Imagined Savage: The American Indian and the New England Mind, 1620–1675.* Washington University, St Louis, PhD dissertation.

57

Robertson, James (1980). *American Myth, American Reality*. New York: Hill and Wang.

Root, Waverly and Richard de Rochemont (1976). *Eating in America: A History*, New York: William Morrow.

Sandburg, Carl (1939). *Abraham Lincoln: The War Years*. New York: Harcourt, Brace.

Stedman, Raymond (1982). *Shadows of the Indians: Stereotypes in American Culture*. Norman: University of Oklahoma Press.

Steinberg, Stephen (1981). Cranberries from a Political Bog', *New York Times*, 26 November.

Steinberg, Stephen (1989). *The Ethnic Myth: Race, Ethnicity, and Class in America*. Boston: Beacon Press.

Stokes, Anson (1950). *Church and State in the United States*. New York: Harper & Brothers.

Trumbull, Benjamin (1797). *A Complete History of Connecticut*. Hartford, CT: Hudson & Goodwin.

Varenne, Hervé, ed. (1986). "Introduction", in *Symbolizing America*, pp. 1–9. Lincoln and London: University of Nebraska Press.

Wallace, Anthony (1966). *Religion: An Anthropological View*. New York: Random House.

Yezierska, Anzia (1923). "America and I", In Gary Colombo et al. (eds) *Rereading America*, pp. 208–17. New York: St Martin's Press, 1989.

Zeuner, Frederick (1963). *The History of Domesticated Animals*. New York: Harper & Row.

58

FUTURE NOTES:

THE MEAL·IN·A·PILL

WARREN BELASCO

6

I have been looking at the future of the food system as it has been represented in a wide variety of texts and arenas, science fiction and serious science, breezy mass journalism and dreary USDA yearbooks, world's fairs and county agricultural exhibitions, Disney's Epcot Center, Hollywood films, ironic cartoons, sober think tank white papers, and so on. When asked how we will be eating 100 years from now, most food scholars divide into two timeworn categories. Neo-Malthusians worry about food shortages wrought by population growth, capitalistic hyper-consumption, and environmental degradation, while Cornucopians forecast an ever-more-sumptuous global banquet catered by biotechnology, industrial agriculture, and the free market.[1] When ordinary people are asked the same question, however, the answer is often much simpler. "Oh, probably pills."[2]

Despite the fact that the Space-Age Jetson family ended their prime time TV run over thirty years ago and that no serious nutritionist or futurist has been advocating the meal-in-a-pill for many years, this professionally discredited notion retained a remarkably strong hold on popular consciousness—much the way generations of science fiction fans have kept the integalactic travel dream alive through space operas like "Star Wars" and "Star Trek" while NASA cannot even get us back to the moon.[3] For example, a random search of "future food" references on the World Wide Web—our contemporary meta-mind of quasi-conscious ruminations, rants, and discourses—turns up diverse suggestive links. No doubt unaware of the American Dietetic Association's disapproval, seven-year old Rachel Evens confidently predicts, "In the future we might have little pills that you can carry in your pocket. Hey, 'Lunch Pockets!'" (Perhaps Rachel was inspired by Nickelodeon's cartoon series, "Rocco's Modern Life," which recently featured a futuristic scenario in which a pill inflates into a full-size cheeseburger.) Poet Liz Thelen worries about "food from the future, small dull pellets . . . that provide a day's worth of nutrition . . . [but] look like dog chow." In "A Shinier, Happier Future?" college student Jamie Tennant wonders whether mail-order "filet mignon tablets" will "remove some angst from high-pressure first dates."[4]

Wary asides in cartoons, jokes, speculative fiction, and films testify to the meal-pill's enduring shelf-life as a staple of taken-for-granted, commonsensical, pop ideology.[5] And the very fact that it must still be refuted testifies to its persistent hold, for if the idea were truly dead, journalists writing about the future of food would not feel compelled to open with disclaimers to the effect that, despite popular belief to the contrary, we probably will not be taking our meals in pill form for some time to come, if ever.[6]

Where did this meal-in-a-pill idea come from? Why does it persist? What does it tell us about popular attitudes toward high-tech solutions to future food needs? Why hasn't it happened—or maybe it has but we don't know it?

Although the meal-in-a-pill fantasy-nightmare sounds very modern, it has archetypal roots in the basic human experience with the life-sustaining embryonic capsules called seeds. Ever since the Neolithic domestication of grains and legumes enabled humans to settle down and proliferate, mythology has been full of references to minute foods with enormous powers. Corn, wheat, and rice are all venerated for founding great civilizations. Beans, too, have rich symbolism in many societies, for these compact pellets are literally packed with life (nutrients) and the life force (reproduction). Indeed, Harold McGee notes that Romans regarded legumes so highly that each of the four major beans lent its name to a leading family: Fabius (faba), Lentulus (lentil), Piso (pea), and Cicero (chick pea). The Iroquois viewed beans as a special gift from the creator to man, while the Kariaks of the Sudan considered the bean the "Mother of Food." Folktales around the world speak of "magic beans" that punish wrongdoers, save the worthy, entertain children, and carry the adventurous to the heavens. Similar powers are associated with nuts, grapes, and olives, for these little fruits yield rich returns, and their intensive culture once represented the essence of Mediterranean agrarian life. Hence, the newly arrived Israelites were ordered first to build houses, then to "plant vineyards and eat the fruits of them." King David's wealth was said to originate in olives, and numerous societies regarded the olive branch as the emblem of pastoral peace and stability.[7]

Underlying these classic connections are other enduring themes. In folklore diminutive charms, gems, and nuggets all possess magical qualities linked to fascination with *miniaturization* and *concentration*, and we still acknowledge this "tiny is beautiful" paradigm when we speak of "pearls of wisdom" and "kernels of truth."[8] By seeking to distill vital essences into a highly condensed "elixir of life," food-pill advocates also echoed ancient dreams of *replication* (the invention of man-made surrogates for nature), and *alchemical transformation* (the conversion of base substances—here, primary chemicals—into precious, life-sustaining food). Above all, the meal-in-a-pill offered a magical fix—an easy solution to that most timeless and universal of human problems, the struggle for food. Reducing feeding to pill-popping would seem to settle once and for all those intractable issues of agriculture, hunger, health, and household labor that have plagued humanity for millennia. This search for the ultimate insurance of food security—and complete freedom from natural limits—is as old as Prometheus. Combining several archetypes, a 1936 *Popular Science Monthly* article on "Life from the Test Tube" predicted that "modern alchemists" of the food laboratory would soon condense the "elixir of life" into "food pills that would contain everything necessary for life—a feat that would render man forever independent of natural resources for his nourishment, and banish fear of crop failure and famine."[9]

While these magic-pellet themes can be found in universal mythology, the actual meal-in-a-pill version seems to have surfaced in the late nineteenth century, a period of enormous economic growth, industrialization, scientific and technological innovation, and rapid changes in everyday social life, especially among thee middle-class urban people who were the audience for the popular literature where the idea was discussed most frequently, primarily in the context of reformist speculation.[10] Several strands came together around this one technology: mobility, radicalism, efficiency engineering, and scientific eating.

★ MOBILITY

In this age of unprecedented exploration, migration, and colonization by European people, pioneering food technologists sought solutions to the logistical problems of life on the road and sea. Thus, inspired by the Donner Party disaster of 1846 (when California pioneers stranded in the Sierras resorted to cannibalism), Gail Borden vowed to create an array of concentrated foods to save future migrants: "I mean to put a potato into a pillbox, a pumpkin into a tablespoon, the biggest sort of watermelon into a sauce. The Turks made acres of roses into attar of roses. I intend to make attar of everything."[11] Borden never got to potato pills, but he did develop concentrated meat biscuits, which proved unpalatable, and then condensed milk (1856), one of the first great triumphs of modern food processing and the precedent for other marketing breakthroughs purporting to cover all nutritional bases in one convenient dish: for example, Kellogg's breakfast cereals, Liebig's infant formulas, Fleischmann's yeast cakes, and Campbell's soup, the last long advertised as "a whole meal in one soup!" Extending the concentrating tendencies suggested by canning, hardtack, and beef bouillon, the pill promised the complete culinary portability deemed essential for maximum geographical mobility. The United States military also investigated food capsules, along with other synthetic edibles, while pursuing ever more compact rations for soldiers in the field. Inevitably, projections of future space travel also included food pills as potential rations for multi-year journeys.[12]

★ RADICALISM

If there was a reigning culinary paradigm in bourgeois Victorian culture, it was abundance. Enormous dining room sideboards were engraved with ornate images of cornucopian excess, while food advertisements depicted plump children, colossal fruits, and huge portions.[13] Such gluttony invited radical backlash; "overnutrition" and fatness became metaphors for social inequities and cultural bankruptcy. Social critics often expressed revulsion against the conspicuous consumption of upper-class banquets, which in turn served as models for middle-class dining rituals. Conversely, reformers linked dietary simplification with visions of wholesale renewal. The rise of "dieting" at the end of the century, Peter Stearns writes in *Fat History*, "was ideally suited to an American need for an implicit but vigorous moral counterweight to growing consumer indulgence." Even before the vogue of calorie-counting, romantic reformers had associated an ascetic, usually vegetarian diet with self-discipline, self-control, and egalitarian values—as, for example, in *Walden*, where Thoreau rhapsodized about the blessed simplicity and self-sufficiency of a diet based on two of nature's more sublime pills, beans and huckleberries. Vegetarianism, like temperance, appealed to Anglo-American radicals of the late nineteenth century because it represented a way to conserve and focus their energies. Thus George Bernard Shaw became a vegetarian in 1880 because "a man fed on whiskey and dead bodies cannot do the finest work of which he is capable."[14]

While male utopians might reject meat as a way to *limit* their disturbing desires and impulses, radical feminists often pondered culinary ways to *expand* women's freedom. Seeking to liberate women from the kitchen, their number-one household burden, some feminists organized cooperative house-keeping networks, fantasized about fully-automated kitchens, or advocated centralized commissaries with home-delivery services.[15] Leaping several steps ahead in her utopian novel, *Mizora* (1880), Mary E. Bradley Lane sketched a male-free Arctic paradise where "parthenogenesis" obviated the need for sexual reproduction and where scientists synthesized fruits and meats that were cheap, chemically "pure," and, perhaps most appealing to middle-class Victorian readers, effortless to prepare. Kristine Anderson writes that "Mizora is a woman's dream of total control—not only of her body, mind, and soul, but of her whole environment," and the well-balanced concoctions of "culinary chemists" was a vital element in that vision of "perfection."[16]

From *Mizora*'s laboratory-assembled breads and fruits it was just one step to perhaps the most complete emancipation from domestic slavery, the meal-in-a-pill. For example, in 1893 the feminist and populist agitator Mary E. Lease predicted that by 1993, agricultural science would allow us "to take, in condensed form from the rich loam of the earth, the life force or germs now found in the heart of the corn, in the kernel of wheat, and in the luscious juice of the fruits. A small phial of this life from the fertile bosom of mother Earth will furnish men with substance for days. And thus the problems of cooks and cooking will be solved."[17] In Anna Dodd's 1887 satirical novel about New York in 2050, *The Republic of the Future*, pneumatic tubes delivered prescription bottles of food tablets directly to kitchenless apartments. While Dodd was a social conservative who deplored feminist aspirations, her spoof closely mimicked the sober tone of the period's reigning utopian literature, which was usually quite serious in addressing the need to "revolutionize" domestic work. Thus, with tongue in cheek, Dodd put the case succinctly: "When the last pie was made into the first pellet, women's true freedom began."[18]

The more affluent housewives of the late nineteenth century may not have baked pies themselves, but they had to deal with the hired cook who did. For them the pill offered a way to bypass the onerous interclass negotiations of "the servant problem"—the focus of "self-service" innovation such as automats, electric household appliances, and processed convenience foods.[19] According to Jane Donawerth, by the 1920s even the apolitical women's writers of "pulp" science fiction frequently allowed for "meat tablets," "liquid foods," and other synthesized "essences" that, "by doing away with eating,…revised women's domestic duties, doing away with shopping for food, gardening, cooking, canning, preserving, cleaning up, and managing servants."[20] Perhaps sensing that true women's liberation required freedom from reproduction *and* housework, the 1930 futuristic musical comedy, "Just Imagine," depicted a New York of 1980 in which young lovers popped pills for meals while automats dispensed infants.[21]

The meal-in-a-pill (or some other form of synthetic food) could thus be considered the first in a series of liberating pills for women: birth control pills disconnected sexuality from reproduction; antibiotics greatly shortened the time mothers spent nursing sick children; and, to be only slightly facetious, antidepressants offered temporary relief from just about every other conflict.[22]

★ EFFICIENCY ENGINEERING

In the wake of Edward Bellamy's wildly popular *Looking Backward* (1888), hundreds of technological utopian novels were written that, while often lacking Bellamy's socialist edge, helped to shape an emerging faith in enlightened engineering and centralized, "scientific" management. If these progressives had a common enemy, it was *waste*—the waste of time, energy, resources, and human potential. Conversely, their common goal was to maximize *efficiency* by rationalizing and consolidating every activity, including housework, shopping, and dining. In addition to developing the modern welfare state, with its central bureaus, this was the era that developed the department store, the modern university, the cafeteria, the public museum, and the amusement park—all amalgamating institutions offering a convenient, one-stop consumption experience under one roof.[23]

In a sense the meal-in-a-pill represented a culmination of the technological utopian's embrace of comprehensive, all-in-oneness. The fact that meal-pills might actually reduce food choices enhanced their efficiency value, for this was the era of Henry Ford, whose celebrated Model T came in "every color as long as it's black." Just as the Model T expressed the "one size fits all" mentality of early mass production, the meal-in-a-pill embodied the efficiency-engineer's determination to reduce costs by concentrating and streamlining essential life processes.[24]

For example, in the 1899 novel *Looking Forward: A Dream of the USA in 1999*, Arthur Bird predicted that scientific management would combine with capitalist enterprise to produce "Ready Digested Dinners." Fulfilling the Taylorist emphasis on prudent time management, meal pills would free busy modern workers from wasteful, lengthy lunches—and the naps that came after heavy lunches. "In order to save time, people [in 1999] often dined on a pill—a small pellet which contained highly nutritious food. They had little inclination to stretch their legs under a table for an hour at a time while masticating an eight-course dinner. The busy man of 1999 took a soup pill or a concentrated meat-pill for his noon day lunch. He dispatched these while working at his desk." As was often the case with technological utopians, Bird combined flat-out gadgetry with social conservatism. Thus, in line with inherently patriachal assumptions, his "fair typewriter" of 1999 preferred feminine "ice-cream pills" and "fruit pellets" to the more masculine "bouillon or consomme pellets."[25]

The meal-pill was closely linked to other key images of technological utopianism: "push-button" farms and factories without sweat, and to what Jeffrey Meikle has called the "damp-cloth utopianism" of the ultra-modern home, where synthetic materials would reduce housekeeping to a mere swipe of a slightly damp rag. World's Fairs have long served as sites for ritualistic enactment of technological utopian visions, and starting with the 1939 Fair in New York, it became customary to bury a "time capsule"—as if the essence of a total civilization could be condensed into a microcosmic torpedo measuring 7½ feet in length by 8⅜ inches in diameter.

And the meal-pill also foreshadowed the nuclear fantasies of the 1930s and 1940s, when popular magazines routinely predicted atomic airplanes, houses, and even cars powered by tiny pellets of uranium.[26] While these "peaceful atom" fantasies never did pan out, the archetypal pursuit of concentration and miniaturization did eventually produce another breakthrough with revolutionary implications, the microchip.

★ SCIENTIFIC EATING

There was a surprisingly short gap between pulp fiction and the futuristic visions of real scientists, particularly the "scientific eating" crusade.[27] This turn-of-the-century movement reflected and reinforced technological utopianism with claims that because science and industry, not tradition and nature, would soon determine what people ate, a diet of meal-pills and other synthetic foods was not at all implausible.

For one thing, the reigning chemical paradigm—established by Justus von Liebig by the 1850s—insisted that all foods could be reduced to a few basic elements. So complete was the chemist's reductionist victory that, as early as 1860 Ralph Waldo Emerson—not otherwise known for modernist affections—could pronounce: "Tis a superstition to insist on a special diet. All is made at last of the same chemical atoms."[28] Since nitrogen is nitrogen, carbon is carbon, bold chemists claimed that man could synthesize anything from basic chemical elements. After developing artificial fertilizers, Liebig also worked on early infant formulas to replace breast milk. As Liebig's successor, the renowned French chemist Marcelin Berthelot, put it in an 1894 preview of "Foods in the Year 2000," "when the milk has left the cow, it is merely a chemical compound and with it physiology has nothing to do." Illustrating the technological utopian penchant for infinite extrapolation of present-day inventions, Berthelot reasoned that because synthetic butter (margarine), sugar (saccharin), vanilla (vanillin), and indigo (alizarin) were already on the market, beefsteak in tablet form (made from coal) was probably just around the corner. "We shall give you the same chemical food, chemically, digestively, and nutritively speaking. Its form will differ, because it will probably be a tablet. But"—in a concession to the emerging capitalist ideology of consumer sovereignty—"it will be a tablet of any color and shape that is desired and will, I think, entirely satisfy the epicurean senses of the future."[29]

Well aware of mounting concerns about food adulteration and contamination, Berthelot argued that synthetic foods would be both tastier and safer than the natural variety—much the way *Mizora*'s cuisine was chemically "pure." "Strange though it may seem, the day will come when man will sit down to dine with his toothsome tablet of nitrogenous matter, his portions of savory fat, his balls of starchy compounds, his casterful of aromatic spices, and his bottles of wines or spirits which have all been manufactured in his own factories, independent of irregular seasons, unaffected by frost, and free from the microbes which over-generous nature sometimes modifies the value of her gifts." In line with mounting pressure for environmental conservation in the more industrialized nations, Berthelot also put a back-to-nature spin on his vision of a "synthetic acadia": by eliminating agriculture, synthetic foods would return the over-farmed countryside to wilderness and save natural resources. "If the surface of the earth ceases to be divided by the geometrical devices of agriculture, it will regain its natural verdure of woods and flowers...."

The favored portions of the earth will become vast gardens, in which the human race will dwell amid a peace, a luxury, and an abundance recalling the Golden Age of legendary lore." Coming from the acknowledged "foster-father of synthetic chemistry" (Liebig was the primary patriarch), Berthelot's prophecy was much quoted and debated over the next forty years, and his argument that only chemistry can "save" nature is still widely repeated by proponents of high-tech food production.[30]

While not necessarily advocating meal-pills, American nutritional scientists such as W. O. Atwater echoed and popularized Liebig and Berthelot's reductionist paradigm. Moreover, in line with the progressive backlash against Gilded Age gluttony, they insisted that people were spending far too much money and effort trying to please their fickle palates at the expense of their stomachs, and that social reform necessitated that people eat to live, not the reverse. In 1913 Belgian chemist M. Effront suggested that foods synthesized from the waste products of breweries and distilleries would ideally be tasteless, because diners would not be tempted to overeat. "It would be a hundred times better if foods were without odor or savor, for then we should eat exactly what we needed and would feel a good deal better." Writing in 1902 on scientific feeding for *Munsey's Magazine*, physician John H. Girdner argued that dining was overrated: "An actual calculation of what is absolutely necessary to nourish the body shows that the compressed food tablet, which has been the dream of scientists is not so far away or as unlikely of realization as some may imagine. It will come when man has conquered his palate and no longer allows it to dictate the quantity and quality of the things he swallows."

Eating enslaved everyone, not just women, Charlotte Perkins Gilman concluded in *Women and Economics* (1898). "The contented grossness of today, the persistent self-indulgence of otherwise intelligent adults, the fatness and leanness and feebleness, the whole train of food-made disorders, together with all drug habits—these morbid phenomena are largely traceable to the abnormal attention given to both eating and cooking."[31] While Gilman pushed cooperative, centralized kitchens—not synthetics—her underlying approach was not all that different from Berthelot's: progress required that food be de-socialized and un-domesticated, that is, divorced from its traditional (and seemingly irrational) associations with home, family, and mothering. In short, at a time when crusader Horace Fletcher was attracting numerous converts to the decidedly antisocial practice of "thorough mastication," and when Americans were already foregoing formal hot breakfasts for pristine cold cereals, including the pellet-sized Grape-Nuts (advertised by C. W. Post as "the most scientific food in the world"), it did not seem such a stretch to contemplate a future of meal pills, especially since Americans were already well acquainted with elixirs, liver tablets, vegetable extracts, and sundry nostrums purporting to cure neurasthenia, dyspepsia, "auto-intoxication," and other diseases of over-civilization.[32]

So if the meal-in-a-pill made so much sense from a progressive scientific point of view, why didn't it take hold? Several reasons, some obvious, some less so, seem to be involved.

★ SOCIOLOGY OF EATING

At some point every food scholar must quote Roland Barthes to the effect that food is more than nutrients; it is also closely tied up with our sense of who we are, where we come from, and how we relate to people.[33] The exchange and sharing of food is so central to group membership that it would be socially disastrous, or at least very destabilizing, to eliminate the rituals of eating. True, these rituals may be inefficient in a time sense, but for the purpose of maintaining relationships, they are highly effective. As my students remind me constantly, it is almost impossible to have a positive social experience without sharing food, even if it is just a cup of coffee or a bag of popcorn. Indeed, even NASA has conceded that astronauts on long-term missions "like to eat at least one of their three daily meals together to socialize and build camaraderie."[34]

The history of technological innovation shows that new inventions succeed best when they are most compatible with the existing social infrastructure. According to Joseph Corn, a true "technological fix" solves problems without changing underlying conventions. Thus automobiles and televisions were enormously popular because they reinforced a prevailing—and essentially conservative— preference for privatized family life.[35] Similarly, while Grape-Nuts and Corn Flakes certainly simplified breakfast rituals, they did not necessarily eliminate morning interactions altogether, and to further ease the transition, cereal marketers wisely balanced claims of "science" and "efficiency" with nostalgic allusions to "nature" and pre-industrial "tradition." On the other hand, meal-pills seemed too radically modernistic; they would disrupt and displace the basic infrastructure of social exchange without presenting an alternative, non-culinary way for people to maintain social ties.

Of course, this is a conclusion based in part on hindsight (meal-pills did not prevail) and scholarly ideology (my fealty to Barthes et al.). What is interesting about the argument for meal-pills is that it happened at all, for it showed that the modern, industrial food era had truly arrived. In a sense, the late Victorian case for the meal-in-a-pill anticipated a central epistemological debate of the ensuing century: what exactly is food? While all societies distinguish between "food" and "nonfood," it can be argued that such distinctions have become increasingly difficult in urban-industrial societies reliant on distant farms and factories. Like so much of modern life, "food" has become essentially an abstraction, since consumers have little knowledge of its natural origins or traditional forms. In a world increasingly dominated by artificial landscapes and "virtual" realities, defining "food" becomes mainly a task of drawing rather arbitrary and indefinite lines that are constantly subjected to redefinition by "experts," politicians, and marketers.[36] In this century the conventional wisdom seem to have drawn a line that excludes pills from the category of "food," but we still remain immensely uncertain about just about everything else—hence the enduring controversies over what is "natural," "organic." and "healthy." We're not even sure what is a vegetable (ketchup?).[37] Berthelot may have lost the battle of the pill, but his chemical-is-a-chemical paradigm still controls the war.

★ AESTHETICS

While confused about origins and composition, people still like "taste," they like variety, and they like amplitude and bulk. (In the 1920s, when nutritionists agreed on the human need for fiber, many synthetic food proponents decided that future foods would be derived from cellulose-rich wood pulp and algae, rather than from the more pristine coal, petroleum, and "air" of Berthelot's day.[38]) Notwithstanding the mounting demand for convenience, people like to work a bit on their food, at least to the extent of heating and chewing. Food marketers and engineers have also concluded that consumers favor products that resemble what is considered to be a natural, traditional form. "Orange drink" needs orange dyes, butter substitutes should be yellow, soy patties should look like hamburgers, and so on. Berthelot's extrapolative leap—that once people accepted something "artificial" like margarine, they would accept *anything* "artificial"—has not played out, yet.[39]

To be sure, consumers also envy the convenience, speed, and "efficiency" offered by pills. So the compromise in the marketplace has been this: a proliferation of easy-to-consume, nutrient-dense products that look and taste like real foods, not "medicine" or "pills"—for example, breakfast cereals, breads, candy bars, juices, milk shakes, and toaster pastries all "fortified" with a day's nutritional requirement. The same dynamic rules the current hyperbole about "nutraceuticals"—foods with conventional appearance and taste but that are genetically engineered to have increased medicinal or nutritional benefits, such as bananas with antibiotics, potatoes with vaccines, cornflakes dosed with anticarcinogenic chemicals from tomatoes. Instead of the meal-in-a-pill, we seem destined to get pills-in-a-meal.[40]

67

We do have vitamin pills, of course, but these are touted as *supplements*, not replacements.[41] Consumer capitalism profits from proliferation and redundancy, not simplification or substitution. In automobiles, Henry Ford's nineteen-year run of all-black Model T's eventually gave way to Alfred Sloan's acutely segmented line extensions and annual model changes. Similarly, the food market caters not to the homogenized lowest common denominator, but rather to ever more discriminating (i.e., picky and fickle) consumers with highly individualized tastes and distastes. As Harvey Green has shown in *Fit for America*, Americans seem almost programmed to be heterogeneous and eclectic in adapting particular health reforms; thus they welcomed John Harvey Kellogg's cereal flakes while *also* expanding the carnivorous habits that so angered Kellogg and his mentor, Sylvester Graham. Purists cringe, but the all-inclusive hypermarket wins.[42] Similarly, rather than simplifying eating, vitamin pills may actually *increase* overall food consumption. Once people feel they have taken care of their nutritional needs by popping the right pills, they may then feel free to treat "real" food as a hedonistic and social experience that extends way beyond mere sustenance—somewhat the way "low fat" and "sugar-free" foods seem to expand, not reduce, waistlines.[43] And with recent discoveries of thousands of phytochemicals, along with the invention of reasonably tasty fat, sugar, and salt substitutes, the potential for the capitalistic propagation of marginally differentiated, "guilt-free" "functional foods" seems almost unlimited.

★ POLITICAL ECONOMY

The food industry is too big, too entrenched, too politically powerful to allow itself to be replaced by a feeding system that is so efficient and rationalized as to threaten millions of jobs. In his 1932 satirical response to those late Victorian technological utopias, Aldous Huxley quipped that the economy of *Brave New World* would never stand for synthetic food because this would idle the third of the work force involved in conventional food production. And by freeing the other two-thirds from food preparation and consumption, the meal-pill would give them more leisure time than they—or the ruling powers—could safely handle. For Huxley's World Controllers, cooking and eating were opiates of the masses.[44]

Sensing the meal-in-a-pill's threat to their basic interests, defenders of the food industry have long argued that Berthelot's dream would be impractical, unhealthy, and, probably the worst thing in a consumer culture, "boring."[45] Yet, in acknowledgment of the progressives' critique of waste, the corporate food industry began, in the 1920s and 1930s, to offer an alternative vision of futuristic "efficiency." This vision was best represented at corporate pavilions at the world's fairs of the 1930s, with their fully automated farms, factories, and "kitchens of the future." Instead of rationalizing the *consumption* of food—the meal-pill's primary appeal—they would rationalize everything else, especially the largely unseen processes of food *production*.[46] But the end product of this newly streamlined, ingeniously value-added food delivery system would still look like traditional food: juicy roasts, steaming mashed potatoes, buttered peas. For, as with so much of consumer capitalism, success in the market place comes through catering to a fundamental ambivalence toward modernism. Marinetti's *Futurist Cookbook* notwithstanding, people want the convenience of the future, and the look (if not quite the taste) of the past.[47]

And yet, despite all these obstacles, many people still believe that meal pills are inevitable, though not desirable. Why so? I see two fatalistic beliefs at work here. In part there is that quasi-Malthusian fear that our propensity for sex will ultimately outrun our capacity for agriculture, so ultimately we may just have to go off-land for our food. A similar, grim apocalypticism seems to motivate the sale of "Emergency Survival Tabs"—"15 Days Food Supply Under A Pound"—in the *Militia of Montana's Preparedness Catalog*.[48]

But I also see another fatalistic tendency: popular fears that scientific rationalization is inevitable even if it is irrelevant to the interests and claims of ordinary citizens. These fears are by no means new—witness the enduring popularity of Mary Shelley's *Frankenstein*, or of Frank Baum's Oz books. Baum was a subtle satirist of the progressive era's over-rationalizing propensities, especially in his sketches of absurdly arch minor characters. In *The Magic of Oz* (1919), Professor H. M. Wogglebug delighted college students by inventing "Tablets of Learning," which reduced a full course of education to a few pills—one for mathematics, another for geography, others for history, handwriting, and so on—thereby freeing students for more important pursuits like baseball and tennis. So far so good, but then the worthy professor—perhaps a sendup of the over-reaching Berthelot—could not leave well enough alone and turned his attention to food. "But it so happened that Professor Wogglebug (who had invented so much that he had acquired the habit) carelessly invented a Square-Meal Tablet, which was no bigger than your little finger-nail but contained, in condensed form, the equal of a bowl of soup, a portion of fried fish, a roast, and a dessert, all of which gave the same nourishment as a square meal." His students objected, however, "because they wanted food they could enjoy the taste of." When the professor persisted, the senior class threw him in the river, where he lay helpless on the river bottom for three days until a fisherman hauled him in.[49]

While I am not so sure that today's students would be quite so rebellious, I do think they would catch Baum's drift. It is my guess that while many people vow and hope that *they* will never rely on pills for food, they fear that future generations will succumb because they believe that "science" marches on to its own beat, deaf or indifferent to human needs for community, relationships, and aesthetics.[50] So if "the scientists" want pills, we'll get pills. While this suggests a rather dreary popular perception of the gap between the lab and real life, it also offers some hope, because that same gap offers a space for resistance to the high-tech wonders that *are* being concocted in lab. People may feel that the lab will *ultimately* win out, but they won't let it happen *on their* watch. Back in 1953 chemical engineer Jacob Rosin lamented that the popular association of food pills with "some crazy scientist in a fiction thriller" was impeding public funding of what Rosin felt was much more viable research: artificial steaks synthesized from algae and yeast.[51] Thanks largely to such popular obstinacy, few, if any, scientists are working on food pills *or* algae today. But many *are* working on genetically modified meat; grain, and vegetables, even though many consumers do not seem happy about actually buying that food. The marketing problems of Calgene's MaGregor tomato and of dairy products laced with Monsanto's Posilac may reflect the same enduring suspicion of overly industrialized food that doomed the meal-in-a-pill. If so, perhaps much of the bioengineered food currently being developed and hyped will meet the same fate as the pill: always a wonder of tomorrow, but never quite of today.[52]

69

NOTES

1. Sampler Malthusian: Lester R. Brown, *Tough Choices: Facing the Challenge of Food Scarcity* (New York: W.W. Norton, 1966). Cornucopian: Joseph F. Coates, John B. Mahaffie, Andy Hines, *2025: Scenarios of US and Global Society Reshaped by Science and Technology* (Greensboro, N.C.: Oakhill Press, 1997).
2 Although not based on scientific polling, this observation is drawn from several hundred open-ended interviews and discussions concerning the future of food with colleagues, students, friends, and strangers. A similar pattern prevails in a recent Delphi-style survey of opinions concerning the dinner of the future. While several dozen food scholars, writers, and professionals divided between Malthusian and Cornucopian visions of the year 2050, the bluntest and possibly most "vernacular" opinion was offered by an octogenarian counterman at New York's Carnegie Delicatessen: "There will be nothing on the plate. You'll eat a pill." "What's for Dinner in 2050?" *Beard House* (Spring 1999), p. 36.
3. A rare exception is the 1999 prediction by Manfred Kroger, professor of food science at Pennsylvania State University, that within 100 years, "it's possible people won't eat meals at all but instead will consume individually designed wafers with just the right amount of fat, protein, fiber, carbohydrates, vitamins, minerals and medicinal herbs to meet their individuals needs." Nancy Hellmich, "Future Food Could Lengthen Your Life," *USA Today*, January 5, 1999, http://www.usatoday.com/hotlines/diet/diet01.htm accessed June 28, 1999. On the relationship between space fantasies and NASA realities: Howard E. McCurdy, *Space and the American Imagination* (Washington, D.C.: Smithsonian Institution Press, 1997).
4. Rachel Evans, "Yesterday, Today, but What about Tomorrow [sic]?" http://www.kidpub.org/kidpub/Yeste... marrow_-Rachel_Evans_POG_html, accessed May 19, 1998; Liz Thelen, "Future Food," 1997, http://www.hort. purdue.edu/super/liz/future.html, accessed May 19, 1998; Jamie Tennant, "A Shinier, Happier Future?" http://www.campus.org.archives/sept95/food.html, accessed April 24, 1997.
5. It is a methodological article of faith in cultural studies that prevailing ideas, images, and values are literally *embedded* in a wide variety of "texts"; hence the disparate types of evidence cited in this article, e.g., web pages, pulp novels, ads, films, and so on. The theoretical literature on popular ideology is voluminous. My starting points include Paul Willis, *Common Culture* (Boulder: Westview Press, 1990); Roland Barthes, *Mythologies* (New York: Hill and Wang, 1978); Richard Wrightman Fox and T. J. Jackson Lears, eds., *The Power of Culture* (Chicago: University of Chicago Press, 1993); Mike Wallace, *Mickey Mouse History and Other Essays on American Memory* (Philadelphia: Temple University Press, 1996).
6. Sharon Begley, "Beyond Vitamins," *Newsweek*, April 25, 1994, p. 49; Edward Dolnick, "Future Schlock," *In Health*, September–October, 1990, p. 22; Liz Brody, "Future Food," *Men's Health*, June 1991, p. 62; "The Future of Foods," *Wired*, 1995, http://www.com/wired/3.01/departments/reality.check.html, accessed May 19, 1998; Sidney Schaer, "For Dessert, Chomp on a Can," *Our Future*, 1999, http://future.newsday.com/Back to the Future, accessed June 28, 1999.
7. On the centrality of grains: Margaret Visser, *Much Depends on Dinner* (New York: Collier, 1986), pp. 22–55, 155–91; Jared Diamond, *Guns, Germs, and Steel* (New York: Norton, 1999), pp. 85–190; Maguelonne Toussaint-Samat, *History of Food* (Oxford: Blackwell, 1994), pp. 45–56, 128, 247–90; Harold McGee, *On Food and Cooking* (New York: Collier, 1984), p. 249; Maria Leach, ed., *Dictionary of Folklore* (New York: Funk & Wagnalls, 1949), p. 123. More recently, the potato has had a similar role as an all-in-one miracle food. See William McNeill, "How the Potato Changed the World," *Social Research* 66 (Spring 1999): 67–83.

8. It is probably not coincidental that the word "tablet" is the diminutive of "table," originally a board covered with food. Etymologically speaking, a tablet might thus be considered a mini-dinner.

9. Robert E. Martin, "Life from the Test Tube Promised by New Feats of Modern Alchemists," *Popular Science Monthly*, June 1936, p. 15.

10. On the primarily middle-class audience for speculative thought: I. F. Clarke, *The Pattern of Expectation, 1644–2001* (New York: Basic Books, 1979); Joseph J. Corn, ed., *Imagining Tomorrow: History, Technology, and the American Future* (Cambridge: MIT Press, 1987); Howard P. Segal, *Technological Utopianism in American Culture* (Chicago: University of Chicago Press, 1985). For an overview of the stresses and dreams of late nineteenth-century, middle-class American culture: Harvey Green, *The Light of the Home* (New York: Pantheon, 1983); T. J. Jackson Lears, *No Place of Grace: Antimodernism and the Transformation of American Culture, 1880–1920* (New York: Pantheon, 1981); James Gilbert, *Perfect Cities: Chicago's Utopians of 1893* (Chicago: University of Chicago Press, 1991).

11. Waverley Root and Richard de Rochemont, *Eating in America* (New York: William Morrow, 1976), p. 159.

12. Jack Goody, "Industrial Food," in *Food and Culture*, edited by Carole Counihan and Penny Van Esterik (New York: Routledge, 1997), pp. 338–56; John F. Mariani, *The Dictionary of American Food and Drink* (New York: Hearst Books, 1994), pp. 256–57.

13. Kenneth L. Ames, *Death in the Dining Room & Other Tales of Victorian Culture* (Philadelphia: Temple University Press, 1992), pp. 44–96; Pamela Walker Laird, *Advertising Progress: American Business and the Rise of Consumer Marketing* (Baltimore: Johns Hopkins University Press, 1998), pp. 101–51.

14. Peter Stearns, *Fat History: Bodies and Beauty in the Modern West* (New York: New York University Press, 1997), p. 60. Thoreau and Shaw quoted in Brigid Allen, ed., *Food: An Oxford Anthology* (New York: Oxford University Press, 1994), pp. 326–27. Also Harvey Levenstein, *Revolution at the Table: The Transformation of the American Diet* (New York: Oxford University Press, 1988), pp. 13–15; Hillel Schwartz, *Never Satisfied: A Cultural History of Diets, Fantasies, and Fat* (New York: Free Press, 1986), pp. 77–111. On earlier reformers: Stephen Nissenbaum, *Sex, Diet, and Debility in Jacksonian America: Sylvester Graham and Health Reform* (Chicago: Dorsey Press, 1988); James C. Whorton, *Crusaders for Fitness: The History of American Health Reformers,* (Princeton: Princeton University Press, 1982); Harvey Green, *Fit for America: Health, Fitness, Sport and American Society* (New York: Pantheon, 1986); Warren Belasco, "Food, Morality, and Social Reform," in *Morality and Health,* edited by Allan M. Brandt and Paul Rozin (New York: Routledge, 1997), pp. 185–200. Urging an entirely streamlined, chemically centered diet F. T. Marinetti waged a similarly righteous war against bourgeois Italian "pastasciutta, an absurd Italian gastronomic religion," in *The Futurist Cookbook* (1932; San Francisco: Bedford Arts, 1989), p. 37.

15. Dolores Hayden, *The Grand Domestic Revolution: A History of Feminist Designs for American Homes, Neighborhoods, and Cities* (Cambridge: MIT Press, 1981); Polly Wynn Allen, *Building Domestic Liberty: Charlotte Perkins Gilman's Architectural Feminism* (Amherst: University of Massachusetts Press, 1988).

16. Kristine Anderson, "Introduction," to Mary E. Bradley Lane, *Mizora: A Prophecy* (1880; Boston: Gregg Press, 1975), p. xii.

17. Mary E. Lease, "Improvements So Extraordinary the World Will Shudder," in *Today Then: America's Best Minds Look 100 Years into the Future on the Occasion of the 1893 World's Columbian Exposition,* edited by Dave Walter (Helena, Montana: American & World Geographic Publishing, 1992), p. 178.

18. Hayden, *Grand Domestic Revolution,* p. 134; Jean Pfaelzer, *The Utopian Novel in America: 1886–1896* (Pittsburgh: University of Pittsburgh Press, 1984), pp. 81–83. For an introduction to late nineteenth-century utopian fiction: Carol Farley Kessler, ed., *Daring to Dream: Utopian Stories by U.S. Women: 1836–1919* (Boston: Pandora Press, 1984); Kenneth Roemer, *The Obsolete Necessity: America in Utopian Writing, 1888–1900* (Kent, Ohio: Kent State University Press, 1976).

19. S. C. Gilfillian, "Housekeeping in the Future," *The Independent,* May 16, 1912, pp. 1060–1062; Levenstein, *Revolution at the Table,* pp. 60–71; Susan Strasser, *Never Done: A History of American Housework* (New York: Pantheon, 1982), pp. 76–84, 162–79.

20. Jane Donawerth, "Science Fiction by Women in the Early Pulps, 1926–1930," in *Utopian and Science Fiction by Women: Worlds of Difference,* edited by Jane L. Donawerth and Carol A. Kolmerten (Syracuse: Syracuse University Press, 1994), p. 138.

21. Joseph J. Corn and Brian Horrigan, *Yesterday's Tomorrows: Past Visions of the American Future* (Baltimore: Johns Hopkins University Press, 1996), p. 15.

22. On other miracle pills: Ruth Schwartz Cowan, *A Social History of American Technology* (New York: Oxford University Press, 1997), pp. 310–24.

23. Edward Bellamy, *Looking Backward* (1888; New York: New American Library, 1960); Howard P. Segal, *Technological Utopianism in American Culture* (Chicago: University of Chicago Press, 1985); Cecilia Tichi, *Shifting Gears: Technology, Literature, and Culture in Modernist America* (Chapel Hill: University of North Carolina Press, 1987); Carolyn Marvin, *When Old Technologies Were New: Thinking about Electric Communication in the Late Nineteenth Century* (New York: Oxford, 1988); Levenstein, *Revolution at the Table,* pp. 44–59, 98–108; Alan Trachetenberg, *The Incorporation of America: Culture and Society in the Gilded Age* (New York: Hill and Wang, 1982); Bradford Peck, *The World a Department Store: A Twentieth Century Utopia* (Lewiston, Maine: Bradford Peck, 1900); Martha Banta, *Taylored Lives: Narrative Productions in the Age of Taylor, Veblen, and Ford* (Chicago: University of Chicago Press, 1993). See Marinetti's *Futurist Cookbook* for a reductio ad absurdum of the efficiency argument.

24. On Fordism: James J. Flink, *The Automobile Age* (Cambridge: MIT Press, 1988), pp. 40–55.

25. Arthur Bird, *Looking Forward: A Dream of the United States of the Americas in 1999* (1899; New York: Arno, 1971), p. 185.

26. Push-button dreams: Thomas A. Edison, "The Woman of the Future," *Good Housekeeping,* October 19, 1912, pp. 436–44; Edwin E. Slosson, "Electric Farming," *Literary Digest,* August 7, 1926, p. 23. Damp-cloth utopi-

anism: Jeffrey L. Meikle, "Plastic, Materials of a Thousand Uses," in *Imagining Tomorrow: History, Technology, and the American Future*, edited by Joseph J. Corn (Cambridge: MIT Press, 1986), pp. 77–96. Time capsules: Folke Kihlstedt, "Utopia Realized: The World's Fairs of the 1930s," in *Imagining Tommorrow*, pp. 97–118. Atomic pellets: Stephen L. Del Sesto, "Wasn't the Future of Nuclear Energy Wonderful?" in *Imagining Tomorrow*, p. 61.

27. Levenstein, *Revolution at the Table*, pp. 72–160. For a parallel case of the interaction between science fiction and real science, see McCurdy, *Space and the American Imagination*.

28. Emerson quoted in *Since Eve Ate Apples*, edited by March Egerton (Portland, Oregon: Tsunami Press, 1994), p. 253. On the reductionist paradigm: Ross Hume Hall, *Food for Nought: The Decline of Nutrition* (New York, Vintage, 1974); Elmer McCollum, *A History of Nutrition* (Boston: Houghton Mifflin, 1957), pp. 84–99.

29. Henry J. W. Dam, "Foods in the Year 2000," *McClure's Magazine*, September 1894, pp. 311, 306. On Liebig: Levenstein, *Revolution at the Table*, p. 311.

30. Dam, "Foods in the Year 2000," p. 312. On saving wilderness through hightech farming: Walter Truett Anderson, "Food Without Farms: The Biotech Revolution in Agriculture," *The Futurist*, January–February 1990, pp. 16–21; Paul E. Waggoner, "*How Much Land Can Ten Billion People Spare for Nature?*" (Ames, Iowa: Council for Agricultural Science and Technology, 1994).

31. "Food from Waste Products," *Literary Digest*, January 4, 1913, p. 16; John H. Girdner, "The Food We Eat," *Munsey's*, November 1902, p. 188; Charlotte Perkins Gilman, *Women and Economics* (1898; New York: Harper Torchbook, 1966), pp. 255, 251.

32. Green, *Fit for America*, pp. 283–317; Levenstein, *Revolution at the Table*, pp. 87–97. Post quoted by Jeremy Iggers, *The Garden of Eating* (New York: Basic Books, 1996), p. 84.

33. Roland Barthes, "Towards a Psychosociology of Contemporary Food Consumption," in *Food and Drink in History*, edited by Robert Forster and Orest Ranum (Baltimore: Johns Hopkins University Press, 1979), p. 166. For recent samplers of food sociology: Alan Beardsworth and Teresa Keil, *Sociology on the Menu* (New York: Routledge, 1997); Steven Mennell, Anne Murcott, and Anneke van Otterloo, *The Sociology of Food: Eating, Diet and Culture* (Thousand Oaks, Calif.: Sage, 1992); Marjorie L. DeVault, *Feeding the Family: The Social Organization of Caring as Gendered Work* (Chicago: University of Chicago Press, 1991).

34. Lori Valigra, "Recipes for Beyond a Small Planet," *MSNBC*, February 18, 1998, http://www.msnbc.com:80/news/144882.asp, accessed February 24, 1998. For an extensive discussion of the virtues of social eating, see "Taste, Health, and the Social Meal," a special issue of *The Journal of Gastronomy 7* (Winter/Spring 1993).

35. Joseph Corn, "Epilogue," in Corn, *Imagining Tomorrow*, p. 221. Ruth Schwartz Cowan argues that feminist utopian community kitchens failed for the same reason: they did not fit the reigning privatistic paradigm. *More Work for Mother* (New York: Basic Books, 1983), pp. 117–19. For an excellent overview of the cultural determinants of technological innovation: Ruth Schwartz Cowan, *A Social History of American Technology* (New York: Oxford, 1997). On the early car culture: Warren J. Belasco, *Americans on the Road* (Cambridge: MIT Press, 1979). On early television: Cecilia Tichi, *Electronic Health: Creating an American Television Culture* (New York: Oxford University Press, 1991).

36. For a compelling discussion of the complexities of modern social constructions: Anne Murcott, "Scarcity and Abundance: Food and Non-food," *Social Research* 66 (Spring 1999), 305–339.

37. On abstract landscapes: Sharon Zukin, *Landscapes of Power: From Detroit to Disney World* (Berkeley: University of California Press, 1991). On definitional vagueness: Warren Belasco, *Appetite for Change: How the Counterculture Took on the Food Industry* (Ithaca: Cornell University Press, 1993), pp. 218–242; Joan Dye Gussow and Paul R. Thomas, *The Nutrition Debate: Sorting Out Some Answers* (Palo Alto, Calif.: Bull Publishing, 1986); Joel Bleifuss, "'Organic' with a Corporate Twist," *In These Times*, February 22, 1998, pp. 11–12.

38. E. E. Slosson, "The Progress of Science," *Scientific Monthly*, October, 1926, pp. 373–84; Warren Belasco, "Algae Burgers for a Hungry World? The Rise and Fall of Chlorella Cuisine," *Technology and Culture* 38 (July 1997): 608–34.

39. There also may be some enduring work ethic involved here. Taking a pill may be appropriate for illness, which is equated with sin, but may be considered "too lazy" when applied to other activities, including eating.

40. Nutraceuticals: Rick Weiss, "Replacing Needles with Nibbles to Put the Bite on Disease," *Washington Post*, May 4, 1998, p. A3; Kathleen Spiessbach, "Are Nutraceuticals the Future of Food?" *Yahoo! News*, http://204.71.177.22/headlines/980130/health/stories/nutra 14_1.html, accessed May 19, 1998; June 30, 1999; David Stipp, "Engineering the Future of Food," *Time*, September 28, 1998, p. 128.

41. Rima Apple, *Vitamania: Vitamins in American Culture* (New Brunswick, N.J.: Rutgers University Press, 1996).

42. On Sloanism: Flink, *Automobile Age*, pp. 229–50. On market segmentation: Richard S. Tedlow, *New and Improved: The Story of Mass Marketing in America* (New York: Basic Books, 1990); Susan Strasser, *Satisfaction Guaranteed: The Making of the American Mass Market* (New York: Pantheon, 1989). I call the trends toward ever greater dietary individualism the "Seinfeld Syndrome," after the impossibly finicky characters on the leading TV sitcom of the 1990s. On the selective and profitable adaptation of health reforms: Green, *Fit for America*, p. 317.

43. Curiously, this was Marinetti's intent in proposing food pills: by taking care of daily metabolic needs with a well-balanced tablet, modern consumers would be free to try a wide variety of aesthetically inventive, but nutritionally empty, creations, like "tactile vegetable garden"—a salad mixture to be rubbed across the face—and "ultravirile," a mysterious dish "designed for ladies." *Futurist Cookbook*, pp. 38, 78, 125.

44. Aldous Huxley, *Brave New World* (1932; New York: Perennial Library, 1969), p. 152.

45. Thomas Edison, "Inventions of the Future," *The Independent*, January 6, 1910, pp. 16–17; C. C. Furnas, *The Next Hundred Years* (New York: Reynal & Hitchcock, 1936), pp. 309–10; Michael Amrine, "Your Life in 1985,"

71

Science Digest, October 1955, p. 26; "Revolution in the Kitchen," *U.S. News & World Report*, February 15, 1957, p. 63.

46. Wheeler McMillen, *Two Many Farmers: The Story of What Is Here and Ahead in Agriculture* (New York: William Morrow, 1929); "New Marvels of Food Factories," *Popular Science Monthly,* July 1934, pp. 20–21; Furnas, *The Next Hundred Years*, pp. 289–319; Harold Pinches, "Engineering's Biggest Job," *Yale Review* 27 (Spring 1938): 496–515; Eve Jochnowitz, "Feasting on the Future: Serving Up the World of Tomorrow at the New York World's Fair of 1939–1940," unpublished Master of Arts Thesis, Department of Performance Studies, New York University, November 1997; Brian Horrigan, "The Home of Tomorrow, 1927–1945," in Corn, *Imagining Tomorrow,* pp. 137–63; Robert E. Rydell, *World of Fairs: The Century-of-Progress Expositions* (Chicago: University of Chicago Press, 1993).

47. On catering to consumer ambivalence about modernity: Belasco, *Appetite for Change*; Donna R. Gabaccia, *We Are What We Eat: Ethnic Food and the Making of Americans* (Cambridge: Harvard University Press, 1998), pp. 1–9, 149–232; Thomas Frank and Matt Weiland, eds., *Commodify Your Dissent: Salvos from The Baffler* (New York: W. W. Norton, 1997); Jennifer Price, "Looking for Nature at the Mall: A Field Guide to the Nature Company," in *Uncommon Ground: Rethinking the Human Place in Nature,* ed. William Cronon (New York: W. W. Norton, 1996), pp. 186–203; David Remick, "The Next Magic Kingdom: Future Perfect," *The New Yorker,* October 20, 1997, pp. 210–24. One current example of the way to profit by streamlining production and distribution while catering to a taste for the past is the success of Amazon.com—a corporation that sells old-fashioned books through the Internet.

48. "Emergency Survival Tabs," http://www.logoplex.com/resources/mom.survtab.html, accessed May 19, 1998.

49. L. Frank Baum, *The Magic Of Oz* (Chicago: Reilly & Lee Co. 1919), pp. 236–37. On Baum's political satire: Henry M. Littlefield, "The Wizard of Oz: Parable on Populism," *American Quarterly* 16 (Spring 1964): 47–58.

50. For a recent example of such fatalism: Charles Arthur, "Food and Drink: Futurology," *The Independent* (London), November 15, 1997, p. 35. Wondering "who let the scientists in" Arthur wearily concludes, "Those films depicting eating in the future as a dreary business, filled with labelled plastic packages so you don't mistake the chicken chasseur for the strawberry pie, weren't so far off. The brave new world is almost on your plate. More helpings of pond scum, anyone?"

51. Jacob Rosin and Max Eastman, *The Road to Abundance* (New York: McGraw-Hill, 1953), p. 36. For alga dreams: Belasco, "Algae Burgers for a Hungry World?"

52. There are, to be sure, at least two other scenarios: In what might be called the Ambivalent Cornucopia scenario, biotechnology may win the battle for the mainstream food market, but nostalgia for "nature" and "tradition" will enrich niche entrepreneurs catering to affluent gourmets. See Coates, Mahaffie, and Hines, *2025,* pp. 368–86. In the neo-Malthusian alternative, relentless economic and population growth will produce a global ecological crash; in the aftermath, *all* survivors may have to return to "nature" and "tradition." See Sidney Mintz, "Eating American," in this volume.

MAKING U.S. FOOD  2

THE AMERICAN RESPONSE
TO ITALIAN FOOD, 1880—1930

HARVEY LEVENSTEIN

7

One can hardly pick up a woman's magazine, daily newspaper, or even the *Wall Street Journal* without being confronted by yet another article on the "ethnic" invasion of American food habits. From the redwood beach houses of the West Coast to the glittering high rises of Manhattan's East Side, taramasalata, hummus, aioli, and Chinese shrimp toast have pushed onion and sour-cream dips from the hors d'oeuvres tray. Dishes that are rejected by all but the poorest peasants in a host of Third World countries grace the finest tables in Indianapolis. Vast franchising operations sell millions of dollars worth of so-called Mexican food to millions of Americans who a bare ten years ago equated tacos and frijoles refritos with stomach cramps and diarrhea.

Pundits offer many reasons for this interest in "foreign" food, ranging from increased foreign travel by Americans through the changing structure of home and family life to renewed immigration since the 1960s. Whatever its origins, however, the phenomenon is widely regarded as a departure from American tradition, and rightly so. Ever since the first Englishmen arrived in America and grudgingly adapted some native products to English methods of cookery, American tastes in food have remained resolutely Anglo-Saxon. Wave upon wave of European, African, and Oriental immigration has washed onto America's shores with remarkably little impact on the food habits of the vast majority of native-born Americans. Within one or two generations the children and grandchildren of the immigrants usually adopted Anglo-Saxon eating habits, often rejecting outright the food preferences of their parents and grandparents. Over the years Americans have added ingredients of overseas origin to their cuisine and have even adopted some foreign methods of preparing and serving food, but they have been relentless in domesticating them, integrating them in ways that did not disturb essentially British palates.[1]

Then there is the exception. One major immigrant group, the Italians, the largest of the "New Immigration" of 1880–1921, managed to survive assimilation with their Old World food preferences and style of eating at least identifiable. Indeed, Italian food was the first major foreign cuisine to find widespread acceptance among native-born Americans. By the 1940s, long before they were making guacamole in their blenders and discussing the relative merits of Szechuan and Hunanese Chinese food, housewives, college students, and professional cooks even in the darkest reaches of Middle America prided themselves on their recipes for spaghetti and meatballs and dined on "Veal Parmigiano" at restaurants with checkered tablecloths and candles mounted in Chianti bottles on the table. Later a seemingly insatiable appetite for pizza would solidify the place of Italian cooking as by far the most popular of the "ethnic" cuisines. Of course, very few Italians in Italy would have recognized any of these dishes in their American form, but millions of Italian-Americans did. Unlike Chinese Americans, for example, who generally found the concoctions served in "chop suey" houses and made-in-Minnesota canned "chow mein" to be abominations, Italian-Americans generally shared the native-born WASP's enthusiasm for the Americanized version of their cuisine. Rather than becoming ashamed of their mothers' cooking, second- and third-generation Italians celebrated it. Indeed, in a community deeply riven by regional and class hostilities, "Italian" food was one of the few sources of pride that the entire community could share, and that pride has subsequently formed a very important bond in keeping their ethnic consciousness alive.

Yet the first generations of Italian immigrants faced tremendous pressure to change their eating habits. The story of how they resisted the forces of assimilation and ended up adapting their food habits to the American environment, creating a cuisine that was distinctive enough to retain the old-country flavors yet attractive enough to turn the tables, as it were, and influence the tastes of the host culture, is an interesting and instructive one, for it gives us some insight into the kinds of forces that cause people to change or retain their food habits.

When the first great wave of Italian immigrants arrived in America in the 1890s and early 1900s, there was no such thing as "Italian food." Italy itself had only recently been unified politically, and the country was marked by profound regional and local differences. The *regionalismo* and *campanilismo* of Italian society were readily apparent in food habits, as they still are today. Although the first generations of immigrants tried to duplicate in the New World the cooking of their particular *paese*, the unavailability of certain ingredients, the relative abundance of others, and the influence of Italians from different regions gradually transformed the large majority's old-country eating habits. Immigrants from Campania, the province of the great port of Naples, and from Sicily formed the two largest groups among the immigrants, and their influence came to be predominant. Theirs was the cuisine of the tomato, onion, oil, cheese, and garlic, so often associated erroneously by Americans with the food of all of Italy. These immigrants, along with sizeable groups from other provinces in the Mezzogiorno, such as Sicily, Calabria, and Abruzzi, whose food preferences were not dissimilar, formed the largest market for imported and domestic Italian-style foods. Imported and domestic foods destined for their tables were thus widely available in the greatest variety and at the most reasonable prices. But their food habits were changing as well, for certain things (some fruits, vegetables, and cheeses) were either unavailable or prohibitively expensive in America, while the poor could more easily afford such items as meat, pasta, and beer.

In the years before the 1920s, however, regional and local influences still ran deep. First-generation immigrants to the cities tended to live in communities dominated by people from their towns and villages in Italy and to shop in stores that specialized in their regional foods. Wherever possible, they tried to grow the grapes, fruits, and vegetables of their *paese* in backyard or rooftop gardens. Many still ate *polenta*, the corn meal mush that was the staple of the poor of northern and central Italy, used lard or butter rather than oil in cooking, and retained other regional or local food preferences.[2]

Whatever their region of origin, Italians arrived in an America that was at best ambiguous about their food habits. On the one hand, in the 1890s the eating habits of wealthier Americans were being influenced by the latest trends in England, whose fancy hotels and country-house kitchens were again being invaded by "Continental" chefs, usually bearing recipes from French haute cuisine. Upper-class American hotels, restaurants, and clubs shifted away from the overwhelmingly "American" and English dishes and meals that had previously characterized their menus. By the turn of the century "Spaghetti Italienne" had joined the extensive choice of American and French items. It was usually served as one of the first courses, along with or instead of chicken livers, sweetbreads, or other relatively light items. But the Italian invasion of elite dining rooms at around this time appears to have halted with spaghetti.[3]

On the surface this is puzzling, for Italians had long since made their mark in the kitchens of America's finer restaurants and hotels. Indeed, Italians had presided over some of America's best-known restaurants, including New York City's Delmonico's, the pinnacle of nineteenth-century haute cuisine. Yet if their star was rising among American elite taste-makers in the 1870s and 1880s, it seems to have been declining by the 1890s and early 1900s. "At first, the Italians outranked the French in popularity," said a 1909 description of the New York City dining scene. "In the old days...the restaurants cherished by *gourmets* were nearly all owned by Italians.... The truth seems to be that Paris is today the mistress of the art of eating.... If an Italian wishes to make a fortune as a *restaurateur*, he gives his place a French name and models his *menu* after those to which Paris devotes so much tal-ent, even genius."[4] The author was somewhat ingenuous in implying that the earlier Italian-run restaurants were popular because they served Italian food, for this does not seem to have been the case. Indeed in 1889, when Alessandro Filippini, Delmonico's famous chef, published his massive cookery book, there were *no* dis-tinctively Italian dishes among its recipes or menus.[5]

However, the author was certainly correct in noting that by the turn of the cen-tury Italians in hotels and restaurants catering to the carriage trade devoted them-selves almost exclusively to French food.[6] While he ascribed the phenomenon sim-ply to patrons who demanded what was in fashion in London and Paris, the fact that the character of Italian immigration into America had changed markedly in the pre-vious twenty years must also have discouraged thoughts of popularizing Italian food among the upper crust. Before 1880 the relatively few Italian immigrants to America had often been skilled people from the north of Italy who were relatively acceptable by native-born White Anglo-Saxon Protestant standards. By 1900, how-ever, as the deluge of unskilled and poverty-stricken immigrants from the Mezzogiorno struck America's cities, Italy no longer merely connoted Rennaissance palaces and happy gondoliers to the native-born mind. More immediate were images of swarthy immigrants in teeming tenements: sewer diggers, railroad navvies, crime, violence, and the dreaded cutthroats of the "Black Hand." Spaghetti could stay on the menu, but only as "Italienne," the French spelling bringing some reassurance that the original Italian dish had been civilized and purified in French hands. (In any event it likely bore little resemblance to anything served in Italy.

Contemporary American recipes called for spaghetti to be cooked to a soggy pulp and served with tomato sauce heavily diluted with broth.) The presumed mediatory role of the French in bringing Italian spaghetti to America made it appropriate that the first major company successfully to market canned spaghetti on a mass scale was the Franco-American Company, whose advertising in its early years emphasized its French recipes and its French chefs.

If the upper class took to French food and at least flirted with Italian and other European dishes in the 1880s and 1890s, the middle classes remained obdurate in their rejection of "foreign" cooking. For gastronomic titillation they might at best be persuaded to try recipes from other parts of the United States. A survey of the recipes in the resolutely middle-class *Good Housekeeping* magazine for 1890 shows virtually no foreign influence.[7] An 1892 article on "Giuseppe's way with macaroni" was exceptional. It said Italian restaurants in America's principal cities cooked pasta "well" but recommended the method of talented Giuseppe and his pretty young wife as the best. Giuseppe's secret for macaroni appears to have been to buy imported pasta in irregular chips (actually a kind of bin-end, which nevertheless cost 10 cents a pound) rather than the long, thin, domestic macaroni, and to add cheese or tomatoes ("a great addition," the author assured skeptical American readers) to the beef stock in which Americans normally cooked pasta. His wife also used hard wheat flour from St. Louis to make "*macaroni a la capellita*" (capelletti or tortellini in much of Italy today), a dish the author found highly attractive, unusual, and tasty.[8] The article demonstrates that although macaroni was well known in middle-class America, the fact that the hard wheat flour of the American Midwest (which Italians call semolina flour) made the finest pasta was not. The reason was likely that semolina flour made pasta that could be eaten *al dente*, whereas Americans ate their macaroni cooked to a pulp. Italian ways of preparing pasta and particularly the many forms of homemade *pasta asciutta* were therefore virtual mysteries.

There is little indication of any growth in interest or appreciation of Italian cookery in the twenty-five years to follow. When Elizabeth Lyman Cabot, a well-educated upper-class Bostonian, toured Italy with her new husband for several months, keeping an extensive journal of all their activities with detailed descriptions of their hotels, nowhere did she even mention the food.[9] Articles on touring Italy in middle-class American magazines extolled the beauties of Rome, Venice, Florence, and Naples, cooed over the simple, smiling natives who always seemed to have a song on their lips and in their hearts, but rarely mentioned their food. Even an article on Venice in a housekeeping magazine managed to avoid describing Italian food. The only culinary reference at all is to some "viands" of an undetermined nature, which made up the author's first Italian dinner. Clearly the author assumed that readers' interest in Italian food would be eclipsed, as hers was, by the Grand Canal and the "gaily dressed party of singers in a brightly lighted gondola" moored at her hotel.[10] In 1913 only ten out of 1200 recipes in the *Around the World Cook Book* could be considered Italian by even a generous-minded reader.[11]

The reluctance of native-born, middle-class Americans to seek out foreign foods and ingredients was reinforced, in the case of Italian foods, by some of the firmly held fears and convictions of the time. The tomato, so important in Southern Italian cooking, was widely regarded in America as harmful throughout most of the nineteenth century. In the late 1880s tomatoes plummeted even further in esteem with the scientific "discovery" that they were carcinogenic.[12] While the cancer scare was short-lived, experts continued to warn that excessive amounts of "oxalic acid" still made tomatoes harmful.[13] Cookbooks often warned that tomatoes should be used only in very small quantities.

Another Italian propensity that found little favor in expert American eyes was an enormous appetite for fruits and green vegetables. Unaware of the existence of vitamins, the first generation of nutritional chemists had found most fruits and vegetables to be composed almost wholly of water and proclaimed green vegetables, in particular, to be of little nutritive value and very overpriced.[14] Pork, the main ingredient in the sausages that were practically a working-class staple, was also out of favor with American middle-class cognoscenti. "As an article of food, pork, of late years, does not generally meet the approval of intelligent people and is almost entirely discarded by hygienists," sniffed *Good Housekeeping* in 1890.[15]

Nor were Italian methods of cooking highly regarded. Zestful spicing was regarded as harmful by many, influenced, it would appear, by a turn-of-the-century recrudescence of the ideas of the early nineteenth-century food reformer William Sylvester Graham, who had warned of the danger of overstimulating the senses and wearing down the nervous system.[16] Prohibitionists, tracing a connection between a taste for spicy food and the excessive consumption of alcohol, warned that one led directly to the other. But prohibitionist or not, almost all Anglo-Saxons regarded garlic with particular horror. Even the Italian love of one-dish meals or mixtures of meat, grains, and vegetables ran counter to American nutritionists' warnings that foods mixed together were difficult to digest and therefore taxing on the system.

As for the native-born working classes, much of Italian cooking ran counter to their prejudice against soups, stews, and cheese. One of the more prominent of the first generation of modern American nutritionists, Mary Hinman Abel, spent much of the 1890s trying to convince American workers that soups and stews (commonly dismissed as "pig wash") were healthful and that cheese, which native-born working-class Americans rarely consumed, was indeed digestible.[17]

Meanwhile, not only were the middle classes decidedly unenthusiastic about Italian dishes in their own homes and restaurants, some were alarmed over the propensity of Italian immigrants themselves to consume Italian food. Upper- and middle-class philanthropists and reformers who were trying to improve the appalling living conditions in the urban slums into which so many of the new immigrants poured, were becoming concerned over its supposedly deleterious economic as well as physical effects on the poor. By the 1890s the idea was gaining currency that the misery of life in the slums could be mitigated if the ignorance of slum dwellers regarding sanitation, personal hygiene, and domestic chores could be overcome. The result was a burgeoning effort to teach "household economics" to slum dwellers, in their homes and in settlement houses. Although subjects involving sewing were usually the most popular among the pupils, the reformers very often regarded those directly involving the kitchen as the most important.[18] Not only did kitchen classes involve elemental health and hygiene, but, because the poor normally spent about half of their income on food, it was hoped that teaching them economy in food purchasing and preparation would provide them with more funds to spend on housing and clothing. But the reformers could not budge Italians on culinary matters.[19] "People of this nationality...cling to their native dietary habits with extraordinary persistence," wrote one public health reformer, reflecting a common frustration of those who tried to help the Italian poor to change their food habits.[20]

There were several reasons for the great difficulty the reformers and social workers encountered in trying to "Americanize" Italian immigrant eating habits. For

79

a start, the preparation and consumption of food played particularly important roles in Italian family life, with a host of highly important symbols attached to the ways in which mothers, daughters, fathers, and sons prepared and consumed it. Moreover, it was extremely difficult either to gain entry into Italian family homes and kitchens or to coax the women out of them.[21] This was especially true for something like settlement house cooking classes. Most women, and even their American-born daughters, retained their confidence in the old tradition of family and community-borne recipes and instruction in cooking. Their conservatism regarding the sources of cooking information was matched by their attitudes toward "American" food, which ranged from mere indifference to absolute disgust. Doctors often complained that Italians refused to be consigned to hospital care because they regarded hospital food as inedible.

The contrast between Italians and other immigrant groups, many of whom were at least interested in learning "American" methods of food preparation for use alongside the traditional methods, was exemplified in the transformation of Denison House, a well-established settlement in Boston's South End. In the 1890s, when the district was mainly Irish, its cooking school was popular. Around 1900, however, when the Irish moved out and Italians and other European groups moved in, only the non-Italian immigrants replaced the Irish in the cooking school. Although Italian men supported the settlement's debating, music, and theater societies, the boys attended its boys' clubs, and Italian women went to sewing classes, they were simply not interested in the cooking classes, even though in 1902 a professional teacher of domestic science was added to the staff.[22] Later, when a separate Italian Department was set up, it did not attempt to deal with food in any way.[23] The North Bennet Street settlement house in what became the "Little Italy" in Boston's North End had a very similar experience. Its first cooking course, given in 1880, before the Italian influx into the neighborhood, drew 200 women and girls to its lectures. By the turn of the century, when Italians had become the predominant ethnic group in the neighborhood, cooking classes were drawing only 11 or 12 students whereas sewing classes attracted close to 100. By 1905, when the neighborhood had become overwhelmingly Italian, cooking classes for adults had been abandoned completely. Cooking was henceforth taught only to children, as part of a domestic science course given for the public schools.[24] The "Housekeeping Center" set up in Rochester, New York, in 1906 seems to have run into similar problems. Apparently, its cooking classes evoked interest among Italians only when combined with sewing classes, and even then it was mainly cake-baking that women wanted to learn.[25]

Repeated failure did not deter the social workers, however, for by the early 1900s many of them were convinced that inadequate diet was a cause of the high death rate among the poor that America's first crude mortality statistics seemed to be exposing. In 1904 Robert Woods, the head of South End House, for many years the most important settlement house among Boston's Italians, expressed his concern in the influential magazine *Charities* over the apparent increase in death rates from the first to second generation of Italians who had settled in New England. Not only was this the result of the change from living outdoors in a sunny land to living in crowded tenements, he wrote, but "their over-stimulating and innutritious diet is precisely the opposite sort of feeding from that demanded by our exhilarating and taxing atmospheric conditions." Changing their diets was therefore "the chief step in bringing about the adaption of the Italian type of life to America."[26] (Others found cruder explanations. In 1901 a Buffalo newspaper reporter blamed high infant mor-

80

tality among Italian children on the unwillingness of Sicilians to touch their savings accounts, no matter what their children might suffer.[27])

Many social workers regarded the Italian way of shopping as one of the major impediments to teaching proper food habits. In 1911 Eva White, head of Boston's Peabody House, lamented that a major barrier to teaching immigrants to cook properly was their insistence on shopping in small stores, usually run by their countrymen. "No matter what inducements the larger stores of the city offer," she said, "they will trade with none but their own people."[28] The Boston Woman's Municipal League circulated fliers warning immigrants against buying food from street markets or from small stores that lacked proper sanitation facilities and allowed in dogs and cats.[29] Leaflets in Italian circulated by the New York Association for Improving the Condition of the Poor warned that produce purchased from ambulatory vendors and open-air stalls was invariably germ-laden.[30]

By 1911 the teaching of immigrants to cook in the American way was becoming a profession in its own right, even—self-styled—a science. Simmons College in Boston now had an expert in that field who traveled from settlement house to settlement house, with Simmons students in tow, teaching the immigrants how to cook and the students how to teach the immigrants.[31] In her influential autobiography of the previous year America's best-known social worker, Jane Addams, had emphasized the importance of public school cooking lessons in "Americanizing" Italians. An Italian girl who had taken them would "help her mother to connect the entire family with American food and household habits," she confidently declared.[32] Winifred Gibbs, the supervisor of household economy work of the New York Association for Improving the Condition of the Poor, taught future teachers of Household Arts at Teachers College, Columbia University, how to try to change Italian diets, warning that "any suspicion of harsh criticism" should be avoided, "as the Italians are very sensitive." In 1912 the association mounted an exhibit in an Italian area in Lower Manhattan showing the residents the supposed deficiencies in their diets. It presented an "Americanized dietary with the deficiencies corrected" and taught "correct" methods of preparation of food. Gibbs's description of the exhibit provides a good example of the air of self-assured superiority with which many of these experts pressed their rather bizarre notions on the immigrants. In this case her views were clouded by the erroneous belief that when various foods were mixed together while cooking, a higher proportion of their food value would be excreted by the body than if they had been cooked, served, and eaten separately, in the approved British and American manner. The "typical" dietary of a local Italian child of twelve was listed on a placard and calculated to cost twenty cents a day. "The breakfast was the inevitable 'bread and coffee,'" she wrote. "The other two meals presented an abundance of caloric values, but because of complexity of combinations the dishes were such as to prove a real tax on digestion." Although the American substitute was "of identical food value" (and cost five cents more), Gibbs proclaimed it superior to the Italian because the food value of the Italian menu "was theoretical only, with too little attention paid to strict assimilation." With placards in Italian proclaiming the superiority of the more expensive American dietary to (likely uncomprehending) immigrants, the two sets of prepared meals were actually laid out before their eyes. Gibbs wrote that the placard explained:

Substitution of cocoa shells for coffee—pleasure.
Introduction of cereal.

81

Separation of one elaborate dish into three simple ones.
Use of oil on salad instead of in frying.
Introduction of milk.[33]

The last two points were favorite themes of those who bemoaned Italian immigrant dietary habits. During the First World War, when imported cheese and olive oil prices rose sharply, investigators from Teachers College would lament finding poor Italian immigrant families "suffering from cold and lack of food, buying 1 and 2 ounces of Roman cheese and small quantities of olive oil. . . . The investigators found many homes in which housewives bought no milk at all because they thought it too expensive and at the same time were buying a small piece of cheese at $1.25 a pound."[34]

These themes had emerged in the Italian pamphlet that the New York association circulated in 1914. It warned that mixing foods together robbed them of their nutritive effects. "It is not right to cook meat, cheese, beans and macaroni together," it said. Rather, the meat should be served alone, and the beans or pasta should be served separately, with cheese. Delicatessens, with their salamis, sausages, pickles, and potato salads, should be avoided, for their spicy foods damaged the stomach without providing any sustenance.[35]

American entry into the world war provided a new impetus to the Americanization effort. Social workers hoped not only that the efforts of the new U.S. Food Administration to conserve food would aid the Allied war effort but that involving immigrants and teaching them how to cook in the American way would heighten their patriotism as well.[36] But the campaign hardly affected most immigrants, and the Italians in particular remained stubbornly immune to outside advice. In part, the Food Administration's problems in reaching Italian and other immigrants lay in its middle-class nature. Under its director, Herbert Hoover, its main thrust was toward voluntary conservation: vast campaigns were mounted to secure housewives' pledges to conserve wheat flour, cane sugar, meat, and other commodities, mainly by substituting other foods for them. These campaigns were usually organized by and around women's clubs and organizations such as the Daughters of the American Revolution, bodies in which immigrants and particularly Italian ones were, to say the least, not particularly prominent. The Food Administration did enlist Jane Addams and other social workers with contacts among the foreign-born to make speeches on behalf of conservation, but their impact was limited. Addams, for example, traveled the country at FA expense, but she spoke almost exclusively to women's clubs, businessmen's clubs, and other middle-class organizations of the native-born, and never, it would seem, to immigrants.[37] The FA did have a Vernacular Press section to reach the foreign-born in their own language, but little of its material was used because it was sent out in English, and most foreign-language papers could not afford to translate its material.[38] That, at least, is what the editors told the FA, but clearly they did not bother to translate it because they also sensed that it would arouse little interest among their readers. And with some justification, for the main reason for the campaign's failure to make a dent among Italian (and other) immigrants would seem to be that in fact there was little they had to learn regarding economy in food preparation and preservation. The realization of this dawned rather quickly on the Food Administration. In September 1917 the Vernacular Press section refused to circulate an article calling for reduced consumption of meat ("We Can Fight Back with Our Teeth") because "practically all the readers of the foreign language press already ate very little meat because they couldn't afford to eat much of it."[39] Lousiana's food administrator reported to Washington that "the poorer part of the [Italian] colony...cannot, it seems to us, be impressed by pleas to conserve a little bread, butter, milk, and fat, since it is forced to economize on these articles all the time."[40]

Neither did the campaign to plant Victory Gardens have any impact. Italians, who had a mania for backyard, front-yard, rooftop, and windowsill gardening, already had a much higher proportion of the cultivatable land near their homes devoted to food production than women's club activists ever conceived of having. As for food preservation, few people could equal the Italians in their late summer and fall orgy of canning, bottling, pickling, and drying, when huge quantities of tomatoes, peppers, cauliflower, and other vegetables (not to mention home-grown grapes preserved in the form of wine) were packed into containers of all kinds and loaded into larders, cellars, and any available space, to be drawn upon during the long winter and spring that lay ahead. It is no wonder, then, that the home economists contracted by the Food Administration to lecture on conservation at social settlement houses in Italian areas had little impact. Indeed the Board of Directors of Boston's Denison House, a settlement with a large Italian clientele, were told that at a number of food conservation demonstrations held over the summer of 1917, "the audience was able to give the teacher instructions."[41]

If the Food Administration had little impact on Italian immigrants' food habits, it did markedly affect the way the native-born middle class regarded Italian food. Some urban home-demonstration agents began to realize that their lectures on food conservation might be better comprehended if they framed their talks in terms of the foods immigrants actually used, speaking of macaroni in explaining carbohydrates to Italian audiences, for example, and trying to portray conservation lessons as things learned from "the food of the allies,"[42] meaning, very often, Italy. More important, thanks in large part to the new emphasis on substituting beans and other legumes for meat as well as the general search for more economical ways of feeding a family as food prices rose, many home economists and writers for middle-class homemakers' magazines began to take a new, more favorable look at the food of Italy. Of course, no one ever admitted that a sharp reversal was taking place. There were no public recantations by nutritionists and social workers, and admissions like "contrary to our former recommendations" were never used. However, by mid-1918 Italian recipes were becoming commonplace in articles on food conservation. "Meatless days have no terror for our Italian friends of California," began a *Good Housekeeping* article on how to make spaghetti and ravioli.[43]

Abetting this new look was Italy's role as an American ally in the war effort, which helped raise the status of things Italian in American eyes. Thousands of Americans heeded Woodrow Wilson's admonition to join Italian-Americans in celebrating Italy Day in May 1918. They commemorated the third anniversary of Italy's entrance into the war by lining the streets of towns such as Oswego, New York, to watch patriotic parades and listen to stirring tributes to Italian immigrants' contributions to the war effort.[44] No longer the foul-smelling sustenance of crime-ridden Little Italies, Italian food was now what fortified America's sturdy ally in the war against the Hun.

"Ravioli, favorite dish of our Italian ally, should be served on every American table," said the above-mentioned *Good Housekeeping* article.[45] One of the first Italian cookery books published in English in America, a slim volume written by a Milwaukee woman married to an Italian, also combined solidarity with the new-found ally and patriotic duty at home. Published to raise money for the families of Italian soldiers, it pointed out that the prototypical Italian meal, with its succession of soup, pasta, rice, vegetables combined with meat, salad, fruit, and coffee, "was in keeping with the suggestions of our Food Administrator that we use a minimum of meats and sweets and a maximum of soups, fruits, vegetables, made dishes and cheese.[46]

Where Italian immigrants had been almost universally condemned by prewar food experts for their use of olive oil, cheese, and other expensive ingredients, they were now praised for their frugality with food. The author of a book defending Italian immigration against those who wished to restrict it wrote that "the housewife will make a cabbage and a knuckle go farther than most native Americans would make a loin of beef and a half dozen vegetables.... Nothing is too coarse or repulsive for the Italian peasant to eat, if it is not absolutely poison." (Indeed, he assured his readers, "squid and octopus, though tough and leathery, are not such hideous things to eat as they are to look at.") There were even more ways of cooking polenta and pasta than there were of cooking eggs, "and each way of cooking it seems a little better than the last."[47] The privations of poverty were now regarded as happy training grounds by enthusiastic converts. "Meatless days to the Italian housewife are no problem," wrote a breathless Grace Selden in the October 1918 *Good Housekeeping*, only one month after another author had used a virtually identical lead sentence. "All her days have been meatless days from her *bambino*-hood up. She can concoct a delicious dinner without meat—soup, varied vegetable dishes toothsome as well as nutritious, a salad that is almost too good to be true, a bit of fruit with cheese and coffee, and there you are. It is a *festa*." Selden even warned against using bottled Parmesan cheese and admonished readers to buy it by the chunk in a "little Italian grocery store in an out of the way street."[48]

During the prewar debate on immigration, restrictionists had emphasized the supposed Italian propensity toward crime, violence, and working for abysmal wages, while defenders had portrayed them as hard-working and frugal, endowed with sunny dispositions and artistic temperaments. Now food writers began to see signs of the latter virtues in Italian food. "What makes Italian cooking so good?" wrote Selden. "Because of the true artist blood in every Italian's veins. Good cooking requires vision, imagination, a sensitiveness to fine shades of flavor, to beauty of color and form and composition. That is where the Latins have the advantage over us."[49]

One manifestation of the new appreciation for Italian food was a tendency among social workers and reformers to reverse their judgments on the food habits immigrants had brought over from Italy. While the overwhelming majority of immigrants from Italy seem to have regarded their diets as having been vastly improved by the move to America, some looked back at those fresh fruits, vegetables, and other foodstuffs of the Old Country which were unavailable in America with the nostalgic longing of men and women who really enjoy eating. Some Americans seized on these reveries, and by 1920 a revisionist tide was in full flow. Now social workers, reformers, and food writers portrayed Italian immigrants as people who abandoned the sunny abundance of a varied and healthful diet for the meager fare of the tenements of America. Their revisionism was reinforced by recent changes in scientific ideas about nutrition, including the discovery of the first vitamins. Now the old standards, which recommended a very high intake of meat and proteins, were being rapidly eroded; milk, cheese, fruit, and vegetables were recognized as containing important vitamins and minerals, and a frantic search began to discover even more of their health-giving properties. Nutritionists, aware that new vitamins might be discovered any day in foods they had discouraged people from eating, increasingly hedged their bets and emphasized variety and "balance" in diet. In early 1921, in place of the usual prewar denunciation of the ignorance regarding proper food habits that Italian immigrants brought with them from the Old Country, an article in the *Journal of Home Economics* began by praising the healthfulness of Italian diets. Even the poorest people of southern Italy had fruits and vegetables in abundance, it said. Goats furnished more than enough milk for the family, and the surplus was made into cheese. The people of northern and central Italy had "a very well-balanced diet.... The occupation of the southern Italians outside the large cities is fishing," it said, which gave these seacoast people "a more varied diet than the other two groups." In America, alas, immigrants had to face much higher prices for milk, eggs, and other staples, and they were forced to do without ample supplies of these healthful items.[50] "The diet of the Italian in his own country is very well balanced," wrote a prominent dietitian-social worker in 1922. "A taste for meat and sweets was acquired in this country. They have milk, cheese, fruit and vegetables in abundance in Italy but these foods seem expensive here and milk is omitted and cheese and greens are used for flavoring to a large extent."[51] Of course, these ideas were just as inaccurate and the conclusions just as wayward as those which underlay the previous, critical stance toward Italians' eating habits. Large quantities of milk were not consumed in Southern Italy, most nonurban Italians were peasants not fishermen, a sweet tooth was not acquired in America, and so on. Nevertheless, some Americans were so affected by the change in attitude toward Italian food that they even advocated abandoning the effort to change immigrant eating habits. "Let the Italians alone," one social worker told Winifred Gibbs of Teachers College. "They have a home life of high standards and a diet rich in energy." "Why grow gray over the home budget of Italians?" an economist asked here. "They are notably frugal, living on simple food and often putting money in the bank."[52]

Although Gibbs and other dietitian-social workers were by no means deterred from their reformist path, their analysis did change in some degree. Some began saying that the problem lay not in the Italian diet itself but in the changes wrought in it by the move to America. They now saw their role as teaching Italians to cook Italian food with American ingredients. "The Italian woman, when she does cook a meal, spends much time and care, and the results are very appetizing," wrote two specialists in the field in 1921. "The raw materials of the Italian diet, many of which were easily procured on their own farms, when combined in home country ways, furnished a cheap well-balanced diet." However, they said, because of the expense of Italian ingredients in America the immigrants often had a poorly balanced diet, "short in some of the most important food elements." Dietitians must therefore teach immigrants how to substitute American ingredients such as vegetable oils for costly Italian ingredients such as olive oil, and to thicken soups with macaroni and rice rather than expensive eggs. "The problem before the dietitian," they said, "is not as much to introduce a complete 'American' dietary as it is to restore the former dietary balance by supplying lost elements."[53]

But Gibbs and her acolytes must have sensed that their endeavor was rapidly being undermined, not only by changes in native-born attitudes toward Italian food but by the dwindling number of immigrants among whom they could spread their unheeded message. The war had effectively closed off most immigration from Europe, including that from Italy; after a renewed influx in 1919 and 1920 the

Immigration Act of 1921 tried to make closure permanent. The Immigration Act of 1924, aimed specifically at immigrants from Southern and Eastern Europe, succeeded in cutting the prewar flood to a trickle. By the mid-1920s interest in changing immigrants' eating habits was on the wane.

Now the influence began to run in the opposite direction. Magazines began to run favorable articles on dining in Italy. "Italian cookery has a tremendous range," said a *Woman's Home Companion* article in 1924. "The peasants and the lower middle-class live with a Spartan rigidity, as far as food goes.... But when you get beyond that you find much elaboration, and many good ideas which are totally unknown to American cooks."[54] An article in the usually chauvinistic *American Cookery* said deep-fried Italian scampi was such a "wonderfully delectable dish" that it had been "pronounced even better than the highly esteemed Long Island scallops of Great Peconic Bay."[55] Of course, one could go only so far: while generally enthusiastic about Italian food, the author echoed the constant refrain of the time, that "the malodorous garlic taints practically everything served, from the salad up, and down. The Italian diet likewise includes a bewildering variety of cheeses and sausages, many of which smell even worse than they look, which is to say a great deal."[56]

Meanwhile, recipes for spaghetti and Italian-style macaroni were becoming much more common in homemakers' magazines and on middle-class tables. Although more closely resembling those of Italy than the prewar ones for "Spaghetti Italienne," they were still normally altered to avoid offending the more delicate palates of Anglo-Saxon readers and would have raised many an eyebrow in Naples or Palermo. For example, rarely was garlic used in the tomato sauce—which was about the only sauce ever mentioned in connection with Italian food. A bit of chopped green bell pepper was as daring as *Good Housekeeping* magazine would go, while *American Cookery* had cooks add a tablespoon of Worcestershire sauce to the two cans of tomato soup that formed the basis of its spaghetti sauce.[57] Nevertheless, the signs are there that "Italian food" was rising in status in American middle-class homes.

Americanized versions of Italian food had also spread to non-Italian tables thanks to the increasing sophistication of the food-processing industry. During the 1920s Franco-American spaghetti was joined by equally bland versions from Campbell's, Heinz, and others. However remote these products might have been from foods of the same name in Italy, they made the idea of dining on spaghetti in tomato sauce commonplace in America. Moreover, their blandness and the ease of digesting them, as well as the sugar that laced their sauces, seemingly made them ideal foods for small children, among whom they became great favorites. At the same time American food processors, witnessing the growing success of Italian-American producers of a large variety of pastas, began to branch out from the soft-flour macaroni with the hole in the middle, which had been well-known in America for many years, to the thinner, hard-flour-based, Italian-style spaghetti and vermicelli that were now being extolled as rich in protein.[58] These were joined on grocers' shelves by canned tomato sauces and, soon, "kits" for making "Italian spaghetti dinners." The kits contained spaghetti, a can or bottle of tomato sauce, and a bottle of grated Parmesan cheese. By 1927 giant Kraft Foods had developed a convenient cardboard container, out of which their version of Parmesan cheese could be poured or shaken, and was playing an active role in promoting the cooking of spaghetti with tomato sauce and its cheese.[59]

Perhaps the ultimate recognition that some form of Italian cooking was filtering down through the kitchens of the nation came in 1933. I. B. Allen, a popular radio cooking teacher in New York City, published a cookbook to be sold exclusively by the Woolworth's chain of 5-and-10-cent stores, whose lunch counters were the almost exclusive preserve of lower-middle and working-class native-born American food tastes. She included a number of Italian dishes in her book, including her versions of gnocchi, polenta (which she called *sopa*), risotto (which she assured readers was the most popular dish that a professor of literature at an old New England college cooked for his students), and a recipe for "Spaghetti Italian" whose tomato sauce actually called for three cloves of garlic as well as one-half cup of olive oil and grated parmesan cheese.[60] As the long years of the Great Depression led to renewed concerns for frugality in the kitchen, "Italian Spaghetti" was well placed to become one of the mainstays of American cooking.

In tandem with this new acceptance was the growth of Italian restaurants specializing in pasta and catering to the non-Italian trade. Space does not permit an analysis of the evolution of the Italian restaurant during the twentieth century or of the changing food habits of Italian-Americans in the 1920s and 1930s,[61] but the following might constitute a reasonable general hypothesis: the restaurants catering to Italian immigrants seem to have gone through a metamorphosis similar to that of immigrants and their children. They began, often as rooming houses, by catering to men from a particular *paese*, serving food cooked in the style of that *paese*; but during the 1920s, as local and regional loyalties began to weaken and feelings of Italian nationality came to the fore, those which had become restaurants tended to abandon their regional identities as well. With restricted immigration, the market among "sojourners," single men who returned to Italy after a temporary stay in America, practically dried up, and an increasing number of first- and second-generation families came to constitute the clientele of those which survived. Restaurants serving the foods of Campania and Sicily, the regions that provided the bulk of the immigration, came to dominate in the large cities.[62] But the process was not quite so simple, for their clientele from other areas were unlikely to have been enamored of many of the southern regional specialities with which they were unfamiliar or which were low-status items in their own *paese*. Few Southern Italian restaurants in America, for example, seem to have relied on the skills of their regions in cooking octopus, squid, and a variety of low-status fishes in *zuppa di pesce*. Rather, customers from various regions of Italy seem to have gravitated toward those items which were well-known and high-status items in most of the peninsula: namely pasta (at best a Sunday dish for many of the poor in turn-of-the-century Italy, coarse bread and polenta being the staple grain foods in most rural areas), chicken, beef, and veal. Thus the emergence of the inevitable triumvirate on the checkerboard tablecloths: spaghetti with meatballs, chicken cacciatore, and veal parmigiano.

Continuing our brief hypothesis: the first Americans to discover this new cuisine in significant numbers were probably those who went to the Little Italies of the major cities during Prohibition to buy alcohol. While boarding house owners may have been hurt by restrictions on immigration, Prohibition provided some economic compensation. They had traditionally made wine and beer and distilled grappa for their boarders and their friends, and now the competition of neighborhood bars and cafes had been eliminated. Many a boarding house lady expanded her production to meet the new demand, leaving Little Italies and their restaurants practically awash with alcoholic beverages during the misnamed Dry Decade. The large number of non-Italians initially attracted to the restaurants of the Italian sections for this reason probably formed a basis for the increasing popularity of Italian restaurants among non-Italians in the 1930s and 1940s.

87

The Great Depression of the 1930s gave a tremendous boost to the new Italian food. Pasta and tomato sauce, meat sauce, or meatballs became favorites in millions of American homes, their economy and meat-stretching attractions supplemented by their ease of preparation. Not only did social workers abandon their attempts to teach the Italian poor how to cook, they began learning from them. The students at Boston's North Bennet Street Industrial School started to stage annual spaghetti dinners, which appreciative social workers and the Boston Brahmin members of the board of directors attended. The social workers published a collection of the neighborhood women's Italian recipes in English as a fund-raising venture.[63]

By the Second World War, then, the circle had turned almost fully. Not only had spaghetti and tomato sauce (or meat sauce or meat balls) become a staple in millions of American homes, but macaroni and cheese had become the nation's great meatless dish. Its consumption was touted as promoting good health as well as food conservation: an Americanized version of exactly the kind of food that the reformers and "Americanizers" of twenty-five years earlier had condemned. "Spaghetti-bender," a term of opprobrium in the 1920s, was losing its bite. Italians, more than any other major non-British immigrant group, had not only succeeded in resisting pressures to "Americanize" their food but were now watching it rise rapidly in status in American homes and restaurants. This success would in turn reinforce their own tendency to use food as a distinctive source of ethnic pride. That the "Italian food" in which they took such pride was a hybrid, arising from interactions among cross-cultural influences within the Italian immigrant community and the opportunities and restrictions of the New World, was of little concern. No matter that "spaghetti and meatballs" in its American form was practically unknown on the Italian peninsula. To millions of Americans, including Italo-Americans, it had come to connote something of which Italians could be proud.

The Italians thus became one of the few ethnic groups in the United States who retained and indeed cultivated distinctively non-Anglo-Saxon modes of cooking and eating through the second and even the third generations after immigration. Clearly, this extraordinary ability to resist cultural assimilation at the dinner table involved many factors, but one of the most important must have been the changes in the "host" culture's attitudes. For reasons likely related to the centrality of food and its preparation to their family life, Italian-Americans were able to withstand the host culture's conscious attempts to change their food habits and to shrug off its denigration of their food. Indeed, they resisted long enough to witness a perceptible change in native-born attitudes toward their food. Meanwhile, they adapted their food to the new environment while retaining its distinctiveness. The positive attitudes of native-born non-Italians toward this new, hybrid food, attitudes that emerged in the 1920s and 1930s, in turn encouraged Italians to value their food highly, keeping it central to their shared family experience. Perhaps it also enabled them to assimilate the values and habits of the dominant culture in many other ways and yet reassure themselves that they were not deserting the culture of their forebears.

It is difficult to conceive of this kind of cultural compromise occurring had American views of Italian food in the 1930s and 1940s remained as they had been in the years from 1880 to 1916. The various modes of acculturation of immigrants appear to be products of the interplay between the "cultural baggage" that immigrants bring from their homelands and the possibilities in the new environment. If this is so, then, in the case of food habits, much more than the physical environment that the immigrants confront must be taken into account. Indeed, in a modern world where it is possible to import almost any food ingredient if people are willing to make the necessary economic sacrifices, the new geographical and agricultural environment takes a back seat to cultural factors. This, at least, would seem to be one of the lessons of the Italian migration to America.

NOTES

1. Waverly Root and Richard de Rochemont made this point in *Eating in America, A History* (New York: Morrow, 1976).
2. The following is a vastly oversimplified description, for space does not permit an analysis of the forces inducing persistence and change in first-generation food habits. A study of the food habits of Italian immigrants to America, on which I am working with Professor Joseph Conlin of the State University of California, Chico, deals with this matter in detail.
3. Restaurant and Hotel Menu Collection, 19th Century Box, Schlesinger Library, Radcliffe College, Cambridge, Mass.
4. Richard Duffy, "New York at Table," *Putnam's* 5, no. 5 (February 1909), 567.
5. Alessandro Filippini, *The Table* (New York: Charles Webster, 1889).
6. At the Culinary Exhibition of Boston's Epicurean Club in 1904, for example, where the professionals in the kitchens of Boston's top hotels, restaurants, and clubs displayed their wares, a good number of the chef/exhibitors were Italian. Yet to a man they presented French dishes as their chefs d'oeuvre: dishes such as Lobster Parisienne. Chaudfroid en Bellevue, Salad Bizantine, Boar's Head Alsacienne, and Salad à La Russe. (The last three were French versions of other foreign, non-Italian, dishes.)
7. *Good Housekeeping*, 10 and 11 (1890).
8. Hester M. Poole, "An Italian Dish," *Good Housekeeping*, 16 (January 1893).
9. "E.L.C. 1st European Trip, 1894," Ella Lyman Cabot Papers, Box 11f, Schlesinger Library, Radcliffe College.
10. Mary Nevins, "Venice, Bride of the Sea," *Everyday Housekeeping*, 23 (November 1906), 254.
11. Mary Louise Barroll, *Around the World Cook Book. The Culinary Gleanings of a Naval Officer's Wife* (New York: Century, 1913).
12. *Good Housekeeping*, 15 (December 1892), 268.
13. J. M. Albahary, *Ann. Falsif.*, 2, no. 5, (1909), 140–44, abstract in U.S. Department of Agriculture, Office of Experiment Stations, *Record*, 22 (January–June 1910), 264.
14. See Harvey Levenstein, "The New England Kitchen and the Origins of American Eating Habits," *American Quarterly*, Fall 1980.
15. *Good Housekeeping*, 10 (15 March, 1890), 229.
16. On Graham, see Stephen Nissenbaum, *Sex, Diet, and Disability in Jacksonian America* (Westport: Greenwood, 1980). On the line from Graham to latter-day Grahamites, particularly Dr. John Harvey Kellogg of Corn Flakes' fame, see James C. Whorton, *Crusaders for Fitness* (Princeton: Princeton University Press, 1982).
17. Mary Hinman Abel, *Practical and Sanitary Cooking Adapted to Persons of Moderate and Small Means* (Rochester, N.Y.: American Public Health Association, 1890).
18. The College Settlement House in New York City, for example, taught cooking to girls from the day of its founding in 1890. So did the Hartley House Settlement on the city's West Side, which had a full-fledged cooking school when it was opened by the New York Association for Improving the Condition of the Poor to teach the poor how to live frugally. See Association of College Settlements, First Annual Report, 1890, and "Hartley House, An Industrial Settlement," both in Settlements Collection, Sophia Smith Collection, Smith College Library, Northampton, Mass.
19. See Levenstein, "New England Kitchen."
20. Rene Bache, "What the Very Poor Eat," *Sanitarian*, 52 (February 1899), 107.
21. See Virginia Yans-McLaughlin, *Family and Community: Italian Immigrants in Buffalo, 1880–1930* (Ithaca: Cornell University Press, 1977), 139–41, for a description of how the settlement houses in Buffalo, with their "diet kitchens" and sewing classes, failed to affect Italians because they misunderstood and undermined the immigrants' values.
22. Reports of the Headworker, 1897–1927, Denison House, Records, Box 2, Folders 6 and 7, Schlesinger Library, Radcliffe College.
23. Reports of Italian Department, 1907–13, Denison House, Settlements Collection, Sophia Smith Collection, Smith College Library.
24. North End Industrial Home and North Bennet Street Industrial Home Reports, 1880–1, 1898–9, 1902–3, 1905, North Bennet Street Industrial School Papers (henceforth NBIS Papers), Series I, Box 1, Folder 1, Schlesinger Library, Radcliffe College. Children continued to be the only ones taught cooking into the 1920s, after the domestic science classes had moved into the public schools. Then the "Little Housekeepers" program at the NBIS taught 7- to 10-year-old Italian children from the large families of this generally working-class neighborhood the arts of upper-middle-class table setting and serving. "The children play father, mother, two guests, and maid and serve what they have cooked," wrote the head of the program with some considerable satisfaction. Adele B. Lewis, memorandum "Little Housekeepers," n.d. [1925?] NBIS Papers, Series II, Box 100, Folder 42.
25. Association of Practical Housekeepers Center, Rochester, N.Y., Annual Report, 1908–9, Florence Kitchelt Papers, Box 1, Folder 6, Schlesinger Library, Radcliffe College.

26. Robert Woods, "Notes on the Italians in Boston," *Charities*, 12 (1904), 81.
27. Buffalo *Express*, 27 August 1901, cited in Yans-McLaughlin, *Family*, 176. Prewar Italian immigrants wishing to save money did look to food expenditures as a place where cuts could be effected, although the link with high infant and child mortality was dubious at best. Not only did food expenditures constitute a large proportion (normally from 40 to 50%) of any poor family's budget but they were also the most flexible item. "Pasta fagioli tutti giorni" (pasta and beans every day) was a favorite maxim describing how to save money, but the dish as often prepared, with salted pork, tomato sauce, onions, and grated cheese, was by no means innutritious, comparing favorably to much of what native-born Americans in similar economic circumstances were consuming, especially when supplemented with the fruits and green vegetables that Italians were often scorned for consuming in such large quantities.
28. Quoted in Boston *Post*, 8 October 1911.
29. Woman's Municipal League, undated flyer, in Eva White Papers, Box 3, Folder 31(a), Schlesinger Library, Radcliffe College.
30. Winifred S. Gibbs, "Dietetics in Italian Tenements," *Public Health Nurse Quarterly*, 6, no. 1, (1914) 46.
31. Boston *Post*, clipping, n.d. (1911?), in White Papers, Box 3, Folder 31 (a).
32. Jane Addams, *Twenty Years at Hull House* (New York: Macmillan, 1915), 253.
33. Gibbs, "Dietetics," 43.
34. Velma Phillips and Laura Howell, "Racial and Other Differences in Dietary Customs," *Journal of Home Economics*, September 1920, 397.
35. Leaflet reproduced in Gibbs, "Dietetics," 45–46.
36. Unidentified newspaper clipping, n.d. (January 1918), in Eva White Papers, Box 3, Folder 32v (a), 10B.
37. Jane Addams File, FA Papers, Box 288.
38. See the voluminous correspondence in this regard in U.S. Food Administration, Records, RG4, 12HM-A3, Box 584, National Archives, Washington, D.C.
39. Memo by F. G. Woodward, 6 September 1917, in ibid., Box 584, File 330.
40. Jno. [*sic*] M. Parker to R. E. Mermelstern, 22 October 1917, in ibid., Box 584, File 12HM-A3.
41. Denison House, Minutes of Board of Directors' Meeting, 15 October 1917, Denison House Records, Box 3, Folder 9, Schlesinger Library, Radcliffe College.
42. Frances Stern to C. F. Langworthy, 10 April 1918, in U.S. Department of Agriculture, Office of Experiment Stations, Records, Record Group 176, Box 595, Entry 5, National Archives, Washington, D.C.
43. Elsinore Crowell, "Peppers and Garlic," *Good Housekeeping*, 65 (September 1918), 63, 121.
44. Luciano Iorizzo, "The Italians of Oswego," in Robert F. Harney and J. Vincent Scarpaci, eds., *Little Italies in North America* (Toronto: Multicultural History Society, 1981), 177.
45. Crowell, "Peppers and Garlic," 121.
46. Julia L. Cuniberti, *Practical Italian Recipes* (n.p., 1917), 4.
47. Francis Clark, *Our Italian Fellow Citizens* (Boston: Small, Maynard, 1919), 174.
48. Grace Selden, "Vegetable Victories," *Good Housekeeping*, 65 (October 1918), 50, 88.
49. Ibid.
50. Michael Davis and Bertha Wood, "The Food of the Immigrant in Relation to Health," *Journal of Home Economics*, February 1921, 67–69.
51. Lucy H. Gillett, "The Great Need for Information on Racial Dietary Customs," *Journal of Home Economics*, June 1922, 260.
52. She replied that the children were still prone to anemia and tuberculosis, and "If there be a full bank account and a depleted health account, whome doth it profit?" Gibbs, "Dietetics," 42.
53. Davis and Wood, "Food of the Immigrant," 73. It is difficult to understand how these experts got the idea that Italians did not thicken soups with pasta and rice and presumably consumed enormous quantities of straciatelli in brodo.
54. Maries Jacques, "Straight from Italy," *Woman's Home Companion*, 5 (April 1924), 64.
55. Antonia J. Stemple, "Eating in Other Lands than Ours," *American Cookery*, 34 (November 1929), 280.
56. Ibid., 279.
57. Katherine Fisher, "Dining in Italy at Your Own Table," *Good Housekeeping*, 92 (October 1931), 85; *American Cookery*, 34 (January 1930). *Good Housekeeping* reserved the Worcestershire (and good English horseradish) for its recipe for the meatballs in its "Italian Spaghetti con Polpette" (meatballs).
58. Department of Cookery, *Good Housekeeping*, 70 (October 1924), 70, 71, 147.
59. Fisher, "Dining in Italy," 85; Peter Borras, "Contriving Spaghetti Dishes That Have a Sure Appeal," *Hotel Management*, 1 (January 1927), 27.
60. I. B. Allen, *The Service Cook Book* (New York: Woolworth's, 1933).
61. This matter too will be dealt with more extensively in my work with Professor Conlin.
62. This was not true of all Little Italies, however. In some smaller cities and towns, such as several in California, people from various Northern provinces formed the dominant cultural groups and had a corresponding effect on the food habits of the communities.
63. A publicity photo for the 1935 spaghetti dinner shows two of the Anglo-Saxon board members with a beaming Italian *mamma*, forks full of spaghetti poised for consumption. While admittedly the male of the threesome, Mr. Theodore Lyman Eliot, does seem to betray a trace of apprehension, his female counterpart, Miss Ethel Forbes, looks positively enthusiastic. Photo no. 10640, Reel 11, microfilm of photos, NBIS Papers. The cookbook, which went through two subsequent editions, was *Specialità Culinare Italiane* (Boston: NBIS, 1936).

THE ORIGINS OF SOUL FOOD IN BLACK URBAN IDENTITY: CHICAGO, 1915—1947

TRACEY N. POE

8

Helen Anglin sits in a high-backed, brown vinyl booth in the southwest corner of her restaurant, Soul Queen, on 91st and Stony Island Drive in Chicago. It is 1997, and this year is Helen's sixty-seventh birthday and the fiftieth anniversary of her business. As she reminisces, she leafs through photographs, tinted brown or faded with age. They are an almanac of the changes she and this neighborhood have been through together since she, along with hundreds of thousands of other African Americans, left the rural South in search of a home where she could "just be herself, without bending down to anybody."

One early picture shows the restaurant's interior, in those days called the H&H Cafe after Helen and her husband Hubert Maybelle. It looks pretty much like any diner in the 1940s—gleaming white Formica countertops, chrome stools with dark leather seats bolted to the floor. A neon sign shines through the window onto the dark sidewalk outside. When deciphered in reverse it reads "Catfish—Louisiana Fried Pies." Other photographs depict Helen, young, proud, and laughing in her waitress's costume, and the restaurant's spotless tables full to capacity with other young, proud, and laughing African Americans, dressed to the nines and out for a good time.

Over the years the outfits change. Pillbox hats become Afros. The cafe's bright postwar gleam gives way to a brown-and-gold, crushed-velvet glamour. Famous faces begin to appear among the anonymous diners. Joe Louis. Martin Luther King, Jr. Sidney Poitier. Muhammad Ali. Jesse Jackson. Nelson Mandela. Looking at them, one begins to realize that the laughing girl in the waitress's dress has become a woman of formidable standing in the world. And yet on this as on any other day, the low-key, motherly presence in the booth is delivering orders to the kitchen and greeting the everyday people who still come in for a piece of that catfish and a bit of pie. Helen Anglin, the seventeen-year-old who moved North from Alabama all those years ago, has become an institution.

We are prone to pass by places like Helen's restaurant without giving them much thought. "Soul food" has become commonplace in American cities, especially in the industrial Midwest. Street corners in African American neighborhoods are crowded with rib joints, chicken takeout stands, and fish markets. Usually one or two of these has a reputation as a "funky" place for white people to go on a Friday night when they cross to the other side of town to hear music. And there might even be a takeoff on a Soul Food kitchen in a white neighborhood, replete with old license plates hanging on the walls and hot sauce on the red-and-white checkered table-cloths.

What we forget, however, is that until 1963, when Malcolm X recorded his life story for "autobiographer" Alex Haley, there was no such thing as "Soul Food."[1] What there was in urban black neighborhoods, was an African American culinary tradition that centered on two principles: Southernness and commensality. The story of how these principles became "Soul Food" is the story of how a transparent and mundane fact of life—food—became a harbinger of an urban, black ethnic identity.

When Helen Anglin said she didn't want to "bend down to anybody," she expressed a sentiment shared, and voiced, by fellow migrants time and again—and by "anybody" she didn't just mean white bosses. The upward percolation of Southern rural culture in Northern black neighborhoods was a direct response to the integrationist aspirations of an established black middle class, as well as to the city's white majority. This Southern rural culture was expressed in many recognizable forms: blues and jazz music and certain language idioms, to name just two. Another is Southern food, now known as Soul Food. African Americans became a "melting pot" unto themselves,[2] absorbing and integrating flavors from various aspects of their African and Southern pasts while, if I may stretch a metaphor, spicing the American consciousness at the same time.

The "discovery" of a distinctly African American cuisine in the middle decades of the twentieth century articulated a multi-dimensional unity among urban African Americans centered on their heritage as Africans, slaves, sharecroppers, and industrial workers. But it also revealed the ambivalence that class and regional loyalties brought to bear on the lives of African Americans, as migrants and urbanites struggled with questions of "respectability" and "authenticity" within the community. As this essay will show, food became one of the issues which illustrated this struggle in material, concrete terms.

Food businesses like Helen Anglin's cafe, as well as grocery stores, butcher shops and bakeries, are especially important to this story because they were the conduits through which an everyday aspect of rural Southern culture, like eating, became remarkable, in a literal sense, in the city. Choices about what to eat and where to spend money on necessities and leisure activities educated migrants in the consumer culture of an urban society they were eager to join, as did the marketing techniques entrepreneurs used to draw people into black-owned businesses. Exercising their freedom to spend hard-earned wages on what they wanted was just one of the ways migrants resisted "bending down."

The process of becoming entrepreneurs and consumers was, paradoxically, a submission to the middle-class values that dominated American society and an expression of individuality and ethnic pride. Using food as a vehicle for displaying Southern identity, migrants made effective use of the free market system without subordinating their new-found freedom to a "soulless" mass culture. In doing so they helped forge a new urban black culture in which all African Americans had a stake.

Chicago was the second- most-popular destination, after New York, for the migrants who left their rural homes during what has become known as the Great Migration. Nearly all migrants to Chicago settled in the area south of downtown known as the "Black Belt," "Bronzeville," or the "Black Metropolis." The geographical and racial isolation of this community, bordered to the north and east by whites, to the south and west by industrial sites and immigrant neighborhoods, makes it a natural site for the studying the development of an urban black community. So does the attention paid to the Black Metropolis and its neighbors by the University of Chicago's School of Sociology during those crucial mid-century decades. Chicago at this time was a virtual laboratory for observing the relationship between ethnic and American cultures and peoples.

In 1920, Chicago was a city of approximately 2.7 million people, 33.9% of whom were classified "foreign-born" or "Negro" by the U.S. Census; 109,000, or 4.1%, of these were African American. A little under half were migrants who had come from the Deep South since 1916 to join the workforce,[3] primarily in the meat-packing, domestic and personal service, and steel industries.[4] As the Depression and World War II slowed immigration to a trickle by the standards of the early twentieth century, African Americans flowed freely northward to make up the difference. By 1944, African Americans made up 9.3% of Chicago's 3.6 million residents. By the end of World War II, there were almost eight times as many migrants in the city's African American population as there were "natives"—people who had been born in or had lived in Chicago before the Great Migration began.

The migration was disruptive for both migrants and natives. Naturally, newcomers experienced some culture shock and were often the victims of conmen and hustlers who saw them as an easy target.[5] But the excitement of the city, the freedom to live without bending down to white people, and the promise of a cash wage were enough to make the hardships worthwhile. Natives, on the other hand, felt besieged. In the twenty-five years prior to the Great Migration, the native black community had developed its own churches, institutions, political base, and class structure. Status was based on a carefully cultivated notion of "respectability" that took its cues from Booker T. Washington's integrationist philosophy. "Middle class" for native black Chicagoans in 1920 was not defined so much by income level as it was by going to sober, moderate churches, supporting appropriate organizations, and exhibiting refined behavior in public.[6] A steady, if not high, income was important, and acceptable leisure habits were essential.[7]

The increase in the number of "backwards" blacks moving into the Black Metropolis was cause for concern in the native community. Most newcomers did not conform to Chicagoans' carefully cultivated standards of respectability, especially in regard to leisure and consumption habits. For urbanized people, eating proper foods in a sanitary, civilized setting such as the home or a restaurant was a social ritual that indicated one's level of respectability. In fact, one of the things on which natives prided themselves was the high level of integration in Chicago restaurants, which they attributed to their unassailable manners and refined tastes. Natives resented it bitterly when migrants' unseemly behavior caused the city's finer establishments to restrict all Negroes.[8] For these reasons, food became prominent in urban African American consciousness.

In the earliest days of the Great Migration, disapproval of migrants' eating habits is most clearly demonstrated in the pages of the *Chicago Defender*, a nationally circulated and highly respected African American newspaper. In advertisements, weekly health and home economics columns, and restaurant reviews, the

Defender's middle-class prejudices were often demonstrated in discussions of food.[9] Feature articles such as one entitled "Pig Ankle Joints" railed against the "unsightly, unsanitary eating places and wagons" which catered to the migrant class's desire for familiar, down-home foods.[10] Less straightforward but more condescending criticism came in the form of "advice." In January 1915, a *Defender* reviewer described the opening of a second location of a popular upscale restaurant, The Elite. "Hundreds and hundreds of Chicago's elite" waited to be let in to the "most beautiful, perfectly appointed" eating place in the Black Metropolis. One of its main attractions, like many swank Chicago restaurants catering to a white clientele, was its Chinese cooks, who were considered exotic and cosmopolitan, even though they prepared the standard steak-and-potatoes middle American fare. "Soon the race will have a Rector's or a Vogelsang's of its own," the reviewer raved.[11] This seems notable in light of the fact that black cooks were prized in the South's finest homes and dining rooms, but the Southern cuisine they created was not considered refined by an urban clientele. The column "The Housekeeper," by Mrs. F. Fletcher, urged African American women to prepare foods that were fashionable in the white women's magazines of the day, emphasizing European dishes (hot cross buns, "violet-colored hard-boiled eggs on lettuce," nasturtium and cucumber finger sandwiches), table settings (the importance of having a French asparagus plate), and rituals (serving tea).

Even more to the point, however, was the prejudice against food practices that smacked of Southernness. Mrs. Fletcher advised against eating vegetables, recommending them "for their laxative effect" only and claiming they "have little nutriment value,"[12] a notion that went against the Southern emphasis on greens, legumes, sweet potatoes, and corn. In 1920 Dr. A. Wilberforce Williams's column on health regularly criticized eating habits associated with Southern food, remarking that heavy meats, excessive carbohydrates, and especially hot sauces and condiments were deleterious to the liver and would cripple the digestive system of anyone over forty. "The normal stomach needs little or no condiments when food is properly cooked," he wrote. These kinds of statements in the publication that was acknowledged as the voice of "The Race" in Chicago contributed to a stereotype of migrants as backwards, unclean, and sorely in need of modernization.

With their sidewalk barbecue pits, "chicken shacks," and public consumption of watermelon, an ugly stereotype of Southern migrants soon developed, no less among the black middle class than among white Chicagoans. Migrants could not understand what the problem was. Southern food was simply dinner. It tasted good and it was traditional. It was a way of preserving something that reminded them of home and family when they moved into the unfamiliar urban environment. And it was healthy. Faced with inexplicable opposition from members of their own race, migrants began thinking of "down-home cooking" as something unique and special. Migration strengthened their desire to preserve their traditions. Migrants' symbolic identification with Southern foodways was reinforced as communal meals continued at family dinners, holidays, and community gatherings. A market was created for the grocery stores, butcher shops, and restaurants that catered to these food preferences and the community that sustained them. Food became a symbolic battleground for the public image of the race, with middle-class native Chicagoans advocating the abolition of Southern food practices while migrants publicly perpetuated them.

In order to understand the significance of foodways in Southern consciousness, it helps to consider the circumstances under which they were established. Southern cuisine was largely created by African American cooks, as an amalgamation of African, European, and early American resources and preparations.

Using foods indigenous to North America but resembling African plants, as the American sweet potato resembles the African yam, and foods imported from Africa and cultivated on American soil like peanuts (known as "guba" on the West Coast of Africa and "goobers" even today in the United States), watermelon, and okra, slave cooks created a new cuisine with the cornmeal and cured pork that were their daily staples on the plantation. Slaves also supplemented this diet when they could by growing some of their own vegetables, such as American leafy greens that resembled African ones, turnips, cabbage, eggplant, cucumbers, tomatoes, onion, garlic, and hot peppers, all of which had been cultivated in West Africa since they were introduced by traders in the sixteenth century. These fruits and vegetables had been important sources of nutrients in the African diet; fortunately, they also grew well in the Southern climate. Hunting small game and fishing provided additional resources. In some cases slaves were allowed to raise their own pigs and chickens.[13]

By combining the foodstuffs and methods of African and Anglo-American cuisines, the lexicon of Southern African American foodways was created: fried chicken and fish; barbecued pork; boiled greens with "pot likker;" roasted sweet potatoes; one-pot dishes which, depending on the region had names such as "sloosh," "cush-cush," or "gumbo;" corn bread, corn fritters, corn pone, cornmeal mush and hominy grits; stewed legumes like black-eyed peas, field peas, and beans and rice; and of course the African-descended watermelon were all typical African American foods. Most significantly, however, black people developed an affinity for the parts of animals normally discarded by whites: entrails, known as "chitterlings" (pronounced "chitlins"); pigs' heads, which were made into "souse," a kind of head-cheese; pigs' and chickens' feet, and so on.

Slaves' meal structure varied from plantation to plantation, or from farm to farm. As a rule, breakfasts were large, in order to fortify workers for a day in the field. Lunch was made of breakfast leftovers carried to the worksite in buckets, and suppers were one-pot meals or "boiled dinners," put on to cook in the morning and served up when people returned to quarters at the end of the workday. On the larger plantations, cooking was usually done by a staff of slaves who prepared meals for the whole group. In other places, slave women were expected to cook for their own families in their cabins during their "time off." In either case, on Sundays and holidays they typically ate large celebratory meals with extended kin-ship groups, sometimes with all the slaves on the plantation or from the surrounding area. This practice had a precedent in the communal style of eating which was, and still is, central to life in African villages. Commensality persisted in the agricultural setting in the form of pic-nics and Sunday dinners after slavery was abolished, establishing itself as one of the most important features of Southern African American culture.

African Americans also invented new rituals that combined African harvest celebrations and American agricultural proce-dures. Hog-killing, in particular, became a time of year for large gatherings centered on eating. Between Christmas and New Year's Day, if the weather was cold enough, the hogs would be slaugh-tered and preserved. Fresh organ meats like the jowl and chitlins were prepared with special side dishes such as black-eyed peas, an indigenous African legume believed to bring good luck for the New

Year. In early July, when the corn was "laid by" and the cotton and hay had been harvested, slaves traditionally indulged in religious meetings in which they thanked God for a good season and consumed a great quantity of fresh chicken, fish, vegetables, and that summer favorite, ripe watermelon. This festival was enhanced in the years after Emancipation by its connection to American Independence Day.[14]

Emancipation from slavery, with all its newfound freedoms, also brought with it harder times on the nutrition front for many black families, as it did for many Southern whites. Except for the rice that was raised in the coastal regions of the Southeast, Southern landowners had focused on profitable agricultural products—tobacco, cotton, and indigo, for example—rather than on sustenance crops.[15] A good deal of the South's food had been imported from the "bread basket" of the North, a situation that had proved crippling during the Civil War.[16] Agricultural problems such as the boll weevil and soil exhausted by nutrient-draining tobacco and cotton crops compounded the issue for sharecroppers who were barely feeding their families on the meager returns from their farming efforts.

96

Additionally frustrating was many white landlords' refusal of tenants' right to farm portions of their land for food. This practice forced some sharecroppers to buy food on credit from landlord-owned stores, compounding their debt and making it nearly impossible to save money.[17] The prospect of using one's money to buy items of one's choice, at the businesses of one's choice, was remote for people caught in the endless debt cycle. The memory of this humiliation was to have significant consequences for migrants when they found themselves in the city earning cash wages.

Former slaves, resourceful as they had always been, made the best of the situation by continuing to live "low on the hog," growing as much of their own small food crops as they could manage, preserving perishables during the harvest season, and relying heavily on small game, foraging and fishing for their sustenance. Communal eating, a hallmark of the slaves' social life, became increasingly important to freemen. Eating traditional foods together forged a spiritual connection between those present and the ancestors of the past, as each family cobbled together what little they had into the great feasts described by Southern black authors like Zora Neale Hurston.[18]

For all these reasons—economic hardship, personal pride, and the concept of commensality—food came to represent the resilience of the African American people in the South. Furthermore, traditional cooking was seen as nutritious. Despite bouts with starvation and disease, when black people had enough food, they felt they could work harder and longer than anybody else. This belief was verified by a U.S. Department of Agriculture study in 1939. The study showed that at least in the summer months, when fresh fruits and vegetables were available, the vitamin, mineral, and protein content of poor, Southern African American families' diets was higher than that of whites who spent the same amount of money on food. Furthermore, it was "established that a large number of Negro urban families handle their food money better than white urban families of corresponding economic status."[19] Black families' justified faith in the food traditions learned from generations of mothers and grandmothers were not likely to be displaced by the nutritional warnings of *Defender* critics like Mrs. Fletcher and Dr. A. Wilberforce Williams.

The economic, social, and nutritional roles that Southern foodways had historically played in the lives of African Americans were not going to be easily cast aside in the city. Quite the contrary; migrants managed to retain their foodways despite opposing forces much more pressing than their new neighbors' disapproval.

Overcrowded housing with scant-to-inoperable kitchens[20] and work schedules that kept many people away from home at mealtimes both could have prevented migrants from continuing time-consuming food preparation and elaborate extended-family dinners.

But nutritional anthropologist Norge Jerome, in her work on African American migrants to Milwaukee, Wisconsin, noted that while the industrial work schedule did cause some changes in the structure of daily meals, it did so slowly and without a great deal of impact on the content of the meal. As a result, migrants' eating habits remained remarkably consistent with their rural Southern roots.[21] Furthermore, Jerome's work indicates that migration enhanced African Americans' awareness of the role of food in their heritage, since the practice of Southern cooking and ritual of the Sunday dinner or church picnic consciously reinforced the cultural connection between the rural South and the urban industrial setting.

Jerome noted two major changes in migrants' daily meal patterns taking place over the course of a two-year period after migration: one, meals became lighter, often excluding some of the high-calorie, high-protein foods that had been so necessary to the performance of heavy manual labor in the South; two, the order in which meals were eaten changed to accommodate urban work and school schedules. Both of these changes, however, occurred within the context of the Southern food lexicon described earlier. The traditional Sunday meal remained unchanged from its Southern model in either content or context.[22]

A few factors in this dietary pattern emerged as significant indicators of the persistence of Southern foodways in Jerome's study. One was the subjects' valuation of the time spent, cost, and variety of dishes in their urban meals, especially Sunday dinners, in order to maintain the quality of the food they had been accustomed to in the South. They did not, for the most part, use canned or convenience foods so readily available in the city to prepare traditional meals, although they had no objection to eating them as "American" food.[23] One exception to this was in the preparation of sweet desserts, which were sometimes prepared from processed ingredients. Another is the persistence of seasonal eating. Migrants continued to eat lighter, vegetable-based boiled dinners in warm seasons and heavy, dried-legume-based dinners in cold seasons, despite the year-round availability of fresh vegetables and dried legumes. Also, Jerome's subjects considered the accessibility of favorite Southern foods, rather than exposure to new foods or more dietary variety, to be one of the chief advantages of moving to the city. This was particularly true of sweets and desserts, once served primarily at special dinners, which became more common in the urban setting with the year-round availability of cake mixes, commercial jellies and preserves, processed sugar, and fresh milk.[24]

Lizabeth Cohen has argued that African Americans contributed to the growth of mass culture in Chicago through their acceptance of brand-name foods and the chain stores that sold them. Contrary to expectation, however, "blacks disappointed those who assumed an integrated American culture would accompany uniformity in tastes."[25] The complexity of Cohen's argument is enhanced when considered in light of the ways in which African Americans' food choices created a dynamic relationship with the marketplace for necessities and leisure goods and services.

As Cohen says, "mass culture...offered blacks the ingredients from which to construct a new, urban black culture."[26] Again, the culinary metaphor is apt. For while the ingredients may have been the same for blacks and whites, the result was something uniquely African American. The combination of the cash wage, which provided liquid spending money; the variety of businesses at which consumers could choose to spend that money; and a visceral attachment to traditional Southern black culture made a potent broth in which urban African American culture as we know it today is steeped. At the center of this newfound consumer power was the idea of freedom. Ralph Ellison's nameless migrant in *Invisible Man* describes the excitement one could feel over its simplest expression, after purchasing a baked sweet potato from a sidewalk vendor.

> I took a bite, finding it as sweet and hot as any I'd ever had, and was overcome with such a surge of homesickness that I turned away to keep my control. I was walking along, munching the [sweet potato], just as suddenly overcome by an intense feeling of freedom—simply because I was eating while walking along the street. It was exhilarating. I no longer had to worry about who saw me or about what was proper. To hell with all that, and as sweet as [it] actually was, it became like nectar with the thought.[27]

98

The pursuit of pleasure was an integral part of migrants' sense of freedom. Drake and Cayton listed "Having a Good Time" as the second "Axis of Life" around which migrants' "individual and community life revolves"—after "Staying Alive," but before "Praising God," "Getting Ahead," and "Advancing the Race."[28] An illustration of this was the home life of "Baby Chile" and "Mr. Ben," two of the sociologists' more colorful characters:

> Baby Chile called us to the kitchen for supper—a platter of neckbones and cabbage, a saucer with five sausage cakes, a plate of six slices of bread, and a punchbowl of stewed prunes (very cold and delicious). Baby Chile placed some corn fritters on the table, remarking, "This bread ain't got no milk in it. I did put some aig (sic) in it, but I had to make it widout any milk"
>
> Though this household represented extreme poverty and social disorganization, its members attempted to maintain a few family rituals...Everyone always said a Scripture verse before meals. Sometimes, Mr. Ben would playfully give as his verse, "rise, Peter, stay and eat," or Slick would quote the shortest verse in the Bible—"Jesus wept."...Christmas, Thanksgiving, Easter, birthdays, or a Joe Louis victory usually called for a special party of some sort.[29]

Along "the Stroll," the section of State Street between 29th and 36th Avenues, leisure activities of all kinds awaited anyone with money in his or her pockets. Music clubs, dance halls, theatres, and movie houses owned by both blacks and whites offered an after-hours escape from the gray world of the factory, as did restaurants that catered to both the refined tastes of the middle class and the more down-home desires of migrants. Even as the middle class emulated urban white culinary trends, enterprising newcomers and their wiser native counterparts were beginning to exploit migrants' spending power.

Business owners began marketing themselves to these new consumers. "When you are walking out stop at the Blue Bird Inn" advertised Mrs. Eva C. Bird in the 1921 edition of *Black's Blue Book*. Owners appealed to the round-the-clock schedules of their customers with signs such as "Open All Night" or "Open from 4:30 A.M. to 1 A.M." Some business owners appealed directly to their Southern clientele's tastes. "Home cooking our specialty" became de rigeur in *Defender* advertisements. "Freshest Fish Received Daily, Live Shrimp and Crabs," announced S. L. Williams's ad, designed to attract clients from the coastal regions of Georgia, Louisiana, and the Carolinas. "Hot Biscuits," "Barbecued Chicken-Barbecued Fish," and "Watermelon," said others.[30]

But having fun was not migrants' only motivation for patronizing black-owned businesses. Migrant entrepreneurs also played a social role in the African American community. New migrants commonly sought out businesses owned by people from their hometowns and congregated with old friends and acquaintances there, just as they had done in the South. Produce and meat markets served as neighborhood meeting places. Since communal eating was characteristic of Southern black food-ways, lunch counters, "chicken shacks," and barbecue wagons took their place alongside urban fixtures such as ice cream shops, hot dog stands, and chili parlors as sites where people ate and socialized together.

In a study of the social world of elderly black men in Chicago's Near South Side neighborhood, University of Chicago sociologist Mitchell Duneier emphasized the role restaurants played in sustaining a sense of a living past being practiced in the context of a modern community:

> If it is impossible to transplant to [the cafe] the particular sounds, smells, and sights of the old neighborhood, at least here black regulars can enjoy the kind of solid food in good company that brings back images of a world that once existed for them . . . just the fact that an inexpensive meal is prepared the old-fashioned way, with natural ingredients on a stove or in an oven satisfies their longings . . . Comments such as "Mamma cooked from the basics" or "Mamma never used packaged stuff" are typical of a generation of black men who feel very much at home in a cafeteria that offers its patrons a kind of food that is symbolic of the integrity of their older way of life.[31]

Ownership of food-related businesses quickly became one of the most popular occupations outside of industry for African American migrants. As early as 1919, migrants made up the majority of black business owners in Bronzeville.[32] A nation-wide study by the Negro Business League in 1928 found that restaurants and gro-ceries were the two enterprises which constituted the largest group of black entre-preneurs, totaling 30% of all black-owned businesses.[33] Among African American women, Restaurateur was ranked first among the "clean" occupations, with two-hundred and thirty-five women claiming that title in 1930.[34] Groceries and restau-rants rated second and fifth, respectively, in Drake and Cayton's assessment of the ten most numerous types of businesses owned by African Americans in Chicago in 1938.[35]

One theory that explains this phenomenon is the relative ease with which migrants could set up shop in the food business. After all, having grown up in an agricultural environment, nearly everyone had firsthand experience producing and preparing food. Selling it didn't seem like too great a leap. Furthermore, it didn't require any specialized education or training, unlike opening a drugstore or beauty parlor, two other popular non-industrial professions in the African American com-munity.[36] Groceries and lunch counters could be opened without a great deal of startup capital, a perpetual problem for minority entrepreneurs.

From the first, the black press promoted Bronzeville residents' patronage of African American enterprise. As early as 1917, the *Defender* ran articles supportive of neighborhood entrepreneurs. Again, though, the prejudices of middle-class lead-ers were apparent. In an article entitled "Patronize Worthy Race Enterprises Along the Stroll," a columnist called "The Wise Old Owl" listed notable restaurants like the

Elite and the DeLuxe, promising that these establishments were "of the highest class." "Any self-respecting person can visit them. A primary virtue of race businesses is that the proprietors keep a close eye on things and won't allow any troublemakers to harass lady customers."[37] It was no secret that middle-class folks thought it distasteful to have to share public space with "lazy, jitterbugging" migrants.[38]

More radical members of the black media took a different approach. When the Depression threatened black entrepreneurs' and industrial workers' livelihoods, papers like the *Whip* encouraged African Americans to show economic solidarity with a "Don't Spend Your Money Where You Can't Work" campaign. The engine of capitalism, however, assured that their efforts had only limited success. Advertising was a major source of these papers' revenue, up to 70% during the worst years of the Depression.[39] And not all— not even most—advertisers were black entrepreneurs. As much as three-quarters of the businesses in the Black Metropolis were owned by non-blacks—mostly Jews, but also Greeks and Italians—and the papers could not afford to alienate this valuable source of revenue.[40]

The fact is, advertising was not something with which migrant entrepreneurs were necessarily familiar. At least in the South, about half the black-owned stores relied on word-of-mouth rather than advertising for their customer base.[41] Some of the more savvy owners figured out early that capitalizing on their Southern roots would bring people in. Advertisements highlighted pointedly Southern names, like "Dixie Fish," "Florida Eat Shop," and "Georgia Food and Fish Hut." Others pointed to their Southern specialties: "Hanson's Chitterling Shack," "Arletta's Creole Food," "Lillian's Old Fashioned Cooking—Hot Biscuits Daily," "Gumbo Our Specialty." Still others offered whole traditional Southern meals. The Subway Lunch Room promised "Wholesome Home-Cooked Meals, Specializing in Boiled Dinners and Hot Biscuits." Geneva's Lunch had a special Sunday dinner "for the whole family," featuring "Expert Southern Style Cookery JUST LIKE HOME."[42]

But owning a business in the Black Metropolis was a challenge, and many hopeful entrepreneurs did not have the resources or the skills to make it work. The lack of training in business principles made it difficult for many less-educated migrants to establish consistent bookkeeping procedures or implement modern marketing techniques. Competition from white-owned businesses, especially chain stores, and lack of investment capital plagued entrepreneurs constantly. Some black consumers were uncertain about shopping at black-owned businesses. And the Depression hit African American businesses and consumers particularly hard.

1924 to 1929 have been regarded as the golden years of the Black Metropolis. The Depression had not yet begun, and seventy-five thousand wage earners supported a prosperous and well-educated professional and business class.[43] By 1929, Chicago outranked New York as the site of the most black-owned businesses in the country.[44] By then, African Americans were spending $39 million annually in the Black Metropolis, $20 million of that on produce, groceries, meat, eggs, and dairy products. Although the total figure rose as migration increased, to $81 million in 1934 and $150 million in 1945,[45] the stability of the market began to break down, making it harder and harder for entrepreneurs to sustain successful businesses for more than a few years.

The stability and financial resources of black-owned businesses was closely related to the banking system. Chicago was in fact the site of two prosperous African American banks. But the infrastructure that should have been built between banks and businesses never was. Small businesses were, frankly, a bad risk. Their fortunes were inclined to shift dramatically with every turn in the economic and personal lives of their owners. Black-owned banks had limited capital to lend. Always speculative by nature, these banks suffered a terrible blow when the Stock Market crashed in 1929. Without them, many small businesses were forced to close down, severely restrict the extension of credit, or turn to white-owned banks, a solution that was denied all but the most established black business owners. This made competing with whites doubly difficult. Problems with the banking system are not adequate, however, to explain black entrepreneurs' financial difficulties. After all, immigrants had to overcome many of the same obstacles and yet they maintained some very successful businesses. Business historians have suggested that a major part of the problem was what E. Franklin Frazier called the "tradition of business hypothesis." The majority of migrants' lack of training in business principles and low levels of education made it difficult for them to establish consistent bookkeeping procedures, marketing plans, and inventory methods.[46]

There was also the problem of location. During the early days of the Great Migration there were plenty of black-owned businesses along State Street, in the heart of the Black Metropolis. But as more and more migrants moved in overcrowding increased, which made commercial space more valuable. Not only did it become more expensive to run a business on State Street, but many landlords, black and white, refused to rent space to people who did not live up to their ideals of respectability. This excluded many migrants. By 1938, in the prime retail district on 47th Street between State and Cottage Grove, only two of the forty grocery stores and eight of the twenty-one restaurants were owned by African Americans.[47] Plenty of entrepreneurs tried to make a go of it in the peripheral areas, but being off the Stroll naturally meant fewer dollars went into African American coffers.

Competition with white shop owners and chain stores was one of the biggest reasons for instability. Many black business owners blamed the problem on lower class peoples' affliction with the "white man's psychology," namely, that migrants had been brainwashed into thinking they had to shop in a white-owned store, either because whites would punish them if they didn't or because white stores were necessarily higher quality than black ones.[48] Whether this was the case or not, there were several other things complicating black consumers' willingness to shop in black-owned businesses. One of these was the prevalence of "Depression businesses." These were "small, poorly stocked back room stores." One man described his shop this way: "When I started this business in 1933...I had a small amount of money and could not find a job so I decided to open a grocery. If worst came to worst, I would at least have something to eat." The seat-of-the-pants mentality of these kinds of owners fostered people's suspicions that they were cheats, as did the dingy conditions of the stores.[49]

There was also the issue of credit. Paying on credit was familiar to migrants who had purchased most of their store-bought food on the system in the South. It also served as a safety net in the event that a family member lost his or her job and cash was not readily available.[50] White small business owners were more likely to have the resources to offer credit to regular customers, which meant black business owners were caught between a rock and a hard place: if they didn't offer credit, they risked losing their customers altogether to someone who could. But if they did offer credit, they risked losing, not just some of their revenue, but possibly all of it. Whether folks were genuinely out of work, or proved to be cheats who sustained themselves by skipping out on bill after bill, a store couldn't just give merchandise away.

Chain stores did not offer credit either, but they did gain some popularity among black consumers. They certainly had a unique advantage in distribution. Chain stores competed aggressively with small businesses in the central distribution depots such as the Water Street and Randolph Street markets, where their high-volume orders cost much less per unit than the wholesale prices paid by small, "one-truck" shops. Numbering only 7,723 in 1920, by the 1930s, grocery chains had added 23,000 stores to their ranks. Most of these were "supermarkets," including meat, fish, dairy, and bakery departments.[51] Although chains were slow to move into poorer neighborhoods like the Black Metropolis,[52] the Depression helped them realize the economic potential inherent in poor communities. Not only did the poor need to buy necessities at the lower prices chain stores could offer, government relief agencies actually encouraged them to shop at chains.[53]

Still, chain stores did not completely corner the market on African American business. True, they offered cheaper goods than local stores. But, contrary to expectations and stereotype, African Americans did not always buy the cheapest goods available. Studies of purchasing decisions in the Black Metropolis and other urban black neighborhoods show that quality, particularly in foodstuffs and clothing, was a primary concern. Of the brand-name products they purchased, like flour, shortening, sugar, baking powder, and coffee, African American consumers preferred the more expensive brands.[54] And although chain stores' pre-weighted, packaged foods did calm customers' fears of being cheated in stores selling bulk goods, chains did not necessarily stock the specialty foods migrants needed to prepare traditional meals.

Small business owners responded to competition from the chains by concentrating on the non-packaged specialty goods and familiar Southern brands the chain stores did not carry. A 1936 study showed that in one week the average black family consumed 2.5 pounds of pork (half that amount was of the salt-cured or offal variety), 1.1 pound of poultry, 1.3 quarts of buttermilk, 1 pound of tomatoes (fresh or canned), 1.2 pounds of cabbage or other greens, and 1.3 pounds of snap beans, in addition to packaged goods like wheat flour, cornmeal, and sugar. Overall a black family consumed 5 quarts less milk, 2 pounds less of white potatoes, and 1 dozen less eggs than a size- and economically-comparable white family (who were statistically more likely to be regular chain-store shoppers), and 1 pound more fresh fish.[55] Smart African American entrepreneurs fought the chains by being aware of their customers' preferences. They stocked live poultry, "Southern-grown" produce, and cold watermelon. They also challenged chain stores with promises like "We are big enough to offer you bargains" and brand-name stock such as Hydrox ice cream and Birdseye Frozen Foods. Like the restaurants, many of the markets touted their Southern connection by noting their Southern specialties like condiments made in Louisiana, Georgia, Alabama, and other Southern states. Some placed prominent ads in the *Defender* using the Alaga syrup tag line "An old favorite in the South" with a tantalizing picture of Alaga over a stack of warm pancakes.[56]

By 1938 African Americans owned half the businesses in the Black Metropolis, but only spent 10% of their consumer dollars in them.[57] Turnover was high. Researchers estimated that between 60 and 95% of the new stores that opened, closed within seven years.[58] Ironically, this does not seem to have discouraged hopeful entrepreneurs. Rather, the Depression stimulated the opening of new restaurants, groceries, and meat and fish markets. In the less prime retail locations around 35th and State, the total number of black-owned businesses jumped from forty-seven to seventy-seven, and at 31st Street it jumped from nine to seventy-one in the first five years of the Depression.[59] Assuming that approximately 30% of these were food-related, as in the 1928 and 1938 studies reported here, about fifty of these would have been restaurants or food markets.

In the 1930s and '40s the number of black-owned food businesses continued to rise. Retail stores suffered a minor setback with the rationing following United States' entrance into World War II. The same forces that worked against groceries and butcher shops, though, bolstered the market for restaurants and lunch rooms, presumably as rationing limited the availability of foods for home cooking, and as women worked longer hours and had less time to spend in the kitchen. Scott's Business and Service Directory reported in 1947 that during the war thirty food stores went out of business while fifty-nine new restaurants, lunch rooms, barbecue, fish, and chicken shacks opened. In fact, the total number of dining establishments had jumped to 442 from 278 in the preceding years, with the number of lunch rooms rising most dramatically, from 92 to 258. Barbecue shacks became numerous enough to warrant a separate section in the directory.

Southern migrants continued to account for most of the African American business ownership in the Black Metropolis, outnumbering native Chicagoans by a ratio of thirteen-to-one by 1947. Mississippians owned most of these businesses, followed by Tennesseans, Louisianans, Alabamans, Georgians, and finally Illinoisians, with entrepreneurs from the less-represented Southern coastal and border states, West Indians,[60] and others from the United States following.[61]

One thing that makes African Americans' continued interest in restaurant and grocery store ownership explicable was the class status and political clout attached to being an entrepreneur, especially in a business with such a strong social dimension. Helen Anglin was a case in point:

> For readers who do not presently understand the connotation of "African American work force" in the year 1939, I hope [I may] bring forth enlightenment. Dishwashing for the Army Corps of Engineers in Memphis, Tennessee, was a step up from the babysitting and other domestic chores which I did [before migration]. This was my initial experience in the restaurant business. Other African Americans who were doing the same or similar sort of work were neither as young nor as uneducated as I was, but their explanation for holding such low-paying jobs was "This is the best job I can get," and the explanation was real. After numerous odd jobs...in Chicago, I returned to the restaurant business as a waitress.... At age 17, I was married and we opened a restaurant. The H&H Cafe did indeed achieve a recognition which led to many significant relationships and experiences in my life... with the local religious, professional, business, and political leaders who were among my customers.[62]

Many entrepreneurs saw themselves as "missionaries of capitalism," whose job it was to lead the black community in realizing the American dream of self-sufficiency. In the South, as in Europe, the aristocratic pretensions of landowners and military leaders had bestowed prestige. But in the industrial North, it was the business people who were exalted.[63] Bankers, insurance company magnates, and store owners had historically been the leaders of the African American community, as they were in other ethnic neighborhoods. Business owners became highly visible, taking out large advertisements featuring prominent photos of themselves, in the black business directories and church bulletins. They also performed a vital philanthropic function, granting credit and taking up collections for the needy. They were employers of other African Americans. As such they were natural spokespeople for The Race.

This prominence of the business class was especially so as the idea of a separate black economy, promoted by the *Whip* and (somewhat) by the *Defender*, grew in popularity. This was not only true for migrants. Even natives, with their faith in Booker T. Washington's integrationist picture, could realistically support a segregated self-help organization like the Negro Business League.[64] This emphasis on cooperation among all African American business owners, native and migrant, and the overwhelming numbers of entrepreneurs with Southern roots, gradually led to an easing of tensions over the social issues that had so disturbed the native middle class in the early days of the Great Migration.

104

By the 1930s the influence migrant business owners wielded in the Black Metropolis began to be felt in the reduction of public clashes between natives and migrants, as a sense of Race solidarity was built. The prejudice migrant foodways once caused faded as Southern food and eating rituals became more normalized within the African American community. As early as 1925 writers to the *Defender* began urging tolerance for Southern eating practices, noting their underlying common sense if not their modernity. In one such article, James M. Davis reprinted a piece from a Brookings, Georgia, white newspaper ridiculing local African Americans for refusing to eat the wild blackberries growing near a spot where pesticides had been sprayed. Their reluctance deprived them of an important, and free, supplement to their summer diet. Davis urges the urban *Defender* audience to see the Southerners' choice not as superstitious or simpleminded, but as wise and demonstrative of agricultural peoples' folk wisdom about food.[65]

Also in 1925, the *Defender*'s children's page began running a cooking column for girls. Although most of the recipes were for the kind of European dishes Mrs. Fletcher favored, occasionally something with a decidedly Southern name turned up. Amid the recipes for Cucumber Sauce, Angel Lemon Pie, and Spanish Potatoes were those for "Mammy's Sweet Potato Pudding," "Southern Fried Chicken," and "Creole Stew." That the latter, unfortunately, was a blend of shellfish, parsley, flour, and salt that no Louisianan would recognize is less significant than the fact that this seems to demonstrate an effort to grant some Southern dishes a bit of respectability, and to acknowledge their role in African American traditions worth passing on to a younger generation.[66]

The degree to which Southern foodways had become mainstream by the middle years of the Great Migration is best illustrated by a 1935 feature article entitled "This Will Be a Warm Dish for Chicago Society." It described the efforts of "Chicago pioneers" Mr. and Mrs. Henry Teenan Jones, owners of that favorite restaurant of the native set, The Elite, to plan a menu for their thirty-seventh-anniversary gala. Mr. and Mrs. Jones reportedly both loathed pork—she "can't look a pig foot in the eye," the article states—but felt obliged nonetheless to include "enough chitterlings (pronounced chittlens) to serve a goodly group of Chicago society." The Joneses only had one problem. "As all good lovers of this delectable dish know, July is not a chitterling month—Neither, for that matter, are April, May, June, August, or September."[67] This article is interesting for its juxtaposition of the iminently respectable Joneses, ignorant about traditional Southern food and too refined to eat pork, and the worldly audience of the *Defender*. With a wink and a nod, readers are presumed to be ignorant enough of a "low class" food like chitterlings to not know how to pronounce it, but knowledgeable enough to know when it is in season. The author's tone, serious about the important occasion about to take place, but humorous about the Joneses' social dilemma, demonstrates the easing of tensions between native Chicagoans and the migrants who made the city their home in such large numbers. By 1940, the *Defender* reports that the NAACP Ladies' Auxiliary is sponsoring a Folk Fest to celebrate Southern heritage through music, dancing, and traditional food, and the Women's Page has a feature on canning and the latest technologies for making preserves at home.[68]

The gradual adaptation of migrant foodways by the mainstream African American community demonstrates the integration of rural Southern culture into urban African American consciousness and the acceptance of migrants not as backwards, unclean, and in need of modernization, but as brothers and sisters with common traditions and heritage. Like European immigrants, Southern migrants developed a sense of ethnic identity around important symbols of rural culture. Food was just one of those symbols, but the primacy of two important ethnic values—Southernness and commensality—were so central to Southern foodways that it made them a natural vehicle for the expression of migrants' sense of individual freedom. Paradoxically, one of the very things that made migrants most visibly ethnic, as far as natives were concerned, was also one of the things that allowed them to integrate most fully into the urban consumer economy. Traditional foodways and food businesses were perfectly matched to assist in the social, economic, and political transformation of rural migrants into urban consumers, and to help them make their mark on urban black consciousness.

105

Ironically, it was the unbridled enthusiasm with which urban African Americans adapted Southern foodways that was to create tension between those who stayed in the South and those who had fled. As urban black identity became more potent, people began exploring the African roots of this familiar cuisine, unearthing the ancient origins of traditions submerged in the daily lives of Southerners. By the time Soul Food was "discovered" in the 1960s, Southerners were already grumbling about the pretensious "uppity cityfolk." A battle over black authenticity ensued, with food once again playing a prominent symbolic role. The continuing story of this tempest in a cast-iron pot is a subject for further study.

NOTES

1. Helen Anglin remembers her mother calling her to the table as a child, saying "Here honey, come get yourself some soul food." But there is no consensus among scholars of culinary and African American history about how and when this phrase came into common usage. Clarence Major, author of *The Dictionary of African American Slang*, says that the term "soul" became common in jazz circles in the 1930s, and meant "essentially the essence of blackness, a feeling for one's roots as demonstrated in black music and culture, a sense of racial history." As to Soul Food, however, Major cites no references to it in print until 1964, in an article in the *New York Times Magazine*, and Malcolm X mentions his landlady cooking soul food in *The Autobiography of Malcolm X, Alex Haley and Malcolm X* (59).
2. Alaine Locke uses this term to describe black migrants to New York in *The New Negro*.
3. Drake and Cayton, 8.
4. Burgess and Newcomb, 59–63.
5. Spear, 147.
6. Grossman, 129.
7. The picture Malcolm X paints of his "high-class, educated, and important" neighbors in Roxbury, Massachusetts, going off to their jobs "in banking," or "in securities"—as janitors—illustrates this point very well. Alex Haley and Malcolm X, 41.
8. Drake and Cayton, pp. 74.

9. *Defender*, January 10, 1920, Editorial page.
10. *Defender*, May 29, 1915, front page.
11. *Defender*, January 23, 1915, "Society" page.
12. *Defender*, March 15, 1915, women's page.
13. There are many excellent sources on slave diets, notably in Eugene Genovese's *Roll Jordan Roll* and Lawrence Levine's *Black Culture and Black Consciousness* but also in the cookbooks of Jessica B. Harris and Kathy Starr, which provide histories of African American food, often handed down orally through these women's families.
14. Cookbook author Kathy Starr remembers her grandmother telling her that the Fourth of July "is our most important holiday. It means freedom to black people, freedom from slavery" (42).
15. Hilliard.
16. James M. McPherson. *Ordeal by Fire: Civil War and Reconstruction.* (New York: McGraw Hill, 1982) 376–380.
17. Jones, *The Dispossessed.*
18. For a particularly vivid account of a Southern black community's food sharing, read Hurston's *Their Eyes Were Watching God*, especially Chapter 5, in which villagers throw a huge picnic to commemorate the lighting of the town's first streetlamp.
19. Table from the Department of Agriculture study is included in Sterner, 122.
20. Spear, 148.
21. Jerome's study was conducted in 1965–66, but there is no question that the food patterns she describes are contiguous with those of the earlier twentieth century. She compares the dietary patterns of her migrant subjects to those collected by Vance in 1932, Cussler and Debive in 1941, and the USDA food consumption report of 1935–36. Jerome, Norge, Randy F. Kandel and Gretel H. Pelto. *Nutritional Anthropology: Contemporary Approaches to Diet and Culture* (NACADC).
22. Jerome, Norge, 1667–1669.
23. Jerome et al., NACADC, 287. Folklorist Anne Sharman, in interviews with urban African American women, discovered that her subjects did make a distinction between "Southern" or "soul" foods and "American food." American food was defined in various ways, but generally referred to "food that white people eat" (remember the distinction between black and white diets in the South) or "foods they might eat if they had unlimited financial resources"—things like steak, fast food, and processed food. Curiously, some respondents also included Chinese and Italian food in this category. "From Generation to Generation: Resources, Experience, and Orientation in the Dietary Practices of Selected Urban American Households," in *Diet and Domestic Life in Society.* (Anne Sharman Janet Theophano, Karen Curtis, and Ellen Messer, eds. Philadelphia: Temple University Press, 1991), 174–203.
24. Jerome et al., NACADC, pp. 293–300.
25. Cohen, 147.
26. Cohen, 148.
27. Ellison, Ralph. *Invisible Man.* New York: Random House, 1952. pp. 258. (originally published 1947).
28. Drake and Cayton, pp. 385.
29. Drake and Cayton, pp. 608–609.
30. All advertising is listed in *Black's Blue Books* of 1917 and 1921 and issues of the Chicago *Defender*, 1915–1935.
31. Duneier.
32. Grossman, 155.
33. Johnson, 101–103.
34. Drake and Cayton, 436.
35. Drake and Cayton, 438.
36. Sterner, 125.
37. Defender, May 8, 1917, 4.
38. Drake and Cayton, 456.
39. Drake and Cayton, 411.
40. Cohen, 426.
41. Edwards, 126.
42. All advertising copy comes from *The Chicago Negro Business Men and Women and Where They Are Located*, 1912 (publisher unknown, located at the Chicago Historical Society Special Collections), *Black's Blue Book, Business and Professional Directory* (Chicago: Ford S. Black, 1917), *Black's Blue Book: Directory of Chicago's Active Colored People and Guide to Their Activities* (Chicago, 1921 and 1923), and *Scott's Blue Book* (Chicago, Illinois, 1947).
43. Drake and Cayton, 78.
44. Cohen, 152.
45. Drake and Cayton, 437.
46. Light, 21.
47. Drake and Cayton, 436.
48. Light, 165.
49. Edwards, 142.
50. Edwards, 135.
51. Lebhar.
52. Cohen, 112.
53. Cohen, 236.
54. Edwards, 56.
55. Sterner, 111.
56. All advertising copy comes from *Scott's Blue Book*, published Chicago, Illinois, 1947.

57. Light, pp. 118.
58. Lebhar, 87 and Cohen, 34.
59. Drake and Cayton, pp. 436.
60. Efforts to find out more about entrepreneurship and foodways among West Indian migrants to Chicago during this period have been singularly unfulfilling. Unlike New York City, which had a large contingent of highly successful foreign black businesses. Chicago did not seem to have been a destination for these immigrants. After the 1964 Immigration Act the West Indian population of Chicago jumped significantly and repeated the pattern of entrepreneurship seen in New York in the 1920s and '30s. Their contribution to the development of Soul Food is, however, outside the scope of this paper. For more on this subject, see Marilyn Halter.
61. Scott's *Business and Service Directory*, 1947. It is unfortunate that the compilers of this interesting list did not note the kinds of businesses owned by these people along with the statistics on states represented so that we could tell whether migrants from certain regions concentrated their efforts in food businesses.
62. Anglin, Helen Maybell. *My Mythical Rubberband*. Chicago: Soul Queen Publishing Company, 1994. pp. 2–3.
63. Heinze, Andrew, 189–90.
64. Cohen, pp. 148.
65. *Defender*, June 21, 1925, Editorial page.
66. *Defender*, February 14, 1925, "Defender Junior" page.
67. *Defender*, July 6, 1935, 6.
68. *Defender*, September 7, 1940, 4.

REFERENCES

Appiah, Anthony K. "The Multiculturalist Misunderstanding," in *New York Review of Books*, Oct. 9, 1997, pp. 30–36.
Archdeacon, Thomas. *Becoming American: An Ethnic History*. New York: MacMillan, 1983.
Brown, Linda Keller and Kay Mussell, eds. *Ethnic and Regional Food ways in the United States: The Performance of Group Identity*. Knoxville, TN: University of Tennessee Press, 1984.
Burgess, Ernest W. and Charles Newcomb. *Data of the City of Chicago, 1920*. Chicago: University of Chicago Press, 1931.
Cohen, Lizabeth. *Making a New Deal: Industrial Workers in Chicago, 1919–1939*. Cambridge: Cambridge University Press, 1990.
Drake, St. Clair and Horace R. Cayton. *Black Metropolis: A Study of Negro Life in a Northern City*. Chicago: University of Chicago Press, 1945.
Duneier, Mitchell. *Slim's Table: Race, Respectability, and Masculinity*. Chicago: University of Chicago Press, 1992.
Eltis, David, David Richardson, Stephen D. Behrendt, and Herbert S. Klein, eds. *The Transatlantic Slave Trade, 1562–1867: A Database Prepared at the W.E.B. Du Bois Institute, Harvard University*. Cambridge University Press, 1998.
Edwards, Paul K. *The Southern Urban Negro as a Consumer*. New York: Prentice Hall, 1932.
Egerton, John. *Southern Food: At Home, On the Road, In History*. Chapel Hill, NC: University of North Carolina Press, 1993.
Fligstein, Neil. *Going North: Migration of Blacks and Whites from the South, 1900–1950*. New York: Academic Press, 1981.
Frazier, E. Franklin. *The Negro Family in Chicago*. Chicago: University of Chicago Press, 1932.
———. *Black Bourgeoisie*. New York: Free Press, 1957.
Gaskins, Ruth L. *A Good Heart and a Light Hand*. New York: Simon and Schuster, 1969.
Genovese, Eugene. *Roll, Jordan Roll: The World the Slaves Made*. New York: Pantheon Books, 1974.
Grossman, James. *Land of Hope: Chicago, Black Southerners, and the Great Migration*. Chicago: University of Chicago Press, 1989.
The Guide to Black Chicago. Chicago: The Guide Group Publishers, 1996.
Haley, Alex and Malcolm X. *The Autobiography of Malcolm X*. New York: Ballantine, 1964.
Hall, Jacqueline. *Like a Family: The Making of a Southern Cotton Mill World*. Chapel Hill: University of North Carolina Press, 1987.
Halter, Marilyn, ed. *Ethnic Enterprise in Massachusetts: New Migrants and the Marketplace: Boston's Ethnic Entrepreneurs*. Amherst: University of Massachusetts Press, 1995.
Harris, Jessica B. *Welcome Table: African American Heritage Cooking*. New York: Fireside, 1990.
Heinze, Andrew. *Adapting to Abundance: Jewish Immigrants, Mass Consumption, and the Search for American Identity*. New York: Columbia University Press, 1990.
Hickman, Nollie. *Mississippi Harvest*. Oxford: University of Mississippi Press, 1962.
Hilliard, Sam. *Hogmeat and Hoecake: Food Supply in the Old South, 1840–1860*. Carbondale, IL: Southern Illinois U.P., 1972.
Hobsbawm, Eric. "Introduction: Inventing Traditions," from *The Invention of Tradition*, Eric Hobsbawm and Terence Ranger, eds. Cambridge University Press, 1983.
Hooker, Richard J. *Food and Drink in America: A History*. Indianapolis: Bobbs-Merrill Inc., 1981.
Jerome, Norge, Randy F. Kandel and Gretel H. Pelto, eds. *Nutritional Anthropology: Contemporary Approaches to Diet and Culture*. Pleasantville, NY: Redgrave Publishing, 1980.
Jerome, Norge. "Northern Urbanization and Food Consumption Patterns of Southern-Born Negroes," *American Journal of Clinical Nutrition*, Vol. 22, No. 12. December 1969, pp. 1667–1669.
Johnson, Charles S. *The Negro in American Civilization: A Study of Negro Life and Race Relations in Light of Social Research*. New York: Henry Holt and Co., 1930.

Jones, Jacqueline. *The Dispossessed: America's Underclasses from the Civil War to the Present.* New York: Basic Books, 1992.

———. *Labor of Love, Labor of Sorrow: Black Women, Work, and the Family from Slavery to the Present.* New York: Basic Books, 1985.

Kiple, Kenneth and Virginia Himmelsteil King. *Another Dimension to the Black Diaspora: Diet, Disease, and Racism.* Cambridge, England: Cambridge University Press, 1981.

Lebhar, Godfrey M. *Chain Stores in America, 1859–1950.* New York: Chain Store Publishing Corp., 1952.

Levine, Lawrence. *Black Culture and Black Consciousness: Afro-American Folk Thought from Slavery to Freedom.* New York: Holt, 1977.

Lewin, Danit. "Race and Class in Soul Food Cookbooks." Unpublished paper: Harvard University, 1997.

Light, Ivan. *Ethnic Enterprise in America: Business and Welfare among Chinese, Japanese, and Blacks.* Berkeley: University of California Press, 1972.

Locke, Alaine. *The New Negro.* NY: Atheneum, 1969 (originally published 1925).

Major, Clarence. *The Dictionary of Afro-American Slang.* New York: International Publishing, 1970.

Philpott, Thomas. *The Slum and the Ghetto: Neighborhood Deterioration and Middle Class Reform, Chicago 1880–1930.* New York, 1978.

Root, Waverly and Richard de Rochemont. *Eating in America: A History.* New York: Ecco Press, 1976.

Sharman, Anne, Janet Theophano, Karen Curtis, and Ellen Messer, eds. *Diet and Domestic Life in Society.* Philadelphia: Temple U.P., 1991.

Sollors, Werner. *Beyond Ethnicity: Consent and Descent in American Culture.* New York: Oxford, 1986.

Spear, Allan H. *Black Chicago: The Making of a Negro Ghetto.* Chicago: University of Chicago Press, 1967.

Starr, Kathy. *The Soul of Southern Cooking.* Jackson, MS: University Press of Mississippi, 1989.

Sterner, Richard. *The Negro's Share: A Study of Income, Consumption, Housing, and Public Assistance.* New York: Harper and Brothers, 1943.

THE NUTRITIONAL IMPACT OF EUROPEAN CONTACT ON THE OMAHA: A CONTINUING LEGACY[1]

CHRISTIANA E. MIEWALD

The Omaha people are not designed to eat European food. The Europeans brought the food over. Their design was to plow the land and they planted their food by plowing and turning the soil over and raising their own domesticated animals such as beef, pork and others. That was their design and they got along with it simply because it is their design. That lifestyle is opposed to Indian living all from the land, living all from the wild animal. So, there's two cultures, two foods and they clashed.

Omaha Tribal Member *(1994)*

The process of colonization of the Americas is linked to disease states among the native populations. Until recently the emphasis has been on infectious disease and its recorded effects on Native American populations. This emphasis on introduced pathogens has tended to ignore the health impacts of political and economic control being placed on native systems. The deliberate destruction of native subsistence patterns through the reduction of land base, elimination of the bison and ecological changes brought on by intensive means of production also had an important impact on the dietary adequacy and health of Native Americans. Current chronic disease states among Native Americans have been found to be associated with the oppressive political and economic conditions which have existed since the formation of reservations. Joe (1991:157), among others, cites the federal government's control of economic and political resources on Indian reservations as helping to perpetuate the persistent poor health of Native Americans through inadequate nutrition and exposure to other health hazards. The nutritional impacts of this relationship were manifested in starvation and malnutrition in the past and are still evident today in the form of certain chronic diseases such as obesity, cancer, diabetes, nutritional deficiencies, and poor dental health (Joe 1991:151).

★ THE OMAHA TRIBE

In 1992, the Omaha tribe of Nebraska reported 4,028 enrolled members, over 2,000 of whom resided permanently within the reservation borders (Omaha Tribe 1993). The Omaha reservation was established by treaty in 1854, which gave the Omaha 300,000 acres or 6 percent of their aboriginal territory. Today, the reservation covers approximately 130,000 acres within the counties of Thurston, Burt, Wayne, and Cumings in Northeastern Nebraska. Within the borders of their reservation, the Omaha are a minority, making up only 35 percent of the population (U.S. Census 1990). The reservation is divided along ethnic lines, with the majority of Omaha residing in the eastern portion and non-Indians further to the west. The current economic situation on the reservation is depressed and jobs are scarce. According to the tribal business office, unemployment was at 64 percent between 1992 and 1993. Both unemployment and underemployment have greatly limited household income. The United States census (1990) estimated that the yearly average per capita income was around $4,765 and that 53 percent of the Omaha was below the poverty line.

Many of the health problems plaguing the Omaha are related to their economic situation. Alcoholism, poor dietary habits, malnutrition and lack of medical attention have contributed to the growing medical crisis. Infant mortality from 1986 to 1987 was nearly thirty-one deaths out of every 1,000 live births, which was one of the highest infant mortality rates in the country. Life expectancy for tribal members is also low, dropping from fifty-eight in 1984 to forty-eight in 1987, compared to seventy-four years for the average in the state of Nebraska (Omaha Tribe 1990b). Contributing to the decline in Omaha health status is an epidemic prevalence of Non-Insulin Dependent Diabetes Mellitus (NIDDM), which affects approximately 35 percent of the adult population. NIDDM is defined as "resistance to the action of insulin, inappropriate insulin secretion, or a combination of the two" (Knowler et al. 1983:108).[2] Defects in the process of glucose use and storage result in high levels of circulating glucose within the body, causing damage to tissue and prohibiting the use of ingested glucose.[3]

Although NIDDM is influenced by genetic predisposition, there is a strong indication that for Native Americans and other non-European populations, diabetes is related to radical changes in diet that occurred via the process of acculturation (Olsen 2001, Ritenbaugh and Goodby 1989). Populations as diverse as Australian Aborigines, Urban Fijian Indians, South African Indians and Mexican-Americans, as well as Native Americans, have all experienced rapid increases in the prevalence of NIDDM over the past several decades, coinciding with significant alternations to traditional foodways (Thornburn et al. 1987, Urdaneta and Krehbiel 1989, Zimmet et al. 1981:213–215). This phenomenon will be explored in the following section which outlines Omaha dietary change over time and argues that a significant increase in the use of non-local foods is associated with the onset of the diabetes epidemic.

While NIDDM is extremely prevalent among Native Americans today, there is ample evidence to suggest that it is a relatively new disease to this population, only occurring in any substantial numbers until the late 1940s. Early ethnographic and health reports make no mention of diabetes or obesity among native peoples. The first comprehensive surveys of Native American health in the *Reports to the Indian Commissioner* describe only two cases of diabetes in 1884 (Department of the Interior 1884:404), four cases in 1886 (Department of the Interior 1886:458), and one case in 1890 (Department of the Interior 1890:507) from a total population of approximately 70,000 Native American patients from all tribes and Indian schools. Even by the 1920s, when health care was more standardized, Native Americans were reported as having fewer cases of diabetes than was found among non-Indians (Department of the Interior 1925:2). Native Americans themselves define diabetes as a new disease, and the fact that there are few medicinal herbs with which to treat it further suggests that it was not a health concern (Kindscher 1992, Lang 1989). Within the last fifty years, the prevalence of diabetes in Native American communities has become significantly greater than among non-Indians, with some tribes, such as the Pima, reporting diabetes rates of over 50 percent (Knowler et al. 1990). It has also been noted that while Native American diets that mimic that of the general United States population are often found in conjunction with elevated rates of NIDDM, those indigenous populations who have retained their traditional diet, such as the Mexican Tarahumara and Canadian Dogrib, are both lean and almost free of diabetes (Schraer et al. 1988). It has therefore been suggested that dietary change associated with acculturation plays a significant factor in the current "epidemic" of NIDDM among Native people.

111

In order to depict the relationship between federal Indian policy, land tenure and nutrition I will focus on Omaha dietary history from the establishment of their reservation until today. For the purpose of identifying the major shifts in Omaha dietary patterns since the creation of their reservation, it was first necessary to define an aboriginal or "traditional" diet for the tribe. This was done using the descriptions of traders, missionaries and other Euroamerican chroniclers in conjunction with Omaha oral history concerning foodways. Interviews and personal histories provided for a greater detailing of changes in Omaha economies and diet over the last 70 years. Finally, by participation in social activities and observation of modern eating habits, modern foodways were delineated.

★ LAND TENURE AND DIETARY CHANGES AMONG THE OMAHA

The changes in Omaha diet exemplify the cultural impacts and adaptations made to new ecological and economic conditions as well as technological and organizational changes brought on by attempts to incorporate the tribe into a Euroamerican system. Like many tribal populations, the Omaha abandoned many of their traditional food habits after moving to their reservation in the 1850s and replaced these with foods of a lower nutritional value. As agricultural production increased and returns from hunting declined, the transition from a subsistence to a cash economy contributed to increased dependence on external food sources. Later in the century, intensive forms of agriculture, cattle raising and increasing development of land along the Missouri would result in further ecological changes, including the reduction of undisturbed areas.

★ THE TRADITIONAL OMAHA DIET

The Omaha (Umoⁿhoⁿ or Upstream People) are a member of the Dhegiha Sioux language family, along with the Ponca, Kansa, Qwapaw and Osage. The identification of a "traditional Omaha diet" is replete with contradictions. Both Omaha history and archeology point to a variety of "traditions" that were adapted to fit changing circumstances. However, the idea of traditional foods remains an important social ideal for the Omaha. In order to reconstruct a traditional diet, I have focused on foods eaten since their arrival on the western side of the Missouri, sometime around 1720. This was done because 1) these settlements coincide with the florescence of Omaha culture and therefore this period is held in deep regard, 2) the Omaha still reside in this area and many of the plants and animals used in the past are still available and 3) many foods used during this earlier time were recorded by ethnographers who provide a fairly accurate record of past food use (see also Reinhard et al. 1994).[4]

Meat, obtained from bison, deer and elk was one of the most important dietary resources to the Omaha. Secondary sources of meat included rabbit, raccoon, squirrel and fowl such as wild turkey or goose. Fish, including catfish, sturgeon, and buffalo fish were either speared or caught with traps (Dorsey 1970:302). Melvin Gilmore (1977), in his study of Omaha ethnobotany, identified approximately 40 species of wild and cultivated plants which were used by the Omaha for food or beverage. Omaha agriculture was typified by a diversity of corn, beans and squash varieties which were adapted to the variable nature of Plains weather patterns.[5] The Omaha also ate wild tubers, greens, fruits, berries, nuts and fungi. Although these plants probably did not contribute the same amount of energy received from game and cultigens, they played an important role in the native diet by providing nutrients. The Omaha collected greens, including milkweed and lamb's quarters. Gooseberry, black raspberry, wild strawberry, buffalo berry, wild grape and red mulberry were eaten fresh in season and dried for use in the winter months. Wild grains, such as rice, and nuts made up an important part of the diet, contributing protein, fat and carbohydrates. Among the most important wild plants were root-producing species such as the prairie turnip, groundnut, hogpeanut, yellow lotus, Jerusalem artichoke, wild onion, and arrowhead (Gilmore 1913a; 1977).

Other foods incorporated into the diet were fungi such as morels and corn smut, which were boiled or roasted; sweeteners made from the sap of the soft maple and boxelder tree; beverages from the leaves of New Jersey tea, wild mint, wild raspberry, wild verbena and red haw (Gilmore 1913a). Salt was obtained from Salt Creek (*Nishki'the ke*), near present-day Lincoln, but slippery elm bark was also used for flavor and to preserve meat (Gilmore 1913a, 1977; Fletcher and La Flesche 1911:342). Finally, some food plants such as wild onion, wild plum, raspberry and wild rose hips were used to treat illness such as stomach ailments, abrasions and eye inflammation (Kindscher 1992).

★ ACCULTURATION AND DIETARY CHANGE AMONG THE OMAHA

The aboriginal territory of the Omaha stretched over an estimated five million acres, extending both west and east of their permanent villages along the Missouri. Prior to their removal to their reservation, the Omaha had been a prosperous tribe, trading pelts with the French, English and Americans for guns, metal implements, silver jewelry, paints, cloth and alcohol (Fletcher and La Flesche 1911:614–661). By 1854, the Omaha were forced to give up three million acres of their territory in eastern Nebraska for a 300,000-acre reservation bordering the Missouri River. Payments for the land included an annual annuity that extended for the following forty years as well as the provisioning of saw and grist mills (Fletcher and La Flesche 1911:623). This treaty agreement also allowed for the discretionary use of Omaha annuities by

112

the federal government for the funding of "civilization" efforts as well as the eventual allotment of Omaha lands (Kappler, Vol. II 1904). The Omaha were assigned an Indian agent to manage the tribe's finances, to oversee their education and to help them to become "yeoman farmers".

The use of traditional foods was neither encouraged socially nor made economically feasible by the colonizing structures placed on the Omaha people. Bison, which was once the mainstay of the Omaha diet, had become scarce on the Western Plains of Nebraska by the mid-1800s and other game became increasingly difficult to find. Furthermore, missionaries, Indian agents, and educators depicted traditional foods as "unclean," lacking in nutrition, or unpalatable. Instead, white foods were given a higher prestige by agents and educators as these items reflected, in their eyes, the move to civilization (for example, see Nurge 1970). The elimination of Omaha traditional foodways, however, was often resisted and contested by the Omaha themselves who viewed their traditional subsistence as both more culturally rewarding and nutritionally sound.

The formation of this reservation meant that the Omaha were largely cut off from their traditional hunting and gathering grounds in western Nebraska. Continued threats from the Sioux, as well as pressure from their agent, occasionally deterred the Omaha in continuing their seasonal round. They continued to trap in the winter, planted their crops in the spring, went on extended hunting trips in the summer and harvested in the fall, a strategy which resulted in adequate food supplies and good health according to the agent's report (Department of the Interior 1863:236).

For the early historic Omaha, food production was divided along gender lines with males primarily responsible for hunting while the women engaged in agricultural activities. During planting, harvesting and preserving of cultigens, Omaha men frequently went on small group hunting trips (Will and Hyde 1962). While on the summer hunt, women were responsible both for the processing of meat and for gathering wild tubers, berries and fruits. Once confined to the reservation, extended hunting trips were discouraged, Omaha men were exhorted to tend to their crops and the women to engage in household chores. According to the farmer hired to assist in Omaha agriculture, "...m any of the men now go into the field with horse and plow, instead, as heretofore, compelling the squaws [sic] to do all the work, and that, too, with the hoe" (Department of the Interior 1864:355). As Omaha men became the primary producers of agricultural products, the economic role of women was moved indoors to pursue activities which were deemed more "proper" by the local non-Indians.

The next major change to Omaha's relationship to their land was the division of previously communal land into individual allotments (see also Swetland 1994, Wishart 1994).[6] Allotment of reservation lands provided Omaha families with 160 acres and individuals with 40 acres, which were to be held in trust by the Federal Government for twenty-five years. During this time the land could not be taxed, encumbered or sold. Allotment, however, did not produce all the positive benefits that had been predicted by Indian reformers. During the middle to late 1800s the tribe continued to farm a relatively small number of acres, usually only enough to support themselves. On the positive side, they were largely self-sufficient and did not need to rely on the poor-quality rations given to other Plains tribes. At the same time, there was constant pressure on the tribe to increase its output, which it did in some years, producing surpluses of corn, wheat and sorghum (Fletcher and La Flesche 1911).

The ability of the tribe to produce surplus, in addition to the annuities they continued to receive, meant that the Omaha could also purchase Euroamerican foods. Early French and Spanish traders probably brought in the first of these foods. Among the initial introductions were sugar and coffee, two easily storable and transportable commodities. These foods quickly became important components of Omaha diet. By the 1820s wheat flour was available to the Omaha (Fletcher and La Flesche 1911) and by the 1880s flour, sugar, coffee, tea, bacon, and other kinds of provisions were incorporated into the diet (Dorsey 1970:272). Despite the accessibility of these Euroamerican introductions, the bulk of the Omaha grain was derived from corn (Dorsey 1970). Given the data on Omaha agricultural production and the depth of information on wild foods, it may be safe to assume that although the Omaha did purchase food from outside sources, it contributed only a portion of the total diet in the 1880s.

1889 saw the first leasing of Omaha land to local whites, an activity that was prohibited under the Dawes Act and done without the approval of their agent (Department of the Interior 1889). Shortly thereafter, leasing came increasingly under the control of the Indian Office. Leasing was first viewed only as a way for those unable to farm due to age (elderly and children) or disability to earn an income (McDonnell 1991). The economic gains which could be made by leasing rather than farming encouraged more Omaha to lease their land. Their agent reported in 1889 that through leasing the Omaha would double their income; a wise business choice given the reduction of government assistance being provided the Omaha for their own production (Department of the Interior 1889).

At its inception, the allotment of tribal lands was viewed as a means to make Native Americans hard-working members of mainstream society by providing private ownership of land. However, only a few years after allotment was completed the federal government felt that the 25-year trust status on allotted land was preventing this goal. The solution was to allow Indians deemed competent to manage their own affairs to have full title to their lands. This "solution," passed as the Burke Act of 1906, brought further loss of land to the Omaha.

Prior to 1890, the Omaha existed in communal villages, with each family tending approximately ten acres of corn, pumpkins, beans, potatoes and other crops. They were largely self-sufficient and were therefore considered a success among Native American tribes (McDonnell 1991:92). Ironically, it was the success of Omaha agriculture that led many to feel that they were one of the most "competent" tribes. In 1910, the Omaha became the test case for the issuance of fee patents to tribal members. Despite the opinion that many members of the tribe were competent to handle their own affairs (even though many did not want fee simple titles), over 80 percent had sold or were swindled out of their titles soon after they were issued. Through deception and outright theft, non-Indian land speculators were able to acquire over 100,000 acres of Omaha lands (McDonnell 1982; 1991).

★ 1920–1945: A COMBINATION OF TRADITION AND NOVELTY

Nutritionally, the period from the 1920s to the United States' involvement in World War II, may be characterized by seasonal hunger and chronic food scarcity. The Omaha continued to survive through self-production of food and some store purchases. It was also a transitional period as residence patterns shifted from rural to urban, and cash income became increasingly important to the family.

While the agricultural market had remained high from 1897 to 1920 enabling some Omaha farmers to remain productive, the post–W.W.I depression resulted in substantially lower return on agricultural production and tougher economic times. After 1920, agriculture in all states ceased to provide adequate incomes for many Native Americans and "bad harvests, droughts and low prices" pushed many to cultivate fewer acres (Carlson 1981:150). The collapse of the U.S. economic system in 1929 had profound effects on Native American subsistence as their dependency on national and world markets had increased. Unable to generate enough income through farming, Native Americans increasingly opted to take wage labor jobs while leasing their land for supplemental income. By the 1930s, declining land base and economic struggles were commonplace among many tribes, further contributing to nutritional insecurity. Overall, the land in Native American possession had declined from 138 to 52 million acres between 1887 and 1934 (McDonnell 1991:121).

The impact of allotment and the Burke Act continued to reduce Omaha land holdings. The policy of issuing fee patents resulted in continued land loss for the Omaha. By 1920, almost 90,000 acres had already been removed from trust, most of the land ending up in non-Indian ownership (Longwell 1961, McDonnell 1982). Between 1920 and 1934, approximately 16,000 more acres were alienated (Longwell 1961). Although the Indian Reorganization Act prevented any further land from being sold, already over 100,000 acres had passed from trust status and were in the hands of non-Omaha so that by 1936 the Omaha tribe owned little more than 30,000 acres (McDonnell 1982).

Economic conditions on the reservation continued to deteriorate between the wars with the majority of income coming from wages, welfare or social security. In 1939, only a small portion of per capita income was derived from farming (Longwell 1961:94). Although the Omaha were able to survive through a strategy of food production, purchase, collection and reciprocity, there were nearly constant seasonal shortages. While few Omaha continued to farm through the 1930s, small gardens and farm animals continued to contribute important quantities of food to the Omaha diet. Gardens were usually large, providing enough produce to be consumed fresh or canned for use during non-productive months. Corn, both "Indian" and sweet was planted; tomatoes, potatoes, squash, beans, and turnips were other mainstays. Gardening was often a means of survival for Omaha, providing a secure supply of food. Elder Omaha frequently mentioned orchards containing apples, as well as wild crabapples, plums and chokecherries. Much of the meat eaten during this time came from hogs, chickens, ducks and a few cattle that were usually kept within the farmstead land. Purchases made at local stores were more infrequent and usually consisted of such necessities as coffee, lard, flour, baking powder, tea and dried fruits. The bulk of the diet, however, was basic, consisting largely of starch and fat from potatoes, oatmeal, biscuits and gravy, corn mush, hominy and the like.

In order to survive through nutritionally precarious periods, the Omaha continued to rely on wild foods as well. Some wild greens, meats, berries and fungi were still in use, especially during the Depression, when cash was nearly impossible to come by. Deer, rabbit and wild fowl were commonly hunted and chokecherries, wild plums, gooseberries, raspberries and blackberries were gathered and either canned or dried. Chokecherries were either made into jam or pounded and made into *wasna*, a mixture of dried berries, meat and fat. Wild onions and garlic continued to be used for flavoring. Wild greens such as lamb's quarters and nettles were used like spinach, cooked with vinegar, boiled eggs and bacon. Prairie turnip, wild rice, arrowhead and yellow lotus, which were once some of the most important wild foods for the Omaha, were rarely collected. This was probably due to environmental changes brought on by intensive agriculture, which destroyed the habitat of these plants, and the introduction of cultivated tubers.

★ 1945—PRESENT: AN ERA OF WAGE LABOR AND WELFARE

By 1945, the Omaha owned approximately 10 percent of their original 300,000 acre reservation. Farming continued to decrease in importance during this period as farm size and production on neighboring lands began to increase. As Omaha agriculture declined, involvement of the tribe in wage labor increased during World War II since large numbers of Omaha men entered the military or took positions in war industries. Thus, the trend continued toward decreasing self-sufficiency and progressive dependence on cash income. Off-reservation jobs also meant adaptation to non-Indian foods.

Of the 130,000-acre Omaha reservation, in 1994 the Omaha people were in possession of 27,697 acres of land, or 21 percent of the total reservation land. As of 1990, all Omaha-owned land has been placed under trust status and can now only be sold with the approval of the Secretary of the Interior. Economically, farming is no longer an important part of the Omaha economy. In the early 1990s, only one Omaha was engaged in the farming, cultivating 580 acres of land, while most of the remaining trust land was rented out for between $30 and $120 an acre (Omaha Tribal Real Estate, personal communication). The tribe also maintained a 3,400-acre farm in Nebraska and Iowa that produced corn, beans and hay (Omaha Tribe 1990a) with the remaining acres either leased or not in use. Tribal land not under agricultural use was used for hunting, fishing and recreation.

Most of the land owned by the Omaha, located along the eastern edge of the reservation, is steeply graded and is largely comprised of poorly or moderately well-drained soils. The land in this area is heavily wooded, consisting of wetlands, mature timber and pioneer willow.

Allotments chosen on other areas of the reservation, where prime farmland exists, have largely passed out of the hands of the Omaha (Longwell 1961). The eastern portion of the reservation is important not only because it is close to the tribal headquarters of Macy but also because it contains the region where old campsites, sacred areas and earlier villages are located.

★ CONTEMPORARY DIETARY PATTERNS

The Omaha diet underwent a variety of changes in terms of content, meal patterning and preparation between 1945 and present day. Wage-labor, off-reservation migration, the influence of schools and the introduction of food aid all served to promote a diet that is radically different from that consumed traditionally. Like many tribal populations such as the Pima, the Omaha gradually abandoned many of their traditional food habits and replaced these with foods of a lower nutritional but greater energy value. The food choices made in the past were based on attempts to provide the family with adequate energy in the face of a declining economy. Given grocery budgets which are constrained by food stamp allotments or tight budgets, many Omaha are still forced to obtain food energy at the lowest cost.

The economic situation on the reservation today has shaped Omaha dietary habits in a variety of ways. Like other Native American populations, the last fifty years have seen a decline in locally produced and gathered foods and increases in store-bought meals, fast food, and commodity distributions (Brenton et al. 1996, Bass and Wakefield 1974, Berkes and Farkas 1978, Lang 1985, Joos 1984, Nurge 1970). While the change in the economy from that based on subsistence and regional trade reduced much of the availability of traditional foods, the entire process of accultur- ation, from social sanctions against some traditional foods to changing the work patterns of women and the forced attendance of children at boarding and day schools, impacted the intake of traditional Omaha foods.

Although there is no one typical Omaha diet, low-cost, high-energy foods such as hamburger, luncheon meats, white bread, macaroni, cake and sweet rolls, chips, kool- aid and pop are common components of most meals. The dietary habits recorded for the Omaha are by no means unique among Native American populations within the United States. In fact, dietary surveys and observations have revealed a startlingly similar pattern (with regional variations) among many tribes throughout the United States (for example, see Joos 1984 for the Seminole; Lang 1985 for the Sioux; Kopp 1986 for the Navajo and Kuhnlein and Calloway 1977 for the Hopi).

Overall, the choice of food for the Omaha is often limited. Many of the foods specifically recommended for weight loss or diabetes are either difficult to obtain or more expensive than other foods. Being on a tight budget or relying on commodity foods is a major constraint on food choice. Recommended foods such as artificial sweeteners, round steak, seafood, "healthy" high fiber cereals and brown rice are expensive and therefore are not typically included in the Omaha diet. Reservation grocery stores, especially those located in Macy, are notoriously poor in quality and more expensive than those in Sioux City, the nearest major shopping area. The majority of space in one Macy store is given to cookies, chips, and frozen desserts, as well as a small kitchen window which serves pizza, fried chicken and fry bread. Fresh fruits and vegetables on the other hand are a scarcity, with only apples, bananas, lemons, tomatoes and oranges being available on a regular basis.

Another important source of food is that provided by government food pro- grams, most notably the Food Distribution Program on Indian Reservations (FDPIR).[7] The commodities distribution center runs a food pantry program that pro- vides commodities and other surplus to any Omaha family in need. Government programs, such as FDPIR, increase the amounts of food available, but fail to build on the nutritional strengths of the traditional Omaha diet (see also Calloway et al. 1974, Calloway and Gibbs 1976, Hug 1994, Wolf and Sanjur 1988).

Dances, giveaways, funerals, and memorials are important events for the pro- duction and consumption of both traditional and modern foods. At every dance, giveaway, funeral, memorial or powwow, food is prepared and served to all atten- dees. Many of these foods contain important cultural meaning and symbolism, which reinforces both Omaha identity and the roles of various segments within the tribe. It is during these events that foods signifying Omaha identity—beef, pork, fry bread, hominy, and beans—are prepared and shared among the attendees. Many of these foods are items that were available to the Omaha shortly after contact with Euroamericans, but which also signal important memories of their past. The Omaha's use of fat, white flour and sugar was said to be a reminder of those times when food was scarce and the acquisition of energy demands overrode those of other nutritional needs. Modern foods, including non-traditional fruits and vegeta- bles, are also incorporated into these events. For example, at one memorial feast the menu included fried chicken, boiled pork, fruit salad, broccoli and cauliflower salad, macaroni salad, mashed potatoes, chicken and rice soup, fresh fruit, radishes, pie, cinnamon rolls, cake, coffee and ice tea.

This is not to say that the Omaha do not utilize pre-contact foods or that they have lost their social importance in Omaha culture. Rather, many Omaha foods used today are a mixture of aboriginal and introduced ingredients. Beef and pork have replaced bison, but beans and corn are included in a number of dishes. The traditional dish of dried corn soup is often flavored with fatback, bacon or beef. Some wild foods, such as prairie turnip, hog peanut, and yellow lotus are no longer collected because they occur in highly specialized environments and therefore are difficult to find. Morel mushrooms, which grow in damp woodlands, and milkweed, which proliferates in old fields, are still seasonally collected and are combined with Euroamerican introductions like eggs and beef. A number of berries, including chokecherries, wild plums, wild rasp-berries, gooseberries, wild grape, mulberries and buffalo berries are still available in undisturbed areas near the Missouri River (known as "the timber") or along road-sides. Instead of being pounded and dried, chokecherries and other berries are made into jams. The reservation continues to supply a good quantity of wild game. Those animals that are mentioned as still being hunted include deer, rabbit, and pheasant. Frequently, the large animals were shared among close family members. The abun-dance of woodlands, forage and water contributes to the abundance and diversity of game still found on the reservation.

Gardening continues to be practiced by some Omaha, but is also constrained by economic and environmental factors. Among the produce grown are tomatoes, onions, peppers, beans and corn; however, very little "Indian corn" is produced. Those with gardens tend to live outside of the HUD housing projects in Macy. Government housing hampers gardening due to the small yard size, close proximity to neighbors and the steep slopes that some houses are built on. Garden harvests are however typically shared among family members who are unable to garden.

★ DISCUSSION AND CONCLUSION

The dietary changes that Omaha people have experienced during their contact with Euroamericans have resulted in a number of health related problems, particularly in an increase in chronic diseases of which diabetes is among the most prevalent. By the time the Omaha had reached the Plains, they were engaged in a mixed economy of hunting, horticulture and gathering. A basic description of their dietary pattern is presented in figure 1.

In contrast, the modern Omaha diet, depicted in figure 2, is strikingly similar to other tribes acculturated to a Western lifestyle. The difference between traditional and modern diets, according to Nabhan (1997) related to the types of foods that are being eaten, not necessarily calorie consumption. For example, when members of the O'odham tribe of Arizona consumed a "mini-mart diet", comprised largely of highly processed foods, their bodies' ability to regulate insulin and glucose worsened.

It was only shortly after these dietary changes occurred that the first incidence of NIDDM was reported among the modern Omaha. According to Indian Health Service records, the first incidence of non-insulin dependent diabetes occurred in 1953 (M. Smith 1993). There are many dietary factors which have been implicated in the rise of NIDDM and obesity among modernizing populations. While Omaha foods

Figure 1: Traditional Omaha Diet c. 1720–1830[8]

Diet based on animal and plant sources
 moderate in carbohydrate
 moderate/high in dietary fiber
 moderate/low in fat
 moderate/high in protein
High energy demands for:
 hunting & warfare
 horticultural activities
 gathering
Seasonal macronutrient shortages

Figure 2: Modern Omaha Diet[9]

Diet based on grocery stores and modern food technology
 high in carbohydrates
 moderate/high in fat
 moderate in protein
 low in dietary fiber
Low energy demands for:
 work and transportation
 sedentary leisure time activities
 potential micronutrient shortages

consumed prior to 1830 were high in fiber, modern staples have had most of their fiber removed through processing. The loss of this fiber is thought to increase intestinal absorption of sugars as well as decrease satiety from foods ingested. Many foods consumed today are high in available carbohydrate and provide small amounts of fiber. This suggests that when these modern foods are consumed, a greater quantity may enter the bloodstream at a higher rate, thus quickly and dramatically elevating blood glucose levels. In addition, many traditional Omaha plant and animal foods are also lower in fat than those commonly consumed today. This is especially true of tubers, greens and fruit that were eaten raw. Bison and other wild game are typically lower in fat than meats available today. While traditional cooking methods usually called for the addition of some fat from meat, these dishes would have also provided fiber, protein and vitamins to the diet.

In many Native American communities there is a growing interest in the revitalization of traditional foodways to prevent or alleviate NIDDM (see Nabhan 1997, Olson 2001). Recent evidence suggests that Native Americans have evolved with gastrointestinal and endocrinological systems better suited for metabolizing "slowly digested" foods found in traditional diets. These diets may therefore be "protective" against diabetes in that they do not produce the glycemic response that often results from modern foods (Nabhan 1997). In one study, Brand et al. (1990) tested the digestibility of traditional Pima foods including mesquite cakes, corn hominy, and acorn and venison stew. They found the glycemic and insulin response to be lower than those produced by Western staples such as potatoes, bread and processed cereal. Conversely, easily digested carbohydrates have been found to elevate glucose and insulin response among the Pima (Aronoff et al. 1977). Today, however, a great proportion of foods consumed by Native Americans are relatively inexpensive and energy dense, but low in the dietary fiber and other components that extend the absorption of glucose into the bloodstream (Nabhan 1997).

These findings have lead Gary Nabhan (1997:204) to comment that "a return to a diet similar to their traditional one is no nostalgic notion; it may, in fact, be a nutritional and cultural imperative." Thus, in order to alleviate NIDDM and other dietary related problems, it is not only necessary to increase screening and treatment of diabetes, but also to look for ways of preventing this illness through a close examination of traditional Omaha diet and lifestyle. Or in the words of one Omaha man,

> I think we need to develop a lifestyle of eating to prevent diabetes. Prevention to me is much better than treating the disease. It would be greater if we didn't have the disease. That's what I'm looking at. Let's go back to where we left off. We missed something on our trail here. On our journey of life we overlooked a few things and so we, as Indian people, need to go back and backtrack our mistakes and find where we went wrong.

The possible roles of traditional Omaha foods within the culture are varied, depending on its past and present use, cultural value, availability, and acceptability. Some foods, such as traditional cultigens or bison, may be revitalized through personal or tribal production. Others may be used to teach about Omaha heritage.[10] In general, the traditional Omaha diet can serve as a culturally meaningful model for modern dietary habits. What is clear is that the Omaha continue to value their traditional foodways, an asset that has the potential to play a variety of roles in diabetes prevention and care.

The process of dietary change described for the Omaha is neither unique among tribal populations nor can it be considered a benign result of acculturation. The loss of land, resources, and political and economic power associated with these losses means that the Omaha were and continue to be in a situation of nutritional dependence. They are presented with few options to feed themselves and are therefore forced to rely on government supplied foods. Local stores also provide them with high-calorie foods which satisfy their basic energy requirements but do little to alleviate malnutrition. The Omaha's reliance on fat, white flour and sugar may be a reminder of those times when foods were scarce and the acquisition of energy demands overrode those of other nutritional needs. This dietary pattern is also encouraged by the economic problems still facing the Omaha today. Still, for many Omaha, feeding oneself and one's family continues to be a struggle given current economic constraints.

Without social and economic improvements leading to a greater range of dietary options the Omaha will continue to suffer from chronic nutritional disease with little hope of alleviation. The goal of Omaha people and health care professionals on the reservation today is to reverse the general trend in food use and incorporate a greater degree of traditional foods into the diet. Traditional Omaha foods and preparation methods are increasingly incorporated into diabetes education and there is a growing interest among many Omaha in reviving the use of wild meats and cultigens. For many, this is the only way to reverse the unrelenting process which has forced the Omaha from a healthy, self-sufficient tribe into one suffering from the effects of nutritional dependency.

NOTES

1. This chapter is an abridged version of an earlier article that appeared in *Great Plains Research* (Miewald 1995).
2. Insulin is a hormone produced by the pancreas that assists in converting glucose to energy. If energy is not immediately required insulin assists in storing glucose as glycogen within muscle tissue or converting it to triglycerides that are stored in fat cells.
3. While NIDDM is usually a manageable disease, untreated or poorly managed it can result in a variety of serious secondary complications and death. Among these are retinopathy leading to blindness, neuropathy or nerve damage which may increase the risk of sores, gangrene and amputations, hypertension and cardiac arrest, and kidney damage requiring dialysis.
4. See Miewald (1995) for a more detailed description of traditional Omaha foodways.
5. Five different varieties of corn were grown including flint, flour, dent, sweet and popcorn (Gilmore 1977), of which there were white, yellow, blue, spotted and red variations (Dorsey 1970, Will and Hyde 1917). The Omaha also planted approximately fifteen varieties of garden bean which varied in size and came in varieties of dark red, black, dark blue, and white, with variations or mixtures of these colors (Dorsey 1970:308). While Gilmore (1977:65) claims that the Omaha grew eight types of squash, Dorsey (1970:306) identifies only five, three native and two introduced.
6. Although the allotment of tribal land was part of their 1854 land cession treaty, this was not actually completed until 1884, two years after the passage of the Dawes Act of 1882 provided for the allotment of all Native Americans lands within the United States.
7. This program provides surplus food to low-income households residing on Native American reservations. Basic elements of FDPIR distributions include canned meats, peanuts and peanut butter, canned vegetables, dried potatoes, cheese, dried or evaporated milk, rice or macaroni, dried fruits, cereals and oil. The foods that are part of the commodities program are largely made up from surpluses, which the government prevents from entering the market.

   Omaha attitudes about commodity foods are mixed. Some Omaha have voiced concern over the dependence on outside food sources, claiming that it prevents the Omaha from eating traditional foods. Many expressed doubts about the nutritional quality of commodity foods, especially the canned meats, which have been described as "full of fat". Indeed, many of the canned meats are in fact defined by Indian Health Service booklets as being "high fat" (IHS 1990). Others felt that the provisioning of commodities is an important part of the government's obligation to the tribe, although rations were not supplied to the tribe during the 19th century.
8. Adapted from Jackson (1994) and Ritenbaugh and Goodby (1989). 1830 marks the first reduction in Omaha land, when the tribe, along with the Yankton and Santee Sioux, Iowa, Oto-Missouri, and Sauk and Fox, gave up over two million acres of land in western Iowa for which they received $25,000 paid over ten years (Fletcher and La Flesche 1911, Royce 1972). Although the Omaha continued their hunting and farming subsistence pattern well into the reservation period, they were increasingly constrained by both Euroamericans and other tribes vying for access to land.
9. Adapted from Ritenbaugh and Goodby (1989).
10. In 1995, the Winnebago tribe, whose reservation borders the Omaha, began their own bison herd. Today, the tribe has two refuges with approximately 50 animals (*The Daily Nebraskan* 2001). For more on diabetes prevention among the Winnebago Tribe of Nebraska, see Miewald (1994).

121

REFERENCES

Aronoff, S.L., P.H. Bennett, P.I. Gordon, N. Rushforth and M. Miller. 1977. Unexplained Hyperinsulinemia in Normal and "Prediabetic" Pima Indians Compared with Normal Caucasians: An Example of Racial Differences in Insulin Secretions. *Diabetes* 26:827–840.

Bass, M.A. and L.M. Wakefield. 1974. Nutrient Intake and Food Patterns of Indians on Standing Rock Reservation. *Journal of the American Dietetic Association* 64:36–41.

Berkes, F. and C. S. Farkas. 1978. Eastern James Bay Cree Indians: Changing Patterns of Wild Food Use and Nutrition. *Ecology of Food and Nutrition* 7: 155–172.

Brand, Janette C., B. Janelle Snow, Gary P. Nabhan, and A. Stewart Truswell. 1990. Plasma Glucose and Insulin Responses to Traditional Pima Indian Meals. *American Journal of Clinical Nutrition.* 51: 416–420.

Brenton, B.P., Sly-Terpstra D. and C.E. Miewald. 1996. Return of the Buffalo and the All-You-Can-Eat Buffet: Native American Dietary Change in the Age of Casinos. Paper presented at the ninety-fifth Annual Meeting of the American Anthropological Association, San Francisco, CA.

Calloway, D.H., R.D. Giauque and F.M. Costa. 1974. The Superior Mineral Content of Some American Indian Foods in Comparison to Federally Donated Counterpart Commodities. *Ecology of Food and Nutrition* 3:203–211.

Calloway, D.H. and J.C. Gibbs. 1976. Food Patterns and Food Assistance Programs in the Cocopah Indian Community. *Ecology of Food and Nutrition* 5:183–196.

Carlson, L.A. 1981. *Indians, Bureaucrats and Land: The Dawes Act and the Decline of Indian Farming.* Westport: Greenwood Press.

The Daily Nebraskan. 2001. Winnebago Tribe takes healthy approach to diabetes. University of Nebraska: Lincoln.

Department of the Interior. 1859–1922. *Annual Report of the Commissioner of Indian Affairs.* Washington: Government Printing Office.

Dorsey, J.O. 1970. *Omaha Sociology.* Third Annual Report of the U.S. Bureau of Ethnology, Smithsonian Institution, 1884. Reprinted by New York: Johnson Reprint Corporation.

Fletcher, A.C. and F. La Flesche. 1911. *The Omaha Tribe.* Smithsonian Institution, Bureau of American Ethnology, 27th Annual Report.

Gilmore, M. 1913a. A Study in the Ethnobotany of the Omaha Indians. *Nebraska State Historical Society* 17:314–357.

———. 1997. *Uses of Plants by the Indians of the Missouri River Region.* Lincoln: University of Nebraska Press.

Hug, L. M. 1994. Diet and Disease on the Plains: Diabetes among the Omaha. *Great Plains Research* 4(2): 271–292.

Jackson, M.Y. 1994. Diet, Culture and Diabetes. In *Diabetes as a Disease of Civilization: the Impact of Culture Change on Indigenous Peoples*, ed. J. Joe and R.S. Young, 382–406. Berlin: Mouton de Gruter.

Joe, J. 1991. The Delivery of Health Care to American Indians: History, Policies and Prospects. In *American Indians: Social Justice and Public Policy*, eds. D.E. Green and T.V. Tonnesen, 149–179. Madison: University of Wisconsin.

Joos, S. K. 1984. Economic, Social, and Cultural Factors in the Analysis of Disease, Dietary Change and Diabetes Mellitus Among the Florida Seminole Indians. In *Ethnic and Regional Foodways in the United States: The Performance of Group Identity*, eds. L.K. Brown and L. Mussell, 111–128. Knoxville: The University of Tennessee.

Kappler, C. 1904. *Indian Affairs: Laws and Treaties, Vols. I & II.* Washington: Government Printing Office.

Kindscher, K. 1987. *Edible Wild Plant of the Prairie: An Ethnobotanical Guide.* Lawrence: University Press of Kansas.

Knowler, W. C., D. J. Pettitt, and R. C. Williams. 1983. Diabetes Mellitus in the Pima Indians: Genetic and Evolutionary Considerations. *American Journal of Physical Anthropology* 62:107–114.

Kopp, J. 1986. Crosscultural Contacts: Changes in the Diet and Nutrition of the Navajo Indians. *American Indian Culture and Research Journal* 10(4):1–30.

Kuhnlein H.V. and D. H. Calloway. 1977. Contemprary Hopi Food Intake Patterns. *Ecology of Food and Nutrition* 6:159–173.

Lang, G. 1985. Diabetes and Health Care in a Sioux Community. *Human Organization* 44(3):251–260.

Longwell, A.R. 1961. *Lands of the Omaha Indians.* Lincoln: Unpublished Masters Thesis.

McDonnell, J. 1982. Land Policy on the Omaha Reservation: Competency Commissions and Forced Fee Patents. *Nebraska History* 63:399–412.

———. 1991. *The Dispossession of the American Indian: 1887–1934.* Bloomington: Indiana University Press.

Miewald, C.E. 1994. Attitudes and Awareness of Winnebago Parents Concerning Acanthosis Nigricans and Diabetes Risk. Report presented to the Winnebago Diabetes Project, Winnebago, NE.

———. 1995. The Nutritional Impacts of European Contact for the Omaha: A Continuing Legacy. *Great Plains Research* 5(1):71–114.

Nabhan, G.P. 1997. *Cultures of Habit: On Nature, Culture and Story.* Counterpoint: Washington, D.C.

Nurge, E. 1970. Dakota Diet: Traditional and Contemporary. In *The Modern Sioux: Social Systems and Reservation Culture*, ed. Ethel Nurge, 35–91. Lincoln: University of Nebraska Press.

Olsen, B. 2001. Meeting the Challenges of American Indian Diabetes: Anthropological Perspectives on Prevention and Treatment. In *Medicine Ways: Disease, Health and Survival among Native Americans*, eds. C.E. Trafzer and D. Weiner, 163–184. Walnut Creek: Altamira Press.

Omaha Tribe. 1990. *The Omaha Tribe of Nebraska Overall Economic Development Plan.* Macy: Privately printed.

———. 1993. "Omaha Tribe of Nebraska: Economic Data for 1992–1993", mimeograph copy.

Reinhard, K.J., L. Tieszen, K. L. Sandness, L. M. Beiningen, E. Miller, A. M. Ghazi, C. E. Miewald, S. V. Barnum. 1994. Trade, Contact, and Female Health in Northeast Nebraska. In *In the Wake of Contact: Biological Responses to Conquest*, eds. Clark S. Larsen and George R. Miller, 63–74. New York: Wiley-Liss.

Ritenbaugh, Cheryl and Carol-Sue Goodby. 1989. Beyond the Thrifty Gene: Metabolic Implications of Prehistoric Migration into the New World. *Medical Anthropology* 11:227–236.

Schraer, C. D., A. P. Lanier, E. J. Boyko, D. Gohdes, and N. J. Murphy. 1988. Prevalence of Diabetes Mellitus in Alaskan Eskimos, Indians, and Aleuts. *Diabetes Care* 11(9):693–700.

Smith, M. 1993. "Diabetes Among the Omaha Indians: Omaha Children at Risk". Paper presented at the Annual Meeting of the Society for Applied Anthropology, San Antonio, Texas, March 10–14, 1993.

Swetland, M.J. 1994. "Make-Believe White-Men" and the Omaha Land Allotments of 1871–1900. *Great Plains Research* 4(2):201–236.

Thorburn. A. W., J. Brand, K. O'Dea, R. Spargo and A. S. Truswell. 1987. Plasma Glucose and Insulin Responses to Starchy Foods in Australian Aborigines: A Population Now at High Risk. *American Journal of Clinical Nutrition* 46:282–285.

United States Bureau of Census. 1990. Census of Population and Housing Summery, Tape File 3A. Washington D.C.:U.S. Government Microfilms.

Urdaneta, Maria Luisa and Rodney Krehbiel. 1989. Cultural Heterogeneity of Mexican-Americans and Its Implications for the Treatment of Diabetes Mellitus Type II. *Medical Anthropology* 11:269–282.

Wedel, W. R. 1978. Notes on the Prairie Turnip (*Psoralea esculenta*) among the Plains Indians. *Nebraska History* 59(2):155–179.

Will, G. F. and G. E. Hyde. 1917. *Corn among the Indians of the Upper Missouri.* Lincoln: University of Nebraska Press.

Wishart, D.J. 1994. *An Unspeakable Sadness: the Dispossession of the Nebraska Indians.* New York: Garland Publishing.

Wolfe, W.S. and D. Sanjur. 1988. Contemporary Diet and Body Weight of Navajo Women Receiving Food Assistance: An Ethnographic and Nutritional Investigation. *Journal of the American Dietetic Association* 88(7): 822–827.

Zimmet, P., S. Whitehouse, J. Kiss. 1979. Ethnic Variability in the Plasma Insulin Reposes to Oral Glucose in Polynesian and Micronesian Subjects. *Diabetes* 28:624–628.

CONSUMER CULTURE AND PARTICIPATORY DEMOCRACY: THE STORY OF COCA-COLA DURING WORLD WAR II

MARK WEINER

As a foreign traveler can attest, the relation between food and national identity is close and strong, as deeply intertwined, perhaps, as the twin yearnings of hunger and love. Not only do citizens of most nations come to perceive some aspect of their cuisine as distinctive, nations themselves are typically associated with particular foods. Consider the people of Japan, whose collective identity is firmly based on their shared consumption of rice, or those of Scotland, who take pride in their distinguished tradition of distilling fine whiskey. These national symbols, of course, are far from arbitrary; the food that represents a nation is frequently said to reveal the special values of the people who live there. A carafe of wine, for example, often serves as the national symbol of France, in part because the complex fragrance of the beverage is a powerful reminder of French concern for aesthetic subtlety. Similarly, a steaming cup of hot tea recalls the nation of England, partly because the leisurely manner in which it must be consumed brings to mind British ideals of civil discourse. Countries are what they eat, or at the very least, people tend to think of nations in culinary terms.

The United States is hardly unique in possessing a national icon drawn from the world of comestibles. Symbolically unifying its diverse, multiethnic society, Coca-Cola is what Roland Barthes has called a "totem-drink," and more than any other food (except, perhaps, hamburgers, with which it is often served), this beverage has come to symbolize the American nation.[1] Speak with people in India, China, Austria, or Egypt, just about anywhere, and many will tell you that Coke and the United States are closely associated, if not synonymous. But while a Bordeaux recalls the celebrated complexity of the French palate, and tea the special esteem in which the British hold polite conversation, Coca-Cola *is* special among patriotic symbols in at least one important respect: the national characteristic it represents is a political one, a democratic vision of consumer abundance known as the "American Way of Life." Inexpensive, simple for the palate, and providing a sweet, caffeinated release, Coca-Cola indeed not only embodies the egalitarian, self-directed spirit of consumer society in the United States, but also explicitly served as an international symbol of that society during the Cold War. This cultural status is reflected in documents as diverse as Billy Wilder's comedy film classic *One, Two, Three*, the renowned "World and Friend" cover of Henry Luce's *Time* magazine, and Stanley Kubrick's *Dr. Strangelove*.[2]

Because Coca-Cola has served as an icon of American consumer society, it also possesses another quality unique among foods: the emotional hostility it arouses. Other culinary symbols have certainly caused great anger when they were removed from stores (one thinks of the recent shortage of domestic rice in Japan, or of Gorbachev's ill-fated attempt to curtail vodka consumption in the Soviet Union). But no other foods, except Coca-Cola, have aroused such strong negative feelings when they were merely introduced to the open marketplace, for in serving as a primary symbol of the "American Way of Life," Coke often is viewed not simply as a food but also as a social danger. Coca-Cola may be inexpensive, critics announce, but it also is the same everywhere, and so intimates the approach of cultural uniformity. The drink may be simple for the palate, easily enjoyed by all, but it also is sold from machines, and so exists outside of sanctioned locations of community ritual. Coca-Cola may provide an innocent, sweet release, but that sweetness seems to conceal the fact that Coke is manufactured by a single multinational corporation, a major locus of economic power. Such criticisms animated what Mark Pendergrast has characterized as the series of "threats and rumors [Coke faced] at midcentury around the world," including French protests of the late 1940s and early 1950s, and such criticisms continue to undergird the cynicism many direct toward Coke today.[3]

How was Coca-Cola forged into this hotly contested symbol? That story began in the 1920s, when company president Robert Woodruff initiated a series of reforms important for the growth of his organization, including an increased emphasis on the sale of Coca-Cola in bottles, especially from gasoline stations, as well as a campaign to standardize the beverage, to make certain that "every bottle and fountain drink [would] taste exactly the same across the United States."[4] In the 1930s Coke deftly employed film and radio to market cheap distraction to people enduring difficult times, utilized new methods of electric refrigeration in its sales (Coca-Cola tastes best over ice), and used Madison Avenue to emphasize the critical role the beverage played in the culture of the drugstore soda fountain—which, at the time, lay "at the heart of America's social activity."[5] But while the 1920s saw Coke become portable, accessible and uniform, and the 1930s witnessed how Coke became more widely consumed, and "increasingly...performed a social function," in order to understand how Coca-Cola became deeply linked with *American* identity, one must look to World War II.[6] For it was only during the war, when savvy business executives placed Coke within the smithy of global conflict, within its peculiar cultural and psychological circumstances, that this already popular beverage was transformed into an icon of *national* values.

This essay examines that transformation and the tactics The Coca-Cola Company used to create it, in order to explore a widely held political judgment of the consumer society Coke represents.[7] Scholars generally believe that consumer society is hostile to the republican ideal of participatory democracy, which valorizes the active involvement of citizens in public decision-making. Many assert not only that the self-focused ethic of consumerism diminishes commitment to the common good, the foundation of a democratic republic, but that the fluid meaning of commodities masks the concentrated, anti-democratic power of capital. Recently, scholars have developed and periodized this judgment by focusing their attention on the 1930s and 1940s, especially on World War II, when a "far-reaching ideological redefinition of polity and society [allegedly] began to take hold." This redefinition, which ushered in "the social contract of cold war liberalism," reconceived consumer items as one of the primary rights of citizenship and so refigured citizenship, in the words of Jean-Christophe Agnew, "in the seemingly innocuous language of soft drinks, arms, and household appliances."[8] This transition formed an anti-democratic turning-point in American history because civic self-perceptions were altered in a way that privatized political consciousness, and the fluid language of commodities in which those self-perceptions were articulated served to conceal corporate power.

Although I agree that historical evidence supports this perspective, I believe that the story of Coca-Cola during World War II can also support a somewhat different conclusion. During the war, certainly, Coca-Cola did come to play a role in how Americans understood their identity as citizens, and The Coca-Cola Company did become tightly intertwined with the American state, setting the stage for its enormous postwar expansion. But the wartime tale of Coke may not be simply one of declining democratic politics, for the history of Coca-Cola also reveals how a consumer item, a product of concentrated economic power that appealed to individual desires, could be used by the people who drank it for ends that were not private but communal. Coca-Cola was unique among most consumer products in being a *food*, an item whose meaning is rarely fluid but is instead created through social practice; but it is partly for this reason that I believe the story of Coca-Cola suggests a different evaluation of consumer society as a whole from that held by many critics. This evaluation, which I discuss in my conclusion, is sensitive to the ways in which consumer goods can be used in morally profound interactions between individuals and within communities, as suggested by the work of Lizabeth Cohen. It also incorporates the scholarship of those who consider goods as being "good to think," especially Timothy Breen's analysis of non-importation and the American Revolution.[9]

I have divided the following discussion into four primary parts, the first three of which deal with the history of Coca-Cola during World War II. In the first, I discuss the distribution of Coke to American servicemen, describing the extensive intermingling of Coca-Cola and the U.S. government, a relation dramatically embodied in the work of company representatives known as "T.O.'s." In the second, I examine Coca-Cola advertising, placing one particular Coca-Cola campaign within the national propaganda context in which it was produced, and that facilitated its success. And in the third section, I explore how G.I.'s actually felt about Coke, their emotional attachment to the drink, using a letter from Coca-Cola company archives to establish how American servicemen associated the beverage with both private, personal experience, and national civic identity. After discussing these three aspects of Coke's past, I briefly sketch how Coca-Cola could be used to foster participatory politics by gesturing toward the role the beverage played in the African-American Civil Rights Movement. This final section uses anecdotes whose emotional power, I believe, suggests that under certain circumstances, consumer goods, like food in general, could serve in the formation of a beloved community, even despite the largely antidemocratic forces operating within consumer society. In doing so, they also reveal how the nature of food can illuminate the nature of "the culture of consumption."

★ DISTRIBUTING COCA-COLA OVERSEAS

During World War II, American business faced a problem. The war had dramatically increased average family income, but it also had created a shortage of consumer goods, and this lack threatened to erode brand loyalty. How could an organization protect its long-term marketing interests during the course of global conflict, emerging from a period of economic belt-tightening into one of increased sales? The solution was for businesses to keep their products in the public eye by symbolically associating them with the Allied cause. As Richard Polenberg notes, with the availability of consumer goods limited by economic rationing, "businessmen were not primarily interested in motivating people to buy more, but by linking their product[s] with the war they hoped to keep alive brandname preferences, build up postwar demand, and maintain good will."[10] Over the course of World War II, then, business engaged in a variety of campaigns that linked their products with hopes of American victory; for instance, they publicly encouraged employees to purchase defense bonds, hosted company salvage drives, and spread patriotic messages over the radio and through magazines. Businesses also promised that while military conflict would temporarily create economic scarcity, it also would lead to the development of futuristic household gadgets after V-Day. In the language of Madison Avenue, one might say that businesses viewed the war as an opportunity for product placement and public relations, as well as for national public service.

The Coca-Cola Company was no exception. Like other corporations, for instance, Coke contributed to the national collection of scrap metal, especially tin, conducting salvage drives in its local bottling plants and, occasionally, helping to coordinate scrap collections for the beverage industry as a whole.[11] And by 1942, Coke had produced, at its own expense, a number of short, patriotic slide-films to be shown to businesses and civic clubs. One of these films, "The Free American Way"—which promoted the War Savings Program by contrasting "the life of those in Axis-ruled nations" to conditions of material abundance "here in America"—became extremely popular, generating numerous requests for copies from across the nation.[12] The real importance of such work, of course, should not be underestimated, nor should the genuine patriotism of Coca-Cola be subject to doubt. Still, such activities allowed Coke to use the circumstances of military crisis to advance its corporate image at home, to dutifully serve a nation-at-arms while helping to ensure its own postwar sales. Times may have been hard, but like other companies, Coca-Cola knew that patriotism would offer an excellent financial return on its investment.

While Coca-Cola was not unique in its desire to maintain its image through wartime marketing, it was exceptional in promoting itself among one influential group of consumers: American G.I.'s. Certainly, every astute business sought to associate its products with soldiers and sailors; if a consumer item could be symbolically linked to men surrounded by an aura of national honor, its manufacturer stood to increase sales among civilians. But Coca-Cola hoped not only to *associate* its product with servicemen, but also to become an important part of their *lives*, and it did so in two specific ways. The first was relatively simple: the company implemented a series of recreational programs to help soldiers enjoy their time off. For example, Coca-Cola coordinated a domestic tour of popular musicians, known as the "Victory Parade of Spotlight Bands," and distributed card and board game sets to military personnel. (As one naval commander wrote, expressing thanks for three-hundred "Coca-Cola Game Kits" on behalf of those "defending the American way of life," such an "expression of loyalty [helped] make life a little easier for fighting Americans in far-off corners of the world."[13]) The second way Coke tried to become part of servicemen's lives, though, was far more audacious, and here, in a tale that involves the deep interpenetration of The Coca-Cola Company and the U.S. government, is the crux of the story.

Shortly after December 7, 1941, Robert Woodruff made an astounding promise: that his organization would "see that every man in uniform gets a bottle of Coca-Cola for five cents, wherever he is and whatever it costs our company," so that Coke would be "within arms reach of desire" of *every* soldier. Woodruff had set a difficult goal. Even without the special obstacles posed by global conflict (shipping space was largely dedicated to war material and sugar rationing was in effect), the distributional problems of such an effort were extremely complex. Still, although Coca-Cola never became as ubiquitous a presence in the field as Woodruff had predicted, "the Boss" was able to place the beverage in the hands of an enormous number of military personnel—in part because of the extensive influence Coca-Cola maintained in the halls of Washington (James Farley, head of The Coca-Cola Export Corporation, had been Postmaster General, and former Coke executive Ed Forio was a member of the federal sugar rationing board).[14] By August 1943, when the amount of Coke produced for the military reached its apex, over 95 percent of Ship's Service Stores and Post Exchanges had served the drink. In that month alone, the company shipped eight million cases of Coke to the armed forces, part of over five billion cases sent to the military over the course of the war. In the world of name-brand food, only Wrigley's gum and Hershey chocolate held such prominent places in the American military diet. Woodruff had fulfilled his pledge, with government help.[15]

Relations between Coke and the American state were so close, in fact, that Woodruff typically had no need to wield direct political influence to achieve his goals; instead, the state often freely sought to assist *him*. In 1942, for example, FDR defended a controversial policy that gave soft drink producers large quantities of scrap metal as payment for participating in salvage drives by asserting that "soft drinks...are part of our way of life" and that companies needed metal to produce bottle caps.[16] More importantly, top military leaders greatly facilitated distribution of Coke by deeming availability of the beverage an important part of the war effort. These military officers, including Gen. Eisenhower, feared that a lack of Coca-Cola among American troops would "cause an increase in the consumption of alcohol," and also viewed Coca-Cola as a tool that would sustain morale.[17] In this regard, military officers were not interested in serving *any* soda, but in serving Coca-Cola in particular, for just as servicemen frequently requested a specific brand of tobacco when asking for cigarettes, so they often asked expressly for Coke when they wanted a soft drink. In 1944, the War Department officially encouraged such selective consumption, authorizing overseas commands to order beverages by "name or description" for their supplies, further tightening the link between the state and manufacturers of brand-name products through the rules of military requisition.[18]

The assistance the United States government rendered Coca-Cola was embodied most clearly, though, in those responsible for physically bringing Coke to American G.I.'s, the 148 Coca-Cola representatives known in company parlance as "T.O.'s." These men were charged with establishing bottling plants and soda dispensers wherever American troops traveled, and their moniker reflected the dual status they held as agents of both Coke and Uncle Sam: the military gave them the status of "Technical Observers." Dressed in military uniform, T.O.'s moved with Allied forces across the Middle East, up the boot of Italy, and through the jungles of the South Pacific, satisfying military thirst while simultaneously laying the foundation for Coke's postwar expansion. The conditions in which T.O.'s worked were primitive (like others in the field of combat, they faced supply shortages, poorly trained labor, and the physical dangers of war), but they nevertheless managed to establish a total of *sixty-three* bottling plants in cities around the globe, including plants in Tripoli, Aden, Dongalla, Florence, Reykjavik, Khorramshahr, Marseilles, Frankfurt, Amsterdam, Okinawa, and Kobe. This was business-government cooperation in its highest incarnation, and at its most efficient.[19]

Coca-Cola T.O.'s were the human base of Coke's overseas development and their stories, therefore, are highly instructive. First, T.O. narratives (documented in the company magazine *T.O. Digest*), reveal how Coke could have assumed largely negative social meanings among those encountering it for the first time, because T.O.'s frequently acted with that problematic innocence often associated with Americans abroad. For example, on one hand, T.O. stories are filled with situations in which men face tremendous obstacles to achieve what they believe is right, sincerely laboring against the odds in order to get a job done. "I had quite an interesting day yesterday," wrote a T.O. from the Philippines in 1945.

> One of the combat divisions sent a dispatcher down for me to accompany him to their operations to set up five jungle units for their division.... The forward line was just about three hundred yards from us and a little action was going on. The dispenser was out but the ice machine was operating. I got the dispenser operating just as the line company was relieved in the hills where they had been for quite some time. It was the first time that I have sincerely felt that I had accomplished something. Those boys lined up and passed through the line twice and I acted as the dispenser. I managed to fix the five units for the division and got back about ten p.m. It was quite a picture watching the fire power of our units by the flashes. This is the real thing and we even pack a gun into mess when up there with the boys.[20]

On the other hand, as moving as such accounts may be, T.O. narratives are also animated by a callous ethnic prejudice based upon the same earnest view of the world. "To begin with," wrote one T.O. from Cairo in 1945,

> we have about 40 natives employed and they are a constant source of both laughs and headaches. In the beginning they were very shy of the machinery and now they are very intrigued by it and their childlike love for turning switches off and on without warning is going to make the Arab death rate go way up, if it doesn't stop damned soon.[21]

T.O.'s thus exhibit in their emotions the connection between naiveté and intolerance many associate with Americans' relations with foreign peoples, a connection that some consider to be present in the nature of Coca-Cola itself, which is nonalcoholic, pleasingly sweet and full of empty calories, but is also a troubling harbinger of cultural colonization.

But T.O. stories reveal more than the nature of America's relations abroad during wartime; they reveal the nature of wartime America itself. For when the state not only allowed military officers to request Coca-Cola for their personnel, but also directly assisted the distribution of the beverage by dressing Coca-Cola representatives in military uniform and charging them with quasi-military duties, it implicitly transformed Coke into a symbol of the very cause for which Americans were fighting. After all, the state, including a significant portion of its military apparatus, was guaranteeing the availability of Coke among its most essential citizens, thereby implying that what it meant to be an American was intricately bound with the ability to enjoy a pause that refreshes, and that it was the duty of government to ensure that this ability would not be infringed. In their dual role as Coca-Cola Men and Government Men, T.O.'s therefore suggest that during the war, the state underwent a qualitative change, becoming less an organ for the exercise of republican virtue than a provider of mass-market consumer products; it literally became an institutional source of "soft drinks, arms and household appliances." In the lives of Coca-Cola T.O.'s, we seem to witness one manifestation of the "ideological redefinition" Agnew has described: the quiet steady refiguration of American identity in the language of commodities. As one group of Navy seamen tersely stated, "If anyone asked us what we are fighting for, we think half of us would answer, 'the right to buy Coca-Cola again—as much as we want.'"[22]

★ **COCA-COLA AND WARTIME ADVERTISING**

In order to ensure that servicemen perceived Coca-Cola in this manner, Woodruff's organization did more than distribute its product overseas, thereby implicitly refiguring American identity in the language of Coke. It also undertook a series of sophisticated advertising campaigns which surrounded Coke with the language of American identity. The company used advertising to associate its product with the symbolism suggested by the institutional status of Coca-Cola T.O.'s. Discussing the social significance of advertising, of course, is an endeavor rife with problems. When examining the works of Madison Avenue, for instance, it is easy to fall into the error of what Alan Trachtenberg has called "culturism," in which culture is characterized "as a giant mechanism, a machine not only for total explanation in light of a single dominating pattern, but a machine of total determination."[23] As Roland Marchand has documented, advertisements ultimately tell scholars more about the minds of the people who created them than of those at whom they were directed.[24] Nevertheless, because The Coca-Cola Company has long dedicated a significant portion of its general budget to advertising, and because initial popularity of the beverage was created largely by ingenious marketing, in the following section of this analysis, I examine a particular advertising campaign for Coca-Cola that appeared in a variety of publications throughout World War II. In discussing this campaign, which was based on the semiotic use of the = symbol, I hope to offer a rough architectural sketch of Coke's cultural meaning, especially its status as a consumer good with associations at once private and public.

Before we begin, we first need to consider a special feature of American wartime propaganda: the unprecedented extent to which it used the strategies of advertising in films, broadcasts, and publications. In particular, propaganda created by the Office of War Information, as well as by independent corporate institutions, portrayed the need for people to do their part in the war effort not through discussions of international legal rights or deep political questions, but by appealing to personal self-interest. For example, as Allan Winkler notes, one OWI booklet distributed to merchants involved in campaigns to raise and share food "pointed out the need to 'remind people of the pleasure and deliciousness... of having all the dewy-fresh vegetables they want,'" and discouraged discussing the abstract and imper-sonal concept of national duty. This "positive approach," claimed the pamphlet, "which quickly answers the instinctive human question 'What is in it for me?' seems to be the *surest* way to get people to take action." Another booklet similarly advised those involved in conservation campaigns not to stress "the general, national patri-otic 'why'" but the "*private* 'why.'" The drive behind these admonitions was to "sell" the war by showing that participation in it would improve consumers' *personal* lives; citizens implicitly were to "purchase" the Allies (or so derisive critics of the OWI claimed) in the same manner as they might buy a bottle of soda. Thus, when a number of OWI members balked at the increasing influence Madison Avenue held over their organization, some satirized the nature of OWI policy by producing a poster that depicted the Statue of Liberty holding four bottles of Coke; the poster's caption read, "The War That Refreshes: The Four Delicious Freedoms."[25]

Despite the prominence of such personal, consumerist appeals, the messages of American propaganda were not solely those of privatization. The OWI and other information organs also used the techniques of Madison Avenue to link the private components of Americans' lives to issues of *national* significance. Most important, wartime propaganda frequently used visual juxtapositions to argue that objects of peaceful domestic use were intricately tied with objects employed on the field of battle, so the consumption of those objects in the United States tied individuals to remote people and events. This theme of what one might call the *moral equivalence* of consumer products was especially evident in propaganda concerning food. In one film cited by William Chafe, for instance, a wounded G.I. on Bataan exhorted his family not to be wasteful in the kitchen. "We haven't had anything but a little horse-meat and rice for days," pleaded the G.I. "And kitchen fats mom. Don't waste any. Kitchen fats make glycerin and glycerin makes explosives. Two pounds of fat can fire five anti-tank shells."[26] Other food-related propaganda presented similar mes-sages. "Can HE save more grease THAN YOU?" asked one poster that depicted a scowling Nazi diligently scraping fat from a pan. "There's *Ammunition* In *This* Kitchen." "Save waste fats for explosives," advised another, which depicted a pan pouring grease over a panoply of falling bombs. "Take them to your meat dealer."[27] By creating such visual connections, these images associated the mundane objects of personal life with the matériel of national combat, thereby symbolically trans-forming what was private into what was public—an ontological movement of tremendous significance.

Perhaps the most affecting examples of U.S. wartime propaganda as a whole ini-tiated such symbolic transformations by linking objects of personal importance not simply with *objects* on the field of battle, but with *people*. Again, propaganda about food was especially notable in this regard. Over the course of the war, OWI and cor-porate publications frequently depicted food as a stand-in for those physically sep-arated from the consumer; in the case of soldiers, food was depicted as being morally equivalent to distant civilian friends, and for civilians, food was linked with servicemen. For example, a promotional from the National Dairy Products Corporation depicted a prisoner of war opening a small package and exclaiming, "Honest-to-gosh American food!" "Put yourself behind German barbed wire," invites the text, linking in its short narrative the POW, domestic foodstuffs, and readers themselves.

You're hungry and homesick. Into your hands comes an 11-pound package of food. It's all yours. Raisins, sugar, coffee, oleo, corned beef, biscuits, ham, salmon, orange concentrate, milk chocolate, cheese, powdered milk, soap and cigarettes. Familiar cans and packages. Labels that look *like old friends*. Can you imagine the *gratitude*?[28]

Such a representation of food is significant, because it suggests how American propaganda facilitated Woodruff's drive to transform Coke into a symbol of national life. For if OWI and other patriotic appeals encouraged citizens to associate private consumer goods not only with the public matériel of war but also with *individuals* outside the boundaries of the self, then citizens were well accustomed to perceiving mass-market products as bridging the gap between personal and civic. And this division, naturally, was already blurred for a company deeply implicated in the institutional workings of the collective effort.

Arguably the most powerful use of the theme of moral equivalency in wartime advertising appeared in a series of promotionals for The Coca-Cola Company beginning in 1943. Based on the semiotic use of the = symbol, the promotionals seem odd today for the manner in which they so clearly reveal the intent of the advertiser: to associate Coke with interactions that are not private but have *communal* significance. In one typical ad, a soldier on leave relaxes at a drugstore lunch counter, telling stories of battle to an admiring boy, who is flanked by the smiling figures of his mother and sister. All are sipping Coke, and they seem to be joined in their talk by a prominent red Coke dispenser and a series of unfilled Coca-Cola drinking glasses. As the man stares intently into the boy's eyes, his hands form two parallel lines that suggest the movement of a plane or vehicle in combat, lines that also appear to place a subliminal = sign between the soda dispenser and the boy and his family. The headline above this warm, patriotic image states plainly, "Have a Coca-Cola = Howdy, Neighbor," while the subhead explains, ". . . or greeting friends at home and abroad."[29] Another advertisement from the campaign depicts two sailors greeting a civilian family containing a mother, father, and two admiring blonde daughters. While one of the sailors looks on and smiles, the other reaches his hand left, across the center of the image, to shake that of the father, who bows slightly. Almost directly below the point where the civilian and military hands meet is a table bedecked with sweets and Coca-Cola. The headline of the image states, "Have a 'Coke' = You're invited to our house"; the subhead notes ". . . or how to make sailors feel at home."

The number and variety of Coke advertisements that employed the juxtapositional force of the = is overwhelming, and a search through any popular middle-class magazine of the time will uncover scores of them. Even here, through mere written description, one can easily imagine their emotional force. G.I. letters in Coca-Cola archives, in fact, testify to that intensity, expressing in indignant tones the frustration that followed when The Coca-Cola Company seemed to promise the public more than it could deliver. "As staunch but frustrated Coca-Cola fans," wrote one group of bitter seamen from North Africa, for instance,

> we are a little puzzled by your new advertising policy. In your ad of the July 24 issue of the POST, is that Marine in the desert seeing a mirage? Must be, for we have the palm trees, the sand, but no cokes. . . . Here's to the fulfillment of your mirage. Don't just "tell it to the marines."[30]

Viewed together as a steady stream of images, Coca-Cola promotionals reveal the power and clarity with which Coke associated its very private product with communal life—how within the larger context of U.S. propaganda, the company provided its beverage with meanings that were not restricted to the "private 'why'" but instead were more broadly national. For when Coke used the techniques of advertising to associate its product with a variety of intimate rituals constituting American social life (as well as with the notion of American cultural ambassadorship), it also asserted by implication that American social life depended upon Coca-Cola for its very existence. And the implication of *that* assertion was clear enough: that the United States, as it was known and loved, was almost inconceivable without Coke. During World War II, the masters of persuasion were fast attempting to become the masters of American identity.

★ COCA-COLA AND THE MEMORY OF HOME

But did soldiers actually come to perceive Coke as a symbol of the United States or of their own identity? The evidence in the third part of my discussion suggests that they did. The headquarters of The Coca-Cola Company in Atlanta, Georgia, contain extensive archival holdings concerning the history of company products, materials intended largely for in-house marketing use. Among these astonishingly rich documents are scores of letters from American soldiers pleading with company executives to send packages of Coke to specific regiments in the field, correspondence that testifies to the special place the beverage held in the minds of servicemen abroad. These letters were created within a peculiar psychological context, and it is important briefly to consider that context before discussing them in any detail. In particular, we should remember that, like all wars, World War II was a *lonely* endeavor. Not only were men forced to encounter the horror of mechanized death on an unprecedented scale, they were taken from their families and sent across an ocean to foreign lands. Afraid, deprived of sex, and most of all, terribly homesick, the impoverishment faced by soldiers and sailors was material, but more important, it was emotional. As any reading of wartime memoirs will reveal, the popular language of World War II was based not on masculine fantasies of adventure or visions of national glory, but on solitude; its words signified loss.

The fact that servicemen were lonely becomes significant when we recall that food often serves as a cathexis for emotions, and that familiar foods can ease a troubled heart. As the work of Paul Fussell indicates, when soldiers used their diaries to comment on foods they enjoyed, which they did extensively, they were expressing more than simple physiological pleasure with what they had been served at mess. Instead, they implicitly were using the opportunity of a meal to recollect the distant comforts of civilian life. "Sometimes [servicemen's diaries] almost make you weep," writes Fussell.

The American sailor James J. Fahey notes in his diary in July, 1944: "We had Jello for chow at noon, this was the first time we had it in about a year." And eleven months later, another red-letter day: "This morning we had something for breakfast we never had before. When they gave us fried eggs we almost passed out. This was the first time we ever had fried eggs while in the navy," he writes, and he's been in it for years.[31]

Or consider Ernie Pyle's description of the best-cooked powdered eggs he encountered during his wartime travels: "Rogers cooked with imagination," writes Pyle.

Here's how he made powdered eggs for approximately a hundred men: He took two one-gallon cans of egg powder, poured in sixteen cans of condensed milk and four quarts of water, mixed it up into a batter, then dipped it out with a ladle and fried it in boiling lard. The result looked like a small yellow pancake. It was frizzled and done around the edges like well-fried egg, and although it tasted only vaguely like an egg still it tasted good. And that's all that counted.[32]

Despite its self-consciously comic focus on quantity and technique, Pyle's description suggests his poignant attempt to console himself with thoughts of home; in the Biblical cadence of his concluding sentence, one hears Pyle's appreciation for innovative cooking, but also something more. In Pyle's work, fried eggs implicitly become a touchstone of civilian life.

While other comestible items seem to have played a similar role in servicemen's lives, especially milk and ice cream, apparently none were so powerful as Coca-Cola.[33] Reading G.I. correspondence about the beverage, in fact, can be a deeply moving experience, for it paints a highly charged portrait of Coke as the only stable object in a world of total chaos, as the one familiar point-of-reference in acutely disorienting situations. "No ice cream, no milk, no eggs, no white bread, no butter, punk coffee, tea, tea, tea, no chicken, no steaks, no vegetables, no fruit, warm beer," wrote one soldier from England, where shortages were especially severe. "[But even here] I can buy ICE COLD COCA-COLA!!! Ain't it a wonderful world?"[34] "I always thought it was a wonderful drink," wrote another soldier from the South Pacific, "but on an island where few white men set foot, it is a God-send...I can truthfully say that I haven't seen smiles spread over a bunch of boys' faces as it did when they saw the Coca-Cola in this God-forsaken place."[35] For men in the field, Coca-Cola was a firm rock in a sea of cultural confusion, a morale-boosting token of a place that seemed exceedingly remote.

Indeed, servicemen's writings indicate that Coke was such a powerful talisman of the United States that it reminded them of *actual moments* of their experience as civilians. Coca-Cola triggered memories of the *specific* events in their prewar lives. Most importantly, G.I. letters attest that Coke was a potent, even Proustian conjurer of the social life of the drugstore soda fountain, in which the beverage had played an increasingly important role since the 1930s. Again and again, soldiers noted the connection between Coca-Cola and their local gathering place. "The ole 'Coke' sign," wrote one serviceman from Sicily, "brings every soldier back to his moments in his favorite drug store, where he sat and conversed with his friends."[36] "The Officers' Club, we call it 'Tony's Tavern,' was merely a tent pitched on the sand," wrote another, "but in there, with a blue ribbon tied around it, the 'Coke' would always draw such comments as, 'Boy I'd give a month's pay for an ice-cold Coke.' The shape of the bottle, the memory of the refreshing taste, brought to mind many happy memories."[37] Even General Eisenhower, a noted Coca-Cola aficionado, told reporters, "Being a general is a lonely life. I wish I could be home and go down to the cafe this morning and have a coke with the gang."[38] Countless newspaper articles about G.I. life tell a similar story. "The first thing Colonel Moore did after leaving the station," observed a reporter for *Life*, "was go uptown in Villisca to his old drugstore and buy a Coke and a hamburger, the first in 16 months."[39] In other words, soldiers seem to have perceived Coke as a part of the peaceful rituals of domestic fellowship, and it recalled for them the friends they had cultivated within those folk conventions.

Unsurprisingly, then, servicemen also associated the beverage with American women—with what Col. Robert Scott called The American Girl—because drinking Coke had been a part not only of friendly camaraderie, but also of wholesome romantic courtship.[40] As one Coca-Cola employee noted, "You want to know what makes Coke so romantic to so many people?...Well, maybe that starry-eyed kid who lives next door to you was sitting in a drugstore booth with his girl one night, and maybe they were drinking Coke, and maybe while they were drinking that Coke was the first time that girl let that boy put his hand on her leg."[41] Thus, in numerous letters, G.I.'s refer to bottles of Coke in the same manner they might discuss the opposite sex, though using hyperbolic language appropriate to situations of psychological stress. Consider the words of one soldier to his mother, which reveal an obsession well understood through a Freudian interpretive framework:

> While obtaining the life jackets in the warehouse a sailor came in who was carrying a Coke around in his hip pocket. After eyeing it till I could stand it no longer I asked him if I might buy it from him. I explained to him that I had not had one since I left the States. Whereupon he was so benevolent as to give it to me. It was hot and he apparently did not want it himself in that condition. I carried it around with me all over town and nursed it like so much gold, all the while getting longing glances at it from the soldiers and sailors whom we passed on the streets. I started out of the galley with it to take it to the wardroom to consume but seeing that I was going to be mobbed passing through the crew's mess I went back and wrapped it in a towel. I then crept out [reclined] on the transom in the wardroom and tasted for the first time since I left the States "Nectar of the Gods." It was celestial bliss and I feel now that I have been restored to my former self.[42]

Or consider the following humorous message sent to The Coca-Cola Company by twelve weathermen in 1943:

> We are twelve men, tired yet true, here in the deserts of North Africa and for the past many months our tongues have been parched for something better than the hard and saline water that we have to drink. It may be paradoxical to say this, but being weathermen our thirst mounts faster than normal in the summer heat. As we are swinging a psychrometer or watching a balloon mount into the hot and dusty sky, we are watching with feverish eyes the rising temperatures, and praying that it will stop before the thermometer bursts. This situation besides contributing to a mental case due to sunstroke and worry also does much to increase our thirst and desire for a "Pause that Refreshes," but what do we have—I ask you, what do we have? Even a mirage cannot slack our thirst, and we must fall back on those dreams of yesteryear, when we moved up to the soda fountain and sighed contentedly—cherry coke, large glass, plenty of ice! The bubble bursts as sweat dims our eyes, and again our dream castle fades and we realize we are back in Africa de Nord.
>
> Now Sir, surely by now you can, you must, realize what we are about to ask you? Is it possible that one of your fairer members, willing to do her part for men and country, could pack and send a container of coca cola concentrate and don't worry about our mixing the materials, necessity is always the mother of invention—need we say more!
>
> We assure you and her that we shall thank you from the bottom of our hearts and will be glad, delighted and ready to pay the price and postage and whatever else is necessary.
>
> Trustingly yours...
>
> P.S. If you cannot make it in cokes, we will accept a bottle of scotch.[43]

Such correspondence often reached The Coca-Cola Company not through G.I.'s themselves, but through their wives, who begged the organization to help fulfill their husband's earnest requests.[44] "Dearest Liz," wrote one G.I. in a letter ultimately forwarded to Atlanta,

You know you've been sending me packages now for quite some time, and you've covered just about everything I could use, regardless of whether or not I've asked for it. But, of all the things you have sent me so far, *there is one item that I've wanted you to send* which probably you'd never have thought of, and would not think of sending unless I'd of told you what it was. You might think me nuts or maybe a bit silly, but when you haven't seen one like this for almost a year now and then suddenly see one in front of you, that you know is all yours, it kind of makes you think of all the times you could've gotten it, but didn't, because you had just about all you wanted then, when you were in the States... Well, I guess you want to know now what it is that *I want so much, outside of you. Well Darling, it is a bottle of Coca-Cola.* Yes, exactly as you read it. One bottle of Coca-Cola.[45]

Food and identity, hunger and love, all blend together in servicemen's writings, a testament to the talismanic personal importance Coca-Cola had for soldiers overseas.

Moreover, while G.I. letters reveal that Coke was important to servicemen on a personal level, that it reminded them of their own private stories, they also exhibit that soldiers perceived the beverage as an equally evocative symbol of the American polis, of the United States as an abstract political entity. Letters housed in Coca-Cola archives, in fact, suggest that soldiers understood Coke as a symbol of civic significance precisely because it was so closely connected with their individual experience. In servicemen's writings, for example, we find numerous seemingly paradoxical statements that link conceptions of communal, national sacrifice with the noncommunal, antipolitical desire to drink a sweet, fizzy beverage. "Since I've come across," wrote one enthusiastic soldier to his parents, "I've met and talked with some of the greatest men in the world, *real men who have gone through Hell and come out again, but would go back for a cold Coca-Cola.*"[46] "An American airman may be able to carry 'plenty of thunder to the Japs,'" one officer told a local reporter, "provided he can have... a Coca-Cola to drink occasionally, to help him keep in touch with the American way of life."[47] These sentiments indicate precisely what Agnew's historical portrait would predict: that Coca-Cola did play a role in American civic consciousness, that soldiers did come to describe their own identity as citizens using "the language of soft drinks." Soldiers' letters seem to tell us, in other words, that under the special psychological conditions of war—at a moment when men craved the comfort of the familiar—Woodruff's patriotic promise refigured not only Americans' conceptions of government, but also their inner lives.

★ COCA-COLA AND PARTICIPATORY POLITICS?

The transformation of Coke into a national icon, we have seen, contained a number of separate but related components: first, the cooperation between the American state and Coca-Cola, embodied in the story of T.O.'s; second, as revealed in advertising, the attempt of Coca-Cola to associate its product with the mundane but meaningful aspects of daily life, a project facilitated by its rhetorical use of the = sign; and third, the emotional response of American servicemen to Coke, a beverage that for many was strongly linked to peaceful, civilian life. If Coca-Cola became a national icon under these circumstances, did that icon advance a democratic, participatory vision of society or did it serve to hinder the republican political ideal many of us find so compelling? If we live in the "World of Coca-Cola," if we are, as The Coca-Cola Company implicitly claims, a "community" brought together around a mass-market good, then how might we characterize that community in regards to the civic responsibilities felt by its members? These issues concern the more general debate over consumer society I raised at the start of this discussion and invite the question: When American soldiers claimed to be fighting for the right to purchase Coke, were they in fact fighting for an impoverished notion of political life?

I would like to suggest that they were and that they were not. That the politics implicit in Coca-Cola is an impoverished vision of politics, inimical to the type of participatory political vision on which the United States was founded strikes me as a reasonable position to take. A strong body of scholarly literature certainly exists that reveals how a privatized, consumerist understanding of national life can have a disastrously corrosive effect upon civic fellowship. This literature, which bears much in common with the literature of philosophical antiliberalism, asserts that the "commodification of politics," embodied in the story of Coca-Cola, offers little hope of a future communitarian social order. Instead, consumer society conceals the antidemocratic relations of economic power on which it is based, and encourages an ethic of individual self-focus incompatible with republican ideals of virtue and community. In regard to Coke, such criticisms seem not only immanently valid but also functionally linked. For if Woodruff's promise induced servicemen to consider one of the most important functions of the state to be to supply brand-name consumer products to its citizens, then that allegedly "patriotic" commitment to fulfill individual desires seems simultaneously to have concealed the *institutional* machinations it presupposed. As Agnew has noted, of those servicemen who asserted that they were fighting to preserve their ability to drink Coca-Cola, how many also saw themselves as fighting for The Coca-Cola *Company*? During the war, the business of America remained business.[48]

But there are other ways of understanding the role of consumer goods in society and the story of Coca-Cola as well. For instance, Timothy Breen, in his challenging analysis of eighteenth-century commercial culture, suggests that everyday consumer items provided Americans with a shared "language of consumption" that ultimately served as a "language for revolution," that consumer goods became "good to think" in political ways.[49] More specifically, Breen focuses his attention, as we have here, on a particular beverage—tea—explaining how it served as a medium through which nationalist consciousness grew and ultimately exploded into revolutionary action. The reason why Americans displayed such marked political solidarity beginning in 1773, writes Breen, a solidarity not evident during the Townshend protest, was that the Tea Act "affected an item of popular consumption found in almost every colonial household," an item very much like Coca-Cola which "appear[ed] on the tables of the wealthiest merchants and the poorest labourers." In creating a *material* commonalty among Americans, tea became an ideal medium through which "to transmit perceptions of liberty and rights," and a way in which "*ideological* abstractions acquired concrete meaning."[50] Breen's analysis suggests that commodities generally can provide "a shared framework of consumer experience" that allows individuals to "reach out to distant strangers, to perceive, however dimly, the existence of an 'imagined community'" and then to take political action when the liberties and rights of that community are infringed.

Similarly, Lizabeth Cohen's powerful analysis of Chicago working-class culture from 1919 to 1939 richly illustrates how commodities have not always served as forces of privatization, but, at times, have reinforced group identities. In particular, Cohen's discussion of how Americans of varied ethnic backgrounds "encountered" mass culture "at the grassroots"—a discussion that centers, in part, on a study of grocery stores—suggests that mass-market goods are not consumed by isolated individuals, but by groups of people in acts of shared experience. In doing so, Cohen suggests that goods can create situations in which morally profound loyalties are formed and sustained. "A commodity," she writes, "could just as easily help a person reinforce ethnic or working-class culture as lose it. What mattered were the experiences . . . that the consumer brought to the object."[51] Speaking of shopping at local groceries, for instance, Cohen notes that in acts of consumption, buyers brought "their own values to every exchange" and thus, while "ethnic workers [during the 1920s] came to share more in the new consumer goods" they did so "in their own stores, in their own neighborhoods, and in their own ways."[52] Cohen's analysis implies, in other words, that consumer goods can have potentially democratic political significance because their meanings are not based solely on the associations ascribed to them by Madison Avenue, but instead are rooted in a history of sentimental interaction between the people who buy them. Consumers form *real* communities around what they purchase, communities that hold affective and even political meanings for their members.

We ignore these meanings at our intellectual peril, and we ultimately harm our chances of achieving a more progressive national life when we turn a blind eye to how civic language modeled on the language of consumption can lead to democratic political change. Here we might usefully consider the role that Coca-Cola played in the African-American struggle for civil rights.[53] Of the many ways black Americans advanced their political power and mobilized others to act on their behalf, one of the more symbolically enduring was their use of images of *non*-consumption in venues associated with the sale of food, and especially with the sale of Coke: lunch counters. Just as the rebels of the American Revolution fostered national consciousness through the commodity of tea, so the students who demonstrated at Woolworth stores across the South used the image of *denied* hamburgers and Cokes to urge citizens on to great sacrifice. Sit-ins advanced liberal politics not only by politicizing consumer goods, but by employing a language of consumerism as a language of justice. If Coke was an essential part of the American Way of Life, so their logic implicitly stated, then its refusal to those who held U.S. citizenship was tantamount to a denial of both formal and substantive liberty—and a very persuasive symbol of injustice for those who felt that the war had been fought so that Americans could return to the drugstore and drink Coke again. The Civil Rights Movement seems to indicate, in other words, that a struggle for freedom grew *in part* on a foundation we typically would consider antidemocratic, the development of consumer goods into items of quasi-political entitlement.[54]

Not surprisingly, the story of racial struggle in postwar America has often been remembered in consumerist language, and frequently using stories that represent Coke as a medium through which "ideological abstractions acquired concrete meaning."[55] For instance, Henry Louis Gates, Jr., recently described to a National Public Radio audience one of the ways he experienced discrimination as a child in the South. "It was frustrating," explained Gates, "because of segregation when we couldn't sit down with the other kids at the local hang-out, the cut-rate, the drugstore where you'd go after basketball games, and one of the doctors would set the whole team up with Coca-Colas, and all the white kids would sit down and drink out of glasses and all the black kids would stand up drinking out of paper cups."[56] More significantly, consider the words of James Forman of the Student Non-Violent Coordinating Committee, describing in *The Making of Black Revolutionaries* how he first came to social awareness. He was a young boy, at midcentury, visiting relatives in Mississippi from his home in Chicago, and he wanted a Coke. "I went to the drugstore," Forman writes, "and hopped on one of the leather-covered stools":

> There were about six or seven of them and they were all empty. I spun around on the stool several times, waiting for the fountain clerk. I took out my nickel, twirled it around and around on the black marble counter. There was a crack in it and I began moving my nickel along the crack. Finally the fountain clerk appeared. She was an elderly woman, rather fat, without a smile. "What do you want?" "I want a Coke and a glass, please."

We can imagine what happened next: the manager came and told the young Forman that he could not drink his Coke at the fountain, that he must drink it in the back of the store. The boy was left crying, wondering "who this man was, what right he had to tell me where I had to drink my Coke."[57] As Forman well knew, the power of his narrative rests, in part, on the nature of the beverage involved. It certainly would not have altered the formal quality of the injustice in Forman's account had he asked for and been refused, a glass of orange juice; but it would have significantly altered its emotional content. Drawing on a tradition of cultural commonalty, Forman's depiction of a small incident of racial injustice can make readers angry even today because it uses as its foundation a symbol Americans recognize, especially since 1945, as an icon of national citizenship.

Here we find the most enduring legacy of Woodruff's promise, and the most powerful testament to its effect: that Coke has become such a basic part of American life that it now plays a role in our *memory* of major national events. I have spent much of this analysis describing the lives of American soldiers, and so it seems fitting, on this note, to close with the words of one of those men. His name was Clarence Dickinson, and he was shot down over Hawaii during the Japanese bombing of Pearl Harbor. Approximately one year after the attack, Dickinson narrated his harrowing experience to *The Saturday Evening Post*.[58] As a remembrance of things past, one in which food plays a notable function, the story illustrates how Coke could symbolically divide those who fell within and outside the protections of American citizenship. After he was shot down, Dickinson stopped a passing car and asked to be driven to Pearl Harbor. The couple driving agreed and offered the flyer a drink of their whiskey. "I didn't take any," writes Dickinson, "because I figured I would have to fly again that day." Along the road, Dickinson spotted a general store, and he asked the couple to stop. "As far as I was concerned," he writes, "the war was going to have to wait until I had a coke." The store Dickinson had spotted was no ordinary Anglo market, however, it was operated by Japanese residents of the island for "Jap and Filipino laborers of the cane and pineapple plantations." The flyer entered the establishment (the front was "draped with dried fish") and asked for his Coke. At which point, supposedly, an extraordinary exchange took place. "The kid in charge of the store," writes Dickinson, "who was about nineteen, was looking up at the Jap planes and laughing."

> He turned a smirking grin on me. I asked for a coke twice before he moved. He fiddled around and half opened the lids of two chests, pretending he didn't have what I wanted. I looked in the first box. There, in plain sight, were several bottles. Scowling, I seized one, wrenched off the cap and started out. He was just behind me at the front when I whirled on him and shook the bottle in his face. "This one," I said, "is on the house."

Through such instances of recollection, in the minds of those who endured the special circumstances of global conflict, Coca-Cola became the totem drink of the American nation. It became the hallmark of a people who would be asked to bear many of the burdens of the war's political aftermath.

NOTES

This essay is adapted from "Democracy, Consumer Culture, and Political Community: The Story of Coca-Cola during World War II," which was presented at "Eating for Victory: American Foodways and World War II," held at the University of Colorado-Boulder, 8–9 October 1993. I wish to thank Philip Mooney and Brookie Keener of The Coca-Cola Company, who offered invaluable access to historical materials and provided a model of corporate openness to scholarly inquiry; my anonymous reviewers for their criticism and advice; Amy Bentley, Meg Jeffrey, and Mark Pendergrast for their assistance; and, though he was not party to writing this essay, Jean-Christophe Agnew for his indispensable teaching.

1. Roland Barthes, "Wine and Milk," *Mythologies*, trans. Annette Lavers (New York: Hill and Wang, 1972), 58.
2. Billy Wilder, *One, Two, Three* (1961); "World and Friend," *Time* (15 May 1950), front cover; Stanley Kubrick, *Dr. Strangelove, or How I Learned to Stop Worrying and Love the Bomb* (1964). See also Dusan Makavejev, *The Coca-Cola Kid* (1985), Jamie Uys, *The Gods Must Be Crazy* (1982), and the variety of works of American literature in which Coca-Cola plays an iconic role, for example, Arthur Miller, *Death of a Salesman* (1949), and Saul Bellow, *Seize the Day* (1956). On Coca-Cola as icon and as folklore, see Christia Murken-Altrogge, *Coca-Cola Art: Konsum, Kult, Kunst* (Munich: Klinhardt und Biermann, 1991), and Paul Smith, "Contemporary Legends and Popular Culture: 'It's the Real Thing.'" *Contemporary Legend: The Journal of the International Society for Contemporary Legend Research 1* (1991): 123–52. See also E. J. Kahn, Jr., *The Big Drink: The Story of Coca-Cola* (New York: Random House, 1960), 3–12.
3. Mark Pendergrast, *For God, Country and Coca-Cola: The Unauthorized History of the Great American Soft Drink and the Company That Makes It* (New York: Charles Scribner's Sons, 1993), 244. On French protest, see Richard Kuisel, *Seducing the French: The Dilemma of Americanization* (Berkeley: The University of California Press, 1993). See also Kahn, *The Big Drink*, 20–44.
4. Mark Pendergrast, *For God, Country, and Coca-Cola*, 169. General information about the history of Coca-Cola can be obtained from Pendergrast's extensive work. See also Frederick Allen, *Secret Formula: How Brilliant Marketing and Relentless Salesmanship Made Coca-Cola the Best Known Product in the World* (New York: Harper Business, 1994).
5. Ibid., 178. For evocative though non-scholarly comments on soda fountain culture, see Paul Dickson, *The Great American Ice Cream Book* (New York: Atheneum, 1972). See also John J. Riley, *A History of the American Soft Drink Industry: Bottled Carbonated Beverages 1807–1957* (Washington: American Bottlers of Carbonated Beverages, 1958).
6. Pendergrast, *For God, Country, and Coca-Cola*, 178.
7. For an early examination of the place of Coca-Cola in World War II, see John Morton Blum, *V Was for Victory: Politics and American Culture during World War II* (San Diego: Harcourt Brace Jovanovich, 1976), 38, 107–8. See also Kahn, *The Big Drink*, 12–19. My analysis differs from the work of Blum, Pendergrast, Allen, and Kahn in being driven primarily by the theoretical concerns raised in Jean-Christophe Agnew, "Coming Up for Air: Consumer Culture in Historical Perspective," *Intellectual History Newsletter* 12 (1990): 3–21; Robert Westbrook, "'I Want a Girl, Just Like the Girl That Married Harry James': American Women and the Problem of Political Obligation in World War Two," *American Quarterly* 42 (December 1990); and Robert Westbrook, "Fighting for the American Family: Private Interests and Political Obligations of World War II," in *The Power of Culture: Critical Essays in American History*, ed. Richard Wrightman Fox and T. J. Jackson Lears (Chicago: The University of Chicago Press, 1993), 195–221.
8. Agnew, "Coming Up for Air," 14.
9. Lizabeth Cohen, *Making a New Deal: Industrial Workers in Chicago, 1919-1939* (New York: Cambridge University Press, 1990); Timothy Breen, "'Baubles of Britain': The American and Consumer Revolutions of the Eighteenth Century," *Past and Present* 119 (May 1988): 73–104. On goods as "good to think," see Mary Douglas and Baron Isherwood, *The World of Goods* (New York: Basic Books, 1979).
10. Richard Polenberg, *War and Society: The United States 1941–1945* (Philadelphia: J. B. Lippincott Company, 1972), 135.
11. See, for example, E. J. Farina, Chairman, Contra Costa Salvage Committee to James G. Hamilton, Secretary, Industry Salvage Central Committee (11 August 1942), Archives Department, The Coca-Cola Company. Unless otherwise indicated, all following citations refer to manuscripts placed in uncatalogued binders housed in The Coca-Cola Company archives. See also C. H. Luebbert, Executive Secretary for Virginia, War Production Board, to Harrison Jones, President, The Coca-Cola Bottling Company (25 January 1943).
12. "Film Is Shown at Kiwanis Meeting," *Bushville Telegram* [Bushville, Indiana] (2 September 1942). "Have had inquiry from Detroit General Motors Public Relations," telegramed one agent of The Coca-Cola Company soon after the film was released. "Asking possibility their purchasing one hundred prints and records "Free American Way" which they wish put in hands every G M Plant in country.... Hope these requests not becoming nuisance to you but we can't seem to shut them off" (Elaine Nagle, Jam Handy Organization, to Frank W. Harrold [19 August 1942]).

139

13. H. M. McKinley, Commander, USNR, District Staff Headquarters, Twelfth Naval District, San Francisco, California, to R. C. Fowler, Vice President, The Coca-Cola Bottling Company (13 August 1943).

14. Pendergrast, *For God, Country, and Coca-Cola*, 199–217. See also Allen, *Secret Formula*, 245–78. On problems faced by the soft drink industry during the war, see also John J. Riley, *Organization in the Soft Drink Industry: A History of the American Bottlers of Carbonated Beverages* (Washington: American Bottlers of Carbonated Beverages, 1946), 202–72.

15. Jim Kahn, "Coca-Cola in World War II" (unpublished company manuscript, ca. 1946), 2, 5–6. Kahn's manuscript was commissioned for print by The Coca-Cola Company; however the corporation ultimately chose to leave it unpublished, in part from concern that the public would look with disfavor on Coke's close cooperation with the United States government during the war. See Harrison Jones, The Coca-Cola Company, to Steve Hannagan, Publicity (22 January 1946). On Wrigley and World War II, see Blum, *V Was for Victory*, 108–10.

16. "President's Scrap Plea Stresses Mill Needs," *The Washington Post* (16 September 1942). See also "White House Yield Is 5 Tons of Scrap," *The New York Times* (16 September 1942).

17. See, for example, Ralph McT. Pennell, Major General, Office of the Representative of the Military Governor of the Territory of Hawaii to War Production Board, San Francisco, California (28 May 1942).

18. Gen. George C. Marshall, Chief of Staff, "War Department Circular No. 51" (25 February 1944), 1. According to typescript copy scheduled to appear in The Coca-Cola Company magazine *The Red Barrel*, a survey by *The American Legion Magazine* of 5,000 World War II veterans indicated that "63.67 per cent insisted that Coca-Cola was their preference [among soft drinks] and no mistake about it. In fact, the preference was so pronounced that the nearest competitor received but a 7.78 per cent vote" ("Veteran's Preference," *Red Barrel* typescript [ca. 1945]). On brand-name preference for cigarettes, see, for example, Ernie Pyle, *Brave Men* (New York: Henry Holt and Company, 1944), 26.

19. Jim Kahn, "Coca-Cola in World War II," 16.

20. *T.O. Digest* 1, 4: 6. The Coca-Cola Company has requested the names of T.O.'s remain unpublished in scholarly works. I have complied with this request here and throughout my analysis.

21. *T.O. Digest* 1, 1:4.

22. [Seven servicemen of the USS 1st Flotilla, North African Waters] to The Coca-Cola Company (8 September 1942). The Coca-Cola Company has requested the names of servicemen who wrote the organization remain unpublished in scholarly works. It should be noted that occasionally, the nature of Coca-Cola archives makes it unclear whether their holdings represent the letters actually written by servicemen or are instead retyped transcripts. Unless otherwise indicated, I have assumed that letters housed by The Coca-Cola Company represent original G.I. correspondence, and that any transcriptions represent faithful copies.

23. Alan Trachtenberg, "Myth and Symbol," *Massachusetts Review* 25 (Winter 1984): 672.

24. Roland Marchand, *Advertising the American Dream: Making Way for Modernity, 1920–1940* (Berkeley: University of California Press, 1985).

25. Allan M. Winkler, *The Politics of Propaganda: The Office of War Information 1942–1945* (New Haven: Yale University Press, 1978), 62, 64.

26. William H. Chafe, *The Unfinished Journey: America Since World War II*, 2d ed. (New York: Oxford University Press, 1991), 5.

27. *With Weapons and Wits: Propaganda and Psychological Warfare in World War II: Heroic Leaders and Heroic Unknown Warriors in Their Finest Hour* (Lexington: Museum of Our National Heritage, 1992), 53.

28. "Honest-to-gosh American Food!" *Time* (20 December 1943), 3. First emphasis added.

29. "Have a Coca-Cola = Howdy, Neighbor," *Life* (5 June 1944), back cover.

30. [Seven seamen stationed in North African waters] to The Coca-Cola Company (8 September 1943).

31. Paul Fussell, *Wartime: Understanding and Behavior in the Second World War* (New York: Oxford University Press, 1989), 199.

32. Ernie Pyle, *Brave Men*, 114.

33. On milk, ice cream, and Coca-Cola, see for instance Hedda Hopper, "The Lusty Laughton," *The Washington Post* (21 October 1943); "Little Hard Liquor Available in Africa," *Herald-Courier* [Bristol, Virginia] (28 November 1943); and "U.S. Flyers Crave Ice Cream, Soft Drinks," *The Baltimore Sun* (17 November 1943). On the significance of ice cream in American cultural history, see Dickson, *The Great American Ice Cream Book*, and Patricia M. Tice, *Ice Cream for All* (Rochester: Strong Museum, 1990).

34. Whitey [soldier stationed in England] to Ronnie (1 August 1943).

35. Corp. Richard E. Storekman, "Coca-Cola in South Pacific: Letter Tells of Joy it Brings to Soldier There," *Republican-Register* [Mt. Carmel, Illinois] (16 July 1943).

36. Louis [soldier stationed in Sicily] to The Coca-Cola Company (10 September 1943).

37. John [Captain, Army Air Force] to Advertising Manager, The Coca-Cola Company (3 August 1943).

38. "Mother of 'Ike' Tells Hope," *New York Journal American* (10 November 1942). Eisenhower's comments were widely printed in publications of the time.

39. "Col. Moore's Homecoming," *Life* (16 August 1943).

40. Robert L. Scott, Jr., *God Is My Co-Pilot* (New York: Charles Scribner's Sons, 1943), 166. "First of all," writes Scott, "I don't know exactly what a democracy is, or the real, common-sense meaning of a republic. But as we used to talk things over in China, we all used to agree that we were fighting for The American Girl. She to us was America, Democracy, Coca-Cola, Hamburgers, Clean Places to Sleep, or The American Way of Life." On servicemen, Coca-Cola, and American women, see also Thomas R. St. George, *C/O Postmaster* (New York: Thomas Y. Crowell Co., 1943), including the image on p. 65; for a humorous cartoon on women and Coca-Cola see John R. O'Donoghue, "What! No Coca-Cola?" *The Stars and Stripes: Africa* (2 October 1943).

41. Kahn, *The Big Drink*, 11.

42. W. P. [Lieutenant] to his mother, transcribed excerpt (undated).

140

43. [Twelve soldiers stationed in North Africa] to The Coca-Cola Company (5 August 1943).
44. "I have a problem that confronts me," wrote the wife of one serviceman, "and it happens that the Coca-Cola Co. may be able to help solve it. My husband is stationed in Africa, with the army, and in several letters stated his desire for a 'coke.' I thought this would be easy to send and this morning I bought a dozen bottles of Coca-Cola, and I find it is not easy to pack to meet postal requirements. Then, too, he may not receive them and I would not like to disappoint him." [Wife of serviceman in Chicago, Illinois] to The Coca-Cola Bottling Company (5 September 1943).
45. Harry to Mildred (3 October 1943).
46. Tommy [somewhere in Australia] to Mom and Dad (7 February 1943), transcribed copy.
47. "Lieut. Thomas R. Waddell Jr. Smuggles Pup as Jungle 'Pal': Former Local Youth Describes Activities of Air Combat Units," *The Florida Times-Union* (16 July 1943).
48. Agnew, "Coming Up for Air," 16. For a discussion of some of these issues in the context of corporate historical presentations, see also Mark Weiner, "We Are What We Eat; or, Democracy, Community, and the Politics of Corporate Food Displays," *American Quarterly* (June 1994), 227–50.
49. Breen, "'Baubles of Britain,'" 76.
50. Ibid., 98, 104. Emphasis added.
51. Cohen, *Making a New Deal*, 106.
52. Ibid., 116.
53. For a different perspective on the role of The Coca-Cola Company in the Civil Rights Movement, see Allen, *Secret Formula*, 279–317.
54. Indeed, the Civil Rights Movement also seems to suggest that, in the case of Coke, the concentration of wealth democrats abhor was in fact a necessary precondition for the drink becoming a symbol that encouraged civil participation.
55. This seems to be the case of wartime remembrances as well. In narrating their experience in a Jim Crow army, black former servicemen have described the indignity they felt at not being allowed in Post Exchange stores; being barred from outlets of purchasing was a powerful symbol for them of the failure of the United States to live up to its democratic ideals. See Mary Penick Motley, ed., *The Invisible Soldier: The Experience of the Black Soldier, World War II* (Detroit: Wayne State University Press, 1975), 70, 162, and Philip McGuire, *Taps for a Jim Crow Army: Letters from Black Soldiers in World War II* (Santa Barbara: ABC-Clio, 1983), 19–20.
56. Robert Siegel, "A Visit with Henry Louis Gates, Jr.," National Public Radio (18 May 1994). Emphasis added.
57. James Forman, "Childhood and Coca-Cola," *The Making of Black Revolutionaries: A Personal Account* (New York: The Macmillan Company, 1972), 18–19.
58. Lt. Clarence Dickinson, U.S.N., with Boyden Sparks, "I Fly for Vengeance," *The Saturday Evening Post* (10 October 1942).

141

"FARM BOYS DON'T BELIEVE IN RADICALS": RURAL TIME AND MEATPACKING WORKERS

DEBORAH FINK

11

The IBP pork plant where I worked outside of Perry, Iowa, in 1992 pulsated with cockroaches. Trying to contain them, IBP had laid down sanitation rules controlling all food brought into the plant. To no avail. Feeding on the rich layer of lard that oozed over everything each day, the cockroaches marched across the walls, they crawled up our sleeves and into our pockets, and they eavesdropped in restroom crannies. They had won their rights and enjoyed their freedom with little harassment from the humans who shared their quarters.

But just when I had been on the job long enough to learn cockroach tolerance, we got an announcement that IBP was fumigating the plant. We were to empty our lockers and leave them open on Saturday evening so the exterminators could have everything cockroach free by Monday morning.

What turned IBP from détente to open cockroach warfare?

Roaches had invaded the time clock on the kill floor. The drill was for workers to draw their green plastic identification cards through the slot on the time clock to check in or out, but with cockroach intervention, no identification number would flash to connect or disconnect workers from company time. This was an unforgivable provocation.

IBP was a strange mix of rigor and indifference. The overriding concern with roaches in the clock rather than on the meat or the workers was but one example of the priority of time discipline as a means of controlling workers and maximizing profit in packinghouses of the 1990s. While line speed and time-and-motion analyses are also aspects of modern exploitation of meatpacking workers' time, this paper will deal with time control in terms of the number of hours that companies required of their workers. I root the analysis of 1990s packinghouse time discipline in the way that family farms exploited rural workers' time in the first half of the century. The struggle for free time became a central point of resistance as workers distanced themselves from farm labor. While meatpacking operations have a long history in rural settings such as Perry, the control of the industry was in midwestern cities until the late twentieth century. The center of gravity of the meatpacking industry began to shift to rural locations after 1960, allowing new-breed meatpackers such as IBP to bypass unions, in part by drawing on the history of rural labor.[1]

★ WORKER TIME IN RURAL MIDWESTERN HISTORY

While the owner-operated family farm is commonly considered the economic base of the rural Midwest, wage work was historically an indispensable and theoretically neglected support to every successful family farm. Nonfarm labor in construction, transportation, and agricultural industry was as fundamental to midwestern agro-industrial development as farm labor, and it was conditioned by its close association to the farm. Farmwork was sometimes irregular, but its nature and the geographic isolation of farms meant that a hired farmworker typically ceded all of her time to the employer. Long hours of work are a leading complaint in virtually every description of a rural farmhand's existence from the early 1990s. Although a farmhand may have been able to take off Saturday nights, his recreation depended on begging a ride from the farmer, as workers had no transportation of their own. Farm wages were low, but low wages were only part of the distress that led workers steadily away from the farm. A farmhand had little, if any, life outside of his job.[2]

Abe Mohr, was one such worker living in rural Iowa outside of Perry in 1930. His working day on the farm started at 5 A.M., when he arose to milk cows and feed and water other livestock. Work in the fields and in maintaining farm machinery and equipment continued until nightfall, when he finished with another round of animal chores before going to bed. Abe, his wife, and their baby lived on the farm, where his wife did housework and chores for the farm family. For a farmworker, eating and sleeping were refueling and recharging rather than relaxation. Abe and his wife did not have even their own chair, table, or bed in which to unwind.[3]

They wanted off the farm badly. In 1931, when Abe learned that the Perry meatpacking plant would be hiring workers on a particular day, he walked to the plant early enough to be one of ten to twelve workers hired, edging out six to seven hundred other job-hunting men. As a packinghouse worker, he put in a sixty-hour week processing offal. The job, which involved collecting stray body parts from the kill floor and processing them into a stew, was hard. He quit in exhaustion after several years and developed a niche doing part-time railroad work, tinkering, digging basements, wiring, painting, and roofing. Such work was grueling, and one cannot look back on the "casual" setting as a rural utopia, at least from the perspective of a rural worker such as Abe. Yet Abe never seriously considered the option of returning to farm labor. The difference between digging a basement with a shovel and tossing hay with a pitchfork was not that throwing dirt was easier or more pleasant than throwing hay. The major difference was that in town, Abe rented his own home—albeit without electricity or water—and kept a small piece of his life free from his jobs. For him, the family farm meant regimentation and loss of control rather than freedom.

Far from offering a platform for resistance, Abe's farm experience predisposed him to be thankful for almost any work that took him away from the farm. As consuming and destructive as packinghouse work was in the 1930s, it was less so than farmwork. Wage workers like Abe preferred a dense distillation of their working time and a separation of work and leisure over the mix that they found on the farm, where work permeated their lives and seeped into every corner of their existence.

Only after an immersion in plant culture did workers such as Abe pick up the struggle for shorter hours and better working conditions.[4]

In fact, the 1930s federal labor legislation, which prohibited child labor, regulated the length of the work week, established a minimum wage, and eased the way for unions in nonfarm industries, excluding agriculture. States such as Iowa, which were dominated by farm politics, retained right-to-work laws that impeded union organizing and held wages low. Iowa developers cultivated the image of the state's rural culture and love of hard work and long hours. In 1950, for example, a thinly veiled anti-union message of the Iowa Development Commission stated, "There are no Big City political bosses or machines in Iowa....These Iowa ex-farm boys are just plain God-fearing Sons of Toil....Farm boys don't believe in radicals. They expect to do a real day's work and be paid for it."[5]

★ EXTREMELY MODERN TIMES

This history of rural work culture had renewed significance for many late-twentieth-century workers, thanks to IBP. IBP was born in 1960 as Iowa Beef Packers. The first plant was built outside of Denison in 1961 with a starting small business loan. From here, the company made an end run around both the old-line meatpacking giants and the unions. Rural location was a cornerstone of IBP strength, as it totally rewrote the rules of meatpacking operations. It became the world's largest beef producer by 1970. In 1982, it dropped the "Iowa" and "Beef" from its name, having moved its headquarters to rural Nebraska, and set its sights on pork. From that point, it was simply the letters "IBP." IBP rapidly rose to the top of the pork industry, replaying its mastery of the beef industry. Central to IBP's approach to packing-house work was a retooled work ethic that allowed it to combine the long work hours of the rural past with the intense work hours of factories. Being a backyard rural company, IBP was a good way down the road before industry leaders took serious notice of the threat the new meatpacker posed.[6]

"Those simple barefoot boys from Iowa Beef," the title of a laudatory 1981 article in *Forbes*, suggested rural, no-frills operations as the basis of IBP success. The article outlined the IBP program of transferring skill from workers to management and machines. "Processing was done not by skilled butchers, but by a succession of relatively unskilled workers performing a number of elementary tasks—removing the hoofs or tail, splitting open the abdomen or halving a carcass, making a single cut with an electric saw...IBP was able to replace the highly skilled and high-cost packing-house butcher with relatively low-cost assembly-line labor."[7] As an IBP official stated, "We wanted to be able to take boys right off the farm and we've done it."[8] Rural labor was cheap, and it was identified with a work ethic that subordinated personal time to the enterprise. Robert B. Peterson, a college dropout who became IBP's CEO in 1977, epitomized the gritty, single-pointed pragmatism that made IBP soar. Proud of subordinating his life to the business of meatpacking to the exclusion of all else, he set the tone and pace for the rest of IBP's employees: "Six days, sometimes seven, it ought to be ten to twelve hours a day. You give it all you've got, and we drive a hard bargain."[9] Sixty-hour work weeks became an IBP trademark, and Peterson attributed the success of IBP to the intense time discipline that squeezed the last drop of productivity from everyone from himself to janitors: "I know people who are hardly working when they think they're working hard. I'm serious about this. There are many companies where lunch time is the most important period of the day...I know most companies don't work on Saturdays."[10] IBP did, with the CEO leading the way.

The first agreement that IBP exacted from me when I applied to work at the Perry plant was sixty-hour weeks: ten hours a day, six days a week on the production floor. As it turned out, that was and was not the deal. IBP had the right to use me for sixty hours of work each week. In fact, an IBP work week might be even longer. Overtime was semivoluntary, and it was often sought because the pay rose to time-and-a-half after forty hours each week. For many workers, it was overtime that lifted them above poverty-level income. One worker told me that in order to make a down payment on a mobile home, he had worked as many as 120 hours in one week, doing a double shift. On the other hand, if kill numbers were off, workers might get thirty or fewer hours with no warning. With IBP, you never knew. When we worked a five-day week, workers did not get the usual Saturday free, which would have allowed them to play with school-age children, attend family reunions, or watch Saturday sports on television. Even when production was off and we had five-day weeks, we still worked Saturdays. Rather than having a Saturday free, we would be off on Monday, typically a low point for social or recreational opportunities. Moreover, lest we be tempted to plan something in advance on a Monday, the announcement of whether or not we would be free the following Monday was made only on the preceding Friday afternoon. This made it hard.

Extra work-related hours were tacked onto the officially acknowledged and paid work day. My commute added two more hours to my work day, and other workers had longer drives. There was little housing that IBP workers could afford in or around the town of Perry, so workers lived in Des Moines, in abandoned farmhouses or other small towns within a fifty-mile radius. Virtually no one was within walking distance of the plant. For those who drove, the time and expense of keeping a car going added to work time and detracted from income. IBP ran a daily bus to bring workers to and from Des Moines. Although Des Moines was only forty minutes from the plant by car (for those who had a working car), taking the bus might add four hours to their work days. My Des Moines friend who started work at 7:30 A.M. was forced to catch a 5:30 bus in order to be on the production floor in time. In addition to our commutes, lunch break, clothes changing, and showering in the plant were also unpaid and uncounted, but they detracted from the time we were free of IBP.

Attendance rules at IBP were Draconian, and missing work was grounds for dismissal. Attendance was one of the major points stressed during orientation, and all absences were to be verified. If you called in sick but were later not at home when a supervisor telephoned or showed up at your residence, you would be fired. One worker who was late because of a flat tire was required to take his supervisor to the parking lot and show him the flat tire in the car trunk. Being excused from work involved ingratiating yourself to your supervisor, which further circumscribed your actions on the job. No one was officially entitled to vacation days until she had worked in the plant for one year, which excluded most workers. Further, vacation schedules (for those who had them) were negotiated and subject to plant contingencies; they were not given on demand. A worker who requested and was refused permission to attend the funeral of his wife's grandmother called in sick in order to go to the funeral. He was fired.

The vehemence with which IBP pursued the attendance issue betrayed its most serious management problem. Workers stayed away for all reasons, and IBP— chronically short of labor—would not fire everyone. Many of us would take a day off on our own once in a while. Latino workers were especially prone to simply not come in. Supervisors did not speak Spanish and would probably not understand the cultural context of Latino lives if they took the time for a detailed translation of the reasons for their absences, but generally these went unexplored. Latino workers did or did not get fired for reasons that were unrelated to why they did not come to work. Roberto, one of my Mexican friends who had worked himself into a key job in his eighteen months in the plant, was craving unstructured time and unable to negotiate it with his supervisor. He finally took ten days off, sitting on the banks of the Racoon River that flows by the plant, thinking about his life. During this time, he also tried unsuccessfully to get a better job. His departure caused disruption on the production floor, as no one else was able to get into the rhythm of Roberto's job (calling into question the "unskilled" label). His supervisor was finally reduced to hunting for him, begging him to come back, and offering him a bonus to make up for his lost pay. Other workers would ask for and receive attendance favors from their supervisors, who might also joke with them over feigned illnesses that kept them off the job. But still other workers, particularly those who were more expendable, those who had been injured and would cost the company money for medical bills, or those who for some reason had gotten on the bad sides of their supervisors, were given no leeway. They had no recourse when pleading for their jobs, because they had broken the rules. Nor did they receive unemployment compensation when they were fired.

No one found it harder to juggle IBP time with commitments outside the plant than mothers with young children. One former IBP worker who was a single mother with a baby explained to me that she had had to be at the plant at 5 A.M. six days a week, and she would not be home until anywhere from 4:30 to 6:00 P.M. She talked about the dilemmas she had faced:

> I was not getting any time hardly at all to spend with her [the baby]. One day a week. I couldn't seem to get all the things done that I needed to do . . . To finally get some time off, it was like pulling teeth. [When] I had to take her to the doctor, I'd schedule it for after my shift. I'd have to leave right afterwards and I'd get all sorts of crap about leaving early sometimes. Because once in a while I would have to leave about fifteen minutes early to take her to the doctor.

In the three to four hours after work she played with her baby, shopped, cooked, cleaned, did laundry, read mail, paid bills, and tended her car. She was chronically short of sleep, behind in everything, and unable to maintain a social life outside the plant.

If this was extreme, it is nevertheless indicative of time conflicts we all faced as IBP workers. In 1987, worker Chris Lauritsen expressed the tradeoff of time for money: "You know, you work enough hours, you make a lot of money. But the fact is that they're killin' off our people doin' it. You're makin' $20,000 a year workin' six days a week, fifty weeks a year."[11] Except by 1992, many IBP workers were working fifty-one or fifty-two weeks a year if they could survive it.

As IBP workers, we were to receive a paid fifteen-minute break mid-mornings, and we were allowed thirty minutes unpaid time to eat lunch in the plant. Workers were disciplined for returning seconds late to their work stations, production being coordinated so that any missing worker created a hole in the line. Even going to the bathroom became an issue. While I was working at IBP, the U.S. Supreme Court ruled that an employer could not deny workers reasonable bathroom breaks. Eventually IBP decided that workers could go to the bathroom at most two times a week outside of paid breaks and unpaid lunch periods. Sometimes a supervisor would time a worker's bathroom break; at least once a supervisor went to the bathroom with one of the workers to monitor him. However, some workers, including myself, continued to take liberal bathroom breaks.

Workers resisted. They quit. They denied having telephones and gave impossible-to-find rural addresses so that they could "be sick" without being checked. They managed to find ways to smuggle time from out of the grips of IBP. Despotic systems are notoriously inefficient and arbitrary, and IBP is no exception. Nevertheless, all of us who signed onto IBP discipline—from the CEO to production workers—had trouble maintaining outside lives. Out of approximately 500 UFCW members, a monthly union meeting would draw something like five attenders. Iowa's celebrated presidential caucuses, the time every four years when what Iowans think and do matters to the world, came when I was working at IBP. I heard no one in the plant discuss the caucuses, and as far as I know, I was the only worker who attended one. For even those workers who were citizens, the idea of democratic participation came from another planet. For those enmeshed in the world of the plant, the tendency was for outside existence to wane so that the only remaining reality was IBP.

148

Throughout the twentieth century, rural workers drifted away from farms to jobs that offered them not just more money but the promise of personal time and broader options. The rural relocation of the meatpacking industry in the late twentieth century drew on an early rural work history and enabled corporations to revive agricultural work schedules. A desire for free time finds little resonance in the rural middle-class culture of family farms or other small businesses.

The trend in the 1990s was toward tighter time discipline, replicating some of the long hours of early farm labor but with all the intense and alienating qualities that modern industrial technology can deliver at its worst. By appropriating disproportionate segments of workers' mental and physical resources, meatpacking time discipline increasingly deprives workers of even their lives outside the plants. The changes have been technological, but they also rest on the particular social and political history of the rural Midwest.

NOTES

1. Deborah Fink, *Cutting Into the Meatpacking Line: Workers and Change in the Rural Midwest* (Chapel Hill: University of North Carolina Press, 1998).
2. For an analysis of the interconnection between agriculture and manufacturing in midwestern history, see Brian Page and Richard Walker, "From Settlement to Fordism: The Agro-Industrial Revolution in the American Midwest," *Economic Geography* 67 (1991): 281–315. On farm labor, see Cecilia Danysk, *Hired Hands: Labour and the Development of Prairie Agriculture, 1880–1930* (Toronto: McClelland and Steward, 1995); William T. Ham, "Farm Labor in an Era of Change," in *Yearbook of Agriculture*, 1940 (Washington, D.C.: Government Printing Office, 1940), 910; Toby Higbie, "Indispensable Outcasts: Harvest Laborers in the Wheat Belt of the Middle West, 1890–1925," *Labor History* 38 (1997): 393–412. Paul S. Taylor, "The American Hired Man: His Rise and Decline," *Land Policy Review* (Spring 1943): 3–17; Kenneth Harry Heitmann, "An Examination of Hired Farm Workers on Iowa Farms" (M.S. thesis, Iowa State University, 1969); Curtis Harnack, *We Have All Gone Away* (Ames: Iowa State University Press, 1981), 91–101.
3. Fink, *Cutting*, 161–64; Jarvis Hiles interview, Estherville, Iowa, November 11, 1982, Iowa Labor History Oral Project, State Historical Society of Iowa, Iowa City.
4. On rural antipathy to union organizing, see Wilson Warren, *Struggling with "Iowa's Pride:" Labor Relations, Unionism, and Politics in the Rural Midwest since 1877* (Iowa City: University of Iowa Press, 2000), 9, 72–3; Kate Rousmaniere, "The Muscatine Button-Workers' Strike of 1911–12: An Iowa Community in Conflict," *Annals of Iowa* 43 (1982): 243–62; Fink, *Cutting*, 164–66.
5. Iowa Development Commission, *Iowa... Land of Industrial Opportunity* (Des Moines, 1950), A-5, C-8.
6. Fink, *Cutting*, 57–60, 179, 195; "IBP," in *Electrical and Electronics-Food Services and Retailers*, vol. 2 of *International Directory of Company Histories*, ed. Lise Mirabile (Chicago: St. James Press, 1990), 516.
7. James Cook, "Those Simple, Barefoot Boys From Iowa Beef," *Forbes* (22 June 1981): 34.
8. Quoted in Mirabile, "IBP," 515.
9. Quoted in *Des Moines Register*, 2 September 1988.
10. Quoted in Barbara Young Huguenin, "Old Song, New Tune," *National Provisioner* (June 1996): 25
11. Chris Lauritsen interview, Denison, Iowa, July 22, 1987, Iowa Labor History Oral Project, State Historical Society of Iowa, Iowa City.

12

THE RISE OF YUPPIE COFFEES AND THE REIMAGINATION OF CLASS IN THE UNITED STATES

WILLIAM ROSEBERRY

Let us begin at Zabar's, a gourmet food emporium on Manhattan's Upper West Side. We enter, make our way through the crowd waiting to place orders in the cheese section, move quickly past the prepared foods, linger over the smoked fish, then arrive at the coffees. There, in full-sized barrels arranged in a semicircle, we find a display of roasted coffee beans for sale—Kona style, Colombian Supremo, Gourmet Decaf, Blue Mountain style, Mocha style, French, Italian, Vienna, Decaf Espresso, Water Process Decaf, Kenya AA—and a helpful clerk waiting to fill our order, grind the beans to our specification, and suggest one of a small selection of flavored syrups.

Given Zabar's reputation for quality and excess, this is a rather modest selection as coffee now goes. The evidence of plenty and waste can be found in the size of the barrels and the quantity of roast beans available for sale and spoilage. But the real spot to spend money is upstairs, where the brewers, grinders, and espresso coffeemakers are sold—from simple Melitta drip cones and carafes to the more serious Krups Semiprofessional Programmatic ($349) or the Olympia Caffarex ($1,000). Zabar's collection of coffee is not especially distinguished. They eschew the trend toward flavors (raspberry, almond, chocolate, amaretto, vanilla, and the like, in various combinations), offering instead a few prepackaged coffees in flavors and small bottles of flavored syrups for those customers who prefer them. But only two of their coffees are sold as specific varietals, Colombian Supremo and Kenyan AA. The rest are "styles" that suggest a geographic place without having anything to do with it. Kona style can include beans from El Salvador, Blue Mountain style, beans from Puerto Rico, and so on.

If I visit the deli across the street from my apartment, I can choose from a much wider variety of coffees, 43 in all, including Jamaican Blue Mountain, Venezuela Maracaibo, German Chocolate, Swedish Delight, Double Vanilla Swedish Delight,

Swiss Mocha Almond, and Decaf Swiss Mocha Almond, to name just a few. These are displayed in burlap bags that take up much more space than coffee sections used to occupy when my only choices were Maxwell House, Folgers, Chock Full o' Nuts, El Pico, and Medaglia d'Oro. And they require the assistance of a clerk to weigh, bag, and grind the coffee.

As I walk down the street, virtually every deli offers a similar variety, generally in minibarrels, though sometimes the barrels are distributed in apparently casual abundance throughout the store so that I can also select breads, spreads, teas, chocolates, and cheeses as I decide which among the many roasts, varietals, styles, or flavors I will choose this week. I no longer need the gourmet shop—though such shops, which proliferated in the 1980s, continue to thrive, concentrated in cities but also present in suburban towns and shopping malls—to buy what coffee traders call "specialty" coffees; nor do I need to be a gourmet to buy and enjoy them (or better said, I need not be a gourmet to look, act, and feel like one). I can go to the corner deli or the major supermarket, where even Maxwell House and A&P have joined the "specialty" trend.

Surely these developments are "good." Specialty coffees taste better than mass-market coffees. They offer pleasure in many ways: the aroma, ambience, and experience of the coffee shop or even the deli itself (indeed, part of the experience of a place like Zabar's is the succession of smells); the casual conversation with the shop owner or dinner guest about varietals, roasts, preparation methods; the identification with particular places through consumption—Copenhagen or Vienna, Jamaica or the Celebes; or the inclusion of coffee purchasing, preparation, and consumption in a widening spectrum of foods—including wines, beers, waters, breads, cheeses, sauces, and the like—through which one can cultivate and display "taste" and "discrimination." Moreover, the expansion of specialty coffees marks a distinct break with a past characterized by mass production and consumption. The move toward these coffees was not initiated by the giants that dominate the coffee trade but by small regional roasters who developed new sources of supply, new modes and networks of distribution that allowed, among other things, for consumers to buy coffee directly (well, not *directly*) from a peasant cooperative in Chiapas or Guatemala. New coffees, more choices, more diversity, less concentration, new capitalism: the beverage of postmodernism.

Proper understanding of the proliferation of specialty coffees requires consideration of the experiences and choices of the consumer in the coffee shop and at the dinner table, but it also requires consideration of the methods, networks, and relations of coffee production, processing, distribution, and sale in the 1980s, as well as a placement of those methods, networks, and relations within a wider history.

This essay concentrates on that second range of questions, on what might be termed the *shaping* of taste. I begin with two historical issues—first, the complex relation between the recent rise of specialty coffees and an earlier period characterized by standardization and mass-marketing, and second, the specific history of specialty coffees themselves. In considering both, I deal with coffee in particular, but what was happening with coffee marketing and consumption was not at all unrelated to what was happening with many other food commodities. I then turn to a range of questions that might be termed sociological: How has the turn toward specialty coffees been organized? What has been the position and role of the giant corporations that dominated the coffee trade during the period of standardization? Who have been the innovators and "agents" of change in the move toward specialty coffees? How have they organized themselves? How have they reimagined and reorganized the market? What kinds of class and generational maps of United States society have they used in their reimagination of the market? How have they imagined themselves, and the class and generational segments they target as their market niche, in relation to a wider world of coffee producers?

These more historical and sociological questions raise issues for anthropological interpretation. Can the study of changing marketing and consumption patterns of a single commodity at a particular moment—even a mundane commodity produced for everyday and routine consumption—shed some light on a wider range of social and cultural shifts? We have a good example of such an analysis in Sidney Mintz's *Sweetness* and *Power* (1985), an exploration of the growing and changing presence of sugar in the English diet from the 17th through 19th centuries, linked—explicitly and necessarily—to industrialization and the growth of a working class, changing modes of life, consumption, and sociality in growing cities in England, and to the establishment of colonial power, plantation economies, and slave labor in the Caribbean. The range of issues considered here is more modest, but it shares Mintz's conviction that "the social history of the use of new foods in a western nation can contribute to an anthropology of modern life" (1985:xxviii).

A distinctive feature of this essay is that the data come largely from two trade journals, *World Coffee and Tea* (*WC&T*) and *Coffee and Cocoa International* (*C&CI*). These journals raise several questions, the first of which is methodological—the use of trade journals in relation to other possible methods and sources, including ethnographic ones. The journals give us access to the preoccupations, diagnoses, and strategies of a range of actors in the coffee trade—growers, traders, roasters, distributors, and retailers large and small, in producing as well as consuming countries. In one sense, they share a common interest: to increase coffee consumption and maximize profits. In many other senses, their interests and their stakes in the coffee trade differ.

If we are trying to understand these actors—their interpretations and intentions, their images of the social world in which they act, their disagreements and disputes, and their actions—trade journals constitute a central, readily available, and underused source. But their use raises a second related and interesting issue of the trade journal as text. The articles in the journals speak to a particular kind of public—in this case, to an assumed community of "coffeemen." The anthropologist who would use these articles for other purposes has the strong sense that he (in this case) is eavesdropping, or—to return to the text—peering over the shoulder of the intended reader.

★ CONNECTIONS AND CONTRASTS

We understand and value the new specialty coffees in relation to "the past," though in fact more than one past is being imagined. On the one hand, specialty coffees are placed in positive relation to the past of, say, two decades ago, when most coffee in the United States was sold in cans in supermarkets, the roasts were light and bland, the decaffeinated coffees undrinkable, the choices limited to brand and perhaps grind, and the trade dominated by General Foods and Procter and Gamble. On the other hand, the new coffees seem to connect with a more genuine past before the concentration and massification of the trade. The identification of particular blends and varietals recalls the glory days of the trade; the sale of whole beans in barrels or burlap bags recalls that past (for a present in which the "containerization" in international shipping has rendered such bags obsolete) at the same time that it gives the late-20th-century gourmet shop the ambience of the late-19th-century general store. This identification is further effected with the tasteful display of old coffee mills, roasters, and brewing apparatus on the store shelves. Coffee traders themselves share these identifications. Alan Rossman, of Hena "Estate Grown" Coffee, explained to *World Coffee and Tea* in 1981:

> I am a second generation coffeeman and, through direct experience, remember when there was a certain pride in the coffee business. We used to wonder why, in earlier days, there were so many second generation coffeemen around. And it was because there was an art to coffee then.... Today, the ballgame has changed and suddenly the password in coffee has become 'cheaper, cheaper!'
>
> All of a sudden...comes along somebody who's interested in quality. He doesn't care that he may have to sell it at twice the price of canned coffee, he's only interested in quality. All we're doing today is copying what our fathers and grandfathers did years and years ago.... Specialty coffee has revived the pride that was lost somewhere along the line and it is the main reason why I, who was born and raised in the coffee business, really enjoy now being part of that business. [*WC&T* 1981b:12]

In the same issue of *World Coffee and Tea*, the journal enthused:

> And so it seems that the coffee trade in the U.S. has come full circle, returning to its roots and the uncomplicated marketing of coffee in bins, barrels and the more modern method of lucite containers. As they did in the early days of coffee consumption, American consumers, in ever-growing numbers, are blending their own coffee, grinding it at home and brewing it fresh each day. [*WC&T* 1981b:12]

Similarly, the journal notes that specialty coffees appeal to consumers who prefer "natural," "whole," and "fresh" foods. Imagining yet another past, the same journal nervously tracks the latest government reports on the effects of caffeine or methylene chloride. But to what extent is the new also a return? Upon what pasts have the specialty coffees actually built?

In an important essay, Michael Jimenez (1995) describes the processes through which coffee was transformed from an elite and expensive beverage, with annual per capita consumption in the United States at three pounds in 1830, to a relatively inexpensive drink consumed in working-class homes and at factory "coffee breaks" across the country by 1930. Much of his analysis concerns the first three decades of the 20th century, by which time coffee was widely distributed and consumed.

Of special relevance is Jimenez's analysis of the emergence of a more concentrated and consolidated coffee trade in the first three decades of this century, one that had developed a central directing (though not controlling) authority and imposed standardized notions of quality and taste in the creation of a national market. Jimenez shows that we cannot understand transformations in the coffee trade without understanding a broad range of economic and social transformations in the history of American capitalism—the industrial revolution of the late 19th century and the creation of a more homogeneous proletariat; the development of national markets and modes of distribution; the revolution in food production, processing, and distribution that resulted in the creation of the supermarket, among other things (indeed, the histories of the supermarket and of standardization in the coffee trade are contingent); the revolution in advertising; the concentration and consolidation of American industry; and so on. In all this, the particular history of the stan-

Table 1: Percentage of U.S. population drinking coffee, 1962–88. Redrawn and simplified after WC&T 1989a.

Year	Percentage drinking
1962	74.7
1974	61.6
1975	61.6
1976	59.1
1977	57.9
1978	56.7
1979	57.2
1980	56.6
1981	56.4
1982	56.3
1983	55.2
1984	57.3
1985	54.9
1986	52.4
1987	52.0
1988	50.0

dardization of coffee for mass markets is not unrelated to the history of standardization, indeed "industrialization," of foods in general in the 19th and 20th centuries (see Goody 1982:154–174).

The process of standardization and concentration begun before the depression was consolidated over the succeeding decades, especially after World War II, during which we can locate two new developments. The first involved the creation of international control instruments and agreements, beginning in World War II and culminating in the creation of the International Coffee Organization and an International Coffee Agreement signed by producing and consuming countries, through which export quotas were imposed upon producing countries. Though room was allowed for new producers (especially from Africa) to enter the market, entry and participation were controlled. With such instruments, and with the widening production and consumption of solubles, the trend toward coffee of the lowest common denominator continued.

The second postwar development involved the long-term decline in consumption beginning in the 1960s. Through the 1950s, consumption was essentially flat, with minor fluctuations. From 1962, one can chart a consistent decline. In that year, 74.7 percent of the adult population was calculated to be coffee drinkers; by 1988 only 50 percent drank coffee (see Table 1). Even those who drank coffee were drinking less. In 1962, average coffee consumption was 3.12 cups per day; by 1980 it had dipped to 2.02 cups and by 1991 had dropped to 1.75, which represented a slight increase over the 1988 low of 1.67 (*WC&T* 1991:14). Worse, in the view of "coffeemen," consumption was increasingly skewed toward an older set. At the beginning of the 1980s, they worried that they had not been able to attract the 20- to 29-year-old generation, who seemed to identify coffee drinking with the settled ways of their parents and grandparents. According to their calculations, 20- to 29-year-olds drank only 1.47 cups per day in 1980, while 30- to 59-year-olds drank 3.06 cups, and those over 60 drank 2.40 (*WC&T* 1980:22).

★ DIFFERENTIATION AND THE IDENTIFICATION OF MARKET NICHES

The long-term trend toward decline was exacerbated by the effects of the July 1975 frost in Brazil, after which wholesale and retail prices rose precipitously. In response, various consumer groups began to call for boycotts, and coffee purchases declined sharply. Congressional hearings were called to investigate the coffee trade, and the General Accounting Office conducted an official inquiry and published a report.

At the beginning of the 1980s, then, many "coffeemen" had reason to worry. Kenneth Roman Jr., president of Ogilvy & Mather, a major advertising and public relations firm which carried the Maxwell House account, offered them some advice. In an interview with the editors of *World Coffee and Tea*, he commented,

> Coffee is a wonderful product. I believe, however, that we have got to stop selling the product on price. We must sell coffee on quality, value and image. I believe coffee has a potential for this marketing approach and I know we can do it. But we must get started now....
>
> Once you start selling a product on price, you end up with a lot of money being put into price promotions...and you forget the basic things like the fact that coffee tastes good, that it smells and looks nice, that it's unique....
>
> We are entering the 'me' generation. The crucial questions 'me' oriented consumers will ask, of all types of products, are: What's in it for me? Is the product "me"? Is it consistent with my lifestyle? Does it fill a need? Do I like how it tastes? What will it cost me? Is it necessary? Can I afford it? Is it convenient to prepare? How will it affect my health? [*WC&T* 1981a:35]

In a speech to the Green Coffee Association of New York, Roman suggested fictitious couples and individuals who could serve as markers of distinct market niches and suggested that "coffeemen" should develop different coffees to appeal to specific niches. The first couple was "the Grays," a dual-income couple in their midthirties, for whom coffee is a "way of life" and who prefer to buy their coffee in a gourmet shop. Others included "the Pritchetts," in their late fifties and watching their pennies, for whom price is the most important question; "Karen Sperling," a single working woman in her thirties who does not want to spend much time in the kitchen and for whom a better instant coffee should be developed; "the Taylors," in their sixties and worried about caffeine, for whom better decaffeinated coffees should be developed; and "Joel," a college student who does not drink coffee. "We don't know yet what to do about Joel....Finding the right answer to that question will be the toughest, and probably the most important task coffee marketers will face in the 80s" (*WC&T* 1981a:76–77).

Kenneth Roman was inviting "coffeemen" to envision a segmented rather than a mass market, and to imagine market segments in class and generational terms. In his scheme were two groups that were to be the targets of specialty coffee promotions—the yuppie "Grays" and the mysterious "Joel," who prefers soft drinks. These two segments mark what were to become two strains of an emerging specialty business—the marketing of quality varietals, on one hand, and the promotion of flavored coffees, the equivalent of soft drinks, on another.

Roman was describing the virtues of product diversification to a trade that had grown on the basis of standardization. Yet the standardization itself was a bizarre development, having been imposed upon a product that "naturally" lends itself to diversity. Even during the period of concentration among roasters and packagers, the export-import trade was organized around a complex grading hierarchy, first according to type (arabica or robusta), then according to place, processing methods, and shape, size, and texture of the bean. Coffees are graded first according to a hierarchy from Colombian arabica, other milds, Brazilian, to robustas. They are traded and may be sold by the place of their origin or export (varietals such as Guatemalan Antigua, Kona, Blue Mountain, Maracaibo); once traded, they may be blended with coffees from other locales or of other grades. Both varietals and blends can then be subjected to different roasts, imparting different, more or less complex aromas and tastes to the coffee. From the point of production through traders, export firms, importers, warehousers, roasters, and distributors, the grading hierarchy with significant price differentials prevails. In their attempt to capture and service a mass market in the 20th century, the giant roasters had bought their coffee through these grading differentials, then proceeded to obliterate them in the production of coffee of the lowest common denominator.

The giants had never controlled the whole trade, however. In addition to the major roasters and their distribution network through grocery stores, smaller "institutional" roasters were scattered throughout the country, servicing restaurants, cafes, offices, vendors, and the like. At the beginning of the 1980s, fewer than 200 roasting and processing companies operated in the United States, with four of them controlling 75 percent of the trade (*C&CI* 1982:17). In addition, a small network of specialty, "gourmet" shops could be found, primarily in coastal cities like New York and San Francisco. In the retrospective view of "coffeemen," these shops began to attract new customers and expand business in the wake of the 1975 freeze, when coffee prices expanded across the board and consumers faced with paying $3 a pound for tasteless coffee began searching for something "better" and found that "quality" coffee that used to cost three times supermarket prices was now only about a dollar more.

This, in turn, provided stimulus for others to enter the gourmet trade, perhaps including specialty coffees as one of a range of foods in a gourmet shop. For this expanding number of retailers, supply was a problem. They were dealing in small lots of a product that was imported, warehoused, and sold in bulk, and were entering a trade that was highly concentrated. As the specialty trade expanded, the critical middlemen were the roasters, who could develop special relationships with importers willing to deal in smaller lots. The roasters, in turn, would supply a network of specialty stores. Location mattered, as a relatively dense concentration of specialty traders, roasters, retailers, and customers developed on the West Coast, especially in Seattle and the San Francisco Bay Area. The roasters best situated to take advantage of the situation were institutional roasters who began to develop specialty lines as subsidiaries of their restaurant supply business. These regional roasters, and others new to the trade, quickly became the control points of an expanding gourmet trade, developing new supplies, roasts, and blends; taking on regular customers among shop owners; running "educational" seminars to cultivate a more detailed knowledge of coffee among retailers, expecting that they in turn would educate their customers; and so on. An early gourmet-market idea popular with retailers was the "gourmet coffee of the day," sold by the cup, allowing the retailer to drain excess inventory and acquaint customers with different blends and roasts at the same time.

One of the most important difficulties for the roaster was the establishment of a regular supply of green coffee. Here the problem was less one of quality than of quantity: major importers and warehousers were reluctant to break lots into shipments below 25 to 50 bags (of 60 kilograms each), but a small to medium-sized roaster dealing with several varietals needed to buy in lots of about 10 bags each. While a collection of green coffee traders in the Bay Area (B. C. Ireland, E. A. Kahl, Harold L. King, Royal Coffee) specialized in the gourmet trade and traded in smaller lots, New York traders were slow to move into the new markets (Schoenholt 1984a:62). As late as 1988, Robert Fulmer of Royal Coffee complained, "Demand for quality has happened faster than producers can react. The New York 'C' market is becoming irrelevant, because it's not representative of what people want" (*C&CI* 1988a:18–22).

Although the trend still represented a very small percentage of total coffee sales in the United States by the early 1980s, traders and roasters had begun to take notice. A scant seven months after Kenneth Roman discussed the need to identify a segmented market and diversify coffee products, *World Coffee and Tea* issued a report on "the browning of America," pointing to an exponential growth in the segment of the coffee trade devoted to specialty lines, with annual growth rates approaching 30 to 50 percent. The journal estimated total U.S. sales of specialty coffees for 1980 to be 14 million pounds (*WC&T* 1981b:12). Over the 1980s growth was phenomenal: *Coffee and Cocoa International* reported sales of 40 million pounds in 1983 (*C&CI* 1985), after which further reports were presented in value of the trade rather than the number of bags—$330 million in 1985 (*C&CI* 1986), $420 million in 1986, $500 million in 1987, by which time specialty coffee constituted 8 percent of total trade, and so on (*C&CI* 1988b).

The expansion of specialty coffees was coincident with a number of technological and commercial developments that require brief mention. First, the "containerization" revolution in international shipping has drastically cut the amount of time coffee is in transit from producing countries to consuming countries (from 17 to 10 days for a typical Santos–to–New York run), and has transformed warehousing practices in the United States, cutting warehouse storage times from an average of six months to an average of 10 to 14 days. Speed in transfer and the development of direct and immediate relationships with roasters have become critical, and the widespread use of containers has allowed distributors to relocate from the coasts to interior cities, enhancing flexibility in supply and distribution (Coe 1983).

Changing relationships between roasters, traders, and bankers were also involved in the gourmet boom. The combination of high inflation and interest rates of the late 1970s and early 1980s affected the way in which "coffeemen" could think about financing their trade. By the early 1980s, banks were less willing to finance purchases of large lots that would be warehoused for several months and encouraged their clients to buy smaller lots and maintain lower inventories. "It's a different world now," Mickey Galitzine of the Bank of New York commented to *World Coffee and Tea* (1983a:21), "and I'm not sure we can go back. People have adjusted to this new situation and are now buying in a different pattern. They're simply used to buying less."

They were buying less, but still buying in lots that were large and risky enough to concern the specialty roaster. Institutional roasters could roast, grind, and package large lots and not worry about freshness. Specialty roasts, to be sold in whole beans, required freshness and had to be distributed and sold quickly. The roaster therefore had to develop an extensive network of retailers but was limited to particular regions because of the difficulties in shipping whole roast beans and maintaining freshness. Here the development of valve packaging made it possible for roasters to keep roasted beans fresh longer, extending the time available for shipping, storage, and selling. The beans could be packed in 250-gram bags for direct retail sale or in 15- or 25-pound bags for retail storage. Indeed, the deli across the street from me buys its 43 varieties from a single roaster in 15-pound valve bags, transferring the coffee to burlap bags for presentation and sale.

★ NEW ACTORS, NEW INSTITUTIONS

Throughout the 1980s, the "quality" segment of the coffee market, highest in prices and profit margins, was booming while total coffee consumption declined. This constitutes such a perfect response to market decline, and such an obvious response to the suggestions of Kenneth Roman, that we might expect a central directing power—"Capital," or at least "The Coffee Interest." But the initiative toward specialty coffees occurred outside of and despite the controlling interests of the giants like General Foods, Procter and Gamble, and Nestlé, who ignored the growth of specialty coffees and seemed to regard them as a fad until they captured a significant percentage of the market. Their reticence might be explained by the fact that the giants were part of large food conglomerates likely to be less threatened by a long-term decline in coffee consumption than the smaller institutional roasters, who were forced to develop new markets in order to survive.

This is not to say that the emergence of specialty coffees was completely free from direction and organization. I have pointed to *some* of the larger commercial, financial, and technological changes with which the move to specialty coffees was associated. In addition, the coffee trade viewed the new developments with interest and excitement. We have seen the notice taken by trade journals from the early 1980s. *World Coffee and Tea* began tracking developments quite closely, with frequent reports on the trade and profiles of particular roasters or retailers. In 1984, the journal also began an irregular column, "The Gourmet Zone," by Donald Schoenholt, followed in the early 1990s by a regular column with various contributors, "The Specialty Line." *Coffee and Cocoa International* viewed developments from a greater distance but enjoyed profiling particular gourmet retailers for their readers. Most important, a group of roasters and retailers formed the Specialty Coffee Association of America (SCAA) in 1982. As with the earlier formation of the National Coffee Association (and later the International Coffee Organization), the importance of such trade associations needs to be emphasized. They provide an important directing organization that can lobby the government, speak for the trade, identify economic and political trends, engage in promotional campaigns, provide information and training for entrepreneurs entering the trade, and so on.

In association with the National Coffee Service Association, the SCAA appealed to the Promotion Fund of the International Coffee Organization and received a $1.6 million grant to promote specialty coffees, especially among the young (*WC&T* 1983b). The money was funneled through the Coffee Development Group (CDG), which promoted specialty coffees throughout the 1980s. One of their early activities involved joint sponsorship of coffeehouses on college campuses (Columbia

University being one of the first), at which coffee brewed from specialty roasts and blends would be sold. The CDG would specify the amount of coffee that had to be included in each pot brewed (*WC&T* 1988). Some, such as the shop at the University of Southern California, even experimented with iced cappuccino, sold in cold drink "bubblers" (*WC&T* 1989b).

In addition to promotional efforts, the SCAA has pursued other goals as well, including the dissemination of information on green market conditions and the development of networks among roasters, retailers, and traders. By 1989, the group held its first convention, and each annual convention demonstrates the phenomenal growth of the association. Its conventions now attract over 3,000 people, and it claims to be the largest coffee association in the world.

Many of the association's members are new to the coffee trade, and they bring with them a formation quite unlike that which characterized second- and third-generation "coffeemen." For one thing, many begin with a lack of knowledge about the basics of coffee production, processing, and marketing. This is reflected in a new tone in *World Coffee and Tea*, which increasingly offers articles giving basic and introductory information of various aspects of the coffee trade, recently advising new entrepreneurs that "historic and geographic background is an essential element to a comprehensive knowledge of coffee. If you're selling Colombian coffee, you should have some idea about where Colombia is located and what kinds of coffee it produces" (McCormack 1994:22). It is also reflected in the kinds of workshops and training sessions offered at annual conventions of the SCAA, popularly known as Espresso 101 or Roasting 101 or Brewing 101.

The presence of new entrepreneurs is also reflected in new sets of social, political, and ethical concerns that would have been anathema to earlier generations of "coffeemen." Among them is a growing interest in social and environmental issues and the creation by coffee roasters of such organizations as Equal Exchange and Coffee Kids, and companies like Aztec Harvests ("owned by Mexican co-op farmers"). As the founder of Coffee Kids, Bill Fishbein, expresses the problem:

> This disparity that exists between the coffee-growing world and the coffee-consuming world is rooted in the centuries and remains the true inheritance of 500 years of colonialism. Although no one in today's coffee industry created the existing situation, everyone, including importers, brokers, roasters, retailers, and consumers, is left with this legacy either to perpetuate or address. [Fishbein and Cycon 1992:14]

William McAlpin, a plantation owner in Costa Rica, gives voice to an older generation that dismisses these concerns along the paternalistic lines one expects from a plantation owner proud of the livelihood he has provided for "our residents," but also observes:

> I am always amused to see that many of these same people, who are involved in the final stages of selling specialty coffee, while proclaiming that they support this or that charity or political action squad, are careful to avoid mentioning that the usual mark-up by the specialty coffee trade is from 400% to 600% of the price paid for delivered green coffee....
>
> From the producer's point of view, it seems truly ironic that a product that takes a year to grow, and that requires thousands of worker hours of difficult, delicate, and often dangerous work, should be so remarkably inflated by someone who simply cooks and displays the coffee. [McAlpin 1994:7]

In any case, both dimensions of the formation of the new coffee men and women find expression and are given direction by the SCAA. In addition to the workshops and training seminars, one can see this in their annual choice of a plenary speaker. At its second convention, held in San Francisco, the SCAA arranged a group tour of wineries and invited a wine merchant to give the plenary address, in which he offered advice based on the success of a beverage that the trade journals have most frequently taken as the model to be emulated. For the 1993 convention, the association invited Ben Cohen of Ben and Jerry's Ice Cream. Of his address, *World Coffee and Tea* reported:

> Ben Cohen urged the members of the coffee industry to integrate the 1960s values of peace and love with running their businesses....
>   Cohen pointed out that coffee is a very political commodity and called on the members of the special coffee industry to:
>
> • purchase coffee from the Aztec Cooperative because a high percentage of the money goes back to the farmers; "buy it, tell your customers about it, and let them choose whether or not they want to pay the higher price," Cohen said.
> • buy organic coffees; and
> • participate in Coffee Kids by using a coin drop or donating a percentage of sales.
>
>   "Use these steps to build your image as a socially conscious business," Cohen explained, "and make it your point of difference in a highly competitive business." [*WC&T* 1993:7]

★ FLEXIBILITY AND CONCENTRATION

As the smaller roasters captured the new market niche, they expressed both surprise and concern about the activities of the giants, sometimes assuming that the market was theirs only as long as the giants stayed out (e.g., *WC&T* 1984:12). Some of the roasters' and retailers' fears were realized in September 1986 when both General Foods and A&P introduced specialty lines for sale in supermarkets— General Foods with Maxwell House Private Collection and A&P with Eight O'Clock Royale Gourmet Bean in 14 varieties, "all designed to appeal to the former soft drink generation." At the time, Karin Brown of General Foods commented, "Gourmet is the fastest-growing segment of the market—large enough to make sense for General Foods' entry now" (*C&CI* 1986:9).

By the time the giants began to enter the market, the groundwork for a certain kind of standardization and concentration among the newcomers had already been laid. In coastal cities, the isolated gourmet food shop was already competing with chains of gourmet shops operating in minimalls, which could, if they chose, develop their own roasting capacities. In addition, some roasters (the best known and most aggressive of which has been Starbucks of Seattle) had begun to move beyond regional distribution chains and develop national markets. While structural changes, from the technologies of shipping, warehousing, and packaging to the credit policies of banks, were significant, we need to also consider some of the characteristics of the gourmet beans themselves.

As the gourmet trade expanded, participants viewed two new developments with excitement or alarm, depending on their respective commitment to traditional notions of "quality." As noted above, the quality of coffee "naturally" varies according to several criteria—type of coffee tree and location of cultivation (varietals), method of processing, size and texture of bean, and degree of roasting. With the expansion of the specialty trade, two new modes of discrimination were introduced—"styles" and "flavors." Because the availability of particular varietals is uncertain (a hurricane hits Jamaica, wiping out Blue Mountain coffee, or a trader cannot provide Kenya AA in lots small enough for a particular roaster because larger roasters can outcompete, and so on), and the price of varietals fluctuates accordingly, roasters attempt to develop blends that allow them flexibility in using a number of varietals interchangeably. "Peter's Blend" or "House Blend" says nothing about where the coffee comes from, allowing the roaster or retailer near perfect flexibility, but so again does the sale of "Mocha style" or "Blue Mountain style." At the beginning of this trend, J. Gill Brockenbrough Jr. of First Colony Coffee and Tea complained, "It is more and more difficult all the time to find the green coffee we need....But there really is no such thing as a 'style' of coffee, either *it is or it isn't* from a particular origin" (*WC&T* 1981b:15). Donald Schoenholt of Gillies 1840 elaborated in his column, "The Gourmet Zone," in *World Coffee and Tea*:

> In the past I have pointed out the practice of labeling "varietals" with the code word "style," a habit which has come to replace good judgment too often these days. But now it appears we have a new phenomenon added to the good-humored diversity of specialty coffee labeling: the gentle art of selling the same coffee by whatever varietal label the customer orders.
>
> One well-known trade executive states his customers understand that substitutions are made from time-to-time when varietals are unavailable. A well-known roaster/retailer avoids buying varietal selections, following instead the accepted tradition of buying for cup qualities alone. He offers his patrons distinctive tastes in varietal labeled blends—Colombian Blend, Kenya Blend, Jamaica Blue Mountain style, etc.
>
> Where the wholesale or retail clientele understand a merchant's practices and honorable intent, both the above-mentioned methods of labeling have been accepted. The problem arises where a merchant's intent is to mislead, through unbridled use of a stencil machine, creating labels just for the sake of inventing variety where none exists. Where no effort or skill is used, the public is presented with cut-rate mislabeled coffees.
>
> A recent inspection of a grocer in the New York area sadly proved a point: Virtually every American roast coffee on display was the same item under different label, purchased from a discount roaster offering all American roast beans, regardless of origin, in the same $2.60 per lb. price range. [Schoenholt 1984b:39]

A second, related development was the emergence of coffee flavors that can be sprayed on recently roasted beans. C. Melchers and Company of Bremen began operating in the United States in 1982, offering an ever-expanding variety of liquid flavors for coffee and tea. Each flavor is composed of 20 to 60 "natural" and "artificial" (chemical) ingredients, and Melchers is adept at developing different combinations to produce "unique" flavors for particular roasters (*WC&T* 1983c:16, 18). Viewing this trend, Larry Kramer of Van Cortland Coffee observed, "Specialty coffee is becoming the Baskin Robbins of the specialty food trade." Actually, as we have seen, it turned out that Ben and Jerry's would have been more to the point. Some roasters and retailers refused to deal in such coffees. Complained Paul Katzeff of Thanksgiving Coffee, "People who drink good coffee drink it because they enjoy the flavor of real coffee....I doubt that flavored coffees bring in drinkers who never drank coffee before" (*WC&T* 1982:20). Despite such expressions of dismay, the move toward flavored coffees has continued apace; roasters and retailers alike recognize that flavors are popular, that they are attracting new coffee drinkers, especially among the "former soft drink generation" that had seemed lost to coffee consumption at the beginning of the 1980s—Kenneth Roman's "Joel," about whom "we don't know yet what to do." Increasingly popular in both retail shops and espresso bars are flavored syrups that, in addition to imparting an apparent "Italian" elegance, grant the small retailer more flexibility. A smaller number of blends, varietals, and roasts can be kept in stock, along with a few bottles of syrup, and customers can add or mix their own flavors.

Style and flavor can, in turn, be combined in various ways, so that one can buy Blue Mountain style vanilla or almond, Mocha style chocolate cream or amaretto, and so on. If we further combine with different roasts, throw in the possibility of caffeinated or water process decaffeinated, the possibilities for variety are almost endless. Critically important, however, is that the variety is *controllable.* To the extent that roasters and retailers are able to create criteria of variability and quality that are removed from the "natural" characteristics and qualities of the coffee beans themselves, they generate for themselves extraordinary flexibility. In extreme cases, they "invent variety where none exists," as Schoenholt complains. Here we find a consumer who acts and feels like a gourmet but is buying coffee that is not far removed from Maxwell House Private Collection. More generally, they create, define, and control their own forms of variety. Specialty "coffeemen" constantly emulate and consult wine merchants and hope that consumers will select coffee with the same discrimination and willingness to spend money they demonstrate when buying wine, but the Baskin Robbins (or Ben and Jerry's) model may not be too much of an exaggeration.

Ironically, controllable variety also makes the specialty trade subject to concentration, whether from the outside as giants create their own "Private Collection" and "Royale Gourmet Bean" lines or from internal differentiation, expansion, and concentration among smaller roasters. Variety, too, can be standardized, especially if the varieties have little to do with "natural" characteristics.

★ **THE BEVERAGE OF POSTMODERNISM?**

In his study of the transformation of coffee production and consumption in the early 20th century, Michael Jimenez suggests that coffee is the beverage of U.S. capitalism. Indeed, as we consider the place of coffee as a beverage of choice in working- and middle-class homes and in factory canteens, the role of coffee traders in the emergence of a practical internationalism, and the processes of standardization and concentration that restructured the coffee market, we see that the coffee trade was subject to and participant in the same processes that made a capitalist world.

This is not to suggest, of course, that coffee exists in some sort of unique relationship with capitalism, but that it provides a window through which we can view a range of relationships and social transformations. The processes of standardization and industrialization were common to many foods in the 20th-century United States, and coffee would therefore be one of many foods through which one could examine the transformation industrialization wrought in such broad areas as the structure of cities, the remaking of work, and domestic life and organization, or more specific concerns, such as the rise of advertising or the supermarket. Here, Jimenez's work on coffee in the United States complements Mintz's work on sugar in

England (1985). Yet coffee and sugar belong to a small subset of commodities that can illuminate capitalist transformations in other ways in that they link consumption zones (and the rise of working and middle classes that consumed the particular products in ever increasing numbers) and production zones in Latin America, the Caribbean, Africa, and Asia (and the peasants, slaves, and other rural toilers who grew, cut, or picked the products). For these commodities once inadequately termed "dessert foods" and now increasingly called "drug foods," Sidney Mintz offers a more arresting phrase—coffee, sugar, tea, and chocolate were "proletarian hunger killers" (1979).

Might we, in turn, now consider coffee to be the beverage of postmodernism? That is, can an examination of shifts in the marketing and consumption of one commodity provide an angle of vision on a wider set of social and cultural formations and the brave new world of which they are a part? That I can walk across the street and choose among a seemingly endless variety of cheeses, beers, waters, teas, and coffees places me in a new relationship to the world: I can consume a bit of Sumatra, Darjeeling, France, and Mexico in my home, perhaps at the same meal. Such variety stands in stark contrast to the stolid, boring array of goods available two decades ago. We live now in an emerging era of variety and choice, and the revolution in consumption seems to indicate, and in some ways initiate, a revolution in production. As with coffee, so with other food products: the moves toward product diversification often came not from the established and dominant corporations but from independents whose initiatives have undercut and undermined the established practices and market share of those corporations. We might see this as the extension of the Apple Computer model of entrepreneurialism to other realms.

David Harvey elaborates:

> The market place has always been an "emporium of styles"... but the food market, just to take one example, now looks very different from what it was twenty years ago. Kenyan haricot beans, California celery and avocados, North African potatoes, Canadian apples, and Chilean grapes all sit side by side in a British supermarket. This variety also makes for a proliferation of culinary styles, even among the relatively poor....
>
> The whole world's cuisine is now assembled in one place in almost exactly the same way that the world's geographical complexity is nightly reduced to a series of images on a static television screen. This same phenomenon is exploited in entertainment palaces like Epcot and Disney-world; it becomes possible, as the U.S. commercials put it, "to experience the Old World for a day without actually having to go there." The general implication is that through the experience of everything from food, to culinary habits, music, television, entertainment, and cinema, it is now possible to experience the world's geography vicariously, as a simulacrum. The interweaving of simulacra in daily life brings together different worlds [of commodities] in the same space and time. But it does so in such a way as to conceal almost perfectly any trace of origin, of the labour processes that produced them, or of the social relations implicated in their production. [1989:299, 300]

A more complete understanding of coffee marketing and consumption in the 1980s and 1990s requires that we make some attempt to examine the world of production concealed by the emporium of styles. We might begin by maintaining an understanding of coffee as "the beverage of United States capitalism" but placing the history of that beverage within two periods of capitalist accumulation.

In David Harvey's view, much of 20th-century capitalism was dominated by a "Fordist" regime of accumulation; since the mid-1970s a new regime has emerged, which he labels "flexible accumulation." The Fordist regime can be seen to begin in 1914, with the imposition of assembly line production, and it has dominated the post–World War II period. The Fordist regime was founded on mass production and industrial modes of organization, based in a few key industries (steel, oil, petro-chemicals, automobiles), characterized by the presence of both organized management and organized labor with negotiated, relatively stable pacts between them. These industries, in turn, were subject to state regulation and protection of markets and resources, and they produced standardized commodities for mass markets. With the financial crises of the 1970s, the stabilities of the Fordist regime came to be seen as rigidities. Harvey sees the regime of flexible accumulation emerging in partial response. His description of the innovations characteristic of flexible accumulation concentrates on many features that we have already encountered in our discussion of specialty coffees—the identification of specialized market niches and the production of goods for those niches as opposed to the emphasis on mass-market standardized products; the downsizing of plants and production processes; the shrinking of inventories so that producers purchase smaller quantities and practice just-in-time production; the revolution in shipping and warehousing technologies to cut shipping times; the reconfiguration of financial markets; and so on.

In this regard, it is interesting to place the period considered by Jimenez and the period examined in this essay next to each other. Both concern decades that saw, if we follow Harvey's analysis, experimentation with new regimes of accumulation. But if we return to a history more specific to coffee, both also began with a perceived problem—stagnation in consumption in the first, long-term decline in the second. Both began with evident consumer dissatisfaction and governmental investigation (in the form of congressional hearings). In both, the coffee trade, in the individual actions of its fragmented members and in the programs of its directing centers, devised strategies to respond to perceived crises that, as it happens, neatly correspond with the forms, methods, and relations of emerging regimes of accumulation.

As I visit the gourmet shop, it might be a bit disconcerting to know that I have been so clearly targeted as a member of a class and generation, that the burlap bags or minibarrels, the styles and flavors of coffee, the offer of a "gourmet coffee of the day," have been designed to appeal to me and others in my market niche. But such are the circumstances surrounding my freedom of choice. In an influential essay on the global cultural economy, Arjun Appadurai has suggested the emergence of a new "fetishism of the consumer" and claims that commodity flows and marketing strategies "mask...the real seat of agency, which is not the consumer but the producer and the many forces that constitute production.... The consumer is consistently helped to believe that he or she is an actor, where in fact he or she is at best a chooser" (1990:307). While I think Appadurai's larger claims regarding the radical disjuncture between the present global cultural economy and earlier moments and forms require careful and skeptical analysis (Roseberry 1992), the recent history of coffee marketing and consumption seems to support his understanding of consumer fetishism.

That is to say, my newfound freedom to choose, and the taste and discrimination I cultivate, have been shaped by traders and marketers responding to a long-term decline in sales with a move toward market segmentation along class and generational lines. While I was thinking of myself as me, Kenneth Roman saw me as one of "the Grays." How many readers of this essay have been acting like "Joels"? This is not, of course, to say that we enter the market as mere automatons; clearly, we have and exercise choices, and we (apparently) have more things to choose from than we

163

once did. But we exercise those choices in a world of structured relationships, and part of what those relationships structure (or shape) is both the arena and the process of choice itself.

Another, inescapable part of that world of structured relationships is a set of connections with the world of production and of producers. My vicarious experience of the world's geography is not *just* a simulacrum; it depends upon a quite real, if mediated and unacknowledged, relationship with the rural toilers without whom my choice could not be exercised. How has the brave new world of choice and flexibility affected them?

For both Fordist and flexible accumulation regimes, the mode of mobilizing labor is critical—the importance of a stable core of organized labor and labor relations under Fordism and its virtual opposite under flexible accumulation, which seems to remove labor as much as possible from core to peripheral (temporary, seasonal, occasional, or contracted) labor supplies that can be engaged and disengaged as needed. Some of the innovations that I have discussed in relation to the coffee market have involved such shifts in labor relations (e.g., the move toward containerization in international shipping, which revolutionized distribution in the United States and allowed importers to bypass the docks and warehouses of coastal cities, cutting the need for labor and the power of the unions of longshoremen and warehousemen).

As we turn from the United States to the manifold points of production, we find that the changes can be quite dramatic, though their shape and consequences remain uncertain and can only be suggested here. Throughout the post–World War II period, the coffee trade was regulated by a series of international coffee agreements, the first of which was the Pan American agreement during the war, and the longest lasting of which was the International Coffee Agreement (ICA) administered by the International Coffee Organization (ICO), formed in 1963. Through the agreements, producing and consuming countries submitted to a series of quotas that could be adjusted and even suspended from year to year—as particular countries suffered hurricanes, droughts, or frosts or other countries entered the market and signed the agreement—but that nonetheless imposed a series of (let us call them Fordist) rigidities on international trade. They also provided a series of protections for individual producing countries and regions, regulating both prices (which fluctuated but with highs and lows that were less dramatic) and market share.

The agreements were never especially popular among "coffeemen," who profess a free trade philosophy, and they encountered increasing opposition in the 1980s. Specialty traders wanted to develop new sources of supply, emphasizing arabicas and deemphasizing robustas, which had an important place in mass-market blends and soluble (instant) coffees but found little acceptance in specialty markets. Unfortunately for the specialty traders, the percentages of arabicas and robustas offered on the world market were fixed by the ICA; fortunately for robusta producers, their livelihoods were relatively protected by that same agreement.

The ICA was due for renewal and extension in 1989, but the various members of the ICO encountered difficulties in resolving their differences. Two countries were especially insistent on their needs—Brazil, which wanted to maintain its 30 percent share, and the United States, which pressed two concerns: (1) the troublesome practice among producing countries of discounting prices to nonmember consuming countries (essentially those within the then-existing socialist bloc), and (2) the inflexibility of the quotas that, they argued, prevented traders and consumers from acquiring more of the quality arabicas. Because the differences could not be resolved, the ICA was suspended in mid-1989, ushering in a free market in coffee for the first time in decades.

The immediate effects were dramatic for producing countries. Prices plummeted and quickly reached, in constant dollar terms, historic lows. Exporting countries that could do so expanded exports in an attempt to maintain income levels in the face of declining unit prices, and importers took advantage of the low prices and expanded stocks. In addition to the general price decline, robusta producers were especially disadvantaged, as prices for robusta dipped below $.50 per pound and farmers faced a world market that no longer wanted their product. Robusta is grown primarily in Africa, and African producers and economies were devastated.

By 1993, under the leadership of Brazil and Colombia, along with Central American arabica producers, a coffee retention plan was signed that called for the removal of up to 20 percent of production by participants in the plan. The plan was the first step toward a new Association of Coffee Producing Countries in which both Latin American and African countries participated, and it has succeeded in spurring a price recovery. It remains a fragile coalition, however, and by the time it had been formed the market had been completely restructured. Most important, because market prices had fallen below the level of production costs, only the strong—those who could weather a prolonged depression—survived. The weak disappeared from the coffee scene.

The free market vastly increased the flexibility of coffee traders and "peripheralized" the labor of coffee growers in a direct and immediate way. My freedom to choose in the deli across the street or the gourmet shop a few blocks away is implicated with the coffee trader's freedom to cut off the supply (and therefore the product of the laborer) from, say, Uganda or the Ivory Coast. To the extent that "coffeemen" have been successful in creating styles, so that I think I am drinking coffee from a particular place but the coffee need not have any actual association with that place, I will not even be aware of the processes of connection and disconnection in which I am participating. "The beverage of U.S. capitalism," indeed!

★ CONCLUSION

Resolution of the issues raised by this analysis would take us beyond our sources. My aim is to draw out certain implications and perspectives resulting from the angle of vision pursued herein, but also to point toward questions and perspectives that could be pursued in supplementary and complementary analyses—other chapters, so to speak.

This essay's perspective on the shaping of market trends and taste may raise the specter of manipulation by unseen, but powerful, forces. In an important discussion of the Frankfurt School's approach to culture industries in general and to consumption patterns in particular, Stephen Mennell observes:

> The problem with the use of words like "manipulation" by the Frankfurt School and other critics is that it suggests that those in powerful positions in industry—the culture industry or the food and catering industries—*consciously* and with malevolent intent set out to persuade people that they need and like products of inferior or harmful quality. It fails to draw attention to the unplanned, unintended, vicious spiral through which supply and demand are usually linked. [1996:321]

There is, of course, plenty of evidence from the trade journals that conscious action on the part of a range of actors in the coffee trade to persuade people that they need and like certain products—leaving aside the question of intent and the quality of the products—is *precisely* what they do. But it is also clear from the sources that they do not act in concert, that there is no single controlling interest (despite obvious power relations), that there has been ample room for new interests and actors, that these actors, big and small, often do not know what they are doing, and that in their bumbling experimentation they have stumbled on some strategies that work. They work not because there is a manipulable mass out there waiting to be told what to drink but because there is a complex, if specific, intersection between the shaping actions of various actors in the coffee trade and the needs, tastes, and desires of particular groups of consumers and potential consumers.

We gain access to that intersection by means of a discussion of *class*. We have seen that Kenneth Roman preached market segmentation along class and generational lines. His own suggestion of segments was relatively simple, even crude—divided by very broad distinctions of class and generation, with some sense of gender differentiation, but each of the segments was implicitly white. Theorists of niche marketing have since gone much further in dividing national populations into class, racial, ethnic, and generational groups than Roman would have imagined in the early 1980s, as books like *The Clustering of America* (Weiss 1988) make clear. That these distinctions, however crude, are being made, and that they *work* for the purposes for which they are intended, is worth some reflection.

The point, of course, is that when market strategists *imagine* a class and generational map that includes people like "the Grays" and "Joel," they are not trying to create categories out of thin air. They are doing—for different purposes—what sociologists and anthropologists used to do: trying to describe a social and cultural reality. The imagined map works only if there are indeed such groups "out there," so to speak, and that the map needs to work is the whole point.

That there is a complex relationship between class and food consumption is often remarked, first in the obvious sense that particular groups occupy differential market situations in terms of their ability to purchase certain foods, and second in the uses various groups make of foods and food preferences in marking themselves as distinctive from or in some sense like other groups. In the case of specialty coffee, one of its interesting features is that it is *not*, or is not meant to be, a "proletarian hunger killer." Looking further afield, it is worth comment that the other proletarian hunger killers of the 19th and 20th centuries—with the exception of sugar, which does not lend itself to such multiple distinctions except in combination with other substances—are also caught up in the move toward variety and at least the illusion of quality. In one sense this signals the return to "dessert food" status, but there are other senses that need to be considered.

The original market segment toward which specialty coffee, tea, and chocolate were directed was that of "the Grays"—urban, urbane, professional men and women who distinguished themselves through consumption and who consumed or hoped to consume variety and quality, as well as quantity. If they fashioned themselves through consumption, an interesting feature of the movement is that among the commodities in which they demanded variety and quality were the old proletarian hunger killers. In doing so, they almost certainly did not imagine themselves in connection either with proletarians or with the rural toilers who grew, cut, or picked what the yuppies chose to consume.

The identifications they were making were rather more complex and may connect with the commodities' "prehistory," as it were, representing a kind of preindustrial nostalgia. Each of the proletarian hunger killers entered European social history as expensive goods from exotic locales, affordable and consumable only by a privileged few, not in homes but in the courts, or, increasingly in the 17th and 18th centuries, in coffee houses (Schivelbusch 1992; Ukers 1935). They became proletarian hunger killers as their costs of production, processing, and shipping dropped, as available quantities increased dramatically, and as they became items of domestic and routine consumption. The class and cultural identification of this yuppie segment, then, is not so much bourgeois as courtly, genteel, cosmopolitan. It could be seen to represent an attempt to re-create, through consumption, a time before mass society and mass consumption. It could be seen, then, as a symbolic inversion of the very economic and political forces through which this particular class segment came into existence. Here, close attention to class-conditioned patterns of consumption can provide another window onto the cultural history of U.S. capitalism.

But the story does not end here. Over the past decade, the consumption of yuppie coffees has broken free from its original market segment, as the coffees are more widely available in supermarkets and shopping malls and are more widely consumed. We have seen that the processes of production and distribution have been subject to concentration and centralization from above and below as Maxwell House and Eight O'Clock Coffee have introduced gourmet coffees and as new chains as different from each other as Starbucks and Gloria Jean's move into central positions at the coffee shop end. This movement, in which a class-conditioned process of marketing, promotion, and consumption escapes class locations, and apparent variety and quality are standardized and mass-marketed, has obvious limits. Gourmet coffees can be standardized, and their processes of production and marketing concentrated, but it is unlikely that these coffees will ever become truly mass-market coffees. Their continued success will depend upon the processes of social and cultural differentiation they mark, even as the social locations of groups of consumers are blurred. It will also depend upon the continued existence, at home and abroad, of a world of exploitative relationships, evidenced in the social relations through which coffee is produced, the engagement and disengagement of coffee-producing regions under free-market conditions, and the processes of standardization and concentration to which gourmet coffee production and marketing have been subjected. Coffee remains, as Ben Cohen expressed it, a "very political commodity."

NOTES

Acknowledgments. An early version of this article was presented at the session "Histories of Commodification: Papers in Honor of Sidney Mintz," at the 91st Annual Meeting of the American Anthropological Association, San Francisco, November 1992. I thank Ashraf Ghani for inviting me to participate in the session and Richard Fox for his astute commentary. I have also benefited from a stimulating discussion among sociologists and anthropologists at the University of California at Santa Barbara, for which I thank Elvin Hatch and Roger Friedland, and a discussion among historians at the State University of New York at Stony Brook, for which I thank Brooke Larson and Paul Gootenberg. For their useful suggestions, I thank as well the reviewers for *American Anthropologist* and Talal Asad, Kate Crehan, Nicole Polier, Deborah Poole, Rayna Rapp, and Kamala Visweswaran.

REFERENCES

Appadurai, Arjun. 1990. Disjuncture and Difference in the Global Cultural Economy. *Theory, Culture and Society* 7:295–310.
Coe, Kevin. 1983. Changes in Store. *Coffee and Cocoa International* 10(5):39–41.
C&CI (Coffee and Cocoa International). 1982. High Hopes for the Promotion Drive. *Coffee and Cocoa International* 9(2):14–17.
———. 1985. Major Growth Seen for Gourmet Coffee Market. *Coffee and Cocoa International* 12(1):5.
———. 1986. Giants Clash in Specialty Brands War. *Coffee and Cocoa International* 13(5):9.

———. 1988a. The California Trade: A West Coast View. *Coffee and Cocoa International* 15(5):18–22.

———. 1988b. $500m Gourmet Market to Expand, Says Study. *Coffee and Cocoa International* 15(6):6.

Fishbein, Bill, and Dean Cycon. 1992. Coffee Kids. *World Coffee and Tea*, October:14–15, 28.

Goody, Jack. 1982. *Cooking, Cuisine, and Class: A Study in Comparative Sociology.* Cambridge: Cambridge University Press.

Harvey, David. 1989. The Condition of Postmodernity. Oxford: Basil Blackwell.

Jimenez, Michael. 1995. From Plantation to Cup: Coffee and Capitalism in the United States, 1830–1930. In Coffee, Society, and Power in Latin America. William Roseberry, Lowell Gudmundson, and Mario Samper Kutschbach, eds. Pp. 38–64. Baltimore, MD: Johns Hopkins University Press.

McAlpin, William J. 1994. Coffee and the Socially Concerned. World Coffee and Tea, July:6–7.

McCormack, Tim. 1994. Teaching Consumers about Coffee. World Coffee and Tea, July:21–23.

Mennell, Stephen. 1996. All Manners of Food: Eating and Taste in England and France from the Middle Ages to the Present. 2nd edition. Urbana: University of Illinois Press.

Mintz, Sidney. 1979. Time, Sugar, and Sweetness. Marxist Perspectives 2:56–73.

———. 1985. Sweetness and Power: The Place of Sugar in Modern History. New York: Viking.

Roseberry, William. 1992. Multiculturalism and the Challenge of Anthropology. Social Research 59:841–858.

Schivelbusch, Wolfgang. 1992. Tastes of Paradise: A Social History of Spices, Stimulants, and Intoxicants. New York: Vintage.

Schoenholt, Donald N. 1984a. The Gourmet Zone. World Coffee and Tea, September:62–63.

———. 1984b. The Gourmet Zone. World Coffee and Tea, November:39.

Ukers, W. H. 1935. All about Coffee. 2nd edition. New York: The Tea and Coffee Trade Journal Company.

Weiss, Michael J. 1988. The Clustering of America. New York: Harper and Row.

WC&T (World Coffee and Tea). 1980. U.S. Coffee Drinking Slips after Slight Gain; Young Still Not Drinking. World Coffee and Tea, November 21–22.

———. 1981a. Ad Man Cautions Coffee Men to Modernize Coffee's Image; Sees Coffee as Drink of '80s. World Coffee and Tea, January:35, 76–78.

———. 1981b. America's Coffee Renaissance Explodes with Excitement as Specialty Coffee Trade Booms. World Coffee and Tea, August:10–15.

———. 1982. Specialty Coffee '82: A Look at Some Trends. World Coffee and Tea, August:16–28.

———. 1983a. Bankers Cite Changes in Coffee Business Due to World Economy. World Coffee and Tea, November:20–22.

———. 1983b. CDG Receives ICO Grant: Specialty Coffee Task Force Formed. World Coffee and Tea, August:11.

———. 1983c. Coffee, Tea Flavorings Play Important Role in U.S. Gourmet Scene. World Coffee and Tea, August:16–18.

———. 1984. Quality, Fresh Product Keep Sales Booming in the Gourmet Segment. World Coffee and Tea, August:8–14.

———. 1988. College Coffeehouses Flourish. World Coffee and Tea, August:10.

———. 1989a. United States of America, Percentage Drinking Coffee, 1962 to 1988. World Coffee and Tea, March:14.

———. 1989b. Decaffeinated and Soluble Constantly Experiment to Improve Market Share. World Coffee and Tea, March: 1—15.

———. 1991. Depressed Prices Lead to Continued Building of Stocks by Consumers. World Coffee and Tea, September:12–16.

———. 1993. SCAA '93—The Largest Coffee Event in History! World Coffee and Tea, June:6–7.

COMPLEXITIES OF CONSUMPTION

3

ISLANDS OF SERENITY: GENDER, RACE, AND ORDERED MEALS DURING WORLD WAR II

13

AMY BENTLEY

In 1943, illustrator Norman Rockwell's *Four Freedoms* series appeared in the *Saturday Evening Post*. Its warm, intimate scenes of American life concretely represented the abstract reasons President Roosevelt offered for the country's involvement in the war. The United States, the president told the American public, was fighting to preserve at home and extend abroad the liberties Americans held most dear: freedom from fear, freedom of worship, freedom of speech, and freedom from want. The public immediately embraced the series of paintings, to such an extent that it seemed as if the paintings had inspired the themes they were intended to illustrate.[1] These paintings, reproduced by the millions, conveyed what was at stake for American families in this global battle against fascism. *Freedom from Want*, for example, gathers up images of domesticity and material plenty. An older man, presumably the patriarch of this extended, Euro-American family, sits at the head of the table, dressed in his Sunday best, and gazes down in obvious pleasure at the oversized, succulent turkey his aproned wife has placed in front of him. Other family members, seated on both sides of the table, eagerly await the feast. They smile broadly at each other; one even looks toward the viewer as if to invite her or him to join the festivities. The table is replete with all the trimmings. The room is warm and comfortably furnished. Yet *Freedom from Want* was controversial as well as popular. Some, particularly U.S. allies, found the lavishly dressed turkey an inappropriate symbol during a global war which left so many hungry and undernourished.[2] Most Americans, however, identified with the scene because of its familiarity and idealism. *Freedom from Want* seemed to embody the best of what the United States stood for—stable and extended families, abundant material wealth, familiar rituals, non-denominational and patriotic celebration.

That so many Americans enthusiastically embraced *Freedom from Want* makes it a tableau of wartime values. Rockwell's depiction of a Thanksgiving dinner,

America's famous and perhaps most ritualized meal, functioned as a visual metaphor for prescriptive notions about expectations of abundance, societal order and stability, and maintenance of the status quo. The scene illuminated the "inalienable right" of Americans to eat their familiar and abundant foods in their traditional ways, and not just at Thanksgiving. Rockwell's image, along with countless similar illustrations of Americans sitting down to dinner, is part of what I call the icon of the "ordered meal." Image-makers and citizens alike intuitively recognized meals as "not only a symbolic language but...a cultural performance."[3] The "A + 2B" representation of a hot dinner of meat, potatoes, and vegetable, served by a white or black woman, reassured Americans that despite mandatory wartime food rationing the United States was still a land of unparalleled abundance and they were still a "people of plenty."[4] However, the image of the ordered meal with red meat as the centerpiece, so seemingly central to Americans, was at odds with such realities as the chronic existence of an American underclass, as well as with certain wartime realities. While American agricultural abundance remained a constant during the war—American farmers produced food at record-breaking levels—mandatory government rationing, a tightened domestic food supply (though not dangerously so), and government attempts to persuade Americans to put their red-meat eating habits on hold "for the duration," portended tensions that the status quo ideology embedded in Rockwell's painting could not consider.[5]

Freedom from Want is important not only for the abundance it portrays, but for the social and familial relations it conveys. Whether or not consciously understood, the "traditional" manner of eating has meant in part that family meals are organized according to gender-specific roles: men as presiders and presenters, women as coordinators and servers.[6] During the war, media depictions of bountiful meals with women as servers and cooks connoted stability to many Americans, in large part because the images reinforced the status quo of traditional gender roles. By masking the significant social changes occurring in society as a result of the war, *Freedom from Want* and similar illustrations not only were icons of abundance during a time of restricted consumption, but also functioned to naturalize gender and racial hierarchy. The image of the ordered meal unquestioningly promoted the long-held assumption that women, as wives, mothers, and domestics, would serve nutritious and abundant meals for their families, despite the fact that more and more women were involved in work outside their homes as "Rosie the Riveters" or in other, more traditionally feminine kinds of work, both voluntary and paid.[7] Although African-Americans were for the first time moving out of their prescribed and oppressive places in society—particularly black women leaving domestic service in droves for better-paying jobs—they were commonly portrayed as the preparers and servers of the ordered meal, images that in part conveyed a desire to maintain race segregation and domination. Media representations of the Southern kitchen, featuring black "mammy" figures contentedly cooking and serving, assuaged some Americans' anxieties about the defection of a black domestic workforce lured by the prospect of employment in higher-status war jobs.

★ **WAR AND CHANGE**

Scholars of the American home front have well documented the significant changes wrought by World War II as soldiers went off to war, families separated, millions moved to cities in search of war work, and women and African-Americans in significant numbers moved into higher-paying and higher-status jobs.[8] Over 10 percent of the population, nearly thirteen million people, left family and friends to enter the armed services; of these, the war claimed three hundred thousand American lives, and left almost seven hundred thousand physically and psychologically wounded.[9] To build a nation's "arsenal of democracy," the wartime government mobilized private industry on a phenomenal scale as factories shifted production from consumer items to wartime matériel. To meet the employment needs of this expanding industrial economy, government and private industry recruited all able-bodied civilians, including those it had previously ignored such as women and African-Americans. Thus, an estimated six million women entered the workforce for the first time during the war, most of whom were married and had children. At the peak of wartime industrial expansion, the number of women employed in the United States was 47 percent higher than in 1940.[10] Further, after much prodding by the U.S. government, including the establishment of the Fair Employment Practices Committee, private firms reluctantly began to hire African-Americans in significant numbers, and over one million additional blacks entered the workforce (six hundred thousand of them were women).[11] While African-Americans comprised just 3 percent of all war workers in 1942, three years later the number was 8 percent, and the number of skilled black workers had doubled.[12]

173

While not all Americans were affected equally, these wartime changes generated significant social upheaval.[13] Millions poured into cities from the countryside in search of war work, often moving from job to job in search of the highest wages, and leaving rural areas suffering from a labor shortage. The heavy influx of migrants strained city services. Housing became tight or even nonexistent, especially for African-Americans confined to small segregated segments of cities, and transportation proved woefully inadequate. Tension and even violence resulted among groups vying for the same living quarters and lucrative jobs, producing in its extreme form riots in Detroit, Baltimore, Los Angeles, and elsewhere. The status of women shifted during the war as well, as more women were seen in public places without chaperones, felt more independent with wages earned, and generally reveled in the freedom the wartime home front provided. But women's lives became more difficult as they shouldered the burden of extra wartime responsibilities while being responsible as before for all the cooking, cleaning, and child care. Moreover, women of comfortable means no longer had their black cooks and maids on whom to depend. During the war the number of black women working as domestics dropped by about half, and though many returned to domestic work after the war, about 20 percent left domestic employment permanently.[14]

These changes, combined with the horrors of war and the loss of loved ones, for many Americans brought on feelings of anxiety and a sense of impending social and familial chaos. After the long depression decade, and then the war, many feared the country's stability might be gone forever. Historian Richard Polenberg writes that although World War II created for the United States "no physical destruction, no redrawing of territorial lines, no change in the outward structure of government . . . in more subtle ways the war exerted a profound impact upon the American people and their political, social and economic institutions."[15] Public opinion polls bear out this anxiety about the war and social change, indicating that many Americans were worried about domestic shortages, high inflation, and job security. Half of those polled in 1946 indicated the war had changed their lives "a great deal," for some in negative ways, such as shortages, death, and the disruption of family life, and for others in positive ways, including improved education and financial situations.[16] For many, especially African-Americans and women, the changes were a welcome event that brought hope of permanent change and equality. For others, such as working- and middle-class men afraid of losing their positions or white women worried about household management, the change was unsettling and threatening.

That African-Americans were slowly making their way into higher-paying and higher-status jobs as a result of wartime labor shortages created anxiety for many white Americans, as revealed in public opinion polls. A May 1944 poll asked: "After the war, if Negroes could get more kinds of jobs than they can now, do you think there would be fewer jobs for white people?" While 45 percent responded "No, [there] would not be fewer," 40 percent responded affirmatively. In 1946, 49 percent of whites questioned agreed that white people should have first chance at any kind of job over African-Americans; a 1944 poll indicated 61 percent thought whites should have the first chance at jobs over those of Japanese descent. Another 1944 poll indicated that many feared changes in employment would affect the culture at large. Sixty-five percent of those questioned agreed with the statement "If Negroes could get more kinds of jobs than they can now, do you think they would want to go more places white people go?" Of these respondents, 40 percent "would not like it if they did want to go more places where whites would go."[17] Other evidence also illustrates the anxiety some felt over increasing opportunities for blacks. Despite the well-known Nazi doctrine of Aryan supremacy, the South Carolina state legislature passed a resolution declaring that American soldiers were "fighting for white supremacy."[18] While many whites dreaded a more integrated society, African-Americans saw such changes with hope. For example, Americans were asked in 1942: "Five years after the war is over, do you think we Americans will be leading about the same sort of life as we did before the war, or will it be a better life, or a worse life?" While those with more positive outlooks about the future had higher incomes, the group most hopeful of a better life in postwar United States were "Negroes," an indication of their expectation that the war would induce long-term social improvements.[19]

Although the proportion of married women in the wartime workforce was relatively small (26 percent), their increasing numbers also generated anxiety among many. Social scientists, journalists, and others warned that women in the public sphere led to "distortion of values, irregular family routines, promiscuity, lack of respect by men [for women], and a rejection of feminine roles."[20] While 40 percent of women not employed in war industries indicated they would be willing to take a full-time job running a machine in a war plant (another 17 percent agreed, with qualifiers), 55 percent of men polled said they would not be willing to have their wives take this sort of full-time job. Seventy-two percent of women, but only 64 percent of men, thought women should always be paid the same as men for doing exactly the same jobs. Moreover, because more women were employed outside the home, increases—imagined and real—in juvenile delinquency among unwatched and unsupervised American youth became a nationwide concern.[21]

Besides these social and cultural anxieties, Americans had specific fears about personal and family safety. Many Americans worried about Axis attacks on the United States, especially immediately after the bombing of Pearl Harbor. Days after the attack 65 percent of those polled thought it was "very" or "fairly probable" that the Pacific Coast would be bombed within the next few weeks, while in March 1942, half of those questioned thought it was probable that the enemy would bomb the East Coast.[22] Decades of prejudice, journalistic irresponsibility, political ambitions, and a failure of the nation's leaders to protect loyal American citizens, combined with public anxieties at the war's outbreak to be manifested in the forced relocation of 110,000 Japanese-Americans, two-thirds of them U.S. citizens, from the West Coast to concentration camps inland. Unsubstantiated claims of "military necessity" persuaded a majority of the Supreme Court, the Roosevelt Administration, and most Americans that internment was not an unreasonable response to the attack on Pearl Harbor, and through ignorance, fear, and prejudice, they justified the abolishment of these Americans' civil rights.[23] While fear that the United States could be attacked—from within or from without—subsided over time, the threat always loomed near, and each town and neighborhood assigned air-raid wardens to search the skies for enemy aircraft. Americans also worried about the Axis powers winning the war and gaining control over the United States. Even before the United States entered the war, almost three-fourths of those polled thought that if Hitler won the war, the effect on the future well-being of the United States would be "very serious." In March 1942, 70 percent of those questioned thought that if Germany and Japan won the war "they would keep their armies over here to police the United States." Seventy-one percent thought the Germans would "take a lot of our food away so they would starve most of us."[24]

To combat American's perception of and anxieties about their unsteady society, the United States government, in coordination with private industry, employed pamphlets, posters, films, magazines, and radio broadcasts to portray the American home front as stable, unified, healthy, and ready for battle. Historian Allen Winkler and others have described in detail the government's efforts at producing and controlling wartime propaganda, and the private sector's wholehearted participation in publicizing and promoting U.S. war aims.[25] Until Congress cut its funding dramatically, the Office of War Information (OWI) provided eight hundred newspapers around the country with four cartoons a week on wartime themes. Additionally, it sent out ideas for storylines, photographs, posters, recipes, and purchasing and canning tips to promote wise use of rationed foods. The OWI especially targeted American housewives, as the prime consumers in American families, with these wartime messages.[26] The government-supported Committee on Food Habits (CFH), comprised of prominent social scientists, sought to understand the diverse cultural and social aspects of food consumption in order to incorporate the principles of good nutrition into American food habits. The CFH was charged with determining how best to improve Americans' nutrition and ensure the public's support of the war despite domestic food shortages. Through its research the Committee on Food Habits determined what Madison Avenue already knew: the most effective way to alter Americans' food habits, as well as persuade them to comply relatively cheerfully with the government's wartime food campaign, was to work through women.[27]

Historian George Roeder persuasively argues that an explicitly stated goal of the Roosevelt Administration from the onset of the war was "to encourage widespread participation in the war effort while minimizing concern over disruptions to the social order." Visual imagery played a key role in these efforts. While the wartime imagery often promoted harmony, depicting America as a melting pot with citizens from different backgrounds joining together for the good of the war effort, government officials and those in the private sector were nonetheless keenly aware of the sharp and divisive prejudices existing in the United States, and were very careful not to upset the status quo, especially regarding race. Roeder explains, "Imagery often served as a substitute for, or one barrier to, more substantive changes in the distribution of opportunity within the U.S. Few images sharply criticized existing discriminatory practices.... Virtually all images, whether questioning or affirming existing social relations, share one thing in common: they suggested that the point of view to which they gave visual support served the needs of the war effort."[28] For example, while one of Frank Capra's famous *Why We Fight* films carefully celebrated America's pluralistic family and the strength it derived from its diversity of immigrants, images of Americans of Japanese descent are nowhere to be seen. Moreover, the few brief shots of African-Americans clearly portray them as inferior. A minor *Life* magazine article noting blacks' contributions to the war effort generated swift and angry responses by whites, who accused the magazine of promoting racial strife and division.[29]

★ FOOD RATIONING AND THE ICON OF THE ORDERED MEAL

While President Roosevelt assured Americans they would have freedom from want, and Norman Rockwell and OWI illustrators provided reassuring images of abundance, nonetheless many Americans were anxious about possible food shortages. Mandatory rationing and price control, after all, were new to Americans. Two decades earlier, in the First World War, the government had instituted limited control over food production and distribution, but deliberately excluded compulsory food rationing for civilians. Instead, it encouraged the equitable distribution of meat and wheat, and placed limits on the production of alcoholic beverages, soft drinks, candy, and other "nonessential" uses of sugar. It asked Americans to observe voluntarily one meatless and one wheatless meal each day, to abstain fully from these foods one day each week, and to limit consumption of sugars and fats in general.[30]

World War II was a different war, with different imperatives. As the United States was thrust full force into the Second World War, the tremendous volume of goods required to wage war in both the Pacific and European theaters meant shortages of food as well as of steel, nylon, tin, wool, cotton, and soap—even with the unprecedented production levels of U.S. factories and farms. With demand exceeding supply, government officials immediately recognized the need for rationing programs and price controls, especially for food, to offset spiraling inflation, undermine black markets, and ameliorate the inequitable distribution of goods. When the government, through its Office of Price Administration (OPA), instituted ten major rationing programs, most Americans were willing to comply with the measures; American business and agriculture complied more reluctantly. Tires were the first items to be rationed, and other essential items followed: sugar, coffee, shoes, gasoline, butter and other fats, canned goods, and red meat.[31] Theoretically, rationing accompanied by price control would do two things. First, it would help combat the high inflation that was sure to come with low unemployment, higher pay, and too few places consumers could spend their cash. Price controls and rationing would keep prices down, allowing all, not just the wealthy, to afford food that otherwise could command exorbitant prices. Rationing would ensure a more equitable allocation of scarce resources. The U.S. government needed all its citizens, rich and poor alike, to support the war effort, and Americans with pantries and bellies filled democratically and equitably were more likely to do so.

While sugar and eventually coffee were rationed according to the stamp method, under which consumers would relinquish a single stamp to purchase five pounds every few weeks, the government introduced a more complicated point system for rationing meat and processed foods.[32] The point system maintained government control over rationing, but at the same time allowed the consumer a reasonable amount of control over her family's diet.[33] The OPA issued each person monthly five blue and six red stamps worth ten points each, a total of fifty blue points for processed foods and sixty red points for meats, fats, and some dairy products, to spend on rationed items.[34] Each item, canned pineapple or pork chops, for instance, was assigned a point value determined by both availability and consumer demand. The point values were periodically reevaluated and changed accordingly. For instance, in 1943 the OPA lowered the point value of peaches to encourage increased consumption of that summer's bumper crop of the fruit. With such a system a consumer could choose to spend some of her family's points on more desired or scarcer items with high point values, such as beefsteak, knowing that she would have fewer points left over that month to buy other meats and fats. And since points had indefinite expiration dates, consumers could save up points over a period of time for a special occasion.

It is startling to realize how quickly the government dismantled rationing at the war's end, especially considering that in 1945 supplies were at their leanest. Most rationing restrictions were lifted the day after the Japanese surrendered in August 1945. The OPA terminated the rationing of meat and fats several months later in November, though shortages would continue for months. Sugar rationing, by contrast, was the only type of food control that existed until well after the war.[35]

While many American citizens, and most in business and agriculture, celebrated the cessation of mandatory rationing, others viewed the abrupt and speedy dismantling more soberly. With food shortages and famine across much of the world, many believed the government had prematurely ceased rationing.[36]

Evidence suggests that while wartime food rationing had a significant psychological impact on Americans, their eating habits and the structure of their meals did not change significantly.[37] In a May 1943 opinion poll, almost two-thirds said their meals were no different since extensive rationing had gone into effect; three-fourths indicated the size of their meals had remained the same. In 1944, 90 percent of women felt rationing provided all the meat they and their families needed. Seventy-five percent felt sugar rations were adequate. More than one-third of Americans could not use up their allotment of canned-goods stamps before they expired. Although Americans could not get as many choice cuts of red meat as before the war, they did have other, less-desired cuts to choose from, as well as unrationed but more limited supplies of chicken, fish, eggs, and cheese. Moreover, while quantity remained fairly consistent, the quality of foods Americans consumed during wartime declined only moderately.[38] There is compelling evidence that the wartime diet of many Americans, including those with low incomes, increased both in quality and quantity.[39]

What clearly changed, however, was Americans' *perception* about food and its abundance during wartime, a perception that in the realm of politics and symbols often substituted for reality. Americans worried that food rationing combined with tight domestic supplies might lead to severe food shortages and hence inadequate nutrition. In a February 1942 poll, 82 percent agreed that the government should have the right to instigate rationing as it saw shortages developing. To a similar poll asking: "Do you think we ought to start right now to ration all materials in which shortages may develop, or do you think we ought to wait until there really is a shortage?" 73 percent of respondents said "Ration right now." In response to another poll's question "What worries you most [at the present time]?"

the answer "Nourishment, food" came in third behind "clothes, shoes" and "every-day requirements."[40] The perception of shortages added to the anxiety already created by the war's impact on society in general, and did in fact help create shortages by spurring the hoarding of coffee, sugar, and red meat; when word came of a new shipment of coffee at the local grocer's, people rushed to snap up all they could buy. Moreover, many wondered with government-mandated rationing and domestic shortages affecting the food they consumed everyday, whether some of their most important rituals and habits would be altered as well.

The structure of any meal includes such elements as which foods are served and how they are prepared, where one sits, who is served first, who gets to eat what. Mealtime rituals and patterns, such as the "alpha male" sitting at the head of the table or the housekeeper eating her dinner in the kitchen, often designate a person's place in a larger society and maintain and mediate the social hierarchy among different groups of people. As cultural historian John Kasson has explained, the "civility" of the upper and middle classes—their assumptions about culture and about their rightful place as guardians of society—depends in part on the existence of an underclass designated to perform such activities as cooking and serving meals. In times of uncertainty and chaos, the middle and upper classes, in particular, accord extra importance to ritualistic social patterns, especially those surrounding food. Adhering to and even accentuating such rituals help assuage their growing uncertainty about society and their place in it, particularly if that place is threatened by social instability. Thus, these rituals often become more prominent and rigid during times of social and economic transition, such as nineteenth-century industrialization and immigration and, as I argue, the Second World War.[41] During wartime, the disruption of familiar and ritualistic meal patterns coupled with the resignation of those, such as black women, "assigned" the duties of domestic caretakers, compounded feelings of cultural instability for many white middle- and upper-class Americans.

Since the government needed to ration the U.S. civilian food supply for the duration, officials also needed to make Americans feel there was plenty of food available during wartime. Part of this crucial psychic security had arguably as much to do with the rituals and structure of family meals as it did with nutrients and calories. Anthropologist Carl Guthe, chair of the Committee on Food Habits, astutely observed:

> The home management of meals symbolizes family solidarity. The variety and quantity of food symbolizes economic status. Table manners symbolize social status.... In food consumption, as in other aspects of our society, symbolic values, sanctions, and taboos are very real social forces which, however, are not based upon scientific fact or logical reasoning. They are the result of traditions and customs of long standing which are accepted without conscious evaluation by the majority of the members of our society.[42]

"It is a well-known principle," Guthe went on, "that when any force threatens the equilibrium of well-established social values, the response is an emotional one, in defense of deep-seated, almost subconscious motivations." Altering the way people ate, Guthe suggested, even presenting the possibility of such change, might weaken a whole host of other cultural beliefs and practices, threatening family stability, parental control, even loss of community, and commitment to the war. Americans' fears of shortages, and the actual reduced availability of certain high-status foods, made it more important than ever to portray meals in idealized terms. This was particularly true of dinner, the most symbolic and ritualized of the three daily meals.[43] The iconographic ordered meal of a large cut of red meat with accompanying smaller servings of vegetables was held up in the government-sponsored media as an ideal connoting the stability, familiarity, and abundance Americans had long believed their country symbolized.

Cultural anthropologists and others have explored the ordered meal. Mary Douglas describes this standard dinner as an "A + 2B" meal: a larger portion of a higher-status food, usually meat but sometimes eggs or cheese, with two complementary foods served in smaller quantities, most often breads and vegetables.[44] While it is of British origin, Douglas's "A + 2B" structure of cuisine—meats and vegetables cooked and served distinctly, instead of mixed together in a soup or a casserole, for instance—can also be identified as peculiarly "American." Indeed, until recently middle America has been prejudiced against "mixed" or spicy foods. One-pot soups and stews, and anything containing garlic or chili pepper, were reminiscent of peasant status. In earlier years Americans' prevailing notions about such foods were that they were harder to digest and contained fewer nutrients than the same foods separated on a plate.[45] Higher-status food such as meat and vegetables prepared and served separately seemed more proper, more appealing, and more respectable to most Americans, especially the middle classes, who were more anxious about their status and the structure of their meals than those below (or above) them on the socioeconomic scale. Thus meals are more than just ingesting needed nutrients. Meals necessitate, as Sidney Mintz has observed, "a search for consensus [and] compromise through attending to the needs of others."[46] A family eating food from the same communal bowl demands great cooperation and, in fact, may be an influence on (or reflection of) larger family dynamics; a household's ability to distribute food equally and in a congenial manner may indicate the state of their relationship in general.[47] Meals require coordination, interaction, and cooperation among family members or others sitting down together.

It follows, then, that the practice of ordered meals is one largely circumscribed by class, since on the whole the middle class, and people aspiring to be "middle class," according to Pierre Bourdieu, are more concerned with appearance, respectability, and decorum than is the working class. Bourdieu has explained that "the style of a meal people offer is a good indication of the image they wish to give or avoid giving to others." For the middle and professional classes, according to Bourdieu, form is perhaps more important than content, and dinner is the most symbolic and important because of its highly structured form.[48] Middle-class Americans in the mid–twentieth century had internalized such notions. These understood, if not consciously articulated, rules gained added meaning during the war, when society seemed to function precariously and Americans sought a sense of control and order.[49]

During the Second World War, pamphlets, posters, newsreels, advertisements, and radio programs depicted the icon of the ordered meal, but the images contrasted sharply with the government's calls for Americans to reduce their consumption of choice cuts of meat.[50] The government, in a booklet sent to American journalists, advised, "Consumers should be told when they 'eat out' in restaurants, hotels, etc., to cooperate with the new meat rationing program by voluntarily accepting a smaller serving of meat than they've been accustomed to." A magazine article, "Variety Meats: They Are Good, Abundant, Highly Nutritious," berated those Americans who begrudged G.I. Joe his hefty allotment of choice red meat: "The steak, chops, and roasts which have been standard fare on most tables are now being served to the men in uniform at home and abroad. . . . The army does not want the 'variety meats' because they spoil easily, take time to prepare and the men don't like them. These objections, valid for the Army, make no sense when cited by civilians."[51]

Thus, government messages were somewhat at odds with each other: some told Americans to downscale their accustomed meals, while others told them that an abundant meal with a huge cut of meat as the centerpiece still symbolized the American way of life. In reality, food rationing compelled women to serve many meatless and one-pot meals. To counter the notion that such meals were inferior, nutritionists and writers did their best to infuse "non-A + 2B" meals with the same kinds of symbolic connotations of security, love, and abundance that the "A + 2B" meal contained. For example, Lola Wyman, in her 1943 cookbook *Better Meals in Wartime*, identified the sections on soups as "specifically planned for the busy housewife, the employed woman, or the woman who gives much of her time to war activities."[52] Wyman urged women to go back to one-pot soups and stews, even though the busy wartime woman would have to make them from scratch. Serving such a homemade meal, Wyman explained, would harken back to the old-fashioned one-pot meal, providing a warm and comforting (though it is implied, perhaps inferior) substitute for the idealized meat-and-potatoes dinner. Similarly, radio spots, frequently written by the Office of War Information, attempted to promote the virtues of a "non-A + 2B" meal. In one, listeners heard a young girl tell of the "delicious soybean casserole" she was serving for supper. "Tonight's my night to get supper, cause Mom's doing war work," she cheerily announces.[53] The government's attempt to infuse dishes such as soybean casserole with the same meanings as a meat-and-vegetable dinner were feeble and ineffective. Efforts to change the public's negative perception of non-meat-based meals did not work, as numerous studies conducted by the Committee on Food Habits revealed. Moreover, messages promoting meat substitutes paled next to the plethora of posters, advertisements, films, and pamphlets the public witnessed regularly featuring reassuring images of the meat-dominated ordered meal.[54]

★ NUTRITION AND ORDERED MEALS

The promotion of soybean casseroles and other curiously "non-American" dishes was not accidental, but part of the government's effort to improve Americans' nutrition. After all, a total war required a healthy and strong population at home as well as on the battlefront. Americans by World War II were moderately familiar with principles of nutrition. For several decades home economists had emphasized proper nutrition and eating habits, while the Great War and after spurred the "Newer Nutrition," discovery of vitamins, and emphasis on eating a diversity of foods to attain optimum health.[55] But most Americans still knew little about specific components of good nutrition. In 1941, for instance, 84 percent of those polled could not explain the difference between a vitamin and a calorie.[56] It was during the war that the National Research Council's Food and Nutrition Board first established minimum daily requirements and guidelines for good eating.[57] To translate these guidelines into a compelling and eye-catching symbol for the public, the government designed what they called the Basic Seven food groups. Although nutritionists constructed the Basic Seven from "hard" scientific evidence, in retrospect it is clear that this organizing principle was determined as much by contemporary cultural norms as by objective science.

The Basic Seven—a forerunner of the more recent four food groups and the 1992 "pyramid" guide to nutritious eating—outlined the different foods Americans should eat daily for optimum health.[58] They consisted of

1. Green and yellow vegetables
2. Oranges, tomatoes, and grapefruit
3. Potatoes and other vegetables and fruits
4. Milk and milk products
5. Meat, poultry, fish, or eggs
6. Bread, flour, and cereals
7. Butter and fortified margarine[59]

Government officials regarded the Basic Seven as a way housewives could learn about proper nutrition without having to know much about specific nutrients. Vitamin C was the dominant vitamin in the second group, for example, and foods high in the B vitamins were in group six. Those consuming foods from each group every day, Americans were told, would receive all the necessary nutrients. The Basic Seven accurately assessed the need for different vitamins but gave no clues about the amounts of fat, for instance, one should consume daily, primarily because scientists were not yet aware of the dangers of excessive amounts of fat and salt in people's diets. That butter had a category of its own, for instance, is telling.[60]

The Basic Seven food groups were conceived as the building blocks of the ordered meal, and the graphics representing the seven categories connoted the familiar wartime notions of strength and order. The icon around which the Basic Seven food groups were arranged was the prototypic American family seen so often in government publications and private advertising: father, mother, older boy, younger girl, and above them the slogan, "U.S. Needs US Strong."[61] Unlike other government wartime graphics the Basic Seven icon was aimed at working-class Americans. In marked contrast to advertising's usual upper-middle-class depictions of Americans, in use at least since the 1920s, Father is dressed in work clothes rather than the usual business suit; Mother's dress and shoes are plain and sensible, as are the children's. Officials knew that the higher a family's income and education, the better their health. By October 1942, still early in the war, most Americans had heard radio programs about nutrition "telling people how to eat to keep healthy and that sort of thing." The Basic Seven was a familiar part of the national nutrition campaign, and by January 1944 almost half of those surveyed had heard of the Basic Seven. "Now—the story of nutrition is in the movies!" announced Walt Disney Productions, which produced a movie for the USDA about the Basic Seven titled, "Something You Didn't Eat."[62]

Along with the iconographic American Family, there was another element inextricably tied to the Basic Seven in building good nutrition: women. It was a woman's duty as preparer and server of family meals to account for her family's nutrition. Mildred Lager, in her cookbook *The Useful Soybean*, makes clear who was to cook and serve Basic Seven meals.

> One blessing that has come out of the war is that awakening to the fact that what we eat does make a difference.... We are realizing more and more that the cook holds the health of the family in her hands. It is, therefore, the duty of every mother, housekeeper, and cook to know the fundamental facts of nutrition and to apply these facts to maintaining her family's health whether they know it or not.... The government nutrition program, the rule of the seven basic foods, is beginning to bring results.[63]

★ WOMEN AS MEAL SERVERS

An "ordered" meal practically necessitates some kind of stable household organiza-tion. Someone (or ones) must orchestrate the meal: plan, shop for, and cook the food. In nearly all cultures, it is women who are charged with attending to these requirements.[64] As the war progressed, however, cooking became more difficult and time-consuming. Those women who took on war jobs were still required to cook for their families; many women used to having their housekeepers prepare the meals were now faced with doing it all themselves. At the same time food shortages and rationing made it harder to prepare the accustomed "A + 2B" meals. But, writer Margaret Mills advised women in her cookbook, *Cooking on a Ration: Food Is Still Fun*, "In this troubled universe it's more than ever important to make mealtime loom up as a little island of serenity and contentment . . . it can be done—but it takes wit and wisdom."[65]

Since the nineteenth century in the United States, social and emotional mes-sages concerning status, value, and a woman's love and nurturance for her family have been implicit in the act of cooking and serving meals, and the war accentuated these gendered messages.[66] Government officials and social scientists during the war were concerned that not only the physical, but the emotional well-being of the American family would suffer with so many women working in paid employment. Without women to produce organized meals, it seemed, there would be little chance of maintaining mealtime for family communion. A Committee on Food Habits memo warned of destructive consequences to the nuclear family if, for instance, an emer-gency evacuation forced communal dining:

> Unless care is taken to make the meal a family meal, the cafeteria situation may con-tribute to the breakdown of family ties. If father, mother, and children are to eat in a cafe-teria, small tables, family tickets, adequate allowance for young children, should all be made. Otherwise, the children, assured of meals, may form gangs and break away from parental control which is no longer reinforced by the ritual of family meals.[67]

Ironically, the government forced these exact disruptions on Americans of Japanese descent by "relocating" them from their homes to the communal barracks of intern-ment camps. These people, who were not provided small tables and family tickets, found their family lives profoundly disrupted, including mealtime rituals and social-ization, as they dined in communal dining halls on food prepared in the barracks kitchen.[68]

It seemed not to occur to those writing about mealtime and food habits during the war to recommend that Father help with meal preparation, since that would be yet one more disruption of gender roles and family dynamics. However, there was plenty of advice for women on how to cope with the double duty of war work and housework, and still get in what the next generation would term "quality time" with their children. The main way to do this was through meals. A wartime child-care book for working mothers suggested, "Let the children have their main meal at night with you. In this way you can make sure they are getting a balanced diet. . . . At the same time you will have an opportunity to foster that feeling of family unity which is so important to a child's happiness."[69] The Office of War Information, in its campaign to conserve food and promote food rationing, effectively employed the ideal of women serving the ordered meal. Its propaganda maintained traditional gender roles with women as servers, enhancing the ordered meal's sense of familiarity and stability. A typical OWI cartoon showed a woman with four half-filled plates closing the refrigerator door and calling "Lunch! Everybody come eat what you left on your plates yesterday!"[70]

While mothers were the servers of the ordered meal, fathers were the presiders. The image of father as patriarch over the ordered meal further reinforced gender roles at a time when the war demanded their alteration. An OWI radio script, attempting to explain to the American public why so much food was being shipped overseas, used the metaphor of a family dividing up a meatloaf at dinner time. The image effectively rendered the ideal of the American ordered meal and the assumed gender-based hierarchy of needs it met. The father, as the voice of the text, explained:

> When you divide up a small meat loaf at the table you may give a great big piece to Johnny, who is on the basketball team, a reasonably large piece to yourself, a fair-sized piece to the Mrs., and a tiny one to three-year-old Suzy. That's about the way—on the basis of needs not wants—that the War Food Administration divides the U.S. food supply among the armed forces, civilians, Allies, and other "claimant" groups.... Only the WFA does it on a much bigger scale and calls it "allocations."[71]

Gender is clearly embedded into this illustration of distributing food during wartime according to "needs" (the soldiers, allies, those in formerly Axis-controlled countries) and "wants" (Americans wanting to maintain familiar prewar patterns of consumption). Father explains to listeners that he and Johnny need bigger pieces, the Mrs. and Suzy do not. Although the Mrs. (who is not given a name, only a stated relationship to the speaker) and Suzy may want bigger portions, under current circumstances they may not because the others "need" it more than they do: Johnny is a growing, active boy, and Father presumably needs more nutrients because he is bigger, or because his job requires him to be more active than the Mrs. and Suzy. While there is no question that Americans could afford to sacrifice some of their food supply to those in greater need, the text can be read to imply that when food is apportioned accordingly among family members—when family members assume their "proper" places—all is fair, everyone is content, society is stable. The script may not appear particularly unusual, since numerous societies around the world distribute food, especially high-status foods like meat, according to status and gender: important men get more meat than those less important; women get less than men.[72] However, while custom has dictated that men and boys receive larger portions of nutrient-rich red meat, actual biological evidence shows that the practice has harmful consequences for women and children. Although distributing portions of meat according to gender might seem logical given average differences in weight or (perhaps) activity level among men and women, numerous studies show that vitamin and protein needs for infants, children, and lactating and pregnant women are actually higher than those for adult men.[73] Thus, the ad's (and society's) gender-based hierarchy of assumptions about needs—"not wants," as the script explains—is a custom that physiologically is not well founded and is potentially destructive to the society at large.

"You're at the head of the table...but you have some hungry guests!" read a similar advertisement aimed clearly at men. While this ad illustrating overseas food distribution contains the same emphasis on gender hierarchy (the father once again presides over the table and is addressed by the narrator), the image is modified to represent the idea in a less-restrictive manner than the radio script. The illustration shows a soldier, a sailor, a marine, and in "traditional" dress a Russian, a Britisher, and a Mexican, help Father, Mother, Johnny, and Suzy consume the ordered meal.[74] Here the icon of the ordered meal connoting abundance and security is not restricted to the home front and the nuclear family but is extended to those abroad, illustrating the American commitment to feed others as part of defending its international community of "friends." In a gesture unusual in wartime rhetoric for its inclusive spirit, through the ordered meal the American Family is enlarged to include war allies, citizens of formerly occupied countries, and those generally in need.[75]

★ RACE AND THE PROBLEM OF ORDERED MEALS

Not only were messages about gender implicit in the icon of the ordered meal, but so were notions about race. As thousands of American blacks during the war emigrated from the rural South to northern cities in search of better opportunities, racial tensions increased among groups vying for the same scarce housing, as well as the same high-paying war work. Black women working as domestics saw in the war a great opportunity to quit their low-paying, often demeaning housekeeping jobs for higher-paying work with fewer, more regular hours. This too created racial tensions and anxieties, as white women complained how hard it was "to find good help these days" and grumbled about the higher wages they had to pay.[76] While blacks looked toward these economic and social changes with hope, many whites eyed the changes with trepidation. Many white women believed their cooks and maids were members of subversive "Eleanor Clubs," groups of black women led by the President's wife who supposedly disrupted the status quo by refusing to perform certain tasks for their white employers, or who demanded that after cooking their employer's family dinner, the white woman reciprocate by cooking dinner for the housekeeper's family. According to another rumor circulating among whites, black women on prearranged days conspired to "bump into" white women while shopping.[77] Some feared that if this "breakdown" of society continued after the war, the United States would be a much different place—precisely the scenario American blacks hoped for. A University of Pennsylvania sociologist declared that one of the greatest postwar challenges facing Americans was to lead women and blacks back into the realm of domesticity. "There is a sizeable group of household employees," Dr. J. H. S. Brossard wrote, "who since the outbreak of war have doffed their aprons to don overalls . . . it is in the public interest that they return to their former occupations." "American home life needs an efficient servant class," Brossard explained, "and this element in the population must have positions in domestic service if any program for their peacetime employment is to be realized."[78]

Part of whites' fears were exhibited in issues of food, primarily the cooking and serving of it. As Joan Jacobs Brumberg explains, "The question of who gathers and prepares food is a critical problem in gender [and race] politics . . . because the production, consumption and distribution of food always involves issues of power and cultural authority." Historian Phyllis Palmer put it another way: "Much of the feeling of greatness [of power] comes from being served."[79] Blacks held a subservient position to whites, and who served whom denoted this social hierarchy and was a powerful reminder of the distinct and unequal places each occupied. Natalie Joffe and Tomannie Walker, authors of a wartime report analyzing African-American food habits, reminded government officials, "The symbol of status involved [in the cooking, serving, and eating of food] is freighted with emotion."

> The fact that Negroes prepare food, serve it, and even feed it to Whites in some instances is thoroughly accepted, and food is not regarded as "contaminated." Nevertheless, throughout the South, and in many places in the North, the two groups may not sit together to eat. If a Negro is served, the dishes may be ostentatiously destroyed in his presence.[80]

During the war, then, when many blacks were challenging long-held racial prescriptions, the images (and realities) of blacks cooking and serving food powerfully reinforced existing racial hierarchies. For many whites, this was how an "ordered" society should be structured.

The federal government, needing every able-bodied person to participate in the war effort, was concerned about maintaining the loyalty and support of African-Americans. Officials realized blacks were angry and frustrated with their status as second-class citizens. Though the Office of War Information was careful in its publications to present African-Americans in a favorable light, and urged others to do the same, little progress was made in reducing racial prejudice and combating racial stereotypes during the war.[81] In the quest to mute racial stereotypes some affiliated with the government attempted to understand black women's complicated roles as family food providers and, if working as domestics, as food preparers and servers to another's family. Joffe and Walker's report discusses in detail the importance of black women as meal providers and servers. Not surprisingly, the study notes that providing family meals was just as important to a black woman as it was to a white woman. African-American women took less time to prepare their families' meals than did white housewives, primarily because so many worked as domestics and cooks in others' (white women's) homes. "Where there are many women who work long hours," the report described, "the mother makes some attempt to provide food for her children when she is away. Real anxiety is manifest if these arrangements fail."[82]

Stereotypical images of black women as "Aunt Jemima" or "Mammy," widely employed in the 1940s, particularly in the South, were in part an unconscious attempt to maintain the racial status quo. While these images portraying African-American women as large-bodied domestics and cooks had long existed, they took on added meaning as the number of available black domestics shrank considerably during the war.[83] Sociologist K. Sue Jewell describes how the mammy image of a well-fed, strong, humorous black woman functioned in the antebellum South to counter the accusation that slavery was harsh and exploitative. After the Civil War the mammy stereotype (along with the young seductress "Sapphire" image) was used to keep black women at a lower socioeconomic level. "It is tenable," Jewell argues, "that the cultural images of African American women were important to the economic order to keep African American women and others outside the economic mainstream.... [T]he economic motivation for images that define African American women as domestics, and consign them to perform menial tasks that others in society are reluctant and unwilling to perform, is significant as such images lead to societal perceptions and expectations."[84] At all times, Jewell explains, the mammy stereotype served to elevate the status of others, namely white women, by representing the antithesis of idealized white womanhood, whose characteristics included being small in size, pale, demure, dependent, and well groomed.

185

Many in the government, including the OWI, sought to dispel these kinds of stereotypes in part because doing so would help maintain African-Americans' loyalty and support for the war. Joffe and Walker's report cautioned against using these stereotypes when appealing to African-Americans. "No specific appeals to Negroes should be made on the basis of being Americans or winning the war," they warned.

> A very large number of Negroes have been disaffected.... There should not be pictures of the "Aunt Jemima" type, which means no bandana on the heads of women who are neither young nor slim. Women should be neat, prettily but not too brightly dressed, and in decent surroundings. When they are shown with Whites, they should not be in menial positions with reference to the Whites.[85]

In the South, however, the authors deemed equal representation as too radical and dangerous. Joffe and Walker went on to warn of regional differences regarding societal "order." "For use in the North, pictures of Whites and Negroes on equal social planes may be used, but in the South these might be omitted."

Cookbooks, most often artifacts of the middle class, can reveal elements of a culture's norms and habits, and numerous war-era cookbooks employed the mammy icon either on the cover or as an accompanying illustration. The mammy image in these cookbooks functioned to connote such positive characteristics as good, home-cooked food prepared and served with love, but the image is wrapped in decidedly inferior overtones, as Jewell argues, to maintain black women in subservient positions.[86] For example, on the front of the cookbook, *Kentucky Fare: A Recipe Book of Some of Kentucky's Mouth Watering Specialties*, a mammy stirs something in a big cast-iron pot over a wood fire while looking down the road at a big house, presumably the plantation owner's. While the introduction describes several countries' cuisines as forerunners of Kentucky fare, including the cooking of England, France, Spain, and even Native American Indians, it makes no mention of culinary traditions brought and maintained by slaves from Africa (like the mammy pictured on the front cover).[87] In Daisy Breaux's war-era cookbook, *Famous Recipes of a Famous Hostess*, Breaux invokes the pejorative image of the illiterate mammy who, although she cooked magnificently, was unable to follow recipes:

> In the deep South the good old Southern cooks, many of them not knowing how to read or write, and who cooked entirely by taste and instinct, when asked for the recipes of their delectable concoctions have given this proverbial reply: "Well, I jes takes a little pince ob dis, and a little dash ob dat til I gets de right tase, an' das all." But I am going to endeavor to give you the correct proportions of "this and that" to make otherwise dull dishes delicious.

Throughout the cookbook Breaux makes casual references to "Mom Hannah," "my old cook in Charleston," giving the distinct impression that most of these famous old Southern recipes were not Breaux's but her cook's. It did not occur to Breaux to give Mom Hannah any credit.[88]

War-era cookbooks also depicted scenes of African-Americans serving food, an act whose hierarchical connotations were more pronounced, perhaps, than were those of black women cooking. In her *New Orleans Recipes*, Mary Moore Bremer wrote about coffee:

> When first you open your eyes in the morning, if you are fortunate enough to see a kind brown face beaming down at you while she holds a tray on which is a small sized cup of

black coffee, you have started the day right. The Creoles say that this early cup lengthens the span of life.[89]

Bremer implies that not just coffee in bed, but coffee served by a beaming, kind, brown face, starts the day off right, psychologically as well as physiologically.

Black men as well as women were affected by stereotypes regarding food preparation and service.[90] For men of any color the occupation of chef, preferably in a fine restaurant, is regarded as an acceptable occupation. However, during World War II black men in the military were assigned to kitchen duty and other noncombatant positions in grossly disproportionate numbers, and deeply resented being put in this decidedly subordinate, and traditionally female, position.[91] An article in the Baltimore *Afro-American* newspaper illuminated this frustration. It described a black soldier's contempt at his white commanding officer's note congratulating the all-black-and-male kitchen crew. "[Y]ou are doing excellent work in our kitchen," the officer's note read, "we have not forgotten you boys in the kitchen." The *Afro-American* commented: "The language in which the [officer's] letter was couched is resented bitterly by many of the men on the post, some of whom are college graduates, already irked by their assignment to jobs as menials in spite of their educational qualifications."[92] Changes wrought by the war provided an opening for black men to protest uses of stereotypical images and nicknames. Nash Thompson of Baltimore successfully demanded that the offensive name "Rastus" be removed from under the image of the black chef on the Cream of Wheat box. "Rastus is Dead," declared the *Afro-American* triumphantly. It is interesting, however, that stereotypical images of African-Americans as mammies existed even in the *Afro-American*. For example, in 1942 the newspaper printed a cartoon sketch of a mammy, with the limerick underneath: "A cheerful old mammy named Hannah; Who'd lived eighty years in Savannah / Said—'Sho-nuff, I'll buy / Defense Bonds, 'cause I / Am in love with the Star Spangled Bannah!'" But by 1944 such caricatures, no doubt in response to growing black resentment of and action against their inferior status, had all but disappeared. Despite minor successes, both black men and women during the war resented their lack of options; the number of black women who left domestic work suggests that many women as well as men felt limited by the careers to which they were relegated, including that of cook, professional or domestic. A cartoon in the *Afro-American* illustrated, with biting irony, the fate of educated black women and their limited options for the future, revealing as much about restrictions by gender as by race. The two women in the cartoon are wearing graduation caps and gowns, as one says to the other: "Here I am graduating with the highest honors in the class, and I'll probably spend my life cooking for some dumb man."[93]

Faced with social upheaval at home as a result of the war, many middle- and upper-class white Americans (unconsciously or consciously) used food and the serving of food as a way of maintaining hierarchies of gender and race. Yet the war's collapse of the separate spheres at the level of lived experience produced a backlash of considerable proportion in the realm of cultural iconography. On the home front, the need to rearticulate the distinction between men's labor and women's work and to reassert the dominant role of the white family and the subordinate place of the black domestic, preserved the illusion that American middle-class identity could withstand the vicissitudes of global conflagration and emerge unchanged. Even as the war was forcing a second look at the existing dynamics of race and gender, the media and others presented images of what meals were supposed to be, and of who was to prepare and serve them. The images no doubt reassured those who benefited most from the preexisting hierarchies of gender and race. Not surprisingly, after World War II American society in many respects exhibited a sharp return to a prewar ordering of society, including patterns of consumption. As Americans resumed familiar food habits and rituals, postwar consumption of red meat rose sharply, and "A + 2B" meals dominated Americans' diets for decades. Just after the war, for instance, for most Americans the "perfect" meal was an elaborate version of "A + 2B," consisting of fruit or shrimp cocktail for an appetizer, vegetable soup or chicken broth, steak, mashed or french-fried potatoes, peas, vegetable salad, rolls and butter, with apple pie à la mode and coffee for dessert. Their second choice in meat was roast beef, and roast chicken was their third.[94] This resumption of eating habits reflects a larger desire to return to a prewar societal status quo, in which women would relinquish wartime jobs and return to full-time homemaking or more traditional (lower-paying) occupations. Many did so happily, but others felt the pain of the "problem that has no name," as Betty Friedan described middle-class white women's sense of malaise, leading eventually to the women's movement of the sixties and seventies. African-Americans, too, experienced postwar forms of discrimination and attempts to restore the prewar social hierarchy of race, but by then the germ of the Civil Rights Movement had taken root. The prewar "ordered" society of gender and race—with "everyone in place and a place for everyone," according to some people's estimation—would never permanently return.[95]

Finally, the metaphor of the ordered meal and its abundance neglected to acknowledge the existence of an American underclass, a group of "have-nots" in a land characterized by its "haves," who were a testament to poverty and malnutrition existing within the country's own borders. What the metaphor more accurately represented was that in general, through rationing, the United States had food enough (though not large quantities of the highest-status foods), not only to last the war but to feed people in other countries as well, although its domestic distribution did not necessarily reflect this situation. Norman Rockwell's *Freedom from Want* embodied prominent symbols of abundance, order, power, and, no less important, unity. All Americans, the image claimed, could take part in the American dream. All were strong and healthy enough, and the country's abundant resources would physically satisfy their hunger. At this time when a vision of unity and strength was so important to the war effort, it was a prescription the government promoted and one many Americans believed. But Rockwell's painting of Americans' greatest ordered meal did not hint at the reality of contemporary society. Rockwell did not feel a need to paint the black woman in the kitchen who had cooked the succulent feast. During this war waged to administer America's Four Freedoms to all parts of the world, many Americans were, literally and figuratively, barred from sitting at the table and partaking of the meal.

NOTES

1. Norman Rockwell, *Norman Rockwell: My Adventures as an Illustrator* (New York: Abrams, 1988); Arthur L. Guptill, *Norman Rockwell, Illustrator* (New York: Watson-Guptill Publications, 1946, 3d ed. 1970), p. 140.
2. Rockwell, p. 315. Rockwell himself never much liked *Freedom from Want*. Of the four scenes, his favorite was *Freedom of Speech*, which portrayed a young man speaking up in a citizens' town meeting.
3. Patricia Curran, *Grace Before Meals: Food Ritual and Body Discipline in Convent Culture* (Urbana and Chicago: University of Illinois Press, 1989), p. 101.
4. David M. Potter, *People of Plenty: Economic Abundance and the American Character* (Chicago: University of Chicago Press, 1954). While Potter's book is an important and relevant analysis of American culture, it has been criticized as neglecting to consider the fact that there has always been an American underclass who has not partaken of the fruits of U.S. abundance. See Giles Gunn, *The Culture of Criticism and the Criticism of Culture* (New York: Oxford University Press, 1987), p. 163.

5. For a discussion of U.S. farm production, see Walter W. Wilcox, *The Farmer in the Second World War* (Ames, Iowa: The Iowa State College Press, 1947). For a general discussion of the U.S. government's attempt to portray a unified home front through visual images, see George H. Roeder, Jr., *The Censored War: American Visual Experience during World War Two* (New Haven: Yale University Press, 1993), chap. 2.

6. Margaret Visser, *The Rituals of Dinner* (New York: Grove Weidenfield, 1991), pp. 133, 272, 274; Marjorie DeVault, *Feeding the Family: The Social Organization of Caring as Gendered Work* (Chicago: University of Chicago Press, 1991).

7. The most thorough study of women and work during the war is Ruth Milkman, *Gender at Work: The Dynamics of Job Segregation by Sex During World War II* (Urbana: University of Illinois Press, 1987). See also Karen Anderson, *Wartime Women: Sex Roles, Family Relations, and the Status of Women during World War II* (Westport, Conn.: Greenwood Press, 1981), esp. chaps. 1 and 2; Maureen Honey, *Creating Rosie the Riveter: Class, Gender and Propaganda during World War II* (Amherst: University of Massachusetts Press, 1984). For a discussion of the important icon of Rosie the Riveter, see Melissa Dabakis, "Gendered Labor: Norman Rockwell's 'Rosie the Riveter' and the Discourses of Wartime Womanhood," in *Gender and American History since 1890*, ed. Barbara Melosh (New York: Routledge, 1993), pp. 182–204.

8. Books on the U.S. experience of World War II include: John M. Blum, *V was for Victory: Politics and American Culture during World War II* (New York: Harcourt Brace Jovanovich, 1976); David Brinkley, *Washington Goes to War* (New York: Ballantine Books, 1988); Richard Lingeman, *Don't You Know There's a War On?: The American Homefront, 1941–1945* (New York: G.P. Putnam's Sons, 1970); Susan Hartmann, *Home Front and Beyond: American Women in the 1940s* (Boston: Twayne, 1982); Neil Wynn, *The Afro-American and the Second World War* (New York: Holmes and Meier, 1976); Russell Buchanan, *Black Americans in World War II* (Santa Barbara: Clio Books, 1977).

9. Blum, *V was for Victory*, p. 333; "Fact Sheet: World War II" (prepared by the 50th Anniversary of World War II Commemoration Committee, HQDA, SACC: Pentagon, Room 3E524, Washington, D.C. 20310-0107); Richard Polenberg, *War and Society: The United States, 1941–45* (Philadelphia: J. B. Lippincott Company, 1972), p. 132.

10. Anderson, *Wartime Women*, p. 4; Chester W. Gregory, *Women in Defense Work during World War II* (New York: Exposition Press, 1974), p. 3; Eleanor F. Straub, "United States Government Policy toward Civilian Women during World War II," *Prologue* 5, 4 (Winter 1973): 242–43.

11. Wynn, *The Afro-American*, p. 132.

12. Polenberg, *War and Society*, pp. 105–23.

13. See Amy Bentley, "Wages of War: The Shifting Landscape of Race and Gender in World War II Baltimore," *Maryland Historical Magazine* 88 (Winter 1993): 420–43.

14. Anderson, *Wartime Women*, pp. 34, 172.

15. Polenberg, *War and Society*, p. 239.

16. Hadley Cantril, ed., *Public Opinion, 1935–1946*, prepared by Mildred Strunk (Princeton: Princeton University Press, 1951), p. 1121.

17. Ibid., p. 510; Roeder, *The Censored War*, p. 122.

18. Roeder, *The Censored War*, p. 45.

19. Cantril, *Public Opinion*, p. 141. The responses were broken down into the revealing categories of "Prosperous," "Upper middle," "Lower middle," "Poor," and "Negro."

20. Elaine Tyler May, *Homeward Bound: American Families in the Cold War Era* (New York: Basic Books, 1988); Anderson, *Wartime Women*, p. 91.

21. Cantril, *Public Opinion*, pp. 1045–46, 1051. See also James B. Gilbert, *Cycles of Outrage: America's Reaction to the Juvenile Delinquent in the 1950s* (New York: Oxford University Press, 1986).

22. Cantril, *Public Opinion*, pp. 1067–68.

23. Polenberg, *War and Society*, chap. 2; Sandra C. Taylor et al., *Japanese Americans: From Relocation to Redress* (Salt Lake City: University of Utah Press, 1986).

24. Cantril, *Public Opinion*, pp. 1119–20.

25. Allen M. Winkler, *The Politics of Propaganda: The Office of War Information, 1942–45* (New Haven: Yale University Press, 1978); Brett J. Gary, "American Liberalism and the Problem of Propaganda: Scholars, Lawyers, and the War on Words, 1919–1945" (Ph.D. diss., University of Pennsylvania, 1992); Mark H. Leff, "The Politics of Sacrifice on the American Home Front in World War II," *The Journal of American History* 77, 4 (March 1991): 1296–1318; Garth Jowett, *Film: The Democratic Art* (Boston: Little, Brown, 1976).

26. Roeder, *The Censored War*, p. 55.

27. For more discussion of the Committee of Food Habits, see Rebecca Spang, "The Cultural Habits of a Food Committee," *Food and Foodways* 2 (1988): 359–91; Carleton Mabee, "Margaret Mead and Behavioral Scientists in World War II: Problems in Responsibility, Truth and Effectiveness," *Journal of the History of the Behavioral Sciences* 23 (January 1987): 3–13. See also chapter 2 of my "Eating for Victory: United States Food Rationing and the Politics of Domesticity during World War II" (Ph.D. diss., University of Pennsylvania, 1992).

28. Roeder, *The Censored War*, pp. 44, 64.

29. Frank Capra, *Why We Fight: America Enters the War* (1944); Roeder, *The Censored War*, p. 45.

30. William Clinton Mullendore, *History of the United States Food Administration, 1917–1919*, with an introduction by Herbert Hoover (Palo Alto: Stanford University Press, 1941), p. 12. The closest the government came to rationing any food during World War I was issuing certificates limiting sugar purchases to all industrial manufacturers, wholesale producers, and retailers—everyone, in fact, except domestic consumers. The retailer was then urged to limit voluntarily sugar sold to customers to two pounds at a time for city dwellers, and five for those in rural areas. Ibid., pp. 112–114. It is interesting to compare this with the government's priority for distributing sugar during World War II, where industrial and institutional users received much more generous allotments.

31. Relatively little has been written about U.S. rationing. For the most complete account of U.S. rationing see Harvey C. Mansfield, *A Short History of OPA* (Washington, D.C.: U.S. Government Printing Office, 1947). See

189

also Ayers Brinser, "A History of the Administration of Rationing in the United States during the Second World War" (Ph.D. diss., Harvard University, 1951).

32. At first sugar and coffee were rationed at one pound per stamp. The amount was then raised to five pounds per stamp. In February 1943 Ration Book Number 2 was issued for the rationing of meat, fats, and canned and frozen foods. Also issued through the public schools, Book 2 was bigger and more elaborate than Book 1. Mansfield, *Short History*, p. 173. People had to bring Book 1 in order to qualify for the second. Coffee stamps were taken out of the books of children under the age of fifteen, and as with sugar, Book 2 was "tailored" to the number of canned goods one already had on hand to prevent hoarding, though many simply lied to keep the extra stamps.

33. As an OPA pamphlet explained, "The individual consumer—usually the housewife—obtains her rationed foods by giving up stamps from the ration books which have been issued to each member of the family," taking for granted that it would be women who would do most of the point juggling.

34. "Change" (in case the point value of an item did not equal a multiple of ten) was made in red and blue tokens, which could be used even after the specific stamps had expired. A system of "ration banking" was worked out to simplify the system for the local boards. Citizens registered at local boards for ration "currency" (stamps and tokens), which they then spent at merchants' establishments (giving the retailer both money and ration currency). The merchants then deposited the currency in "bank accounts" at their local banks and wrote "checks" to rationing officials for their own allotments of the rationed goods, whether sugar, processed foods, meats and fats, coffee, gasoline, fuel oil, or shoes. "The Mechanics of Consumer Rationing," RG 188, Box 659, File: "Education." National Archives, Washington, D.C. (NA).

35. The extended control served to ensure that no shortages ensued for Americans. Briefly, controls remained because it was in business's best interest. Mansfield, *Short History*, pp. 193–96. Rent controls also remained in place until 1948.

36. For more on postwar famine and U.S. food rationing, see Amy L. Bentley, "Uneasy Sacrifice: The Politics of United States Famine Relief, 1945–1948," *Agriculture and Human Values* 11, 4 (Fall 1994): 4–18.

37. This is not to say that food rationing during World War II was not needed; on the contrary, as up to 50 percent of some foodstuffs were being sent overseas to the military and allies, mandatory food rationing assured Americans that they would get their fair share of the nation's food supply. See Bentley, "Eating for Victory," chaps. 1 and 7; Mansfield, *Short History*; Brinser, "History of . . . Rationing."

38. Cantril, *Public Opinion*, pp. 166–67, 436, 731, 835. Three-fifths of those questioned said their meals were of the same quality, almost 10 percent said they were better in quality, but 31 percent thought their meals were poorer in quality since rationing began. In December 1943, 20 percent said they were getting less nourishment from their meals. Another poll indicated that 20 percent were eating smaller meals. Nineteen percent had lost weight since food rationing began, but at the same time 44 percent indicated that their health would be better if they ate less anyway. Twenty-five percent thought their health would be the same, 27 percent thought it would be worse. *The Gallup Poll: Public Opinion, Volume I, 1935–1948* (New York: Random House, 1973), pp. 395, 569. Of course, it is not known if the people who thought their health would be better if they ate less were the same ones who noted that they were eating smaller meals with rationing. Although polls indicated that food rationing had not significantly changed either the quantity of food consumed or the quality of meals for almost two-thirds of Americans, it is important to use caution when relying on results of opinion polls. Since pollsters questioned only those who had telephones, the results may be skewed in favor of those with a steadier income. Certainly poorer people, those with the greatest chance of suffering from a lack of food during the war, were the most likely to be excluded from such opinion polls. Even so, the results still support the claim that most Americans' eating habits did not change markedly with the advent of rationing.

39. Bentley, "Eating for Victory," chaps. 5 and 7.

40. Cantril, *Public Opinion*, pp. 729, 1189.

41. John F. Kasson, "Rituals of Dining: Table Manners in Victorian America," in *Dining in America, 1850–1900*, ed. Kathryn Grover (Amherst: University of Massachusetts Press, 1987), pp. 134, 139. See also Visser, *Rituals of Dinner*, pp. 21–22, 24; Pierre Bourdieu, *Distinction: A Social Critique of the Judgement of Taste* (London: Routledge & Kegan Paul, 1984); Mary Douglas, "Deciphering a Meal," *Daedalus* 101, 1 (Winter 1972): 61–81.

42. Carl Futhe, "Comments on the National Nutrition Campaign," 1 October 1942 (1–2). Records of the Committee on Food Habits (CFH), Archives of the National Research Council, Division of Anthropology and Sociology, National Academy of Sciences, Washington, D.C., Fol. CFH 1942 Reports: General. See also, James H. S. Brossard, "Family Table Talk—An Area for Sociological Study," *American Sociological Review* 8 (1943): 295–301; and Spang, "Cultural Habits," pp. 359–91.

43. Bourdieu, *Distinction*, p. 196.

44. Douglas, "Deciphering a Meal," p. 69. In her study of British food habits, Douglas found "with an entirely monophagous and unstructured diet we would have been surprised to find a structured family life." See Mary Douglas, "Food as a System of Communication," *In the Active Voice* (London: Routledge & Kegan Paul, 1982), pp. 85–86.

45. Harvey Levenstein, "The American Response to Italian Food, 1880–1930," *Food and Foodways* 1 (June 1986): 38–39 (reprinted in this volume); Octavio Paz, "Eroticism and Gastrosophy," *Daedalus* 101, 4 (Fall 1972): 74–75; see also Norbert Elias, *The Civilizing Process*, trans. Edmund Jephcott (New York: Urizen Books, 1978).

46. Sidney Mintz, *Sweetness and Power: The Place of Sugar in Modern History* (New York: Viking, 1985), p. 201.

47. Susan Strasser, *Never Done: The History of American Housework* (New York: Pantheon, 1982), p. 296. Serving dishes placed on the table, in comparison, allow each person to take the desired (though still socially determined) portion to his or her individual plate or bowl. See Amy Shuman, "The Rhetoric of Portions," *Western Folklore* 40, 1 (1981): 72–80. Dining in a restaurant, by contrast, where each person orders an individual preference, requires even less cooperation.

48. Bourdieu, *Distinction*, pp. 79, 196, 199. In contrast, the working class, Bourdieu argues, focuses on content more than form.

49. The Army too was well aware of the importance of ordered meals as promoting good morale, and listed many tips on how to serve attractive meals. *The Army Cookbook* gave this advice: "Under the direction of the mess sergeant, the senior cook on duty is responsible for the service of meals; that is, that foods are ready at the proper time and placed on serving dishes in an attractive manner. It is of little use to exercise great care in cooking a food if it is to be sent to the mess table presenting an unattractive appearance. On the other hand, the plainest foods become appealing when served in an attractive manner." *The Army Cook technical manual* (Washington, D.C.: War Department, 24 April 1942), in collections of Schlesinger Library, Radcliffe College, Cambridge, Mass.

50. Examples of meals portrayed with meat as the centerpiece are found in *A Call to Action* and *We Waste Not the Meat*, National Archieves, Suitland, Md. (NA-S), RG 208, Entry 66, Box 5, Fol. FFFF general.

51. "The Campaign Against Black Markets in Meats," prepared by the USDA, in cooperation with the OPA and OWI, 26 April 1943, Government Documents, University of Colorado at Boulder; "Variety Meats: They Are Good, Abundant, Highly Nutritious" (from unidentified magazine), MS 2010, Box 71, File: CMC "F" Scrapbook. Maryland Historical Society, Baltimore, Md. (MHS).

52. Lola Wyman, *Better Meals in Wartime* (New York: Crown, 1943), p. 30.

53. One-minute dramatized announcement, "Food Fights for Freedom," for broadcast week of 17 January [1944], NA-S, RG 208, Entry 66, Box 6, Fol. Food Fights for Freedom—master file / Industrial Nutrition.

54. Kurt Lewin, "Forces behind Food Habits and Methods of Change," *The Problem of Changing Food Habits*, CFH, Bulletin 108 (Washington, D.C.: National Academy of Sciences, National Research Council, 1942), pp. 35–65; Patricia Woodward, "Attitudes toward the Use of Soybeans as Food." CFH, Fol. CFH Reports, General, 1943. See also Bentley, "Eating for Victory," chap. 2; William Graebner, "The Small Group and Democratic Social Engineering, 1900–1950," *Journal of Social Issues* 42 (1986): 137–54.

55. Several interesting studies of the development of principles of nutrition have been written, including Harvey Levenstein's *Revolution at the Table: The Transformation of the American Diet* (New York: Oxford University Press, 1988), especially chaps. 9–13.

56. *Gallup Poll*, p. 310. In a November 1941 USDA survey 61 percent correctly answered the question, "What foods are richest in the vitamins we need?" "Background material for 26–27 April 1942 meeting," CFH, Fol. Meetings, 1942.

57. Joan Dye Gussow and Paul R. Thomas, *The Nutrition Debate* (Palo Alto, Calif.: Bull Publishing Company, 1986), p. 67. See Bentley, "Eating for Victory," chap. 2 for a discussion of the Food and Nutrition Board.

58. "Uncle Sam's Groceries: How Dietary Recommendations Have Changed," *New York Times*, 3 May 1992.

59. *Victory Bulletin* (October 1943), p. 20.

60. More recent controversies over similar guidelines to proper eating give much evidence about the extent to which they were culturally influenced. The attempt to alter the "Four Food Groups," to de-emphasize meat and dairy products and emphasize fruits, grains, and vegetables, was defeated largely due to the lobbying of the meat and dairy industries. See "USDA Wilts under Pressure, Kills New Food-Group Pyramid," *San Francisco Chronicle*, 27 April 1991; "The $855,000 Pyramid," *Washington Post*, 28 April 1992. It has been since reinstated.

61. Roland Marchand, *Advertising the American Dream: Making Way for Modernity, 1920–1940* (Berkeley and Los Angeles: University of California Press, 1985), pp. 191–92.

62. "Provisional Plan of Action," 28 February 1941, CFH, Fol. Activities 1942–45; Frank G. Boudreau, "Social and Economic Implications of Freedom from Want of Food," *Proceedings of the American Philosophical Society* 87, 2 (16 August 1943): 131; Cantril, *Public Opinion*, pp. 166, 527; RG 208, Entry 66, Box 5, NA.

63. Mildred Lager, *The Useful Soybean: A Plus Factor in Modern Living* (New York: McGraw-Hill, 1945), p. 175.

64. Astri Riddervold and Andreas Riddervold, eds., *Food Conservation: Ethnological Studies* (London: Prospect Books, 1988); Thomas A. Adler, "Making Pancakes on Sunday: The Male Cook in Family Tradition," *Western Folklore* 40, 1 (January 1981): 45; Ruth Schwartz Cowan, *More Work for Mother: The Ironies of Household Technology from the Open Hearth to the Microwave* (New York: Basic Books, 1983), p. 213; Marvin Harris and Eric B. Ross, eds., *Food And Evolution: Toward a Theory of Human Food Habits* (Philadelphia: Temple University Press, 1987), p. 21.

65. Mills, *Cooking on a Ration: Food Is Still Fun* (New York: Houghton Mifflin, 1943), p. 4.

66. For the well-documented connection between food and nurturance see Cowan, *More Work for Mother*, chap. 4; Phyllis Palmer, *Domesticity and Dirt: Housewives and Domestic Servants in the United States, 1920–1945* (Philadelphia: Temple University Press, 1989), p. 23; DeVault, *Feeding the Family*, p. 79.

67. "The Relationship between Food Habits and Problems of Wartime Emergency Feeding" (May 1942), pp. 4–5, CFH. "This consideration applies to every type of wartime feeding, including provisions for feeding industrial workers where the mother is working," the report also stated.

68. Lecture given by Mr. Tom Masamori, 7 October 1993, Boulder, Colorado. Notes in my possession. See also Roger Daniels, *Concentration Camps: North American Japanese in the United States and Canada during World War II* (Malabar, Fla.: Kreiger Publishing Co., Inc., 1981). One can only speculate whether an intended goal of internment was disruption of the tight Japanese-American social order.

69. Milton J. E. Senn and Phyllis Kraft Newill, *All About Feeding Children* (Garden City, N.Y.: Doubleday and Co., 1946), p. 245.

70. Cartoons found in NA-S, RG 208, Entry 66, Box 7, Fol. FFFF.

71. NA-S, RG 208, Entry 66, Box 7, Fol. FFFF.

72. Eric Ross, "An Overview of Trends in Dietary Variation from Hunter-Gatherer to Modern Capitalist Societies," pp. 19–23, and Marvin Harris, "Foodways: Historical Overview and Theoretical Prolegomenon," p. 73, both in *Food and Evolution*, ed. Harris and Ross.

73. Anna Roosevelt explains: "It turns out that male adults may not need large and well-balanced ratios of amino acids . . . nor . . . vitamin intake . . . [T]he amount and quality of protein and vitamins in the diet does indeed matter very much for pregnant and lactating women, infants, and young children. The requirements of these

groups per unit weight are higher than those of adult men, but the ethnographic and archaeological record seems to show that these groups generally get less of their requirements than do adult men, possibly because of their lesser ability to secure nutrients in a context of scarcity." Anna Roosevelt, "The Evolution of Human Subsistence," in *Food and Evolution*, ed. Harris and Ross, p. 570. See also pp. 19–23, 73. Giving the largest amounts of protein to adult males and depriving women and children from adequate amounts (contributing to the higher mortality rates) in some societies acts as a population control. See also Amartya Sen and Martha Nussbaum, eds. *The Quality of Life* (New York: Oxford University Press, 1993).

74. NA-S, RG 208, Entry 66, Box 5, Fol. FFFF general.

75. Robert Westbrook, "Fighting for the American Family: Private Interests and Political Obligations in World War II," in *The Powers of Culture: Critical Essays in American History*, ed. Fox and Lears (Chicago: University of Chicago Press, 1993), p. 216.

76. Bentley, "Wages of War."

77. Patricia A. Turner, *I Heard It through the Grapevine: Rumor in African-American Culture* (Berkeley and Los Angeles: University of California Press, 1993), p. 44; Polenberg, *War and Society*, p. 110.

78. J. H. S. Brossard, "Family Problems of the Immediate Future," *Journal of Home Economics* 37, 7 (September 1945): 387.

79. Joan Jacobs Brumberg, "Feed Your Head," *Nation* (9 April 1990), p. 496; Palmer, *Domesticity and Dirt*, p. 159.

80. Natalie Joffe and Tomannie Thompson Walker, "Some Food Patterns in the U.S. and Their Relationship to Wartime Problems of Food and Nutrition" (1944), p. 24, CFH, Fol. CFH 1944 Reports: General.

81. John Hope Franklin, "Their War and Mine," *Journal of American History* 77, 2 (September 1990): 576–79; Neil A. Wynn, "Black Attitudes toward Participation in the American War Effort, 1941–45," *Afro-American Studies* 3 (1972): 13–19; Clayton R. Koppes and Gregory D. Black, *Hollywood Goes to War: How Politics, Profits, and Propaganda Shaped World War II Movies* (New York: Free Press, 1987); Winkler, *Politics of Propaganda*, pp. 56–57.

82. Joffe and Walker, "Some Food Patterns," pp. 11, 17. For descriptions of domestics' traditionally long hours see Palmer, *Domesticity and Dirt*, and David M. Katzman, *Seven Days a Week: Women and Domestic Service in Industrializing America* (New York: Oxford University Press, 1978).

83. K. Sue Jewell, *From Mammy to Miss America and Beyond: Cultural Images and the Shaping of U.S. Policy* (New York: Routledge, 1993), pp. 21, 24–25, 37–44; Trudier Harris, *From Mammies to Militants: Domestics in Black American Literature* (Philadelphia: Temple University Press, 1982), chap. 1; Marvelyne H. Styles, "Soul, Black Women and Food," in *A Woman's Conflict: The Special Relationship Between Women and Food*, ed. Jane Rachel Kaplan (Englewood Cliffs, N.J.: Prentice-Hall, Inc., 1980), pp. 164, 168; Bentley, "Wages of War," p. 14.

84. Jewell, *From Mammy to Miss America*, p. 56. See also, pp. 21–25, 37–44, 55.

85. Joffe and Walker, "Some Food Patterns," p. 74. Not until the 1970s was Quaker Oats' Aunt Jemima image changed on pancake boxes and syrup bottles. Her kerchief was replaced by a head band, her skin lightened, and her exaggerated grin replaced by a less prominent smile. In the late-1980s this image was further altered: her headband was removed and the hairstyle changed to an above-the-shoulder bob. Jewell, *From Mammy to Miss America*, p. 183.

86. Lynne Ireland, "The Compiled Cookbook as Foodways Autobiography," *Western Folklore* 40, 1 (January 1981): 107–14; Jewell, *From Mammy to Miss America*, pp. 55–56.

87. "We, who live in the United States, are fortunate to live in a country so rich in culinary heritages. The Indians, then the Spanish, English, German, Scandinavian and French settlers, and later immigrants from all parts of the world, have each contributed a share in making American food famous." Margaret M. Bridwell, *Kentucky Fare: A Recipe Book of Some of Kentucky's Mouth Watering Specialties* (1944), p. 1. For African contributions to American, particularly Southern, cuisine, see Charles Joyner, *Down by the Riverside* (Urbana: University of Illinois Press, 1984), chap. 3.

88. Daisy Breaux, *Famous Recipes of a Famous Hostess* (Washington, D.C.: Polytechnic Publishing Co., 1945), pp. 1, 49.

89. Mary Moore Bremer, *New Orleans Recipes* (New Orelans: Dorothea Forshee, P.O. Box 158, 1944, 10th ed.), p. 5.

90. In my survey of mainstream women's magazines during wartime, the very few portrayals of black men and women are as cooks, maids, butlers, and railroad porters.

91. Adler, "Making Pancakes," p. 46; Franklin, "Their War," pp. 576–79.

92. "Our Soldiers Resent Being Called 'Boys in Kitchen,'" Baltimore *Afro-American*, 14 October 1944.

93. Baltimore *Afro-American*, 22 April 1944; 21 March 1942; 22 July 1944.

94. *Gallup Poll*, p. 636. See Harvey Levenstein, *Paradox of Plenty: A Social History of Eating in Modern America* (New York: Oxford University Press, 1993), and Warren J. Belasco, *Appetite for Change: How the Counterculture Took on the Food Industry* (New York: Pantheon, 1989), for discussion of postwar American eating habits.

95. See William Chafe, *The American Women: Her Changing Social, Economic, and Political Roles, 1920–1970* (Westport, Conn.: Greenwood Press, 1981), p. 4; Anderson, *Wartime Women*; Hartmann, *The Home Front*; Harvard Sitkoff, *The Struggle for Black Equality, 1954–1980* (New York: Hill and Wang 1981); Richard Dalfiume, "Stirrings of Revolt," in *Segregation Era, 1863–1954*, ed. Allen Weinstein and F. O. Gatell (New York: Oxford University Press, 1970), pp. 235–47.

THE PASSOVER SEDER:
RITUAL DYNAMICS, FOODWAYS,
AND FAMILY FOLKLORE

SHARON R. SHERMAN

14

Food, family, and ethnic identity are at the core of the Passover ritual. Despite a lengthy and strong tradition governing the formal observance of Passover, the meaning given to each of these elements changes with each enactment, building on earlier interpretations (both "official" and family-generated ones). Such family folklore thus appears to be not merely "a creative expression of a common past"[1] but rather the reflection of a constantly evolving process. To understand this process better and to appreciate more fully the nature of my family's celebration of Passover, I studied the behaviors of members of my own extended Gershenowitz family during two Passover Seders held in Toronto by Stan and Brenda Kates.[2] Many of the events described in this chapter relate to that festive occasion, but my study of changes in one family's Seder has continued to evolve, along with my own participation in that family's Seders, in subsequent years. By their levels of participation in the family Seder, participants define their relationships within the family. The meanings of those relationships arise then from the rich mix of the generations within the family, the varying intensities of their involvement in Judaism, the differing sorts of family membership, as well as their experiences with previous Seders.

One might assume that a "common past" does exist for the Gershenowitz family as for other Jews, and, indeed, most Jews see the Passover event as a symbol for the Jewish people or Jewish "family" as a whole.[3] One of the rituals connected with the yearly cycle of seasons, Passover creates a sense of *communitas* with Jews throughout time—from the Exodus upon which it is based to the present. Added to this diachronic dimension, Jews sense the synchronic simultaneous celebration of the event with all Jews at one specific time of the year throughout the world. On a more intimate level, Jews mark the celebration as one which has symbolic meanings acquired within individual families.

Since "Seder" means "order," the Haggadah, or prayer book for this holiday, has a definite structure which must be followed, giving the Seder ritual, therefore, an ingrained continuity. As the leader of a Seder once remarked to me, the Seder is oriented "to bring the tradition along, year after year after year." Certain passages of the Haggadah text, for example, are commonly read by most families, yet other sections allow for familial improvisation. Thus, the Seder integrates both continuity and change. Beatrice Weinreich, in "The Americanization of Passover," has described generalized cultural transformations in the Passover Seder resulting from external change (such as mechanization, urbanization, and cross-cultural acculturation) and internal change ("adaptations to internal historical events," such as the Holocaust and "a general trend toward secularization").[4] The changes she describes have affected the ritual for most North American Jews of East European ancestry, but Weinreich does not analyze change within a specific family, the multi-layered dynamics of prescribed and personal food symbolism, or the family inter-relationships which underlie the Seder ritual and serve to shape the event.

194

Although religious studies scholars have researched the origins of Passover to pre-Exodus rituals, these early symbols, reinterpreted in the light of the Exodus event, are generally ignored by many contemporary Jews. Indeed, when I mentioned their historical significance during a family Seder, I was met with uneasy short comments and a quick shifting of topic. These rituals were "too primitive" to consider as foundations for an event which had acquired immediate relevance to each year's current world situation.

Nevertheless, we do know that two nature festivals predate the Exodus.[5] In ancient times, Jews who lived as nomadic shepherds in the desert sacrificed a sheep or goat from their flocks during the spring month when the lambs and kids were born. The animal's blood was smeared on the tent posts to ward off misfortune and ensure good luck for the coming year. This festival, observed within family groups, was called "Pesach," derived from "paschal offering."

The agricultural Jews who lived in Palestine also celebrated the cutting of the grain in the spring with a Festival of Matsos or Unleavened Bread. They first removed all the fermented dough and old bread made with the leaven or "chomets" of the preceding year's crop. After this cleaning out was completed, the first new sheaf of grain, the "omer," was cut and sacrificed to God by a priest, while the entire community attended. According to other scholars, agricultural groups also baked their freshly harvested grain into unleavened cakes eaten in a special ceremony to thank God for the harvest.

These early nature rituals eventually merged and came to symbolize the exodus of the Jewish people from Egypt—an event which had occurred in the first spring month (Nisan) of the year—reinterpreting the Pesach sacrifice. When the Angel of Death slew the first-born of the Egyptians in the tenth plague sent against the Pharaoh (who refused to release the Jews from bondage), the Jews marked their doors with the blood of the sacrificed animal so the Angel would pass over their homes. The earlier meaning of the Festival of Matsos (or Matzo) came to symbolize the bread of affliction since the Jews did not have time for their bread to rise when fleeing Egypt.

Because spring was a busy season, many Jews could not travel to the faraway Temple in Jerusalem, the national center, the only place where the sacrificed lamb could be killed. Thus blood was no longer smeared on the doorposts, and Passover became, and still is, a home-centered festival. After the Romans destroyed the

Second Temple (around 70 C.E.), the Pesach sacrifice was totally discontinued, but re-emerged in symbolic form as roasted shankbone on the Seder plate.

Passover signals the beginning of spring and a celebration of freedom—a unique paradigm for a historically oppressed people. The eight-day holiday,[6] starting on the evening of the fourteenth of Nisan (calculated by the Jewish lunar calendar, which explains its variation from a fixed secular date), begins with a ritual meal called a Seder, the symbolic foods of which lead Jews to experience the past and bring the story of the Exodus into the present. Indeed, according to the Torah, parents have a duty to tell the tale to children; in every generation each Jew must tell as if he or she personally came out of Egypt.

In contemporary times, Passover has numerous connotations. The celebration of freedom, for example, brings to mind not only the Exodus, but the pogroms of Russia and Poland, the Holocaust, the Warsaw Ghetto uprising, the establishment of the State of Israel, the plight of the Ethiopian Black Jews (or "Falasha" [outsiders] as they are called by other Ethiopians), and the situation of today's Soviet Jews (to whom matzo is smuggled for Passover). All of these events become part of the tale and add new dimension for families whose members may have lived through such acts and now relive them in memories evoked by the Seder. For example, Doris, a member of the family studied, commented upon her daughter-in-law's parents who survived the Holocaust: "Sheri's family—her mother was in the camps—her father was in the camps—and they had gone through so much hardship and they can come out of that experience and still believe in God, and still have so much religious faith. It's marvelous to see." Another family member, Tittle, who fled Poland before the Nazi occupation, remarked: "This, in essence, is the idea behind Passover—that you went out of slavery and tried to get into freedom, and what you had to pay for it.... It seems the more you are repressed, the stronger your roots come through."

Ruth Gruber Fredman, in *The Passover Seder: Afikoman in Exile*, has pointed out the structural oppositions balanced by the Seder and argues that Jewish culture attempts to create order, placing it eternally in transition. Thus, the Seder becomes a means of expressing *galut*, an in-between state which illuminates "the experience of the individual Jew."[7] The ordering exhibited by the Seder can also be seen as being symbolic of the ordering of family. Like Seder, "family" connotes order. And, like Seder, families exhibit change. Just as the Haggadah does not explicate everything which must be done during the Seder,[8] mere family membership does not guarantee the rules and roles demanded for family participation, particularly because a family consists of individuals who constantly combine and recombine their experiences. In participating in the dynamics of this disordering and reordering, a sense of family emerges.

For instance, most of the people at the Kates's Seder have participated in Seders dating back to the last Seder held by Pearl Gershenowitz, my maternal grandmother. The memory of that Seder provides a point of reference for the current Seder members and a symbolic common link. But everyone who attended remembers the Seder for different reasons. For example, Pearl's daughter-in-law, Doris, whom I interviewed, sees that Seder as an initiation into the Gershenowitz family and as an introduction to a "real" Passover Seder.

> We always had Passover in our house but we never really had a Seder.... My father
> was more Canadianized, my mother was more European, so we just had Kiddush and
> we had someone read the four questions but we never had a full Seder, and we did-

n't start having a full Seder, I remember, until we went to your Grandmother's. Do you remember? Well, anyways, when your grandmother had the first Seder and Joel [Doris's son] was just a baby at the time and that was very, very memorable because we had the whole family together and we had a full Seder, and I didn't know what a Seder was until then.

For Brenda, however, it was the death of her grandmother that she associates with that Seder:

My grandmother had a Seder and, um, that Seder I remember for different reasons because my grandmother was very sick and then, that was the last Seder she was here for.... I don't associate my grandmother with Seders that much, partly because she died when I was thirteen and partly because she really didn't have many Seders. She may have had them before I was born, but I only remember one Seder at her place and that was just before she died. And I associate the Seder with the family all being together. But not as much as a Seder...The Seder that my grandmother and grandfather made doesn't stand out as a Seder; it stands out for other reasons.

Pearl's daughter, Trudy, remembers the Seder not only because of its traumatic aspects but because she realized that the responsibility for the Seder would now shift to her generation:

The one that stands out in my mind the most is about the last Passover that I had at my mother's home before she passed on.... She'd been home from the hospital about a month and I was making dinner for everyone that was coming in from out of town, and for our family, when Mother said, "Next year we will have a bigger Passover and we will invite all my brothers and sisters and their offsprings." And I started to cry because I knew there wasn't going to be a next year, and she said, "Why are you crying?" and I said, "Well, it's the onions that I'm cutting." So that is the Passover that has stayed...been outstanding in my mind ever since.

At that Seder, my sister Suzanne and I, both Pearl's grandchildren, were six and eleven years old. For us, Grandma's Seder also stood out in memory, although I am certain we did not know she was dying. Perhaps the Seder was highlighted in our memories because it became the model for subsequent Seders. Over thirty years of Seders have come and gone, but this *one* Seder is spoken of each year and has become part of Passover for all in the family who participated. Although the narrative may appear to function as a means of creating solidarity for the family, at the same time it also functions differently for each person who tells it; for those who did not attend Grandma's Seder, the telling is an introduction to the Gershenowitz family Seder.

The dynamics of a family can frequently be illuminated by its foodways, especially of the Seder. The Seder ritual has a break during which a festive and relaxed meal is served. For the Gershenowitz family, the "rules" for what may be eaten are based not only on prohibitions against *chometz* (leavened foods), but also on the family's notions of acceptability, derived from the foods served by Pearl. As is true for most Ashkenazic Jews, the foods recall Eastern European meals. Pearl, who immigrated to Canada from a small village in Poland, continued to prepare foods common in the "old country": chicken soup with matzo, *knadlach* (dumplings), roast chicken, beef brisket, potato *kugel* (pudding), and *tzimmes* (cooked carrots, prunes and apricots in a rich, thick, honeyed sauce). Thus, these foods are always served by the family. However, no one eats the *tzimmes* and every year someone mentions that it should not be included in next year's menu. A year later, *tzimmes* again appears and Pearl's family tradition is upheld.

The meals for the two nights vary, but some items remain the same. Gefilte fish (made from chopped whitefish and pike, formed into ovals), sometimes referred to as "Jewish fish" on Russian and Polish restaurant menus, was an economical dish in Eastern Europe, and is now traditionally served for Passover by most families. Available at supermarkets in jars packaged by Jewish food suppliers, gefilte fish is usually served cold and needs no further preparation. Pearl's daughter, Trudy, however, remembers her mother's painstaking cooking and thus boils the already cooked fish in a broth with carrots, celery, and spices, chills the fish, and serves it on lettuce with a slice of carrot as garnish. On the second night, tomato juice is substituted as an appetizer for either the fish or the chicken soup.

Beef brisket, prepared by Trudy or her daughter (trained to make it the "same" way), is served the first night, along with *kishka* (also East European in origin)—intestine stuffed with flour, fat, crumbs, and minced onion filling which is then roasted with the brisket. Brenda buys a standing rib roast for the second night, an innovation, but the roast is rarely cooked since so much food remains from the prior night's feast (except the *kishka*, which disappears immediately despite Brenda's dislike of it). The second night's menu also includes two capons to add to any leftover chicken.

Who prepares or brings certain dishes is supposedly open but nevertheless a pattern has been re-established each year. Doris brings chicken or turkey for the first night. Trudy, who stays at Brenda's home during Passover, prepares the fish and brisket, fills the silver salt and pepper shakers, cuts and arranges a pickle tray, and hardboils dozens of eggs. A fertility and springtime symbol, the egg (now often associated with Easter but whose ritual use is ancient) is served in a bowl with salt water as the first course. Salad, another appetizer and a contemporary, health-conscious addition, is always brought by someone of Brenda's generation. Great Aunt Lil, Pearl's sister-in-law, always brings a cake, usually a sponge cake made with matzo flour—a very traditional Passover dessert. Guests who do not prepare food bring Passover chocolate, small gifts, or freshly cut flowers.

Brenda's responsibility for food preparation has changed because of the vast marketing of Passover foods, especially in cities like Toronto, where large numbers of Jews live. In fact, some companies, such as Coca-Cola and Canada Dry, and many local dairies in Toronto, have their entire stock made "kosher for Passover" to simplify bottling and distribution during the holiday. Traditional foods, such as matzo, chicken soup, sponge cake mix, horseradish, and beet borsht, are packaged and available in the major supermarkets. Kosher butchers not only stock the standard items and meat cuts, but will cook chickens, *tzimmes*, potato *kugel*, *kishka*, and soup. Brenda orders all of these items already cooked; the brisket is one of the few foods actually made in the house. Nevertheless, neighborhood availability and what is served are of paramount importance to Brenda. She commented,

> I take for granted the fact that I can get all of these Jewish products, whether they're prepared or whether I have to prepare them and they're just the materials for preparing them.... And it's important for me to live in the kind of neighborhood where all of these things are accessible to me.

I can order the traditional dishes and we cook certain things ourselves. Trudy does a lot of work...helping me prepare the way, ah, I was going to say the way my grandmother used to, but that isn't true. I mean obviously we have made certain changes even in the foods. But we do try to stick to the traditional things that we remember.

Tillie recalled how much things had actually changed from what was done when the family lived in Europe:

You made all the food by yourself and...there was a limited range of food. Foods that you use now that are considered to be, oh, how should I say, kosher for Pesach, weren't considered kosher at that time. You had fish and you had meat, like, ah, geese, ducks, chickens, and, um, roasts, veal or beef....You used fish, you used matzo, you used eggs and, you know, certain fruit you were allowed, and certain staples like carrots, potatoes, onions...a limited selection because they weren't sure whether it's right or wrong. They figured, you know, it's best not to use certain things so then you know you're doing the right thing.

She underscored that matzo was made by hand and not sold in boxes:

All matzo at that time years ago was made by hand and it was round; it wasn't made on a machine, where it's put through, ah, on an assembly line way. It was made by hand. It wasn't packaged. It came, oh, you bought it by the pound and mostly it came in big wicker baskets that you bought so many pounds. Mostly it was a lot and, um, that's the way it was delivered to you. It wasn't packaged. And it wasn't square. It was round and it was all made by hand.

The situation Brenda finds herself in is radically different—and she is pleased to find herself living where Jewish stores are common. The older generation has not quite adjusted to these changes. Doris pointed out:

The only thing about Seder or Passover that upsets me is the fact that some of the shop-keepers seem to take advantage—just like Christmas, it's too commercialized. And prices go sky high and the women, when you go shopping, get a little hyper, and you want to buy your fish or chicken or whatever—it's quite an ordeal [laugh].

Stan, not dependent on memories of past Gershenowitz Seders, is free to create his own role. He assumes responsibility for the foods on the Seder plate and for setting out the wine glasses, refilling the decanter, and leading the Seder. Passing pieces of the various Seder plate foods from hand to hand down the table, rather than distributing them on a dish, he consciously chooses to act as a pivot for the meanings applied to the Seder by the participants. All of these actions and attitudes of the various generations define appropriate behavior and create a notion of *communitas*.

The newest generation sees the Passover Seder from a completely different perspective from that of their parents (Pearl's grandchildren). The children are preoccupied with learning the basics of the Passover Seder: how to ask the four questions, open the door for Elijah, and steal the Afikomen. All the adults take responsibility for educating the children, but the roles accompanying grandmother, mother, and grandchild are not generationally restricted. The grandmother, Pearl, who passed away in 1954, is ever present in the minds of her children. But, as children of each new generation are born, the mothers also become grandmothers in their role as transmitters for a family tradition. Pearl's daughter, Trudy, is now the grandmother of my son Mikey. Trudy's daughter Suzanne, now in her late thirties, remained the child who asked the four questions until she assisted Mikey in learning this skill. That these generations overlap is exemplified by the joint responsibilities undertaken by both Suzanne and Mikey to insure that the four questions are asked. Until Mikey began attending Seders at the age of three, my sister Suzanne always asked the questions. The 1983 and 1984 Seders demonstrated that this phase was in flux. Mikey asked the questions with Suzanne in 1982, attempted to ask them himself with some help in 1983, and by 1984 learned not only how to ask them without assistance, but surprised the group by reciting them in Hebrew (which he became motivated to do after watching his visiting Israeli cousins do so the previous year). Thus Suzanne's role finally shifted from child to adult.

Areas of folklore which invariably function to bind the children together as active participants and the adults as an encouraging audience occur at places where the Haggadah lacks commentary, thus providing an open interpretative frame for certain portions of the Seder, such as explanations for Elijah's entry and the importance of the Afikomen. Each adult reveals his/her interpretations of the rituals. The following exchange about opening the door for Elijah the prophet illustrates how meanings for familiar themes arise. The family discusses who Elijah is, how he will arrive to announce the coming of the messiah, visit families on Passover, and take a sip of wine from a cup reserved especially for him. The children then are placed in charge of opening and closing the door and are joshed about the level of wine diminishing (someone will often jiggle the table as well). Stan points out, "This cup is for Elijah the prophet. When you opened up the door we think he was in the neighborhood and came in and had a drink. We didn't see him, but, you see, the glass was full before . . . ." Another cousin interrupts: "Did you see him at the door?" Brenda notes, "You don't have to be afraid of him because he's a good prophet." Amy's grandmother joins in, "He's a good prophet, he's a friend." Mikey repeats, "A friend." Stan says, "So we think he came in and took a sip of wine." "You don't believe it, right, Amy?" asks Brenda. "I don't know," Amy responds. Stan points, "The glass was full before we started." "I don't know," Amy repeats, as Mikey stares at the wine goblet, and the service continues. Here, despite the lack of commentary in the Haggadah, all family members share in the recitation and acting out of an ancient story which is transformed into a family tradition in its own right.

Hiding the Afikomen is another family event that is not commented on in the Haggadah. The edition used by this family makes no mention of the activity but rather states, "After the meal, the Afikomen is distributed." The Afikomen, or dessert matzo, must be eaten before the service commences following the meal. During the dinner, as courses are served and cleared, the adults urge the children to steal and hide this matzo when Stan is not looking. Several adults whisper at one time: "Don't eat it, don't eat it." . . . "Wrap it in a napkin." . . . "Go hide it somewhere, go hide it together." . . . "Under the tablecloth, in front of your seat." "Here?" "Yeah, underneath." . . . "Lift up the tablecloth." "Hurry up." . . . "Did you hide it?" . . . "OK, that's all. OK, now you can go play." "OK, put your napkin on top of it so it won't be noticeable." "We'll call you."

After the children leave the room, the adults laugh at the obvious hiding place. "And the thing I like is . . . you can't even tell it's there," Brenda laughs. "Well, children have so much faith. They don't question things, thank God," says Amy's grandmother.

This little interchange is a prime example of family participation in a food-centered ritual of their own making. Likewise, the ransoming of the Afikomen follows the family's tradition rather than any command in the Haggadah. Stan always calls everyone's attention back to the service, and then reaches ceremoniously for the Afikomen, now mysteriously missing. "Which one of you guys has got the Afikomen?" he asks. Everyone chimes in, "Oh oh; who hid something?" The children always claim that they don't have it and don't know where it is. Finally, the adults encourage them to make a deal with Stan, and ask him how much it's worth to him. Amidst much laughter and bantering, a deal is struck. This part of the Seder will often take twenty minutes, involves everyone, and is family folklore which adheres to an almost identical structure each year. (If the children have gone to sleep, an adult represents them.) Such folklore is shared, follows the childhood experiences adults recall, and, although it marks a "change" from the Seder ritual, it conforms to family expectations.

Because the bargaining event is not prescribed by the Haggadah, it serves as a point in the ritual where change may occur. For Stan and Brenda, the host and hostess of this Seder, it represents one example of a blend of family traditions now experienced by the group as a whole. As Brenda pointed out, "When the children steal the Afikomen at our Seder, they do get little presents for it, and I remember that as a child. . . . Stan doesn't remember getting anything for stealing it. He likes, though, combining this because he feels that this makes it nicer for the children." Here one family's tradition has been merged with another's through marriage. Just as Brenda has retained the tradition of gift-giving, Stan has brought elements of his childhood Seder to his new family's Seder. For example, instead of using parsley for the green vegetable on the Seder plate, he provides onion (acceptable since it grows green above the ground). Thus both continuity and change are promoted as one would expect with folkloric manifestations, and as the above examples demonstrate.

One might assume that the Seder plate, constituting a table of ritual foods which correspond in the text to the deliverance from Egypt, would be static. The foods on the Seder plate have acknowledged and deeply ingrained meanings. A piece of roasted lamb shank bone (although any roasted meat bone may be used) represents the Pesach sacrifice. A roasted egg, called "*chagigoh*," symbolizes a second animal sacrificed in Jerusalem. The first animal had to be entirely eaten before the dawn of the first day. Because the group was large, some only received a small bite, so a second animal (not sacrificed in the Temple) was used for the second night. "*Charoses,*" a kind of fruit salad from the early Spring festival, consists of nuts, cinnamon, wine, and apples; it is often said to symbolize the mortar mixed by Jewish slaves for the Pharaoh's buildings in Egypt. It also represents the hope of freedom. Bitter herbs or "*moror,*" usually a piece of horseradish, symbolize the bitterness of the Jews' lives in Egypt. Greens, often parsley, lettuce or watercress, dipped in salt water (representing tears) stand for the coming of spring and the hope of redemption.[9] The table setting includes a plate with three pieces of matzo, each wrapped separately within a folded cloth. The matzo has three meanings: (1) the bread which the Jews took with them on fleeing Egypt that had not risen (including the dessert matzo or "afikomen"); (2) the bread of poverty; and (3) the bread of the simple life in the desert. A wine decanter and wine glasses for each person are also set on the table. Participants drink four glasses of wine: one for Kiddush (thanks to God for the fruit of the vine); one after the first part of the Seder ends and before the festive meal is eaten; one after grace following the meal; and one at the end of the Seder. These glasses of wine are said to match the fourfold promise of redemption given by God to the Jewish people.[10] Lastly, an empty wine glass or cup is set for Elijah, the prophet. It is not filled until the end of the meal.[11]

As is obvious from this description of the background and meanings attributed to the foods which are displayed and discussed during the Seder, a Seder is multilayered like all ritual events. On the surface, it appears to be a "text," with historical commentary, liturgical readings, symbolic foods, and obligatory roles to be played by the dramatis personae of a family. However, scholars' assumptions about reducing events to "texts" or conceptions about common meanings for groups of individuals engaged in events have to be challenged when one examines the significance of the Seder and its foods as symbolic for the Jewish people at large and then narrows that examination to one extended family and the individuals which make up that family.

For example, in eight interviews in which I asked a question about the personal or religious importance of the ritual foods as signifiers, only two people mentioned specific foods. Doris initially said, "No," when I asked if there were symbols that were most important to her. After a brief pause, she continued:

> I guess when you think of the *moror*, the bitterness and everything, you realize how lucky we are here to be living in Canada, to be in a free country.... We can imagine what it is to be a slave but it must have been terrible for them, and to have survived all these things and now we live in Canada, we should really appreciate it 'cause we have a marvelous life here. We really do.

Stan singled out matzo because it identified him as a Jew:

> I think matzo is the most important because that's the most obvious. That's the one that not only we as Jews see but non-Jews are very much aware of it, and they're aware that there's a holiday going on. Because I remember, even at school, during the Passover period, that instead of having sandwiches, we would have hardboiled eggs and pieces of matzo with butter in them, and that was, again, very symbolic as something different was happening. So all of my non-Jewish friends would be aware that I was celebrating or partaking of something that was different from what they were used to. And they, of course, wanted to taste it, and that sort of made me special at that time.

I was surprised that Stan, as the leader of the Seder, did not remark about the other ritual foods. I asked, "Is there anything about the bitter herbs...?" He quickly replied:

> Those things are intellectually symbolic, I think, rather than emotionally symbolic. The matzo's very emotional. The bitter herbs and the egg and the neck of the chicken, these are all very intellectual kinds of things and I guess have been created by the rabbis through the ages and...they're interesting symbols, but you don't *feel* them as much as you do the matzo.

Joel's comment about the foods in general point out their functional aspects:

> Well, the whole idea of the symbolism of the various objects, the fact that, you know, there's physical things there to point at, to keep...to draw people's attention to...to keep people interested. I mean, it's not particularly a very long thing, but you know it is before supper,

201

during and after, and you know it's at night, people can get very bored, but I think it's good because you have the various things to look at and to describe and it keeps everybody involved.

Other participants shifted the topic to concerns about the Seder as a whole. Tillie, for example, remarked that some people "eat a fancy dinner," but do not think about the underlying idea—freedom. Trudy noted that the symbols stand for "what the Jews had gone through" and "everything that is going on today."

Common themes run through these comments, but particular references do not recur. Circumscribed meanings give way to individualized and personalized "texts." Because each Seder builds on past events, overall messages and individual memories create a different "text" for each participant. Food is perhaps more important for the memories it triggers than for its ritual qualities. Although the Seder represents a major past event for all Jews, Stan's recollections emphasize how much the Seder foods bring the individual's past into the present.

> I think Passover is probably the most symbolic of all the holidays . . . we celebrate as Jews. It's the one that . . . I remember as being the happiest when I was a child. We would have . . . Seders at my Grandparent's home or my Grandmother's home and . . . as a child I remember running around and . . . taking . . . bits and pieces of the special foods and it was a holiday that had the smell of cooking, it was a holiday that . . . had a lot of people around, and it wasn't focused on the synagogue, it was focused on the home more than anything else. And I think that was nice, and I remember meeting my cousins, and meeting my uncles and my aunts, and . . . having all sorts of good times. So to me it's one that . . . is filled with a lot of very pleasant early childhood memories, and those memories go back to, you know, when I was four or five years old. I remember crawling underneath the table as the Seder was being conducted and that . . . has nice memories for me. I remember playing with my cousins, and I remember the taste of various foods. I remember the taste of matzo, and I remember the taste of the *charoses* and as a kid we were allowed to have wine, and that was fun. Very nice and warm and very symbolic kind of holiday.

Like the foods, family relationships mark changes and make every Seder a different "text." But, under the surface, the changes are not merely a signal for the ever-shifting dynamic of folklore ritual. One's knowledge of how to effect changes within unstated family rules can function to define roles within the family. For blood relatives, incorporation in the family is automatic. Growing up within its confines and rituals, family members learn to fit in. Those who marry into the family must actively seek entry. Their success or failure may be determined by how well they understand and help shape family folklore.

Michael, who is Suzanne's husband, is younger than she by two months, but is not asked to assist in the four questions. His lack of participation is revealed in a traditional family interchange: Stan tells Mikey, "You can say it with Suzanne because she's young too." Suzanne replies (as she does every year), "I'm older than Michael" (referring to her husband). Brenda responds (also every year), "You say that all the time." Suzanne is a blood relative of the inner family circle. Michael has married in. He was often criticized because he attended only the first Seder night until his daughter was born. "For me, one night is enough, and I don't consider myself to be a hypocrite, and to me it was hypocritical to come two nights and spend that much time with something I'm not really that fond of and don't believe in that much." Yet

Michael also said that Passover was his "favorite holiday because of the Seder—not for the Seder itself, but because the entire family gets together...." Michael's aloofness from this family's Seder is due to his positive experiences with his own family. He has ambivalent feelings about his role in this Seder since his responsibilities are not clearly delineated, as they were in his "blood" family.

Amy, the child of a Jewish father and a non-Jewish mother, does not want to ask the questions although she has attended the Seders since she was a baby and is three years older than Mikey. Amy's reluctance may be due to her own sense of not fully belonging. Although family members encourage her and attempt to make her comfortable with the Seder ritual, they also are concerned about her lack of Jewish identity.

Alan, about to marry a cousin in the family, broke the "rules" by arriving in the midst of the 1984 Seder. He explained that he had to participate in his own family's Seder. Despite his somewhat intrusive behavior, he added to the Seder by bringing in a special prayer. In many families it is now customary to say an extra prayer for oppressed Jews. Often the prayer is for Soviet Jewry, although prayers for the Ethiopian Jews are recent additions. Seder leaders will pencil in a note in their Haggadahs to insert the prayer at a certain point. Stan commented that his father did not recite such a prayer, but he does: "That's my personal choice. It's not something that has been said 'do this.'" Alan instinctively knew that he could add a prayer to the Seder and brought one commemorating the forty-year anniversary of the Warsaw Ghetto uprising. Not yet particularly close to Alan at this point in their relationship, family members treated him with new respect for his attempt to fit into their ritual.

Stan considers himself part of this intensely matriarchal family. Again, past experiences are significant in shaping such behavior. "I guess from about age eighteen to twenty-five, I had a very poor relationship with my own personal family...and when Brenda and I got married, the Hertz and Gershenowitz family seemed to adopt me, and...they became very much my first family." One way Stan was able to effect this shift was by taking over the host and Seder leader role, and blending many of his own family's traditions with his new one in an acceptable way. When the generation preceding his was ready to give over the role of leading the Seders, Stan was ready and willing to take on the task. Amy and Mikey, even at their young ages, demonstrate the importance of one's acceptance of generational roles. Their budding knowledge of family lore and levels of participation make one child a guest and one child a central figure in the family.

However, the idyllic picture of a cohesive family, all sharing the same folklore, is modified if not shattered when we consider individual differences. Not only does one's generational and host/guest role color one's perception of and role in the event, but one's sense of responsibility for continuity of the tradition, one's level of participation, and one's personal experiences with Judaism and previous Seders are all motivations which decide the particulars of traditional involvement. Even the mix of family members on a given night can significantly influence the event. As well as focusing on the similarities in the content, as folklorists usually do, we must look at differences in the behaviors and performances of individuals as well as other, perhaps larger, social changes in the form of the event. In this particular setting, foodways (i.e., participation in the preparation and consumption of Seder meals) can be as important as the underlying ritual itself in the determination of *communitas*. Moreover, in this family, folkloric behavior actually defines who is in control, who the "guests" really are, and, ultimately, who is and isn't "family."

203

NOTES

This article is an expanded version of a paper presented at the annual meeting of the American Folklore Society in San Diego, October 1984.

1. Steven J. Zeitlin, Amy J. Kotkin, and Holly Cutting Baker, *A Celebration of American Family Folklore* (New York: Pantheon Books, 1982): 2.
2. The results of that fieldwork project appear on videotape as *Passover: A Celebration* (B & W, 28 min.), 1983, distributed by the Folklore and Ethnic Studies Program, University of Oregon, Eugene, Oregon. For details of the fieldwork and videotaping processes and the problems inherent in studying one's own family, see Sharon R. Sherman, "That's How the Seder Looks: A Fieldwork Account of Videotaping Family Folklore," *Journal of Folklore Research* 23 (1986): 53–70.
3. The Passover Seder commemorates the deliverance of the Jewish people from bondage in the land of Egypt, their exodus into the desert, and the journey to the Promised Land—an event which occurred over three thousand years ago. Each year, Passover is celebrated by Jews with varying levels of religious observance and, more than any other holiday, is enjoyed by both religious and secular Jews.
4. Beatrice S. Weinreich, "The Americanization of Passover," in *Studies in Biblical and Jewish Folklore*, ed. Ralphael Patai, Francis Lee Utley, and Dov Noy (Bloomington: Indiana University Press, Indiana University Folklore Series No. 13:1960): 342.
5. See Hayyim Schauss, *The Jewish Festivals: History and Observance* (New York: Schocken Books, 1962 [originally published in 1938]): 38–85, for a detailed description of Passover's origins as well as different observances in various places through time.
6. The Torah specifies a seven-day observance (Exodus 12:15; 13:6). An exiled people, the Jews added an extra day to ensure correct observance for many holidays since people were notified by bonfires lit on mountains and the possibility for error was great. Because a reliable calendar exists, Reform Jews and all Jews in Israel celebrate for seven days. Conservative and Orthodox families, having followed an eight-day holiday for centuries, continue the ancient practice. Thus, they have two Seder nights, whereas Reform Jews and those in Israel have one.
7. Ruth Gruber Fredman, *The Passover Seder: Afikoman in Exile* (Philadelphia: University of Pennsylvania Press, 1981): 34. In analyzing the metaphoric and symbolic characteristics of the Seder, Fredman also presents the Seder plate as one that summarizes oppositions to achieve balance or ordering.
8. One would assume that, at the least, continuity would be exhibited by the Haggadah, since it is written text. All participants at a Seder read from individual Haggadahs placed before them. Haggadah means "telling" and the booklet contains directions for how to organize the Seder plate, and is a blend of legends, prayers, commentary, questions, and songs set in an order for following the ritual. Parts are from the Mishnah and parts from the Talmud. Although Haggadahs vary in translation and tone, the order is constant. Thus, even if as many as five different versions are used at one table, readers will be able to recognize the similarity between the portion of the text being read aloud by another participant and the portion in their own Haggadahs. As the evening progresses through four glasses of wine, variations in the texts may lead to questions and laughter about the differences. Scholars assume the Haggadah and the Seder were instituted after the destruction of the Second Temple, with the Haggadah added to the prayer book, but much of it was recited as early as the days of the Second Temple. In the thirteenth century the Haggadah appeared as a separate volume and new editions continue to appear every year, reflecting changing times and interpretations.
9. Greens were commonly dipped once in a tart sauce at regular meals and after washing one's hands at banquets (which, like Passover, also began with wine).
10. "I will bring you out; I will deliver you; I will redeem you; I will take you to me for a people." The number "four" is a constant throughout the Seder: four glasses of wine, four questions, four sons, four matriarchs of Israel, four promises, and four Pesach symbols.
11. Several explanations have been offered for the existence of the cup of Elijah or "fifth" cup. Elijah is said to have gone, living, to Heaven in a chariot of fire. Many tales are told about his magical feats while on earth. Popular belief is that Elijah will return and announce the coming of the Messiah and lead the Jewish people to a new deliverance as Moses did in ancient days. At a point late in the Seder the door is opened for Elijah to enter. Opening the door was once done at the beginning of the Seder so any traveling or hungry Jew could join the ritual, but as Jews began living in areas with non-Jews (often hostile ones), opening the door was shifted to the conclusion of the Seder. Another explanation is that a fifth cup of wine was disputed by the Talmudists. "Let Elijah decide" was the solution offered and the fifth glass became his. In the family studied, any extra chair or place set by accident is always referred to as Elijah's in-jokes throughout the year.

204

CONTINUITY AND CHANGE IN SYMPTOM CHOICE: ANOREXIA

JOAN JACOBS BRUMBERG

RUTH STRIEGEL-MOORE

The post-1960 epidemic of anorexia nervosa can be related to recent social change in the realm of food and sexuality.
—Joan Jacobs Brumberg (1988, p. 268)

In the past two decades, anorexia nervosa has become an increasingly prevalent disease in the United States, and eating disorders are regarded as commonplace among women students on our nation's campuses. Patients with anorexia nervosa are drawn largely from the middle and upper classes; they are Caucasian, female, and largely adolescent and young adult. Despite many confusions (and lapses) in the historical epidemiology of the disorder, most medical and mental health observers agree there has been a real rise in incidence in the number of patients with anorexia nervosa since the 1960s. Since the 1970s, the number of women patients seeking help with eating disorders has increased steadily in clinical settings across the country (Brumberg, 1988).

These changes in incidence and presentation of symptoms are of concern to social historians and mental health professionals. For historians and psychologists, the current situation prompts an important theoretical question: Why does a psychopathology become more prominent in one time period than another? What one thinks about the causes or etiology of this particular disease will obviously determine an answer. For the purposes of this essay, however, we will set aside the discussion of etiology and proceed from the following shared assumptions.

First, in mental illness, basic forms of cognitive and emotional disorientation are expressed in behavioral aberrations that mirror the deep preoccupations of a particular culture. Second, anorexia nervosa is a multidetermined disorder involving biology, psychology, and culture. We regard these three etiological components as interactive and reciprocal; no one model can be used in isolation (Brumberg, 1988; Garner, Garfinkel, & Bemis, 1982). For purposes of studying the disorder, however, we follow a two-staged conceptualization of the disease (Brumberg, 1988) that is useful for clarifying the relationship of sociocultural influences to individual bio-logical and psychological variables.

In Stage 1—*recruitment*—sociocultural factors play a critical role. In this period, dieting and the pressure to be thin are extremely salient. Not eating, or eating very little, is culturally sanctioned among elite women in the West (Brumberg, 1988; Chernin, 1981). Individual psychological and biological variables, however, ulti-mately explain why some women but not others move from chronic dieting to the full-blown clinical psychopathology. (Does the symptom have some larger meaning in the patient's emotional and family life? Does starvation actually make her feel good and energetic?) Then, in Stage 2—*career or acclimation*—we see biological and psychological responses to starvation: these physical and psychological responses are relatively uniform from patient to patient and from time to time and serve to per-petuate the illness (Garfinkel & Kaplan, 1985). The study of Stage 2 is within the realm of medical science (broadly defined), but Stage 1, recruitment, represents an important arena for historical inquiry in collaboration with clinical, developmental, and social psychology.

In this essay we explore change and continuity in the meaning of the primary behavioral symptom in anorexia nervosa—refusal of food—and comment on how the symptom constellation in this disorder has changed over time. Our analysis is based on a comparative investigation of patients with anorexia nervosa in the late nineteenth century and clinical and research experience with contemporary anorectics. Admittedly, our methodology is highly qualitative, and, because of the limitations of the historical material, it has been based on only about a dozen cases. Yet, we have been able to compare our "patients" on a number of important dimen-sions, particularly the issue of presentation and symptomatology.

For the psychologist, the historical material did, of course, have a striking limi-tation: in nineteenth-century case records, doctors concentrated on somatic issues and said little about the psychology of their anorectic patients. Moreover, there is virtually no primary source material—diaries or letters—written by Victorian anorectics explaining their behavior. Thus, it is very difficult, if not impossible, for the historian to explain why a particular individual developed anorexia nervosa. As a result, we are unable to say a great deal about the psychodynamics of individual cases in past time. This is a frustration, but also an important reality, in collabora-tive research between historians and clinical psychologists.

If the individual psyche was hard to approach from a historical perspective, the family was somewhat easier. Again, historians of medicine generally do not have pri-mary materials that describe the daily functioning and emotional environment of the families of individual patients. Yet, because of the importance of intrafamilial dynamics in explaining contemporary anorexia nervosa, we felt that we must try to penetrate the family world of the nineteenth-century anorectic. By coupling what we knew about patterns of Victorian middle-class nurturance (culled from primary and secondary historical literature) and the psychodynamics of modern anorectic families (described by Sargent, Liebman, & Silver, 1985; Strober & Humphrey, 1987; and Yager, 1982), we did come to some understanding of the emotional milieu that surrounded anorexia nervosa in the nineteenth century.

★ A BRIEF HISTORY

Anorexia nervosa was named and identified in the 1870s by William Gull and Charles Lasègue in England and France. This is not to say that it had not existed before.

Published reports from at least one American asylum, as early as the 1850s, reveal that there were adolescent girls, aged 16 to 23, from "good families," who refused to eat their food and suffered no other physical or mental disorder. At that time, American anorectics were classed as "sitomaniacs," those who feared or loathed their food (Brumberg, 1988). These patients clearly did not have commonplace "wasting diseases" such as tuberculosis or consumption; nor were they explicitly delusional or insane.

Because wasting diseases were so prevalent and so critical in the nineteenth century, the doctor's first task was to determine the source of emaciation. In general, nineteenth-century physicians concentrated on the problem of differential diagnosis (how to tell one disease from another) and on the cure of physical symptoms. Because of the somatic emphasis in nineteenth-century medicine, not much attention was paid to the psychology of anorexia nervosa or to the question of the patient's motivation. Before Sigmund Freud, the meaning of noneating was not explored; few questions were asked about "feelings." A cure was accomplished when the patient gained weight, or "added flesh," and appeared to be out of physical danger. In essence, anorexia nervosa was a relatively rare disorder, and therapeutics in that day centered on relieving the primary physical symptom: emaciation.

The rarity of anorexia nervosa as well as the pattern of treatment in the nineteenth century makes the task of historical documentation and analysis particularly difficult. In the nineteenth century, young women of respectable social backgrounds were generally not treated in public institutions of any kind. Anorectic patients were most often treated in their own homes or on an ad hoc basis. Some went to private "hysterical homes" for a brief respite; others took extended recuperative trips and sea voyages. The bias against institutionalization of respectable girls means that few records were kept. Consequently, documentary materials on this disorder are scant and hard to come by.

Having acknowledged these problems of documentation, a great deal can still be garnered from a comparative study of anorexia nervosa in past and present. Using published and unpublished case reports, the social historian of medicine can assess the nature of the Victorian anorectic's presentation, the involvement of her family, and the nature and pattern of her symptoms. The historian can also move beyond case materials on individuals to the larger cultural milieu that surrounded bourgeois Victorian girls, specifically to the language of food and the body in that era.

We argue that to understand and treat anorexia nervosa, some attention must be paid to the meaning of food and eating in female identity in both the Victorian and the contemporary world. Ultimately, our joint investigation illustrates two basic but important points for the behavioral sciences: first, that the same psychopathology may change over time despite numerous continuities; and second, that symptoms and symptom constellations are quite responsive to culture.

★ **THE LANGUAGE OF PRESENTATION**

The nineteenth-century patient understood implicitly that the doctor was primarily interested in the physical signs and sounds of disease. As a result, the Victorian anorectic presented somatically rather than psychologically. "I have no appetite" or "It hurts when I eat" were the most common explanations of noneating in the Victorian era.

Today, in a medical world that is becoming increasingly more sensitive to psychological issues—particularly among adolescents whom we expect to see struggling with issues of sexual maturation and autonomy—anorectics present their refusal of food in a quite different way. Today, the formulaic statement is "I do not need to eat" or "I am too fat." Often, the modern anorectic denies that her eating behavior is unusual. She maintains that she is not ill or sick and that her jogging, swimming, and aerobics are proof of her good health. Typically, she denies her problem and her need for professional help or therapeutic intervention.

Today, her therapist is likely to see her problem as a developmental one: the eating disorder typically emerges during adolescence, a life stage that ushers in several developmental tasks. These tasks include coming to terms with the physical changes of puberty, establishing stable peer relationships while becoming increasingly independent from one's family, and developing a cohesive personality structure (Attie & Brooks-Gunn, 1989). Although girls *and* boys experience these challenges, achieving mastery is more difficult for girls because they are faced with ambiguous messages or ideals. Acceptance of the mature female body, for example, has to be accomplished in a cultural context that values the prepubertal shape more than the mature female shape. Furthermore, appearance plays a more central role in peer relationships for girls than boys; popularity figures more prominently into girls' self-esteem than it does for boys. Finally, girls receive conflicting messages about the ideal female personality: although they are encouraged to be autonomous, they also are urged to be empathic, caring, and helpful to others. Developing an autonomous self is difficult for girls who have been raised to be obedient and conformist, personality characteristics often ascribed to anorectic girls (Friedlander & Siegel, 1990). Dieting represents a seemingly "ideal" solution for the adolescent girl who is struggling to live up to our culture's developmental tasks. By reducing her weight, the adolescent girl can approximate the beauty ideal and hope for popularity among her peers; by restraining her food intake, she signals to others and to herself that she is in control of herself and her life, that she is "mature."

By contrast, in the Victorian era, the ideal of female fragility and debility was incorporated into personal identity, family interactions, and medical assessment. Ill health in women had a certain currency and social value. Women who suffered were admired; robust women were considered uncouth or déclassé. Consequently, Victorian ideas about the superior moral and aesthetic sensibilities of frail women underlay presentations that stressed physical pain and suffering. An adolescent daughter who did not eat was a source of enormous concern to the middle-class family. In an age of medical somaticism that concern was legitimated by complaints of organic discomfort and gastrointestinal or digestive pain. Although some nineteenth-century doctors (such as Lasègue) saw anorectics who denied their illness, the general cultural milieu promoted discussion rather than denial of ill health in women and dependence rather than autonomy in relation to medical personnel. In essence, anorexia nervosa was a medical rather than a psychological problem of adolescent development.

208

★ FAMILY DYNAMICS

Although we recognize that the psychogenesis of anorexia nervosa is not strictly familial, historical materials confirm the continuing influence of family and class factors. In the earliest nineteenth-century case reports, there is a connection between socioeconomic class and anorexia nervosa. Anorectic girls did not work outside the home; many had formal schooling well into late adolescence; they came from families able and willing to expend financial resources on them. Today, as in the late nineteenth century, anorexia nervosa is confined largely to middle- and upper-class young women in the West, a phenomenon that explains its classification as a "culture-bound syndrome" (Prince, 1985).

The emergence of anorexia nervosa as a modern disease entity was intimately linked to the emergence of modern adolescence. By the late nineteenth century, family life had intensified as a result of social and economic changes that accompanied industrialization, urbanization, and class stratification (Brumberg, 1988). Families became smaller, corporal discipline declined and "spoiling" increased; and children lived at home with their parents well into their late teens and early 20s. In this environment of material and emotional privileging, adolescence and anorexia nervosa were "born." Thus, anorexia nervosa has been and remains largely an adolescent disorder for reasons that are social and historical as well as developmental.

In fact, the middle-class families described in nineteenth-century clinical case records appear to have been "enmeshed" much in the manner Salvador Minuchin and other family systems theorists describe. *Enmeshment* refers to a style of family interaction characterized by an overinvolvement of family members in each other's affairs. Needs and moods of others are often inferred; family members are highly sensitive to one another. The good of the whole is often put above the needs of the individual. Criticism is discouraged because it threatens an ideal of harmony and unity. Although parent-child enmeshment is functional when the child is young, failure to disengage gradually undermines the child's development of an autonomous self. For example, in enmeshed families exploration and independent problem solving are discouraged, depriving the child of the opportunity to experience a sense of self-efficacy (Minuchin, 1974; Sargent et al., 1985).

The nineteenth-century middle-class family appears to have another characteristic hypothesized to play a role in the development of anorexia nervosa among women today. According to Minuchin and colleagues (Minuchin et al., 1975; Minuchin, Rosman, & Baker, 1978), families with an anorectic daughter exhibit relationships characterized by overprotectiveness. Family members feel a strong sense of vulnerability and respond by being overly protective and unable to take risks or allow for risk taking. Highly nurturant interactions dominate, at the expense of constructive criticism and the chance for the development of a sense of mastery and autonomy.

In terms of intrafamilial psychodynamics, the historical evidence for enmeshment and overprotection is highly suggestive but not altogether conclusive: nineteenth-century doctors had a sense that the family was implicated in the disorder, but they were imprecise about the nature of the emotional involvement. Although the Victorian physician recognized that the family played a role in the maintenance of the anorectic symptomatology, this assessment led to blaming the parents for failed moral leadership rather than to understanding the family from a systems perspective.

For example, doctors almost always considered both parents overly solicitous and indulgent in relation to anorectic daughters. It is important to understand that middle-class parents in the Anglo-American world prided themselves on their ability to protect their daughters and that their protectiveness set them apart from "heathens" and the working class (Brumberg, 1982). Middle-class physicians observing middle-class families regarded parental overprotectiveness in a positive way but often described the daughters as "spoiled" and in need of a firm moral authority.

At the same time, in a number of cases, the doctor observed "hostility" between the indulgent mother and her emaciated daughter. Unfortunately, the specific issues between mother and daughter are not usually elaborated. In at least one case, however, the patient told her girlfriends that her mother complained that she was too fat, suggesting that there were parental expectations and pressures surrounding the girl's body and her social persona. The unwillingness of the parents to follow medical orders—that is, to separate from their daughters—was a theme in early reports. At least one death from anorexia nervosa was attributed by the doctor to his inability to keep the patient isolated from a "nervous" mother. According to this 1895 case report, the concerned mother continued to visit her daughter in the hospital on a daily basis despite orders to the contrary. As a result, the effects of medical intervention were negated (according to the doctor) and the patient died.

The middle-class families of Victorian anorectics were, by virtue of their single-minded focus on their daughters' health, child-centered to a fault. The pursuit of health for the daughter was a centerpiece of the family's social activity. Lasègue noted that every visitor to an anorectic's family was expected to talk earnestly and continually about the girl's food and eating. Although William Gull never said anything explicit about the psychology of the disorder, he (and many others) advocated removal of the anorectic girl from her family, what is now called a "parentectomy." Once the patient was away from home, in a "new moral environment," the girl was expected to improve and return to normal eating. In fact, Gull's clinical reports suggest success after separation from the nuclear family.

In sum, bourgeois family life in the Victorian era was child-centered, overprotective (especially with girls), and sometimes indulgent. Not surprisingly, in this materially and emotionally privileged environment, some young women chose to express their unhappiness in a "ladylike" symptom—not eating—that clearly disturbed the family without being as flamboyantly disruptive as a tantrum or quarrel. The evidence suggests that Victorian anorectics were then, as they are today, extremely "nice" adolescent girls whose behavior combined overcompliance with hostile symbolic behavior.

Despite these striking behavioral continuities, we propose that enmeshment and overprotectiveness were motivated differently in the Victorian era than today precisely because contemporary parents have different expectations for themselves as well as for their daughters. For the Victorian mother, the central task was to ensure that a daughter was "marriageable." A daughter with social graces (the ability to make polite conversation, a restrained appetite, and a moral reputation) was visible proof that mother had performed her maternal role. Costanzo and Woody (1979) argue that when parents are highly invested in a domain of a child's life, they tend to use a restrictive parental style (including overinvolvement) to influence the child in that domain. Thus, by being overly involved with her daughter's social life, a Victorian mother was able to exert control with the expectation of achieving what her role as mother prescribed: launching her daughter into a proper marriage.

Mothers in the 1990s have different developmental needs and social expectations from their Victorian counterparts. A mother's expectations for herself as well as for her daughter are more diverse, possibly giving rise to anxiety about her performance as a mother. In fact, launching a daughter into marriage and/or career no longer signals that mother has reached a developmental milestone and can now retire. Modern mothers are expected to continue to have active lives, to be attractive, and, most of all, to remain young; at the same time that they aim for these personal goals, they may be ambivalent about what the "emptying nest" implies for their own lives and future achievement.

In contemporary society, a mother's overinvolvement in her daughter's life may be motivated in part by a desire to participate in her daughter's experiences and thus be a part of the younger generation. Mother-daughter relations around clothing provide a telling example. As much as being able to wear her mother's clothes signals that the adolescent girl is growing up, wearing her daughter's clothes proves that mother is not aging. It seems quite unlikely that a Victorian girl would have worn her mother's clothes and even more inconceivable that the mother would have chosen to wear her daughter's clothes. In all probability, the Victorian mother and daughter differed in size (as a function of repeated child-bearing as well as cultural acceptance of a matronly form). In this milieu, sharing clothes would not have been possible, even if mother or daughter desired to do so. Today's mother and daughter commonly have a number of clothes items that are interchangeable; mother is as busy trying to look young as the adolescent is trying to look sophisticated.

211

Thus, although it is useful to underscore the continuity of enmeshment as a contributing factor in the genesis of anorexia nervosa, we must also consider how new social arrangements and personal expectations have changed the motivational dynamics that underlie enmeshment. From a clinical perspective, we have little idea of what new parental values, styles of parental behavior, or family interactions may be contributing to the current "epidemic" (post-1960).

The literature on recent family change provides few clues and concentrates on structural issues such as divorce and remarriage or number of children. But there is no positive correlation between divorce and anorexia nervosa, suggesting that we push for more intense investigation of parental inputs within stable, nuclear families. This question suggests that students of the family and the life course take a closer look at the parents of the anorectic generations in terms of their personal achievement values and parental styles.

Efforts are needed to assess more carefully the role of fathers in the etiology of anorexia nervosa because an expanded research focus reduces the likelihood of blaming just mothers. Certainly the role of fathers in relation to daughters has changed considerably.

In the seventies, our culture seemed to have "found" fatherhood, as exemplified by the numerous popular and scientific books on fathers and fathering. Our culture now upholds an ideal of fatherhood that encourages men to be more involved in parental activities and to expand the father role to include caring for the emotional needs of one's children. How this ideal relates to modern anorexia nervosa remains to be explored. It appears that being male no longer is a guarantee of freedom from body-image concerns. In fact, even though women continue to be more likely than men to feel fat (Silberstein, Striegel-Moore, Timko, & Rodin, 1988), survey data suggest that men are catching up with women (Cash, Winstead, & Janda, 1986; Striegel-Moore & Kearney-Cooke, 1991). At this point, we can only speculate about the significance of fathers' increased preoccupation with appearance and shape for their daughter's body esteem. Research has already established a relationship between mothers' dieting and food behaviors and the severity of the daughters' disordered eating (Drewnowski, Yee, & Krahn, 1988). It is quite plausible that fathers' attitudes as well as dieting and exercise efforts may also contribute to the development of eating disorders in adolescent daughters. Thus, although the overt behavioral symptom (food refusal) has remained the same, the social and personal dynamics that underlie enmeshment may be quite different because both parents have changed.

★ THE LANGUAGE OF FOOD AND THE BODY

In societies where food scarcity is not a problem, the appetite appears to become more of a social and emotional instrument (Brumberg, 1988). Moreover, food is an important analog of the self. Food choice is a form of self-expression made according to aesthetic, literary, and social ideas as well as economic and physiological requirements (Barthes, 1975; Lévi-Strauss, 1966). In anorexia nervosa, today and in the past, young women use the appetite as a voice, as a way of saying something about personal identity.

Ideas about food and eating circulating in popular culture are central to the anorectic experience today and in the Victorian era. The Victorian anorectic was likely to say, "I cannot eat because I have no appetite" or "When I eat, I feel bad." The modern anorectic generally says, "I am too fat and I need to be very careful with my food." Although we recognize these statements as rationalizations for the symptom's deeper emotional meaning, it is useful to understand the changing language of food and the body because the language provides an important context for understanding a disorder such as anorexia nervosa.

In Victorian society, food and feminity were linked in such a way as to promote restrictive eating among privileged adolescent girls. According to the bourgeois perspective, only peasant or working-class women ate with gusto; their bodies were robust. By contrast, privileged women and girls cultivated "birdlike" appetites and slim bodies that marked them as ethereal and spiritual. Meat eating was considered an inflammatory or socially aggressive act among privileged young women; many women thought it was necessary to hide their eating from public view. Doctors reported that many adolescent girls became phobic about certain foods and about eating itself. Displays of appetite became problematic for young women who understood appetite to be both a sign of sexuality and an indication of lack of self-restraint.

We live in a social and cultural environment where food is also loaded with complex meanings. In our society, some young women fear normal food and eating because eating constitutes the first step on the way to being fat. In this obesophobic culture, rigid dieting constitutes a popular form of perfectionism and competitiveness. For example, anorectic clients report that when they enter a room at a party they immediately rank all the women in the room in terms of body weight. The anorectic experiences her greatest satisfaction if she ranks lowest; if she has not achieved the prized place in the order, she feels despair. Many anorectic clients talk about how they compete with a sister over who is thinner.

Moreover, today the act of eating may no longer induce feelings of shame because of a sexualized meaning of food. However, eating may evoke shame because of the anticipated consequence of gaining weight (Silberstein, Striegel-

Moore, & Rodin, 1987). Not uncommonly, women talk about their embarrassment about eating in public, particularly in front of others whose opinions they value. "Eating lightly" is a culturally prescribed strategy to attain the thin body ideal and is clearly linked to femininity. Data from social-psychological experiments suggest that women who "eat lightly" are perceived to be more feminine than women who eat normal meals (Mori, Chaiken, & Pliner, 1987). Furthermore, women appear to adjust their eating behavior to the social context in which it occurs, presumably in the service of "impression management." For example, women ate significantly less when asked to interact with a desirable man than when they interacted with an undesirable man or another women. In contrast, the eating behavior of men was not influenced by the attractiveness of their women partners (Mori et al., 1987). Hence, modern women seem to be aware that their eating and weight serve as a primary form of communication about their femininity.

In addition, our society is characterized by an extraordinary amount of attention, particularly in the educated middle and upper classes, to the notion of "right" foods. Food cultists and food fads are coupled with a constant stream of new diet regimens aimed at promoting beauty, health, and happiness. Clinically, today we see a fair number of anorectic and bulimic women who are vegetarians (Kadambari, Gowers, & Crisp, 1986). In effect, it is easy to see how a young woman can become preoccupied with food and, in the name of purity and health, begin to restrict her food repertoire to a small number of foods or maybe even to a single item eaten only at one specific time of day.

In fact, the ritualistic intensity with which the anorectic diets suggests that the disorder has obsessive-compulsive features (Rothenberg, 1986; Solyom, Freeman, Thomas, & Miles, 1983; Strober, 1980; Strober & Humphrey, 1987). A central characteristic of individuals who display obsessive-compulsive symptoms is a preoccupation with control. Impulses, wishes, fears, or fantasies unacceptable to the individual are controlled by means of obsessional thoughts and compulsive behaviors. In this case, weight regulation serves as a metaphor for self-regulation and self-control as the patient confronts various sources of adolescent anxiety: a changing and maturing body, the mandate to develop interpersonal relationships, and the expectation to become autonomous.

It appears that the typical obsessive-compulsive individual, today and in the Victorian era, exhibits excessive perfectionism, stubbornness, and rigidity, along with a preoccupation with order and cleanliness (Rothenberg, 1986). In the late nineteenth century, women showed they were in control of themselves by being asexual, meticulous about cleanliness, restrained, and slim. This package implied a superior spirituality.

Today, the same characteristics also imply a superior morality and a high degree of control. (Cleanliness is less central because it is taken for granted.) Being in control implies being able to get what one wants to get. Modern concepts of control include being able to restrain one's needs in the service of long-term goals (e.g., career achievement) as well as satisfying one's needs instantly (e.g., buy now, pay later). Thus, our contemporary culture holds up an ideal for women that may be more complicated to actualize, in part because it entails contradictory components. This ambiguity may give rise to considerable anxiety, which in turn may feed the development of compulsive rituals—such as obsessive dieting—as a way of managing anxiety.

★ THE CHANGING SYMPTOM CONSTELLATION

In the history of anorexia nervosa, food refusal represents a basic continuity: anorectics in both the Victorian and modern eras do not eat, although they articulate different reasons for their behavior. There are, however, two "new" symptoms: hyperactivity and bulimia (bingeing and purging). Our final collaborative effort assesses the sources (and consequences) of these new symptoms in light of historical evidence and clinical practice. We argue here that the new symptom constellation is a function of changed social opportunities and greater options for young women as well as of the cultural environment in which they find themselves.

Hyperactivity was not a central feature of anorexia nervosa in the Victorian era, although some published clinical case reports do describe anorectic girls who insisted upon taking long solitary walks, playing at badminton all day, or doing somersaults in bed until late at night. The Victorian physician generally regarded frenetic physical activity on the part of the anorectic patient as a form of "moral perversity" (Brumberg, 1988). Clearly, jogging, swimming, and aerobics were not culturally sanctioned for women a century ago. Doctors in that era also observed anorectic patients who were frenetic about doing charity and philanthropy work (Albutt & Rolleston, 1905).

For contemporary women, exercising is a socially sanctioned and prescribed way to control weight. Not surprisingly, more women than men report that their primary reason for exercising is to control their weight (Klesges, Mizes, & Klesges, 1987; Silberstein et al., 1988). Over the past two decades, exercise studios have sprung up throughout the United States, and women who represent the ideal of American beauty (e.g., film stars, media celebrities, and models) promote different exercise regimens that have kept them healthy, young, and trim. The current fitness movement has also brought about a redefinition of female beauty so that some muscularity is now seen as desirable. Freedman (1986) argues that this creates a double burden for women that generates even more anxiety. For most women, aspiring to be fit is a thinly veiled effort to achieve thinness. That women who exercise religiously are admired for their efforts explains our tolerance for behavioral extremes in this area and also serves as a source of satisfaction to the hyperactive anorectic.

Yet, the symptom of hyperactivity has received relatively little empirical attention despite its being a central feature of anorexia nervosa in our time. In clinical treatment, we see a pattern of excessive and compulsive running, swimming, and exercise that persistently accompanies not eating and diminishes with successful treatment (Kaye, Gwirtsman, George, Ebert, & Petersen, 1986). The more one runs and the less one eats is the prevailing moral calculus in contemporary anorexia nervosa.

Clinical experience suggests that hyperactivity serves a number of functions for the anorectic. For example, excessive exercise provides a way to regulate body weight, to manage the fear of weight gain, and to make up for real or feared transgressions in one's diet. Aside from these weight-related functions, excessive exercising may constitute a compulsive symptom that serves to contain feelings of anxiety by providing a distraction. Furthermore, hyperactivity serves as an achievement ritual to the anorectic, who seeks to compensate for her profound sense of ineffectiveness by aspiring to perfection (Druss & Silverman, 1979). Compulsive exercising also provides a way of punishing oneself and punishing the body that has become the focus of the anorectic's discontent with herself. These examples show a variety of ways (that are not mutually exclusive) in which the role of hyperactivity can be understood in an individual case. Regardless of the particular reason, the contemporary anorectic's frantic physical activity occurs in a climate of acceptance, admiration, and even envy.

The issue of bulimia in anorexia nervosa is more difficult to explain. Since the 1980s, an increasing number of patients appear to "mix" bulimia with anorexia nervosa. This condition may be referred to as *bulimia nervosa* or *bulimarexia* (American Psychiatric Association, 1987; Boskind-White & White, 1983; Russell, 1979). In the historical material that Brumberg examined, there was no evidence of bulimia in anorexia nervosa. Victorian doctors did identify and write about "hysterical vomiting," but that was a different phenomenon altogether and did not involve the same patient group. It could be that bulimia was a hidden or covert activity, kept secret from parents and physicians. Yet, we hypothesize that covert bulimia was unlikely on the basis of what we know about Victorian girls, their families, and their homes.

First, the degree of privacy needed to support covert bingeing and purging was not generally available to young women in the Victorian era. If there were an indoor toilet with plumbing facilities, it would be shared with parents, siblings, and guests so that chronic regurgitation and its telltale signs and smells would be hard to hide on a regular basis. To eliminate all traces of regurgitation, a flush toilet of some kind is required, but in the late nineteenth century many homes still used chamber pots where the "evidence" collected.

Second, eating in the nineteenth-century middle class was a highly visible and interactive activity, arranged for certain times of the day, and organized around a fixed center of sociability: the family dinner table. The kitchen (in contrast to the dining room) was the territory of domestic servants, and leftovers from the family were for servants to eat. It is difficult to conceive how the Victorian girl could have acted autonomously enough to secure large amounts of food on her own and, then, have had the time to eat it undetected. Where did she binge? (At the family table? At teatime while visiting an aunt or neighbor?) Where did she secure large amounts of easily digestible foods? (Did she raid the larder when everyone was in bed? Was she able to purchase food items for herself whenever she wanted?) On historical grounds, we argue that these opportunities were simply not available to Victorian young women and that bulimia nervosa was probably not part of the symptom repertoire of the earlier age.

Bulimia in anorexia nervosa seems to be a recent development suited to the pace and psychology of our contemporary society. To a large extent, the characteristic bingeing and purging of the modern bulimic depends on personal freedom, a desocialized eating environment, lack of supervision, and the availability—at almost any time—of food for purchase. Personal reports from bulimic women include regular mention of picking up "fast" or prepared foods in supermarkets or convenience stores and eating alone in cars or other solitary settings. Brumberg (1988) suggests the ways in which the contemporary epidemic of eating disorders may be related to (1) the availability of food in our society; (2) desocialized eating, particularly on college campuses where rates of anorexia and bulimia are quite high; and (3) "learning" the behavior from others who know how to do it (Striegel-Moore, Silberstein, & Rodin, 1986).

The emergence of bulimia as a symptom may also be related to two other important but essentially contradictory aspects of our culture: the extraordinary emphasis on dieting (a form of denial) and the equally powerful push for instant gratification. Many current psychological theories of bulimia nervosa propose that the increasingly thin beauty ideal plays a major role in promoting bingeing and purging. The data on the effects of starvation on mood and behavior make a compelling argument for a link between dieting and binge eating (Polivy & Herman, 1985). In other words, the emphasis on the former makes the latter possible. Astute clinicians increasingly discern that chronic denial around food sets the stage for bulimic behaviors.

Despite this pervasive American preoccupation with dieting, our society also promotes instant gratification and the notion that "you can have it all." Traditionally, Americans admired persons who attained success through hard work. Today we admire and envy those who are happy and successful without observable effort. We are told to "work smarter, not harder" (Machlowitz, 1980). At the same time, the ability to indulge oneself—in exotic foods, an elegant perfume, a massage, or a sensual vacation—is now regarded as a sign of mental health, whereas once these same self-indulgences generated moral indignation if not vilification.

The bulimic symptomatology mirrors these contemporary cultural characteristics. Bingeing behavior—almost always involving easily digestible foods high in carbohydrates, sugar, and fat—is based on instantaneous gratification. There are no appetizers to tease the palate and no delays between courses. A lot of food (as much as 10,000 calories at one sitting) is consumed as quickly as possible (Abraham & Beaumont, 1982; Fairburn, Cooper, & Cooper, 1986). In the act of regurgitating this food, the bulimic finds a temporarily efficacious compromise: a way to offset the caloric implications of indulgence without the hard work of chronic dieting. In effect, she has found a way, albeit a dangerous one, to beat the metabolic system.

The two "new" symptoms we describe seem to have real physical consequences for anorectic patients and for treatment. Anorexia nervosa is a more dangerous disease than ever before because of the extraordinarily low weights of its victims. An index of body mass in anorexia nervosa hospital admissions since the 1930s shows a marked decline over time, suggesting that more patients with severe weight loss are being admitted today than were admitted 50 years ago. In short, today's anorectic is thinner than ever before (Agras & Kramer, 1983). The severity of anorexia nervosa today could be the result of delays in treatment or more extended outpatient therapy before hospitalization, but this scenario is unconvincing given our current sensitivity to the disease. We suggest that the severity of current cases probably reflects the patients' zealous commitment to both exercise and diet as well as peer, parental, and/or medical tolerance for thinner bodies. And, quite importantly, bulimia in anorexia nervosa complicates the therapeutic picture: clinical data suggest a worsening of symptomatology once a young woman begins to engage in regular vomiting as a way of undoing the caloric effects of her binges (Garfinkel & Garner, 1982).

★ CONCLUSION

The modern symptom constellation in anorexia nervosa—chronic refusal of food, hyperactivity, and bulimia—did not (and could not) exist a century ago. Although individual and family variables contribute to the psychogenesis of anorexia nervosa, our present cultural infatuation with extremely thin women, our preoccupation with exercise, and our desocialized style of eating have all contributed to an acceleration in the number of women who are at risk for anorexia nervosa (and bulimia nervosa). Our joint investigation suggests, however, that more than incidence is at stake here. In fact, the past two decades have witnessed the expansion of the symptom repertoire in a manner altogether in keeping with the spirit and direction of contemporary culture.

For the purposes of our collaboration, we had to put aside the individual psyche and focus instead on patterns of symptoms and family life. We have not done "psychohistory" as it is usually practiced because we offer no analysis of the psychogenic origins of anorexia nervosa in any particular person. Yet, it is our contention that the collaboration of psychology and history can be quite fruitful, particularly in understanding psychopathologies that are clearly linked to particular stages of development and/or socially constructed sex and gender roles.

Ultimately, history serves psychology as an important vehicle for understanding the pattern and variability of psychiatric symptoms, and psychology serves history as a suggestive model for interpreting human behavior. Both disciplines gain from a fuller understanding of this fact: today, as in the past, psychopathologies exist in reciprocal relationship to the culture in which they occur. It is our hope that clinicians can incorporate this insight as they work to understand how individual patients construct their reality and that social psychologists will begin to take seriously the issue of social contagion, particularly as it affects adolescent women.

217

REFERENCES

Abraham, S.F., Beamont, P.J.V. 1982. How patients describe bulimia or binge eating. *Psychological Medicine* 12, 625–635.

Agras, W.S. and Kramer, H.C. 1983. The treatment of anorexia nervosa: Do different treatments have different outcomes? *Psychiatric Annals* 13, 928–929, 932–935.

Albutt, T.C. and Rolleston, H.D. (eds.) 1905. *A system of medicine.* Vol 3. *Diseases of obscure origin. Alimentary and peritoneum.* New York: Macmillan.

American Psychiatric Association. 1987. *Diagnostic and statistical manual of mental disorders: DSM-III-R* (3rd ed. Rev.) Washington, D.C.: Author.

Attie, I, and Brooks-Gunn, J. 1989. Development of eating problems in adolescent girls: A longitudinal study. *Developmental Psychology* 25, 70–79.

Barthes, R. 1975. Toward a psychosociology of contemporary food consumption. In *European diets from pre-industrial to modern times,* ed E. Forster and R. Forster. New York: Harper and Row.

Boskind-White, M. and White, W. 1983. *Bulimarexia: The binge/purge cycle.* New York: Norton.

Brumberg, J.J. 1982. "Ruined" girls: Changing community responses to illegitimacy in Upstate New York, 1890–1920. *Journal of Social History* 18, 147–272.

Brumberg, J.J. 1988. *Fasting girls: The emergence of anorexia nervosa as a modern disease.* Cambridge, MA: Harvard University Press.

Cash, T.F., Winstead, B.A. and Janda, L.H. 1986. The great American shape-up. *Psychology Today* 20, 30–37.

Chernin, K. 1981. *The obsession: Reflections on the tyranny of slenderness.* New York: Harper and Row.

Costanzo, P.R. and Woody, E.Z. 1979. Externality as a function of obesity in children: Persuasive style or eating-specific attribute? *Journal of Personality and Social Psychology* 37, 2286–2296.

Drewnowski, A., Yee, D.K., and Krahn, D.D. 1988. Bulimia in college women: Incidence and recovery rates. *American Journal of Psychiatry* 145, 753–755.

Druss, R.G. and Silverman, J.A. 1979. Body image and perfectionism of ballerinas. Comparison and contrast with anorexia nervosa. *General Hospital Psychiatry* 1, 115–121.

Fairburn, C.G., Cooper, Z. and Cooper, P.J. 1986. The clinical features and maintenance of bulimia nervosa. In *Handbook of eating disorders: Physiology, psychology, and treatment of obesity, anorexia, and bulimia,* ed. K.D. Brownell and J.P. Foreyt. New York: Basic Books.

Freedman, R.J. 1986. *Beauty Bound.* Lexington, MA: Lexington Books.

Friedlander, M.L. and Siegel, S.M. 1990. Separation-individuation difficulties and cognitive-behaviorial indicators of eating disorders among college women. *Journal of Counseling Psychology* 37, 74–78.

Garfinkel, P.E. and Garner, D.M. 1982. *Anorexia nervosa: A multidimensional perspective.* New York: Brunner/Mazel.

Garfinkel, P.E. and Kaplan, A.S. 1985. Starvation based perpetuating mechanisms in anorexia nervosa and bulimia. *International Journal of Eating disorders* 4, 651–665.

Garner, D.M., Garfinkel, P.E., and Bemis, K.M. 1982. A Multidimensional Psychotherapy for Anorexia Nervosa. *International Journal of Eating Disorders* 1, 2, 3–46.

Kadambari, R., Gowers, S. and Crisp, A. 1986. Some correlates of vegetarianism in anorexia nervosa. *International Journal of Eating Disorders* 5, 539–544.

Kaye, W.H., Gwirtsman, H., George, T., Ebert, M.H. and Petersen, R. 1986. Caloric consumption and activity levels after weight recovery in anorexia nervosa: A prolonged delay in normalization. *International Journal of Eating Disorders* 5, 489–502.

Klesges, R.C., Mizes, J.S., and Klesges, L.M. 1987. Self-help dieting strategies in college males and females. *International Journal of Eating Disorders* 6, 409–417.

Lévi-Strauss, C. 1966. The culinary triangle (P. Brooks, Trans.) *Partisan Review* 33, 586–595.

Machlowitz, M. 1980. *Workalcoholic: Living with them, working with them.* Reading, MA: Addison-Wesley.

Minuchin, S. 1974. *Families and family therapy.* Cambridge, MA: Harvard University Press.

Minuchin, S., Baker, L., Rosman, B.L., Liebman, R., Milman, L. and Todd, T.C. 1975. A conceptual model of psychosomatic illness in children. Family organization and family therapy. *Archives of General Psychiatry* 32, 1031–1038.

Minuchin, S., Rosman, B.L., and Baker, L., with Liebman, R. 1978. *Psychosomatic families: Anorexia nervosa in context.* Cambridge, MA: Harvard University Press.

Mori, D., Chaiken, S., and Pliner, P. 1987. "Eating lightly" and the self-presentation of femininity. *Journal of Personality and Social Psychology* 53, 693–702.

Polivy, J and Herman, C.P. 1985. Dieting and binging. A causal analysis. *American Psychologists* 40, 193–201.

Prince, R. 1985. The concept of culture-bound syndromes: Anorexia nervosa and brain-fag. *Social Science and Medicine* 21, 197–203.

Rothenberg, A. 1986. Eating disorder as a modern obsessive-compulsive syndrome. *Psychiatry* 49, 45–53.

Russell, G. 1979. Bulimia nervosa: An ominous variant of anorexia nervosa. *Psychological Medicine* 9, 429–448.

Sargent, J., Liebman, R., and Silver, M. 1985. Family therapy for anorexia nervosa. In *Handbook of psychotherapy for anorexia nervosa and bulimia,* ed D.M. Garner and P.E. Garfinkel. New York: Guilford Press.

Silberstein, L.R., Striegel-Moore, R.H., and Rodin, J. 1987. Feeling fat: A woman's shame. In *The role of shame in symptom formation,* ed H.B. Lewis. Hillsdale, NJ: Erlbaum.

Silberstein, L.R., Striegel-Moore, R.H., Timko, C., and Rodin, J. 1988. Behavioral and psychological implications of body dissatisfaction: Do men and women differ? *Sex Roles* 19, 219–232.

Solyom, L., Freeman, R.J., Thomas, C.D., and Miles, J.E. 1983. The comparative psychopathology of anorexia nervosa. Obsessive-compulsive disorder or phobia? *International Journal of Eating Disorders* 3(1), 3–14.

Striegel-Moore, R.H., and Kearney-Cooke, A. 1991. *Exploring the determinants and consequences of parents' attitudes about their children's physical appearance.* Manuscript submitted for publication. (Department of Psychology, Wesleyan University, Middletown, CT.)

Striegel-Moore, R.H., Silberstein, L.R. and Rodin, J. 1986. Toward an understanding of risk factors in bulimia. *American Psychologist* 41, 246–258.

Strober, M. 1980. Personality and symptomatological features in young, nonchronic anorexia nervosa patients. *Journal of Psychosomatic Research* 24, 353–358.

Strober, M., and Humphrey, L.L. 1987. Familial contributions to the etiology and course of anorexia nervosa and bulimia. *Journal of Consulting and Clinical Psychology* 55, 654–659.

Yager, J. 1982. Family Issues in the pathogenesis of anorexia nervosa. *Psychosomatic Medicine* 44, 43–60.

"A WAY OUTA NO WAY":

EATING PROBLEMS AMONG AFRICAN-

AMERICAN, LATINA, AND WHITE WOMEN

BECKY WANGSGAARD THOMPSON

16

Bulimia, anorexia, binging, and extensive dieting are among the many health issues women have been confronting in the last 20 years. Until recently, however, there has been almost no research about eating problems among African-American, Latina, Asian-American, or Native American women, working-class women, or lesbians.[1] In fact, according to the normative epidemiological portrait, eating problems are largely a white, middle-, and upper-class heterosexual phenomenon. Further, while feminist research has documented how eating problems are fueled by sexism, there has been almost no attention to how other systems of oppression may also be implicated in the development of eating problems.

In this article, I reevaluate the portrayal of eating problems as issues of appearance based in the "culture of thinness." I propose that eating problems begin as ways women cope with various traumas including sexual abuse, racism, classism, sexism, heterosexism, and poverty. Showing the interface between these traumas and the onset of eating problems explains why women may use eating to numb pain and cope with violations to their bodies. This theoretical shift also permits an understanding of the economic, political, social, educational, and cultural resources that women need to change their relationship to food and their bodies.

★ EXISTING RESEARCH ON EATING PROBLEMS

There are three theoretical models used to explain the epidemiology, etiology, and treatment of eating problems. The biomedical model offers important scientific research about possible physiological causes of eating problems and the physiological dangers of purging and starvation (Copeland 1985; Spack 1985). However, this model adopts medical treatment strategies that may disempower and traumatize women (Garner 1985; Orbach 1985). In addition, this model ignores many social, historical, and cultural factors that influence women's eating patterns. The psychological model identifies eating problems as "multidimensional disorders" that are influenced by biological, psychological, and cultural factors (Garfinkel and Garner 1982). While useful in its exploration of effective therapeutic treatments, this model, like the biomedical one, tends to neglect women of color, lesbians, and working-class women.

The third model, offered by feminists, asserts that eating problems are gendered. This model explains why the vast majority of people with eating problems are women, how gender socialization and sexism may relate to eating problems, and how masculine models of psychological development have shaped theoretical interpretations. Feminists offer the culture of thinness model as a key reason why eating problems predominate among women. According to this model, thinness is a culturally, socially, and economically enforced requirement for female beauty. This imperative makes women vulnerable to cycles of dieting, weight loss, and subsequent weight gain, which may lead to anorexia and bulimia (Chernin 1981; Orbach 1978, 1985; Smead 1984).

Feminists have rescued eating problems from the realm of individual psychopathology by showing how the difficulties are rooted in systematic and pervasive attempts to control women's body sizes and appetites. However, researchers have yet to give significant attention to how race, class, and sexuality influence women's understanding of their bodies and appetites. The handful of epidemiological studies that include African-American women and Latinas casts doubt on the accuracy of the normative epidemiological portrait. The studies suggest that this portrait reflects which particular populations of women have been studied rather than actual prevalence (Andersen and Hay 1985; Gray, Ford, and Kelly 1987; Hsu 1987; Nevo 1985; Silber 1986).

More important, this research shows that bias in research has consequences for women of color. Tomas Silber (1986) asserts that many well-trained professionals have either misdiagnosed or delayed their diagnoses of eating problems among African-American and Latina women due to stereotypical thinking that these problems are restricted to white women. As a consequence, when African-American women or Latinas are diagnosed, their eating problems tend to be more severe due to extended processes of starvation prior to intervention. In her autobiographical account of her eating problems, Retha Powers (1989), an African-American woman, describes being told not to worry about her eating problems since "fat is more acceptable in the Black community" (p. 78). Stereotypical perceptions held by her peers and teachers of the "maternal Black woman" and the "persistent mammy-brickhouse Black woman image" (p. 134) made it difficult for Powers to find people who took her problems with food seriously.

Recent work by African-American women reveals that eating problems often relate to women's struggles against a "simultaneity of oppression" (Clarke 1982; Naylor 1985; White 1991). Byllye Avery (1990), the founder of the National Black Women's Health Project, links the origins of eating problems among African-American women to the daily stress of being undervalued and overburdened at home and at work. In Evelyn C. White's (1990) anthology, *The Black Woman's Health Book: Speaking for Ourselves*, Georgiana Arnold (1990) links her eating problems partly to racism and racial isolation during childhood.

Recent feminist research also identifies factors that are related to eating problems among lesbians (Brown 1987; Dworkin 1989; Iazzetto 1989; Schoenfielder and Wieser 1983). In her clinical work, Brown (1987) found that lesbians who have internalized a high degree of homophobia are more likely to accept negative attitudes about fat than are lesbians who have examined their internalized homophobia. Autobiographical accounts by lesbians have also indicated that secrecy about eating problems among lesbians partly reflects their fear of being associated with a stigmatized illness ("What's Important" 1988).

Attention to African-American women, Latinas, and lesbians paves the way for further research that explores the possible interface between facing multiple oppressions and the development of eating problems. In this way, this study is part of a larger feminist and sociological research agenda that seeks to understand how race, class, gender, nationality, and sexuality inform women's experiences and influence theory production.

★ METHODOLOGY

I conducted 18 life history interviews and administered lengthy questionnaires to explore eating problems among African-American, Latina, and white women. I employed a snowball sample, a method in which potential respondents often first learn about the study from people who have already participated. This method was well suited for the study since it enabled women to get information about me and the interview process from people they already knew. Typically, I had much contact with the respondents prior to the interview. This was particularly important given the secrecy associated with this topic (Russell 1986; Silberstein, Striegel-Moore, and Rodin 1987), the necessity of women of color and lesbians to be discriminating about how their lives are studied, and the fact that I was conducting across-race research.

To create analytical notes and conceptual categories from the data, I adopted Glaser and Strauss's (1967) technique of theoretical sampling, which directs the researcher to collect, analyze, and test hypotheses during the sampling process (rather than imposing theoretical categories onto the data). After completing each interview transcription, I gave a copy to each woman who wanted one. After reading their interviews, some of the women clarified or made additions to the interview text.

Demographics of the Women in the Study

The 18 women I interviewed included 5 African-American women, 5 Latinas, and 8 white women. Of these women, 12 are lesbian and 6 are heterosexual. Five women are Jewish, 8 are Catholic, and 5 are Protestant. Three women grew up outside of the United States. The women represented a range of class backgrounds (both in terms of origin and current class status) and ranged in age from 19 to 46 years old (with a median age of 33.5 years).

The majority of the women reported having had a combination of eating problems (at least two of the following: bulimia, compulsive eating, anorexia, and/or extensive dieting). In addition, the particular types of eating problems often changed during a woman's life span. (For example, a woman might have been bulimic during adolescence and anorexic as an adult.) Among the women, 28 percent had been bulimic, 17 percent had been bulimic and anorexic, and 5 percent had been anorexic. All of the women who had been anorexic or bulimic also had a history of compulsive eating and extensive dieting. Of the women, 50 percent were compulsive eaters and dieters (39 percent) or compulsive eaters (11 percent) but had not been bulimic or anorexic.

Two-thirds of the women have had eating problems for more than half of their lives, a finding that contradicts the stereotype of eating problems as transitory. The weight fluctuation among the women varied from 16 to 160 pounds, with an average fluctuation of 74 pounds. This drastic weight change illustrates the degree to which the women adjusted to major changes in body size at least once during their lives as they lost, gained, and lost weight again. The average age of onset was 11 years old, meaning that most of the women developed eating problems prior to puberty. Almost all of the women (88 percent) consider themselves as still having a problem with eating, although the majority believe they are well on the way to recovery.

★ THE INTERFACE OF TRAUMA AND EATING PROBLEMS

One of the most striking findings in this study was the range of traumas the women associated with the origins of their eating problems, including racism, sexual abuse, poverty, sexism, emotional or physical abuse, heterosexism, class injuries, and acculturation.[2] The particular constellation of eating problems among the women did not vary with race, class, sexuality, or nationality. Women from various race and class backgrounds attributed the origins of their eating problems to sexual abuse, sexism, and emotional and/or physical abuse. Among some of the African-American and Latina women, eating problems were also associated with poverty, racism, and class injuries. Heterosexism was a key factor in the onset of bulimia, compulsive eating, and extensive dieting among some of the lesbians. These oppressions are not the same nor are the injuries caused by them. And certainly, there are a variety of potentially harmful ways that women respond to oppression (such as using drugs, becoming a workaholic, or committing suicide). However, for all these women, eating was a way of coping with trauma.

Sexual Abuse

Sexual abuse was the most common trauma that the women related to the origins of their eating problems. Until recently, there has been virtually no research exploring the possible relationship between these two phenomena. Since the mid-1980s, however, researchers have begun identifying connections between the two, a task that is part of a larger feminist critique of traditional psychoanalytic symptomatology (DeSalvo 1989; Herman 1981; Masson 1984). Results of a number of incidence studies indicate that between one-third and two-thirds of women who have eating problems have been abused (Oppenheimer et al. 1985; Root and Fallon 1988). In addition, a growing number of therapists and researchers have offered interpretations of the meaning and impact of eating problems for survivors of sexual abuse (Bass and Davis 1988; Goldfarb 1987; Iazzetto 1989; Swink and Leveille 1986). Kearney-Cooke (1988) identifies dieting and binging as common ways in which women cope with frequent psychological consequences of sexual abuse (such as body image disturbances, distrust of people and one's own experiences, and confusion about one's feelings). Root and Fallon (1989) specify ways that victimized women cope with assaults by binging and purging: bulimia serves many functions, including anesthetizing the negative feelings associated with victimization. Iazzetto's innovative study (1989), based on in-depth interviews and art therapy sessions, examines how a woman's relationship to her body changes as a consequence of sexual abuse. Iazzetto discovered that the process of leaving the body (through progressive phases of numbing, dissociating and denying) that often occurs during sexual abuse parallels the process of leaving the body made possible through binging.

Among the women I interviewed, 61 percent were survivors of sexual abuse (11 of the 18 women), most of whom made connections between sexual abuse and the beginning of their eating problems. Binging was the most common method of coping identified by the survivors. Binging helped women "numb out" or anesthetize their feelings. Eating sedated, alleviated anxiety, and combated loneliness. Food was something that they could trust and was accessible whenever they needed it. Antonia (a pseudonym) is an Italian-American woman who was first sexually abused by a male relative when she was four years old. Retrospectively, she knows that binging was a way she coped with the abuse. When the abuse began, and for many years subsequently, Antonia often woke up during the middle of the night with anxiety attacks or nightmares and would go straight to the kitchen cupboards to get food. Binging helped her block painful feelings because it put her back to sleep.

223

Like other women in the study who began binging when they were very young, Antonia was not always fully conscious as she binged. She described eating during the night as "sleep walking. It was mostly desperate—like I had to have it." Describing why she ate after waking up with nightmares, Antonia said, "What else do you do? If you don't have any coping mechanisms, you eat." She said that binging made her "disappear," which made her feel protected. Like Antonia, most of the women were sexually abused before puberty; four of them before they were five years old. Given their youth, food was the most accessible and socially acceptable drug available to them. Because all of the women endured the psychological consequences alone, it is logical that they coped with tactics they could do alone as well.

One reason Antonia binged (rather than dieted) to cope with sexual abuse is that she saw little reason to try to be the small size girls were supposed to be. Growing up as one of the only Italian Americans in what she described as a "very WASP town," Antonia felt that everything from her weight and size to having dark hair on her upper lip were physical characteristics she was supposed to hide. From a young age she knew she "never embodied the essence of the good girl. I don't like her. I have never acted like her. I can't be her. I sort of gave up." For Antonia, her body was the physical entity that signified her outsider status. When the sexual abuse occurred, Antonia felt she had lost her body. In her mind, the body she lived in after the abuse was not really hers. By the time Antonia was 11, her mother put her on diet pills. Antonia began to eat behind closed doors as she continued to cope with the psychological consequences of sexual abuse and feeling like a cultural outsider.

Extensive dieting and bulimia were also ways in which women responded to sexual abuse. Some women thought that the men had abused them because of their weight. They believed that if they were smaller, they might not have been abused. For example when Elsa, an Argentine woman, was sexually abused at the age of 11, she thought her chubby size was the reason the man was abusing her. Elsa said, "I had this notion that these old perverts liked these plump girls. You heard adults say this too. Sex and flesh being associated." Looking back on her childhood, Elsa believes she made fat the enemy partly due to the shame and guilt she felt about the incest. Her belief that fat was the source of her problems was also supported by her socialization. Raised by strict German governesses in an upper-class family, Elsa was taught that a woman's weight was a primary criterion for judging her worth. Her mother "was socially conscious of walking into places with a fat daughter and maybe people staring at her." Her father often referred to Elsa's body as "shot to hell." When asked to describe how she felt about her body when growing up, Elsa described being completely alienated from her body. She explained,

> Remember in school when they talk about the difference between body and soul? I always felt like my soul was skinny. My soul was free. My soul sort of flew. I was tied down by this big bag of rocks that was my body. I had to drag it around. It did pretty much what it wanted and I had a lot of trouble controlling it. It kept me from doing all the things that I dreamed of.

As is true for many women who have been abused, the split that Elsa described between her body and soul was an attempt to protect herself from the pain she believed her body caused her. In her mind, her fat body was what had "bashed in her dreams." Dieting became her solution, but, as is true for many women in the study, this strategy soon led to cycles of binging and weight fluctuation.

224

Ruthie, a Puerto Rican woman who was sexually abused from 12 until 16 years of age, described bulimia as a way she responded to sexual abuse. As a child, Ruthie liked her body. Like many Puerto Rican women of her mother's generation, Ruthie's mother did not want skinny children, interpreting that as a sign that they were sick or being fed improperly. Despite her mother's attempts to make her gain weight. Ruthie remained thin through puberty. When a male relative began sexually abusing her, Ruthie's sense of her body changed dramatically. Although she weighed only 100 pounds, she began to feel fat and thought her size was causing the abuse. She had seen a movie on television about Romans who made themselves throw up and so she began doing it, in hopes that she could look like the "little kid" she was before the abuse began. Her symbolic attempt to protect herself by purging stands in stark contrast to the psychoanalytic explanation of eating problems as an "abnormal" repudiation of sexuality. In fact, her actions and those of many other survivors indicate a girl's logical attempt to protect herself (including her sexuality) by being a size and shape that does not seem as vulnerable to sexual assault.

These women's experiences suggest many reasons why women develop eating problems as a consequence of sexual abuse. Most of the survivors "forgot" the sexual abuse after its onset and were unable to retrieve the abuse memories until many years later. With these gaps in memory, frequently they did not know why they felt ashamed, fearful, or depressed. When sexual abuse memories resurfaced in dreams, they often woke feeling upset but could not remember what they had dreamed. These free-floating, unexplained feelings left the women feeling out of control and confused. Binging or focusing on maintaining a new diet were ways women distracted or appeased themselves, in turn, helping them regain a sense of control. As they grew older, they became more conscious of the consequences of these actions. Becoming angry at themselves for binging or promising themselves they would not purge again was a way to direct feelings of shame and self-hate that often accompanied the trauma.

Integral to this occurrence was a transference process in which the women displaced onto their bodies painful feelings and memories that actually derived from or were directed toward the persons who caused the abuse. Dieting became a method of trying to change the parts of their bodies they hated, a strategy that at least initially brought success as they lost weight. Purging was a way women tried to reject the body size they thought was responsible for the abuse. Throwing up in order to lose the weight they thought was making them vulnerable to the abuse was a way to try to find the body they had lost when the abuse began.

Poverty

Like sexual abuse, poverty is another injury that may make women vulnerable to eating problems. One woman I interviewed attributed her eating problems directly to the stress caused by poverty. Yolanda is a Black Cape Verdean mother who began eating compulsively when she was 27 years old. After leaving an abusive husband in her early 20s, Yolanda was forced to go on welfare. As a single mother with small children and few financial resources, she tried to support herself and her children on $539 a month. Yolanda began binging in the evenings after putting her children to bed. Eating was something she could do alone. It would calm her, help her deal with loneliness, and make her feel safe. Food was an accessible commodity that was cheap. She ate three boxes of macaroni and cheese when nothing else was available. As a single mother with little money, Yolanda felt as if her body was the only thing she had left. As she described it,

225

> I am here, [in my body] 'cause there is no where else for me to go. Where am I going to go? This is all I got...that probably contributes to putting on so much weight cause staying in your body, in your home, in yourself, you don't go out. You aren't around other people...You hide and as long as you hide you don't have to face...nobody can see you eat. You are safe.

When she was eating, Yolanda felt a momentary reprieve from her worries. Binging not only became a logical solution because it was cheap and easy but also because she had grown up amid positive messages about eating. In her family, eating was a celebrated and joyful act. However, in adulthood, eating became a double-edged sword. While comforting her, binging also led to weight gain. During the three years Yolanda was on welfare, she gained seventy pounds.

Yolanda's story captures how poverty can be a precipitating factor in eating problems and highlights the value of understanding how class inequalities may shape women's eating problems. As a single mother, her financial constraints mirrored those of most female heads of households. The dual hazards of a race- and sex-stratified labor market further limited her options (Higginbotham 1986). In an article about Black women's health, Byllye Avery (1990) quotes a Black woman's explanation about why she eats compulsively. The woman told Avery,

> I work for General Electric making batteries, and, I know it's killing me. My old man is an alcoholic. My kid's got babies. Things are not well with me. And one thing I know I can do when I come home is cook me a pot of food and sit down in front of the TV and eat it. And you can't take that away from me until you're ready to give me something in its place. (7)

Like Yolanda, this woman identifies eating compulsively as a quick, accessible, and immediately satisfying way of coping with the daily stress caused by conditions she could not control. Connections between poverty and eating problems also show the limits of portraying eating problems as maladies of upper-class adolescent women.

The fact that many women use food to anesthetize themselves, rather than other drugs (even when they gained access to alcohol, marijuana, and other illegal drugs), is partly a function of gender socialization and the competing demands that women face. One of the physiological consequences of binge eating is a numbed state similar to that experienced by drinking. Troubles and tensions are covered over as a consequence of the body's defensive response to massive food intake. When food is eaten in that way, it effectively works like a drug with immediate and predictable effects. Yolanda said she binged late at night rather than getting drunk because she could still get up in the morning, get her children ready for school, and be clearheaded for the college classes she attended. By binging, she avoided the hangover or sickness that results from alcohol or illegal drugs. In this way, food was her drug of choice since it was possible for her to eat while she continued to care for her children, drive, cook, and study.

Binging is also less expensive than drinking, a factor that is especially significant for poor women. Another woman I interviewed said that when her compulsive eating was at its height, she ate breakfast after rising in the morning, stopped for a snack on her way to work, ate lunch at three different cafeterias, and snacked at her desk throughout the afternoon. Yet even when her eating had become constant, she was still able to remain employed. While her patterns of eating no doubt slowed her productivity, being drunk might have slowed her to a dead stop.

Heterosexism

The life history interviews also uncovered new connections between heterosexism and eating problems. One of the most important recent feminist contributions has been identifying compulsory heterosexuality as an institution which truncates opportunities for heterosexual and lesbian women (Rich 1986). All of the women interviewed for this study, both lesbian and heterosexual, were taught that heterosexuality was compulsory, although the versions of this enforcement were shaped by race and class. Expectations about heterosexuality were partly taught through messages that girls learned about eating and their bodies. In some homes, boys were given more food than girls, especially as teenagers, based on the rationale that girls need to be thin to attract boys. As the girls approached puberty, many were told to stop being athletic, begin wearing dresses, and watch their weight. For the women who weighed more than was considered acceptable, threats about their need to diet were laced with admonitions that being fat would ensure becoming an "old maid."

While compulsory heterosexuality influenced all of the women's emerging sense of their bodies and eating patterns, the women who linked heterosexism directly to the beginning of their eating problems were those who knew they were lesbians when very young and actively resisted heterosexual norms. One working-class Jewish woman, Martha, began compulsively eating when she was 11 years old, the same year she started getting clues of her lesbian identity. In junior high school, as many of her female peers began dating boys, Martha began fantasizing about girls, which made her feel utterly alone. Confused and ashamed about her fantasies, Martha came home every day from school and binged. Binging was a way she drugged herself so that being alone was tolerable. Describing binging, she said, "It was the only thing I knew. I was looking for a comfort." Like many women, Martha binged because it softened painful feelings. Binging sedated her, lessened her anxiety, and induced sleep.

Martha's story also reveals ways that trauma can influence women's experience of their bodies. Like many other women, Martha had no sense of herself as connected to her body. When I asked Martha whether she saw herself as fat when she was growing up she said, "I didn't see myself as fat. I didn't see myself. I wasn't there. I get so sad about that because I missed so much." In the literature on eating problems, *body image* is the term that is typically used to describe a woman's experience of her body. This term connotes the act of imagining one's physical appearance. Typically, women with eating problems are assumed to have difficulties with their body image. However, the term body image does not adequately capture the complexity and range of bodily responses to trauma experienced by the women. Exposure to trauma did much more than distort the women's visual image of themselves. These traumas often jeopardized their capacity to consider themselves as having bodies at all.

Given the limited connotations of the term body image, I use the term *body consciousness* as a more useful way to understand the range of bodily responses to trauma.[3] By body consciousness I mean the ability to reside comfortably in one's body (to see oneself as embodied) and to consider one's body as connected to oneself. The disruptions to their body consciousness that the women described included leaving their bodies, making a split between their body and mind, experiencing being "in" their bodies as painful, feeling unable to control what went in and out of their bodies, hiding in one part of their bodies, or simply not seeing themselves as having bodies. Binging, dieting, or purging were common ways women responded to disruptions to their body consciousness.

Racism and Class Injuries

For some of the Latinas and African-American women, racism coupled with the stress resulting from class mobility related to the onset of their eating problems. Joselyn, an African-American woman, remembered her white grandmother telling her she would never be as pretty as her cousins because they were lighter skinned. Her grandmother often humiliated Joselyn in front of others, as she made fun of Joselyn's body while she was naked and told her she was fat. As a young child, Joselyn began to think that although she could not change her skin color, she could at least try to be thin. When Joselyn was young, her grandmother was the only family member who objected to Joselyn's weight. However, her father also began encouraging his wife and daughter to be thin as the family's class standing began to change. When the family was workin- class, serving big meals, having chubby children, and keeping plenty of food in the house was a sign the family was doing well. But, as the family became mobile, Joselyn's father began insisting that Joselyn be thin. She remembered, "When my father's business began to bloom and my father was interacting more with white businessmen and seeing how they did business, suddenly thin became important. If you were a truly well-to-do family, then your family was slim and elegant."

As Joselyn's grandmother used Joselyn's body as territory for enforcing her own racism and prejudice about size, Joselyn's father used her body as the territory through which he channeled the demands he faced in the white-dominated business world. However, as Joselyn was pressured to diet, her father still served her large portions and bought treats for her and the neighborhood children. These contradictory messages made her feel confused about her body. As was true for many women in this study, Joselyn was told she was fat beginning when she was very young even though she was not overweight. And, like most of the women, Joselyn was put on diet pills and diets before even reaching puberty, beginning the cycles of dieting, compulsive eating, and bulimia.

The confusion about body size expectations that Joselyn associated with changes in class paralleled one Puerto Rican woman's association between her eating problems and the stress of assimilation as her family's class standing moved from poverty to working class. When Vera was very young, she was so thin that her mother took her to a doctor who prescribed appetite stimulants. However, by the time Vera was eight years old, her mother began trying to shame Vera into dieting. Looking back on it, Vera attributed her mother's change of heart to competition among extended family members that centered on "being white, being successful, being middle class,... and it was always, 'Ay Bendito. She is so fat. What happened?'"

The fact that some of the African-American and Latina women associated the ambivalent messages about food and eating to their family's class mobility and/or the demands of assimilation while none of the eight white women expressed this (including those whose class was stable and changing) suggests that the added dimension of racism was connected to the imperative to be thin. In fact, the class expectations that their parents experienced exacerbated standards about weight that they inflicted on their daughters.

228

★ EATING PROBLEMS AS SURVIVAL STRATEGIES: FEMINIST THEORETICAL SHIFTS

My research permits a reevaluation of many assumptions about eating problems. First, this work challenges the theoretical reliance on the culture-of-thinness model. Although all of the women I interviewed were manipulated and hurt by this imperative at some point in their lives, it is not the primary source of their problems. Even in the instances in which a culture of thinness was a precipitating factor in anorexia, bulimia, or binging, this influence occurred in concert with other oppressions.

Attributing the etiology of eating problems primarily to a woman's striving to attain a certain beauty ideal is also problematic because it labels a common way that women cope with pain as essentially appearance-based disorders. One blatant example of sexism is the notion that women's foremost worry is about their appearance. By focusing on the emphasis on slenderness, the eating problems literature falls into the same trap of assuming that the problems reflect women's "obsession" with appearance. Some women were raised in families and communities in which thinness was not considered a criterion for beauty. Yet, they still developed eating problems. Other women were taught that women should be thin, but their eating problems were not primarily in reaction to this imperative. Their eating strategies began as logical solutions to problems rather than problems themselves as they tried to cope with a variety of traumas.

Establishing links between eating problems and a range of oppressions invites a rethinking of both the groups of women who have been excluded from research and those whose lives have been the basis of theory formation. The construction of bulimia and anorexia as appearance-based disorders is rooted in a notion of femininity in which white middle- and upper-class women are portrayed as frivolous, obsessed with their bodies, and overly accepting of narrow gender roles. This portrayal fuels women's tremendous shame and guilt about eating problems—as signs of self-centered vanity. This construction of white middle- and upper-class women is intimately linked to the portrayal of working-class white women and women of color as their opposite: as somehow exempt from accepting the dominant standards of beauty or as one step away from being hungry and therefore not susceptible to eating problems. Identifying that women may binge to cope with poverty contrasts the notion that eating problems are class bound. Attending to the intricacies of race, class, sexuality, and gender pushes us to rethink the demeaning construction of middle-class femininity and establishes bulimia and anorexia as serious responses to injustices.

Understanding the link between eating problems and trauma also suggests much about treatment and prevention. Ultimately, their prevention depends not simply on individual healing but also on changing the social conditions that underlie their etiology. As Bernice Johnson Reagon sings in Sweet Honey in the Rock's song "Oughta Be a Woman," "A way outa no way is too much to ask/too much of a task for any one woman" (Reagon 1980).[4] Making it possible for women to have healthy relationships with their bodies and eating is a comprehensive task. Beginning steps in this direction include ensuring that (1) girls can grow up without being sexually abused, (2) parents have adequate resources to raise their children, (3) children of color grow up free of racism, and (4) young lesbians have the chance to see their reflection in their teachers and community leaders. Ultimately, the prevention of eating problems depends on women's access to economic, cultural, racial, political, social, and sexual justice.

229

NOTES

1. I use the term *eating problems* as an umbrella term for one or more of the following: anorexia, bulimia, extensive dieting, or binging. I avoid using the term *eating disorder* because it categorizes the problems as individual pathologies, which deflects attention away from the social inequalities underlying them (Brown 1985). However, by using the term *problem* I do not wish to imply blame. In fact, throughout, I argue that the eating strategies that women develop begin as logical solutions to problems, not problems themselves.
2. By trauma I mean a violating experience that has long-term emotional, physical, and/or spiritual consequences that may have immediate or delayed effects. One reason the term *trauma* is useful conceptually is its association with the diagnostic label Post Traumatic Stress Disorder (PTSD) (American Psychological Association 1987). PTSD is one of the few clinical diagnostic categories that recognizes social problems (such as war or the Holocaust) as responsible for the symptoms identified (Trimble 1985). This concept adapts well to the feminist assertion that a woman's symptoms cannot be understood as solely individual, considered outside of her social context, or prevented without significant changes in social conditions.
3. One reason the term *consciousness* is applicable is its intellectual history as an entity that is shaped by social context and social structures (Delphy 1984; Marx 1964). This link aptly applies to how the women described their bodies because their perceptions of themselves as embodied (or not embodied) directly relate to their material conditions (living situations, financial resources, and access to social and political power).
4. Copyright © 1980. Used by permission of Songtalk Publishing.

REFERENCES

American Psychological Association. 1987. *Diagnostic and statistical manual of mental disorders.* 3rd ed. rev. Washington, DC: American Psychological Association.

Andersen, Arnold, and Andy Hay. 1985. Racial and socioeconomic influences in anorexia nervosa and bulimia. *International Journal of Eating Disorders* 4:479–87.

Arnold, Georgiana. 1990. Coming home: One Black woman's journey to health and fitness. In *The Black women's health book: Speaking for ourselves,* edited by Evelyn C. White. Seattle, WA: Seal Press.

Avery, Byllye Y. 1990. Breathing life into ourselves: The evolution of the National Black Women's Health Project. In *The Black women's health book: Speaking for ourselves,* edited by Evelyn C. White. Seattle, WA: Seal Press.

Bass, Ellen, and Laura Davis. 1988. *The courage to heal: A guide for women survivors of child sexual abuse.* New York: Harper & Row.

Brown, Laura S. 1985. Women, weight and power: Feminist theoretical and therapeutic issues. *Women and Therapy* 4:61–71.

———. 1987. Lesbians, weight and eating: New analyses and perspectives. In *Lesbian psychologies,* edited by the Boston Lesbian Psychologies Collective. Champaign: University of Illinois Press.

Chernin, Kim. 1981. *The obsession: Reflections on the tyranny of slenderness.* New York: Harper & Row.

Clarke, Cheryl. 1982. *Narratives*. New Brunswick, NJ: Sister Books.

Copeland, Paul M. 1985. Neuroendocrine aspects of eating disorders. In *Theory and treatment of anorexia nervosa and bulimia: Biomedical, sociocultural and psychological perspectives*, edited by Steven Wiley Emmett. New York: Brunner/Mazel.

Delphy, Christine. 1984. *Close to home: A materialist analysis of women's oppression*. Amherst: University of Massachusetts Press.

DeSalvo, Louise. 1989. *Virginia Woolf: The impact of childhood sexual abuse on her life and work*. Boston, MA: Beacon.

Dworkin, Sari H. 1989. Not in man's image: Lesbians and the cultural oppression of body image. In *Loving boldly: Issues facing lesbians*, edited by Ester D. Rothblum and Ellen Cole. New York: Harrington Park Press.

Garfinkel, Paul E., and David M. Garner. 1982. *Anorexia nervosa: A multidimensional perspective*. New York: Brunner/Mazel.

Garner, David. 1985. Iatrogenesis in anorexia nervosa and bulimia nervosa. *International Journal of Eating Disorders* 4:701–26.

Glaser, Barney G., and Anselm L. Strauss. 1967. *The discovery of grounded theory: Strategies for qualitative research*. New York: Aldine DeGruytler.

Goldfarb, Lori. 1987. Sexual abuse antecedent to anorexia nervosa, bulimia and compulsive overeating: Three case reports. *International Journal of Eating Disorders* 6:675–80.

Gray, James, Kathryn Ford, and Lily M. Kelly. 1987. The prevalence of bulimia in a Black college population. *International Journal of Eating Disorders* 6:733–40.

Herman, Judith. 1981. *Father-daughter incest*. Cambridge, MA: Harvard University Press.

Higginbotham, Elizabeth. 1986. We were never on a pedestal: Women of color continue to struggle with poverty, racism and sexism. In *For crying out loud*, edited by Rochelle Lefkowitz and Ann Wilborn. Boston: MA: Pilgrim Press.

Hsu, George. 1987. Are eating disorders becoming more common in Blacks? *International Journal of Eating Disorders* 6:113–24.

Iazzetto, Demetria. 1989. When the body is not an easy place to be: Women's sexual abuse and eating problems. Ph.D. diss., Union for Experimenting Colleges and Universities, Cincinnati, Ohio.

Kearney-Cooke, Ann. 1988. Group treatment of sexual abuse among women with eating disorders. *Women and Therapy* 7:5–21.

Marx, Karl. 1964. *The economic and philosophic manuscripts of 1844*. New York: International.

Masson, Jeffrey. 1984. *The assault on the truth. Freud's suppression of the seduction theory*. New York: Farrar, Strauss & Giroux.

Naylor, Gloria. 1985. *Linden Hills*. New York: Ticknor & Fields.

Nevo, Shoshana. 1985. Bulimic symptoms: Prevalence and ethnic differences among college women. *International Journal of Eating Disorders* 4:151–68.

Oppenheimer, R., K. Howells, R. L. Palmer, and D. A. Chaloner. 1985. Adverse sexual experience in childhood and clinical eating disorders: A preliminary description. *Journal of Psychiatric Research* 19:357–61.

Orbach, Susic. 1978. *Fat is a feminist issue*. New York: Paddington.

——. 1985. Accepting the symptom: A feminist psychoanalytic treatment of anorexia nervosa. In *Handbook of psychotherapy for anorexia nervosa and bulimia*, edited by David M. Garner and Paul E. Garfinkel. New York: Guilford.

Powers, Retha. 1989. Fat is a Black women's issue. *Essence* Oct., 75, 78, 134, 136.

Reagon, Bernice Johnson. 1980. Oughta be a woman. On Sweet Honey in the Rock's album *Good News*. Music by Bernice Johnson Reagon; lyrics by June Jordan. Washington, DC: Songtalk.

Rich, Adrienne. 1986. Compulsory heterosexuality and lesbian existence. In *Blood, bread and poetry*. New York: Norton.

Root, Maria P. P., and Patricia Fallon. 1988. The incidence of victimization experiences in a bulimic sample. *Journal of Interpersonal Violence* 3:161–73.

——. 1989. Treating the victimized bulimic: The functions of binge-purge behavior. *Journal of Interpersonal Violence* 4:90–100.

Russell, Diana E. 1986. *The secret trauma: Incest in the lives of girls and women*. New York: Basic Books.

Schoenfielder, Lisa, and Barbara Wieser, eds. 1983. *Shadow on a tightrope: Writings by women about fat liberation*. Iowa City, IA: Aunt Lute Book Co.

Silber, Tomas, 1986. Anorexia nervosa in Blacks and Hispanics. *International Journal of Eating Disorders* 5:121–28.

Silberstein, Lisa, Ruth Striegel-Moore, and Judith Rodin. 1987. Feeling fat: A woman's shame. In *The role of shame in symptom formation*, edited by Helen Block Lewis. Hillsdale, NJ: Lawrence Erlbaum.

Smead, Valerie. 1984. Eating behaviors which may lead to and perpetuate anorexia nervosa, bulimarexia, and bulimia. *Women and Therapy* 3:37–49.

Spack, Norman, 1985. Medical complications of anorexia nervosa and bulimia. In *Theory and treatment of anorexia nervosa and bulimia: Biomedical, sociocultural and psychological perspectives*, edited by Steven Wiley Emmett. New York: Brunner/Mazel.

Swink, Kathy, and Antoinette E. Leveille. 1986. From victim to survivor: A new look at the issues and recovery process for adult incest survivors. *Women and Therapy* 5:119–43.

Trimble, Michael. 1985. Post-traumatic stress disorder: History of a concept. In *Trauma and its wake: The study and treatment of post-traumatic stress disorder*, edited by C. R. Figley. New York: Brunner/Mazel.

What's important is what you look like. 1988. *Gay Community News*, July, 24–30.

White, Evelyn C., ed. 1990. *The Black women's health book: Speaking for ourselves*. Seattle, WA: Seal Press.

——. 1991. Unhealthy appetites. *Essence*, Sept., 28, 30.

DIABETES, DIET, AND NATIVE
AMERICAN FORAGING TRADITIONS

17

GARY PAUL NABHAN

The consumption of "wild" foods has been interpreted as an adaptive strategy for periods of seasonal, other irregularly episodic, and long-term catastrophic shortages of cultigens. The very pursuit of wild foods generally can be construed as adaptive since, in that quest, individuals learn about new ecologies.

—*Nina L. Etkin,* Eating on the Wild Side

"It was this way, long time ago," explained the old Indian lady. She was a member of the binational Hia C-ed O'odham tribe that is scattered across Sonora and Arizona. A distant relative was translating her words for me: "The People were like a cultivated field producing after its kind, recognizing its kinship; the seeds remain and continue to produce. Today all the bad times have entered the People, and they [the O'odham] no longer recognize their way of life. The People separated from one another and became few in number. Today all the O'odham are vanishing."

Candelaria Orosco sat in a small clapboard house in the depressed mining town of Ajo, Arizona, recalling the native foods that she had hunted, gathered, and harvested before the turn of the century. Her leg hurt her, for the sores on it were taking a long time to heal because of the adult-onset diabetes that came to her late in life. Today this is a common affliction among her people, the O'odham, who suffer one of the highest incidences of diabetes of any ethnic population in the world. Orosco was trying hard to describe how her kin, the migratory Hia C-ed O'odham, had lived prior to such afflictions, when roughly five hundred of them had obtained their living from what outsiders consistently regard as a "hopeless desert." Around the time of Orosco's birth, a U.S. Indian agent had visited the O'odham and described their habitat in this way: "Place the same number of whites on a barren, sandy desert such as they live on, and tell them to subsist there; the probability is that in two years they would become extinct."

Yet Orosco was invoking a litany of plant and animal names in her native language, names referring to herbs and seeds and roots, birds and reptiles and mammals that had once formed the bulk of her diet. Even when English rather than O'odham words are used for these nutritional resources, the names of the native foods that once filled her larder still have an alluring ring. For meat, her family ate desert tortoises, pack rats, bighorn sheep, hornworm larvae, desert cotton-tails, pronghorn antelope, Gambel's quail, mule deer, whitewing doves, Colorado River squawfish, black-tailed jackrabbits, and occasional stray camels. Although the unpredictability of desert rains kept her people from harvesting crops on a regular basis in many places, they did successfully cultivate white tepary beans, Old Lady's Knees muskmelons, green-striped cushaw squash, sixty-day-flour corn, Spanish watermelons, white Sonora wheat, and Papago peas. They gathered a much greater variety of wild plant foods: broomrape stalks, screwbean mesquite pods, plantain seed, tansy mustard, amaranth, cholla cactus buds, honey mesquite, povertyweed, wolfberries, hog potato, lamb's-quarters, prickly pears, ironwood seed, wild chiles, chia, organ-pipe cactus fruit, old woman's cactus seed, and sandfood. When Orosco mentioned sandfood—an underground parasite that attaches to the roots of wind-beaten shrubs on otherwise barren dunes—my facial expression must have given me away.

"What's that?" she asked in O'odham.

I stammered, "Sandfood... are you saying that the old people knew how to find it, and they once told you how it tasted?" Few people alive today have ever seen this sandfood, let alone tasted it, for it is now endangered by habitat destruction.

"I said that I ate it. I wouldn't have told you that it had a good sweet taste if I hadn't eaten it myself. How could I explain to you what other people thought it tasted like or how to harvest it? Because it doesn't stick up above the ground like other plants, I had to learn to see where the little dried-up ones from the year before broke the surface. That's where I would dig."

She described how you can steam succulent plants in earthen pits, boil down cactus fruit into jam or syrup, roast meat over an open fire, and parch wild legume seeds to keep them for later use. Orosco spoke matter-of-factly of such work, the customary tasks of desert subsistence. There was no romanticism about the halcyon days of her youth, but it was clear that she felt some foods of value had been lost.

Her concerns about the loss of gathering and farming traditions were shared by her tribesman, the late Miguel Velasco, in an interview with Fillman Bell in 1979:

> We are from the sand, and known as Sand Indians, to find our way of life on the sand of the earth. That is why we go all over to seek our food to live as well. We cover a large portion of land in different harvest seasons to gather our food to store in time of winter season. Long time ago, this was our way of life. We did not buy food. We worked hard to gather foods. We never knew what coffee was until the White People came. We drank the desert fruit juices in harvest time. The desert food is meant for the Indians to eat. The reason so many Indians die young is because they don't eat their desert food anymore. They would not know how to survive if Anglos stopped selling them food. The old Indians lived well with their old way of life.

Oral accounts such as these are often regarded as "nostalgia for the old ways," even by eminent ethnobotanists such as Peter Raven, who used this phrase to dismiss my exploration of the value of Native American subsistence strategies,

Enduring Seeds. If by "nostalgia" we mean a longing for experiences, things, or acquaintances belonging to the past, we may indeed include under its rubric some of the statements made by Indian elders. Consider, for instance, this commentary by Chona, recorded by Ruth Underhill in *The Autobiography of a Papago Woman* during the early thirties:

> We always kept gruel in our house. It was in a big clay pot that my mother had made. She ground up seeds into flour. Not wheat flour—we had no wheat. But all the wild seeds, the good pigweed and the wild grassess...Oh, how good that gruel was! I have never tasted anything like it. Wheat flour makes me sick. I think it has no strength. But when I am weak, when I am tired, my grandchildren make me a gruel out of the wild seeds. *That* is food.

Chona was clearly referring to foodstuffs that had formed a greater proportion of her dietary intake in the past than they did at the time she spoke with Underhill. Yet these foods were not exclusively relegated to the past, because they retained their functional value when she was sick, providing her with nourishment that mainstream American foods could not. Moreover, in Chona's mind, the wild desert seeds had remained the quintessential foods, embodying her cultural definition of what food should be. Because she did not consider the value of her people's traditional diet to be obsolete, Chona's respect for that diet should not be relegated to the shelf holding antiquarian trivia.

This point was brought home to me again by Candelaria Orosco. After we spent several hours looking at pressed herbs, museum collections of seeds, and historic photos of plants that I had presumed to be formerly part of her culture's daily subsistence, she brought out several of her own collections. She rolled out from under her bed two green-striped cushaw squashes that she had grown in her postage-stamp–sized garden. Then she reached under her stove and showed me caches of cholla cactus buds and some wild tansy mustard seeds she had gathered. These foodstuffs were not simply for "old times' sake"; they had been the fruits of her efforts toward self-reliance for more than ninety years.

Cynics or self-described "realists" might still dismiss the relict consumption of native foods by Chona or Candelaria Orosco as nostalgic and trivial, and they might dismiss my interest in Candelaria and Chona as a misguided attempt to elevate these women to the status of "ecologically noble savages." Because the plants and animals these women mentioned now make up such a small portion of the diet of contemporary Indians, few contemporary anthropologists even study them, claiming that such traditional foods now play no significant functional role in Native American nutrition or culture. If a Navajo man eats more Kentucky Fried Chicken than he does the mutton of Navajo-Churro sheep, is it not true that ecologically and nutritionally speaking, he is more like an urban Kentuckian than he is like his Diné ancestors? If an O'odham woman eats more fry bread than cholla cactus buds, is she not more pan-Indian than she is a part of her own tribe's historic trajectory?

The answer may be a qualified yes. I interpret many of the O'odham elders' statements as warnings to their descendants that the younger generations are abandoning what it means to be culturally and ecologically O'odham. This concern is explicit in the following statement by the late great O'odham orator Venito García:

> The way life is today, what will happen if the Anglos discontinued their money system? What will happen to our children? They will not want to eat the mountain tur-

tle, because they have never eaten any. Maybe they will eat it if they get hungry enough. I think of all the desert plants we used to eat, the desert spinach we cooked with child....If we continue to practice eating our survival food, we may save our money we do receive sometimes....The Chinese, they still practice their old eating habits. They save all their money. The Anglos don't like this. They [the Chinese] like to eat their ant eggs [rice]. They even use their long sticks to eat with, picking the ant eggs up with their long sticks and pinning it to their mouths. This is their way of life.

To be Chinese is to be one who eats rice with chopsticks, according to García's view as an outsider; likewise, an outsider should be able to recognize the desert-dwelling O'odham by their consumption of cactus, amaranth greens, or mesquite. Although such dietary definitions are too restrictive for ethnographers to take seriously, traditional peoples often use culinary customs as primary indicators of a particular culture.

O'odham elders relate their culinary traditions to their health and survival. The elders not only recall "survival foods" used during times of drought and political disruption but they also remember the curative quality of the native foods that were a customary component of their diets. These presumed curative qualities are now being scientifically investigated, for, in a real sense, native foods may be the best medicine available to the O'odham. The O'odham metabolism evolved for several thousand years under the influence of a particular set of native desert plant foods with peculiar characteristics that formerly protected the people from certain afflictions now common among them.

Through the 1930s, native desert foods contributed a significant portion of Pima, Desert Papago, and Sand Papago diets; mesquite, acorns, chia, tepary beans, cacti, and mescal were eaten as commonly as foods introduced by Europeans. At that time, the O'odham were generally regarded as lean, active people who worked hard at obtaining a subsistence from one of the most unpredictable but biologically diverse deserts in the world. Then government work projects and World War II came along, and rather than persisting with their own foraging traditions, the O'odham became cheap labor for extensive irrigated cotton farms in Anglo communities near their reservations. Others went off to the war and became accustomed to a cash economy and canned food.

When these people returned to their villages in the late forties, their gathering grounds and fields were overgrown or eroded due to lack of care, and off-reservation opportunities were still calling. Government advisers termed their ancient farming and foraging strategies risky and unproductive and offered no assistance in renovating the fields that for centuries had remained fertile under periodic cultivation. Instead, the tribal governments were encouraged either to develop their own large farms using the corporate model or to lease tribal lands to non-Indian farmers for them to do the same. Fewer than a tenth of the traditional farms of the O'odham survived these economic and social pressures. As the droughts of the fifties came and went, subsistence farming went by the wayside, while hunting and gathering remained activities for only a small percentage of them.

Before the war, diabetes had been no more common among the O'odham than it was among the population of the United States as a whole. Yet twenty-five years later, the O'odham had a prevalence of diabetes fifteen times that of the typical Anglo-American community. The average young O'odham man in the early 1970s weighed 44.1 pounds more than his 1940s counterpart and was considered overweight verging on obese. Since obesity is correlated with susceptibility to diabetes, pathologists at first concluded that the "escape" of the O'odham from their primitive, feast-or-famine cycle of subsistence had made calories more regularly available year-round; hence, they had gained weight and diabetes had set in.

The only flaw in this theory was that the modern wage-earning O'odham individual was not necessarily consuming any more calories than the traditional O'odham or, for that matter, than the average Anglo. The difference, I believe, was not in the number of calories consumed but in the kinds of wild and cultivated plants with which the O'odham had coevolved.

A few years ago, I sent a number of desert foods traditionally prepared by the O'odham to a team of Australian nutritionists, who analyzed the foods for any effects they might have on blood-sugar and insulin levels following meals. High blood-sugar levels are of concern because they stress the capacity of the pancreas to keep pace with insulin production. If stressed repeatedly, the pancreas essentially becomes poisoned. Insulin metabolism becomes permanently damaged, and the dangerous dysfunctional syndrome known as diabetes develops. Yet when a person is fed acorns, mesquite pods, and tepary or lima beans, the soluble dietary fiber, tannins, and insulin in these foods reduce blood-sugar levels and prolong the period over which sugar is absorbed into the blood. Insulin production and sensitivity are also improved. In short, these native foods may protect Indian diabetics from suffering high blood-sugar levels following a meal. Mesquite pods and acorns are among the 10 percent most effective foods ever analyzed for their effects in controlling blood-sugar rises after a meal. Unlike domesticated plant foods, their fiber, tannins, or complex carbohydrates have not been genetically removed by crop breeders or milled away by industrial food technologists' machinery. Historically, the O'odham were consuming more than 120 grams of these "slow-release" soluble fibers a day; now they consume less than a third of that volume.

Recent studies suggest that many desert foods contain mucilaginous polysaccharide gums that are viscous enough to slow the digestion and absorption of sugary foods. Such slow-release gums have probably evolved in many desert plants to slow water loss from the seeds, seedlings, and succulent tissues of mature plants. The O'odham metabolism may, in turn, have adapted to such qualities after centuries of dependence on the foods containing these gums—foods such as prickly pear fruit and pads, cholla cactus buds, plantain seeds, chia seeds, mesquite pods, and tansy mustard seeds. All were former seasonal staples of the O'odham; all are nearly absent from their diet today. Together with Australian nutritionist Jennie Brand, I have advanced the hypothesis that these foods served to protect indigenous people from the diabetic syndrome to which they were genetically susceptible.

For O'odham families who remained on a traditional diet, their genetic predisposition to diabetes was not likely to be expressed. But diabetes-prone Indians on a fast-food diet of fried potatoes, soft drinks or beer, sweets, and corn chips find their insulin metabolism going haywire. Obtaining highly milled grains or finely processed root starches further aggravates the problem. At the Phoenix Indian Hospital, Boyd Swinburn compared the responses of twenty-two patients who changed from a traditional O'odham diet (which I reconstructed from historic accounts) to a fast-food diet consisting of virtually the same number of calories. When they switched to what we nicknamed the "mini-mart diet," their insulin sensitivity to glucose worsened, as did their glucose tolerance. Swinburn concluded, "The influence of Westernization on the prevalence of [adult-onset] diabetes may in part be due to changes in diet composition." For the O'odham and other indigenous peoples whose diets were recently Westernized to highly bred, industrially processed foods, a return to a diet similar to their traditional one is no nostalgic notion; it may, in fact, be a nutritional and cultural imperative.

Recently, I assisted nurse practitioners who were screening Seri neighbors of the O'odham for early warning indicators of diabetes. The Seri have persisted with a traditional diet far longer than the O'odham were able to. When a Seri tribal elder asked why we were recording the genealogies of those Seri women who did have high blood-sugar levels, I tried to explain the genetic component of diabetes to him—that among O'odham, diabetes is known to "run in families." The Seri elder, Alfredo Lopez Blanco, thought about this notion that we call "genetic predisposition" for a moment, and then rejected it as irrelevant.

"Look," he said, shaking his head, "their grandparents weren't overweight in the old days, and I don't think they had this sickness you call diabetes. They're sick now not because of their blood [inheritance] but because their diet has changed. They hardly eat mesquite or cactus or desert tortoise anymore. They eat white-bread sandwiches, Coke, sweets from the stores, and the pork rinds we call *chicharrones*. You don't need to know our family histories so much as you need to remind us to keep eating our desert foods!"

In desert villages where native food plants were formerly gathered, the majority of the O'odham are now classified as unemployed or underemployed. Because their income levels are so low, many Native American families are eligible for government surplus commodity foods, nearly all of which are nutritionally inferior to their native counterparts. At the same time, the hyperabundance of these federally donated foodstuffs serves as a disincentive for local food gathering. As one O'odham woman lamented, "Why gather different kinds of beans when someone delivers big bags of pinto beans to our house every month?" The demise of local foraging, the indulgence in a welfare economy, and a worsening of health and self-esteem are linked. This syndrome is not restricted to the O'odham; because of their high Mexican and Indian population, by the year 2000 Arizonan and Sonoran health programs will spend at least two billion dollars annually on their four hundred thousand citizens suffering from diabetes.

Is it not ironic that at the same time, more than a half million agricultural acres in the Sonoran Desert have been left barren owing to excessive irrigation costs of producing water-consumptive, conventional crops? The sowing of native food plants, some of which require a third to a fifth as much water as conventional crops to obtain the same food yields, has not been given due consideration as a feasible option for the management of these lands. The society to which the food industry caters is simply not accustomed to the tastes, textures, and preparation techniques associated with these wild and semidomesticated foods. And so the transplanted agriculture has damaged the health of the land, at the same time that it has diminished the land's capacity to produce the plant foods needed to sustain our own well-being.

I only wish that we had heeded the words of ethnobotanist Melvin Gilmore, who began his work among Native American farmers and gatherers seventy years ago, before the tide of diabetes and agricultural desolation had swamped them:

> We shall make the best and most economical use of our land when our population shall become adjusted in habit to the natural conditions. The country cannot be wholly made over and adjusted to a people of foreign habits and tastes. There are

large tracts of land in America whose bounty is wasted because the plants that can be grown on them are not acceptable to our people. This is not because the plants are not useful and desirable but because their valuable qualities are not known.... The adjustment of American consumption to American conditions of production will bring about greater improvement in conditions of life than any other material agency.

NOTES

Earlier versions of this essay appeared in the *Journal of Gastronomy* 5, no. 2 (Autumn 1989), reprinted in Robert Clark's edited collection, *Our Sustainable Table* (San Francisco: North Point Press, 1990). I have since realized that the O'odham metabolic preference is for wild foods rich in soluble fiber, tannins, and insulins, not for native crops per se.

The epigraph is from Nina L. Etkin's introduction to her edited volume, *Eating on the Wild Side* (Tucson: University of Arizona Press, 1994).

The Chono interview is in Ruth Underhill's *Autobiography of a Papago Woman* (Menasha, Wisc.: American Anthropological Association, 1936). The first interviews of Candelaria Orosco and Miguel Velasco ever published were included with other O'odham oral histories in Fillman Bell, Keith Anderson, and Yvonne G. Stewart, *The Quitobaquito Cemetery and Its History* (Tucson: Western Archaeological Center, National Park Service, 1980). I have since recorded Candelaria Orosco several more times; she is now well over one hundred years of age.

Recent analyses of the value of wild foods in controlling blood-sugar and insulin levels challenge the National Institute of Health's view that this disease should be treated genetically, instead of as a cultural, nutritional dilemma. See Janette C. Brand, B. Janelle Snow, Gary P. Nabhan, and A. Stewart Truswell, "Plasma Glucose and Insulin Response to Traditional Pima Indian Meals," *American Journal of Clinical Nutrition* (1989). See also A. C. Frati-Munari, B. E. Gordillo, P. Alamiro, and C. R. Ariza, "Hypoglycemic Effect of Opuntia Streptacantha Lemaire in NIDDM," *Diabetes Care* 11 (1988): 63–66, and Charles W. Weber, Radziah B. Arrifin, Gary P. Nabhan, Ahmed Idouraine, and Edwin A. Kohlhepp, "Composition of Sonoran Desert Foods Used by Tohono O'odham and Pima Indians," *Journal of Ecology of Food and Nutrition* 26 (Summer 1996).

I assisted National Institutes of Health researchers in reconstructing a historic Piman diet for the study by B. A. Swinburn, V. L. Boyce, R. N. Bergman, B. V. Howard, and C. Bogardus, "Deterioration in Carbohydrate Metabolism and Lipoprotein Changes Induced by a Modern, High Fat Diet in Pima Indians and Caucasians," *Journal of Clinical Endocrinology and Metabolism* 73 (1): 156–64 (1991).

Janette Brand and I have compiled but have not completed editing an anthology, *Parallel Evolution of Australian Aborigines and Native Americans? Diet, Lifestyle, and Diabetes*, from an international workshop held at Kims Toowon Bay, New South Wales, Australia, 10–13 May 1993. Copies are available to read at the Native Seeds/SEARCH library, Tucson.

I end with a quote from Melvin R. Gilmore, "Uses of Plants by Indians of the Missouri River Region," *Bureau of American Ethnology Annual Reports* 33 (1919): 43–154.

THE CONTEMPORARY SOUP KITCHEN

IRENE GLASSER

18

It was snowing the day of George's memorial service. Most of the twenty or so people present were from the Tabernacle Soup Kitchen. The service was held in the small chapel above the soup kitchen, in Saint Mary's Church. George had died the previous week, and his obituary consisted of two sentences: one announcing his death, the other identifying the minister who would officiate at the memorial service.

George was a soup kitchen "regular." He was a black man in his fifties, tall, thin, with long matted hair and torn clothing. His eyes were always bloodshot, his beard grew in many directions, his gait was slow, and he stuttered. Often he could be seen walking on the streets between the west end of town and Main Street. He liked to stop and rest on the low stone wall of the First State Bank. George had been receiving dialysis treatment several times a week at a hospital in a neighboring town, and white gauze was visible around his wrists, under his oversized coat. I first met him in the spring of 1983 at the soup kitchen. I remember how solemn and dignified he seemed, and at the time I was conscious of trying not to disturb his meal; I sensed, and later confirmed, that this was to be his sole meal of the day.

At George's memorial service, the minister faced the group and said that we were gathered together to commemorate George Smith's life and death. Since the minister had not known him personally, he read from small pieces of paper people had given to him to remember George: "I will always remember George's friendly smile and soft giggle as he greeted people from the wall of the bank." "I will always remember that as down and out as George looked and seemed to be, he always carried himself with respect and dignity."

Jane, a woman who had a severe motor impairment and was considered mentally slow, had taken the morning off from her sheltered workshop to attend the service. She read a psalm to the group. Alan, a balding thin man with a large bump on his forehead, gave the eulogy. He said that George's friendliness was outstanding, and he even liked the way George mispronounced his last name (referring to

George's speech problems). At that point I noticed a large young man with long red hair, who usually sat by himself at the soup kitchen and was considered violent by the rest of the guests. He was seated several pews in front of me and was shaking all over throughout the service. Although I had never seen the man speak with George, he too was there to mourn George's death. Barbara, a soup kitchen worker on welfare, whose upper arms were tattooed with flowers, appeared to be an organizer of the ceremony. She handed everyone a copy of "Amazing Grace," which we sang at the end of the service. None of George's family seemed to be there.

After the ceremony, as people were leaving to go back downstairs to the soup kitchen, I tried to find out if anyone knew how George had died. No one did. Once downstairs, a group of men continued discussing his death. One said he thought the weather must have contributed to it.

What is the nature and significance of the soup kitchen, which had become in George's life and death the very center of his social existence? The soup kitchen may be seen as a particular adaptation to contemporary North American life, serving as an ecological niche for a segment of the poor who are considered "marginal" to the dominant culture. This marginality takes the forms of little income, long-term unemployment, debilitating physical conditions, serious mental illness, and a separation from family relationships. Because of these conditions, soup kitchen guests lack the sources of human contact that most of us take for granted in work, family relationships, and consumer activities. The soup kitchen functions as a symbolic living room for this segment of people in poverty, in a manner reminiscent of "Tally's Corner" for a group of urban men in Washington, D.C. (Liebow 1967), and the tavern for alcoholic men (Dumont 1967: 938–45).

The Tabernacle Soup Kitchen (a pseudonym) began in 1981 and is one of the thousands that have emerged in the United States in the last ten years. It is located in Middle City, a small industrialized city of 20,000 people in a New England state. The soup kitchen serves a hot meal to approximately one hundred men, women, and children six days a week, fifty-two weeks a year. The doors of the soup kitchen are open from 8:30 A.M., when the large pot of coffee is first turned on, to 1 P.M., when the kitchen workers put the chairs on the table and the soup kitchen is over for the day. It is housed in the basement of a church, which gives it an underground quality in both a figurative and a literal sense. In Philip Slater's terms (1970: 21), the soup kitchen guests are out of sight and out of mind for the rest of the community.

The soup kitchen offers its guests a unique configuration of physical comforts and opportunities for sociability and acceptance in ways that are culturally congruent with its diners' lifestyles. It provides such physical comforts as doughnuts, coffee, a hot meal, and bathrooms, along with a public meeting place where people can come together and leave at will. The guests are known to each other and the staff on a first-name or street-name basis. The soup kitchen is one of the few examples of a "hassle-free" or "problem-free" service in our society (Rousseau 1981). The people, or "guests" as they are called in the soup kitchen nomenclature, know that the soup kitchen offers shelter for the morning and a hot meal at noon, yet there are no forms to fill out, no eligibility requirements to meet, no demands to "reform," "gain insight," or change.

★ THE SOUP KITCHEN AS AN URBAN CULTURE

The goal of this study is to describe the main features of the culture that emerges from the daily coming together of the guests in the dining room of the soup kitchen.

Anthropology in particular has been concerned with the description and analysis of culture, or the ways in which people view their world, define reality, and organize their behavior (Spradley 1970). A useful characterization of culture is provided by Ward Goodenough, who states: "A society's culture consists of whatever it is one has to know or believe in order to operate in a manner acceptable to its members." (Goodenough 1957: 167). In working within modern, pluralistic societies, the term *subculture* is often used, recognizing that individuals also share the attributes of the dominant North American culture, as well as that of their own group. I will continue the tradition of many urban anthropologists (see, for example, Spradley 1970) and refer to the patterns of behavior in the soup kitchen dining room as a culture.

The culture of the soup kitchen is created as guests interact within the confines of the dining room, in what Anthony F. C. Wallace (1970: 26) calls *repetitive patterns of reciprocal interaction*. These patterns are created in part by the guests and in part by the staff, who enact the numerous rituals of daily soup kitchen life, including making coffee, serving doughnuts, announcing the menu, serving the meal, and socializing within the dining room. New guests are enculturated and learn proper soup kitchen behavior as they sit and observe the daily rituals of passing time and eating in the dining room. The soup kitchen culture then becomes one of the many cultures of an individual's repertoire.

★ REVIEW OF WORKS IN URBAN ANTHROPOLOGY

When anthropologists and other social scientists have entered the world of the poor in our society, they have often made discoveries and presented descriptions that have challenged stereotypes and had important social policy implications. One of the earliest examples of an in-depth study of people outside the mainstream of society was William Foote Whyte's classic *Street Corner Society* (1943). Whyte was able to form in-depth relationships with members of a group of young Italians in a street corner gang of an eastern city in the 1930s. Unlike earlier writers who characterized this type of community as "disorganized," he found a high degree of organization and activity. His personal relationships with the people moved Whyte and his readership beyond facile descriptions of them as clients of social agencies or criminals in the court system, to see them as individuals who had been inventive in their struggles for survival.

In the 1960s Elliot Liebow focused on the world of black men in a lower-class ghetto. Previous research had portrayed the black male as "absent" from community life. Liebow was able to chart the day-to-day life of the group of men he found at "Tally's Corner" (1967). He challenged the popular stereotype of the black male as being unmotivated to work, and in detail unearthed the realities of employment and unemployment for men in the black ghetto.

In a different vein, James Spradley (*You Owe Yourself a Drunk*, 1970) presented the cultural scene of the homeless men of Seattle's skid row, a group that is either avoided or stereotyped by the rest of society. Spradley referred to the men as urban nomads and tried to understand the insider's point of view. This cultural description made more comprehensible the "revolving-door" relationship that men charged with public drunkenness had with the jails and treatment centers to which they were sent. More recently, Ellen Baxter and Kim Hopper in *Private Lives/Public Spaces* (1981) directed attention to the contemporary homeless people of urban areas. Contrary to the belief that the homeless do not want shelter, they found that the men and women they came to know on the streets would indeed accept shelter if it was safe and offered with dignity. The Baxter and Hopper report is now frequently cited in discussions of homelessness.

The soup kitchen can be viewed as a social center and so has a role in the lives of the guests similar to that of the Jewish Community Center described in the work of Barbara Myerhoff in *Number Our Days* (1978). Myerhoff demonstrated the importance of the Jewish Community Center in the lives of elderly men and women. Her study viewed the Center through the eyes of its members, for whom it had become a surrogate family and surrogate village. In the Center the elderly tried to re-create the memories of their lives in the shtetls and ghettos of Eastern Europe of almost a century ago. So too, I hypothesize that the present-day soup kitchen is a temporary surrogate family and community for a segment of the poor in a small city in New England.

Perhaps the most controversial work arising out of contemporary urban anthropology is that of Oscar Lewis and his characterization of the "culture of poverty" (1966). Lewis attempted to generalize about people living in poverty, using his studies in urban Mexico, Puerto Rico, and New York as a base. He tried to explain what he saw as pervasive feelings of helplessness, pessimism, and despair. He hypothesized that the general tendency of the poor, especially those in industrialized, capitalistic nations, is to develop a particular set of cultural attributes as an adaptation to their lack of money, their high rates of unemployment, and their crowded and generally inhospitable living conditions. These characteristics then became self-defeating and self-perpetuating. He described the major characteristics of this "culture of poverty" as "the lack of effective participation and integration of the poor in the major institutions of the larger society...a minimum of organization beyond the level of the nuclear and extended family...an absence of childhood as a specially prolonged and protected stage in the life cycle...a strong feeling of marginality, of helplessness, of dependence and of inferiority" (Lewis 1966: 51–53).

The problem came about when the poor were seen to have family instability, a lack of effective participation in society's major institutions, and a sense of helplessness *because* of culturally transmitted values, rather than because of the economic and social processes of the larger social system. This focus on the "culture of poverty" implied that the burden of doing something about poverty was on the poor themselves, absolving the rest of society from considering the general economic and social system as a basic cause of poverty. The culture-of-poverty concept also tended to gloss over many of the variations that exist among low-income families. The soup kitchen may be seen as one culture within poverty that in fact is not self-defeating, but is a positive adaptation that cushions some of the harsh realities of life for its guests.

The majority of the guests of the soup kitchen are unemployed and are victims of what Daniel Bell (1973) has called the postindustrial society, in which technical and interpersonal skills have replaced willingness to work as the key to success in employment. In the postindustrial society, there is an illusion of advancement based solely on merit (meritocracy), so that poor people are made to internalize their "failures" in the competitive economic world. Many of the soup kitchen diners *never* had the chance to compete educationally, economically, or socially with the larger society. Cut off from the social life of school or work (and, for many, of family), the soup kitchen becomes a temporary, alternative way to fill their days without the success of employment, school, or money.

The soup kitchen diner may be seen as a member of a stratum of society that has been called the *underclass*—a word that Gunnar Myrdal introduced to the

242

English-speaking world in the 1960s as a translation of the Swedish *underklasse* (Lawrence 1986; Myrdal 1962: 34). The *underclass* refers to people who are increasingly isolated from the rest of society, and who lack the education, employment experience, and literacy skills essential for upward mobility. What makes the underclass distinct from other low-income people is the *permanence* of their situation and their separation from others. The term *underclass* is a particularly useful one in that it transcends the traditional categories of welfare mothers, deinstitutionalized mentally ill, long-term unemployed, and inner-city minority youth that are used to describe groups in poverty in America. The term also distinguishes the contemporary poor from the poor of an earlier era who had the protection of a strong family (Auletta 1982). There is in addition a group of *new underclass*. This is the group of downwardly mobile people whose parents were members of the working class (Loewenstein 1985: 35–48). This new underclass has come about in large part because of the shift of the economy away from the predominance of low-skilled jobs to an increasing concentration on technical skills and communications fluency in the work force.

The site of the Tabernacle Soup Kitchen gives us an opportunity to see the underclass in a small urban area. Middle City is a former textile center in New England. Its population of 20,000 identifies it as an "urban locality" in the words of the U.S. Census for 1980. Middle City may be viewed as a small-scale metropolitan area, with all of the problems of crime, unemployment, poor housing, and unequal access to education and social and health services, though it contrasts sharply with some aspects of big city metropolitan conditions. Although Middle City is culturally diverse it has a very small black population. The diners of the Tabernacle Soup Kitchen add to our understanding of the composition of the underclass.

★ CULTURAL THEMES OF THE SOUP KITCHEN

Soup kitchens serve an overt nutritional function for their guests. Beyond that are the important latent *social* functions they serve. In an effort to explore the various levels of meaning of the social life of the soup kitchen, I have identified three related but distinguishable themes that permeate the social interactions of the guests in the soup kitchen. These themes are sociability, acceptance, and the opportunity for some to become a part of a social network.

Sociability

For the group of people who are its guests, the soup kitchen provides an important focal point for the development of social contact and human interaction to meet basic needs of sociability. This general desire for human contacts, as distinguished from longer-term relationships, has been conceptualized by Georg Simmel (Wolff 1950) as "sociability." Sociologist Regina Kenen, in paraphrasing Simmel, defines sociability as "interaction that exists for its own sake, that is spoiled if its content grows significant or its emotional impact too strong, and that is separated from interaction solely geared to providing or receiving information.... The "sociability drive" is imperative for social life to flower and because even though sociability is not the equivalent or substitute for community, it may promote a feeling of community even when this is lacking" (Kenen 1982: 163).

The search for human interaction and sociability that occurs in the soup kitchen has recently been documented in other contemporary urban settings such as the neighborhood laundromat (Kenen 1982), and the secondhand clothing store (Wiseman 1979), and among groups of former and current drug addicts who loiter around methadone-maintenance clinics (Goldsmith et al. 1985). The soup kitchen, then, can be viewed as creating a modified, ephemeral, and temporary community, where feelings of connectedness with others can be expressed, however tentatively and guardedly. That is, a certain minimal level of social interaction is achieved, without strong ties or deep involvement. For some, this sociability can lead to the development of a more permanent and involved social-support network.

The soup kitchen contains some of the key elements that environmental psychologists have identified as being conducive to strangers approaching each other (Mehrabian and Russell 1975). This tendency to approach strangers, or to affiliate, can be identified when people previously unknown to each other have eye contact, smile, nod, greet one another, and begin a conversation. These beginnings of sociability can be seen occurring repeatedly in the soup kitchen setting. Moreover, at least two of the environmental attributes that Mehrabian and Russell identify as leading to affiliation—pleasure and "arousal"—appear to exist in the soup kitchen for the diners. The soup kitchen can be seen as a pleasant setting, in contrast to the single rooms and cramped apartments of most of the guests. The availability of doughnuts, coffee, bathrooms, and the permission to smoke, all lead to positive social feelings among the guests. The arousal factor is the anticipation of the meal to be served. It is interesting to note that as soon as the meal is served and the guests have eaten, everyone quickly departs, not often stopping to chat and socialize at the exits. It is as though the soup kitchen has been defined by the meal, and that once the meal is over, the spell is broken.

In many ways, a soup kitchen is ideally suited to creating an ephemeral sense of community. The highlight of the day in the Tabernacle Soup Kitchen is the hot noontime meal, and food and companionship are intimately related. In their work on the anthropology of food and eating, Farb and Armelagos (1980) point out that the very word *companion* derives from French and Latin "one who eats bread [pain] with [com] others." People who eat together have a relationship with each other from the act of eating. The foods people eat, and the patterns of who eats with whom, capture some of the most important aspects of any society. Food and eating, then, are symbolic of the social position and social relationships of the individual. Perhaps it is symbolic of the rest of a person's life that the food of the soup kitchen is the leftovers of the rest of society, and that the food is eaten in the company of a temporary community of strangers.

Acceptance

The tendency to sociability in the soup kitchen is enhanced by a general atmosphere of acceptance of a great variety of behavior that would be seen as "deviant" in other settings. Although many of the guests have visible physical, mental, and social handicaps, these features are rarely noted or commented on by staff or other guests. There are no interviews held to assign diagnostic labels, as routinely occurs in health-care settings, for example. One never hears soup kitchen staff say "that alcoholic over there" or "the psychotic at that table." There are no case conferences held, and people are not treated as specimens or cases of some disease entity or other. This lack of labeling and categorizing, so unusual in contemporary America, has been called *deprofessionalism* (Scheper-Hughes 1983). The word d*eprofessionalism* connotes a conscious omission of professionalism. The atmosphere of peaceful coexistence of a variety of "deviant" behaviors and conditions has also been seen as *benevolent anarchy* (Scheper-Hughes 1983). Anarchy reigns in the soup kitchen because there is little effort to impose a structure on the guests. It is benevolent, since the lack of structure is meant to convey a respect for the guests as adults who do not need to be infantilized by the rules and labels found in welfare offices and other agencies that serve the poor. The two rules that exist in the Tabernacle Soup Kitchen—no drinking alcohol or using drugs in the soup kitchen (though people may enter drunk or high), and no fighting—both seek to ensure that the atmosphere of the soup kitchen is a safe one, and that the "anarchy" remains benevolent.

The deprofessionalized ambiance of acceptance brings to mind the original meanings of the words *sanctuary* and *asylum*, both signifying a place of refuge and protection from the outside world. The soup kitchen is indeed a temporary sanctuary and asylum for those outside the flow of life of the majority of the United States population. It is perhaps no accident that the common usage of the word *sanctuary* is religious, and the common usage of the word *asylum* connotes a place of refuge for the mentally ill. The soup kitchen is tied to concepts of religiosity and is a type of community setting (a temporary asylum) for many who have severe psychiatric problems.

Social Networks

The atmosphere of sociability and acceptance enables at least some of the guests to begin to affiliate in fairly consistent, predictable ways, forming social networks with each other. These networks are most dramatically indicated by the groupings around tables at which the guests regularly sit.

Social networks may be defined as a "set of linkages among a defined set of persons" (Mitchell 1969: 2). The term is related to but not identical with the concept of social support, which is the subjective evaluation of the social network in terms of benefits received by the individuals (Schaefer, Coyne, and Lazarus 1981: 381–406). These benefits, or support, may take the form of tangible, emotional, or informational help received from members of the social network.

The study of social networks became important as anthropology moved from the study of traditional, tribal cultures, where kinship relationships dominated people's behaviors, to urban settings where kinship ties hold a less central place (Wolfe 1978). The social network approach to the study of community was pioneered by John Barnes (1954), in his study of a fishing village in Norway, and Elizabeth Bott (1957), in her study of families in London.

The concepts of social network and social support have received a great deal of attention in the recent social science literature (Mitchell and Trickett 1980: 27–44) because of the strong association believed to exist between both concepts and physical and mental well-being. The soup kitchen is an important natural setting in which to study the emergence of social networks and social support. If indeed the dining room is a place in which networking and support flourish, this discovery may point to a previously untapped resource for self-help within a segment of the poor.

★ CONCLUSION

Soup kitchens have not been, to date, the subject of long-term, in-depth ethnographic study, despite their pervasiveness in American society. My book, *The Ethnography of a Soup Kitchen*, continues the anthropological tradition of exploration and analysis of cultural patterns in economically and socially marginal popu-

245

lations. The study examines the meaning of the soup kitchen in the lives of the guests and the place of the soup kitchen in contemporary society. It utilizes a qualitative and quantitative methodology that is consonant with the nonthreatening ambiance of the setting. This research suggests that in many ways the soup kitchen is ideally suited to meeting some of the social needs of America's underclass, and that the soup kitchen setting has the potential for giving the more traditional health and social service providers a *model* of service that is congruent with the needs of this group of people. The research also gives us an opportunity to view how diverse groups of poor people interact when they regularly meet within the closed space of a dining room. The soup kitchen, therefore, represents a rather unique opportunity to study emergent patterns of social interaction and communication among individuals with widely diverse backgrounds in terms of age, sex, parenthood, ethnicity, and mental and physical states of health and illness.

For George Smith, the Tabernacle Soup Kitchen became the site of life's ultimate rite of passage, just as in life it had become the center of his social existence. For another hundred people who are without work, are physically or mentally ill, live in unfriendly or dangerous surroundings, and exist on the meager incomes of welfare programs, the soup kitchen creates a culture in which the desire for sociability, acceptance, and social support may be at least fleetingly realized.

REFERENCES

Auletta, K. 1982. *The Underclass.* New York: Vintage.

Barnes, J. 1954. Class and Committees in a Norwiegan Island Parish. *Human Relations* 7, 1:39–58.

Baxter, E., and K. Hopper. 1981. *Private Lives/Public Spaces: Homeless Adults on the Streets of New York City.* New York: Community Service Society.

Bell, D. 1973. *The Coming of the Post-Industrial Society.* New York: Basic Books.

Bott, E. 1957. *Family and Social Network.* 2nd ed. London: Tavistock.

Dumont, M. 1967. Tavern Culture: The Sustenance of Homeless Men. *American Journal of Orthopsychiatry.* 37:938–45.

Farb, P. and G. Armelagos. 1980. *Consuming Passions: The Anthropology of Eating.* Boston: Houghton Mifflin.

Goldsmith, D. et al. 1985. An Anatomy of Loitering: Social Behavior around Methodone Programs. Unpublished Paper.

Goodenough, W. 1957. Cultural Anthropology and Linguistics. In P. Garvin, ed. *Report of the Seventh Annual Round Table Meeting on Linguistics and Language Study.* Washington, D.C.: Georgetown University Monograph Series on Language and Linguistics.

Kenen, R. 1982. Soap Suds, Space and Sociability: A Participant Observation of the Laundromat. *Urban Life* 11,2: 163–83.

Lawrence, F. 1986. Personal communication with native Swedish-speaker.

Lewis, O. 1966. *La Vida.* London: Panther Books.

Liebow, E. 1967. *Tally's Corner: A Study of Negro Street Corner Men.* Boston: Little, Brown.

Loewenstien, G. 1985. The New Underclass: A Contemporary Sociological Dilemma. *Sociological Quarterly* 26, 1:35–48.

Mehrabian, A., and J. Russell. 1975. Environmental Effects on Affiliation among Strangers. *Humanitas* 11:219–30.

Mitchell, J., ed. 1969. *Social Networks in Urban Situations.* Manchester, England: Manchester University Press.

Mitchell, R. and E. Trickett. 1980. Task Force Report: Social Networks as Mediators of Social Support. *Community Mental Health Journal* 16, 1:27–44.

Myerhoff, B. 1978. *Number Our Days.* New York: Simon and Schuster.

Myrdal, G. 1962. *Challenge to Affluence.* New York: Pantheon.

Rousseau, A. 1981. *Shopping Bag Ladies: Homeless Women Speak about Their Lives.* New York: Pilgrim Press.

Schaefer, C., J. Coyne, and R. Lazarus. 1981. The Health-Related Functions of Social Support. *Journal of Behavioral Medicine* 4,4.

Scheper-Hughes. 1983. A Proposal for the Aftercare of Chronic Psychiatric Patients. *Medical Anthropology Quarterly* 14,2.

Slater, P. 1970. *The Pursuit of Loneliness: American Culture at the Breaking Point.* Boston: Beacon.

Spradley, J. 1970. *You Owe Yourself a Drunk: An Ethnography of Urban Nomads.* Canada: Little, Brown.

Wallace, A. 1970. *Culture and Personality.* 2nd ed. New York: Random House.

Whyte, W. 1943. *Street Corner Society.* Chicago: University of Chicago Press.

Wiseman, J. 1979. Close Encounters of the Quasi-Primary Kind. *Urban Life* 8:23–51.

Wolfe, A. 1978. The Use of Network Thinking in Anthropology. *Social Networks* 1, 1:53–64.

Wolff, K, ed. 1950. *The Sociology of George Simmel.* New York: Macmillam.

FOOD SIGNIFYING IDENTITIES

4

THE SIGNIFYING DISH:
AUTOBIOGRAPHY AND HISTORY IN TWO
BLACK WOMEN'S COOKBOOKS

RAFIA ZAFAR

19

The Black woman cook—overweight, decked out in snowy apron, undisputed genius of the American kitchen—is an image too well inscribed on the collective American unconscious. One southern culinary historian, John Egerton, concisely describes this difficult-to-eradicate stereotype:

> They [Black women chefs] were "turbaned mammies" and "voodoo magicians" and "tyrants" who ruled the back rooms with simpleminded power; they could work culinary miracles day in and day out, but couldn't for the life of them tell anyone how they did it. Their most impressive dishes were described as "accidental" rather than planned. Their speech, humorously conveyed in demeaning dialect in many an old cookbook, came across as illiterate folk knowledge and not to be taken seriously.[1]

These buffoonish characters were the fictive counterparts of legions of unknown culinary workers, African Americans whose legacy and labor shaped much of what we eat to this day.[2] Yet these historical chefs continue to be overshadowed by the long-running specter of the mammy-cook.[3] As folklorist Patricia Turner asks, in her analysis of the production and reproduction of "mammy" kitchen artifacts: "What price has been exacted from the real black women who have been forced to make their way in a culture that pays homage to a distorted icon?"[4] This disjunction—between the spurious worship of an unlettered genius Black cook[5] and that figure's long absence within what I call the "kitchens of power"—leads to still another question, posed by Quandra Prettyman: If "Black cooks are familiar figures in our national mythology as well as in our national history. . . . [why is it] so few have produced cookbooks"?[6] The beginnings of an answer lie in the difficulty of writing a book that engages simultaneously with the shadows of Black slavery, servitude, and oppression, the persistence of stereotypes, and the practicalities of cooking.[7]

To write and to cook—to participate in a national discourse about food and eating—leads the Black woman into territory loaded with conflicting meanings: for a twentieth-century African American female publicly to announce herself as a cook means that she must engage with the reigning ghosts of American racism; she must tackle literally visceral ideas with metaphor, individual agency, and historical memory. The Black woman cook must always engage with these sites of memory—or *lieux des memoires*—when writing about specific foods. As Geneviève Fabre and Robert O'Meally observe, such African American *lieux des memoires* "prompt both the processes of imaginative recollection and the historical consciousness . . . [they] stand at the nexus of personal and collective memory."[8] Meanings are assigned by people, and those items can be specific places or foods common to many. Each recalled or re-created dish in a community's cuisine signifies mightily, and the multiple readings of a simple dish of rice, greens, and meat reveal past and present worlds in which race and culture define our very taste buds. In this lies the quandary of the Black woman who would write a cookbook: even if Aunt Jemima's image on the pancake-mix box has been updated, has the consciousness of American consumers been similarly revised? Popularly held misconceptions about Black cooks haunt, consciously or not, the African American woman, whether she is a chef or an author. When negotiating the intersections of memory, history, food, and creativity, well might the Black woman author ask: In writing a recipe, can one also right history?

In the 1970s, following the crest of the Black Power movement, two works appeared that take on the figure of the Black woman cook and her problematic heritage, Vertamae Smart-Grosvenor's *Vibration Cooking: Or the Travel Notes of a Geechee Girl* (1970) and Carole and Norma Jean Darden's *Spoonbread and Strawberry Wine: Recipes and Reminiscences of a Family* (1978).[9] These two cookbooks, which have now attained near-cult status, help us understand how a recipe collection functions as an articulation of a personal and/or communal identity. Each text works as autobiography and history in addition to engaging, obliquely or not, the linked issues of Black stereotyping and class. They also operate simultaneously on gastronomic *and* historical levels. Both illustrate the ways Black culinary traditions can be imagined or inscribed—by the author, by her readers—as a way of enacting the cultural, expressive, and historical agenda of the African American female. Along with *how-tos*, the Dardens and Smart-Grosvenor give us *whys*; presenting these cookbooks to a national audience, Smart-Grosvenor and the Dardens enact a gastronomic Black Reconstruction.

A little background first, for a reconstruction implies a previous edifice. The first cookbook by a Black woman, Abby Fisher's ghostwritten *What Mrs. Fisher Knows about Old Southern Cooking*, appeared in 1881. Despite the straightforward culinary instruction explicit in a cookbook, Fisher's personal life and historical situation as a Black woman intrudes. Autobiographical and historical information comes in the form of asides, as when the former southerner concludes her last recipe with the words "I have given birth to eleven children and raised them all, and nursed them with this diet. It is a Southern plantation preparation."[10] However firmly Abby Fisher tried to keep out the world beyond her kitchen, her life as a Black woman erupted into her professional presentations. In the twentieth century, the setting down of recipes grew beyond Fisher's early efforts to keep it simple to recipes unabashedly presented alongside community histories, family memoirs, and autobiography.

Increasingly, Black cookbooks written after the 1940s function as recoveries or recastings of an African American world. The National Council of Negro Women sponsored a number of such culinary celebrations of community, beginning in 1958 with the *Historical Cookbook of the American Negro.*[11] In the post–World War II era, authors find food, politics, and history increasingly hard to separate from one another.[12] The civil rights movement of the 1950s eventually led to the massive civil disobedience and increasingly aggressive activism of the 1960s; this upswing in political activism led to a burgeoning market for Black subjects. The subsequent increase in African American–owned presses after 1960 attests to the growing market for books by and about African Americans.[13] With this increased number of Black publications overall came a rise in the genres published—and a growing number of African American cookbooks. Latter volumes, such as *A Good Heart and a Light Hand: Ruth L. Gaskins' Collection of Traditional Negro Recipes* (1968), often explored and celebrated group identity through relatively straightforward collections of recipes.[14] But two works that followed *A Good Heart and a Light Hand* encapsulate the era's heady mix of politics and the personal.

The Dardens and Smart-Grosvenor volumes engagingly reflect the creative and political consciousness of the 1960s. The well-worn cliché of the women's movement—the personal *is* political—becomes more than an assertion of *female* rights when in *Vibration Cooking* the forthright Smart-Grosvenor unrestrainedly asserts that for too long Caucasians have been dictating who's in charge of the American kitchen: "White folks act like they invented food and like there is some weird mystique surrounding it—something that only Julia [Child] and Jim [James Beard] can get to. There is no mystique. Food is food. Everybody eats!" (p. 3). At the same time Smart-Grosvenor notes that whites have heretofore controlled the kitchen economy, she points out that all people must eat. Implicit in this leveling observation is her assertion that one group does not "own" a set of recipes, despite the apparent primacy of plantation cookbooks over "soul food" collections. Anne E. Goldman reaches a similar conclusion when she observes that in the kitchen, women of different races and classes do not easily fall into sisterhood.[15] Although less confrontational in approach than Smart-Grosvenor, the Dardens, in *Spoonbread and Strawberry Wine*, also do not fail to inform their reader-cooks that the legacy of slavery and racism affects even the foods we remember: despite the numerous family members the Dardens could contact for recipes, they "could not trace [their] family roots past [their] grandparents...such was the effect of slavery and its resulting destruction of family ties" (p. xi). But if the Dardens and Smart-Grosvenor similarly weave a love of cooking and eating around the markers of slavery, family pride, and the civil rights movement, the differences between the two cookbooks demonstrate generational shifts within the Black community as well as the class divisions that have become more marked at the end of the twentieth century: the Dardens can be seen as showcasing the elegant side of southern cooking along with more informal cooking styles, while Smart-Grosvenor's folksy tone and simplified recipes seem to privilege classic soul food, although her volume is far more complicated than that rubric would imply. These two cookbooks demonstrate that African America was, by the 1970s, quite diversified in terms of class, educational achievement, and region.[16]

Yet the class issue remains for Black women cooks and authors, whatever their educational achievement and household income. In a society long arranged around a binary opposition between white and Black, free and slave, the middle-class status of African Americans continues to be contested in any number of arenas. Because of this long-standing link between racial (e.g., Black) and economic (e.g., lower) status in the United States, Black women and their cookbooks come across as less "high culture" than the popular American guides to French or Italian cuisine which crowd the "Cookery" shelves of bookstores and libraries.[17] There are class issues hidden within the very existence of a cookbook, an artifact commonly held to be a "woman's thing" in general. Although such works are said largely to appeal to "women" as a group, women themselves are stratified in terms of race and class as any number of feminist scholars have argued. Individual working-class women (and men), as for many generations were the vast majority of African Americans, are less likely to write, compile, or even read recipe books, if only because their work and financial situations militate against leisure-time activities like "gourmet" cooking.[18] African American women cooks, then, operate within overlapping systems—mainstream, or "white" and culturally specific, or "Black"—that define their class positions in contradictory ways.

Both the Dardens and Smart-Grosvenor recognize that there is neither a monolithic Black culture nor a single African American cuisine, although each of their productions play up and against prevalent notions of what "Black" food is (and is not). The subtitles of each book reveal their individual and distinctive agendas: *Spoonbread and Strawberry Wine: Recipes and Reminiscences of a Family* invites us into a procession of middle-class homes for fruit wines, hot baked goods, and comfortable living. *Vibration Cooking, or, the Travel Notes of a Geechee Girl* heralds the author's unorthodox approach to life: Smart-Grosvenor cooks with tradition and intuition together, with a global roster of recipes enhancing her picaresque adventures in the rural South, inner-city Philadelphia, France, and Cuba. The Dardens deliver a gastronomic social history of African America, emphasizing nineteenth- and early-twentieth-century ideals of racial uplift in the face of adversity. As Anne E. Goldman has noted that "if the Dardens are intent on providing their own middle-class status with an historical precedent, they are equally interested in providing ignorant readers with lessons in nineteenth-century American history."[19] Smart-Grosvenor offers an idiosyncratic, wisecracking, personal narrative of the changes wrought in contemporary Black America. If *Vibration Cooking*'s unabashed first-person narrative creates an autobiography through meals, *Spoonbread and Strawberry Wine*'s text, with sepia-toned pictures, can better be called a keepsake or an archive. Each set of culinary reminiscences captures a moment in Afro-American history. *Spoonbread and Strawberry Wine* can, at times, seem an idealized version of Black life—the now-familiar lament that segregation had its positive side, in the enforced closeness of Black community life, comes to mind. *Vibration Cooking*, on the other hand, comes across like a Zora Neale Hurston of the culinary set.[20] As the late 1970s arrived, desegregation had been achieved—at least as far as the courts were concerned—and increasing numbers of African Americans entered the enclaves of formerly all-white institutions. *Spoonbread and Strawberry Wine* and *Vibration Cooking* can therefore be seen as late-twentieth-century Black cultural events, expressions of the prevailing winds of change.

Vibration Cooking, the first of this pair of cookbooks, comes as a high-water mark of the nexus of Black Power and cuisine.[21] Smart-Grosvenor consciously counterwrites those generations-old images of overweight Black geniuses who presided over generations of southern kitchens with nary a written-down recipe.[22] Before she offers a single how-to, the author engages pointedly with these ever-present myths, when she dedicates her work "to my mama and my grandmothers and my sisters in appreciation of the years that they worked in miss ann's kitchen and then came home to TCB in spite of slavery and oppression and the moynihan report" (p. v).[23] Whom the U.S. mainstream would categorize and pigeonhole, Smart-Grosvenor will liberate through scathing commentary, family history, humor, and personal letters. Her recipes, related in a contemporary African American vernacular, place the Black cook in a community of women who like to whip things up—for themselves, for their families, for their lovers. These recipes are not for Miss Ann's kitchen: cooking as domestic service is invoked only to be scorned.

Vibration Cooking impresses upon the reader the necessity to eradicate culinary racism along with other kinds of bigotry. In the introduction, entitled "The Demystification of Food," Smart-Grosvenor writes:

> In reading lots and lots of cookbooks written by white folks it occurred to me that people very casually say Spanish rice, French fries, Italian spaghetti, Chinese cabbage…with the exception of black bottom pie and niggertoes [Brazil nuts], there is no reference to black people's contributions to the culinary arts. (p. 3)

253

The introduction to the second edition extends the above critique to tell us that "the white folks were on my case" about the original edition of *Vibration Cooking*. Mainstream readers seemed puzzled, Smart-Grosvenor avers, by the frank mixing of culinary and political motives. Her cookbook includes a more than ancillary running commentary on Black life in the white United States, whether complaining about "the segregation of ethnic foods in supermarkets…[w]hy can't the mango juice be with the tomato juice [and not in] some 'exotic' section" (p. 197) or including an entire chapter about the Black person's inability to hail a taxicab in Manhattan (pp. 95–97). Preceding a recipe for her paternal uncle's corn muffins, Smart-Grosvenor's readers hear why her father was called "a *bad* nigger" by a southern white and how a racial slur can actually amuse, if not left-handedly compliment, the father and his child (pp. 42–43). In a chapter entitled "Name-Calling," she enumerates the culinary imperialism inherent in the renaming of foods like okra (the original African word is gombo) or succotash (Smart-Grosvenor uses an Indian spelling, "sukquttash"). Although she includes in that chapter a recipe for "Cracker Stew," whose ingredients perform a veritable culinary dozens, Smart-Grosvenor admits she does not generally "call people out of their name" (p. 85). Her disdain for things "white" is complicated, for she can not simply dismiss European culture. Instead, when and wherever possible, she asserts the superiority of the African American.

That desire to refocus American gastronomic history leads Smart-Grosvenor to invoke and then to discard the legacy of expatriate American cookbook author and memoirist Alice B. Toklas. Both Smart-Grosvenor and Toklas can be termed "unconventional" if we agree they each lived in defiance of white middle-class heterosexual U.S. culture: Toklas as a lesbian whose lifelong partner was the writer Gertrude Stein; Smart-Grosvenor as a Black American refusing to be channeled into either the stuffy respectability of the American Negro middle class or the still-segregated bohemian life of the American abroad. When Smart-Grosvenor mimics white readers asking, "Was I trying to be a black Alice B. Toklas?" she snaps, "the only thing I have in common with Alice B. Toklas is that we lived on the same street in Paris [the rue de Fleurus]. I lived at #17 and she at #27" (p. xvi).[24] That backhanded reference to Toklas makes the comparison between two American cooks living on the rue de Fleurus unavoidable: Parisian-dwelling, American expatriates, Smart-Grosvenor and Toklas each record a smart set of renowned visitors and their amusing anecdotes. Despite their differences in social class, both women moved in a vigorous and exhilarating community of expressive artists.[25] As opposed to Toklas, whose text often included the sayings of Gertrude Stein, Smart-Grosvenor never alludes directly to her husband or any other long-term partner. In lieu of a famous lover's words she records her own *bon mots* and wisecracks and those of her children, Chandra and Kali ("My daughter said, 'My mamma cook like Aretha Franklin sing!'" (p. xv)). Her sense of worth, most decidedly, does not turn on being an observer of the greats and near-greats of U.S. cultural history.[26] Yet recipes and commentary in *Vibration Cooking* and *The Alice B. Toklas Cookbook* invite their readers to be impressed by the writers' creative connections. Both authors make a connection between gastronomy and artistic achievement: meals celebrate novelists, "Chicken Carlene Polite" (*Vibration Cooking*, p. 165); painters, "Oeufs Francis Picabia" (in Toklas); or musicians—Virgil Thomson contributes a recipe for "shad roe mousse" (in Toklas) while Donald Hubbard worries about a "soul food party…in Rome" (*Vibration Cooking*, p. 74).[27] By writing about African American food in such venues as France and Italy, Smart-Grosvenor implicitly acknowledges European connections and affiliations. Yet like many other African Americans, she tries to keep a distance from "white" ancestry. To affirm "down-home" food in the belly of "Western civilization" thus keeps Smart-Grosvenor's priorities as Black activist clear.

Smart-Grosvenor's reluctance to admit kinship with Toklas stems not from an inability to admit a connection with a white predecessor—she does refer to her, after all—but from her much greater desire to form a chain of Black women forebears.[28] When she introduces a "white" dish and then replaces it with a "Black" analogue, Smart-Grosvenor performs a Black female signifying (or, she might say, a "hurting") on white gourmet foods: her comparisons of crepes with her grandmother's hoe cakes and "Pancakes Smith St. Jacques" exemplify this culinary revisionism (pp. 22, 23). She would have us recognize that it is from *Black* women cooks and writers that she draws her courage and inspiration; the geechee girl's kitchen and life frankly seek out connections with women, with all peoples, of the African Diaspora. Smart-Grosvenor acknowledges those who have come, and cooked, before her. African American culinary colleagues like Edna Lewis and Ruth Gaskins receive high praise; so too does she praise the famous, if less self-consciously aesthetic, *A Date with a Dish: A Cookbook of American Negro Recipes*. A scandalized Smart-Grosvenor notes that few cookbooks by Afro-Americans appeared before the first edition of *Vibration Cooking*—this despite the fact that "Afro-American cooking is like jazz—a genuine art form that deserves serious scholarship" (p. xviii).[29] Her assertion that cooking, like other forms of nonliterate artistic expression, merits scholarly attention anticipated scholarship in women's and cultural studies of African America. Still, the multiple genres of *Vibration Cooking*—its letters, its recipes, its narrative excursions—assert Smart-Grosvenor's personal agenda over a strictly academic or historical one.

In *Spoonbread and Strawberry Wine*, the Darden sisters take their cooking less autobiographically—or, I should say, more historiographically. If the welter of different texts offered by Smart-Grosvenor presents an individual's unique experiences along with her recipes, the carefully researched and kitchen-tested recipes of several generations of Dardens and Sampsons attest to a belief that the individual is inextricable from the larger community and continuum of Black folks.[30] So when a

254

friend of the two sisters inquires, "didn't their black American *family*, deeply rooted in the experiences of slavery and rural life, have rich material on genuine American cookery?" the sisters answer yes (p. ix; emphasis mine). Further realizing that many of the wonderful dishes they "had taken for granted" were more real to them than the relatives dispersed across generations and regions, they decided to put together a cookbook. For these women, a compendium of loved foods would be inextricable from recapturing past African American life; to do so properly would result in a "thick description" of a past age.[31] Thus, *Spoonbread and Strawberry Wine* is literally "a testimonial to those who lovingly fed us and at the same time gave us a better sense of ourselves by sharing themselves" (p. xi).

Unsurprisingly, along with those earliest remembered bites came their identity as African Americans.[32] Northern raised and Sarah Lawrence educated, the two sisters must recapture their culinary and familial antecedents through travel to distant relatives, specifically referring to their travels as "our pilgrimage 'home'" (p. xi). They visit neighbors in small southern towns; pick through boxes of photographs; and collect, try out, and standardize old recipe cards. As one might expect from a cookbook cum history, statements from historical personages abound—except here the statements come from surviving relatives and old friends of the family. Rather than Smart-Grosvenor's savory stew of old and new recipes, letters from friends, and bohemian Black arts hobnobbing, the Dardens re-create course by formal course a lived experience they see vanishing with increased social mobility, desegregation, and distance from slavery. Theirs is not an autobiography in the sense of a telling of their own, individual cooking stories, although some of those are included—we have only to compare the number of recipes culled from older relatives with the ones the Dardens themselves contribute to see where the emphasis in *Spoonbread and Strawberry Wine* lies. As the youngest contributors to the volume, the Dardens subsume their culinary narratives within a larger history, that of their maternal and paternal ancestors—and by extension, within the greater context of African American history.

Within the covers of their cookbook the sisters divide one side of the family from another, mapping out their genealogy and giving credit for each recipe where due (each branch of the Sampsons and the Dardens is neatly delineated). Carefully planned, every chapter refers specifically to a family member; accompanying photographs and reminiscences heighten the succulence and significance of the recipes within. Following a brief biography of the only grandparent they ever knew, the sisters append adaptations of granddad Sampson's honey-based recipes—"Fruited Honey Chicken," "Honey Duck," "Honey Custard," even "Cough Syrup" (pp. 148–51). Memories of their travels in the segregated South as young girls precede a picnic menu; dishes by various friends, old and new, who gave them food and shelter are provided as well—"Hot Crab Meat Salad" and "Edna Neil's Pan-Fried Blowfish" (pp. 248, 249). That so many of those whose recipes are included, or to whom chapters are dedicated, were elderly or deceased at the time of the book's composition lends an elegiac tone to the cookbook. Although far from a eulogy for a vanished African America, *Spoonbread and Strawberry Wine* strikes a nostalgic note absent from *Vibration Cooking*.

> Thoughts of [our uncle] J.B. conjure up images of big shiny cars, polished two-toned shoes, straw hats tipped to the side, and the continual party that always seemed to be going on around him...he was a cook [who]...preferred to eat his "dinner" first thing in the morning...(p. 53)

The wistful tone struck in more than one entry could almost lead one to believe that this cookbook was specifically aimed at those who attended northern and/or integrated schools, grew up away from an extended Black family, and who acknowledge an ever-widening gap between the Black working class and the bourgeoisie.[33] Although segregation of a different character remains, the current dilemma leaves African Americans of the poorest families almost as insulated from the middle-class Black world as the two races had once been. That separation leads to a key, if almost prosaic, agenda of these cookbooks. Along with the invocation of time past or a radical manifesto, *Spoonbread and Strawberry Wine* and *Vibration Cooking* must offer specific remedies and recourse for those readers yearning to (re)create Black community, if not an African American identity, through gastronomic venues.

There are those, however, who have neither the time nor the knowledge to prepare the labor-intensive and classic dishes of African American cuisine with which the Dardens concern themselves. Working parents with attenuated links to an older generation—and restricted free time—might just as soon purchase precooked African American food as prepare it themselves; they might also limit time-consuming, home-cooked meals to Sunday dinners.[34] The owner of an Atlanta chain of drive-in chitlins restaurants notes that "doctors, lawyers, all kinds of people...remember" this and other foods of their youth and come to buy.[35] Others far from Georgia's drive-ins with "the yearning for collard or turnip greens" can now "pick a few cans off the [supermarket] shelf": at least two companies, including a side venture of New York City's famed Sylvia's restaurant, offer Black culture in a can.[36] Do not such businesses thrive in part not just because busy people appreciate the convenience of prepared foods but also because growing numbers of African Americans no longer know *how* to cook chitlins (and other gastronomic relics)? Perhaps, too, the younger members of contemporary Black America do not want to eat foods identified with the past and privation: "I don't know what they are, but they're something nasty."[37] As older Black women turn away from the stereotypes of the Black cook, so might younger African Americans eschew meals associated with want.[38] Some Black folks turn to takeout, adjusting in that way to the fact that "soul food" and "home cooking" may no longer appear under the same roof. Others, with the time or the inclination, will go to the elongating shelf of Black cookbooks—where *Spoonbread and Strawberry Wine* and *Vibration Cooking* now have the status of brand names.

The ways the Dardens and Smart-Grosvenor treat a traditional African American holiday, New Year's Day, and its signature soul food dish, Hoppin' John, illustrate what each offers to the reader in search of community and cuisine. (Such New Year's celebrations, as expressions of an African American identity, date back to the early nineteenth century.)[39] The homely dish of Hoppin' John has been said to be named after a limping New Orleans slave who sold the dish, or the children who hopped around the table begging for a taste.[40] The making of this plain fare sends the Dardens and Smart-Grosvenor down parallel memory lanes. The two sisters tell us:

> On New Year's Day we always have Open House at our father's home. It is a leisurely day, designed to give us an opportunity to unwind from the frenzy of New Year's Eve...Black folklore has it that hoppin' john brings good luck in the coming year, so we always serve this...with all the essential trimmings. (p. 223)

As is typical, the Dardens link food, history, and folklore; their Hoppin' John, which they take care to subtitle "Black Eyed Peas and Rice," contains rice, peas, red and black pepper, ham hocks, bay leaf, onions, celery stalk, and salt. By placing the dish in the context of Black American culture, as well as providing exact instructions, the Dardens hope to ensure that their readers' attempts at gastronomic and ethnic revival will turn out successfully.

Smart-Grosvenor also does not fail to connect black-eyed peas and rice with New Year's Day, although the link she forges does not necessarily connect folklore and family. Instead, she recollects

> those New Year's open houses I used to have and everyone I loved would come. Even Millie came from Germany one year. She arrived just in time for the black eyes and rice. And that year I cooked the peas with beef neck bones instead of swine cause so many brothers and sisters have given up swine. I had ham hocks on the side for the others. . . . If you eat . . . (Hopping John) on New Year's Day, you supposed to have good luck for the coming year. Black people been eating that traditional New Year's Day dinner for years. That's why I'm not having no more open house on New Year's Day. I'm going to try something new. (pp. 5, 6)

For this cook, strict adherence to tradition should not overrule the spirit of the occasion. Accordingly, Smart-Grosvenor's ingredients and recipe can be included in four short lines:

> Cook black-eyed peas.
> When they are almost done add rice.
> Mix rice and peas together.
> Season and—voila!—you got it. (p. 6)

So although she gives you a recipe for Hopping John, she prefaces it with her explanation of why she omits the pork (mainly because the prevailing Black ethos eschewed pig meat as the food of poverty and antithetical to a Muslim lifestyle), leaves the seasoning up to her audience (because she and the reader should cook by vibration), and intimates, more or less, that she plans to skip it entirely on subsequent Firsts (because she won't be bound by the past). Smart-Grosvenor wants to ensure continuity, the cook's own sense of integrity, and innovation simultaneously.[41] Still, she will not break with some traditions—nothing so newfangled as Teflon "can't fry no fried chicken" (p. 4). For this cook, only the cast-iron pots, if not the classic dishes, of her girlhood will do.[42]

Once, in response to an earlier version of this article, a colleague replied testily, "Who ever thought 'African American food' was 'just grits and greens' anyway?" Although there may be some who believe African Americans subsist on corn meal and leafy vegetables, that remark speaks as much to intragroup notions about the food of rural Black southerners (not to mention urban Black northerners) as to that of the Dardens' or Smart-Grosvenor's implied readership. To deny that these items were common because of the poverty-stricken conditions of much of African America is to deny the past. It is also to deny a link with the continent. To identify greens as a cornerstone of Black cuisine doesn't mean that there is one African American culinary tradition. Jessica B. Harris, noted scholar of African diasporic cuisine, has delineated two "major African-American culinary traditions . . . that of the dirt-poor, hardscrabble Deep South . . . [and the one that] harked back to the kitchens of Virginia plantations manned by house slaves who turned spits, put up preserves, and served elegant meals."[43] (She would agree that there are further minor and regional variations.)

Both major traditions incorporate cooked greens as a standard dish. So although Black American cuisine is certainly more than "grits and greens," those "lowly" dishes signify mightily. The eating of collards has meaning in ways analogous to the eating of parsley from a modern-day seder plate: for Jews and Blacks alike, the ingestion of bitter greens serves as a near-literal taste of slavery. With each group's shared food comes a shared identity, if not a shared fate. As Pierre Bourdieu has observed: "Taste is *amor fati*, the choice of destiny, but a forced choice, produced by conditions of existence which rule out all alternatives as mere daydreams and leave no choice but the taste for the necessary."[44] Ironically, and sometimes triumphantly, what we have to eat we come to prefer.

For most African Americans, greens have a content beyond B vitamins and iron: "greens are undeniably one of the United States' best known African inspired foods"; they "go into the pot boiling on the back of the stove in a traditional Black American household."[45] Unsurprisingly, the Dardens present their readers with three headings under greens: Mixed Greens, Collard Greens, and "Pot Likker." Noting that their father "eats greens every day, so he always makes them in quantity and reheats them during the week" (p. 136), the Dardens offer recipes that yield between twelve and sixteen servings. By not dividing the recipe for their readers, the sisters implicitly affirm the foundational place of cooked greens in Black American cuisine. Going on to speak of the value of pot likker, the leftover cooking liquid, the sisters remark: "It is renowned for its nutritional value and can be used as an excellent vegetable stock for soups, as a soup in its own right, or traditionally to dunk corn bread" (p. 137).[46] Giver of vitamins and representative of folk custom, greens serve as side dish and symbol.

Smart-Grosvenor, who could well be called a gastronomic Afrocentrist, celebrates greens in a mixed message of nutrition and nationalism. In a chapter titled "Collards and Other Greens" she discusses the various aspects of this food. They are, "according to the *National Geographic* . . . prehistoric. The Romans took them to France and England. The Romans are said to have considered them a delicacy. I know I consider them a delicacy. They are very rich in minerals and vitamins" (p. 139). Two exchanges occurring during greens-buying expeditions further illustrate her conflation of provender and politics. When shopping in her Lower East Side Manhattan neighborhood, Smart-Grosvenor has an unpleasant déjà vu when the person of color wrapping her greens (in her adulthood it is a Puerto Rican man; in her childhood it was a Black man) does not also take her money. That the white store owner deems this employee good only to wrap vegetables offends his proudly Black customer: she vows to shop in Harlem for her greens henceforth, even if it means taking a long subway ride (p. 141). The echo of boycotts, of lunch-counter sit-ins, would not have been missed by her contemporaries—nor should we. In a second incident, when a white shopper asks, "How do you people fix these [greens]?" Smart-Grosvenor wields humor, not her spending power, as a lance. The woman's patronizing epithet, "you people," provokes a mischievous reply. Our intrepid chef announces, with a straight face, that African Americans make salad with collards using "Italian" dressing. Nearby, "a black woman . . . looked at me as if I had discredited the race" (p. xvii). With eleven recipes given for these common vegetables, *Vibration Cooking* affirms the author's belief in the tastiness, curative powers, and unshakable place of greens in Black American life.

"Black" foods like collards and Hopping John may be prepared differently from year to year, and what might be considered "soul food" has indeed changed from its inception.[47] Nevertheless, the entity known as African American cuisine persists.

Put another way, the way anthropologist Fredrik Barth would see it, the "boundaries" of culinary Black America may alter (in this case, foods or styles of preparation), but the site itself remains identifiable, both by practitioners of that cuisine and others.[48] Ethnographers often depend on a reading of what we eat to understand how we construct a self around the axes of food and other cultural "stuff."[49] Soul food, that phrase long used by African Americans to refer to their common cuisine, underscores the link between psychic identity and eating. Food habits and tastes constitute some of the strongest factors of group identity. Their significance in creating a bedrock, ethnic self has been acknowledged by anthropologists: "[F]oodways seem particularly resistant to change.... It has been suggested that this is because the earliest-formed layers of culture, such as foodways, are the last to erode."[50] So if eating "Black" functions as one of the primal determinants of an individual's life, we can see how the productions of the Dardens and Smart-Grosvenor take up the task of re-creating that primal, gastronomic entity as their group identity becomes ever more fragmented, stratified, and diverse.

In the end, the simple act of eating cannot be separated from the personal, the literary, or the social. Neither can you remove the preference for, or preparation of, certain foods from a historical context. When the Dardens describe the box lunches with which they and other Black Americans traveled, their memories demand we acknowledge the Jim Crow transportation and hotel industry, which barred African Americans from public-eating places and restricted their movement on common carriers (pp. 245–46). Smart-Grosvenor writes a different kind of culinary history when, fired up by white author William Styron's rewriting of the life of noted slave insurrectionist Nat Turner, she finds evidence that "Nat's last meal [was] roast pork and apple brandy" and creates a new recipe, "Nat Turner Apple Pork Thing" (pp. 182–83). Thus, the Dardens' book works like an encyclopedia of recipes with history, while Smart-Grosvenor's autobiography with recipes regards modern Black cookery as an agent of change. One cannot say that the Dardens enshrine their heritage never to partake of it. Yet because Smart-Grosvenor writes almost exclusively of her own life and the place food and cooking hold within it, while the Dardens record the manner in which their mother, father, and older relatives ate, these two "Black" cookbooks differ remarkably. The three see their roles, if not their dishes, dissimilarly, approaching from complementary angles the "stuff" of African American culture: their gastronomic *lieux des memoires* are in turn personal and communal, individual and historical. Each book places African American cuisine in a political context, records a social history that must not be forgotten, and relates the lived experience of the writer and/or her family.[51] Much more than grits and greens, the signifying dishes of the Dardens and Smart-Grosvenor provide us with a taste of where we've been, who we are, and where we should be going.

NOTES

I would like to thank all who have provided me with encouragement and critical feedback: the editors and readers of *GRAAT* (of University of Tours, France), especially my friend and colleague Claudine Raynaud, as an earlier version of this article appeared in *GRAAT* 14 (1996); the Culinary Historian Societies of Ann Arbor, Michigan, and Cambridge, Massachusetts; John Egerton; the Program in American Studies at the University of Texas, Austin; the editors and anonymous readers for *Feminist Studies*; and Doris Witt.

1. John Egerton, *Southern Food: At Home, on the Road, in History* (1987; reprint, Chapel Hill: University of North Carolina Press, 1993), 16.
2. As one historian has written, "the spread of southern cooking to the North in our own day, like the spread of so much else in southern culture, has represented, above all, the triumph of its black component." See

Eugene D. Genovese, *Roll, Jordan, Roll: The World the Slaves Made* (1974; reprint, New York: Vintage Books, 1976), 543.

3. The popular Charleston [South Carolina] Junior League's *Charleston Receipts* (Charleston: Junior League of Charleston, 1950), a community cookbook organized by a white women's volunteer organization, has perpetuated these stereotypes for five decades. A "Southern" cookbook, *Charleston Receipts* depends for its renowned gentility on the recipes, ingredients, and labor culled from the Blacks who labored in white kitchens. Cuisine elements deemed simple when offered elsewhere by African American practitioners here become classic when presented by white upper-middle-class employers. Sometimes thanked directly and sometimes not, the Black cooks are demeaned via quaint illustrations and even more quaint dialect; they become, in Patricia Yaeger's words, "edible labor." See her "Edible Labor," *Southern Quarterly* 30 (winter–spring 1992): 150–59, especially her remarks on the effaced Black cook/server (156). I have made an analogous observation elsewhere of how the politically vanquished become the rhetorically cannibalized. See Rafia Zafar, "The Proof of the Pudding: Of Haggis, Hasty Pudding, and Transatlantic Influence," *Early American Literature* 31 (1996): 133–49.

4. Patricia Turner, *Ceramic Uncles and Celluloid Mammies: Black Images and Their Influence on Culture* (Berkeley: University of California Press, 1995), 43.

5. Much of culinary tradition and method is handed down orally, whatever the society. That cookery is "embodied knowledge" in Lisa M. Heldke's words, whether practiced by white or Black women, accounts for its denigrated status in a society that privileges pure reason; see Lisa M. Heldke, "Foodmaking as a Thoughtful Practice," in *Cooking, Eating, Thinking: Transformative Philosophies of Food*, ed. Deane W. Curtin and Lisa M. Heldke (Bloomington: Indiana University Press, 1992), 203–29, esp. 218–20. The doubly low status of the Black woman predicts their nearly subterranean level in U.S. society, and by way of a corollary, the belief in their gastronomic labors as unworthy of notice.

6. In addition to the Darden sisters and Vertamae Smart-Grosvenor, Prettyman's essay discusses Black women chefs Edna Lewis and Cleora Butler; we arrive at some of the same conclusions. See Quandra Prettyman, "Come Eat at My Table: Lives with Recipes," *Southern Quarterly* 30 (winter–spring 1992): 131–40.

7. As Doris Witt has remarked, "The cookbook is a privileged textual site among blacks because of their overdetermined over representation in American kitchens, both public and private"; she also discusses the mammy figure with particular reference to turn-of-the-century American culture. See "In Search of Our Mothers' Cookbooks: Gathering African-American Culinary Traditions" [indexed as Doris Smith], *Iris: A Journal about Women* 26 (fall/winter 1991): 22–27.

8. Geneviève Fabre and Robert O'Meally, *History and Memory in African-American Culture* (New York: Oxford University Press, 1994), 7. In their introduction, Fabre and O'Meally extend and apply French historian Pierre Nora's term *lieu de memoire* to African American culture.

9. Vertamae Smart-Grosvenor, *Vibration Cooking: Or the Travel Notes of a Geechee Girl* (1970; reprint, New York: Ballantine Books, 1986, 1991); subsequent references (all to the 1991 edition) appear in parentheses in the text, unless otherwise noted. Carole and Norma Jean Darden's *Spoonbread and Strawberry Wine: Recipes and Reminiscences of a Family* (New York: Doubleday & Co., 1978) is also in paper, but I have used the original hardcover. Subsequent citations to this edition appear in parentheses in the text. The continued popularity of these two works can be attested to by their publication history: *Spoonbread and Strawberry Wine* has been in print pretty much continuously since its first publication; *Vibration Cooking* is now in its third edition. Much anecdotal evidence indicates hardcover first editions of *Vibration Cooking* are often borrowed from, and never returned to, their original owners.

10. [Abby Fisher] *What Mrs. Fisher Knows about Old Southern Cooking* (1881; reprint, with notes by Karen Hess, Bedford, Mass.: Applewood Books, 1995), 72.

11. The National Council of Negro Women, *Historical Cookbook of the American Negro* (Washington, D.C.: Corporate Press, 1958).

12. Emblematic of a kind of ripple effect, similar celebrations of one's origins, as well as one's political activism, arose in other groups. In terms of cultural origins, the impetus to celebrate one's identity came to be known in the 1970s as the "ethnic revival"; along with this rise in various Americans' perceptions of themselves as "Italian" or "Greek" came a corresponding interest in ethnic cookbooks and restaurants. (Ethnic cookbooks, as such, appeared well before the 1970s.) In terms of a political affiliation expressed through an alternative venue, cookbooks and/or food also became a way to express a certain lifestyle and/or social change. One volume that provides examples of both impulses is Ita Jones's *The Grubbag: An Underground Cookbook* (New York: Vintage, 1971), a cookbook that grew out of a column in the Liberation News Service; Jones refers to her upbringing in Texas and her search for ethnic origins. For discussions of such politically oriented endeavors, see Warren Belasco, *Appetite for Change: How the Counterculture Took on the Food Industry* (Ithaca, N.Y.: Cornell University Press, 1989, 1993); and Curtin and Heldke.

13. Fewer than fifteen books were published by Black presses in the first part of the 1960s, while about 160 books by similar firms appeared between 1970 and 1974. Donald Franklin Joyce's research on the Black press demonstrates this sharp rise in the number and output of Black-owned presses post-1960; he also discussed the exchanges and competition between white- and Black-owned publishers. See his *Gatekeepers of Black Culture* (Westport, Conn.: Greenwood Press, 1983), esp. 78–79, and 147.

14. Ruth L. Gaskins, *A Good Heart and a Light Hand: Ruth L. Gaskins' Collection of Traditional Negro Recipes* (Annandale, Va.: Turnpike, 1968). Although Quandra Prettyman's essay and Howard Paige's *Aspects of Afro-American Cookery* (Southfield, Mich.: Aspects Publishing Co., 1987) each provide bibliographies in their publications, Doris Witt's *Black Hunger: Food and the Politics of U.S. Identity* (New York: Oxford University Press, 1999) provides the most complete bibliography to date on Black cookbooks (the bibliography was compiled with the assistance of David Lupton).

15. See Anne E. Goldman "'I Yam What I Yam': Cooking. Culture, and Colonialism" in *De/Colonizing the Subject: The Politics of Gender in Women's Autobiography*, ed. Sidonie Smith and Julia Watson (Minneapolis: University of Minnesota Press, 1992), 169–95, esp. 171–73, which takes issue with Susan J. Leonardi's invocation of a female-centered, cross-class recipe exchange. See Leonardi's "Recipes for Reading: Summer Pasta, Lobster à la Riseholme, and Key Lime Pie," *PMLA* 3 (May 1983): 340–47, for the origins of this debate.

16. Despite the growing numbers of Black Americans in the professional and middle classes, the percentage of Black poor remains too large for any American to feel complacent. That there has long been an identifiable "middle" or "upper" class in African America is undeniable: see Jessica B. Harris's "Heirloom Recipes from a Southern Family: A Big-Flavored Meal in the African-American Tradition" (*Food and Wine*, February 1991) for a gastronomic exegesis of this phenomenon.

17. Think, for example, of the "high-class" volumes of Julia Child, with their implication that the cook will spend hours in the kitchen and frequently use expensive ingredients; note again Smart-Grosvenor's above-quoted remark on this implied distinction between "white" and "Black" food—"white folks act like...there is some weird mystique [about food]" (3).

18. Exceptions could be found in the collectively authored community or "charity" cookbooks, volumes compiled by a group of women whose initial motives were often financial (to rebuild a church, to raise funds for relief organizations) but whose final product could speak to both individual desires for recognition and an acknowledgment of woman's worth. See Marion Bishop, "Speaking Sisters: Relief Society Cookbooks and Mormon Culture," in *Recipes for Reading: History, Stories, Community Cookbooks*, ed. Anne L. Bower (Amherst: University of Massachusetts Press, 1997), 89–104. In the same volume, Ann Romines's essay, "Growing Up with the Methodist Cookbooks" (75–88), attests that such community cookbooks were the most-used texts her family owned. Bower's fine anthology collects a number of essays on community cookbooks—as autobiographies, as cultural histories, as women's alternative media.

19. Anne E. Goldman, *Take My Word: Autobiographical Innovations of Ethnic American Working Women* (Berkeley: University of California Press, 1996), 42.

20. Anne E. Goldman also finds the irreverence and sass of Smart-Grosvenor similar to Hurston's; see *Take My Word*, 47–49.

21. *Black Hunger* discusses the evolution of Smart-Grosvenor's volume over its three editions and two-plus decades.

22. In a well-known moment of gastronomic essentialism, the fictional Chloe of *Uncle Tom's Cabin* exclaims: "look at my great black stumpin hands. Now, don't ye think dat de Lord must have meant me to make de piecrust, and you [Mrs. Shelby, the slave's "mistress"] to stay in the parlor?" (Harriet Beecher Stowe, *Uncle Tom's Cabin* [1852; reprint, New York: Harper Classics, 1965], 27).

23. Doris Witt's "'My Kitchen Was the World': Vertamae Smart-Grosvenor's Geechee Diaspora," in *Black Hunger*, refers to other works by Smart-Grosvenor, notably "The Kitchen Crisis" and *Thursdays and Every Other Sunday Off. A Domestic Rap* (Garden City, N.J.: Doubleday, 1972) that are specifically concerned with the status of domestic servants.

24. An expatriate social set and culinary doings are the well-known subjects of Alice B. Toklas's *The Alice B. Toklas Cookbook* (1954; reprint, New York: Harper Perennial, 1984).

25. Toklas may have had more entrée into French society than Smart-Grosvenor by virtue of being white, but the African American counts wealthy people among her set as well. On the other hand, Smart-Grosvenor was not, early on, immune from heterosexism. In the preface to the second edition (1986) she decides not to excise a homophobic remark; in the most recent printing (1991), the offensive sentence—"I wouldn't pay no faggot six hundred dollars to dress me up like a fool" (page 152 in the 1986 edition)—is expunged.

26. So sure is Smart-Grosvenor of her value as an author and person, rather than as a "mere" cook, that she includes an entire chapter of her correspondence, a move Robert Stepto might refer to as self-authenticating.

27. For the Toklas recipes, see pp. 30 and 230 in *The Alice B. Toklas Cookbook*. Those of us who cook from the books we read will notice at least one divergence in philosophy, if not in method, in the two works. Although Toklas and Smart-Grosvenor share a respect for their audience-cooks' expertise and common sense, Smart-Grosvenor insists: "I never measure or weigh anything. I cook by vibration...The amount of salt and pepper you want to use is your own business" (p. 3).

28. In this, Smart-Grosvenor can be said to anticipate Alice Walker's well-known claiming of Black women foremothers, in *In Search of Our Mother's Gardens: Womanist Prose* (New York: Harvest/HBJ, 1984); see esp. 3–14.

29. Freda de Knight, *A Date with a Dish: A Cook Book of American Negro Recipes* (first published in 1948; revised and reprinted as *The Ebony Cookbook: A Date with a Dish* [Chicago: Johnson, 1962, 1973]). Thanks to Doris Witt for the dating. References to *A Date with a Dish* and several other Black cookbooks are absent in the 1991 preface, although she does refer to John Pinderhughes. Smart-Grosvenor may not have been aware of the existence of Black cookbooks, in part due to the relative obscurity of many such works; Witt and Lupton's Black culinary bibliography (in *Black Hunger*) lists about forty Black-authored cookbooks before 1970; a good number were published by small presses or brought out by the authors themselves.

30. Although it may not need saying, I'll note it anyway: the positions I sketch out here, between individual and community, between Smart-Grosvenor and the Dardens, are not absolute; elements of each outlook are found in both texts. Perhaps it's best to say that each cookbook emphasizes a different authorial stance.

31. The term "thick description" is Clifford Geertz's; for amplification, see "Thick Description: Toward the Interpretive Theory of Culture" in Clifford Geertz, *The Interpretation of Cultures: Selected Essays* (New York: Basic Books, 1973), 3–30.

32. Susan Kalcik has explored the transmission of ethnic identity through food, as I will return to shortly. Elizabeth and Paul Rozin have noted that flavor may function symbolically: having ethnic "tastes" places an

individual within a specific group; similarly, foods with a particular taste identify themselves as belonging to a particular community. See Elizabeth Rozin and Paul Rozin, "Some Surprisingly Unique Characteristics of Human Food Preferences," in *Food in Perspective: Proceedings of the Third International Conference on Ethnological Food Research, Cardiff, Wales*, ed. Alexander Fenton and Trefor Owen (Edinburgh: John Donald Publishers, 1981).

33. Irma McClaurin reminds me that the book was published in 1978 and so before the current suburbanization of the Black middle class. That *Spoonbread and Strawberry Wine* remains in print, and has even been transformed into a play in the 1990s, may speak to its continuing, *reinvented* appeal as a nostalgia item for the contemporary Black bourgeoisie.

34. The food pages of *Essence* attest to the bind between the need for quick, easy meals and the desire for "heritage" recipes; thanks again to Irma McClaurin, for reminding me of the continuing, if changing, significance of Sunday dinner.

35. Chitlins, or chitterlings, are pig intestines; they "are testament to the down-home doctrine that nothing in the hog is inedible." See Rick Bragg, "Atlanta Journal: A Delicacy of the Past Is a Winner at Drive-Ins," *New York Times*, 10 Nov. 1996, Final edition, sec. 1, p. 20.

36. See Lena Williams, "Preparing Soul Food Can Now Be as Easy as Opening a Can," *New York Times*, 26 May 1993, C3.

37. Quoted in Bragg, 20. Latter-day proscriptions against pork by Muslims and others in Black America wishing to separate themselves from a slave past may also have effected the turn away from pork products.

38. The avoidance of certain foods on the part of younger people speaks in part to a related desire to distance themselves from hardship and social ostracism. See my remarks on Pierre Bourdieu and his concept of the "foods of necessity," n. 44.

262

39. "[In 1808] Congress finally prohibited the slave trade. Absalom Jones and other black preachers began delivering annual thanksgiving sermons on New Year's Day, the date of the prohibition of trade and also the date of Haitian independence in 1804." See Gary B. Nash, from *Forging Freedom*, quoted in Ntozake Shange, *If I Can Cook/You Know God Can* (Boston: Beacon Press, 1998), 6.

40. Howard Paige, "African American Emancipation Day Celebrations," informal talk, August 1991, Greenfield Village Museum, Dearborn, Michigan.

41. Compare my observation with a similar one of Doris Witt's, on the handling of greens by the same cook: "Grosvenor manages to recreate the social context of recipe exchange, yet she simultaneously refuses to give us anything but thoroughly imprecise and unscientific suggestions on what to, and not to, do with greens. She offers a nuanced analysis of the social forces which come into play in the economy of recipe exchange." See "In Search of Our Mothers' Cookbooks," 25.

42. Surprisingly, although intent on recapturing the exact tastes and smells of the past, the Darden sisters show less resistance to modernization.

43. Harris, "Heirloom Recipes from a Southern family," 50.

44. Pierre Bourdieu, *Distinction: A Social Critique of the Judgement of Taste*, trans. Richard Nice (Cambridge: Harvard University Press, 1984), 178. His discussion of "the paradoxes of the taste of necessity" (177–79) has relevance beyond his original control group of French women and men.

45. Jessica B. Harris, *Iron Pots and Wooden Spoons: Africa's Gifts to New World Cooking* (New York: Atheneum, 1989), 15, 11.

46. That the practice is fading I surmise from the few student hands raised in response to my query "Do you know what pot likker is?" I, on the other hand, having lived with a grandmother who was raised in part in a southern Black community, was frequently admonished to drink my pot likker.

47. Cookbooks in the late 1990s regularly suggest smoked turkey wings as substitutes for pork in various dishes; baked macaroni and cheese, a staple at Black American family functions, can not be traced back to West Africa.

48. For a discussion of how ethnic groups persist as such and yet change in composition and style, see Fredrik Barth, introduction to *Ethnic Groups and Boundaries: The Social Organization of Culture Difference* (Boston: Little Brown, 1969), 9–30.

49. For example, Benedict Anderson, in *Imagined Communities: Reflections on the Origin and Spread of Nationalism* (London: Verso, 1983), notes that "communities are to be distinguished, not by their falsity/genuineness, but by the style in which they are imagined" (15). Although Anderson goes on to write of the ways groups construct themselves around print media, one can extrapolate his ideas to the manner in which a Black cultural identity is re-created, or created, through cookbooks.

50. Susan Kalcik discusses this phenomenon in her essay, "Ethnic Foodways in America: Symbol and the Performance of Identity," in *Ethnic and Regional Foodways in the United States: The Performance of Group Identity*, ed. Linda Keller Brown and Kay Mussell (Knoxville: University of Tennessee Press, 1984), 37–65, esp. 39.

51. The writings of Jessica B. Harris, John Pinderhughes's *Family of the Spirit Cookbook: Recipes and Remembrances from African-American Kitchens* (New York: Simon & Schuster, 1990), Cleora Butler's *Cleora's Kitchens and Eight Decades of Great American Food: The Memoir of a Cook* (Tulsa: Council Oak Books, 1985), and other, more recent books all display similar literary/historical/culinary instincts. Although each presents food and its role in the author's life differently, all cooks choose to collect, compile, and record recipes taken from family, travels, friends, or an individual career as chef and caterer. All take care to explain why one might want to conflate a cookbook with a historical or personal narrative.

"TO EAT THE FLESH OF HIS DEAD MOTHER":

HUNGER, MASCULINITY, AND NATIONALISM

IN FRANK CHIN'S *DONALD DUK*

EILEEN CHIA-CHING FUNG

★ 20

> Certainly the relationship between the experience of Otherness, of pleasure and death, is explored in the film "The Cook, the Thief, His Wife and Her Lover" [...] The [dark skinned] cook tells her that black foods are desired because they remind those who eat them of death (in the film, always and only by white people), the cook as native informant tells us it is a way to flirt with death, to flaunt one's power. He says that to eat black food is a way to say "death, I am eating you" thereby conquering fear and acknowledging power. White racism, imperialism, and sexist domination prevail by courageous consumption. It is by eating the Other [...] that one asserts power and privilege. (36)
> —bell hooks, Black Looks: Race and Representation

Throughout Asian American literature, the acts of eating and cooking have been productive metaphors for the poetic process. These acts associated with food reveal a complex and sometimes contradictory cultural economy that links identity politics to the production of labor and the exchange of commodities for social values. Implicit in the roles of the cook and the eater is their embodiment of cultural enterprise: they are not only symbolic bodies that assign meaning and value to their work, they also bear information for developing personal and communal identities. For Asian Pacific Americans who have been historically deprived of the symbolic value of their history and their subjectivity, constructing meaningful labor as identity represents a popular avenue for seeking self-affirmation. For example, many Asian Pacific American texts incorporate the metaphor of culinary activity as positive social work that produces a cultural nationalist vision of an Asian American subjectivity. However, the affinity between eating and ethnic subject formation, noted by Asian American literary scholar Sau-Ling Wong, elicits other concerns about gender, class, and sexuality. "Eating is one of the most biologically deterministic and, at the same time, socially adaptable human acts" (18) through which cultural and sexual agendas are repeatedly inscribed. Frank Chin's *Donald Duk* offers some of the most lucid material for exploring the problematics of constructing a cultural hero through the language of cooking and eating. Chin's story, a *bildungsroman* of a Chinese American boy learning about his ethnicity through his father's participation in food preparation, festivity, and storytelling in San Francisco's Chinatown, is explicit in the author's intent to create a positive masculine identity. In his narrative, Chin manipulates cultural signs of culinary productivity to define a cultural nationalist hero who, consequently, also signifies a "rebirth" of an Asian American masculinity. While I sympathize with Chin's frustration and understand the urgency to assert Chinese American visibility, I am concerned about his chosen avenue for reaching his goal: why is his project inflated within a capitalistic economy which animates a consumerist desire where one's gain is exchanged for another's loss?

Chin's masculinization and nationalization of domestic metaphors elicits questions about the power relations between men and women in his narrative, especially when the men in the text subsume the domestic space that traditionally has been gendered female while excluding the women as participants. Here, the ethnic men are both laborers and consumers, displacing the ethnic women from both public and domestic work as well as denying them their consumption.[1] As the men construct a kind of social reality based on the context of market economy and nationalist discourse, the women, like food, embody exchange and fetishistic values. In other words, the process of producing and consuming food constructs complex power dynamics based on gender and class differences that ultimately lead to a language of legitimacy and exclusion: namely, deciding who gets to obtain, cook, and/or eat food signals an economy of power, exchange, and desire. In fact, Chin's text reveals a nationalist investment in patriarchal and heteronormative practices within the social institution of family. The acts of cooking and eating construct a nation and a national subject by creating symbolic labor, values and commodity within the familial and domestic realm. On the other hand, women, excluded from labor and left out of the social network of economic systems, become commodities that can be desired and consumed. They are commodities of and witnesses to a discourse of nationalism and heterosexuality, disguising sexual anxiety and homosocial community among the men in the text.

★ THE DISCOURSE OF FOOD AND THE POLITICS OF GENDER

To analyze the affinity among eating, identity politics, and domination is to understand the pleasure of locating Asian American masculinity in the Asian American cultural "kitchen." To articulate a need for a rebirth of Asian American male identity and community is to imagine a lack and a sense of loss. The articulation of dispossession stems from decades of anti-Asian sentiment and racist and sexist ideologies in the United States. Beginning with the dire condition of the early railroad laborers and migrant workers, exclusionary immigration laws, antimiscegenation laws, Japanese internment camps, and the continuous representation of the "Yellow Peril" in media, Asians in America have experienced an oppressive and exclusionary history that has defined a certain specificity of Asian Pacific American social and cultural conditions. The need for culturally inspirational and affirmative representations has driven many artists and scholars to construe a sense of identity from other places and times, because few positive representations were offered and legitimated by American society. Emasculated by sexual, political, and economic discrimination, Chinese American men experience an invisibility both in American history and mass culture. Along with racism and their long absence in American history, the lack of ideal images of role models—authority figures—in both political and literary arenas has often led to a rhetoric of mourning, nostalgia and recuperation in Asian American narratives.

The language of mourning, according to Freud, is about loss. To experience loss is to imagine a prior time when the lost object was possessed, and the moment when it was lost. Returning to an origin is about learning to recover through representation. However, the problem with locating an originary moment through representation, as I will argue in this essay, is one of gender trouble and sexual violence. In *Beyond the Pleasure Principle*, the "fort-da game" becomes a story of loss in which the mother's absence—as the child mourns for her—is mastered through representation. The child's "artistic" play can be negotiated through the disappearance of the mother. However, the mother, denied entry into language and signification, remains outside the game itself. With the mother exiled outside the symbolic realm of language, her body becomes simply matter serving metaphors that sustain the myth of paternal productivity. She is the very object to be desired and reclaimed, through the recuperation of which men can achieve representation. Such recovery and its problematic end result necessitate a process of domination and self-consumption. The rhetoric of loss and nostalgia is transfigured into a language of work. The kinship between labor and the issue of power has been noted by Catharine MacKinnon: "Work is the social process of shaping and transforming material and social worlds, creating people as social beings as they create value. It is that activity by which people become who they are. Class is its structure, production its consequence, capital its congealed form, and control its issue" (65). Likewise, Fredric Jameson, in *The Political Unconscious*, also refers to the nature of violence in the birth of a subject. The initiation of subjectivity, according to Jameson, precedes an ultimate alienation of the Being from the Self; this separation and the loss of human collectivity become fundamental to identity formation in historical and cultural contexts. In other words, the birth of individual consciousness depends on the violent emergence of sex, race and class divisions. Chin's narrative seems to reinscribe a similar process of the birth of identity: the boy's turning thirteen years old signifies a beginning of manhood; Donald's becoming a "man" depends upon a set of cultural laws and social regulations policed by the paternal figures in the novel. Chin's narrative of a historical identity first enforces a process of alienation and separation, which in turn individualizes, compartmentalizes, and commodifies human relations in a materialist economy.

A consumer society is dependent on a division of the subject/self from the object/other, supporting a system of hierarchy and domination. The project of historicizing a masculine identity, not unlike Jameson's vision of "primitive communism"[2] in human history, is nostalgic for a possible "unfallen" state of Chinese American "manhood." Thus, a paradox resides in the narrative itself. The process of reconstructing prelapsarian moments for Chinese American manhood and Chin's desire for a historical subjectivity are contradictory in nature: seeking an individualized historical subject demands a *fragmentation* which cannot be equated to a moment of *totality* in the history of Asian American manhood, if it ever existed. Ultimately, Chin's narrative ends in division and domination—even the historically constructed subjects, both King Duk and Donald Duk, are in danger of being consumed in the cultural materialistic economy set up by the narrative.

265

The materialist economy is defined in *Donald Duk* by the culinary activities in which both those who cook and those who eat participate. Cooking and eating, inscribed with political and masculinist agendas, express and organize the social positions and relations between characters. Since the consumptive practice signals Donald's initiation into his ethnic and sexual identity, it is crucial to identify the active agents of culinary labor. This relationship takes our reading to the location and the source of food production—the home/restaurant and the role of the cooking father and the nonlaboring mother. As Jameson observes that the system of family relations emerges as a private space under the surge of bourgeois capitalism, the semiotics of sexual desires in the domestic sphere become the workings of a consumeristic desire upon which the modern historical consciousness has founded itself. Thus, the link between historical identity formation and capitalist materialism intensifies our interest—perhaps even anxiety—about the constructed relationship between Donald's search for a subjectivity and the labor divisions between his parents in the kitchen. Indeed, the home and restaurant—sometimes they cannot even be differentiated in the novel—represent the factories of "eating," constructing not only a material fetishism, but also a central agency of a masculine discourse. In one of Chin's short stories, "The Eat and Run Midnight People," he reiterates his belief that culture is consumable: "We were the dregs, the bandits, the killers, the get out of town eat and run folks, hungry all the time eating after looking for food. Murderers and sailors. Rebel yeller and hardcore cooks. Our culture is our cuisine" (11).

The political agenda is obvious: food becomes a discourse of a masculine culture which reinscribes male aggression and domination. The questions here are disturbing: who are those that are "eaten" by the "hunger" of the bandits, the killers, and the murderers? And if "our culture is our cuisine" and our cuisine produces the food—the object of the consumptive desire—then does the Chinese culture/tradition produce desirable food for a masculine hunger? And is this hunger for food a sexual hunger? And most important, who is the feeder and what—or who—is the food? This complex reading of eating and desire in the text directs us to a masculinization of eating. Food has become the fetishized object of a masculine desire. Chin's political agenda for creating an acceptable male identity in both Chinese and Western cultures is thus translated into the multicultual meals that Donald consumes:

> Fettuccini Alfredo with shark's fin. Poached fish in sauces made with fruit and vegetables. Olives on toast that taste like rare thousand-dollar caviar. Chocolate, bananas, yellow chili peppers, red chili oil and coconut milk go into one sauce over shredded chicken and crab meat to be eaten rolled up in hot rice paper pancakes with shredded lettuce, green onions and a dab of plum sauce. (64)

King Duk's cuisine, "wonderful, strange and tasty," is an eroticized and fetishized representation of multiculturalism. The multicultural identity of Donald becomes the manifestation of both the "salad bowl" and the "melting pot" theory; the "Fettuccini Alfredo with shark's fin" legitimizes the possibility of the American dream in which different cultures can retain and combine their individual "flavors" without being subsumed by a dominant culture. If the novel valorizes aggregation over assimilation, then, it fails to control its own aggressive desire to metabolize and incorporate the feminine other. Since Donald's self-recognition and establishment as a multicultural male subject depends upon his consumption of the fetishized objects (i.e. King Duk's cuisine), the "cooking" demonstrates the central masculine economy which excludes the participation of women. The father's role as the Chinese cook then resembles the producer of cultures—the benefactor of his son's eventual achievement of masculine subjectivity. Furthermore, the act of cooking becomes ritualized into a hypermasculine activity: "Dad uncovers a wok. Dad's hawk-eyes flash through the rising mounds of steam. He looks like a hawk above the clouds, a cosmic chef playing the music out of live food and dried food" (67). The figure of the father establishes the realm of the Symbolic: he sets up the laws of Order and the Norm. A Lacanian reading would translate the process as the acquisition of language when the child separates from the Mother and the Law of the Father intervenes. The excessively ethnicized father, in the absence of the "ethnic" mother, bestows the power of a cultural language on Donald. In a family where both the public and domestic labors revolve around the activity of cooking, the mother is denied the identity of a productive member, even in the sphere of the home which has been traditionally privatized for women. This unequal division of labor—the maximized labor of the father and the "non-labor" of the mother—frames the relationship of both domestic and public authority in this constructed capitalistic economy in the narrative.

267

Indeed, the men's activities in the kitchen also demonstrate a political market economy which assigns power to those who work and consume. As I previously argued, the men, especially Donald's father and his uncle, are perceived as productive members of a consumer society who equate cooking and eating rituals with cultural authentication, while women remain passive and excluded from all modes of production. Baudrillard discusses such dialectical play between labor and commodities in the political economy of signs. The exchange system sets up in the novel a linear and non-reciprocal exchange which inevitably establishes a pattern of social and sexual hierarchy:

> the consumption of goods (alimentary or sumptuary) does not answer to an individual economy of needs but is a social function of prestige and hierarchical distribution [...] Goods and objects must necessarily be produced and exchanged (sometimes in the form of violent destruction) in order that the social hierarchy be manifest. (30)

King Duk's consumer society is well defined in the narrative by the abundance of his food supplies for his family and community. His feeding of the poor and other eaters in his restaurant—he is the only cook, thus the only provider—again valorizes his Master position in the hierarchical economy. In other words, the "servant" and the women may consume food, "but in the name of the Master (vicarious consumption); their indolence and their superfluousness testify to his wealth and grandeur" (Baudrillard 31). Luce Irigaray describes the unequal dynamics between the men and women in the male economy where "men make commerce of [women], but they do not enter into any exchange with [men]" (172). Here, the expected hierarchies of Master and Slave, Man and Woman in a one-way exchange system reiterate the rhetoric of capitalist division. For example, "two old Chinatown sisters"—bag ladies—are found right outside the father's kitchen:

> Twins. Scrunched up old Chinatown women who have exactly the same eyes. Frog eyes. Their eyes seem to bulge out of their heads. They wait outside Dad's restaurant

when the garbage is put out. Now and then, when Dad knows they are out in the alley, he gives them a fresh catfish to take home [...] Donald Duk calls the old twins "the Frog Twins." He thinks they look like frogs. He says they look like they eat flies. (10)

This passage not only reiterates the wealth of the father as the provider, it also points to the exclusive eating community inside the affluent kitchen of the father juxtaposed with the sisters outside by the garbage. The mother, the sisters, and the Frog Twin sisters are all excluded from the material wealth and cultural affluence. Thus, the material poverty of these women—their non-participation in and exclusion from the labor economy—signals their cultural poverty. The juxtaposition here articulates an unequal power relationship among the "haves" and the "have-nots." Richard Schmitt puts it well in his account of power and control in the social community of capitalism: "The relations between people—the questions of who is rich and who is poor and how they relate to each other and, similarly, who has power and who not and how the powerful exercise that power over the weak—are in a capitalist society presented as relations among things" (88).

268

This kind of male domination in the form of class division, as Luce Irigaray would argue, continues in the representation of sexuality. The cultural poverty of the mother—her lack of recognition as a cultured body—goes beyond merely the problem of how others may "speak of or about" her, but is an evident sign of sexual oppression: "[the question] may always boil down to, or be understood as, a recuperation of the feminine within a logic that maintains it in repression, censorship, non-recognition" (78). Her unrecognizability or lack of an ethnic identity is justified by the fact that she is American born; thus Crawdad Man, King Duk's friend, reminds Daisy Duk of her ignorance of the Chinese culture: "'It's the real Chinese story [...] Everybody knows it. Ah-Daisy, you're born here, your folks are Christians. You don't hear the Chinese stories like Chinese children. That's why you don't understand more of the opera'" (164). Furthermore, her subjectivity—if there is any sense of that at all—stems from her theatrical impersonations of performers in American cinema (i.e. Greta Garbo, Katharine Hepburn), which further reinforces her distance from Chinese traditions and culture. She represents the "whitewashed" generation of Chinese Americans. Like their Americanized mother, the twin daughters, Penny and Venus, who always speak in cartoon-like dialogue, avoid any ethnic sensitivity. Their identities, as constructed in the narrative, are always displaced by TV or cinematic personalities; they can only understand the world through the American mass media. Chin in several scenes pokes fun at their artificial TV personifications, further fortifying the lack of a genuine individual—and clearly defined—identity:

"Gee!" Venus says, "Mom! You sound just like Connie Chung..."
"...doing her impression of Annette Funicello," Penny says in Venus's voice as if Venus hasn't stopped.
"...doing her impression of Shirley Temple," Venus continues.
"...saying Don't you dare hurt my grandfather, You!" Penny finishes....
"Oh, I love the way Mom speaks Spittoon," Venus says.
"Oh, thank you," Penny says. "She learned her Spittoon from early morning instructional TV. You would love Mom, except she's been institutionalized in Fog Bank Bubble Gardens ever since Annette Funicello started anchoring the NBC weekend news." (105)

The attack on the superficiality of Connie Chung's personality is obvious. Connie Chung's reputation of being the "fake" Chinese American face on TV is transposed onto the body of the mother whose Americanized "fake" Asian identity is also criticized in the novel. The scene above not only illustrates an erasure of a distinct identity for the mother—she is only an imitation of the multiple theatrical voices—but the fusion of the twin's voices also implies a lack of individuality in their characterizations. The artificial impositions of different voices through the electronic tubes (i.e. TV) onto the mother and daughters deny them any sense of human authenticity. This artificializing of the mother and the daughters becomes a way to de-legitimate women. They are, in Baudrillard's term, simulations of a "hyperreal" social order construed outside the father's ethnic kitchen and his cultural stage as a foil to the "real" material economy that forms the male community.

★ BODY POLITICS, SEXUAL VIOLENCE AND FOOD COLONIALISM

269

Indeed, Chin's text narrates a masculine national community landscaped by male heroism and female abomination. His adaptation of the *Water Margin* myth valorizes masculinity at the expense of women—the story of the seductive and treacherous woman, Lee Shi Shi, and the eaten mother, along with the reference to the masculinized sword woman, are the only examples of womanhood. The novel's references to the outlaw heroes of the *Water Margin* and the performance of Donald's father as Kwan Kung reiterate Chin's militant solution to the problem of the feminized stereotypes of Asian men. Here, Chin argues for a connection between heroism and masculinity in the Chinese culture, again identifying a Chinese hero with only male aggression and fraternal loyalty. Such a vision of Chinese heroic revival dictates and even justifies the sacrifice and exclusion of the Chinese woman. His notion of cultural heroism vindicates violence, more specifically, consumptive violence, against women. Aside from the mother's and daughter's simulated images of non-authentic identity, there are other women's bodies in the narrative who, like food, represent the fetishized materiality that can be commodified and consumed: Lee Keuy's mother and the "Ten Feet of Steel" woman in Chin's readaptation of the Chinese classic the *Water Margin*, and finally the girl dancer in Donald's dream exemplify the fetishized bodies that help maintain the institution of heterosexuality and the discourse of nationalism in the narrative.

The consumption of the fetish in Chin's text signifies on two levels: embodiment of certain social values and affirmation of heterosexual practices by misrecognizing desire. First, fetishism, in terms of Marxist ideology, stems from the language of religion and magic that is used to help imagine a capitalist reality. A capitalist fetishism is about one's own fascination with signs and commodified social values. In other words, the desire of consumption is about consuming not the actual commodity but the meanings which the commodity embodies. In a parallel conceptualization of the fetish, Freud articulates a connection between transgressive desires (in terms of the oedipal love for the mother and/or homosexual love for another man) and the origin of the fetish. Freud's notion of fetishism argues that in order to combat homosexual tendencies of the boy/child who is confronted with the dilemma of either giving up his identification with the mother as a love object or losing the penis, women are endowed with desirable characteristics to act as tolerable substitutes for the phallus (154). Thus women must become fetishes, which both distracts the boy/child from his own obsession with his phallus and valorizes his own image (via the missing phallus) as authority and power. This will become significant when Chin's narrative ends in a symbolic self-incorporation, representing the symbolic return of a boy/child to the originary state of completion and wholeness.

The problematics of consuming female bodies as fetishized commodities in Chin's text is most visible in this infamous statement. "I am the only one to eat the flesh of his dead mother, because I was hungry and knew she loved me" (160–61). In Frank Chin's reinterpretation of the Chinese myth, the *Water Margin*, Lee Kuey's cannibalistic act is deemed heroic and justified by the necessity of survival, the assurance of his mother's love, and his vow of blind loyalty to the outlaw brotherhood in the marshes. Indeed, the most visible act of literal consumption is cannibalism; the object of Lee Kuey's cannibalistic desire is his mother's flesh while the source of his justification is his blind loyalty to justice and his faith in her love for him. Her love then signifies her willingness to sacrifice for her men and her nation. In "The Eat and Run Midnight People," the desire to incorporate the maternal body does erupt into a visible narrative violence in the discourse of nationalism. The transgressive act is textualized into a theme of male inhabitation of the feminine body: "I tell her being a Chinaman's okay if you love having been outlawborn and raised to eat and run in your mother country like a virus staying a step ahead of a cure and can live that way" (11). The speaker/Chinaman's identification as a "virus" feeding on the nourishment of the body of a "mother country" visibly demonstrates a parasitic relationship, not unlike Lee Kuey's consumption of his mother's flesh for survival. The metaphor of the "male" virus eating away the maternal body signals a grotesqueness that emphasizes the double nature of the body politics in the discourse of nationalism. While the institution of a nationalist language is dependent on the social construction of desire for female bodies, women also remain a threat to the gender purity of a nationalist community. Thus, female bodies provoke both desire and horror. According to Kristeva, the foreboding co-existence of desire and horror in regard to the maternal body is an inevitable conflict. Both the repulsion and attraction to the body of the mother, or the "abject" mother, produce male distress. In order to protect the order of the Symbolic realm of the paternal laws, the narrative responds to the urgency to repress—to make absent—the very object of desire of the child/subject, the maternal body.[3] Woman as impurity, a topic to which I will return later in this paper, becomes more detectable towards the end of the story, when Donald's father equates sexual intercourse with ethnic defilement.

Interestingly, the paradoxical nature of the mother—who both attracts and repulses—resonates with the colonizer's sentimentality towards the colonial object. It resembles the complex relationship in which a national subject must negotiate with the strangeness of the Other's cuisine as well as the myth that ethnic knowledge can be consumed through the mouth. Ethnic food has long been debated as a site for colonialization: the eroticization and mythification of ethnic food and the cultural enclave (i.e. Chinatown) where the food is produced all appear exotic to the white gaze. Uma Narayan makes a powerful argument about the link between food and colonialism. "Food colonialism" and "culinary imperialism," she points out, reveal a complex relationship between social meaning and ethnic food in the context of colonial domination. Her example of curry in Britain tells us about the colonial subtext in the act of cooking and eating:

> The incorporation of curry into "British" cuisine in England, and of Indian artifacts into English homes, was in striking contrast to the attitudes of British colonialists resident in India [. . .] Making curry part of native British cuisine in England did not

expose British curry eaters to the risk of "going native." Incorporating things Indian was an easier task for those resident in England, who did not have to work at distinguishing themselves from their colonial subjects. (165–66)

Domesticating foreign-ness through the mouth is a way to fabricate multiculturalism; it is an act which emphasizes the polarity of otherness and sameness. Interestingly, Chin's novel suggests dangerous parallels to white fascination with the yellow culture: Donald guides Arnold through Chinatown where Arnold is enchanted and enthralled with the Chinese culture constructed by the *Water Margin* myth and King Duk's elaborate preparation of food. Chin appears to be aware of the relationship between cuisine and colonialism. In the same short story mentioned above, he hopes to de-mythologize the eroticism of "Oriental food" by naming food sources without ethnicization: "We eat toejarn, bugs, leaves, seeds, birds, bird nests, treebark, trunk, fungus, rot, roots, and smut [...] fingering the ground, on the forage, embalming food in leaves and seeds [...]" (11). However, there is always the problem of counter-productivity: that by emphasizing the foreign-ness of elements used in ethnic food, the food remains alien and exoticized to the gaze of the white eater. The father's elaborate "melting pot" and "salad bowl" cuisine also fails to escape the colonial subtext when the protagonist and his friend both consume it as cultural knowledge and power. It resembles Lee Kuey's cannibalistic act of consuming the mother for the survival of male valiance.

In summary, food and the maternal body, then, must be read as semiotic codes of linguistic systems that both animate and disrupt the production of a masculine subjectivity.[4] To sum up the problematic dynamics of food and maternal bodies in Chin's narrative is to recognize that Donald's subjectivity can only be found in a masculine economy regulated by the Law of the Ethnic Father. On one hand, the food is marked with signifiers of cultural meanings which are produced by the Symbolic father and consumed by the son. This process of production and consumption signifies the completion of cultural acquisition for Donald. On the other hand, the unethnicized mother becomes the anti-projection of the hyper-ethnicized father, actively reinforcing the masculine community which only allows the participation of masculine labor and productivity.

Here, in order to understand the problematic role of the mother completely, I will complicate my discussion of labor by examining the mother's *only* sign of productivity in the story. While the narrative denies her any cooking activity in the kitchen, she is assigned the task of building the paper plane "Ten Feet of Steel," commemorating a woman warrior who joined the outlaws in Leongshan Marshes to avenge her father's death. At first, Daisy's participation in the paper plane-building and the naming of an admirable woman from the myth seem to allow women a certain agency in the narrative. Yet, the "Ten Feet of Steel" woman is a "male" woman. Her character is very much masculinized—she enters the male community because her swordmanship demonstrates a masculine aggression: "Ten Feet of Steel charges into battle with her horse's reins between her teeth and one of her swords in each hand. She can carve her way through a thousand men. On foot she can fight off a thousand men" (49). Chin also fails to mention that this one—and only—beautiful and virtuous woman warrior appears to be a passive victim in the original myth. She ultimately becomes a commodity in the masculine exchange in which she is married off as a peace-offering by the leader of the Outlaws to an unflattering and unfaithful warrior in Leongshan, not to mention that her death occurs almost immediately after the marriage.[5] The mother's labor here is thus a reminder of the misogyny and the tragedy of the sword woman who has to act as a man to enter the masculine community of the outlaws only to become a "peace weaver" in order to maintain the camaraderie between the men.[6] Despite her show of "masculine" aggression, she still cannot escape her gendered status and the social expectation of her gendered body—a material object to be exchanged by two men. Most significantly, she is a victim of male violence and tradition.

It is evident that not only the maternal body but all female bodies represent manifestations of exclusion and violence: in the novel, female marginalization—even colonization—results not only from literal consumption but also through incorporation by the male gaze. King Duk's "dark piercing" hawk eyes again translate heroic militarism; Donald compares his father to a hawk who "looks pissed, wanting a fight, like his dad" (61). His father teaches Donald the power of the male gaze so Donald can "zap them with [his] eyes, and they had better nod at [him] or look away" when dealing with gang kids in Chinatown (4). While the father's instruction is meant as a defensive strategy for a young boy in a tough neighborhood, the gaze proves to be more lethal than a strategic move for self-defense. Women again become the targets for such masculine aggression. Notwithstanding the urgency to subvert the stereotypical feminization of the Asian men, the affirmation of such masculine desire sacrifices only women in return. The story the father tells Donald about the actor who disobeys the "Law" by sleeping with his girlfriend before he plays Kwan Kung is the perfect example of the female sacrifice—for "when he takes the stage his girlfriend's hair turns white and she has a miscarriage" (68). The masculine Law enforcer here is also the transgressor. The gaze is phallic in that it obtains the transgressive pleasure; at the same time, it destroys the object of desire in order to reaffirm the boundaries of cultural "Law" legislated by the gazer.

Furthermore, the emphasis on the vegetarian diet and the prohibition of sexual intercourse with women before playing Kwan Kung also disguises a problematic agenda. The parallel here is clear. Both the eating of meat and the entering of female bodies, while representing acts of power and domination, also signify pollution and, ironically, emasculation. King Duk's celebration of Donald's turning thirteen—the age of manhood—with a vegetarian dinner at the New Year guarantees Donald's purity. The eating of meat is also a reminder of eating the flesh of the dead mother: the violence again has sexual resonance. Thus, Donald's fear of Lee Kuey is not only Lee Kuey's fierce appearance but Donald's anxiety about his own desire to consume.

★ HUNGER AND HOMOSOCIALITY

If the existence of the women in the text brings on such anxiety, then the logical question is, why are women written into the text at all? This leads to the detection of certain interesting digressions of masculine desire in the narrative. While I agree that the presence of culturally "meaningless" women has served to further project and illuminate omnipotent figures of masculine cultural legacy, feminine bodies, more importantly, mask possible transgressive desires for homosocial love. However, Donald's desire for another of the same sex is constantly contested by the heterosexual gaze of the Father. I confront a paradox in my study. While the rituals of eating and gazing in masculine cultural economy exclude women, Donald's homosocial desires enforce a double exclusion. The homophobia of the paternal laws ironically must manipulate the bodies of women into policing any transgressive desire out of the narrative to pacify the homophobic F/father under the assumption that only a heterosexual man can be "masculine."

In other words, while the identities of women are threatened in such masculine commerce, they exist to prevent a different yet visible danger for the male subjects themselves. If both King Duk's and Donald's subjectivities are constructed by "consumed" bodies, they are ultimately consumed by the same desire in order to protect and maintain the masculine economy which exclusively fosters male friendship and masculine lineage. The women must exist for the men to safely play out the community of fellowship without anxiety about male bonding. For example, the act of eating constructs a community that is clearly homosocial. Donald's collective eating scenes with Arnold, his white school friend who is more interested in the cultural production prepared by King Duk than Donald himself, are invested with more complexity than a simple sharing of meals. Arnold, the readers are told, would "join Donald in the kitchen. The boys sit on Chinese stools at two places set on the kitchen chopping block and challenge the extent of Dad's knowledge of food and cooking" (9). The boys' sharing of the same hunger, nourishment, and tasting—later even sharing a bed—commemorates a homosocial love which excludes the participation of women. This masculine economy of the same, what Eve Sedgwick calls homosociality, disguises homosexuality as "sociocultural endogamy"—"they openly interpret the law according to which society operates" (62). Homosocial bonds in the canonical discourse on male friendship serve both to reaffirm masculine economy or order and to deny women agency so that they remain commodities.

Chin's narrative valorizes such male economy, not only through Donald and Arnold's friendship, but in his choices of cultural myth and the historical scene with the railroad project. However, the text struggles to repress a visible paranoia that these traces of homosocial love will erupt into homosexuality. The source of the "homosexual panic" (Sedgwick's term) is the F/father himself. Although King Duk encourages the camaraderie between Donald and Arnold,[7] Donald senses his father's uneasiness about his friendship with another boy. King Duk's anxiety about his son's sexual identity is manifested in the episode of the visitation to the herbalist in Donald's dream. The herbalist's inquiry about Donald's interest in girls and his crucial question, "Do you think about boys the way boys think about girls?" marks the narrative anxiety about homosexuality (91). The father's visible relief—"Whew!"—at Donald's immediate denial is deliberately constructed to contest the apparent homosocial bonds which, ironically, the male subject, Donald, has been taught to internalize as the very core of masculinity from the beginning.

Thus, the recognition of the father's obvious role as the homophobic law-enforcer intensifies a curiosity about the presence of the nameless girl in Donald's dream. If Chin has constructed specific moments to contest any sexual transgression, then it is possible to read the nameless girl as another feminine body exploited by the gaze of male observers. Both Donald and Arnold see her in the dream which they again share; the girl becomes the object of heterosexual desire and under the male gaze, she is a seductress:

273

> In and out from inside the lion's head, he dances and kicks after the girl. She makes dangerous scary moves at the lion, pokes and whacks with her staff pretty as the flight of a hummingbird. Donald Duk feels his heart thumping, galloping easy, and his eyes seeing everything a little crazy. (112)

While Arnold watches (we are under the assumption that Arnold sees what Donald sees), Donald dances with the lion as the girl teases it, inflaming Donald in his desire for her while reminding the reader that Donald is essentially heterosexual (and very much ready to become a "man"). The plot of this triangulation of desire—Donald, no name girl, and Arnold—responds again to the homophobia in the narrative by prohibiting and controlling any possible readings of transgressive desire between Donald and Arnold.[8] The body of this nameless girl—her identity is not important, because it is her gendered body that the narrative needs—signifies at once an assurance and insertion of a masculine, now heterosexual, male identity.

In the course of examining the semiotic language of feminine bodies, I discover that the lurking danger of identifying male agency is a consumerist history and culture. In other words, the project of writing or rewriting history and ritualizing a cultural myth which is essentially misogynistic can never escape a consumerist economy. It has to reiterate the relations of domination and exclusion. The desire to consume is endless. The narrative is forever trapped in a nostalgia for a lost utopian moment in history when Asian American manhood can be made whole and complete. The final New Year celebration in *Donald Duk* attempts to restore and immortalize the nostalgic ideal of Asian manhood (as perceived by Chin in Kwan Kung): "They already treat him [the F/father] as Kwan Kung, as if his eyes will kill...He looks into his mirror and sees Kwan Kung. 'It's been a long time'" (168–69). While women's bodies are out of sight both figuratively and literally, the body of the father itself is the object of masculine gaze and desire. Symbolically, in the father's melancholia for the loss of Asian manhood, he consumes himself in order to incorporate the lost masculine ideal. The narrative, thus, leads to the ultimate consumption of the male subject himself. The internal incorporation of a male subject implies a male communion of homosociality.

Montaigne's "De L'Amitie," as Carla Freccero tells us, suggests that cannibalism "may be said to (re)appear around the question of friendship and the incorporation of the [male] (love) object into the self" (8).[9] Eating the other and being eaten by him signifies the "most lofty intersubjective communion between men, or rather, of subjectivity itself" (8). King Duk's final self-consumption has two significances. On one hand, male economy is completed and reinstated—nothing is more pure than a self-incorporation of the male subject; on the other hand, the masculine, heterosexual father commits the very act he himself struggles to prevent and repress—the creation of another homosocial economy inscribed onto the body of the F/father himself.

★ **"ANYBODY HUNGRY" FOR NATIONALISM?**

Appropriately, the narrative ends with the father asking "Anybody hungry?" at the dining room table (173). The father has incorporated and consumed, with his mouth and his gaze, both the other and himself. In his obsession with hunger (perhaps the author's as well), he is forced to cannibalize his own body. In an attempt to construct a mythical hero and a national origin, Chin inscribes a subtext about nation-making through the process of eating that ultimately signals a systematic act of violence against others and even oneself. The danger in a heroic quest for national identity, as Richard Slotkin suggests in his book *Regeneration through Violence*, depends upon a colonialist move to locate the Other and to justify the domination of the Other. The hero is the hunter, the frontier man, the soldier, and the colonialist who baptizes combat/violence in the fabrication of American mythology. This highlights the problem Chin faces in attempting to parody an Asian American hero within the Western tradition of mythogenesis, creating an Asian American frontier myth that celebrates a narrative about domination and colonialism. Food and female bodies become the frontier—the romanticized terrain—of Chin's Asian American mythology making. The final narrative hunger in *Donald Duk* perpetuates the consumerist desire in which food remains gendered (though now, more ambiguously) and nationalized. The narrative concludes with an acute consciousness of the passing of time and history through a vow to immortalize food, forcing it to remain coded with cultural urgency and consumerist violence: "it begins and ends with *Kingdoms rise and fall, Nations come and go*, and *food*" (173, emphasis mine). This narrative leaves behind disturbing implications. A Chinese American male subjectivity must be defined solely upon gender polarization, consumerist strategies, and systems of exchange. If one believes that the birth of a male subject in history, prophesied by Jameson, proceeds from a set of capitalistic and consumptive violence, then it ultimately leads to a destruction of the (female) Other as well as the (male) Self.[10]

NOTES

1. I am using labor in terms of the Marxist notion of the labor power in a commodity-producing society in *Capital*. I will argue that in Chin's narrative, only specific people control and own the means of production as the productivity of labor; in this case, domestic labor becomes socially meaningful. Food, the product of the labor, is also commodified and consumable by a select few. The language of cooking and eating clearly develops a power relation between persons who are allowed to participate in the market economy and those who are denied participation.

2. Jameson envisions primitive communism to be the stage before relations of domination emerged in human society. It is similar to Hegel's notion of Being as yet un-negated and estranged from its own self-identity. The intrusion of bourgeois capitalism brings on the end of the Edenic state of unity; humans begin to differentiate from each other in race, class, sex, and age.

3. Julia Kristeva in *The Power of Horror* discusses the psychoanalytical status of the mother. She argues that before the "beginning" of the symbolic there must have already been moves, by way of the drives, towards expelling/rejecting the mother. The symbolic, the intervening Law of the Father, is not strong enough to ensure the separation of the mother and child; it depends on the mother becoming abjected. Yet, the subject/child, though he fears "castration," still desires the maternal body. Thus, abjection, or the abject mother, remain fundamentally "what disturbs identity, system, order" (4).

4. The politics and the poetics of the body treat the body as a site for cultural signification. Despite the appearance of lack in meaning, the body is a part of the semantic project of the narrative and can be semiotically retrieved. Thus, Donald's mother, though her body lacks any ethnic recognition, bears semiotic meanings in that very absence.

5. Many Chinese critics have long debated and criticized the misogyny in the *Water Margin* myth. For example, Su argues in *The History, Psychology, and Artistry of the Water Margin*:

   > There is no doubt that everyone who has read the *Water Margin* would be suspicious of the author's prejudice against women [. . .] this is a male-centered book and good women are rare in the story. And nine out of ten women are dishonorable. [W]e always hear [. . .] the author call the young beautiful women "sluts" and "bitches" [. . .] full of hatred and balefulness [. . . .] [T]he percentage of women's dying rate is much higher than that of men [not to mention the brutal ways they die; one woman's breast is cut open so her heart can be retrieved, and another woman is decapitated]. (32–33, translation mine)

6. The no name girl in Donald's dream also parallels this analysis of the "Ten Feet of Steel" woman. Her show of "masculinism" in taking over Donald's position in the Lion Dance illustrates again that her only agency is to take a man's place. However, the longer discussion about the "woman warrior" figures may distract from my

main argument. Thus, I refrain from conducting a detailed analysis of the two women here, though one should keep them in mind in order to examine the constructions of womanhood in the overall framework of Chin's novel.

7. King Duk's militant attitude about life—"History is war"—is also invested in his guidance of the friendship of the two boys. He expects the same loyalty from them as that of the relationship between the outlaws from the marshes.

8. Sedgwick in "Homophobia, Misogyny, and Capital: Our Mutual Friend" discusses the central preoccupation in novels where they

> site an important plot in triangular, heterosexual romance—in the Romance tradition— and then [change] its focus as if by compulsion from the heterosexual bonds of the triangle to the male-homosocial one, here called "erotic rivalry." In these male homosocial bonds are concentrated the fantasy energies of compulsion, prohibition, and explosive violence; all are fully structured by the logic of paranoia. (162)

This Girardian triangulation exemplifies the tradition of displacing a homosocial love with a heterosexual romantic triangle where a woman's presence contains and hides the transgressive love between two men.

9. Freccero points out the affinity between cannibalism and "homosociality" in Montaigne's elegy:

> Montaigne's melancholic elegy to his dead friend, Etienne de La Boetie, thematizes an uncanny merging enacted, as absence, by the (missing) inclusion of de La Boetie's poetic corpus. The merging Montaigne describes between himself and his friend is accompanied by metaphors of nourishment, hunger, tasting, communion. (8)

10. I am grateful to Rowena Tomaneng for her professional and personal support through the numerous revisions of this draft. I would also like to thank Wei-Ming Dariotis for her thoughtful reading and Vanessa Shieh for reference checking.

276

REFERENCES

Chin, Frank. *Donald Duk*. Minneapolis: Coffee House Press, 1991.
———. "The Eat and Run Midnight People." *The Chinaman Pacific & Frisco R.R. Co.* Minneapolis: Coffee House Press, 1988. 8–23.
Baudrillard, Jean. *For A Critique of The Political Economy of the Sign*. Trans. and Introd. Charles Levin. St. Louis, MO: Telos Press, 1981.
Freccero, Carla. "Cannibalism, Homophobia, Women: Montaigne's 'Des Cannibales' and 'De L'Amitie.'" *Women, 'Race,' and Writing in the Early Modern Period*. Ed. Margo Hendricks and Patricia Parker. London: Routledge, 1994. 73–83.
Freud, Sigmund. *Beyond the Pleasure Principle. The Standard Edition of the Complete Psychological Works of Sigmund Freud*. Ed. James Strachey. Trans. James Strachey et al. Vol. 18. London: Hogarth, 1953–74.
———. "Fetishism." *Standard Edition*. 1927. 152–57.
hooks bell. *Black Looks: Race and Representation*. Boston: South End Press, 1992.
Irigaray, Luce. *This Sex Which Is Not One*. Trans. Catherine Porter with Carolyn Burke. New York: Cornell University Press, 1980.
Jameson, Fredric. *The Political Unconscious: Narrative as a Socially Symbolic Act*. Ithica, NY: Cornell University Press, 1981.
Kristeva, Julia. "Approaching Abjection." *Powers of Horror*. New York: Columbia University Press, 1982. 13–15, 135–36.
MacKinnon, Catharine. "Feminism, Marxism, Method, and the State: An Agenda for Theory." *Feminist Social Thought: A Reader*. Ed. Diana Tietjens Meyers. New York: Routledge, 1997.
Narayan, Uma. *Dislocating Cultures: Identities, Traditions, and Third World Feminism*. New York: Routledge Press, 1997.
Sedgwick, Eve Kosofsky. *Between Men: English Literature and Male Homosocial Desire*. New York: Columbia University Press, 1985.
Schmitt, Richard. *Introduction to Marx and Engels*. Boulder: Westview Press, 1987.
Slotkin, Richard. *Regeneration through Violence*. Middletown, CT: Wesleyan University Press, 1973.
Su, Shu Yu. *The History, Psychology, and Artistry of the Water Margin*. Taipei: Wu Chun Press, 1981.
Wong, Sau-ling Cynthia. *Reading Asian American Literature: From Necessity to Extravagance*. Princeton: Princeton University Press, 1993.

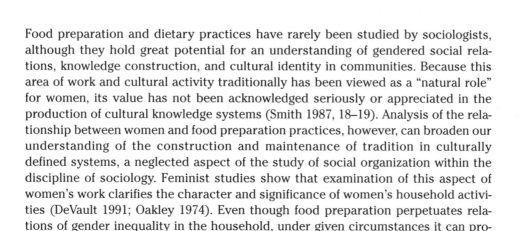

"WE GOT OUR WAY OF COOKING THINGS":

WOMEN, FOOD, AND PRESERVATION OF   21

CULTURAL IDENTITY AMONG THE GULLAH

JOSEPHINE BEOKU-BETTS

Food preparation and dietary practices have rarely been studied by sociologists, although they hold great potential for an understanding of gendered social relations, knowledge construction, and cultural identity in communities. Because this area of work and cultural activity traditionally has been viewed as a "natural role" for women, its value has not been acknowledged seriously or appreciated in the production of cultural knowledge systems (Smith 1987, 18–19). Analysis of the relationship between women and food preparation practices, however, can broaden our understanding of the construction and maintenance of tradition in culturally defined systems, a neglected aspect of the study of social organization within the discipline of sociology. Feminist studies show that examination of this aspect of women's work clarifies the character and significance of women's household activities (DeVault 1991; Oakley 1974). Even though food preparation perpetuates relations of gender inequality in the household, under given circumstances it can provide a valued identity, a source of empowerment for women, and a means to perpetuate group survival (DeVault 1991, 232).

This article illuminates how women, as primary actors responsible for managing and preparing food in the household and the community, contribute to our understanding of the formation and continuance of food-related cultural practices in Gullah communities. I argue that although food preparation, under pressure of dominant cultural practices, may be viewed as a measure of gender inequality and of women's subordination in the household, it also can promote resistance and strengthen cultural identity in marginalized cultural groups.

By drawing on the analytical constructs of an Afrocentric value system (self-reliance, women-centered networks, the use of dialogue and connectedness with community, spirituality, and extended family), Black feminist studies provide a framework for conceptualizing knowledge construction and cultural identity from the perspective of Black women's lives (Gilkes 1988; Gray White 1985; Collins 1990;

Reagon 1986; Steady 1981; Terborg-Penn 1987). These studies show that cultural beliefs, values, and traditions are transmitted largely in women-dominated contexts such as the home, the church, and other community settings.

The work of scholars such as Angela Davis (1971, 7) illuminates how African American women have contributed to the formation and continuance of African American cultural institutions. Davis argues that under slavery, cultural beliefs and practices were transmitted largely by the performance of nurturing and caregiving roles, which enslaved women provided primarily in the family and the community. Although caregiving activities may have reinforced women's oppression in the household, these roles were significant in that they provided women with the only meaningful opportunity to influence their families in ways not immediately subject to control by their oppressors.

In discussing women's role in more recent struggles affecting African Americans, Johnson Reagon (1986, 79) argues that African American women have helped to create and maintain a cultural identity in their communities that is independent of the dominant culture. For example, she contends that if women did not teach these traditions to younger members of their communities, the youths would never know how far African Americans had come, or the depth of that struggle. Hill Collins also stresses the importance of viewing the Black woman as "the something within that shape[s] the culture of resistance and patterns of consciousness and self-expression in the Black community" (1990, 142). She postulates that Black women may seem to conform to institutional rules of the dominant culture, but closer examination reveals that historically they have resisted such structures by promoting their own self-definitions and self-valuations in safe spaces that they create among other Black women.

This article contributes to this discourse by examining the significance of cultural practices related to food and the role of women in forming and continuing these practices in Gullah communities in the coastal region of Georgia and South Carolina. I give particular attention to the significance of the natural environment as a primary food source in the culture, the centrality of particular foods such as rice, the rituals and norms of food preparation, and efforts to preserve these practices under pressure of social change and intrusion by the dominant culture.

Historically in Gullah communities, both men and women have played a vital role in procuring and preparing the food necessary for their families' survival. Studies, however, reveal very few examples of men's activities in domestic food preparation. Food preparation in Gullah households tends to be gender-specific and organized around particular tasks; each successive task is more highly gender-stratified. Although men are more likely to engage in activities such as hunting, fishing, gardening, and preparing meat and seafood for cooking and barbecues, women also participate in these activities when they choose to do so. Although most men are knowledgeable about cooking, and most mothers seem to teach both their sons and daughters how to cook, men rarely cook regularly in the household. Women more often take responsibility for cooking and feeding, and they appear to be the custodians of food rituals and practices that perpetuate the group's survival.

★ DATA SOURCES AND ANALYSIS

This study uses ethnographic data based on my field observations and semi-structured interviews with 22 Gullah women in the Sea Islands and neighboring mainland communities in South Carolina (Wadmalow, St. Helena, John's, Edisto, and

Coosaw Islands) and Georgia (Sapelo and St. Simon's Islands, and Harris Neck community) over several visits made between 1989 and 1992. My research interest in this region stems from my background as an African scholar who was raised in a West African rice-cultivating society; later I conducted research on rural households and rice cultivation in that society. As a result, I felt that I was uniquely prepared to examine historical and cultural connections in the food practices of West African and Gullah rice cultures. To collect naturalistic observational data on the significance of Gullah food practices, I arranged to stay with selected families in two of the communities I studied. I also kept a journal of my daily experiences and observations while living with my host families.

Women participating in the study were drawn from each of the communities mentioned above. The criteria for selection were that they were descendants of formerly enslaved African Americans from these islands and that they had been raised there. I found participants through key individuals and community organizations. Through snowballing and by a process of proving my credibility as an African woman researcher interested in making cultural connections between the rice culture of West Africa and the rice culture of the Gullah, I selected a number of women willing to work with me as study participants.

279

Semistructured interviews were designed to give the participants an opportunity to voice their opinions and experiences in their own terms. Although the interviews followed guidelines, they allowed ample opportunity for women to elaborate or to introduce issues they considered relevant. Interviews with each participant usually were completed in one and a half to two hours, although in some cases subsequent interviews were necessary. Interviews focused on participants' knowledge of Gullah food practices and rituals, management of food practices in the home and community, and their role in preserving and transmitting these practices to later generations. About two thirds of the interviews were tape recorded; the others, with women unwilling to be taped, were written down verbatim.

The strategies I used to gain access and establish trust among the participants varied according to the situation of each community. In communities where local residents seemed to be better informed about their African heritage, I worked under the auspices of key individuals and community groups. Sometimes they sent a representative to accompany me to interviews and extended invitations to social events to which I might not have had access otherwise. In other communities, where local residents seemed more reluctant to talk to outside researchers because of negative experiences in the past, it worked to my advantage to distance myself from my university affiliation and to engage myself in the life of these communities. In one community, regular attendance at church services and midday meals at a local community center helped me develop a kinlike relationship with two respected senior women. They taught me the importance of being associated as the guest, relative, or friend of a respected person to gain acceptance among community residents.

Study participants range in age from 35 to 75. They include nine widows living alone or with their children or grandchildren, two single parents, and eleven married women living with their families. Most of the younger women are employed in service or public-sector jobs; the older women are more likely to be homemakers or retired from wage employment. Although the youngest respondent has two years of college education and the oldest has no formal schooling, education for the majority ranges from completion of the third to the twelfth grade. All names used in the study are pseudonyms.

Eight other women whom I asked to interview declined to participate in the study. Most of these women came from one particular community and were the daughters of older women who were participating. They were more ambivalent about my presence than were their mothers because they felt that past experiences with university researchers or journalists had proved to be exploitative. Time constraints from family responsibilities and wage employment also contributed to these women's reluctance to participate.

In analyzing the interviews with study participants, I regarded their narratives both as individual accounts of daily experiences in managing food practices and as a form of custodianship and conveyance of oral traditions about the significance of the Gullah food system. I took this approach because many of the interviews contained an element of reflection about the past as a backdrop for commentary on the present. Although some of this reflection was deliberate because of my interest in establishing historical and cultural connections, the participants and the other community members to whom I spoke also tended to organize their talk so as to provide a background to contextualize their meaning.

The data analysis strategies used in this study are qualitative and inductive. As described by Ariselm Strauss, qualitative research is a form of data analysis that "occurs at various levels of explicitness, abstraction, and systematization" (1990, 4–6). It involves extensive use of field observations and intensive use of interviews as data collection techniques, and emphasizes "the necessity for grasping the actors' viewpoints for understanding interaction, process, and social change" (pp. 4–6).

The data were transcribed almost verbatim, although I did some light editing (such as inserting explanatory or connecting words in a bracket) or excluded small sections of an interview when the material seemed somewhat peripheral to the issue under discussion. After transcribing the taped data, I searched for themes repeated in both taped and untaped interviews, focusing on the rituals and management of food preparation over several stages of the process. My aim was to develop a detailed understanding of these ritual practices in the Gullah household. By looking for detailed, perhaps even mundane, information about each stage of food preparation, styles of cooking, flavors of food, eating practices, and (if possible) the meanings attached to these practices, I hoped to show any variety occurring among households and to establish connections for historical and sociological analysis. I also used my daily journal entries to provide context when analyzing the data.

★ THE SIGNIFICANCE OF THE GULLAH

Gullah communities in the Sea Islands and neighboring mainland regions in Georgia and South Carolina provide a unique opportunity to study some of the distinctive elements of African cultural influences on African American culture in the United States. Despite variations in the demographic structures and economic practices of communities on or near these islands, strong similarities exist in proximity of location and in historical and cultural background. One significant characteristic of these communities, for example, is that most residents are descendants of enslaved Africans who worked on these islands as early as the seventeenth century.

Beginning in that period, Africans were captured and transported as slaves from various regions in Africa, extending from Angola to the Upper Guinea Coast region of West Africa. Between 1670 and 1800, however, Africans from rice-cultivating regions in West Africa, such as Liberia, Sierra Leone, Senegal, Gambia, and Guinea, were sought because of their knowledge of cultivation of rice, which was then a lucrative crop in Georgia and South Carolina (Holloway 1990, 4; Littlefield 1981; Wood 1974). Rice planters were particularly interested in enslaving Africans from the "Rice Coast" of West Africa because the planters themselves lacked knowledge about rice cultivation in tropical conditions. The system of rice cultivation adopted in these coastal regions of Georgia and South Carolina drew on the labor patterns and technical knowledge of the enslaved West Africans (Littlefield 1981; Opala 1987; Wood 1974).

Because of the geographical isolation of these islands, cohesive communities evolved and preserved African cultural traditions more fully than in any other group of African Americans in the United States. These traditions are represented in the Gullah language spoken among Sea Islanders, in birth and naming practices, in folktales, in handicrafts such as grass-basket weaving, carved walking sticks, and fishing nets, in religious beliefs and practices, and in a food culture based on rice (Creel 1990; Georgia Writers' Project [1940] 1986; Jones-Jackson 1987; Opala 1987; Turner 1949).

281

Today the sources of livelihood in these Sea Island communities vary according to available economic opportunities. In communities such as John's, Wadmalow, Edisto, St. Helena, Ladies, and Hilton Head Islands, many inhabitants are engaged in the vegetable track industry; others are involved in fishing, crabbing, and marketing of crafts. Most of the young and the old in these communities garden, fish, hunt, and sell crafts and other services to supplement their incomes (Jones-Jackson 1987, 17). As a result of development of the tourist industry, such as on Hilton Head and St. Simon's Islands, many inhabitants (particularly women) work in minimum wage service positions. Limited employment opportunities on islands still inaccessible by bridge, such as Sapelo Island in Georgia and Daufuskie Island in South Carolina, have led many of the younger or more highly educated community members to seek work elsewhere, causing an imbalance in the age structure of their populations. Sapelo Island, for example, has a population of just 67 people; a disproportionate number are in the economically dependent years, over 60 and under 18.

★ CONNECTIONS BETWEEN THE NATURAL ENVIRONMENT AND GULLAH FOOD PRACTICES

The value of self-sufficiency in food supply is an integral aspect of the Gullah food system. Men and women of all ages are conversant with hunting, fishing, and gardening as ways to provide food. From an early age, both men and women are socialized into the concept and the practice of self-sufficiency as a primary goal of the food system and are encouraged to participate in the outdoor food-procuring activities of parents and other kin or community members. Velma Moore, a woman in her mid-40s and a key participant in my study, became sensitive to environmental causes when, as a child, she accompanied both parents on daily walks in the woods. This experience taught her a variety of survival skills involving the use of the island's natural resources for subsistence and medicine. She learned how and where to collect medicinal herbs, and when and for what purpose they should be used. She also learned various folk remedies that had been passed down in her family for generations, such as life everlasting tea for colds or leaves of the mullein plant for fever. Velma recollected that when she was a child, her mother kept these herbs on hand in the kitchen and stood over a reluctant patient to make sure every sip of the tea was consumed. Now married and the mother of five children, Velma pointed out that she encourages the practice of these traditions among her sons and daughters. She even performs regionally as a storyteller and writes local newspaper articles about the significance of these traditions in her culture.

Grandparents also play an important role in developing children's skills in food self-sufficiency. A typical example was Maisie Gables, a lively and active woman about 70 years of age. When I interviewed Miss Maisie, as she was called, I did not know that our scheduled appointments conflicted with her plans to go fishing with her five-year-old granddaughter, whom she was teaching to fish. Miss Maisie explained later that her granddaughter liked fishing from an early age, so she had decided to cultivate this interest by teaching her the necessary skills, as she had once been taught by her mother. By transmitting these skills, which are part of collective memory, the senior generation of Gullah women fosters and sustains cultural identity intergenerationally, thus broadening the base of cultural knowledge in the community.

While the Gullah depend on their natural surroundings as a reliable source of food, they also have a deep understanding of their coexistence with other living things and believe that the use of these resources should be moderate and nonexploitative. This sense of shared membership in the natural environment stems from Gullah belief systems, which emphasize harmony and social exchange between the human and the natural world. Such a view is influenced by African spiritual beliefs, which are community centered and involve a set of relationships involving God, the ancestors, other human beings (including those yet unborn), and other living and nonliving things. In this complex system of relationships, the well-being of the whole is paramount; individual existence is woven into the whole.[1]

Some aspects of this worldview are reflected in my interview with Velma Moore. She describes herself as a self-taught woman, although "self-taught" does not adequately describe her intelligence, strong will, and vast knowledge of Gullah history and culture. During one interview, she revealed that she, like many Gullah women, had been taught to hunt and would do so if necessary. Even so, she considered herself a keen environmentalist, with concern for the protection of nature, and would not engage in such activities for recreation because "it is not sporting to go up and kill animals that can't shoot you back." In other words, although she would rely on these resources for survival, anything beyond that purpose would threaten the harmony with nature.

Velma also expressed concern about the threat of environmental destruction in the region, a result of increasing tourism and economic development. She conceptualized this problem in connection with the struggle to preserve her own endangered cultural heritage:

> I always felt that if you don't deal with one and the other, if you just strictly deal with one, then you're losing the rest of it. Because you cannot have stabilization in a minority community in this area here unless you recognize the culture and the environment. And if you mess up the environment, and you move the people away because the environment is not right, then you are taking away their culture at the same time. So if you take away their land, you are also taking away the culture when you move the people, and so forth. (Velma Moore, 1991)

In making this connection between the threat of environmental destruction and the survival of her own cultural heritage, Velma reveals an awareness of her relationship, represented by culture, with other living beings, both human and nonhuman. She does not distinguish between the two because she perceives them as natural allies in a struggle to protect tradition from the intrusion of dominant cultural practices. Because both are woven into her existence, the survival of one depends on that of the other and must be defined and challenged from this standpoint.

Interviews with Gullah women suggest that engagement in fishing, gardening, hunting, and other outdoor activities is not based strictly on gender role divisions. Although many of the outdoor activities related to food procurement are men's domain, women are more likely to be associated with these activities than men are with activities regarded as women's domain. In other words, it seems that at each successive stage of food preparation (which can overlap somewhat), work activities become more gender-specific. This is true, for example, of role expectations in some fishing activities, such as men's use of the cast-net method and women's use of the reel and rod method.

I observed, however, that women make judgments about what is appropriate for them, which give them some flexibility in choosing activities they wish to pursue. In the Moore family, for instance, Velma's husband and son were responsible for planting vegetable crops for their garden, while Velma took responsibility for weeding and maintaining the garden. Velma, however, also expected their help in weeding because she did not want to be burdened with an activity that is monotonous and unpopular among men. Similar attitudes were revealed in my discussions with these women:

> *Interviewer:* Do you both do the same type of fishing?
> *Velma Moore:* Well, yes and no. We both fish with the reel rod and he fishes with the cast net more than I do, although occasionally I go fishing with the cast net, too. But he basically does that.
> *Interviewer:* But you do cast-net fishing, too?
> *Velma:* Oh yeah. Most of us women here can. Most—I retract that—most of the older women here can.

> *Interviewer:* You mean you still go hunting?
> *Willietta Davies:* Um hum. Like we [self and husband] go hunting for coon and things in the night. We goes with the truck. We usually go at night anywhere around the island. I use an A-22 gun and a flashlight. I like to take the light and blind their eyes. I catch the eyes of that raccoon, and I stop and shoot.
> *Interviewer:* What do you catch?
> *Willietta:* Raccoon, possum.
> *Interviewer:* I can't believe that (laugh).
> *Willietta:* That's the only two sport I like now. I don't go dancing and I don't drink. I like to go [hunting] and fishing, and that's the truth. I love it.

★ THE CENTRALITY OF RICE IN GULLAH CULTURE

Dependence on rice as a staple food is the most significant way the Gullah express cultural identity through food practices. Rice is the main food that links Gullah dietary traditions with the food traditions of West African rice cultures; women play a primary role in fostering the continuance of these practices. In such cultures a person is not considered to have eaten a full meal unless rice is included.

283

Although most Gullah families no longer cultivate rice regularly, people are still conscious of its significance. Rice was described as the central part of the main family meal by at least 90 percent of the women I interviewed. Typical were responses like

> It's the one that makes us fat because we go to sleep on it.... My father used to say, "Eat something that sticks to your rib." (Velma Moore, 1991)

> Many people feel if rice isn't cooked, they haven't eaten. Take my grandson, for instance. No matter what you cook, whether it's potatoes or macaroni, you have to prepare a separate portion of rice for him. Otherwise he'll feel like he hasn't eaten. (Carla Bates, 1989)

> Rice is security. If you have some rice, you'll never starve. It is a bellyful. You should never find a cupboard without it. (Precious Edwards, 1992)

> Well, they have to have that rice 'cause, see, they be working hard at the farm and they have to have something to give them strength. They don't hardly bother with too much grits. They eat that grits in the morning now. But when dinnertime come they have to have that rice. They always say that Black people like too much rice. They don't eat like the white people. I don't know why they always say so. (Wilma Davies, 1991)

Because of Gullah women's daily involvement in food preparation in the home, they are very conversant with the stories and traditions passed down in their families about the significance of rice to their culture. On the occasions when I stayed as a guest in study participants' homes and helped prepare evening meals, women often shared stories and folktales with me, as well as songs and dances connected with their rice culture. On Sapelo Island I learned about formerly enslaved women who prepared special rice cakes made with honey for their families on particular days and months of the year, in observance of Muslim religious festivals.[2] Women also told me about folk traditions such as a song called "Blow Tony Blow." This accompanied a traditional dance still performed by Gullah women at cultural festivals to demonstrate how rice grain was removed from its husk with a flat, round, woven grass-basket called a fanner.

Several elderly women also recalled a time when rice held such a special place in their communities that children were not permitted to eat it except on Sundays or special occasions:

> They have folklore on rice down here. One of the things we grew up with, for instance, after the birth of a child you wasn't given rice—no rice. Because rice is supposed to been too starchy for the newborn baby to digest through the mother's milk, and so you wasn't given rice to eat at all. (Velma Moore, 1991)

> Some of the old folks believe that rice was also a cure for sick chickens, believe it or not. If your chicken were looking like they were kind of sick, you was to feed them raw rice, and it supposed to make them feel better. So they will take raw rice and toss them in the chicken yard. (Velma Moore, 1991)

> I've known people to parch rice and make their coffee. Put it in the frying pan or something, and you toss it lightly and keep shaking it lightly until it brown—you mix it and you can drink it, and you put water and you make [it] like coffee. (Velma Moore, 1991)

These accounts are distinctive because of choice of words and expressions used to communicate custodianship of these traditions. For example, the use of terms such as "security," "strength," "bellyful," "makes us fat" helps us to understand the role of this food not only as a means of survival when families are on the brink of economic disaster but also in times of plenty. Recollections of folklore traditions similarly enable us to explore the versatility of the culture, as expressed in the ability to transform rice into a form of coffee or a cure for animal ailments.

It is also significant that these recollections are narrated by women, because through such stories we learn how marginalized cultural groups construct a familiar and identifiable world for themselves in a dominant cultural setting. This point is addressed in Orsi's (1985) study of the role of popular religion in an Italian Catholic community in Harlem between 1880 and 1950. Orsi contends that identity is often constructed through a people's ability to discover who they are through memory. Although pressure from a dominant culture may weaken their ability to reproduce their knowledge and perceptions of themselves and of their world, the ability to remember and to create a communion of memory in the group provides the foundation for establishing membership and continuity of that group (p. 153). A parallel can be drawn in the role of Gullah women in maintaining a sense of shared tradition through food practices. Through their recollections of stories and songs and in their performance of dances and enactments of past traditions, they create a frame of reference alternative to those promoted in the dominant culture, while at the same time transmitting collective memory to the next generation.

One way of promoting an alternative frame of value reference through food practices is in the daily observance of strict rituals of rice preparation. In Gullah and West African rice cultures, for example, it is typical to commence the preparation of rice by picking out any dirt or dark looking grains from the rice before washing it. Then the rice is washed vigorously between the hands a number of times before it is considered clean enough for cooking. As a girl growing up in Sierra Leone, I was taught to cook rice in this way. I still follow this practice faithfully, even though most of the rice available for sale today in the United States is labeled as prewashed.

Whenever Gullah women speak of cooking rice, they distinguish between the various types of grains before explaining which cooking method will be most appropriate for a particular grain. They also take pride in describing the proper texture and consistency of a well-cooked pot of rice, although the suggestion that food must have a particular appearance to be satisfying is as culturally specific to the Gullah as to other ethnic groups.[3] Indeed, the belief that well-cooked rice must be heavy to be filling to the stomach is a cultural trait that the Gullah share with many African societies that eat heavy staple foods (Bascom 1977, 83; Friedman 1990, 83).

Gullah women also control the interaction of their food practices with those of the dominant culture by emphasizing the preferred place of rice in the main meal. For example, even though foods associated with other ethnic groups are generally eaten in Gullah families (e.g., lasagna, pizza, hamburgers), the women I interviewed tend to categorize such foods as snacks, not meals. To illustrate this point, the following discussion took place between me and one participant.

> *Betty:* Well, occasionally there is, you know, maybe lasagna. That is an occasional thing. Um, pizza is something that the kids love. And we have that like—that is never a meal. That's like if you have a bunch of guys dropping over and you are

going to have pizza and pop, or tea, and a salad, you know, something like that. But it is never a meal, never.

Interviewer: For you it is like a snack.

Betty: Yeah, it is more like a snack. Yeah, definitely. It's like a snack... You need to have some type of rice. (Betty Smith, 1992)

In the following accounts of how various women cook a pot of white rice, we see how Gullah women establish cultural boundaries by situating rice at the center of their food system:

Interviewer: How do you like to prepare your rice?

Maisie: Well, I scrub it real good with water. With my hands scrub all that dirt off it.

Interviewer: Yes, that's how we do it too back home.

Maisie: I know, I'd say most Black people [do that]. Some Black people don't wash it you know, they try to take the vitamins from it. How can you eat all them germs? [If] I can't wash it [then] I don't want it. Then I put [the rice] in my pot and just put enough water, you know, to steam it without draining it off. I don't drain my rice. That's it. (Maisie Gables, 1991)

Two others commented

Well, I don't like it real dry and I don't like it real soft. Just medium. Some people, they cook their rice so that all the grain just fall apart, but I don't like it real dry. I wash all that stuff off. Pick those strings and things out of it 'cause you have to take all that out. So we wash it good. Now the one that you plant and beat yourself has more starch on it than the one you buy at the store. And you have to wash it real good. [Then] I average the water, put a little soda in it. I don't use so much salt now. And if it have too much water on it, I pour it off. Then I let it boil according to what kind of heat—now that you have electric or gas stove, now you see you turn it down medium until it soak down. I don't wait until it get real moist. Even up [turn the heat] on it to steam it down. (Willietta Davies, 1991)

and

Gosh, some of that depends on the rice too because you got short grain rice, you got long grain rice. And sometime you tend to fix one a little different from the other. I basically starts mine in cold water, I wash it in the same pot. I will just pour it in the pot. We don't measure it. So I just pour it in the pot what I think the amount I need. I go to the sink and I'll wash it . . . twice to clean it off. Pour the necessary water back on it and salt it and put it on the fire, and let it come to a full boil. The heat is usually reduced about three times, 'cause it's high until it starts boiling, then the middle, you let it cook a little normally for a while, then once all the water has evaporated or boiled into the rice, then you turn it real low so that it stay back there and soak and get just right. (Velma Moore, 1991)

Each of these examples reflects a sense of continuity of tradition as each stage of the process is described. For example, measurements are not discussed. This means that such recipes have been handed down by word of mouth and depend to some extent on one's particular taste. Also, each person emphasizes that the rice has to be washed well and that it must be cooked in just enough water to allow it to steam on its own, without the interference of draining or stirring. All of these descriptions might be said to follow a common tradition handed down from the period of slavery and still practiced in present-day West African rice cultures.[4]

These examples also reveal that the task of cooking rice is laborious and time-consuming. The Gullah, however, are fairly conservative in accepting innovations that might alter some of their existing practices. For example, labor-saving devices such as rice cookers, now in common use, do not seem to be used in the Gullah households I visited. One possible example of this cultural conservatism can be demonstrated in the story of a rice cooker I gave to a family with whom I often stay and with whom I had shared the joys of a rice cooker when they visited my home. Although they appreciated the gift and showed it off to neighbors and family members, on two subsequent visits I noticed that it was still in its box and that rice was cooked in the familiar way. The family's reluctance to use the cooker more regularly might imply a lack of respect for custom, as well as fear of jeopardizing the survival of a tradition that is already endangered.

Such a line of reasoning is developed in Williams's (1985) analysis of the role of tamales in the food practices of Tejano migrant families. Williams suggests that in the wider context of Tejano culture, the preparation of tamales symbolizes the Tejanos' sense of who they are in an alien cultural setting and is a means of strengthening interpersonal bonds within the community. Tejano women play a key role in this process by monopolizing the traditional skills and knowledge necessary to enhance understanding of the significance of this food in their group identity (Williams 1985, 122–23). In the case of the Gullah, one could argue that by conforming to the traditional rice-cooking practices, women serve as a medium to control the limits of interaction between their food practices and those of the wider dominant culture. As shown by their covert reluctance to use my gift, which is a major time-saving device for those who prepare rice daily, my friends may interpret a change in their way of cooking to mean the eventual loss of skills and practices they are striving to keep alive for future generations of their people.

287

★ RITUALS AND NORMS OF MEAL PREPARATION

Gullah culture is influenced strongly by rules and norms of West African food preparation. Many women who cook perpetuate these practices daily. One of these practices involves the selection, the amounts, and the combination of seasonings for food. These elements differentiate Gullah cooking practices from those of other cultures, according to many women I interviewed. Although the Gullah identify certain foods as their own, such as Hoppin' John (rice cooked with peas and smoked meat), red rice, rice served with a plate of shrimp and okra stew, and collard greens and cornbread, the interaction between European American, Native American, and African American food systems in the South has carried these popular southern dishes across ethnic lines. One way in which Gullah women try to control cultural boundaries in their way of cooking these foods, as distinct from other southern practices, is to assert that although similar foods are eaten by others in the South, their style of preparation and the type of seasonings they use are different. Just as West African cooking is characteristically well seasoned with salt, pepper, onions, garlic, and smoked meat and fish, Gullah food is flavored with a combination of seasonings such as onions, salt, and pepper, as well as fresh and smoked meats such as bacon, pigs' feet, salt pork, and (increasingly) smoked turkey wings (to reduce fat content). The Gullah women's views are expressed clearly in the following statements:

> Interviewer: As an African American living in this area, what do you think makes the food you eat different?

> Culture and what's available to you. I call it a "make do" society on Sapelo because you can't run to the supermarket to get things. We are plain cooking. We use salt, pepper, and onion as basic additives. Our flavoring comes from the type of meat we put in it. Bacon is white folks' food, pig tails, neck bones, and ham hock is what we use. Soul food is what other Americans call it, but we consider these to be foods we always ate. We never label ourselves or our food. (Velma Moore, 1991)

> On Sapelo you got things like red peas and rice. You know, they cook the same things on that side over there too, but we assume that we have the monopoly on it, that nobody cooks it the way we cook it... although they call it the same thing, the ingredients may be a little different than they use, or the taste is definitely different. So it's considered Sapelo food. I mean very few places you go [where] they cook oysters and rice or they cook clam and gravy the way we do, and stuff like that. So we got our way of cooking things. So we pretty proud of calling it Sapelo food. Yes. (Vanessa Buck, 1989)

By claiming these features of the food system as their own through daily cooking practices, and by situating this knowledge in the community through the use of such words as "we" and "strictly ours," the Gullah women maintain the credibility and validity of a familiar and recognizable tradition in resistance to pressure to conform to dominant cultural practices.

A strong preference for food produced and prepared from natural ingredients is another norm of Gullah food practice. In many of my interviews, women stated that much of the food they prepare for their families is grown locally and naturally. When asked to comment on what makes Gullah food distinctive, Betty Smith, who is married, in her mid-40s, and an active community and church member, explains:

> A lot of what we eat is locally grown. Not the rice, but everything else. We dabble in other things that are imported, but... I guess the type of food we eat is indigenous to this area. It's what we have kind of grown up on. Most of my food is still prepared traditionally. My rice is usually boiled. I don't buy parboiled rice. I don't buy too many processed foods.

Annie Willis, who is in her 70s and also is active in church and community activities, lamented the demise of locally grown foods and expressed concern about the quality, taste, and health implications of store-bought foods:

> When I was a child coming up, we never used to put fertilizer in our crop to rash up the food. Food used to taste much better then than now. The old folks didn't have as many health problem as we are having and they ate all those forbidden foods. I think it's the fertilizers and chemicals they put in the food now. Seem to me that children were more healthy in those days than they are now. (Annie Willis, 1989)

The suggestion that the younger generation of Gullah may no longer prepare food strictly from naturally produced sources implies that the Gullah way of producing and preparing food is symbolically significant and a mark of their difference from other cultures. These statements also reflect a concern for the customs and traditions threatened by the influence of urban development in the region. By recalling a past that their foremothers and forefathers created, these women set a context in which the values of their community can be understood and reclaimed for future generations of Gullah.

The women's statements also reveal concern about the expectations of custom and tradition and how these can be accommodated to the demands of present-day family life and employment. Certainly many of the traditional foods eaten by the Gullah must be time-consuming to prepare, and one cannot always prepare them regularly if one has a full-time job or other commitments. How do women cope in these circumstances? Several women employed outside the home admitted that they had made some adjustments. Pat Forest, a 43-year-old woman who is employed full time as a nursing aide in a local health clinic, lives with her husband and four children, who range from 10 to 22 years of age. Because of the demands of her job and her role as primary caregiver in the family, I was not surprised to learn that she prepares red rice by using a precooked tomato-based sauce rather than cooking from scratch. Traditionalists in the community would frown on this type of cooking, however. Some women told me that they often save time by preparing part of the meal the night before serving it or that they might prepare traditional meals only on specific days of the week such as Saturday and Sunday. Some women even said that they simply do not set a time for the main evening meal until it is prepared to their satisfaction. Several also mentioned that they had taught their sons and daughters to take on some of the basic responsibilities of cooking, especially the daily pot of rice.

The ways in which these women manipulate time constraints to accommodate the customary demands of their food practices suggest efforts to uphold the central role of these food practices in the home, but also to exercise the flexibility needed for modern living. Although the women show respect for the culture and even express some guilt about failure to conform fully, their actions suggest that they are walking a fine line (albeit rationalized by time pressures): They are maintaining tradition while adjusting to modern influences that potentially might endanger that tradition.

In common with West African cultures, the Gullah tend to prepare excess amounts of food for a meal in case someone should pay a visit. In West Africa, in fact, it would be embarrassing for a host to prepare or send out for food for unexpected guests (Bascom 1951, 52; Finnegan 1965, 67). Even under the economic constraints facing many West African societies today, such a tradition is upheld as strongly as possible because it is still viewed as a mark of prestige for both the head of the household and the cook. Although the Gullah do not necessarily view this tradition as a symbol of prestige, some of its elements are common in many of the homes I visited while conducting this study. As Velma Moore explained to me:

> I'm always able to feed another person in my home. People [here] will automatically cook something more just in case a stranger drops in.

As my study proceeded, I knew that the local residents were beginning to open up to me when, after several visits, I was offered food, whether or not it was mealtime.

★ EFFORTS TO TRANSMIT TRADITIONAL FOOD PRACTICES

Much effort is being made to keep these traditions alive through oral tradition and everyday practice. Observers are pessimistic about what the future holds for a people who now consider themselves an endangered species (Singleton 1982, 38). One of the leading concerns expressed by residents of these communities is that the survival of this coastal culture is threatened by the rapid economic growth and development of tourist centers in the region. According to Emory Campbell, director of the Penn Center on St. Helena Island, South Carolina:

> The Black native population of these islands is now endangered, and we don't have too much time to protect oysters, fish, and crab. Developers just come in and roll over whoever is there, move them out or roll over them and change their culture, change their way of life, destroy the environment, and therefore the culture has to be changed. (Singleton, 1982, 38)

The lack of stable employment opportunities on these islands is also cause for concern, because it has created an imbalance in the age structure; a high percentage of young adults leave for employment elsewhere. Also, it is felt that the drive toward a more materialistic way of life in the region will lead, in the long term, to an array of social problems such as alcoholism, marital conflicts, and youth delinquency (Singleton 1982, 38). The task of transmitting cultural traditions to a rapidly declining younger generation of Gullah poses a challenge to those committed to preserving this way of life. Such transmission will be difficult unless the living context of the culture can be preserved according to Charles Joyner, a folklorist and scholar of Gullah history and culture (Nixon 1993, 56). The women I interviewed also expressed this attitude:

> You've got to have culture in order to make your community stable and stay in one place. And so how else can white people come in and say, "Oh, these people down here speak Gullah or Geechee," and want to learn more about your culture, but at the same time they want to buy your land and push you out. How can you come down and visit me in my area, but I'm hanging on by a thread because you want my area. What do you suppose they'll show their friends and talk about? You know, they'll say, "This used to be a Gullah community, a Geechee community, but now they all live there in the heart of Atlanta or someplace else." It's not going to work. You can't move papa from [here], sit him in the middle of Atlanta, and say, "Make your cast net." Who's he going to sell cast nets to in the middle of Atlanta? ... all of a sudden he'll die. So you can't move the culture and tradition from one area and just plant it in another area... You've got to nurture it here, pass it down, teach children, and so forth. It's a slow process. You've got to know how to do it and you can teach other people how to do it. (Velma Moore, 1991)

In view of these concerns, how does the analysis of women's role as carriers of food preparation practices inform us about cultural survival strategies among the Gullah? How do women transmit knowledge of these practices to the younger generation? How do their strategies relate to emerging themes in the study of Black women?

Perhaps the most relevant context for understanding knowledge transmission among Gullah women may be African-derived cultural practices that stress motherhood, self-reliance and autonomy, extended family, and community-centered networks (Collins 1990; Steady 1981). Each practice is centered in either the home or the community, and the two spheres of activity are mutually reinforcing. Within these domains an alternative framework of identity is constructed and women serve as transmitters of cultural knowledge.

The concept of motherhood illustrates how women use their spheres of activity to transmit cultural traditions. Motherhood among the Gullah is not limited to a biological relationship, but also can embrace other relationships with women termed "othermothers" (women who assist bloodmothers by sharing mothering responsibilities) (Collins 1990, 119). Othermothers may include grandmothers, sisters, aunts, or cousins who take on child care, emotional support, and even long-term responsibilities for rearing each other's children. According to Jones-Jackson (1987), "It is not unusual for a child [in the Sea Islands] to reach adulthood living not more than a block from the natural parent but residing with another relative who is perhaps childless or more financially secure" (p. 24). It is also common to see a neighbor helping to prepare a meal next door or being offered a meal without concern that parental permission would be required.

The concept of family extends beyond the nuclear family to include extended and even fictive family ties. Responsibilities and obligations within the family are defined in this context; they facilitate the development of family communities where relatives live close to each other, and promote cooperative values through shared roles and socialization practices. Women of all generations, as mothers and as extended-family members, play a critical role in fostering self-reliance and a sense of collective memory in their children of both genders. They do so through the daily preparation and eating of traditional foods and by using informal conversation to teach family history and cultural traditions.

291

I learned about the use of informal conversation when I attended a funeral at the home of a Gullah family. In the evening, after the funeral ceremonies were finished and most people had left, all the women of the family sat together in the living room with their children at their feet, eating and telling each other family stories. Someone asked about the people in a family photograph. My hostess described the context in which the photo was taken (which happened to be a family meal) and recalled each family member present, including the wife and mother, who was in the kitchen cooking when the photo was taken. Because children are expected to eventually manage their own lives, both sons and daughters are taught the skills of self-reliance through cooking. Parents believe that their children must know these things to survive in the wider culture.

Much of this socialization takes place around the mother or in the family, but much is also learned from trial and error. Velma Moore recalls:

> I learned to cook by trial and error and mama. Nobody teaches you how to cook, not over here. They allow you to play cook in the kitchen and watch them. Tradition always leaned towards girls cooking, but that boy, if he was hungry, he was expected to go in there and fix something for himself. Not that he had to sit there and starve all week until somebody's sister come home. So he learned how to cook, just like his sisters did. If a parent was home and he was home, they'd come up and ask him, "Hey, you was home all day. How come you didn't put on the rice?" or "How come you didn't boil the beans or something?" And so they would ask him the question that they would ask girls. At least I know mama did [laugh].

Strong bonds between women are also established through women-centered networks, which promote cooperative values in child care and informal economic activities (such as grass-basket weaving and quilting), in the opportunity to share experiences and ideas, and in fostering the development of positive self-images, self-affirming roles, and self-reliance as women (Bush 1986, 120; Collins 1990, 119; Steady 1981, 6). The social exchange of goods and services and the flow of information and ideas that emanate from this type of networking encourage the development of positive self-images and community awareness in the children in these communities. While staying with Gullah families, I often observed exchanging and giving of food and other goods and services among women and their families, although many people commented that this practice was declining. Often when people went fishing or gathered vegetables and pecans, the women sent these foods to neighbors and friends, especially elderly individuals or couples who could no longer move around easily.

Finally, as Jones (1986) points out, preparation and serving of food by Black women in a secular communion of fellowship "symbolize[s] the spiritual component of collective survival" (p. 230). Women who prepare food for church activities play a vital role in helping these community-centered institutions to become sites of cultural preservation and spiritual fellowship, because food is an integral part of the ritual activities associated with spiritual fellowship. During the planning of church functions such as church anniversaries, weddings, and funerals, women who are known for their skills in preparing particular dishes are usually asked to prepare foods such as collard greens, red rice, peas and rice, cornbread, and chicken.

292

> When we go on a church picnic, we have a little cook-out like hot dogs and hamburgers, stuff like that. When we have the anniversary of the church, we cook soul food. And we have collard greens, and string beans, butter beans, fried chicken, some kind of roasts, macaroni and cheese, cornbread, and red rice. (Bernice Brown, 1989)

> We eat our food every day on St. Helena Island, and we also eat it at church anniversaries, weddings, and funerals. When we raise money to help the church, like women's day, the pastor's anniversary, the choir anniversary, we cook our food. (Queenie Moore, 1989)

Some women, including a study participant from Wadmalow Island, also raise funds for their church by preparing meals for sale in their homes.[5] Organizing such a party often involved considerable work in preparing traditional dishes such as red rice, fried fish, barbecued pigs' feet, collard greens, and shrimps and okra served with rice. Usually, my informant's friends and relatives helped her to prepare the food. Members of the church congregation and other community members then were expected to show their support by attending the party and paying for the food, as they would in a restaurant.

By extending food preparation to embrace the church family, the actions of women, who usually do this work, promote a sense of shared tradition and spiritual identity among church members, especially among youths and those who lack the time or talent to practice these traditions. This activity also reinforces community-centered networks by providing a context for dialogue, mutual mentoring, and spiritual development, especially among women in the community (Young 1992, 16).[6]

★ CONCLUSION

Although women in most societies serve as primary preparers of food for the household, this aspect of their daily lives has not received much analytical attention. Not only have women been largely excluded from the process of knowledge construction and validation, the work of food preparation has also been devalued and rendered invisible because of a dominant culture that views it as a "natural role" for women (Collins 1990; Smith 1987). Even in feminist scholarship there is an underlying tension when this issue is discussed because of the dual nature of food preparation as a valued work activity and as "women's work." On the one hand, it provides women with a source of valued identity and empowerment; on the other, it is a means of perpetuating relations of gender inequality and women's subordination in the household (DeVault 1991, 232). Feminists who advocate changes in this sphere usually recommend equitable distribution of housework among household members, cutting back on housework, and creating new family roles for men (Chodorow 1978; Hochschild and Machung 1989; Oakley 1974). DeVault (1991), however, argues that in changing the organization of food preparation in the home, one must be careful not to trivialize its value and its symbolic meaning in the expression of shared group membership. In other words, DeVault advocates preserving the essence of caring that is built into this activity, although in a way that would not maintain relations of inequality for those who perform it (DeVault 1991, 233–35).

I have argued here that through regular food preparation and management of feeding in the family and the wider community, African American women in Gullah communities perpetuate cultural identity and group survival. Cultural preservation through food preparation and feeding is a highly conscious act on the part of these women; it is tied closely to their judgments about when to accept, and when to resist, change. Gullah women, therefore, are willing to take shortcuts in cooking when time pressures demand it, but they seem less willing to compromise their feelings about nature and environmental protection or to tamper with the "unique" seasonings they say are a component of true Gullah cooking.

293

Gullah women devise and transmit alternative ways of understanding their culture by relying on African-derived systems of knowledge, which promote motherhood, women-centered networks, self-reliance, extended family, and community-centeredness. Reliance on these values has enabled Gullah women to resist negative images of their past; they use common but resourceful strategies such as everyday practice, teaching by example, and providing constant recollections of their past through storytelling and other oral traditions. Although present attempts to define and preserve the unique cultural tradition of these communities are threatened seriously by the pace of economic development in the region, Gullah women have learned from their mothers and grandmothers that the observance and practice of the underlying principles of their traditions are vital to the survival and preservation of their culture.

NOTES

1. See Margaret Washington Creel (1990) and Patricia Jones-Jackson (1987, especially 24–28). A good background to African spiritual philosophy is John Mbiti (1969).
2. Former slaves Katie Brown and Shad Hall from Sapelo Island, Georgia, when interviewed by the Federal Writers' Project in the 1930s, vividly described a special rice cake made with honey that their African Muslim grandmother prepared for the family on particular Muslim fast days (Georgia Writers' Project [1940] 1986, 162, 167). Thomas Winterbottom ([1803] 1969), a British physician who worked in Sierra Leone at the end of the eighteenth century, also reported that the Muslims he encountered liked to make cakes of rice and honey.
3. One may find that even when a meal displays the qualities they claim it must have to be satisfying or filling, it still might not be acceptable to a given people if that food is not their preferred staple.
4. See Charles Joyner (1984, 96) for a description of how rice was cooked on some slave plantations in South Carolina, given by Goliah, who was enslaved, on the plantation of Robert F. W. Allston.
5. Interview with May Taylor, Wadmalow Island, 1989.
6. Although I recognize the important contributions of Gullah women in the development of the Black church and in its spiritual leadership and community development activities, they have made this contribution at the expense of holding leadership positions. In the formal authority structure of African American churches, men generally control these positions. Women lack due recognition and status, and they continue to fight to attain a measure of power and influence in many Black churches. At the same time, they have shown differ-

ent patterns of leadership within the church community by fostering a sense of collective autonomy and "woman consciousness" (Gilkes 1988, 228). Like the activities of women who organize voluntary missionary societies, teach Sunday school, raise funds, and become prayer band leaders and church mothers, the activities of women who prepare food for church functions show that women use this sphere of influence in the church to foster a sense of shared tradition and spiritual identity in their communities.

REFERENCES

Bascom, W. 1951. Yoruba food. *Africa* 21:41–53.

———, 1977. Some Yoruba ways with yams. In *The anthropologist's cookbook*, edited by J. Kuper. New York: Universe Books.

Bush, B. 1986. "The family tree is not cut": Women and cultural resistance in slave family life in the British Caribbean. In *Resistance: Studies in African, Caribbean, and Afro-American history*, edited by G. Y. Okihiro. Amherst: University of Massachusetts Press.

Chodorow, N. 1978. *The reproduction of mothering*. Berkeley: University of California Press.

Collins, P. Hill. 1990. *Black feminist thought: Knowledge, consciousness, and the politics of empowerment*. Boston: Unwin Hyman.

Creel, M. Washington. 1990. Gullah attitudes toward life and death. *Africanisms in African-American culture*, edited by Joseph E. Holloway. Bloomington: Indiana University Press.

Davis, A. 1971. Reflections on the Black woman's role in the community of slaves. *Black Scholar* (December): 3–15.

DeVault, M. L. 1991. *Feeding the family: The social organization of caring as gendered work*. Chicago: University of Chicago Press.

Finnegan, R. S. 1965. *Survey of the Limba people of northern Sierra Leone*. London: Her Majesty's Stationery Office.

Friedman, C. G. 1990. Africans and African-Americans: An ethnohistorical view and symbolic analysis of food habits. In *Encounters with American ethnic cultures*, edited by P. Kilbride, J. C. Goodale, and E. R. Amerisen. Tuscaloosa: University of Alabama Press.

Georgia Writers' Project. [1940] 1986. *Drums and shadows: Survival studies among the Georgia coastal Negroes*. Athens: University of Georgia Press.

Gilkes, C. 1988. "Together and in harness": Women's traditions in the Sanctified Church. In *Black women in America: Social science perspectives*, edited by M. R. Alson, E. Mudimbe-Boyi, Jean F. O'Barr, and M. Wyer. Chicago: University of Chicago Press.

Gray White, D. 1985. *Ar'n't I a woman? Female slaves in the plantation South*. New York: W. W. Norton.

Hochschild, A. R. and A. Machung. 1989. *The second shift: Working parents and the revolution at home*. New York: Viking.

Holloway, J. 1990. *Africanisms in American culture*. Bloomington: Indiana University Press.

Jones, J. 1986. *Labor of love, labor of sorrow: Black women, work, and the family from slavery to the present*. New York: Vintage Books.

Jones-Jackson, P. 1987. *When roots die: Endangered traditions on the Sea Islands*. Athens: University of Georgia Press.

Joyner, C. 1984. *Down by the riverside: A South Carolina slave community*. Urbana: University of Illinois Press.

Littlefield, D. 1981. *Rice and slaves: Ethnicity and the slave trade in colonial South Carolina*. Baton Rouge: Louisiana State University Press.

Mbiti, J. 1969. *African religions and philosophy*. New York: Praeger.

Nixon, R. 1993. Cultures in conflict: Sea Island communities are fighting for their survival, stirring new hopes along the coast of South Carolina. *Southern Exposure* (Fall): 53–56.

Oakley, A. 1974. *The sociology of housework*. New York: Pantheon.

Opala, J. 1987. *The Sierra Leone-Gullah connection*. Freetown: USIS.

Orsi, R. A. 1985. *The Madonna of 115th street: Faith and community in Italian Harlem, 1880–1950*. New Haven, Conn: Yale University Press.

Reagon, B. Johnson. 1986. African diaspora women: The making of cultural workers. *Feminist Studies* 12:77–90.

Singleton, V. 1982. We are an endangered species: An interview with Emory Campbell. *Southern Exposure* 10:37–39.

Smith, D. E. 1987. *The everyday world as problematic: A feminist sociology*. Boston: Northeastern University Press.

Steady, F. 1981. *The Black woman cross-culturally*. Cambridge, Mass.: Schenkman.

Strauss, A. L. 1990. *Qualitative analysis for social scientists*. Cambridge: Cambridge University Press.

Terborg-Penn, R. 1987. *Women in Africa and the African diaspora*. Washington, D.C.: Howard University Press.

Turner, L. 1949. *Africanisms in the Gullah dialect*. Chicago: University of Chicago Press.

Williams, B. 1985. Why migrant women feed their husbands tamales: Foodways as a basis for a revisionist view of Tejano family life. In *Ethnic and regional foodways in the United States: The performance of group identity*, edited by L. Keller Brown and K. Mussell. Knoxville: University of Tennessee Press.

Winterbottom, T. [1803] 1969. *An account of the Native Africans in the neighbourhood of Sierra Leone*. London: Frank Cass.

Wood, P. 1974. *Black majority: Negroes in colonial South Carolina from 1670 through the Stono Rebellion*. New York: Alfred A. Knopf.

Young, K. Porter. 1992. *Notes on sisterhood, kinship, and marriage in an African-American South Carolina Sea Island community*. Memphis, Tenn.: Memphis State University, Center for Research on Women.

FOOD AS WOMEN'S VOICE IN
THE SAN LUIS VALLEY OF COLORADO[1]

CAROLE M. COUNIHAN

22

★ INTRODUCTION

This paper is about how a Latina named Bernadette from the small town of Antonito in southern Colorado used food as a voice to speak about gender, class, and ethnic barriers. I tape-recorded food-centered life stories from Bernadette as part of an ongoing ethnographic project I have been conducting since 1996 in Antonito with my husband, anthropologist Jim Taggart (Taggart, this volume; Taylor and Taggart, n.d.). In several informal conversations and tape-recorded interviews, I asked Bernadette questions about her experiences and memories centered around food production, preparation, consumption, and exchange. She spoke about past and present diet, recipes, food preservation, everyday and ritual meals, healing foods, breast-feeding, and food exchanges. These food-centered life stories are like the *testimonios*, which the Latina Feminist Group (2001, 2) defines as "a crucial means of bearing witness and inscribing into history those lived realities that would otherwise succumb to the alchemy of erasure." The stories prone to erasure are those of people like Bernadette, a poor, chronically disabled, working-class Latina from an isolated and ignored region.[2] Her food-centered stories about ethnic, class, and gender barriers express counterhegemonic views and broaden the web of social understanding in the United States.

Because food is so often the work and language of women, food stories emphasize the importance of women and challenge the centrality of men. Because women are sometimes forced to serve and cook for others, food can be a channel of oppression. Yet through cooking, feeding, eating, and fasting, they can express their own views of self and others with creativity and power (Counihan 1999). Food-centered stories are a weapon against the silencing that has always been a central weapon in women's oppression (hooks 1989)[3] and a tool for feminist ethnographers who can collect food-centered *testimonios* and follow Zavella's (2001, 354) goals "to render all of these *testimonios* into a narrative, theorize about their meanings in ways that the subjects would recognize, and make women's lives accessible to wider audiences."

★ THE SOCIOCULTURAL CONTEXT

Bernadette was born and raised in Antonito, a town of 900, six miles north of the New Mexico border in the southern San Luis Valley of Colorado. The population of Antonito is predominantly Latino—of both Spanish and Mexican descent—and contains a smattering of European Americans. Many Hispanics came to Antonito from one of the surrounding riverine hamlets and had roots in farming and sheep or cattle ranching. Bernadette's mother, Carmen, grew up in San Antonio, where her grandfather and uncles were sheepherders. She moved to Antonito after marrying her husband, who worked in a grocery store while Carmen oversaw the household and the five children. In the 1950s and 1960s, they had apricot and apple trees and a big flower and vegetable garden with spinach, rutabagas, turnips, carrots, onions, potatoes, beans, peas, cabbages, tomatoes, and corn. They raised pigs, chickens, and orphaned lambs, and they preserved the meat by freezing it, drying it into jerky, making sausages, and curing ham. The cuisine of Antonito—its widely shared practices of cooking and eating—showed a strong Mexican influence, modified by the cold, dry climate. Potatoes, beans, green and red chile, flour tortillas, and bread had always been staples of the diet, supplemented by game, fish, pork, beef, mutton, and wild and cultivated fruits and vegetables.

By the late 1990s, few people kept gardens or fruit trees, and ranching and agriculture were marginal occupations except for a few large landowners. Most people got most of their food at the supermarkets in Antonito or Alamosa, which rarely sold local produce. Antonito had three restaurants and one food stand, which all served a mix of "American" food like steak, burgers, and chops and Colorado Mexican cuisine like fajitas, burritos, enchiladas, tacos, green and red chile, beans, and red rice. The commercial center of Alamosa, thirty miles away, had fast food outlets of every major chain including McDonald's, Burger King, KFC, and Pizza Hut. People's diets combined traditional foods with lots of fast, processed, junk and commodity food and carbonated soda. Anectotal evidence suggests widespread adult onset diabetes. In many conversations with people in Antonito, food has emerged as a compelling topic and center of social relations.[4]

★ FOOD AND IDENTITY

A major constituent of Bernadette's and other women's identity was cooking and feeding. She said, "The responsibility of providing food was instilled in us. I saw it when my grandmother did it for my grandpa. I saw it when my mother did it for my daddy, and I saw that it was my duty too. That's the cultural thing that you have to do." Because cooking was central to her role, it took on emotional importance: "For me, food is a comfort, I comfort people with food...I love to cook, like for my little ones, my nephews, until they say, 'Oh, Aunt Bernadette, we can't eat any more, we can't eat any more.' I like to cook everything. Everything. And if I can find a new recipe, I'll try it—anything. I just love cooking."

296

But not all women cooked. Some rejected the role and its implicit servitude.[5] Bernadette said, "My sister Anna, who's the baby of the family, she doesn't cook. She says, 'If he ate, he ate. And if he didn't, he didn't.' And she's not going to do it." But most women in Antonito shouldered domestic duties as their lot and relied on female relatives for help and support. Sharing food, recipes, and child-care were important ways women forged familial and extrafamilial relationships. Bernadette expressed connections to her mother and daughter through their macaroni, which was one of her favorite comfort foods:

> Oh my mom made the best. She used to boil the macaroni, and then while it was boiling she'd add canned milk, and then she would put the cheese, and then she would crush up all these soda crackers, and she would put them on top, and then she would stick it in the oven, so that the cheese would melt into the crackers, and then add salt and pepper.
>
> And there is another way to make macaroni. My daughter Gloria makes the best. She fries the macaroni and she toasts it. And then after it's getting toasty she adds water, and then she lets it get soft, and then she puts tomato sauce, and she fries hamburger, and then she puts in the hamburger, and she sprinkles cheese. Oh, that little girl is getting good.

297

Bernadette took pride and pleasure in her mother's and daughter's cooking and kept alive a female-centered family identity (see Beoku-Betts, this volume).

Bernadette described another food that expressed family identity:

> Whenever we get together, the Vigil clan, it seems like all we eat is deviled eggs! For whatever occasion—bring the deviled eggs! I was thinking maybe it's a comfort food. It's associated with the warmness of a family. Deviled eggs themselves means we're all getting together, as a family, as a unit, and that's one of our good foods that we're going to share.

In addition to family identity, food also represented Bernadette's ethnic identity. She said, "To me, I'm *Mexicana*. I associate myself with being *Mexicana*. Because I speak Spanish, I speak the language. And then I eat the food." Although Bernadette used the Spanish word "*Mexicana*," she admitted that others in Antonito did not like that word because they insisted, "We aren't Mexican, we're American." But Bernadette rebutted, "We're all *Mexicanos*. And where in the heck do we get the *frijoles* and the tortillas and all that if it wasn't from the *Mexicanos*? We all eat the same tortillas. We all eat the same way. So what's the big difference between Hispanic, *Mexicano*, and Spanish?"

Bernadette used food not only to enact her Hispanic ethnicity but also to demonstrate her multiculturalism. In describing her family, she said, "We're *Mexicanos*, Irish, Jewish, and all that." She revealed her openness to other cultural traditions through the array of foods she fondly described in her interview, including Puerto Rican rice, chile, macaroni, rice pudding, elk, rabbit, enchiladas, lasagna, sweet-potato-corn-flake-marshmallow croquettes, Chinese chicken, and potatoes—fried, mashed, and abundant. Claiming multiple ethnicities may have been a way to assert a legitimate place in the American melting pot.

Potatoes were the most basic food and staple crop of the San Luis Valley. Bernadette loved them. She said, "And me, I'm a potato person. As long as I have potatoes, I'm all right. My sister Virginia said, 'That must be the Irish in you.'

Because of that potato famine when they all came, they didn't have any potatoes. I go, 'I guess so,' I go, 'Because I've got to have them.'" Potatoes may indeed symbolize the Irish, but they were also central to the San Luis Valley style Mexican-American cuisine that was the heart of Bernadette's culinary passion. She said, "To me the best food is fried potatoes, green chile, or red chile, and sometimes tortillas if you know how to make them."

Red and green chile were at the heart of San Luis Valley and northern New Mexican cooking, and Bernadette described them in loving detail. She made her green chile from fresh hot peppers that merchants would bring from New Mexico in August. She roasted them in a hot oven for about four minutes, turning them constantly, and then peeled them and froze them. She cooked them with pork cubes dredged in flour, fried with onion and garlic, into the renowned green chile. But even more beloved than green chile was red chile, made from the *chile colorado* that the New Mexican vendors sold in beautiful red *ristras*. She cleaned, soaked, and toasted them in the oven. Then she ground the red chile in the blender with cumin, garlic, salt, and a touch of cilantro. Red and green chile were central to her diet and culture. In talking about them, she revealed the value of preparing food correctly, with care and foresight to maximize quality and minimize cost. By continually preparing and talking about these and other central foods, Bernadette contributed to the endurance of her cultural and family traditions.

★ FOOD AND ETHNIC RELATIONS

In Antonito, for much of the twentieth century, Anglos and Hispanics rarely ate in each other's homes. One reason for their scarce interactions was that there were very few Anglos in the largely Hispanic town and they held themselves apart. In Bernadette's high school class, there were only two Anglos out of forty students. She described the ethnic character of her town:

> Antonito is basically Hispanic—you might feel like an outsider because you're almost the only white people that are here.... We're all Hispanic, I mean everybody here. There wasn't a big issue about being white—or whites against us. But you know, even with the few white people that were here, they would try to put the Hispanic people in their place. Because they did have the better jobs. They were better educated.

The Anglos in Antonito claimed higher class status because they were white, relatively wealthy landowners, professionals, and politicians. Except for a few established landowners and teachers, most Hispanics were workers or small farmers. Anglos and Hispanics interacted in the public sphere of commerce and work, but they did not share meals in each other's homes and those who did defined it as an exception. Anglo and Hispanic children mixed at school and sports and Bernadette remembered Anglo as well as Hispanic friends dropping by her house after school because they knew there were always tortillas and a pot of beans on the stove. But while the Anglo kids ate at her house, they did not reciprocate by inviting her to eat at their homes, and thus marked social distance. For eating together forges social connections; not sharing food marks social distance or enmity (Mauss 1967).

But although Hispanic and Anglo women rarely met in the home, food sometimes successfully united them in public places, for example at church suppers. Bernadette described the cooperative cooking of Spanish American and Anglo women when their children had a religious retreat in the local Theatine Fathers' seminary prior to their Confirmation. The mothers prepared all their meals and snacks for two days and had such a great time together that the priest had to come and tell them to quiet down because they were disturbing the children. Cooperative cooking and eating forged temporary ties across ethnic boundaries between women.

But foods associated with mourning the dead marked ethnic borders that Bernadette found difficult to cross. When a Hispanic friend or relative died, Bernadette cooked food for the bereaved family to offer to relatives and friends who visited with condolences. Typically, the mourning family held a big meal at the church hall or at home after the funeral. Some people served sandwiches of cold cuts, but those who wanted to make a good impression had a big dinner of turkey, ham, mashed potatoes, gravy, ice cream and cake, and sometimes Mexican foods like beans and green or red chile.

When I asked Bernadette if Anglos had similar funeral customs, she described a funeral of a local prosperous Anglo family. Since she was friends with the family, she roasted a couple of hens and made mashed potatoes, potato salad, muffins, and cupcakes, which she brought to her friend's house. But at the post-funeral meal, they just served little tea sandwiches, salad, and cake—not the big meal Hispanics had. Bernadette wondered if she had committed an impropriety by bringing abundant food. This occasion underscored the different commensal customs of Chicanos and Anglos, which further reinforced barriers—Chicanos valued abundance and Anglos practiced frugality. Funeral food linked Bernadette to her Anglo friends but also created barriers between them when she found herself unsure about the culturally appropriate behavior for their funerals.

299

FOOD AND CLASS RELATIONS

Hispanics expressed sociability and social equality by sharing food, and marked class differences and borders by not eating together. People in Antonito defined class according to wealth and education. Bernadette described the higher class thus:

> Some of them had a little more money. Their parents were better educated. Education played a big deal, a great deal. Their mothers were volunteers—they would do this, they would do that. They would be involved in a lot of school activities. They would help with the nuns. They were more involved in the church. Things like that.

Hispanics from the laboring classes rarely ate in the homes of the wealthy Hispanic landowners and professionals. Bernadette described the intraethnic class barriers she encountered by telling a food story:

> I was in girl scouts. The [Hispanic] mothers that thought they were better would know that my mother was a good cook. So they would call and say, "Well, Bernadette is in the girl scouts so please bring us five cakes," or, "Please cook us four pies. But since you're not elite like us, just bring us the goodies, but don't come, don't try to associate with us." That kind of attitude.

And my daddy saw that one time when they played it on my mom, Beverly Garcia did; she was my Girl Scout leader. She called up one day on the phone and she told my mom, "Would you make us four cakes?"

And my mom goes, "Sure."

And my daddy asked her, "Why are you making four cakes?"

And my mom said, "Because the Girl Scout leader wants Bernadette to take four cakes for the Girl Scout meeting."

And my dad told her, "Why aren't you going to take them?"

My mom replied, "Well Bernadette's going to take them because they don't want me. I don't go because they don't invite me to go."

And my dad said, "Well that's going to stop right here." So he waited for Mrs. Garcia. And he didn't let my mom bake the cakes. And when Mrs. Garcia came for the cakes he said, "I don't think so. If my wife isn't good enough to associate with you, then you're not good enough to eat her cakes." And that ended that.

Bernadette's father refuted the class subordination expressed through making food for others but not eating with them and thus called into question the class hierarchy that contributed to the lack of unity among Hispanics in Antonito.

★ FOOD AND GENDER RELATIONS

Intraethnic tension also derived from conflictual gender relationships sometimes expressed in expectations that women serve and defer to men by feeding them. Cooking and feeding were central in Bernadette's relationships with men and sometimes fostered connection, sometimes oppression. Her first husband, José, was a Puerto Rican she met and married in Pueblo one hundred miles northeast of Antonito when she was working there. She met José at a dance after she had gotten "thin, real thin" for the first time in her life after a period of misery and homesickness. She had never dated anyone before and had a whirlwind romance with the handsome José, married him, and had a daughter, Gloria. But soon the marriage became increasingly awful as José slid into alcoholism, drug dealing, and violent abuse.

Bernadette's narratives about her marriage used food imagery to communicate both the attraction and the aversion she felt for her husband. Puerto Rican food was different and appealing. Cooking and eating it enabled her to participate in her husband's culture. "I tried to learn a lot—because it's just a really delicious kind of food. That's the only thing I got out of that Puerto Rican culture. It's just really, really good food, and the way they add their herbs and their ingredients, that's what caught my eye." She loved the Puerto Rican *pastelitos* made with meat and garbanzos, which reminded her of the Spanish *empanaditas* her family used to make. She remembered fondly commensal feasts at the park with friends when they roasted a pig flavored with garlic and red pepper in a hole in the ground for hours and then devoured it.

Bernadette appreciated and tried to learn Puerto Rican cooking, but her husband taught her with abuse and dominance:

I learned the hard way how to make rice, let's put it that way. That's about the basic thing. José used to show me, he used to tell me, this is how you make the rice,... but if I didn't get it right, oh, he'd beat me, until I got it right, really. That's how I learned the hard way, eeeh, he'd give me a good one. And it was a brutal kind of way, but hey,

I learned how to cook rice, let me tell you.... And if the food wasn't done the right way, he'd throw it; it would be all over the ceiling. I thought that I was the only one going through that, but I wasn't. There was another little gal, and she had the same problem with her husband. She would cook and she was a good, good cook, and he'd just toss it against the wall if it wasn't just the way he wanted it. And you couldn't very well tell them, "Make it yourself," because you know we were so leery of them, that, hey, we'll learn, we'll learn.

But that's how I learned to make rice, because he'd make me—one night, he made me make eight bowls of rice until I got it right. Now I think all the tears in between, all the tears and all the fear, but that's how I learned how to make rice. I got it right.

Food marked the incompatibilities and power imbalance between Bernadette and her husband and was also a channel for expressing all that was wrong in his life:

I think that when things weren't going his way, and he wasn't happy with the food, that was the way that he showed that he wasn't happy. Because he...wasn't happy with his life to begin with.... I think all of that emotion was in him, and I just met him at the wrong time. He was just like a little volcano waiting to erupt. He had quite a temper. And I think that food was his way of getting out his anger when things weren't going the right way.

José used Bernadette's inadequate cooking as justification for abusing her. Although she tried to please him by cooking Puerto Rican style, he refused her offerings. Rather than allowing food to be a bridge between them, he rejected her cooking and maligned her. His behavior illustrates how culturally sanctioned expectations that women defer to men by feeding them can often threaten gender equality and lead to violence (DeVault 1991, 143–144).[6] José's abuse became so great that Bernadette decided she had to leave. "I didn't want that kind of life for my daughter. I thought no. I would rather live alone. Like there's that saying, *mejor sola que mal acompañada*—better alone than in company with somebody that's bad and evil." She eventually divorced José. Their incompatibility over food reflected and symbolized deeper problems in the marriage.

Several years later, Bernadette married a Mexican migrant worker named Manuel. Again her stories described food as both a bridge and a barrier to cultural communication: "I found that when I married my husband from Mexico, it was the same way, their cooking was really good, with different spices." Bernadette used food to express her appreciation for Mexican culture, yet also its foreignness. Eventually, however, Manuel's foreignness became too much for her. He was kind to Bernadette and her daughter but had trouble finding work, got depressed, did not speak much English, and depended on Bernadette too much. As she became more and more debilitated from an incurable illness, she found it harder and harder to deal with his need:

Finally, I just said, "This is it. I'm sorry, I just can't live with you any more." I told him, "I just can't put up with you."

He was always, "Teach me this, teach me that." I was in so much pain. And I just couldn't do a lot of things—oh, it was just getting to be a hassle. And then, I felt it was my job to get up with him at six o'clock in the morning, or five, fix him his breakfast, his lunch, even though I had to drag myself. And he told me, "Don't get up." But

I had to, it was just something that I felt I had to do. So I would get up and make him breakfast and stuff like that, but it was a killer.

And then finally I told him, "No, it's just not going to work." So we went and we got our divorce.

Bernadette used the language of food to describe her incompatibility with this man who, like her first husband, she had crossed a cultural border to meet in marriage. His neediness and her nurturance were reflected in her feeding him. Repudiation of feeding him represented her decision to stop taking care of a man who was not giving enough back to her. In both her marriages, food became an expression of failed gender relations and the pitfalls of the traditional domestic division of labor when not accompanied by gender equality. With José, Bernadette's food work was the site of her oppression. Food was Bernadette's voice, and her husband tried to silence her by controlling her cooking, by forcing her to make it his way, by shattering her creations against the wall. With Manuel, cooking was a different source of oppression; Bernadette was exhausted by feeding Manuel, when she herself was becoming more and more needy of nurturance. In both cases, the reciprocity essential to gender equality was missing.

Such reciprocity was rare and unlikely unless women had strong socioeconomic positions by virtue of education and earning power, as Bernadette did not have but others in her community did (Counihan 2000). After her second divorce Bernadette moved to a public housing apartment with her daughter, where she lived with failing health on public assistance. She continued to cook and feed others, and used culinary exchanges to recreate ties with her mother, daughter, sisters, and sisters-in-law. She cooked freely and received esteem for her labors through reciprocal relationships with female relatives. Perhaps Bernadette echoed Margaret Randall's words, "Now I cook as a woman, free at last of that feeling of enslavement with which a male culture has imbued the process of preparing food" (1997b, 120).

Bernadette's stories of food gave voice to her counterhegemonic worldview and enabled her to criticize race-ethnic, class, and gender barriers. Voice was an important form of power, central to full citizenship—including the sense of belonging that Flores and Benmayor (1997) have called "cultural citizenship." But many Americans like Bernadette—especially poor women, people of color, and the disabled—lacked a voice in political affairs and media representations. Bernadette was aware of the institutionalized inequalities in her community and her own silencing. She told a story of when she was ten and wrote a letter to the editor of the local paper criticizing a man who was being cruel to animals:

He rebutted me in the paper. And my brother-in-law always remembers that, he calls me the dog lady. That was the only time I ever did anything like that. But I got permission—my daddy said I could go ahead and do it. I think he thought, "Maybe she'll learn a lesson from this," so he went ahead and let me do it.

After being rebuked in the paper and ridiculed by her brother-in-law, Bernadette did learn her lesson and kept publicly silent from then on. Feminist anthropology has sought to give her a voice. In food-centered life-history interviews, stories poured from her like a "long ribbon of laughter, like water,"[7] keeping alive the foods and traditions of her people and affirming her worth against prevailing ideologies that tried to devalue and silence her.

302

NOTES

I presented an earlier version of this paper at the 1998 American Anthropological Association Annual Meeting in the session "The Border Counts: Subjugating Signs and Transnational Agitation." I thank organizers Miguel Díaz Barriga and Matthew Gutmann and discussant Patricia Zavella. I thank my husband, anthropologist Jim Taggart, for sharing fieldwork and commenting on several drafts. I thank Mary Romero for suggesting the San Luis Valley and commenting on an earlier draft. I thank Arlene Avakian and Barbara Haber for suggestions for revisions. Finally, I thank Bernadette for giving me permission to tape-record her stories and write about her.

Bernadette's name and all other names used in this paper are pseudonyms. People in Antonito refer to their Spanish and Mexican identity using a number of terms including Spanish American, Hispanic, Chicana/o, and *Mexicana/o*. Elsasser, MacKenzie, and Tixier y Vigil (1980, xv) discuss terms used in northern New Mexico.

1. On the San Luis Valley, see Deutsch 1987, Simmons 1979, Gutierrez and Eckert 1991, Martinez 1987, Peña 1998, and Weber 1991.
2. Deutsch (1987) writes, "Written history of . . . Chicanas or Hispanic women in Colorado [is] virtually non-existent."
3. Some women who have found a voice through food writing are Fisher 1954, Esquivel 1989, and Randall 1997a. Some feminist studies of food in addition to those in this volume are Adams 1990, Avakian 1997, Bordo 1993, Brumberg 1988, Bynum 1987, Kerr 1988, Chernin 1985, Counihan 1999, DeVault 1991, Paules 1991, and Thompson 1994.
4. Southern San Luis Valley cuisine and culture have roots in northern New Mexico. See Cabeza de Baca 1982, 1994 and Gilbert 1970.
5. See Counihan (2000) for discussion of one Antonito woman whose well-paying job as a school teacher enabled her to escape from many domestic chores.
6. Adams (1990), Kerr (1988, 72), and Ellis (1983) note that men often use dissatisfaction with food as an excuse to abuse women.
7. "The long ribbon of laughter, like water" bubbled from the mouth of Cleófilas, the protagonist of Sandra Cisneros's (1991:56) story "Woman Hollering Creek."

303

REFERENCES

Adams, Carol J. 1990. *The Sexual Politics of Meat: A Feminist-Vegetarian Critical Theory*. New York: Continuum.

Avakian, Arlene Voski, ed. 1997. *Through the Kitchen Window: Women Explore the Intimate Meanings of Food and Cooking*. Boston: Beacon Press.

Bordo, Susan. 1993. *Unbearable Weight: Feminism, Western Culture, and the Body*. Berkeley: University of California Press.

Brumberg, Joan Jacobs. 1988. *Fasting Girls: The Emergence of Anorexia Nervosa as a Modern Disease*. Cambridge: Harvard University Press.

Bynum, Caroline Walker. 1987. *Holy Feast and Holy Fast: The Religious Significance of Food to Medieval Women*. Berkeley: University of California Press.

Cabeza de Baca, Fabiola. 1982 (1949). *The Good Life*. Santa Fe: Museum of New Mexico Press.

——. 1994 (1954). *We Fed Them Cactus*. Albuquerque: University of New Mexico Press.

Charles, Nikki and Marion Kerr. 1988. *Women, Food, and Families*. Manchester: Manchester University Press.

Chernin, Kim. 1985. *The Hungry Self: Women, Eating and Identity*. New York: Times Books.

Cisneros, Sandra. 1991. "Woman Hollering Creek," from *Woman Hollering Creek and Other Stories*. New York: Vintage.

Counihan, Carole. 1999. *The Anthropology of Food and Body: Gender, Meaning and Power*. New York: Routledge.

——. 2000. "I wanted to go my own way": Work, Gender, and Cultural Citizenship in the San Luis Valley of Colorado. 99th Annual Meeting of the American Anthropological Association. San Francisco, CA.

Deutsch, Sarah. 1987. *No Separate Refuge: Culture, Class, and Gender on an Anglo-Hispanic Frontier in the American Southwest, 1880–1940*. New York: Oxford.

DeVault, Marjorie L. 1991. *Feeding the Family: The Social Organization of Caring as Gendered Work*. Chicago: University of Chicago Press.

Ellis, Rhian. 1983. The Way to a Man's Heart: Food in the Violent Home. In Anne Murcott, ed., *The Sociology of Food and Eating*. Aldershot: Gower Publishing, pp. 164–171.

Elsasser, Nan, Kyle MacKenzie, and Yvonne Tixier y Vigil. 1980. *Las Mujeres: Conversations from a Hispanic Community*. New York: The Feminist Press.

Esquivel, Laura. 1989. *Like Water for Chocolate*. New York: Doubleday.

Fisher, M. F. K. 1954. *The Art of Eating*. Cleveland: World Publishing.

Flores, William V. and Rina Benmayor, eds. 1997. *Latino Cultural Citizenship: Claiming Identity, Space, and Rights*. Boston: Beacon Press.

Gilbert, Fabiola Cabeza de Baca. 1970 (1942). *Historic Cookery*. Santa Fe: Ancient City Press.

Gutierrez, Paul and Jerry Eckert. 1991. Contrasts and Commonalities: Hispanic and Anglo Farming in Conejos County, Colorado. *Rural Sociology*, 56, 2:247–263.

hooks, bell. 1989. *Talking Back: Thinking Feminist, Thinking Black*. Boston: South End Press.

Latina Feminist Group. 2001. *Telling to Live: Latina Feminist* Testimonios. Durham: Duke University Press.

Martinez, Ruben. 1991. Chicano Lands: Acquisition and Loss. *Wisconsin Sociologist*, 24, 2/3:89–98.

Mauss, Marcel. 1967. *The Gift*. New York: Norton.

Paules, Greta Foff. 1991. *Power and Resistance among Waitresses in a New Jersey Restaurant*. Philadelphia: Temple University Press.

Peña, Devon, ed. 1998. *Chicano Culture, Ecology, Politics: Subversive Kin*. Tuscon: University of Arizona Press.

Randall, Margaret. 1997a. *Hunger's Table: Women, Food and Politics*. Watsonville, CA: Papier Mache Press.

———. 1997b. What My Tongue Knows. In A. Avakian, ed. *Through the Kitchen Window*. Boston: Beacon, pp. 117–133.

Simmons, Virginia McConnell. 1979. *The San Luis Valley: Land of the Six-Armed Cross*. Boulder: Pruett.

Taylor, José Inez and James M. Taggart. 2002. *"Alex and the Hobo": A Chicano's Narrative*. Austin: University of Texas Press.

Thompson, Becky. 1994. *A Hunger So Wide and So Deep: American Women Speak Out on Eating Problems*. Minneapolis: University of Minnesota Press.

Weber, Kenneth R. 1991. Necessary but Insufficient: Land, Water, and Economic Development in Hispanic Southern Colorado. *Journal of Ethnic Studies*, 19, 2:127–142.

Zavella, Patricia. 2001. *Tenemos que Seguir Luchando*. In *Telling to Live: Latina Feminist Testimonios*. Durham: Duke University Press, pp. 348–355.

FOOD, MASCULINITY, AND PLACE IN
THE HISPANIC SOUTHWEST

JAMES M. TAGGART

23

This paper examines how a Spanish-speaking man from the San Luis Valley in southern Colorado used food to present his masculine moral vision.[1] José Inez Taylor expressed his moral vision when telling his life story in many hours of interviews between 1998 and 2001. I shall draw on the method of food-centered life history and gender theory to interpret how he constructed his moral vision out of his food experiences. Scholars have used food-centered life histories to understand the subjective experience of being a woman (Counihan 1999).[2] The same method can also reveal the subjective experience of being a man. Theories of masculinity focus on a boy's transition from the world of the mother to that of the father (Chodorow 1978; Gilmore 1990, 2001; R. Stoller 1985; Taggart 1997), and Taylor evoked food memories to describe how he made that transition. He presented his masculinity in a moral vision constructed out of his sense of place, his class consciousness, and cultural notions of manhood he learned from his father and mother in accord with his social location (Zavella 1997).

★ GENDER ORGANIZATION OF LABOR

Taylor's role in the gender organization of family labor is crucial for understanding how he recalled his experiences with food that fed his moral vision. Men and women both worked to produce food, but only women tended to cook and feed the members of their families. The contrast between a man's and a woman's perspective on food appears in sharp relief when Taylor's food memories are compared with those of Bernadette, whom Carole Counihan described in her paper in this volume. Bernadette and Taylor lived on the same street and had many things in common. They ate some of the same food, they spoke the same languages—southern

Colorado Spanish ("Mexicano") and American English—and they shared some local webs of meaning that make up their culture (Geertz 1973: 5, 89). Both described Antonito as a socially stratified town with wealthy English-speaking Anglos and Spanish-speaking Hispanic *ricos* at the top. Taylor said many wealthy Anglos and Hispanics lived on "la calle de los ricos" ("the street of the rich ones"), but Bernadette and Taylor lived on other streets in town because they were members of Spanish-speaking families of workers who labored on the farms and in the business of the wealthy Anglos and Hispanic *ricos*.

Bernadette and Taylor did not talk about food—even some of the same foods—in exactly the same way because they occupied different locations in their social structure (Zavella 1997). Although they were members of the same class and ethnic group, they had different positions in their families because of the gender organization of labor regarding food. Bernadette presented herself as a woman who learned how to feed others saying, "The responsibility of providing food was instilled in us. I saw it when my grandmother did it for my grandpa, I saw it when my mother did it for my daddy, and I saw that it was my duty too" (Counihan, this volume). Taylor grew up in a family where men ordinarily did not cook for and feed others. His sister Cordi said, "*Yo creo que no ví a mi dad en la cocina nunca*" ("I don't think I ever saw my dad in the kitchen"). Taylor talked most about producing food in the fields outside of Antonito. His accounts of producing food and Bernadette's descriptions of cooking may apply to other Spanish-speaking persons living in Antonito. The gender organization of labor has historically been flexible in the San Luis Valley and adjacent areas of northern New Mexico (Swadesh 1966; Deutsch 1987), but women were usually responsible for the garden and they worked in the kitchen preserving and processing food (Deutsch 1987: 51–53).

★ FOOD AND PLACE

Taylor's recollections of food experiences as a producer were part of his memories of place and his social location in his community. Food and place are often taken for granted until "we find ourselves living in unfamiliar surroundings" or eating unfamiliar foods (Basso 1996: xiii). I shall regard place as locality imbued with meaning and loaded with memories of lived or imagined experience (Rodman 1987, 1992; Sutton 1998). Men and women may link food to place differently as they blend their distinctive experiences in specific locations into a stew of history, culture, gender, and social position (Rodman 1992; González Turmo 1998).

The San Luis Valley is the site of potato production, and Bernadette as well as Taylor linked food to place by stressing the importance of potatoes in their daily meals. Fried potatoes head Bernadette's list of favorite foods (Counihan, this volume), and Taylor declared that they were part of every meal when he was growing up in Antonito:

> Most of the meals were repeated every, every day. Like fried potatoes and beans and tortillas and chiles. Those were repeated every day. They were broken only maybe on Sundays when you might have had something else like maybe chicken or something different. But most of the days the meals were pretty much the same. Gravy and potatoes and beans and tortillas and spinach, if it was the season for it.

Taylor connected food to place to present his moral vision by comparing several different places in the San Luis Valley. He was born in San Luis, in the valley's southeast corner, and lived with his family in the tiny *plaza* (hamlet) of El Rito in the Culebra Creek basin. El Rito is in a beautiful *vega* (meadow) at the base of the towering Sangre de Cristo mountains. Taylor left El Rito in 1942 when his family moved to Antonito fifty miles west across the stark Río Grande Valley. Taylor's move contributed to what Rodman called a multivocal view of place involving the comparison of memories from several localities (Rodman 1992: 644, 646–647).

Taylor drew a sharp contrast between El Rito and Antonito to explain how he developed his moral vision, acquired class consciousness, and became a union and community activist. He recalled El Rito, where he spent the early years of his childhood, as a hamlet of neighboring and related families who cooperated to produce and process many foods outside of the money economy. Like other Spanish-speakers in the Hispanic southwest (Briggs 1988: 36), he described the El Rito of his past as a place where there was an abundance of good food that allowed his family and neighbors to be comparatively self-sufficient:

> They used to take the fish and they used to steam them like they do salmon, canned salmon. And they used to also do that with meat. They used to take the watermelon rinds and cook them that way too and then they used to make their jellies. *Champes* (rose hips) is the thing that everybody was after, and there were plenty of them over here. *Champes* and *rosa de castilla* (rose of Castile) and the herbs they used to pick in the summer time. *Espárragos* (asparagus) and everything were growing wild.

307

The harsh winters and the short growing season did not permit the cultivation of some crops that Taylor's family and neighbors considered essential to their diet. Among them were chiles that merchants brought in from warmer regions of New Mexico:

> And whatever you didn't get, like your chile and stuff like that, the *chileros*—they used to call them *chameros*—out of New Mexico used to come in and sell you the chile pods, *la ristra de chile*, the red chile.

Taylor recalled that in El Rito he lived in a large extended family household that included his mother's brother, his wife, and their nine children. He noted that as a child, he would play with a gang of over thirty children, all of whom were related by kinship and lived in houses within a short distance of each other.

Nevertheless, Taylor was careful to acknowledge that all was not perfect harmony in El Rito. His maternal grandfather quarreled with his neighbors and lost access to water seriously restricting his ability to grow food. Taylor's father earned a living as a *zapatero* (shoemaker) but did not have a license to practice his trade. Another shoemaker turned him in to the local authorities, and he had to move his family fifty miles across the valley to Antonito where there was no shoemaker and better schools. Taylor's daily play with cousins came to an end when he moved to Antonito, where he had no close kin except his nuclear family. It is possible that the move across the valley may have nourished nostalgia for the past in what John and Jean Comaroff (1992) call the "historical imagination."

★ SOCIAL POSITION IN ANTONITO

Nevertheless, Taylor remembered the Antonito of his youth as a very different place than El Rito, and he grounded his contrast in descriptions of producing, exchanging, cooking, and consuming food. Living with few close family members, Taylor recalled how he started working for wages when he was ten years old in the commercial farms to the north of town. He evoked one particular food experience many times in our conversations that emerged as a key to his moral vision. That experience took place when he was a member of a potato-picking crew a few miles north of Antonito:

> There was this forty-acre field, and it took us a long time to finish that field. They were paying by the half-sack. They'd give us twenty-five half sacks, and they'd give us a little stub to keep track. We finished that field, and then they moved us to another field, and in that field there were potatoes that you wouldn't believe. We were hopping and hollering and saying we were going to get rich on that field. But we suddenly stopped when we were told they were going to pay us by the row. And it would take us practically a whole day to take one row.

Taylor repeatedly brought up this anecdote to explain how he developed the seeds of his class consciousness that later flowered when working for the union in southern Colorado. In the anecdote, the labor contractor's unilateral decision to pay workers by the row in the field loaded with potatoes rather than by the half-sack as in the sparser row was a representative example of how employers exploited workers particularly on the Antonito side of the valley. Taylor merged his class with his ethnic consciousness by pointing out that the labor contractor worked for Anglos. The anecdote revealed how Taylor felt about producing a staple of his diet.

Food memories evoking Taylor's class position converged in another way in his accounts of how different employers treated the workers on their commercial farms and ranches around Antonito. He repeatedly brought up the contrast between the generosity of some employers and the stingy behavior of others:

> I remember this lady that lived over here. Her last name was Ángel [a pseudonym]. And if you went to her house and you took a lunch with you to eat, you were insulting her. That just didn't happen. Not in her house! She was a wealthy lady. She was a well-to-do lady. She'd give you breakfast and she'd give you dinner and, before you left her place, you ate. And then there were the Ángeles over here. Ricardo Ángel [also a pseudonym]. His mom was the same way, but she was from the same family.
>
> And there were others. They'd pick you up and bring you home in the evening. You took your own lunch and you ate your own lunch. And you wouldn't even consider, you wouldn't even think of asking them not even for as much as a drink of water. If there was a well two miles away, you'd just as soon go and drink water at the well than knock on their door and ask them for something to drink.

Taylor's memory of stingy employers who did not feed their workers evokes shades of Bernadette's bitter recollection of her mother being asked to cook cakes for the elite Hispanic women but not being invited to eat with them (Counihan, this volume).

★ THE FATHER AS A GRANJEADOR

Taylor acquired the masculine layer in his moral vision from his father with whom he spent a great deal of time in the cobbler shop after school. Taylor's father, Anastacio, earned his living as a *zapatero* (shoe-maker) and was also an avid fisherman who gave away the fish he caught in the streams and rivers around Antonito:

> He'd give some to every businessman, he'd give some to the priest, he'd give some to the nuns. There were twenty-one nuns here at one time. 'Cause I remember he used to count two fish for each nun. He'd put 'em in a big box with wax paper and, boy, he'd send us over there to take fish to the sisters, take fish to the priest, take fish to the doctor. He was a *granjeador, granjeaba*. He wasn't what you call a *cuzco*. A *cuzco* is a guy that hoards everything. He won't give anybody else anything. He won't share. But my dad, no. If you came to his house, you ate, and if he had something, he'd give it to you.

Rubén Cobos defines the word *granjeador* as someone who is servicable or "who brings or works himself into another's favor" (Cobos 1983: 77). From a histori-cal and comparative perspective, a *granjeador* is someone who carries out what Marcel Mauss called gift exchange according to which the act of giving creates or maintains moral bonds with another person (Mauss 1967). Being a *granjeador* fit being the member of a kin-based society where family loyalties were very important as in El Rito.

It is possible that the *granjeador* principle was less established in the Antonito of Taylor's childhood where the rigid class structure and the widespread use of "estranged labor" created an alienated consciousness (Marx 1964: 106–119). Carole Counihan found that many Hispanic women in Antonito did not recognize the term and it may have been more common in San Luis where gift exchange embodied in the *granjeador* was more common among people of the same class.

Taylor's description of the specific types of fish his father distributed to towns-people in different social categories illustrated the sharp class divisions in Antonito in food terms.

> He used to catch two types of fish. One was the mud sucker and the other one was a trout. Trout he gave to business people, the church, and the school. Anybody else in town that had families could go in and get the mud suckers. Including his own family. Because that's what he used to give us. That's what we ate. But the trout was for the higher class, and the mud suckers were for anybody else who wanted them.

Mud suckers were bottom feeders, their meat had the flavor of mud, and they had a lot of bones. They were very unappealing to trout fishermen and to the members of the Antonito upper class. Thus, to eat a mud sucker was a palpable expression of Taylor's position in a family with no land and little money.

★ **EAT OR BE EATEN**

Taylor acquired an inclination for activism from his father who not only lived by the *granjeador* principle but also stood up to those who abused their power in Antonito. Taylor learned a great deal about his community while spending time in his father's shoe shop (*zapateria*), which was like a little community center:

> People used to come in from New Mexico with their produce, to come and sell it over here. And [a cop would] say, "If you want to sell in my town, you give me so much fruit, so many watermelons, so much this and so much that." That was corrupt. That

309

> was corrupt. And the cop used his authority to steal. That's what it was. Then a lot of these people used to come to my dad and complain. And my dad said, "We know it's true. We know what kind of a man he is." He got a petition to get this man fired. One time he went around and got a petition because he saw the corruption of this man.

Taylor alluded to other, more serious forms of corruption such as the questionable land deals in southern Colorado and New Mexican history.[3] Confronting another with corruption was a risky business in a small town like Antonito, where family loyalties and class boundaries were strong. However, Taylor recalled that his father had the courage and the physical size and strength to confront the corrupt cops who took advantage of the weaker members of the community:

> My dad knew that some of the cops were corrupt. And he wasn't afraid of the cops. He'd go face them. Because they knew better. They couldn't jail my dad. They wouldn't jail my dad. That's just one thing they just didn't do.

310

As he watched his father stand up to corrupt cops in Antonito, Taylor realized that he lived in a world where some men try to dominate others. He used the Spanish phrase "*comerse en vivo*" ("to eat a person live") to express how one person or group completely dominated another. Taylor evoked the expression when recalling how large Anglo baseball players on the Colorado-Kansas border planned to dominate the team of smaller Mexican players from Antonito in the 1950s:

> We went to this place to the east of here, next to Lamar. And we went to play baseball. And we weren't big. And when they saw us, they said, "We'll eat 'em alive. We'll beat them in no time. And then we'll send them back home."
>   (*Fuímos a este lugar que está al este de aquí, junto a Lamar. Y fuímos a jugar béisbol. Y no eramos grandes. Y cuando nos vieron, la gente de allí, Nos los comemos. En un ratito les ganamos. Y luego los dijo mandamos para atrás, para casa.*")

The Antonito team won the game but their victory so angered the town that Taylor and his teammates were blocked from eating a meal before making the long trip back to Antonito. Taylor described on numerous occasions how he needed strength to stand up to others as well as produce the food in the fields around Antonito. When Carole Counihan and I asked Taylor what consuming food meant to him, he replied that he ate to become strong.[4] He also used his strength on the football field, where he played linebacker and fullback, and in fights both on and off the football field.

Brute strength, of course, may not always be the most effective tactic to use against a larger adversary who may try to "eat" and thus dominate a smaller and weaker one. Taylor recalled the case of the folktale hero Juan Chililí Pícaro[5] who used trickery to escape from the clutches of a giant who tried to eat him. The giant caught Juan Chililí trying to steal the giant's parrot, he put the hero into a kettle of water to eat him, and then headed off looking for more firewood, leaving his wife in charge. Juan tricked the giantess into untying him using the ruse that he will fetch more wood for the fire. Once free, Juan tossed the giantess into the boiling kettle and made his escape.

Taylor had moral reservations about using the tactics of a trickster (*pícaro*) whom he defined in his storyteller commentary (Dundes 1965) as a man whose word could not be trusted. When he discussed his community activism, Taylor repeatedly brought up cases of untrustworthy or corrupt managers and town officials who abused their power and dominated others. His ideas about corruption were at the core of his moral vision and of his presentation of masculinity. Central to his moral vision was the idea that the abuse of power developed out of greed. The word he used for greed on several different occasions was the food-related term *goloso/a*, which in northern New Mexican and southern Colorado Spanish is an adjective meaning gluttonous (Cobos 1983: 76; Trujillo 1983: 115). In the Antonito area and possibly elsewhere, it also means greedy (Trujillo 1983: 115).

Taylor considered greed and corruption reprehensible, and he worked against them in many ways. As a union activist he helped organize workers in the Perlite mine south of town, he manned their picket lines, he traveled to food processing plants in southern Colorado delivering speeches in Spanish to mobilize Hispanic workers, and he presented grievances to frequently hostile Anglo management. As he was retiring from the union, he became involved in the bitter Antonito school strike of 1980, taking the side of the teachers and school employees who were fighting a local school superintendent who allegedly abused his power by favoring his relatives and friends with higher wages. Soon thereafter, Taylor helped introduce the Raza Unida party to southern Conejos County and ran successfully for political office. In the early 1990s, he started writing works of fiction in which he depicted the problem of evil in the San Luis Valley (Taylor and Taggart 2002).

311

★ THE MOTHER

Gender studies place the boy's symbiotic relationship with the mother at the core of his masculinity (Stoller 1985; Gilmore 1990). The mother, of course, feeds her infants from her own body and, later on, cooks the food she feeds to the members of her family. It should come as no surprise that some of Taylor's most powerful memories of his mother involve food. Claude Lévi-Strauss drew attention to how cooking transformed raw food with important social and cultural results (Lévi-Strauss 1975). Taylor described how his mother cooked mud suckers spurned by the upper class of Antonito, ameliorating his class position by transforming bottomfeeders into delicious meals and by fostering a feeling of comfort in his family:

> My mom used to skin them, cut their heads off, cut the fins off, and then take boiling water, and that water was boiling, boiling, and she'd take that fish by the tail, and she'd dip it into that boiling water. And all the meat would just come out and she'd take a fork and she'd take all that meat off and leave the bone of the fish and throw that one and do the next one. And then when it was all done, she used to sort of let it boil a little bit. And then after that, she used to take one of those *coladores* (colanders), she'd take it and she'd dump the fish in there. She'd take what was left of the fish in the colander, and she'd pick out the bones that happened to go on in there, which weren't that many, and then she'd take the crackers and she'd grind them in there with pepper and then she'd make patties out of them. And then she'd fry the little patties and to me they were delicious. I was always hungry.

Taylor recalled his mother, who died in 1950, as a very loving woman who comforted him, set good examples, advised him, cradled him in his arms, sometimes intervened when his father wanted to hit him, and shared candy bars with him when he was a small child. I think Joe's mother embodied the *granjeador* principle within the family by providing gifts of delicious, well-prepared food and showing love. Her role in her organization of labor is crucial for understanding why Taylor elected to present his masculinity in moral terms. Taylor expressed on many different occasions, including in his autobiographical written story of "Alex and the Hobo" (Taylor and Taggart 2002), his acute moral awareness. Melford Spiro observed that moral anxiety is not innate but develops out of widespread features of "human socialization systems" (Spiro 1987: 137). Spiro attributed moral anxiety to "agents of socialization" who not only train but also nurture others and thus satisfy a child's important need to be loved. Taylor's mother's love and his fear of the loss of her love were the emotional power of his moral vision.

Taylor, now in his early sixties, has frequently mentioned that it was his mother who held his family together until her tragic death in 1950. He has mellowed with age and embodies some of the ideas of the *granjeador* that he associated with his mother as well as his father. He is an excellent cook and transforms food into delicious meals that he regularly feeds his son and grandsons. His home has become a little community center resembling his father's *zapateria* (shoe shop) where many gather to eat, talk, drink pop, buy and sell "collectables and antiques," and seek Taylor's advice.

312

★ CONCLUSIONS

Theories that define gender as a personal conviction and not as an eternal truth stress the importance of viewing masculinity as a confluence of culture, social experience, and psychology as well as biology (Stoller 1985; Taggart 1997). I have tried to demonstrate that the method of food-centered life histories developed by scholars of food and culture (Counihan 1999) can reveal the subjective experience of masculinity. Taylor's food memories carried him back to the point where his ideas of manliness took form through a merging of his culture, and his social and psychological experiences.

Taylor evoked food memories to present his masculinity in a moral vision and to recall how he made the transition to the world of men. He recalled food memories from his perspective in the gender organization of food labor in his family. He wove those memories in a moral vision that incorporated his ideas of place and expressed his social position as a worker in a highly stratified community. He constructed his moral vision with the cultural concept of the *granjeador*. Exchange embodied by the *granjeador* is different from transactions in capitalism where the purpose is to acquire the product of labor by paying the lowest possible wage to the worker (see Taussig 1980: 124–125). Taylor contrasted the two forms of exchange in his comparison of two places in the San Luis Valley, El Rito, where he spent his early childhood, and Antonito, where he came of age and lived most of his life. While Taylor associated the *granjeador* with his father, he traced the roots of his moral vision to his mother who generously gave love and gifts of deliciously prepared food to the members of her family.

NOTES

1. This paper is based on a long-term fieldwork project that Carole Counihan and I have carried out in Antonito, Colorado, since 1996. See Gilligan (1982) for an interesting but different approach to Anglo-American men's and women's ideas about morality.
2. There are many different approaches to food and gender. For a different kind of study, see Dominique Fournier's (1998) fascinating account of bubbles and femininity.

3. M. Stoller (1985), Sandoval (1985), Peña (1998), and Wilson (1999) for an account of the struggle for the control of the Culebra watershed.
4. Becker (1995) and Sobo (1997) heard similar responses from men in Fiji and Jamaica, and their work illustrates how eating well to become strong is a component of masculinity in other cultures.
5. See Taggart and Taylor (n.d.) for an analysis of the different Spanish-language versions of Juan Chililí, which is Tale Type 328.

REFERENCES

Basso, Keith. 1996. *Wisdom Sits in Places: Landscape and Language among the Western Apache*. Albuquerque: University of New Mexico Press.
Becker, Anne. 1995. *Body, Self, and Society: The View from Fiji*. Philadelphia: University of Pennsylvania Press.
Briggs, Charles L. 1988. *Competence in Performance: The Creativity of Tradition in Mexicano Verbal Art*. Philadelphia: University of Pennsylvania Press.
Chodorow, Nancy. 1978. *The Reproduction of Mothering: Psychoanalysis and the Sociology of Gender*. Berkeley: University of California Press.
Cobos, Rubén. 1983. *A Dictionary of New Mexico and Southern Colorado Spanish*. Santa Fé: Museum of New Mexico Press.
Comaroff, John, and Jean Comaroff. 1992. *Ethnography and the Historical Imagination*. Boulder: Westview.
Counihan, Carole M. 1999. *The Anthropology of Food and Body*. New York: Routledge.
———. 2000 The Border as Bridge and Barrier: Food, Gender and Ethnicity in the San Luis Valley of Colorado. Paper presented at the American Anthropological Association.
Deutsch, Sarah. 1987. *No Separate Refuge: Culture, Class, and Gender on an Anglo-Hispanic Frontier in the American Southwest, 1880–1940*. Oxford: Oxford University Press.
Dundes, Alan. 1965. Metafolklore and Oral Literary Criticism. *The Monist* 50 (4): 505–516.
Fournier, Dominique. 1998. La burbujas y la feminidad. *Estudios del Hombre* 7: 113–132.
Geertz, Clifford. 1973. *The Interpretation of Cultures*. New York: Basic Books.
Gilligan, Carol. 1982. *In a Different Voice: Psychological Theory and Women's Development*. Cambridge: Harvard University Press.
Gilmore, David D. 1990. *Manhood in the Making: Cultural Concepts of Masculinity*. New Haven: Yale University Press.
———. 2001 *Misogyny: The Male Malady*. Philadelphia: University of Pennsylvania Press.
González Turmo, Isabel. 1998. Cocina, territorio e identidad. *Estudios del Hombre* 7: 15–22.
Lévi-Strauss, Claude. 1975. *The Raw and the Cooked: Introduction to a Science of Mythology*, vol. 1. New York: Harper and Row.
Marx, Karl. 1964. *The Economic and Philosophic Manuscripts of 1844*. New York: International Publishers.
Mauss, Marcel. 1967. *The Gift: Forms and Functions of Exchange in Archaic Societies*. New York: W. W. Norton and Company, Inc.
Peña, Devon. 1998. A Gold Mine, an Orchard, and an Eleventh Commandment. In *Chicano Culture, Ecology, Politics: Subversive Kin*, edited by Devon G. Peña. Tucson: University of Arizona Press.
Rodman, Margaret C. 1987. *Masters of Tradition: Consequences of Customary Land Tenure in Longana, Vanatu*. Vancouver: University of British Columbia Press.
———. 1992 Empowering Place: Multilocality and Multivocality. *American Anthropologist* 94: 640–656.
Sandoval, R. 1985. The San Luis Vega. In *La cultura constante de San Luis*, edited by R. Teeuwen. San Luis: San Luis Museum Cultural and Commercial Center.
Sobo, Elisa J. 1997. The Sweetness of Fat: Health, Procreation, and Sociability in Rural Jamaica. In *Food and Culture: A Reader*, edited by Carole Counihan and Penny van Esterik. New York: Routledge.
Spiro, Melford. 1987. *Culture and Human Nature*. Chicago: University of Chicago Press.
Stoller, Margaret. 1985. La tierra y la merced. In *La cultura constante de San Luis*, edited by R. Teeuwen. San Luis: San Luis Museum Cultural and Commercial Center.
Stoller, Robert. 1985. *Presentations of Gender*. New Haven: Yale University Press.
Sutton, David E. 1998. *Memories Cast in Stone: The Relevance of the Past in Everyday Life*. Oxford: Berg.
Swadesh, Frances León. 1966. Hispanic Americans on the Ute Frontier from the Chama Valley to the San Juan Basin, 1694–1960. Unpublished Ph.D. Dissertation presented to the University of Colorado.
Taggart, James M. 1997. *The Bear and His Sons: Masculinity in Spanish and Mexican Folktales*. Austin: University of Texas Press.
Taggart, James M., and José Inez Taylor. n.d. Class and Ethnic Consciousness in a Giant-Slayer Tale from the Hispanic Southwest. Unpublished manuscript.
Taylor, José Inez, and James M. Taggart. 2002. *"Alex and the Hobo": A Chicano's Life and Story*. Austin: University of Texas Press.
Taussig, Michael. 1980. The *Devil and Commodity Fetishism*. Chapel Hill: University of North Carolina Press.
Trujillo, Luis M. 1983. *Diccionario del Español del Valle de San Luis de Colorado del Norte y de Nuevo Mexico*. Alamosa: O and V Printing.
Wilson, Randall K. 1999. Placing Nature: The Politics of Collaboration and Representation in the Struggle for La Sierra in San Luis, Colorado. *Ecumene* 6 (1): 1–28.
Zavella, Pat. 1997. Reflections on Diversity among Chicanas. In *Challenging Fronteras: Structuring Latina and Latino Lives in the U.S.*, edited by Mary Romero, Pierrette Hondagneu-Sotelo, and Vilma Ortiz. New York: Routledge, pp. 187–194.

313

WHO DESERVES A BREAK TODAY?

FAST FOOD, CULTURAL RITUALS, AND

WOMEN'S PLACE

KATE KANE

Gender differences in culture are usually visible around food. In fast food advertising we can see some of those differences played out as fantasies of consumption. How fast food advertising mediates the real experience of taking a meal, and what that says for symbolic constructions of the body is the subject of this essay. A McDonald's commercial is a text rich in cultural information. I shall argue that McDonald's positions itself as the new Mother in a social order determined by the conditions of contemporary American culture.

When anthropologist Mary Douglas says "Food is not feed" (1977, 7), she refers to the conjunction of the social and the culinary. Food is "a blinding fetish in our culture..." of which "our ignorance is explosively dangerous" (ibid.). Our ignorance is particularly dangerous for women, since feeding is a primary part of women's role in our culture. It is a problematic but central element of femininity, and as such plays a part in the current crisis in gender roles.

★ INTRODUCTION

Food is also an indicator of social status, according to Douglas (1975). This paper examines a McDonald's biscuit commercial for its messages about women's social status. First I shall analyze the commercial itself, and then discuss the issues it raises from the perspectives of history, anthropology, and psychoanalytic theory. Throughout, a recurring theme is alienation.

It is a commonplace among Marxist scholars that workers are alientated from the products of their labor. I am arguing that alienation also operates in the symbolic economy, the system of ideas and values that circulate in the mass media. In regard to women and food, alienation is multiply coded. Fast food signals a double alienation of women from food (displaced as Mothers) and from our own bodies.

Coming from a tradition in which previous generations of women were indoctrinated with the mysteries of home economics, women today confront a profound ambiguity about our gender role as we renegotiate our place in the productive sphere. As Kim Chernin argues in *The Hungry Self* (1985), this ambiguity centers on women's relationship to their mothers (and thus to food and separation). The current proliferation of eating disorders is a manifestation of this identity crisis. Corporate solutions to working women's problems, such as fast food, may momentarily alleviate time pressure. But in the long run, they do little more than that, and may compound women's identity crisis in the following way.

As media scholar Michèle Mattelart observes, "liberal media accept several different ways of conceiving women's role and image, but demand some kind of feminine specificity" (1986, 23). In food commercials, that specificity is an "eternal" feminine that defines women as primarily maternal. Definition of the feminine as essentially maternal underpins an entire edifice of female stereotypes. At base is the virgin-mother-crone (or whore) dialectic. At end is the Child Molester School of Femininity, in which the adolescent female body and mind are held up as models for all women. The pursuit of this false idol distracts women from confronting the injustices done in her name. This is mental alienation.

In the social discourse on gender roles, many voices argue for their definitions of womanhood. In the television commercial, the interests of particular social institutions converge. Those who have the most to gain from the status quo—the corporate sector, the state, the mass media—continue to argue for the "naturalness" of woman's place in the home. Women participate in the workforce outside the home, but in subordinate positions. Further, domestic labor remains "women's work," whether we do it ourselves or see that it is done. This arrangement generates huge profits for corporations and stability for the state. It also perpetuates and legitimates a mode of consciousness based on sexism. Constructions of the feminine in television commercials are used to sell more than products—they are selling cultural values.

★ ICONOGRAPHY OF A MEAL

I shall consider in detail one commercial that is a particularly good example of alienated labor, "Your Biscuit Makers." A twenty-one-shot, thirty-second spot, "Your Biscuit Makers" celebrates alienated labor and its social relations (lyrics and shot breakdown are in the appendix). This commercial presents biscuit-making as a labor of love, not profit.

Description of the Commercial

Three young women (two white, one black) sing and dance with rolling pins in a McDonald's restaurant. They stand in formation, salute, use the rolling pins as though they were guns. The song is in the style of the Andrews Sisters. The women dance in the spaces where customers are allowed—in front of the counter, in the "dining room." These performance shots alternate with close-up shots of biscuits in various stages of production. Biscuit production is performed by a pair of white hands and takes only four shots, three of which occur in sequence. Two white male customers in a pickup truck come to the drive-through (excuse me, drive-thru), where a perky, dimpled, white teenage woman proffers the bag. The older man salutes as he drives off; the woman salutes back.

This commercial masks labor with fun, alienation with social interaction. An army of women makes breakfast. We don't see the generals; the troops are well trained. Eggs marching in formation underscore the "naturalness" of this hierarchy (shot 7). Indeed, eggs are a double code for women and for nature; thus, feminine nature. Men are on their way to work; women are in their place in the kitchen. Not only is there perfect order in this universe, but because everyone is in her/his "natural" place, it is not labor they are performing, it is fun. The harridan wife with a rolling pin weapon has become three cheerful, energetic, nubile teenagers.

While the military metaphor asserts an invisible pecking order, social relations in the workplace here are celebrated as nonhierarchical. Everyone in the place is a private—that is, equal. There is racial "equality" in the makeup of the dancers. The commercial also uses the familiar "you" form of direct address. "We're making biscuits every morning at McDonald's for you." The announcer invites an implied you to "Take breakfast by the hand with a fresh biscuit sandwich," that is, to treat the biscuit as a friend, or perhaps even as a child. In the former sense, McDonald's suggests that "you" the parent solve your breakfast problems at Ronald's house.

McDonald's is a neighborly mother substitute, a friendly place where you get social satisfaction with your meal. Indeed, it is the interpersonal interactions that promise satisfaction. However, there are no interpersonal exchanges among workers. The commercial's social moments mask the alienation of worker from food, worker from consumer, worker from worker. In addition, only food and smiles are exchanged; money is conspicuously absent. McDonald's positions itself as the Mother by association. Who else performs such labor for free? Who else does "it all for you"? Who else "deserves a break today"?

There are some interesting uses of time here. The production of biscuits occurs in close-up, leaving the actual labor offscreen and foregrounding the fun and socializing. Time is of the essence in fast food. Fast service is the obvious motive, but other elements conspire to render fast food an atemporal (= universal = democratic) experience. In its ideal form, fast food is always the same, and so each burger is indistinguishable from any other. The ritualized/standardized procedure, established to minimize time, destroys time. As if to eradicate evidence of one's presence, the fast food consumer throws away empty food containers.

Fast food translates industrial modes of production to the production of food. There is social alienation between the server and the consumer—imagine complimenting the lady behind the counter for the delicious meal, or asking if you can help with the dishes. Indeed, any conversation outside the ritual exchanges ("Is this for here or to go?") would be counterproductive, for it would interfere with the promised speed of service. Industrial values such as efficiency and interchangeability determine the alienated social relations, even though the commercial works to mask alienation. Everyone in the production-consumption equation is interchangeable, except of course Ronald McDonald.

How industrial values made their way into women's education about food is the subject of the next section.

★ RATIONALIZATION OF DOMESTIC LABOR AND THE CAPITALIST MODE OF PRODUCTION

Many of the beliefs we have about food are traceable through the development of the home economics movement, as Laura Shapiro posits in *Perfection Salad: Women and Cooking at the Turn of the Century* (1986). Fast food is the fulfillment of that movement, which sought to rationalize domestic labor, just as assembly-line methods in the workplace were transforming labor. With the growth of industrialization, women were negotiating a new relation to food, setting new boundaries in the kitchen and concomitant ones in the public sphere.

The middle-class women who formed the domestic science movement took as their cause the democratization of American taste. They emphasized nutritional value, predictable results, economy, and appearance in food. Quantification became the order of the day: science had given the calorie as a unit of measure; Fannie Farmer extolled the virtues of level measurement. Armed with scientific analyses of bleach, starch, and baking powder, the new ideal American homemaker was to be a critical consumer. Sanitary kitchens were to produce attractive meals loaded with protein, and working men would be grateful, invigorated, and treat their families properly.

The social formation imposed by industrial society was changing women's relation to men from one based on productive alliances to one based on economic dependence and affectional ties (Ewen 1976). Industrialization split production from reproduction, and assigned gender roles to each. Men exchanged their labor for wages. Women exchanged their bodies in reproductive labor (babies, housekeeping, social maintenance); food was a commodity to exchange in the home. In this sense women stood in the same relations to the products of their labor as did the assembly line laborer—except of course that women had no one at home maintaining them.

Urbanization, a companion to industrialization, further alienated people from their families, creating a void in cultural authority that corporations were eager to fill. Labor-saving technology required new information that grandma could not have provided. Advertising could and did serve as the teacher, in the process creating the role of the consumer "... and establishing a new function for the household in the world of mass production and mass distribution...." (Strasser 1982, 245). Home economists taught classes and wrote advice on how to consume. Industrialization's agenda wrought a new scientific approach to domestic labor.

Fast food signals the absolute acceptance of rational cooking. It is efficient, economical, sanitary (one hopes), and—above all—standard. It also signals the absolute marginalization of discourse on the relationship between food and social relations. Fast food is American taste industrialized and democratized. "Democratic" is used here in its vulgar sense, in which it refers not to egalitarianism but to sameness. Not only are hamburgers and fries standardized, but those who produce them are interchangeable parts. See for example the following recruitment flyer from the Evanston, Illinois, McDonald's:

McDonald's pay mothers for serving breakfast and lunch. If your family doesn't need you to serve breakfast and lunch anymore [sic], we do.

    Come work with us, arrange your hours to fit your schedule and earn extra money. See our manager.

The Mother in the home and the McDonald's server are interchangeable. The flyer implies that the skills women use at home are transferable to the fast food industry. By conflating the mother-at-home and the Mother-server, McDonald's buys the appearance of home cooking. The triumph of form over content is another example of alienation: the illusion masks the slippage between real mother labor of love and McDonald's employee wage labor. This Mother is also a consumer: note that the money she earns is "extra"—not enough to live on, but enough to spend, perhaps taking the family out to eat because she has worked all day and "deserves a break." Her identities as server and as consumer are interchangeable.

So far I have discussed alienation and definitions of the feminine in the text of the commercial and in the historical development of mass production. Next I shall argue for the centrality of gender difference in cultural thought at the mythic level, and finally how that positions this specific commercial within a larger discourse on women and food.

319

★ FOOD, CULTURE, AND GENDER DIFFERENCE

Anthropologists have noted the close relationship of a culture's food practices to the larger social context. While Mary Douglas (1975) emphasizes the symbolic connection of the body human to the body politic, Lévi-Strauss (1983) speaks to the inner workings of language and consciousness. In his analysis of South American myths about the origins of cooked food, he identifies patterns of thought in the stories tribal peoples tell to explain the universe. The myths work on structures based in symbolic oppositions. "The function of signs is, precisely, to express the one by means of the other" (Lévi-Strauss 1983, 14). About food, for instance, he notes a universal distinction between the raw and the cooked. Other basic oppositions, such as gender difference, are interwoven to form symbolic patterns that myths represent on several simultaneous levels.

One such pattern that Lévi-Strauss (1977) identifies is a subdistinction between roast food and boiled food, which invariably revolves around gender difference. The food's relation to the fire is a structuring difference—food that meets fire directly carries one load of signification, food cooked over, but not in, fire carries another. These differences in signification are further coded along gender lines. Men roast and women boil. In some cultures it is the other way around. This opposition is visible in our present-day culture, as in the traditional division of labor that assigns barbequing to men, while women's cooking involves kitchen (indoor, domestic, private) tools that separate food from fire (boiling). The "cave man" myth obtains in associating the masculine with the outdoors (external, public) and an unmediated conjunction of fire and meat.

In American mass culture the roast:boiled distinction appears in the "Burger Wars" ad campaigns for fast food. Burger King, the second-place company in the market, argues that its hamburgers are superior to McDonald's because Burger King "flame broils" its beef. Burger King commercials emphasize the difference between the broiled and the fried. Health considerations aside, this attack is at base a gender difference argument. Symbolically, Burger King positions itself as the masculine player in the competition for fast food dollars. Already coded as masculine by virtue of its name, Burger King seeks to distinguish itself from McDonald's, and does so in the name of "masculine" cookery.

Burger King's campaign is an offensive against the already-positioned first-place McDonald's. McDonald's has achieved its dominant market position in part by constructing itself as a purveyor of social, as well as gustatory, exchange. "We do it all for you" aligns McDonald's with the self-sacrificing eternally nurturing "feminine."

Sexual difference is arbitrary and must be constantly reconstructed in social practice. Commercials are cultural storytelling about food, and their ideological significance touches the very essence of social control—the body. As dominant film practice inscribes woman's body, the male-identified feminine image stands as a sign for male dominance. In this inscription we can see the rhetoric of food as discourse on feminine specificity. No matter how "modern" the times may be, feeding the family is still woman's work. Thus, in its current incarnation, food advertising insists on an "eternal" feminine even as it counsels that women's "equality" is a reality.

Commercials code fast food restaurants as havens of nourishment, but the emphasis is not on nutrition, it is on fun. Food rituals revolve around excitement and individual identity, not sharing or interacting. What that means for the role of women is impoverishment of the food relationship. No longer a privileged one (with all problems that carries), food relations for women are emptied of sanctity but still loaded with hierarchy. This is precisely the crisis point that Kim Chernin (1985) identifies as women's present gender-role confusion.

Commercials exploit the ambiguity inherent in reformulating gender roles to account for women's necessity to participate in the workforce (like our fathers) and at the same time develop a mature female persona (like our mothers). The mass media continue to identify that mature (sexual) female with the adolescent body, thereby maintaining a constant state of tension that can never be resolved. As Chernin says:

> ...we are in urgent need of a ceremonial form to guide us beyond what may well be the collective childhood of female identity into a new maturity of female social development. (Chernin 1985, 169)

As long as the global conditions of food production require that women perform more than their share of unpaid labor, however, it is doubtful that the mass media will provide any support for a "new maturity" for women. The mass media, and the industries whose interest they represent, must continue to insist on a female identity that is fundamentally domestic and dependent. Otherwise we might realize that our labors of love are underwriting their profits.

APPENDIX

"Your Biscuit Makers"

Lyrics
We're making biscuits at McDonald's every morning for you
we're up at dawn
shoopoopydoo

get our aprons on
we're making up the dough
we roll it out
put it in a pan
nobody makes biscuits
like we can
with bacon or sausage
the eggs are fresh
if you say (unclear)
ours are the best
Announcer: take breakfast by the hand with a fresh biscuit sandwich
Song: it's a good time for the great taste of McDonald's

Shots

1. wide shot outside building, sign turns on
2. three women salute
3. open biscuit close up
4. three biscuits close up
5. women spin
6. eggs in formation
7. hands pat dough close up
8. women in dining room flip rolling pins
9. hands roll dough close up
10. cut dough close up
11. biscuits bake
12. women dust hands
13. bacon flips to sausage
14. close up eggs
15. crack egg close up
16. hands take biscuits from oven
17. three-shot through guys in truck to drive-thru window
18. two biscuits
19. hand pats one biscuit
20. older guy salutes, truck drives off
21. girl salutes, smiles

321

REFERENCES

Chernin, Kim. 1985. *The Hungry Self: Women, Eating, and Identity*. New York: Harper & Row.

Douglas, Mary. 1975. *Implicit Meanings: Essays in Anthropology*. London: Routledge & Kegan Paul.

———. 1977. "Introduction." In *The Anthropologists' Cookbook*, ed. J. Kuper. London: Routledge and Kegan Paul.

Ewen, Stuart. 1976. *Captains of Consciousness*. New York: McGraw-Hill.

Lévi-Strauss, Claude. 1977. "The Roast and the Boiled." In '*The Anthropologists' Cookbook*, ed. J. Kuper. London: Routledge and Kegan Paul. 221–30.

———. 1983. *The Raw and the Cooked: Introduction to a Science of Mythology* Vol. 1, trans. J. Weightman and D. Weightman. Chicago: University of Chicago Press.

Mattelart, Michèle. 1986. *Women/Media/Crisis*. London: Comedia.

Shapiro, Laura. 1986. *Perfection Salad: Women and Cooking at the Turn of the Century*. New York: Farrar Strauss & Giroux.

Strasser, Susan. 1982. *Never Done: A History of American Housework*. New York: Pantheon.

FOOD AND THE EMERGING WORLD 5

THE INTERNATIONAL POLITICAL ECONOMY OF FOOD: A GLOBAL CRISIS

HARRIET FRIEDMANN

25

International conflict over agricultural regulation for more than six years threatened to collapse the whole Uruguay Round of the General Agreement on Tariffs and Trade (GATT), and with it an agreement that greatly extends corporate power relative to national (and public) power. At issue, paradoxically, was a type of national regulation of agriculture whose days were already numbered. Even more paradoxically, Europe, cast as defender of the old ways, had committed itself to more basic domestic reform than the United States. Major changes initiated in the European Common Agricultural Policy have gone further than anyone imagined possible at the outset of the Uruguay Round (1). The choice in 1994 is not between "regulation" or "free trade," therefore, but between new forms of implicit or explicit regulation.

In and around the tangled web of national politics, European and North American integration, and international economic competition, new protagonists were taking shape. The contest over new rules and relations for food and agriculture also depends on transnational corporations and popular movements not formally present at the negotiations. Agricultural support programs were put in place roughly half a century ago in response to farm politics. Since then, farms have become suppliers of raw materials within a transnational agro-food sector dominated by some of the largest, most technically dynamic corporations in the world. At the same time, urbanization and the rise of social movements expressing interests of consumers, environmentalists, and others have shifted the focus from farm incomes to other interests.

In the long view, it is clear that the agricultural trade conflicts inside and outside the GATT were the culminations of long-term structural and interstate changes. The rules implicitly governing agro-food relations were established in the years immediately after World War II and worked stably enough for nearly 25 years to justify the idea of a "food regime." However, new relations were forged during that time, which by the early 1970s began to undermine the international relations of food.

In this article, I analyze the rise of a food regime and the emergence of contradictory and conflictual relations within it. First, I define the food regime and its main features. In the second section, I describe the character of the food regime, including its internal tensions, between 1947 and 1973. In the third section I describe the emergence of new relations and new rules after the food crisis of 1972–1973. To simplify the story of the regime and its crisis, in these sections I treat states, particularly the United States, as integral actors. In the final part of this essay, I explore the residual and emergent relations which make possible either new regimes, or the descent into deeper disorder.

★ THE FOOD REGIME: PRINCIPLES AND CONTRADICTIONS

The impasse in international economic relations is centered on agriculture because in the agro-food sector there exists the largest gap between national regulation and transnational economic organization. This gap is the legacy of the post–World War II *food regime*, the rule-governed structure of production and consumption of food on a world scale. The food regime was created in 1947 when alternative international regulation in the form of the proposal for a World Food Board was rejected (2). At the GATT, the only clear positions are those which "decouple" and "deregulate" elements of a food regime that no longer works. The present alternatives for a new regime are not formally proposed. They must be teased out from analyses of the social forces involved in global agro-food restructuring.

The postwar food regime was governed by implicit rules, which nonetheless regulated property and power within and between nations. The food regime, therefore, was partly about international relations of food, and partly about the world food economy. Regulation of the food regime both underpinned and reflected changing balances of power among states, organized national lobbies, classes—farmers, workers, peasants—and capital. The implicit rules evolved through practical experiences and negotiations among states, ministries, corporations, farm lobbies, consumer lobbies and others, in response to immediate problems of production, distribution and trade. Out of this web of practices emerged a stable pattern of production and power that lasted for two and a half decades.

The rules defining the food regime gave priority to national regulation, and authorized both import controls and export subsidies necessary to manage national farm programs. These national programs, particularly at the outset of U.S. New Deal commodity programs, generated chronic *surpluses*. As these played out, they structured a specific set of international relations in which power—to restructure international trade and production in one state's favor—was wielded in the unusual form of subsidized exports of surplus commodities. In this way agriculture, which was always central to the world economy, was an exceptional international sector.

Then, the "food crisis" of the early 1970s, combined with simultaneous money and oil crises, initiated a period of instability from which we have not yet recovered. The sense of crisis in the early seventies stemmed from the sudden, unexpected shift from surplus to scarcity, which sent grain prices soaring and threatened food shortages for poor people and, most of all, for poor countries. In retrospect it is clear that since the shortages came from a one-time explosion of demand and a temporary drop in production, the basic cause of surpluses was bound to reassert itself. Since major states continued to support agricultural prices by purchasing commodities, within a few years farmers produced more surpluses, and states resumed mercantile trade practices to get rid of them.

With the reappearance of surpluses, most commentators abandoned the idea of crisis and focused on ever shorter time horizons. Old policies designed to deal with surpluses once again seemed appropriate, and problems with those policies were not connected to the long trajectory of international food relations since 1947 (for an exception, see 3, pp. 17–30). However, disappearance of the symptom simply masked survival of the disorder. Like a kaleidoscope turning, new relations which had emerged within the regime became significant enough to alter the pattern. Old practices, especially surplus disposal in foreign markets, could not reconstruct the original relations of power and property. Food aid or other forms of export subsidy, which once underpinned the food regime, came instead to express intense international conflicts.

327

★ THE SURPLUS REGIME, 1947–1972

Because the United States protected its own domestic markets, other countries were constrained to adopt similar agricultural policies focused on the national market. U.S. trade restrictions, designed to protect domestic farm programs, encouraged other states to focus on their own national agro-food sectors. States replicated the U.S. regulation of national sectors, but adapted policies to their locations in the food regime. For Continental Europe, this meant shifting the focus of protective agricultural policies away from tariffs, and redesigning trade protection around domestic support for farm prices. For other parts of the world, adaptation of the U.S. model involved parallel shifts in the forms of state agricultural regulation. Thus, the postwar rules did not liberalize national agricultural policy, but created a new pattern of intensely national regulation.

At the same time, the free movement of investment capital tended to integrate the agro-food sectors of Europe and the United States into an Atlantic agro-food economy. This tension framed the new roles of tropical export countries, including former European colonies, in the food regime. This integration, moreover, was uneven. It did not include the countries of the socialist bloc, and, despite high levels of aid and trade, the capitalist countries of Asia were not integrated into transnational agro-food complexes.

Thus the postwar food regime was built on a tension between the *replication* and the *integration* of national agro-food sectors. The tension between replication and integration reflected on an international scale the problem inherent in U.S. farm programs—chronic surpluses.

The United States at the Center

Paradoxically, the main challenge to present rules comes from the source of those same rules in the early postwar years—the U.S. state. New Deal farm programs of the 1930s were retained after World War II despite widespread awareness of the problem of surpluses. Mercantile practices had to be used to dispose of the surpluses and to prevent a flood of imports into the United States. As the dominant economic power after World War II, the United States insisted on international rules consistent with its own national farm support programs. These rules eventually allowed the United States to create an overwhelming preponderance in world agro-food production and trade, far beyond its historic share (4).

Yet mercantilist agricultural policy was in conflict with the larger U.S. policy to promote free movement of goods and money internationally (5). Because of its weight in creating international institutions after World War II, U.S. decisions transferred this tension to the food regime as a whole.

The food regime was created by a series of decisions between 1945 and 1949, which reflected U.S. determination to protect the import controls and export subsidies which, as we shall see, were a necessary complement to its domestic farm policy. U.S. commitment to mercantile agricultural trade practices led to the sacrifice of multilateral institutions which had wide support among postwar governments, not only for regulating food, but also for the pursuit of the larger U.S. agenda for liberal trade. The World Food Board Proposal, which provided for global supply management and food aid through the FAO (Food and Agriculture Organization), was rejected by the United States and Britain at an international conference in Washington, D.C., in 1947. The Havana Treaty creating an International Trade Organization, a 1946 initiative by the U.S. Department of State, was never formally submitted to Congress because it contradicted mercantile clauses in U.S. domestic farm laws. Even the GATT, which began as an ad hoc negotiating forum intended to be subsumed under the formal powers of the anticipated International Trade Organization, and continued as a feeble substitute in its absence, excluded agriculture from its ban on import controls and export subsidies, at U.S. insistence (5).

The need for trade controls stemmed from an odd feature of domestic farm programs, where, instead of direct income support, New Deal price supports tried to raise farm incomes indirectly by setting a minimum price for commodities named in the legislation, and maintaining this price through state purchases. Government purchases to support prices encouraged farmers to produce as much as possible. Legislation to limit production by restricting acreage was never effective. In fact, insofar as they encouraged farmers to remove their worst land from production, acreage controls tended to increase productivity.

Surpluses mounted more persistently with the technological developments involved in the industrialization of agriculture. Industrialization subordinated farms to emerging agro-food corporations, both as buyers of machines, chemicals, and animal feeds, and as sellers of raw materials to food manufacturing industries or livestock operations. Profits in the agro-food sector depended on the larger restructuring of the postwar economy toward mass production and mass consumption (6–8), especially increased consumption of animal products and high value-added manufactured foods, or what might be called "durable foods" (9).

Commodity price support programs both protected family farms and encouraged their relations with agro-food corporations. By supporting prices, the legislation rewarded large family farms. Farms increased productivity and scale through technologies bought from key vehicle and chemical industries. As they became locked onto a technical treadmill, they also became increasingly specialized. The most important shift was the separation of intensive livestock from cereal production, and with it the growth of the two most important crops of the "second agricultural revolution," hybrid maize and soy. Capital-intensive manufacture of soy-maize animal feeds allowed corporations to place themselves between increasingly specialized intensive livestock operations, which were their customers, and maize and soy farms, which sold to them (10). At the same time, mass production of durable

328

foods required standard agricultural raw materials, which corporations obtained through contracts with increasingly specialized and standardized farms (11, 12). As durable foods came to be made from generic ingredients, such as sweeteners, fats, and starches, corporations were able to reduce their dependence on specific products and increase the possibilities for substitution (13).

The key to the persistence of the world food regime was the innovative U.S. policy of foreign aid, combined with import controls. Domestic agricultural price supports required import controls and export subsidies. Without controls, high domestic support prices would attract imports. Apart from its negative impact on hungry people abroad, especially war-torn Europe, this meant that without import controls, the Commodity Credit Corporation, a U.S. government agency, would have to buy ever greater quantities of world supplies to maintain the incomes of U.S. farmers. Moreover, the more it bought, the greater was the gap between support prices and residual "market" prices. Government stocks put a downward pressure on prices by keeping supply (or potential supply) high. This created fiscal problems for the state budget, which had to pay support prices plus storage and disposal costs. Since the destruction of surplus agricultural products was politically unacceptable in a hungry nation (and world), commodity price support programs required a way to dispose of surpluses without lowering prices, that is, outside "markets." These were found through domestic public distribution, such as food stamps and school lunches, and through subsidized exports to other countries in the form of "aid."

Aid allowed the United States to turn the problem of surplus stocks into an opportunity to pursue strategic, welfare, and economic policies. Yet aid did not simply *integrate* donor and recipient. As a mercantile trade practice, aid encouraged recipients and competitors alike to adopt the national regulation of agriculture and trade. Thus *replication* was built into the international food economy at the same time.

In other words, what is frequently called the "export of the U.S. model" of both production and consumption (14–17) was the outcome of specific practices in the postwar food regime. At the same time, these practices also reflected historical experiences, so that the effects were quite distinct in Europe, the emergent third world, and as we shall see later, in Japan. In Europe and the third world, new links with the United States revolved around trade in wheat, animal feeds, and raw materials for food manufacturing.

Europe and the Atlantic Pivot

Marshall aid to Europe simultaneously established the basis for Atlantic agro-food relations, and invented the specific mechanisms of foreign aid which were later adapted to the third world. For European agriculture, the tension between national regulation, with attendant surpluses, and liberal trade was reflected first in Marshall aid and later in the Common Agricultural Policy. The United States supported the European protection of wheat and dairy products, even at the very high level needed to keep out efficiently produced and subsidized U.S. exports. In return, the European Community exempted maize and soy from the import controls of the Common Agricultural Policy (10, 18).

Under the Marshall administration, dumping was secondary to recovery. U.S. legislation required the use of Marshall funds to buy U.S. surplus commodities at specified rates as much as 50 percent below the domestic price; it balanced the contradictory interests of reconstruction and dumping by specifying maximum and minimum quantities to be disposed of in recipient countries. U.S. Marshall adminis-

329

trators, however, minimized agricultural dumping, as they understood it to be (5). The 40 percent of Marshall aid that went to food and agriculture in Europe was concentrated upon imports of feedstuffs and fertilizers for agricultural reconstruction. The balance shifted after 1954, when surpluses were redirected to underdeveloped countries in the form of food aid (19).

However, as soon as agricultural reconstruction showed some success, West European farmers sought U.S. markets for their dairy products. Congress then imposed import quotas on dairy (and a whole range of other) products. This, despite the fact that even with high support prices, imports of dairy products accounted for less than 1 percent of the U.S. market. The ability of special interests to override U.S. interests in trade relations with Europe can only be understood in the ideological context of the Cold War. The farm lobby got its import restrictions not through agricultural legislation but through an amendment in the Defense Production Act of 1950. In 1952, the Act was amended to enable the U.S. Secretary of Agriculture to defend the country against any import which endangered national security, from Danish cheese to Turkish sultana raisins (5).

Despite protection, the openness to direct investment by U.S. transnational corporations helped to integrate European and U.S. agro-food sectors via industrial inputs and processing. Both in promoting meat-intensive diets and in organizing intensive livestock production, agro-food capitals shaped agricultural reconstruction along lines similar to the United States. Most important was investment in an intensive livestock sector relying on industrial feedstuffs composed from soy and maize. This linked apparently national agricultures to imported inputs. Beneath the protected surface, therefore, lay the corporate organization of a transnational agro-food complex centered on the Atlantic economy. It linked North America, especially the United States, to Europe (10).

The combination of the freedom of capital and the restriction of trade shaped agricultural reconstruction so that it created a new relationship between European and U.S. agro-food sectors. A decade later, the Common Agricultural Policy of the European Economic Community introduced a similar form of agricultural support to that in the United States. To achieve import substitution in the face of chronic U.S. surpluses, however, the level of protection required was very much higher. In return for the United States' acceptance of EEC restrictions against wheat and dairy imports (the old products in international trade) the EEC did not restrict the new U.S. exports, maize and soy. The latter soon came to account for greater export revenues than those lost with wheat (20). Both European corporations and subsidiaries of U.S. corporations in Europe contributed to a massive growth of manufactured feedstuffs for intensive livestock production, and a shift from domestic and colonial raw materials, such as flax and cotton meal, to maize and soy imported from the United States. Like other industrial sectors, the apparently national livestock industry rested on a chain of inputs which effectively integrated a transnational sector (10, 20).

Thus European *wheat* replicated the *national* U.S. sector, while specialized European *livestock* farms imported inputs from the United States, creating an integrated *Atlantic* agro-food sector. The price support mechanism for wheat and dairy products eventually replicated the surpluses, and with them the export subsidies to dispose of them. By 1975 the European Community had switched from being a net importer to a net exporter of wheat, and by 1985 France's exports (including to other EC members) were larger than those of the United States (21, p. 45). At the same time, agro-industrial integration allowed European livestock producers to substitute a wide range of feed ingredients for U.S. imports and to diversify trade. Eventually, the Common Agricultural Policy closed the circle by introducing support for domestic oilseed production, an import substitution/replication which eventually brought the United States and EC to the brink of trade war in 1992. Thus, trade restrictions and competitive dumping turned from the founding principle into the enduring friction of the food regime.

The Third World

The Atlantic agro-food economy was the hinge for the reconfiguration of the food relations of Asian, Latin American and African countries. As third world states sought to develop national economies, their agrarian strategies were shaped by the opportunities and limits of world food markets. These gave little reason to question the dominant ideologies—capitalist and socialist; modernization and dependency—which all encouraged states to downplay agriculture except as a contribution to industrial development. For most countries, both the food supply of urban populations and the export revenues for industrial investment were largely sought outside traditional agrarian sectors during the 1950s and 1960s.

For the commercial food supply, U.S. wheat surpluses made imports an attractive alternative to the modernization of the domestic food sector. When the United States lost European wheat markets, which had been virtually the only source of import demand until the 1950s, it sought other outlets for its surpluses. It found them in Japan, and above all in the emerging third world. Third world markets were cultivated, despite lack of foreign exchange, through the use of food aid. The main U.S. food aid instrument, Public Law 480, adapted the specific mechanisms invented for Marshall aid. However, while Marshall administrators in Europe had resisted the Congressional attempts to dump U.S. wheat because it undermined the main goal of agricultural reconstruction (5), there was no such counterbalance for Public Law 480 aid in third world countries. Consistent imports made many third world countries dependent on cheap world wheat supplies (19).

Wheat was both a change from most traditional dietary staples and an efficiently produced, often subsidized alternative to the marketed crops of domestic farmers. Despite the Green Revolution, which *replicated* in the third world the hybrid maize revolution of U.S. agriculture (22) and *integrated* national agriculture into world markets for equipment and chemical inputs, the third world as a whole became the main source of import demand on world wheat markets. Import policies created food dependence within two decades in countries which had been mostly self-sufficient in food at the end of the Second World War.

On the export side, tropical crops faced the notorious problem of declining terms of trade, even when export states tried to manage world supplies (19, 23). Two of the most important tropical export crops, sugar and vegetable oils, were increasingly marginalized by industrial substitutes used as sweeteners and oils. Although changing U.S. (and other advanced country) diets increased the per capita consumption of sugars and fats, these were increasingly consumed in a new form. Sugars and fats became intermediate ingredients in manufactured foods rather than articles used directly by consumers.

Once industrial processes allowed for technical substitutions, the relative costs of crops could determine which would be used as raw materials for durable foods.

The main industrial substitute for cane sugar was high fructose corn syrup, which became economically feasible to use because of U.S. subsidies and surplus stocks of maize. The main substitute for tropical vegetable oils was soya oil, which was a by-product of soymeal for animal feeds. Beyond that, soya oil was the second-largest U.S. food aid item after wheat, and was widely substituted for traditional oils for cooking and for industry, by recipients of U.S. aid from Spain to India (23). Thus the food regime fostered import substitution of tropical oils and sugars in the United States and Europe, the Atlantic hinge of the international food regime.

By the early 1970s, then, the food regime had caught the third world in a scissors. One blade was food import dependency. The other blade was declining revenues from traditional exports of tropical crops. If subsidized wheat surpluses were to disappear, maintaining domestic food supplies would depend on finding some other source of hard currency to finance imports.

The food crisis of 1973–1974 did create a sudden scarcity. It sent prices soaring and dried up aid. Worst of all for dependent third world importers, the food crisis coincided with the oil crisis. The effects included a complex differentiation of the third world based on the new importance of paying for expensive imports of food and energy. The solution was temporary, elegant, and dangerous. The oil revenues deposited in transnational banks by oil-rich states were lent out extravagantly to states desperately in need of financing food (and oil) imports.

★ NEW RELATIONS, NEW RULES, 1972—PRESENT

After two decades, the internal tensions within the food regime had begun to pose serious problems. The *replication* of surpluses, combined with the decline of the dollar as the international currency, led to competitive dumping and potential trade wars, particularly between the European Economic Community and the United States. This eventually made it unbearably costly for small countries, such as Canada or Sweden, to subsidize surpluses or exports. On top of international conflict, transnational corporations outgrew the national regulatory frameworks in which they were born, and found them to be obstacles to further *integration* of a potentially global agro-food sector.

However, the crisis was precipitated externally by an event which permanently breached the boundary between the capitalist and socialist parts of the food regime. The geopolitical context for both Atlantic integration and the reorientation of third world agro-food relations was Cold War rivalry. The catalyst of crisis in the early 1970s, a crisis from which the regime has yet to recover, was the massive grain deals between the United States and the USSR which accompanied Détente. The crisis unfolded through a series of U.S. embargoes in response to feared shortages throughout the seventies, followed by fierce rivalry when surpluses returned in the eighties and nineties.

Détente and the Linking of Blocs

It will take a long time to interpret the effects of East-West relations on capitalism, but their role in the food regime was crucial. The food relations among the United States, Europe, the third world (and as we shall see, the Asian capitalist countries) were only one part, though the dominant part, of the food regime. They were contained by the Cold War dam which, despite leaks, divided the capitalist and the state socialist economies. With Détente, major trade and financial links breached the Cold War dam. It is important to underscore that nearly two decades before the collapse of the socialist bloc and of the Soviet Union, economic ties between blocs had forever altered international food relations.

The Soviet-American grain deals of 1972 and 1973 permanently broke the dam separating capitalist and socialist blocs. Despite leakages, this dam had been a wall containing the surpluses which were the pivot of the food regime. In the 1972–1973 crop year, the Soviet Union bought 30 million metric tons of grain, which amounted to three-quarters of all commercially traded grain in the world (18, p. 227). The scale of that transaction created a sudden, unprecedented shortage and skyrocketing prices. Even though surpluses returned in a few years because the agricultural commodity programs which generated them remained in place, the tensions did not appear, but were intensified by farm debt and state debt, international competition, and the changing balance of power among states.

The sudden scarcity of grains and soybeans precipitated by the Soviet purchases provoked a counterproductive response by the United States. First of all, despite 40 years of experience, the U.S. Department of Agriculture acted as if the chronic surplus problem engendered by commodity price supports had disappeared. With state encouragement, U.S. farmers abandoned conservation and other practices which had reduced acreage erratically since the New Deal. They followed the advice of the Secretary of Agriculture to plant "fence-row to fence-row" to supply foreign demand for wheat, maize, and soybeans. Although the U.S. farm bill of 1973 finally introduced deficiency payments, target prices, and other measures rejected in 1948 as an alternative to simple commodity price supports, the government also raised subsidies (18, pp. 75–77). Hastily treating surpluses as a bad memory, farmers borrowed to finance expansion. In the United States, farm debt more than tripled in the 1970s, fueled by high prices and speculation in farmland (3, pp. 21–22).

Second, the Nixon Administration, already beset by the Watergate scandals and nervous at the prospect of domestic feed shortages, introduced a series of embargoes between 1973 and 1975, which prevented internationally cooperative adjustment to the new conditions. The grain deal of 1972 was the economic centerpiece of its major foreign policy initiative, Détente with the Soviet Union. This focus led to the shift of agricultural trade policy from the Department of Agriculture (as an adjunct to the farm program) to the State Department, where it served U.S. foreign policy as "a lever that . . . has brought back into the world economy some 1.1 billion people" of the Soviet Union and People's Republic of China (Earl Butz, quoted in 18, p. 157). The U.S. government gave the Soviets 75 percent of allocated Commodity Credit Corporation export credits, plus additional subsidies which reduced the export price below the domestic price. When the details became public, another scandal resulted in Congressional inquiries into the "great Soviet grain robbery" (18, p. 75). When soybean prices began to climb the following year, consumers and livestock farmers mobilized, and the United States embargoed all exports in July 1973. Then in 1974 and 1975, fearful of a repeat of the scandals of 1972, the United States embargoed grain to the Soviet Union (18, pp. 146–160).

The embargoes were complete failures. They revealed that the U.S. government could not control trade even when, as for soybeans, the United States had a virtual monopoly over supply. State trading agencies and transnational corporations and their subsidiaries were able to use complex transactions and transshipments to organize trade outside the knowledge, much less the control, of the U.S. government or indeed of any state. Within two months of declaring the second embargo, the United States negotiated the first of a series of five-year contracts with the Soviet Union (18, pp. 159–160). This represented the largest single transaction in the world food economy.

This rapid U.S. shift in 1975 implicitly acknowledged the frailty of U.S. food surpluses as a weapon. The United States reversed course by shifting the focus to economic policy intended to increase export earnings. By 1980 exports of grains and feeds had increased eight times over the 1970 level. The dependence of the United States on agricultural exports was compounded by the fact that a quarter of its maize and about 15 percent of its wheat was bought by the USSR (14, p. 173).

Nonetheless, the Carter administration imposed one last embargo in 1980 (despite its electoral pledge never to do so) in response to the Soviet invasion of Afghanistan. The Soviets bought almost the whole amount of the cancelled contracts on the world market, mostly from Argentina, Canada, and possibly even the United States via transshipments from Eastern Europe. Moreover, the Soviet Union had hard currency from its oil exports with which to buy grain and oilseeds. Consequently, the U.S. embargo gave windfall prices to producers in competing export countries, and windfall profits to the corporate traders which took advantage of the unusual price fluctuations (18, pp. 165–169). The disastrous embargo was one of the woes leading to the defeat of the Carter administration in the next election. Thus, even though the Soviet Union and Eastern Europe together accounted for imports valued at only a third of those of the third world, the United States became dependent on Soviet purchases (24).

334

Yet within less than a decade the Soviet market, having risen to second largest in the world, effectively collapsed. Over the course of the 1980s, Soviet imports began to be sustained by the same U.S. mercantile trade practices which had been applied earlier to Europe, Japan, and the third world. A high level of guarantees and bonuses, that is, subsidies, maintained Soviet purchases from the United States in 1990 and 1991. As late as December 12, 1991, President Bush offered the USSR $1 billion dollars in credit guarantees for feedstuffs. Between 1987 and 1991, the United States gave over $708 million in bonuses for Soviet wheat purchases. By then, subsidized sales by the United States to the Soviet Union were such a large proportion of world trade that each transaction further depressed prices. Indeed, the United States even revived a credit guarantee program via the Export-Import Bank which had been defunct for 16 years in order to offer an additional $300 million in guarantees to the Soviet Union (25). The former Soviet Union is on the list of 28 countries to receive subsidized exports announced by President Bush in September 1992 in his campaign for reelection in farm states. Short of getting the EC to agree to loss of major foreign and domestic markets, U.S. policy now depends on increasing subsidized exports to cash-strapped countries whose prospects of repayment are dim.

Wheat, corn and soybean stocks in the United States rose again in the 1980s, although new policies and expectations kept them in private hands (3, p. 23). When the surpluses returned, they were harder to dispose of than before the boom. The United States had expanded its production and world market share instead of reforming agricultural policy (14). U.S. farmers carried a debt load which could not be supported when falling prices reduced cash flow and deflated land values, and in the 1980s farm failures became as severe as in the 1930s. Farmers had meanwhile lost many of their urban allies and their unity across commodity groups, making room for agro-food corporations to exercise the most effective lobby (18, p. 5).

When the bubble burst in the 1980s, U.S. farmers had lost their monopoly over agricultural exports, and their political weight in U.S. trade policy.

Japan and the Asian Tigers

Just at the time when the United States was becoming dependent on grain and soybean exports, its economic weight was declining relative to the EC and Japan, which were the major markets protected against its products. While the United States and Europe were sliding into a subsidy war, relations between Japan and major exporters began to evolve in distinct ways. With the manifest collapse of the socialist bloc market after 1991, those relations revived the older, prewar competition centered on import demand. These economic relations are deeply subversive of the defining principle of the food regime, namely power based on state supported exports of surplus commodities.

Japan's national agro-food economy began with Marshall aid. The Allied Occupation carried out a land reform and created a large class of small farmers whose interests lay in maintaining high subsidies for rice. Japan's postwar agro-food reconstruction *replicated* the U.S. model, adapted to the circumstances of rice production. Rice producers became politically important to successive governments, and the security afforded by domestic rice supplies became a tenet of national ideology. Subsequent U.S. strategic aid to South Korea and Taiwan had similar effects (26).

Yet replication was *not* balanced by *integration* as in Europe. Despite the similar goals and policies of Marshall aid, the economic and political conditions after the war, plus a lack of historical connections, led U.S. corporations to shy away from significant direct investments in Japan of the sort they were undertaking in Europe (27). Thus compared to Europe, U.S. transnational firms did not create production chains integrating Japan's agro-food sector with that of the United States.

In addition to postwar strategic conditions, the distinctively national character of the Japanese agro-food sector stemmed in part from its distinct diet. Although Japan early became a major importer of grains and soy, they played different roles in consumption and therefore in production. Wheat reflected a dietary change, encouraged by numerous trade missions and specific aid projects, such as provision of school meals. Japan became the largest of the new wheat importers after World War II, the rest being countries of the emerging third world. By incorporating wheat into their diets. Japanese consumers benefited from low world prices and helped clear U.S. surpluses from the market. In this sense, Japan played the same role as third world countries in restructuring international wheat trade around the United States as an export center.

Japan's relation to international soy markets was also different from that of Europe. Since soy was initially used mainly for human diets, it did not enter the economic and technical chains of the feedstuffs industry. The manufacture of soybeans into tofu, miso, and other foods was a distinct, Japanese production. Most important, as human food, soy cannot be substituted in the way that animal feeds can be—and eventually were. By the time Japan began to import significant quantities of soy for animal feeds, the food regime was already changing.

Dependence on U.S. imports was reliable during the stable period of the food regime, when U.S. surpluses led to cheap world supplies. However, the U.S. soy embargo of 1973 changed Japanese perceptions radically and permanently. Although the embargo lasted only two months and all contracts were eventually honored, its effect on the confidence of import states was enduring (14, p. 145). In particular, the embargo fatefully impressed the government of Japan with the unreliability of the United States as a source of virtually all its soy. By 1980, as we shall see, the U.S. share of world soya markets plummeted from its virtual monopoly a decade earlier. U.S. trade negotiations with Japan in the subsequent two decades have included repeated but fruitless apologies for that political blunder almost 20 years ago (28). This may be the reason the U.S. pressure on Japan to reduce agricultural trade barriers in the early 1980s concentrated on beef and citrus products, rather than rice (29).

Japan's investment and trade became a major force in the transformation. Japanese agro-food investments abroad began after the food crisis. If we understand soy and grains to be resources necessary for the domestic economy, then they may fall under the larger resource strategy described for minerals by Bunker and O'Hearn (30). According to their account, Japan and the United States have consistently adopted completely different foreign economic strategies, based on their distinct endowments of natural resources. They argue that without significant domestic production, the Japanese interest is in diversity of supply, which keeps prices down and reduces strategic dependence on any supplier. Japan can best achieve this goal by using the minimum investment necessary to create as many export sectors as possible. Exporters then compete for the Japanese import market, and Japanese importers can pick and choose, and shift from one supplier to another. This contrasts sharply with the longstanding U.S. (and European) pattern of direct foreign investment. Both domestic production by U.S. corporations and foreign production by their subsidiaries are locked into production sites and technologies matched to those sites (30).

Unlike the United States, and even the European Community, Japan is destined to import soy. The component of soy imports used in human diets is not substitutable. With the crucial exception of rice, imports of many agricultural products, and especially soy, are as important to Japan as minerals. In addition to the central tenet of agricultural policy, which continues to be national sufficiency in rice, Japan's interest as an importer lies unambiguously in secure access to necessary imports of grain and soy.

Although Japan is a distant second to the European Community in the volume of its soy and feedgrain imports, its singular foreign economic strategy has the potential completely to undermine the structure of international food relations. Japan began in the early seventies to look for sources of soy supply other than the United States. Its strategy was to change the nature of surpluses from a problem of disposal, which the United States and EC confronted, to an advantage for the buyer. It found a complementary interest among countries of the third world whose national industrial policies created internationally competitive agro-food sectors in the 1960s and after.

New Agricultural Countries

Behind the scenes of the Atlantic conflict which held center stage at the GATT is a new alignment. Trade between Japan (and other commercial importers) and successful new agro-food exporters in the third world continues to destabilize the

Atlantic-centered food regime. The new relations began during the early crisis years of the 1970s.

Soviet-American trade brought skyrocketing prices and new export markets in the seventies. These conditions coincided with the new possibilities for public borrowing created by the oil crisis (31). OPEC states captured a large share of world revenues and deposited them in international banks. The banks in turn pressed these "petrodollars" on borrowers. Many of the borrowers were third world and socialist states, including some which hoped to invest in export agriculture and to use the earnings to repay the loans. Another set of borrowers, on a scale equivalent to third world debt, was U.S. farmers. Seventies lending of petrodollars fueled both buyers and sellers of an expanding world market.

The differentiation of the third world into oil exporters, successful exporters of manufactured products, and those left behind in poverty (sometimes called the "fourth world") began in the early seventies. The new industrial countries, called NICs, were part of a transnational restructuring of industrial production. As we have seen, the technical basis of the U.S. model of agriculture, which was replicated and integrated in different ways in other parts of the world, comprised the subordination of crops and livestock into corporate, often transnational, agro-food complexes and the industrialization of agriculture itself. The successful development of export agriculture was as important as that of manufactures, and created a comparable set of "new agricultural countries," or NACs. Some, such as Brazil, are both NICs and NACs.

Brazil is the most important NAC. Its export capacity was based on a particularly successful development of the industrial agro-food economy in the 1960s, by means of state guided policies of industrialization through import substitution. Starting in the 1960s, the Brazilian state used a strategic mix of agricultural settlement, credit, and taxation policies to create an intensive livestock sector based on nationally produced grain and soya. Not only that, but export taxes on unprocessed soya encouraged national processing, whether by state or private, national or transnational, corporations.

Brazil *replicated and modernized* the U.S. model of state organized agro-food production. It *shifted* the focus of domestic policy from agricultural subsidies to agro-industry, which increased the value of commodities and did not create surpluses. Brazilian export policy replaced the U.S. focus on stabilization of domestic farm programs, with an emphasis on high value-added exports (32).

Within four years of the U.S. soy embargo of 1973, NACs had cut into the previous virtual U.S. export monopoly. By 1977, the U.S. share of world exports of oilseeds and meals, of which soy was the largest, was only 54.6 percent (14, p. 193). Ten years later, the U.S. share of world oilmeal exports had fallen to one-sixth. It exported less than Brazil and only slightly more than Argentina. China, Chile, and India had joined the ranks of major oilmeal exporters (21, p. 52).

Ironically, the United States retained a nearly two-thirds share of unprocessed oilseed exports, while Brazil exported high value-added meal. When Japan, the Soviet Union, and other import countries looked for alternatives to U.S. supplies, Brazil was especially well poised to concentrate on value-added meal rather than unprocessed soybeans. By 1980 Brazilian soybean production was a third as large as that of the United States, and its soymeal production half as large; Brazilian exports of soybeans were 10 percent of U.S. exports, but its soymeal exports were virtually equal. Then within a few years, as we saw, Brazilian soymeal exports exceeded those of the United States (10, p. 16; 21, p. 52).

337

Thus, Brazil's successful adaptation of the U.S. model, which shifted the focus from agriculture to agro-industry and from the management of surpluses to commercial exports, involved a complex web of international and social transformations. It gave Brazil a competitive advantage in a technically evolving and increasingly open international food economy—at a high cost to the victims of capitalist transformation of the agro-food economy of Brazil (33). Most important for international food relations, the NAC phenomenon revived the intense export competition on world markets that existed prior to the postwar food regime, and shifted advantage from exporters to importers.

This fit neatly with Japanese strategies to diversify world supplies with minimal investments and commitments abroad. Like many other states caught in the debt trap, as Bunker and O'Hearn (30) point out, public investments and joint ventures in third world export sectors allowed Japanese capital to gain leverage with minimal direct investment. This link between third world states and (often Japanese) foreign capital supplanted the earlier combination of direct (U.S. and European) foreign investment and state investment and controls favoring import substitution.

Liberalization has created an unstable situation in which importers (with strong currencies) benefit and the larger exporter wields the greatest power in international rule-making. Paradoxically, liberal trade practices now so desperately pursued by the United States to manage short-term deficits reinforce the long-term shift of advantage to (economically strong) import countries. With success at the GATT the United States could find itself in a new game, in which the rules convert export surpluses from a source of power into a source of dependency.

★ THE END OF THE SURPLUS REGIME

The impasse over agricultural subsidies at the GATT reflected the contradictory foundations of the postwar food regime, foundations which are crumbling rapidly. Overt conflict between replication and integration of national agro-food sectors at the end of 1992 was reduced to a few million tons of oilseeds. That it was important enough to jeopardize the comprehensive multilateral agreement to extend corporate power in key areas for future accumulation, such as services and intellectual property rights, testifies to the strength of residual tendencies in the food regime. Even the 1993 agreements to reduce European Community subsidies and end mercantile trade rules do not assure the future envisioned in the larger GATT agreements. The contest will continue between political projects envisioning different futures.

The End of Commodity Programs?

Farm policies were catching up with the collapse of the postwar food regime even before the GATT agreement. Changes in agricultural policy unimaginable at the outset of the Uruguay Round anticipated an end to national surpluses.

The separation of farm income supports from production—that is, the end of price supports—is the likely future for North America and Europe. This would undo the key feature replicated in the food regime—government generated surpluses. In the United States, although farm lobbies gained provisions requiring reinstatement of old measures if the Uruguay Round were to break down, the farm bill of 1985 accelerated the shift from price to income supports—even as it intensified export subsidies. After 1987, fiscal pressures reduced the level of price supports. Most of the U.S. states which are the stronghold of the farm lobby voted Republican in the November 1992 elections, and the Democratic incumbent may feel less beholden to them than the past decade's ruling Republicans. In the EC, reforms of the Common Agricultural Policy initiated in 1988 and intensified in 1991 point more decisively in the same direction. Payments to farmers will support their incomes directly, instead of indirectly through the prices of their commodities. While farmers will no doubt continue to be forced off the land, at least some will be supported as a combined rural welfare and tourism project. Farm income supports may also be tied to management of rural resources and to environmental programs.

The shift to income supports promises eventually to end the mountains and lakes of surplus agricultural commodities disposed of abroad by government subsidies and credits. It is easy to ignore the remarkable consensus on this way of ending an epoch of agricultural policy because (at least to proponents of urgent liberalization) implementation seems glacial (34). Yet the shift is likely to continue, because it confirms in policy what has already occurred structurally. Whatever stocks may be intentionally created for stabilization or security, whatever export subsidies and import controls may be retained or introduced, will have—indeed already do have—effect on the global agro-food sector different from those which shaped the food regime.

The Food Regime Unhinged

The two trade hinges of the food regime are coming unstuck. Countries of the third world and more recently of the former socialist bloc joined the multilateral trade negotiations at the GATT (35). This reflected (and reinforced) the unhinging of Atlantic agro-food integration, and of the U.S.–third world grain trade.

The Atlantic hinge is weakening as Western Europe and the United States are reorienting trade toward their respective continents. The North American Free Trade Agreement of 1992 and the potential expansion of the European Community to Nordic, former socialist, and other countries promise to extend "decoupling" to the continents of North America and Europe. This has been envisioned by corporate policy advocates for some time. As early as 1987, the President of Cargill Ltd. told the *Financial Post* (January 26), the leading Canadian financial journal, "Major agricultural producing countries should concentrate on devising actuarially sound income insurance policies . . . but we must avoid like the plague commodity-specific programs that encourage overproduction or distort land use decisions" (quoted in 36, p. 112). Continental integration is also emerging in Asia, centered on Japanese imports and investment (37, 38). Whether these turn out to be rivals or partners, they replace the U.S. center of the food regime with multiple centers.

The Atlantic hinge held because of the Cold War divide of Europe. The collapse of the socialist bloc was crucial in breaking the impasse over West European farm policy, by separating reform of the Common Agricultural Policy from the conflict with the United States. Prospective incorporation of Eastern Europe (and new Nordic and Alpine members), according to Tim Josling (1, pp. 18–19), was the most compelling reason for the MacSharry reform proposals. The former socialist countries include large fertile regions, which are politically divided, economically underdeveloped, and culturally distinct. Much like the U.S. South in the fifties and sixties, where soy rapidly replaced cotton, it opens a rich hinterland with abundant land and labor for reconstructing original agro-food relations. If stability returns to the former Soviet Union, the indiscriminately maligned state and collective farms may provide ripe pickings for agro-food transnationals (not only European-based, of course), particularly in the livestock sector. Similar openings could include China in Japanese diversification of investment and trade.

The other hinge was between the United States on one side and the third world (and Japan) on the other. The decline of U.S. economic power parallels the transformation of exports from a source of power into a source of dependence. U.S. exports were a source of economic and strategic power. In many underdeveloped countries, the food regime left a legacy of food import dependence, stagnating export revenues, and debt. Later, a few became New Agricultural Countries, whose competitive exports helped to disrupt the food regime. Now, in the twilight of the regime, the export imperative prevails. For strong importing economies, such as Japan, this is an advantage. For the third world as a whole, the transformation of their economies into agricultural export platforms intensifies new global international hierarchies between North and South (39).

The export imperative completely undermines U.S. centrality in the food regime. The "inevitable trend toward export dependence" (18, p. 77), which was built into U.S. farm and export-and-aid programs, has come to fruition. For a decade, Republican governments in the United States have sacrificed long-term restructuring to aggressive export practices. The U.S. zeal to force open commercial markets implicitly recognized the failure of concessional sales, long-term credits and other forms of "aid" to create new markets. Surpluses have come to signify weakness rather than power, a burden rather than an opportunity. The need for markets and the need to restructure domestic agriculture have led to contradictory foreign economic policy—aggressive trade practices combined (since 1987) with insistent demands to abolish such practices.

The accession of former third world countries into the GATT and their sudden conversion to free trade signals the subordination of food restructuring to international debt (39). Promotion of agricultural exports, especially those called "nontraditional" (geared to new niche markets for exotic foods, flowers, and other crops), is an explicit aim of structural adjustment conditions imposed by creditors. They usually intensify social inequalities and conflicts in poor countries. For instance, Brazil, which is a stunning success as measured by investment in agro-food production and exports, is also a nightmare of evictions from the land, displacement of local food systems, hunger, and social unrest (40). As I write, major social unrest has precipitated massive food distribution to the poor. It is certainly less orderly and less integrated with public policy than were the food subsidies abolished in the past decade of austerity. These are part of a string of "IMF riots," frequently over food prices, during the past decade of austerity (41). They reflect the suffering imposed in new centers of accumulation like Brazil, no less than in the vast regions pushed to the margins of accumulation, which include much of the African continent.

Debtor countries are caught in a scissor between the export imperative and import restrictions in Northern markets. They are thus forced to support free trade, however wrenching is the shift from decades of import substitution, controlled flows of goods and money, and state enterprises. Debt repayment, currency reform, and the rest require access to highly protected food markets in North America, Europe, and Japan. Liberal capitalism is the new, externally imposed form of austerity in the late 20th century. It is opposite to the austerity chosen by revolutionary third world states of the Cold War era, which took the form of autarkic socialism. Collectivization regardless of national circumstances was often futile and even disastrous. The same can be said of the creation of agro-food export platforms regardless of national circumstances.

Yet the export imperative, despite the faith in comparative advantage prevailing in expert circles outside Europe, does not create new regime rules. "Decoupling" and "tariffication" are the words used to dismantle farm policies and trade policies which once worked in tandem to regulate the food regime during years—now a distant memory—when it was stable. But if farm incomes are supported for reasons other than agricultural production—social insurance, keeping a lid on unemployment, environmental protection, promotion of tourism—then what will become of agriculture? Direct payments to farmers can address rural poverty and outmigration, can support rural tourist industries, and perhaps mollify farm organizations, but they intentionally *do not regulate agriculture*. Likewise, to increase the "transparency" of trade controls by converting them all to tariffs does not regulate agrofood power or property.

★ WHAT NEXT?

Emergent tendencies have unfolded quickly since the Uruguay Round began in 1986. These prefigure alternative rules and relations. One is the project of corporate freedom contained in the new GATT rules. The other is less formed: a potential project or projects emerging from the politics of environment, diet, livelihood, and democratic control over economic life. Farmers (who are heterogeneous) must somehow ally themselves in the main contest over future regulation: will it be mainly private and corporate, or public and democratic? What international rules would promote each alternative? The answers depend on the ways that emerging agro-food policies are linked either to accumulation imperatives or to demand raised by popular social movements.

Private Global Regulation?

At present, agro-food corporations are the major agents attempting to regulate agro-food conditions, that is, to organize stable conditions of production and consumption which allow them to plan investment, sourcing of agricultural raw materials, and marketing. The new rules defined by the December 1993 GATT agreement significantly empower transnational capital. This empowerment concerns not only the freedom to trade and invest in agriculture (cattle and potatoes), industry (frozen hamburgers and chips) and services (hot hamburgers and chips). Provisions for intellectual property rights also have serious implications for uses of biotechnologies, for control over genetic resources (42), and for standards protecting craft and regional foods (43).

However, transnational agro-food corporations have now outgrown the regime that spawned them. In particular, even U.S.-based corporations have long had interests of their own, not related to those of the U.S. state or national economy, and certainly not to those of U.S. farmers. A major reason why U.S. embargoes never worked, for instance, was corporate collusion with import countries to evade U.S. trade restrictions (18). Even before the food crisis, subsidiaries of U.S. corporations were working independently of U.S. national policy. For instance, in 1970, subsidiaries of Cargill and Continental, assisted by a trade agency of the French government, joined with other major grain companies in a cartel, Francereales, to promote French exports. The cartel was dissolved in 1973, under pressure from public authorities and from excluded competitors, but was revived in 1975 to respond to the new Soviet market (18, pp. 61–63). Because the U.S. state could not control or even monitor shipments by transnational corporations, U.S. policies to increase U.S. food exports at the same time undercut U.S. political power.

Within the limits of international rules, corporate integration of a global agro-food sector has proceeded as quickly and thoroughly as changing technologies permit. A new degree of global sourcing is made possible by feedstuffs that substitute for the standard corn and soy combination of the food regime (44). Three examples may suggest how "substitute feeds" at once integrate agro-food complexes and render substitutable the exports (and farmers) of any nation. First, orange pulp, a byproduct of the frozen orange juice industry, integrates the livestock and durable foods complexes. This adds complexity to the competition between Brazil and the United States, which becomes (among others) an interplay between now-traditional feeds (soy) and durable foods (frozen juice). Second, tapioca, mainly exported from Thailand, directly seizes upon a traditional human dietary staple and converts it into a commercial export feed crop. The expansion of tapioca in Thailand perversely detracts from rather than enhances human diets—but then so does the export of fishery products for human consumption abroad. Third, the most complex relations surround corn gluten as a substitute feed. This produce, which is highly protected by the European Community, is the byproduct of manufacture of high fructose corn syrup. The latter is the main sugar substitute in food manufacture. Without export revenues from gluten feed, the use of corn as a sweetener is too costly, and the domestic U.S. demand for corn will fall considerably. Not surprisingly, this was one of the European import duties most intensely contested by the United States (45).

Meanwhile, as the rules have shifted, so have the commodities central to accumulation. While feedstuffs, the heart of the food regime, are becoming globalized rather than merely internationalized, the completely new markets in "exotic" fruits and vegetables are global from the outset. Any state can enter, and in the push and shove of new markets, there is room for fly-by-night entrepreneurs and instant transnational corporations, as well as the giants of the postwar agro-food regime (46, 47). Rapacious entrepreneurial practices are encouraged by slavish state policies to attract investments and promote exports. The paradise of eternal strawberries and ornamental plants for rich consumers depends on an underworld of social disruption and ecological irresponsibility. While no rules have yet stabilized "nontraditional" export markets, the main corporate agenda points to global sourcing and marketing, that is, the impulse to diversify suppliers and cultivate tastes for "exotic" foods (pears in Mexico no less than starfruit in Canada). Superimposed on the diversification of raw materials for mass-produced durable foods in this post-Fordist nightmare of "flexible specialization" and "niche markets."

Democratic Public Regulation?

Stable rules cannot come from private and competitive organizations, despite the global reach of some corporations. There are two reasons for this. First, the very conditions which allowed for agro-food capitals to become pivots of accumulation have created new social actors and new social problems. Second, agro-food corporations are actually heterogeneous in their interests.

Classes of producers and consumers have changed radically from the time when transnational agro-food corporations were born. The agro-food sector is now focused on food—industry and services—rather than on agriculture. The character of classes, urban and rural, involved in food production has shifted. In meat-packing, for instance, the scale of production has increased dramatically. This has been accompanied by massive restructuring of the labor process and a standardization of products. The main result in the United States over the past two decades has been to replace a native born, male workforce—both disassembly line workers in packing plants and skilled butchers in supermarkets—with new immigrants, often female, recruited in new plants in small cities in the U.S. plains (48, 49). Restructuring is occurring as well in Australia, mainly for export to the Pacific rim, at massive environmental cost (38). Both cases echo in the old centers of accumulation a process that began in NACs, such as Mexico, to create the "world steer" at the expense of the traditional markets for peasant sideline production of cattle (50).

As farmers have declined in numbers and unity, and workers have lost some of their bargaining power with agro-food corporations, food politics have shifted to urban issues, that is, to *food* rather than *agriculture*. Consumers in the food regime have been constructed by agro-food corporations to desire first standard foods, and then exotic foods from the entire globe. Yet contradictions have emerged in the sphere of consumption. Poverty limits access to food and demand for the products of the agro-food economy. In the poorest parts of the world, and the poorest populations of rich countries, many are forced to withdraw from commodity relations into self-provisioning and informal networks. More privileged consumers have come to appreciate the dangers to health and the environment from the dominant practices of agro-food production created by the food regime—mainly the chemical intensive monocultures of farming and the chemical intensive production of durable foods. The most privileged consumers have revived demand for hand-crafted goods, including meals, now expressed in the language of "designer" foods.

A *food policy* is more adequate to present conditions than the farm policies left behind by the waning food regime. It is made possible by the decoupling of farm incomes from agricultural production. The national agricultural policies of the food regime not only support prices and generate surpluses. Through credit and insurance criteria, for instance, they also foster large farms, monocultural practices, and the environmentally destructive use of chemicals and heavy machinery. They also encourage technological and social dependence of farmers on corporate suppliers of packages of chemical inputs and purchasers of contractually (or simply monopoly) specified crops and animals. As national farm policies come under increasing pressure, the possibility arises to create a positive food policy.

The social basis for a *democratic food policy* lies in movements for employment and incomes, for safe and nutritious food, for environmentally sensitive agriculture (including treatment of animals) and for democratic participation. The main social movements concerned with aspects of food focus on poverty, hunger, employment, health, cultural integrity, the environment, rural recreation, and even animal rights. Within this field of issues, agricultural regulation can become part of a comprehensive plan to use the capacities of people and the land to meet the needs of communities for nourishment, cultural expression, and a congenial habitat.

A democratic food policy is quite a different prospect from the implicit policy posited by liberalization of trade and empowerment of transnational corporations. The latter embodies the principles of distance and durability, the subordination of particularities of time and place to accumulation. It moves beyond the global promotion of American diets, such as hamburgers and cola drinks, to the creation of a global diet consisting of an array of manufactured meals and ingredients, called Chinese, Mexican, Middle Eastern, or whatever, in the freezers of supermarkets throughout the world.

343

Democratic principles, by contrast, emphasize proximity and seasonality—sensitivity to place and time. This means the use and development of technologies and markets to facilitate local enterprises in every possible link of agro-food chains. What is increasingly clear is that healthy food and environmentally sound agriculture must be rooted in local economies. These must respond to the capacities and limits of bioregions, including the needs and capacities of the people who dwell there. In other words, food to nourish people and communities can only be linked to agriculture in harmony with nature, by means of chains of commerce and transformation located as much as possible within regions. A democratic food policy can reconstruct the diversity destroyed by the monocultural regions and transnational integration of the food regime. It is also about employment, land use, and cultural expression.

Of course, community Davids cannot contest the power of corporate Goliaths unless they find allies. To act locally entails acting at all levels, up to and including the world economy. National states can protect and link regional projects if pressed to do so. Indeed, some of the most progressive technical possibilities, such as the substitution of fossil fuels by ethanol, depend entirely on the present structure of subsidies and protection. Even if that specific structure cannot be saved, important fractions of capital are engaged in long-term projects, such as Archer-Daniel Midlands in the United States and Ferruzzi in Europe, whose interests, at least in part, lie in public regulation of agro-food economies (45). They are potential allies of popular movements for regional food economies.

344

This possibility could only be pursued through institutions at all levels, from the municipal to the international. In various parts of the world, municipal and regional governments—or popular organizations—are experimenting with ways to support regional agro-food networks. These include community kitchens and links to farms, support for scientific research geared to local industries, and publicly supported community catering in schools and other public institutions.[1] With the exception of Sweden a few years ago, however, no national state has undertaken to create a food policy as a framework for reshaping agriculture to meet environmental and social needs (52). To the contrary, perhaps the most comprehensive national food system in the capitalist world is in an advanced stage of dismemberment in Mexico. A public corporation, whose activities extended beyond regulation of agricultural prices into basic processing, distribution, and provision of affordable food to low income consumers, effectively "decoupled" rights to the land and rights to food from market dictates (53). Against popular resistance whose scale and intensity may not yet be evident, a decade ago new political elites began to dismantle the Mexican system under pressure of negotiated austerity measures and anticipated continental free trade.

Even with national support, the success of regional agro-food systems depends on international institutions. The World Food Board proposal of 1947, which expressed the hopes of a wartorn and hungry world for international cooperation to plan food and agriculture, belongs to the past (2). But it is important to remember that alternatives did exist and choices were made. Despite the multiplication of the number of states since 1947, when many were part of European colonial empires or of the emerging Soviet bloc, virtually all countries have agreed to multilateral economic negotiations. Most are doing so at the very time when national states are being restructured in response to transnational capital (54, 55). The consequences are dangerous for livelihoods and democracy. A better outcome depends on whether, despite their variety and inequality, movements for livelihood and democracy can shape the contest over new international rules, both within and outside the proposed World Trade Organization.

ACKNOWLEDGMENTS

I would like to thank Henry Bernstein, Barbara Harriss-White, Geoffrey Kay, Jean Laux, Philip McMichael, and Mary Summers for critical advice and encouragement in revising earlier drafts, and Yildiz Atasoy for invaluable research assistance.

NOTES

This article is modified from "The Political Economy of Food: A Global Crisis," published in *New Left Review*, No. 197, January/February 1993, pp. 29–57, also published as "The International Relations of Food," in *Food*, edited by Barbara Harriss-White and Sir Raymond Hoffenberg, Blackwell, Oxford, 1994. Earlier versions of this essay were presented at Wolfson College, Oxford, the Agrarian Studies Program, Yale University, and the Department of Political Sciences, University of Toronto.

1. I have in mind examples from northern Italy, Mexico City, and Toronto. For a discussion of the London Food Commission, created by the Greater London Council, see reference 51.

REFERENCES

1. Josling, T. Emerging Agricultural Trade Relations in the Post Uruguay Round World. Paper presented at the Faculty of Political Science, University of Rome, June 1992.
2. Peterson, M. Paradigmatic shift in agriculture: Global effects and the Swedish response. In *Rural Restructuring*, edited by T. Marsden, P. Lowe, and S. Whatmore. David Fulton, London, 1990.
3. Strange, M. *Family Farming, A New Economic Vision*. University of Nebraska Press, Omaha, 1988.
4. Friedmann, H. World market, state, and family farm: Social bases of household production in the era of wage labor. *Comp. Stud. Soc. Hist.* 20: 4, 1978.
5. Rau, A. *Agricultural Policy and Trade Liberalization in the United States, 1934–56: A Study of Conflicting Policies*, pp. 93–121, Librairie E. Droz, Geneva, 1957.
6. Kenney, M., et al. Agriculture in U.S. Fordism: The integration of the productive consumer. In *Towards a New Political Economy of Agriculture*, edited by W. H. Friedland et al. Westview, Boulder, 1991.
7. Berlan, J.-P. The historical roots of the present agricultural crisis. In *Towards a New Political Economy of Agriculture*, edited by W. H. Friedland et al. Westview, Boulder, 1991.
8. Buttel, F. H., and La Ramee, P. The 'disappearing middle': A sociological perspective. In *Towards a New Political Economy of Agriculture*, edited by W. H. Friedland et al. Westview, Boulder, 1991.
9. Friedmann, H. Family wheat farms and third world diets: A paradoxical relationship between unwaged and waged labor. In *Work Without Wages*. SUNY Press. Binghamton, N.Y., 1990.
10. Bertrand, J.-P., Laurent, C., and LeClercq, V. *Le monde du soja*. Éditions La Découverte, Paris, 1983.
11. Gertler, M. E. The institutionalization of grower-processor relations in the vegetable industries of Ontario and New York. In *Towards a New Political Economy of Agriculture*, edited by W. H. Friedland et al. Westview, Boulder, 1991.
12. Friedland, W. H., Barton, A. E., and Thomas, R. J. *Manufacturing Green Gold: Capital, Labor, and Technology in the Lettuce Industry*. Cambridge University Press, Cambridge, England, 1981.
13. Goodman, D., Sorj, B., and Wilkinson, J. *From Farming to Biotechnology*. Blackwell. Oxford, 1987.
14. Revel, A., and Riboud, C. *America's Green Power*. Johns Hopkins University Press, Baltimore, 1986.
15. Tubiana, L. World trade in agricultural products: From global regulation to market fragmentation. In *International Farm Crisis*, edited by D. Goodman and M. Redclift. Macmillan, London, 1989.
16. George, S. *Les Strateges de la Faim*, especially pp. 23–56. Éditions Grounauer, Geneva, 1981.
17. Moore Lappe, F., and Collins, J. *World Hunger, Twelve Myths*, p. 107. Food First, San Francisco, 1986.
18. Gilmore, R. *A Poor Harvest: The Clash of Policies and Interests in the Grain Trade*. Longman, London and New York, 1982.
19. Friedmann, H. Origins of third world food dependence. In *The Food Question*, edited by H. Bernstein et al. Earthscan, London, 1990.
20. Morgan, D. *Merchants of Grain*. Viking, New York, 1979.
21. Hathaway, D. E. *Agriculture and the GATT: Rewriting the Rules*. Institute for International Economics, Washington, D.C., 1977.
22. Kloppenburg, J. Jr. The social impacts of biogenetic technology in agriculture: Past and future. In *The Social Consequences and Challenges of New Agricultural Technologies*. Westview, Boulder, 1984.
23. Friedmann, H. Changes in the international division of labor. In *Towards a New Political Economy of Agriculture*, edited by W. H. Friedland et al. Westview, Boulder, 1991.

24. Organization for Economic Cooperation and Development. *Agricultural Policies, Markets, and Trade*, p. 402, Paris, 1991.
25. U.S. Department of Agriculture, Economic Research Service. *USSR Agriculture and Trade Report*, RS-91-1. Washington, D.C., May 1991.
26. McMichael, P., and Kim, C.-K. The Restructuring of East Asian Agricultural Systems in Comparative and Global Perspective. Department of Rural Sociology, Cornell University, Ithaca, N.Y., 1994.
27. Schonberger, H. B. *Aftermath of War: Americans and the Remaking of Japan, 1945-1952.* Kent State University Press, Kent, Ohio, 1989.
28. Bunker, S. Personal communication.
29. Reich, M., and Endo, Y. Conflicting Demands in US-Japan Agricultural Negotiations. USJP working paper 83-01. Harvard University Center for International Affairs, Cambridge, Mass., May 1983.
30. Bunker, S., and O'Hearn, D. Strategies of economic ascendants for access to raw materials: A comparison of the U.S. and Japan. In *Pacific Asia and the Future of the World System*, edited by R. A. Palat. Greenwood, Greenwich, Conn., 1995.
31. Friedmann, H. Warsaw Pact socialism: Détente and the collapse of Soviet bloc socialism. In *Rethinking the Cold War*, edited by A. Hunt. Temple University Press, Pittsburgh, 1995.
32. LeClercq, V. *Conditions et limites de l'insertion du Brésil dans les echanges mondiaux du soja.* Institut National de Recherches Agronomiques, Études et Recherches No. 96. École Nationale Superieure Agronomique, Montpellier, 1988.
33. LeClercq, V. Aims and constraints of the Brazilian agro-industrial strategy: The case of Brazil. In *International Farm Crisis*, edited by D. Goodman and M. Redclift, pp. 275–291, Macmillan, London, 1989.
34. Organization for Economic Cooperation and Development. *Agricultural Policies, Markets and Trade, Monitoring and Outlook*, pp. 199–200. Paris, 1991.
35. Josling, T. Conflicts between Free Trade and Domestic Policies in Agriculture and the Environment. Paper presented at the Faculty of Political Science, University of Rome, May 1992.
36. Kneen, B. *Trading Up: How Cargill, the World's Largest Grain Company, Is Changing Canadian Agriculture*, NC Press, Toronto, 1990.
37. McMichael, P. Agro-food restructuring in the Pacific Rim. In *Pacific-Asia and the Future of the World-System*, edited by R. A. Palat. Greenwood, Westport, Conn., 1992.
38. Lawrence, G., and Vanclay, F. Agricultural change and environmental degradation in the semi-periphery: The Murray-Darling Basin, Australia. In *Agro-food System Restructuring in the Late Twentieth Century*, edited by P. McMichael. Cornell University Press, Ithaca, N.Y., 1995.
39. McMichael, P. World food restructuring under a GATT regime. In *The Political Geography of Agricultural Trade*, edited by F. Ufkes. Special issue of *Political Geography Quarterly*, 1995.
40. Homem de Melo, F. Unbalanced technological change and income disparity in a semi-open economy. In *Food, State, and International Political Economy*, edited by F. L. Tullis and W. L. Hollist. University of Nebraska Press, Lincoln, 1986.
41. Walton, J. Debt, protest, and the state in Latin America. In *Power and Popular Protest*, edited by S. Eckstein. University of California Press, Berkeley, 1989.
42. Kloppenberg, J. (ed.). *Seeds and Sovereignty: The Use and Control of Plant Genetic Resources.* Duke University Press, Durham, N.C., 1988.
43. Moran, W. Rural Space as Intellectual Property. Unpublished manuscript. 1992.
44. Barkin, D., Batt, R. L., and DeWalt, B. *Food Crops vs. Feed Crops: Global Substitution of Grains in Production.* Lynne Rienner, Boulder and London, 1990.
45. Byman, W. J. New technologies in the agro-food system and US-EC trade relations. In *Technological Change and the Rural Environment*, edited by P. Lowe, T. Marsden, and S. Whatmore, p. 148. David Fulton, London, 1990.
46. Raynolds, L. The restructuring of export agriculture in the Dominican Republic. In *Agro-food System Restructuring in the Late Twentieth Century*, edited by P. McMichael. Cornell University Press, Ithaca, N.Y., 1995.
47. Friedland, W. H. The global fresh fruit and vegetable system. In *Agro-food System Restructuring in the Late Twentieth Century*, edited by P. McMichael. Cornell University Press, Ithaca, N.Y., 1995.
48. Ulkes, F. The Changing Social Structures of Livestock Marketing in Illinois, 1950–1990. Unpublished manuscript. Association of American Geographers, Miami, April 1991.
49. Stanley, K. Industrial change and the transformation of rural labor markets in the US meatpacking industry. In *Agro-food System Restructuring in the Late Twentieth Century*, edited by P. McMichael. Cornell University Press, Ithaca, N.Y., 1995.
50. Sanderson, S. The emergence of the 'world steer': Internationalization and foreign domination in Latin American cattle production. In *Food, the State, and International Political Economy*, edited by F. L. Tullis and W. L. Hollist. University of Nebraska Press, Lincoln, 1986.
51. Jenkins, R. Urban consumptionism as a route to rural renewal. In *The Food Question*, edited by H. Bernstein et al. Earthscan, London, 1990.
52. Vail, D. Economic and ecological crises: Transforming Swedish agricultural policy. In *Towards a New Political Economy of Agriculture*, edited by W. H. Friedland et al. Westview, Boulder, 1991.
53. Grindle, M. S. *Bureaucrats, Politicians, and Peasants in Mexico.* University of California Press, Berkeley, 1977.
54. McMichael, P., and Myhre, D. Global regulation vs. the nation-state: Agro-food restructuring and the new politics of capital. *Capital and Class* 43, 1991.
55. Cox, R. *Production, Power and the World Order.* Columbia University Press, New York, 1987.

346

CHINA'S BIG MAC ATTACK

26

JAMES L. WATSON

★ **RONALD MCDONALD GOES TO CHINA**

Looming over Beijing's choking, bumper-to-bumper traffic, every tenth building seems to sport a giant neon sign advertising American wares: Xerox, Mobil, Kinko's, Northwest Airlines, IBM, Jeep, Gerber, even the Jolly Green Giant. American food chains and beverages are everywhere in central Beijing: Coca-Cola, Starbucks, Kentucky Fried Chicken, Häagen-Dazs, Dunkin' Donuts, Baskin-Robbins, Pepsi, TCBY, Pizza Hut, and of course McDonald's. As of June 1999, McDonald's had opened 235 restaurants in China. Hong Kong alone now boasts 158 McDonald's franchises, one for every 42,000 residents (compared to one for every 30,000 Americans).

Fast food can even trump hard politics. After NATO accidentally bombed the Chinese embassy in Belgrade during the war in Kosovo, Beijing students tried to organize a boycott of American companies in protest. Coca-Cola and McDonald's were at the top of their hit list, but the message seemed not to have reached Beijing's busy consumers: the three McDonald's I visited last July were packed with Chinese tourists, local yuppies, and grandparents treating their "little emperors and empresses" to Happy Meals. The only departure from the familiar American setting was the menu board (which was in Chinese, with English in smaller print) and the jarring sound of Mandarin shouted over cellular phones. People were downing burgers, fries, and Cokes. It was, as Yogi Berra said, déjà vu all over again; I had seen this scene a hundred times before in a dozen countries. Is globalism—and its cultural variant, McDonaldization—the face of the future?

★ IMPERIALISM AND A SIDE OF FRIES

American academe is teeming with theorists who argue that transnational corporations like McDonald's provide the shock troops for a new form of imperialism that is far more successful, and therefore more insidious, than its militarist antecedents. Young people everywhere, the argument goes, are avid consumers of soap operas, music videos, cartoons, electronic games, martial-arts books, celebrity posters, trendy clothing, and faddish hairstyles. To cater to them, shopping malls, supermarkets, amusement parks, and fast-food restaurants are popping up everywhere. Younger consumers are forging transnational bonds of empathy and shared interests that will, it is claimed, transform political alignments in ways that most world leaders—old men who do not read *Wired*—cannot begin to comprehend, let alone control. Government efforts to stop the march of American (and Japanese) pop culture are futile; censorship and trade barriers succeed only in making forbidden films, music, and Web sites irresistible to local youth.

One of the clearest expressions of the "cultural imperialism" hypothesis appeared in a 1996 *New York Times* op-ed by Ronald Steele: "It was never the Soviet Union, but the United States itself that is the true revolutionary power.... We purvey a culture based on mass entertainment and mass gratification.... The cultural message we transmit through Hollywood and McDonald's goes out across the world to capture, and also to undermine, other societies.... Unlike traditional conquerors, we are not content merely to subdue others: We insist that they be like us." In his recent book, *The Lexus and the Olive Tree*, Thomas Friedman presents a more benign view of the global influence of McDonald's. Friedman has long argued in his *New York Times* column that McDonald's and other manifestations of global culture serve the interests of middle classes that are emerging in autocratic, undemocratic societies. Furthermore, he notes, countries that have a McDonald's within their borders have never gone to war against each other. (The NATO war against Serbia would seem to shatter Friedman's Big Mac Law, but he does not give up easily. In his July 2, 1999, column, he argued that the shutdown and rapid reopening of Belgrade's six McDonald's actually prove his point.)

If Steel and his ideological allies are correct, McDonald's should be the poster child of cultural imperialism. McDonald's today has more than 25,000 outlets in 119 countries (see Table 1). Most of the corporation's revenues now come from operations outside the United States, and a new restaurant opens somewhere in the world every 17 hours.

McDonald's makes heroic efforts to ensure that its food looks, feels, and tastes the same everywhere. A Big Mac in Beijing tastes virtually identical to a Big Mac in Boston. Menus vary only when the local market is deemed mature enough to expand beyond burgers and fries. Consumers can enjoy Spicy Wings (red-pepper-laced chicken) in Beijing, kosher Big Macs (minus the cheese) in Jerusalem, vegetable McNuggets in New Delhi, or a McHuevo (a burger with fried egg) in Montevideo. Nonetheless, wherever McDonald's takes root, the core product—at least during the initial phase of operation—is not really the food but the experience of eating in a cheerful, air-conditioned, child-friendly restaurant that offers the revolutionary innovation of clean toilets.

Critics claim that the rapid spread of McDonald's and its fast-food rivals undermines indigenous cuisines and helps create a homogeneous, global culture. Beijing and Hong Kong thus make excellent test cases since they are the dual epicenters of

**Table 1: McDonald's Restaurants
by Country (as of June 30, 1999)**

United States	12,490
Japan	2, 985
Canada	1, 093
Germany	947
Brazil	771
France	744
Taiwan	310
China	235
Italy	211
Hong Kong	158
Other	5, 397
Total	25, 341

China's haute cuisine (with apologies to Hunan, Sichuan, and Shanghai loyalists). If McDonald's can make inroads in these two markets, it must surely be an unstoppable force that levels cultures. But the truth of this parable of globalization is subtler than that.

★ THE SECRET OF MY SUCCESS

How did McDonald's do it? How did a hamburger chain become so prominent in a cultural zone dominated by rice, noodles, fish, and pork? In China, adult consumers often report that they find the taste of fried beef patties strange and unappealing. Why, then, do they come back to McDonald's? And more to the point, why do they encourage their children to eat there?

The history of McDonald's in Hong Kong offers good clues about the mystery of the company's worldwide appeal. When Daniel Ng, an American-trained engineer, opened Hong Kong's first McDonald's in 1975, his local food-industry competitors dismissed the venture as a nonstarter: "Selling hamburgers to Cantonese? You must be joking!" Ng credits his boldness to the fact that he did not have an M.B.A. and had never taken a course in business theory.

During the early years of his franchise, Ng promoted McDonald's as an outpost of American culture, offering authentic hamburgers to "with-it" young people eager to forget that they lived in a tiny colony on the rim of Maoist China. Those who experienced what passed for hamburgers in British Hong Kong during the 1960s and 1970s will appreciate the innovation. Ng made the fateful decision not to compete with Chinese-style fast-food chains that had started a few years earlier (the largest of which, Café de Coral, was established in 1969). The signs outside his first restaurants were in English; the Chinese characters for McDonald's (Cantonese *Mak-dong-lou*, Mandarin *Mai-dang-lao*) did not appear until the business was safely established. Over a period of 20 years, McDonald's gradually became a mainstay of Hong Kong's middle-class culture. Today the restaurants are packed wall-to-wall with busy commuters, students, and retirees who treat them as homes away from home. A 1997 survey I conducted among Hong Kong university students revealed that few were even aware of the company's American origins. For Hong Kong youth, McDonald's is a familiar institution that offers comfort foods that they have eaten since early childhood.

Yunxiang Yan, a UCLA anthropologist, hints that a similar localization process may be under way in Beijing. McDonald's there is still a pricey venue that most Chinese treat as a tourist stop: you haven't really "done" Beijing unless you have visited the Forbidden City, walked around Tiananmen Square, and eaten at the "Golden Arches." Many visitors from the countryside take Big Mac boxes, Coke cups, and napkins home with them as proof that they did it right. Yan also discovered that working-class Beijing residents save up to take their kids to McDonald's and hover over them as they munch. (Later the adults eat in a cheaper, Chinese-style restaurant.) Parents told Yan that they wanted their children to "connect" with the world outside China. To them, McDonald's was an important stop on the way to Harvard Business School or the MIT labs. Yan has since discovered that local yuppies are beginning to eat Big Macs regularly. In 20 years, he predicts, young people in Beijing (like their counterparts in Hong Kong today) will not even care about the foreign origin of McDonald's, which will be serving ordinary food to people more interested in getting a quick meal than in having a cultural experience. The key to this process of localization is China's changing family system and the emergence of a "singleton" (only-child) subculture.

★ THE LITTLE EMPERORS

In China, as in other parts of East Asia, the startup date for McDonald's corresponds to the emergence of a new class of consumers with money to spend on family entertainment. Rising incomes are dramatically changing lifestyles, especially among younger couples in China's major cities. Decisions about jobs and purchases no longer require consultations with an extended network of parents, grandparents, adult siblings, and other kin. More married women in Hong Kong, Beijing, and Shanghai work outside the home, which in turn affects child-rearing practices, residence patterns, and gender relations. At least in the larger cities, men no longer rule the roost. One of China's most popular television shows features a search for the "ideal husband," a man who does the shopping, washes the dishes, and changes the baby's diapers—behavior inconceivable in Mao's heyday.

Most Chinese newlyweds are choosing to create their own homes, thereby separating themselves from parents and in-laws. The traditional system of living with the groom's parents is dying out fast, even in the Chinese countryside. Recent research in Shanghai and Dalian (and Taipei) shows that professional couples prefer to live near the wife's mother, often in the same apartment complex. The crucial consideration is household labor—child care, cooking, shopping, washing, and cleaning. With both husband and wife working full time, someone has to do it, and the wife's mother is considered more reliable (and less trouble) than the husband's mother, who would expect her daughter-in-law to be subservient.

In response to these social and economic changes, a new Chinese family system is emerging that focuses on the needs and aspirations of the married couple—the conjugal unit. Conjugality brings with it a package of attitudes and practices that undermine traditional Chinese views regarding filial piety and Confucianism. Should younger couples strive, irrespective of personal cost, to promote the welfare of the larger kin group and support their aging parents? Or should they concentrate on building a comfortable life for themselves and their offspring? Increasingly, the balance is shifting toward conjugality and away from the Confucian norms that guided earlier generations.

The shift also coincides with a dramatic decline in China's birth rate and a rise in the amount of money and attention lavished on children. The Communist Party's single-child family policy has helped produce a generation of "little emperors and empresses," each commanding the undivided affection and economic support of two parents and (if lucky) four grandparents. The Chinese press is awash with articles bemoaning the rise of singletons who are selfish, maladjusted, and spoiled beyond repair—although psychologists working on China's singletons find them little different from their American or European counterparts.

McDonald's opened in Beijing in 1992, a time when changes in family values were matched by a sustained economic boom. The startup date also coincided with a public "fever" for all things American—sports, clothing, films, food, and so on. American-style birthday parties became key to the company's expansion strategy. Prior to the arrival of McDonald's, festivities marking youngsters' specific birth dates were unknown in most of East Asia. In Hong Kong, for instance, lunar-calendar dates of birth were recorded for use in later life—to help match prospective marriage partners' horoscopes or choose an auspicious burial date. Until the late 1970s and early 1980s, most people paid little attention to their calendar birth date if they remembered it at all. McDonald's and its rivals now promote the birthday party—complete with cake, candles, and silly hats—in television advertising aimed directly at kids.

351

McDonald's also introduced other localized innovations that appeal to younger customers. In Beijing, Ronald McDonald (a.k.a. Uncle McDonald) is paired with an Aunt McDonald whose job is to entertain children and help flustered parents. All over East Asia, McDonald's offers a party package that includes food, cake, gifts, toys, and the exclusive use of a children's enclosure sometimes known as the Ronald Room. Birthday parties are all the rage for upwardly mobile youngsters in Hong Kong, Beijing, and Shanghai. Given that most people in these cities live in tiny, overcrowded flats, the local Kentucky Fried Chicken or McDonald's is a convenient and welcoming place for family celebrations.

For the first time in Chinese history, children matter not simply as future providers but as full-scale consumers who command respect in today's economy. Until the 1980s, kids rarely ate outside the home. When they did, they were expected to eat what was put in front of them. The idea that children might actually order their own food would have shocked most adults; only foreign youngsters were permitted to make their opinions known in public, which scandalized everyone within earshot. Today children have money in their pockets, most of which they spend on snacks. New industries and a specialized service sector have emerged to feed this category of consumers, as the anthropologist Jun Jing has noted in his new book, *Feeding China's Little Emperors*. In effect, the fast-food industry helped start a consumer revolution by encouraging children as young as three or four to march up to the counter, slap down their money, and choose their own food.

In Hong Kong, McDonald's has become so popular that parents use visits to their neighborhood outlet as a reward for good behavior or academic achievement. An old friend told me that withholding McDonald's visits was the only threat that registered with his wayward son. "It is my nuclear deterrent," he said.

McDonald's could not have succeeded in East Asia without appealing to new generations of consumers—children from 3 to 13 and their harried, stressed-out parents. No amount of stealth advertising or brilliant promotions could have done the trick alone. The fast-food industry did not create a market where none existed; it responded to an opportunity presented by the collapse of an outdated Confucian family system. In effect, McDonald's tailgated the family revolution as it swept through East Asia, first in Japan and Hong Kong (1970s), then in Taiwan and South Korea (1980s), and finally in China (1990s). There is no great mystery here, unless one is predisposed to seeing imperialist plots behind every successful business.

★ GRIMACE

In 1994 students protesting against California's Proposition 187, which restricted state services to immigrants, ransacked a McDonald's in Mexico City, scrawling "Yankee go home" on the windows. In August 1999 French farmers dumped tons of manure and rotting apricots in front of their local McDonald's to protest U.S. sanctions on European food imports. During the past five years, McDonald's restaurants have been the targets of violent protests—including bombings—in over 50 countries, in cities including Rome, Macao, Rio de Janeiro, Prague, London, and Jakarta.

Why McDonald's? Other transnationals—notably Coca-Cola, Disney, and Pepsi—also draw the ire of anti-American demonstrators, but no other company can compete with the "Golden Arches." McDonald's is often the preferred site for anti-American demonstrations even in places where the local embassies are easy to get at. McDonald's is more than a purveyor of food; it is a saturated symbol for everything that environmentalists, protectionists, and anticapitalist activists find objectionable about American culture. McDonald's even stands out in the physical landscape, marked by its distinctive double-arched logo and characteristic design. Like the Stars and Stripes, the Big Mac stands for America.

Despite the symbolic load it carries, McDonald's can hardly be held responsible for the wholesale subversion of local cuisines, as its many critics claim. In China's larger cities, traditional specialties are supported by middle-class connoisseurs who treat eating out as a hobby and a diversion. Beijing's food scene today is a gourmet's paradise compared to the grim days of Maoist egalitarianism, when China's public canteens gave real meaning to the term "industrialized food." Party leaders may have enjoyed haute cuisine on the sly, but for most people, eating extravagantly was a counterrevolutionary crime. During the 1960s, refugee chefs kept microregional specialties alive in the back streets of Hong Kong and Taipei, where Panyu-style seafood, Shandong noodles, and Shunde vegetarian delights could be had at less than a dollar a head. Today, many Cantonese and Taiwanese lament the old refugees' retirement and complain that no one has carried on their culinary traditions; the chefs' own children, of course, have become brokers, lawyers, and professors.

Meanwhile, there has been an explosion of exotic new cuisines in China's cities: Thai, Malaysian, Indonesian, French, Spanish, Nepali, Mexican, and Hong Kong's latest hit, Louisiana creole. Chinese-style restaurants must now compete with these "ethnic" newcomers in a vast smorgasbord. The arrival of fast food is only one dimension of a much larger Chinese trend toward the culinary adventurism associated with rising affluence.

McDonald's has not been entirely passive, as demonstrated by its successful promotion of American-style birthday parties. Some try to tag McDonald's as a polluter and exploiter, but most Chinese consumers see the company as a force for the improvement of urban life. Clean toilets were a welcome development in cities where, until recently, a visit to a public restroom could be harrowing. The chain's preoccupation with cleanliness has raised consumer expectations and forced competitors to provide equally clean facilities. Ray Kroc, the legendary founder of McDonald's, was once asked if he had actually scrubbed out toilets during the early years of his franchise: "You're damn right I did," he shot back, "and I'd clean one today if it needed it." In a 1993 interview, Daniel Ng described his early efforts to import the Kroc ethos to his Hong Kong franchise. After an ineffectual first try, one new employee was ordered to clean the restrooms again. The startled worker replied that the toilets were already cleaner than the collective facilities he used at home. Ng told him that standards at McDonald's were higher and ordered him to do it again.

Another innovation is the line, a social institution that is seldom appreciated until it collapses. When McDonald's opened in Hong Kong, customers clumped around the cash registers, pushing their money over the heads of the people ahead of them—standard procedure in local train stations, banks, and cinemas. McDonald's management appointed an employee (usually a young woman) to act as queue monitor, and within a few months, regular consumers began to enforce the system themselves by glaring at newcomers who had the effrontery to jump ahead. Today the line is an accepted feature of Hong Kong's middle-class culture, and it is making headway in Beijing and Shanghai. Whether or not McDonald's deserves the credit for this particular innovation, many East Asian consumers associate the "Golden Arches" with public civility.

★ **HAVE IT YOUR WAY**

At first glance, McDonald's appears to be the quintessential transnational, with its own corporate culture nurtured at Hamburger University in Oak Brook, Illinois. But James Cantalupo, the president of McDonald's Corporation, maintains that his strategy is to become as much a part of local culture as possible and protests when people call McDonald's a multinational or a transnational. "I like to call us multilocal," he told *The Christian Science Monitor* in 1991. McDonald's goes out of its way to find local suppliers whenever it enters a new market. In China, for instance, the company nurtures its own network of russet-potato growers to provide french fries of the requisite length. McDonald's has also learned to rely on self-starters like Daniel Ng to run its foreign franchises—with minimal interference from Oak Brook. Another winning strategy, evident everywhere in East Asia, is promoting promising young "crew" (behind-the-counter) workers into management's ranks. Surprisingly few managers are dispatched from the Illinois headquarters. Yan found only one American, a Chinese-speaker, on McDonald's Beijing management team.

Critics of the fast-food industry assume that corporations always call the shots and that consumers have little choice but to accept what is presented to them. In fact, the process of localization is a two-way street, involving changes in the local culture as well as modifications of the company's standard mode of operation.

The hallmark of the American fast-food business is the displacement of labor costs from the corporation to consumers. For the system to work, consumers must be educated—or "disciplined"—so that they voluntarily fulfill their side of an implicit bargain: we (the corporation) will provide cheap, fast service if you (the customer) carry your own tray, seat yourself, eat quickly, help clean up afterward, and depart promptly to make room for others. Try breaking this contract in Boston or Pittsburgh by spreading out your newspaper and starting to work on a crossword puzzle in McDonald's. You will soon be ousted—politely in Pittsburgh, less so in Boston.

Key elements of McDonald's pan-national system—notably lining up and self-seating—have been readily accepted by consumers throughout East Asia. Other aspects of the Oak Brook model have been rejected, especially those relating to time and space. In Hong Kong, Taipei, and Beijing, consumers have turned their neighborhood restaurants into leisure centers for seniors and after-school clubs for students. Here, "fast" refers to the delivery of food, not its consumption.

Between 3:00 and 5:30 P.M. on Hong Kong weekdays, McDonald's restaurants are invaded by armies of young people in school uniforms. They buy a few fries, pour them out on a tray for communal snacking, and sit for at least an hour—gossiping, studying, and flirting. During the midmorning hours, the restaurants are packed with white-haired retirees who stay even longer, drinking tea or coffee (free refills for senior citizens) and lingering over pancake breakfasts. Many sit alone, reading newspapers provided by the management. Both retirees and students are attracted by the roomy tables, good light, and air-conditioning—a combination not easily found in Hong Kong, Beijing, or Shanghai. In effect, local citizens have appropriated private property and converted it into public space.

The process of localization correlates closely to the maturation of a generation of local people who grew up eating fast food. By the time the children of these pioneer consumers entered the scene, McDonald's was an unremarkable feature of the local landscape. Parents see the restaurants as havens for their school-age children: smoking is banned and (in China and Hong Kong) no alcohol is served, effectively eliminating drugs and gangs. McDonald's has become so local that Hong Kong's youth cannot imagine life without it.

Everyone has heard the story: Japanese little leaguers tour California and spot a McDonald's, whereupon they marvel that America also has Japanese food. Such anecdotes are not apocryphal. The children of visiting colleagues from Taiwan and South Korea were overjoyed when they saw a McDonald's near their temporary homes in the Boston suburbs: "Look! They have our kind of food here," one eight-year-old Korean exclaimed. The stories also work within East Asia: last year, Joe Bosco, an anthropologist at the Chinese University of Hong Kong, took several of his students to Taipei for a study tour. After a week of eating Taiwanese restaurant food, Bosco's charges began to complain that they missed home-style cooking. "Okay," Bosco said, "where do you want to eat tonight?" The students all said, "McDonald's!"

★ NEXT TO GODLINESS

In China's increasingly affluent cities, parents now worry more about what their children eat outside the home. Rumors frequently sweep through Beijing and Shanghai with the same story line: migrants from the countryside set up a roadside stall selling *youtiar*, deep-fried dough sticks eaten with rice gruel for breakfast. To expand the batter, they add industrial detergent to the mix, creating a powerful poison that kills everyone who eats it. Families of the deceased rush back to the scene to discover that the stall has disappeared; the local police are more interested in silencing the survivors than pursuing the culprits. Such stories are, of course, unverifiable, but they carry a "truth" that resists official denials, much like urban legends in the United States. Last summer's food scare in Belgium over dioxin-laced eggs and the recent British mad-cow fiasco were well covered in the Chinese media, feeding the anxieties of urbanites with no reliable system of consumer protection.

McDonald's appeals to China's new elites because its food is safe, clean, and reliable. Western intellectuals may scoff at McDonald's for its unrelenting monotony, but in many parts of the world (including China) this is precisely what consumers find so attractive. Why else would competitors go to such extremes to imitate McDonald's? In Beijing one can find fast-food restaurants with names such as McDucks, Mcdonald's, and Mordornal. In Shanghai a local chain called Nancy's Express used a sign with one leg of the double arches missing, forming an "N." Another popular chain of noodle shops, called Honggaoliang (Red sorghum), advertises itself with a large "H" that bears an uncanny resemblance to the "Golden Arches." All over China, competitors dress their staff in McDonald's-style uniforms and decorate their restaurants in yellow. Corporate mascots inspired by Ronald McDonald—clowns, ducks, cowboys, cats, hamburger figures, mythic heroes, and chickens—parade along the sidewalks of Chinese cities. Local fast-food chains frequently engage in public exhibitions of cleanliness: one worker mops the floors and polishes the windows, all day long, every day. The cleaners usually restrict their efforts to the entryway, where the performance can best be seen by passersby.

★ SO LONELY

During McDonald's first three years in China, Communist Party officials could barely restrain their enthusiasm over this new model of modernization, hygiene, and responsible management. By 1996, however, media enthusiasm cooled as state authorities began to promote an indigenous fast-food industry based on noodles, barbecued meats, soups, and rice pots. Now that McDonald's, Kentucky Fried Chicken, and Pizza Hut had shown the way, party officials reasoned, local chains should take over the mass market. (No such chain has seriously challenged McDonald's, but a Shanghai-based restaurateur has fought a much-reported "battle of the chickens" with KFC.)

Meanwhile, China faces yet another family revolution, this one caused by the graying of the population. In 1998, 10 percent of China's people were over 60; by 2020, the figure is expected to rise to approximately 16 percent. In 2025, there will be 274 million people over 60 in China—more than the entire 1998 U.S. population. Since Beijing has made few provisions for a modern social-security system, the implications are profound. The locus of consumer power will soon shift generations as the parents of today's little emperors retire. Unlike the current generation of retirees—the survivors of Maoism—China's boomers will not be content with 1950s-level pensions, and they cannot expect their children to support them. Like their counterparts in the American Association of Retired Persons, future retirees in China are likely to be a vociferous, aggressive lot who will demand more state resources.

355

So what will happen to child-centered industries? If its experience in Hong Kong is any guide, McDonald's will survive quite handily as a welcoming retreat from the isolation and loneliness of urban life. The full ramifications of China's single-child policy will not be felt for another 20 years. Having one grandchild for every four grandparents is a recipe for social anomie on a truly massive scale. The consequences of China's demographic time bomb can already be seen on the streets of Hong Kong, where the family began to shrink decades ago. Tens of thousands of retirees roam Hong Kong's air-conditioned shopping malls, congregate in the handful of overcrowded parks, and turn their local McDonald's during the midmorning hours into a substitute for the public gardens, opera theaters, and ancestral halls that sheltered their parents. What stands out at McDonald's is the isolation among Hong Kong elders as they try to entertain themselves. Americans may be bowling alone and worrying about the decline of family life, but in early 21st-century Hong Kong, no one even seems concerned about the emergence of a civil society that ignores the elderly.

★ WHOSE CULTURE IS IT, ANYWAY?

Is McDonald's leading a crusade to create a homogenous, global culture that suits the needs of an advanced capitalist world order? Not really. Today's economic and social realities demand an entirely new approach to global issues that takes consumers' perspectives into account. The explanatory device of "cultural imperialism" is little more than a warmed-over version of the neo-Marxist dependency theories that were popular in the 1960s and 1970s—approaches that do not begin to capture the complexity of today's emerging transnational systems.

The deeper one digs into the personal lives of consumers anywhere, the more complex matters become. People are not the automatons many theorists make them out to be. Hong Kong's discerning consumers have most assuredly not been stripped of their cultural heritage, nor have they become the uncomprehending dupes of transnational corporations.

In places like Hong Kong, it is increasingly difficult to see where the transnational ends and the local begins. Fast food is an excellent case in point: for the children who flock to weekend birthday parties, McDonald's is self-evidently local. Similarly, the Hong Kong elders who use McDonald's as a retreat from the loneliness of urban life could care less about the company's foreign origin. Hong Kong's consumers have made the "Golden Arches" their own.

One might also turn the lens around and take a close look at American society as it enters a new millennium. Chinese food is everywhere, giving McDonald's and KFC a run for their money in such unlikely settings as Moline and Memphis. Mandarin is fast becoming a dominant language in American research laboratories, and Chinese films draw ever more enthusiastic audiences. Last Halloween, every other kid in my Cambridge neighborhood appeared in (Japanese-inspired) Power Ranger costumes, striking poses that owe more to Bruce Lee than to Batman. Whose culture is it, anyway? If you have to ask, you have already missed the boat.

REFERENCES

Bestor, Theodore C. 2000. "How Sushi Went Global." *Foreign Policy*, Nov.–Dec. 2000, pp. 54–63.
Davis, Deborah (ed.) 2000. *The Consumer Revolution in China*. Berkely: University of California Press.

China's Big Mac Attack

Friedman, Thomas L. 2000. *The Lexus and the Olive Tree*. New York: Anchor Books.

Guo, Yuhua. "Family Relations: The Generation Gap at the Table." In Jun Jing (ed.) *Feeding China's Little Emporers: Food, Children, and Social Change*. Stanford: Stanford University Press, pp. 94–113.

Charlotte, Ikels. 1993. "Settling Accounts: The Intergenerational Contract in an Era of Reform." In Deborah Davis and Stevan Harrell (eds.) *Chinese Families in the Post-Mao Era*. Berkeley: University of California Press, pp. 307–333.

Jing, Jun (ed.) 2000. *Feeding China's Little Emperors: Food, Children and Social Change*. Stanford: Stanford University Press.

Love, John F. 1995. *McDonald's: Behind the Arches* (revised edition). New York: Bantam. (See, especially, chapter on Exporting Americana, pp. 410–448.)

Lozada, Eriberto. 2000. "Globalized Childhood? Kentucky Fried Chicken in Beijing." In Jun Jing (ed.) *Feeding China's Little Emperors: Food, Children and Social Change*. Stanford: Stanford University Press, pp. 114–134.

Peterson, Peter G. "Gray Dawn: The Global Aging Crisis." *Foreign Affairs*, 78:1, pp. 42–55.

Ritzer, George. 1993. *The McDonaldization of Society*. Thousand Oaks, CA: Pine Forge Press.

Tomlinson, John. 1991. *Cultural Imperialism*. Baltimore: Johns Hopkins University Press.

Watson, James L. 1997. "McDonald's in Hong Kong: Consumerism, Dietary Change and the Rise of a Children's Culture." In James L. Watson (ed.) *Golden Arches East: McDonald's in East Asia*. Stanford: Stanford University Press, pp. 77–109.

Watson, James L. (ed.) 1997. *Golden Arches East: McDonald's in East Asia*. Stanford: Stanford University Press.

Yan, Yunxiang. 1997. "McDonald's in Beijing: The Localization of Americana". In James L. Watson (ed.) *Golden Arches East: McDonald's in East Asia*. Stanford: Stanford University Press, pp. 39–76.

NAFTA AND BASIC FOOD PRODUCTION:
DEPENDENCY AND MARGINALIZATION
ON BOTH SIDES OF THE US/MEXICO
BORDER

27

JAMES H. MCDONALD

The Conasupo imported 2,552 tons of powdered milk from Ireland in order to supplement the domestic market where demand is not met by Mexican dairy producers. [Excélsior, November 18, 1991]

There have been a number of conflicts such as with the farmers in La Chona and Lagos de Moreno, Jalisco who dumped thousands of liters of milk in order to demand a price increase, and to protest the excessive purchases of [imported] powdered milk. [Excélsior, November 21, 1991]

Almost all countries subsidize their principal agricultural products (grains, oilseed, dairy products and sugar).... If no compensation were given, their products would be at a disadvantage vis-á-vis producers in countries who do receive such... In 1987, help to the Mexican domestic agricultural sector diminished notably, both for inputs (loans, fertilizers, pesticides, fuel) as well as for guaranteed prices. [BANAMEX 1991:449–451]

All the subsidies have been removed from agricultural production in Mexico, but not in the United States or Europe. [Excélsior, November 19, 1991]

★ INTRODUCTION

There has been considerable speculation concerning the effects of the North American Free Trade Agreement (NAFTA) on agriculture in both the U.S. and Mexico. We already have a window onto some of the short-term effects on domestic and export production in Mexico, where the federal government led by President Carlos Salinas de Gortari has removed subsidies and support for the agricultural sector over the past two years. In anticipation of NAFTA, the Mexican government has made a number of important agricultural policy decisions that signal a radical shift away from agrarian populism (e.g., heavy subsidies for domestic and export production and support of the *ejido*—peasant farm communities that were created as part of the land reform and redistribution mandated in Article 27 of the 1917 Mexican Constitution) and towards privatization and a reliance on market forces to support Mexican agriculture (Stanford 1991, n.d.). In 1992, the Mexican government revised Article 27 of the Constitution, privatizing *ejido* lands and allowing these communities to enter into financial agreements with outside developers to bring their land and resources into commercial production (see Collier 1994). In short, the Mexican government is no longer in the agriculture business and is placing any hope for the survival of the domestic and export production sectors on foreign investment and the free market.

360

Debt is a source of new relations of dependency between the U.S. and Mexico, and NAFTA is a further institutionalization of those relations. As Barkin et al. (1990) and others contend, Mexican and international agricultural policies have shaped the transformation of agriculture since the 1960s away from basic food crops toward increasing specialization in export and luxury crops. In Mexico, consumer-oriented agricultural policies have resulted in low retail prices for basic foods, which complemented the low wages earned by urban workers. A general trend from the 1960s through the 1980s in low market prices discouraged the expansion of basic food production and, in many cases, resulted in decreased production as farmers produce for their subsistence only (Barkin et al. 1990:110–111).

The first portion of this essay considers the transformation of Mexican agriculture by examining how NAFTA and related policy changes will affect domestic commercial production, especially the dairy industry. In the complex economic trade-offs that are made in the negotiation of international trade agreements, there are indicators that the Mexican government has sacrificed agriculture, especially the production of basic domestic food crops, to foreign import substitution. The confluence of rising costs of production through inflation[1] in conjunction with recent policy changes that withdraw subsidies for basic food crop production has resulted in a sharp drop in basic food production (Appendini n.d., Barkin 1987, Barkin et al. 1990, Stanford 1991, n.d.). One implication is that Mexico will be dependent on the U.S., Europe, Canada, and elsewhere for much of its basic food production. U.S. food exports to Mexico have the potential to be a major U.S. political bargaining chip to ensure that Mexico does not stray far from U.S. interests. Thus, food and politics have the potential to merge under NAFTA.

There are major human/social costs involved with the transformation of the Mexican agrarian landscape as well. Of the estimated 2.3 to 3 million maize farmers in Mexico, between 850,000 and 1.25 million of them will be forced off the land and into already clogged urban centers—or into the U.S. in search of jobs (*El Financiero* 1993, Darling 1992, Calva 1991, Barkin 1987). Consequently, NAFTA will have a direct effect on levels of human suffering, dislocation, and social stability in Mexico.

The second portion of this essay deals with the reaction to NAFTA by U.S. dairy farmers who would, on the surface, appear to benefit from the agreement (or at least not be directly threatened by it) (AFB 1992, USDA 1993, CBO 1993, USITC 1993). Yet, their response has been for the most part stridently negative. I will argue that while NAFTA will potentially benefit the dairy industry as a whole, it may also stimulate the further centralization of dairy production, squeezing out the small-scale producer whose control of this sector has been eroding steadily over the past 15 years. The implementation of NAFTA, then, will further contribute to the destruction of a once-dynamic, small-scale agricultural production sector. This, in turn, could result in the devastation of rural areas of the U.S., including Michigan and other parts of the midwest, whose infrastructure is linked to a local, small-scale dairy industry (see Fitchen 1991).

★ COLLAPSING AGRICULTURAL PRODUCTION IN MEXICO

It is now widely accepted that Mexican agriculture, with the exception of a few production sectors focusing on the export of tropical fruits and vegetables, will be adversely affected by NAFTA. The limitations set by agrarian policy, technology, and the natural resource base make Mexican agriculture uncompetitive on the international market.

361

Even the traditionally lucrative tropical fruit export production has fared poorly under Mexico's recent agricultural reforms. Stanford (1991:73), for example, describes the effects of privatization on cantaloupe production in the humid lowlands of Apatzingán, Michoacán, which historically produced 40–60 percent of the export cantaloupe crop destined for the U.S. Between 1987 and 1990, export production dropped dramatically. During the 1987–88 growing season, 3,145 ha (hectares) of cantaloupe were harvested but only 2,023 ha in 1989-90, a loss of 36 percent. This decline in production is reflected in the volume of export from that region: in 1987–88, 1,616,583 crates[2] of cantaloupe were shipped to the U.S. while only 867,579 crates were exported during 1989–90, a 46 percent drop (Stanford n.d.:9–10).[3] It was hoped that foreign investment would fill the void left by the absence of capital and credit provided by the Mexican government. Unfortunately, this was not the case. Mexican capital is targeted almost exclusively at the importation of basic foods, and foreign capital has not yet entered into the Mexican agricultural sector as expected. Stanford's (1991, n.d.) research highlights the fact that once-prosperous and viable export production sectors are faltering.

The situation becomes even more critical when we turn specifically to the domestic production sector. Barkin (1987), for example, argues that Mexico is importing billions of dollars of basic foods while its own fields stand idle (also see Sosa 1990:43 for detailed figures for the importation of maize, soy, sorghum, and wheat). There has been a trend, supported by Mexican agrarian policies since the 1960s, to produce profitable crops (i.e., high-profit cash crops for the domestic and international markets) rather than necessary staple foods.

Mexico is faced with the dilemma of supporting its underpaid urban wage workers with low-cost food. Rather than grow it, they have maintained a policy of food import substitution. To take one example, cheap powdered milk imports increased 492 percent between 1966 and 1981 (McDonald 1991:305) and 35.5 percent during 1987–88 alone (Sosa 1990:43). Imported powdered milk can be purchased by Mexican milk processors for 25 to 30 percent less than fresh domestically produced milk (AFB 1992:108). As a result, the price of fresh milk has been driven down substantially, to the point where farmers were again dumping milk in Spring 1993 to protest government import substitution policies. Low prices for basic food crops destined for the domestic market provides an inducement to grow higher-profit, nonbasic cash crops for export or domestic elite consumption.

The vulnerability of the domestic production sector is further reflected in recent research by Barkin (1987), Barkin et al. (1990), Collier (1990), Sosa (1990), Appendini (1992, n.d.), Calva (1991), Suárez (n.d.), and Hewitt de Alcántara (1992). Each researcher notes a sizeable drop in basic food crop production throughout Mexico. According to Calva (1991:30–31), for example, between 1982 and 1988 the maize production fell nationally by 43 percent while bean production dropped over 50 percent. The reason for these declines is simple. It costs the average Mexican maize farmer twice as much as a U.S. farmer in per unit production (Darling 1992, Saxe-Fernández 1991). Mexican Secretary of Agriculture and Hydraulic Resources Carlos Hank González noted in 1991 that Mexican producers received a guaranteed price of $200 U.S. dollars per ton for maize, while the international market price was $100/ton (Sepúlveda Ibarra 1991). In August 1993, the guaranteed price for maize was $250/ton, while the international market price was $150/ton. Mexican farmers produce the same amount of maize on 7.7 million ha of land as U.S. farmers produce on 2 million ha, roughly one-quarter of the production of their U.S. counterparts (*El Financiero* 1993).[4] There is a similar story for bean production. In 1991, the Mexican guaranteed price for beans was $600 dollars/ton versus the international market price of $300/ton (Sepúlveda Ibarra 1991), leading Scott (1992:10) to note that "Mexican bean farmers harvest about one-third as much per acre as U.S. farmers. Thus, growing a ton of beans costs almost three times as much in Mexico as in the U.S."

The gap between the Mexican guaranteed price for maize and beans and the international price reflects the heavy subsidies and technology available to farmers in the U.S., Canada, and Europe and the high costs of domestic production in Mexico. Finan et al. (1990:699) show that in countries where small-scale farms predominate, policies supporting production subsidies are essential for their viability and expansion by helping small-scale farmers stay competitive with larger producers. Without subsidies, Mexican farmers will not survive the onslaught of competition from U.S. and other foreign producers. In fact, Calva (1991) projects a Mexican agricultural trade deficit with the U.S. of 6 billion dollars over the next 10 years. This figure is based on a projected U.S. agricultural trade increase of 10 billion dollars, compared with only a 3 billion dollar increase for Mexico, over 10 years (Calva 1991).

Three other factors also contributed to this crisis in Mexican production according to Calva (1991:31): (1) a 17 percent decline in fertilizer use, (2) decline in the number of tractors in use, and (3) a drop in pesticide application from 1985 to 1989. These final factors reflect spiraling inflation resulting in the rising costs of agricultural production—an increase of 18,410 percent between 1980 and 1990 according to the most recent figures released by the Banco de México (1990:104).

Domestic producers are further squeezed by other factors including rising inflation and a shrinking market associated with an approximately 60 percent decline in Mexican consumer buying power between 1982 and 1991 (McDonald 1993b:113). Between 1982 and 1988 alone, the buying power of the average Mexican worker declined over 50 percent (Reding 1989:688). Suárez (n.d.:15) documents a steep decline in domestic consumption over roughly the same period from 1979 to 1989, closely tied to the decline of consumer buying power: 8.9 percent for beans, 19.3 percent for eggs and beef, 33.2 percent for tortillas, and 78.3 percent for milk and cheese. The American Farm Bureau also reports a drop in Mexican fresh milk consumption of nearly 50 percent between 1983 and 1988 (AFB 1992:104).

362

A number of other systemic factors also contribute to the collapse of domestic production in Mexico, as outlined by Calva (1991). Funding for research and extension services dropped 60 percent between 1982 and 1989. In 1981, for example, 355,481 tons of certified high-yield seed was produced in Mexico, and 600,000 tons were projected by 1989. Instead, the tonnage actually dropped to 279,503 by 1989. This drop translates to 3 million ha planted with certified seed in 1982 versus 2 million ha in 1989.

★ THE MEXICAN DAIRY INDUSTRY

The Mexican dairy industry is especially hard hit by the declining economy and rising inflation. Milk has never been an important staple in the Mexican diet, even though it figured into government efforts to raise general levels of nutrition during the 1970s. In the late 1970s, an estimated nearly 90 percent of Mexico's rural population experienced some caloric and protein malnutrition and about half of that group experienced severe malnutrition (Barkin 1987:286). Fueled by the profits from the oil boom, Mexico attempted to make nutritious, high-protein foods such as fresh and powdered milk available to its undernourished rural and urban populations. Over the past 30 years, consumption of dairy products has increased considerably and domestic production has not met this demand for the past 15 to 20 years (McDonald 1991). Nevertheless, the recent drop in dairy consumption by almost 80 percent reflects the fact that milk and cheese are still luxury foods for most people in Mexico and are, thus, the first to be discarded when economic times get tough.

Milk has also never been a lucrative, high-profit product. In fact, milk has consistently lagged behind other staple foods in terms of its profitability (the gap between cost of production and the government mandated cap on wholesale and retail prices) (McDonald 1991). Dairying was not so much a highly remunerative form of production in the 1960s and 1970s as it was a conservative and predictable one in an expanding market. Under stable economic conditions, dairy farmers could easily predict their weekly and monthly profits. In addition, they had cash flow based on the daily sale of their product. Under unstable and inflationary economic conditions, though, dairy farming takes on an altogether different guise. Farmers are saddled with sizeable investments in fixed capital and cannot respond quickly to market changes. Many dairy farmers are sitting on large, fixed capital investments in cattle, machinery, and buildings that are useful only for dairying. Farmers have responded nationally by selling a portion of their herds, but as the economy worsened, it became increasingly difficult to find buyers who were willing to pay a fair market price. (Farmers could sell their cattle for slaughter, of course, but they would do so at a considerable loss.) By 1991, dairy farmers in my field research area in central Mexico had begun selling off their farms altogether at significant losses, and there is no sign that this trend will abate (Jaramillo 1991, McDonald 1991).

There has been some investment of foreign capital in the domestic food processing sector, but not in direct production. In October 1992, for example, a joint Canadian/Mexican dairy project purchased the Ayucan dairy plant in the state of Veracruz. This plant, now known as La Llanura, has the capacity to produce 550,000 liters per day, but currently processes around 40,000 liters of fresh milk and 150,000 liters of powdered milk per day (*Notimex* 1992). Interest in the control of food processing on the part of foreign capital is not surprising since this is an area that offers potentially high profits and relatively less risk than direct production. Therefore, the strategy of foreign capital is long-term and investment is being made with the assumption of greater consumer demand and buying power over the next 10 to 15 years.[5] The short-term survival of many dairy farmers is questionable, however, as they face the risk of inflating production costs in an unstable economy.

In sum, although there is some limited indication of foreign investment in the Mexican dairy sector, that investment appears to center on the food processing industry rather than on direct production. We can draw two conclusions from this investment pattern. First, foreign investment is targeting the highest profit area of the domestic dairy industry, while leaving the farmer to absorb all the risks of production. Second, foreign capital is investing in an area that has traditionally marketed to the Mexican elite, who have grown accustomed to consuming processed yogurt, cheese, milk, and ice cream.[6] Overall, the short- and long-term prospects for the domestic dairy industry appear quite discouraging from the perspective of the Mexican dairy farmer. These two factors have prompted many U.S. analysts to suggest potential benefits for the U.S. dairy industry, which will easily out-compete its Mexican counterpart, especially as the general collapse of the Mexican domestic dairy production sector appears imminent (AFB 1992, Darling 1992).

364

★ DAIRY FARMING IN MICHIGAN AND THE FEAR OF NAFTA

In Michigan as elsewhere in the U.S., farmers are concerned about the impact of NAFTA on their livelihood. Farming is the number two industry in the state, behind automobile manufacturing, generating 37.5 billion dollars annually (Foren 1992). Some labor-intensive agricultural sectors in the state fear the competition of Mexico's export agricultural sector, which has access to a large and inexpensive labor pool. Michigan farmers producing asparagus and sugar beets cannot afford to shift to mechanized harvesting to lower their costs (Foren 1992). Dry bean growers in Michigan, on the other hand, produce one-third of the total U.S. bean exports to Mexico, and they anticipate greater export potential as the Mexican domestic agricultural sector collapses (Foren 1992).[7]

Michigan dairy production ranks seventh nationally, just behind Texas which has a significantly larger dairy heard (MASS 1992:55). Dairy farmers here and elsewhere are solidly opposed to NAFTA. On the surface, this opposition would appear to be a counterintuitive response. Most sources see NAFTA providing at least some benefit to the U.S. dairy industry (AFB 1992, USITC 1993, USDA 1993, CBO 1993).[8] Additionally, the Mexican dairy industry has always been small and relatively weak. Furthermore, it has never been able to meet the historically rising demand for milk products (McDonald 1991). Even if the Mexican dairy industry were able to maintain its current levels of production, U.S. farmers apparently would be well positioned to take advantage of a market with so much potentially unmet demand. U.S. dairy farm lobbyists contend that their product is currently competitive on the world market but requires subsidies to remain so. Furthermore, they claim that U.S. dairies will relocate to Mexico and flood the market with inexpensively processed dairy products (*Flint Journal* 1992). As one Michigan dairy farmer expressed his fears, "It hurts me to say it, but dairy farmers make a living off of other peoples' problems. The export of dairy products can only thrive when there is trouble else-where in the global dairy industry, because we produce far too much for the domes-tic market. But I don't know about the free trade agreement. Dairy processors may just relocate to Mexico and leave us behind."

The fears of lost subsidies and industrial relocation speak more to trends in the global economy than to NAFTA itself. The first concern about subsidies seems directed more toward the current negotiations with the European Community, which maintains high levels of subsidy for its farmers than with Mexico, which has removed virtually all subsidies from its agricultural production (Calva 1991, McDonald 1991). While the U.S. has reduced many of its subsidies, there is little indi-cation that all will be removed as Mexico has done. Nevertheless, the lowering of U.S. subsidies through NAFTA negotiations does make U.S. farmers less competitive with their more heavily subsidized European counterparts who have historically been major suppliers of cheap powdered milk to Mexico (McDonald 1991, AFB 1992:114).

The second concern speaks more directly to the shift in processing and manu-facturing that opponents of NAFTA claim will occur as U.S. industries take advan-tage of cheap Mexican labor. These fears, I will argue, are attached to broader polit-ical-economic processes that favor the centralization of agricultural production, whether it is in the U.S. or Mexico. The resistance of dairy farmers to NAFTA has more to do with these processes, in other words, than with NAFTA itself. For dairy farmers, NAFTA has become a convenient way of articulating the struggle between small and large capital.

Dairy farming is one of the last arenas of agrarian struggle between small and large capital in the U.S. (McDonald 1993a). There is a powerful trend in the dairy industry away from small-scale, family farming toward large-scale, corporate dairies. This shift has had a devastating impact on states where the family farm has traditionally been the backbone of dairy production. In Wisconsin, Minnesota, and New York, the multiplier effect of dairy farm closings on local infrastructures (e.g., small businesses, the tax base, health care) has impoverished rural communities (Manchester 1983, Fitchen 1991, Schminkle 1992). These traditional dairy states will be replaced by California, Texas, and Florida as the major producers (Schminkle 1992). The shift to corporate dairies in the southeast and southwest in part reflects shifting population centers in the U.S. However, it also reflects federal agricultural tax codes that were in place prior to the 1986 Tax Reform Act, and which favored large-scale expansion of dairy and other agribusinesses (Strange 1989:154–156). Prior to 1986, investors could deduct farm losses from the profits gained through unrelated, outside business ventures (McDonald 1993a:26, Young and Newton 1980:157). Additionally, it was also possible to receive large tax breaks as an incen-tive for the construction buildings and investment in other large, fixed capital items. The 1986 agricultural tax code reforms have taken away some of the tax-based incentives encouraging the formation of corporate dairies. Nevertheless, Strange (1989:160) notes that those tax reforms were not complete and still encouraged tax-motivated investment through the continuation of corporate tax rates, cash accounting procedures, capital gains, investment tax credit, and accelerated depre-ciation, all of which favor agribusiness. Furthermore, President Bill Clinton is already suggesting that he may reinstate investment tax credits similar to those in the pre-1986 agricultural tax code. These proposed changes by Clinton will have the effect of undermining family farms by providing tax credits for investments that expand farm size, further intensify production, and the like (Hassebrook 1993).

These corporate dairy farms are unlike any we have known. Typically, small-scale capitalist operations, whether in the U.S. or Mexico, have 50–75 cows and attempt to be relatively self-sufficient in labor and feed for their animals (McDonald 1991, Borton et al. 1990:9). The corporate dairy may have 1,000 cows and employ management techniques that are so sophisticated that cows produce well above the national average of 14,500 pounds of milk per year.[9] These farms not only have higher yielding cattle, but they also take advantage of economies of scale. Consequently, they produce more milk for less money than their small-scale counterparts. Not surprisingly, one out of every three U.S. dairy farms shut down its business during the 1980s, translating into the closure of 21,000 dairy farms in Minnesota and Wisconsin in that period (Schminkle 1992:C4). Control of the dairy industry is being concentrated into fewer, larger-scale operations, a trend already well established in most other farming sectors (Browne et al. 1992:20).

While rarely clearly articulated as such, it appears that dairy farmers are making a conceptual linkage between NAFTA and the further concentration of dairy farming in the hands of large-scale producers. This conclusion is quite logical, if poorly clarified by these threatened farmers. If we assume that Mexican dairy producers will neither meet future increases in domestic demand nor successfully compete with U.S. producers, then there is a further source of stimulus for the creation of these new, economically efficient, large dairy operations in the states bordering Mexico (Pugh 1992:5). Thus, NAFTA may simply speed up the process of the concentration of dairy production by large capital, especially in those border states that are geographically well positioned to take advantage of new markets in Mexico.

★ CONCLUSION

Discussions of NAFTA and agriculture from a Mexican perspective commonly focus on two themes: export production and the future of the *ejido*. Little attention is placed on the effects of NAFTA on the commercial domestic production of basic foods in Mexico outside of the *ejidal* context. This inattention is due in large part, as Luiselli (1989:91) notes, to the structure of the discourse on development in Mexico: "The right in Mexico, the political right, the academic right, wants to present the agrarian problem as one of the *ejidos* versus private property: the inefficient socialist utopia in the *ejido* versus the efficient family farm."

The political and academic left has spent equal amounts of energy defending the *ejido* and examining in detail the loss of food production and self-sufficiency in Mexico, especially in terms of maize and bean production (Appendini 1992, Barkin 1987, 1990, Hewitt de Alcántara 1992, McDonald 1993b). What has been created is in many ways a false debate. What is critical is that we examine NAFTA and agricultural privatization as it affects different agrarian sectors, regions, and forms of land tenure at the local level.

I have argued that NAFTA is a further institutionalization of dependency relations that will result in the collapse of the domestic private, commercial production sector in Mexico. These trends are already firmly in place as a result of new agricultural policies, instituted by the Salinas government, that emphasize privatization and a reliance on foreign capital to fund the agricultural sector. As a result, thousands of hectares of formerly productive land have already been left fallow by farmers who cannot farm at a profit or find credit (Barkin 1987, Sosa 1990, Suárez n.d., Stanford 1991, n.d.). These trends threaten Mexico's very sovereignty by making it completely dependent on foreign, and especially U.S., food production.

While NAFTA further crystallizes relations of dependency between the U.S. and Mexico, it also threatens to forge similar kinds of relations in the rural U.S. It does so by further stimulating the concentration of wealth, power, and production, thus impoverishing large areas of rural America by putting small-scale farmers out of business. The ensuing multiplier effect of small farm collapse on rural business and other infrastructures further plunges rural areas into a marginal, dependent status (Fitchen 1991). Consequently, whether NAFTA stimulates an actual shift in dairy production to Mexico or the U.S. southeast and southwest, is really a moot point for the dairy farmers in the upper midwest, who already are being forced out of business. NAFTA, thus, supports the further economic colonization of Mexico, but ironically, it also stimulates similar processes in parts of the rural U.S.

If we take the perspective of institutional economics, further implications can be drawn from these data. The new agrarian reforms in Mexico may, in fact, have similar effects on both *ejidal* and small-scale commercial farmers. The revisions of Article 27 permit communities to privatize their holdings and allow individual property holders to sharecrop, rent, mortgage or sell their land, as well as enter into a number of different types of joint ventures with outside investors (see Collier 1994). Thus, the *ejidos* (especially those with richer sets of natural resources) will be privatized and come to have a land tenure structure similar to that of already private, small-scale commercial family farms.

Christy and Vandeveer (1989:293) note, for example, "that different institutional arrangements enable different structures of property rights." As the institutional context in which farms exist changes, so do individual farmer's decisions about what and when to plant, whether to sell or lease their land, and so on. If we turn to the agricultural sector as a whole, the economic performance may be radically altered by these new institutional arrangements. Christy and Vandeveer (1989) look at one aspect of new institutional arrangements in the U.S. in the 1980s that is strikingly similar to the current situation in Mexico: the relationship between credit availability and changing forms of farm ownership. As access to credit became increasingly constricted and reserved for only the larger U.S. farms, there was a marked shift towards sharecropping, tenant farming, and other types of joint arrangements between larger, capital-rich farms and smaller operations. An important conclusion drawn by Christy and Vandeveer (1989:293–295) is that not only did land tenure patterns shift from one characterized by full owners to one characterized by part owners, but these new sharecropping and tenant farm arrangements often led to poor, inefficient farming techniques and a decrease in productivity due to the misallocation of farm resources. Whether Mexican farmers come from former *ejidos* or existing family farms, they face institutional problems of credit access similar to those faced by U.S. family farmers in the 1980s. We must question whether these changes in agrarian policy in Mexico will not only alter the structure of land tenure in the countryside but also lead to yet further degradation of Mexico's agricultural productivity.

★ 2001 UPDATE

When this paper was originally published in 1994, Mexico had been going through a prolonged economic restructuring dating back to the economic crisis of 1982 when the country's debt, in conjunction with the crash of the world oil market, brought the country to the brink of bankruptcy. President Miguel de la Madrid (1982–1988) began to slowly institute neoliberal reforms (e.g., lowering tariffs and opening the economy to foreign competition, privatization of state-run industries, the marked reduction of spending on social welfare programs, and an overall shrinking of government) at the behest of the World Bank in order to induce that body to restructure Mexico's outstanding loans. During the administration of Carlos Salinas (1988–1994) the process of neoliberal economic reform was far more aggressively implemented, and the outlook for most agrarian sectors in Mexico was grim at best. Ernesto Zedillo (1994–2000) continued with Salinas's general neoliberal economic reforms, but his administration also showed some concern for social welfare. The Zedillo administration, for example, implemented *Alianza para el Campo* (Rural Alliance) as a mechanism to direct development money to rural farmers. Farmers were encouraged to organize and achieve greater efficiency through economies of scale. In return they would have the opportunity to receive much-needed credit and other resources. The program's success at channeling money to smaller farms has been variable from state to state—in Guanajuato it has worked reasonably well while in Michoacán money and other forms of patronage continue to go to powerful local elites with political connections (McDonald 2001). Also during the Zedillo era, states formed private NGOs (non-governmental organizations) that worked closely with government in rural development. Finally, Zedillo will be remembered as the last president in the Institutional Revolutionary Party's (PRI) 71 years of unbroken rule. Zedillo's successor, Vicente Fox (2000–2006), won the 2000 presidential election backed by the pro-business, right-wing National Action Party (PAN). All indications are that Fox will continue with the basic neoliberal policies of his PRI predecessors that include a corporate approach to rural development emphasizing government–private sector alliances along with a desire to transform small farmers into entrepreneurs (see McDonald 2001:257).

The cross-border political-economic analysis and predictions outlined in this article have, on the whole, stood up well to the test of time. This is, of course, most unfortunate for small-scale farmers on both sides of the U.S.-Mexico border. In the U.S., the dairy industry continues a process of centralization and concentration where tax structure and policy continue to overwhelmingly favor large-scale agribusiness, a long-term trend whose devastating results on rural livelihood and community were recognized early on by anthropologist Walter Goldschmidt (1947) in his groundbreaking critique of corporate agriculture. Goldschmidt's legacy can be found in a wide array of recent work on contemporary American agriculture and rural society (see, for example, Durrenberger and Thu 1998). This growing concentration of farms in the hands of increasingly fewer people is, in fact, a pronounced trend worldwide (for an excellent overview of the global restructuring of the dairy industry, see Schwarzweller and Davidson 2000).

U.S. dairy farmers' fears of competition from what we might refer to as "milk maquiladoras" in Mexico has not, however, materialized. Nevertheless, transnationals have an increasing presence in the Mexican dairy industry (e.g., Nestlé, Dannon, Parmalat), but they have focused almost exclusively on the domestic market. A lack of competitive prices in conjunction with sanitary and phytosanitary restrictions imposed by the U.S. on foreign agricultural imports have kept most Mexican dairy products out of U.S. markets. In response to being blocked from entry into the U.S. market, large commercial dairies in Mexico have recently begun to exhort farmers to produce with greater quality, efficiency, productivity, self-reliance, and the like. They realize that they will not be able to compete domestically against foreign imports, let alone on the international market, unless they are able to produce high-quality products inexpensively. This will be put to an extreme test in 2003 when all Mexican dairy tariffs will be dropped according to NAFTA provisions and U.S. dairy products will flow freely into the country.

Those new demands on farmers have come at a cost, and resulted in a marked clash between local culture and the outside forces (large commercial dairies and government officials) who seek to modernize the Mexican dairy industry. In this process, state and local relations are being reshaped in important ways. On the basis of work in the highlands of Michoacán in West-Central Mexico, which has a long-standing small-scale, peasant-like dairy economy, I have explored the changing political economy of the regional dairy industry through the concept of "quality" (McDonald 2000). I found, for example, that the owners of large dairies and government officials, as well as local farmers, have equally situated and relativistic notions of milk quality. On the one hand, new notions of milk quality have filtered down through a hierarchical web of agents to the local level. Commercial dairy owners and government staff employ a quantitative understanding of milk quality, and they value such things as a high percent of milkfat and low bacteria counts in their effort to create products competitive with those coming into Mexico from Europe, the U.S., Canada, and even Argentina, Brazil, and Costa Rica. On the other hand, local farmers have a qualitative understanding of milk quality constructed through their relationship with local cheese makers. And they claim that their milk is always of sufficient quality to make the uncooked white cheese found ubiquitously throughout the region. As a result of this clash of cultures, local farming practices, day-to-day activities, and relationships are being reconfigured; in sum, local culture, identity, and social organization are undergoing rapid change (McDonald 1999, 2000, 2001).

It is also important to consider the diversity of the Mexican dairy industry when gauging the local effects of globalization and change. García Hernández et al. (2000) note that some areas, such as the Laguna Region of Torreón, Coahuila in North-Central Mexico, have transformed rapidly and become internationally competitive with farms of similar size and technological capacity as those found anywhere in the U.S. Mexico's top dairy producing region, the Jalisco highlands in West-Central Mexico, is conversely characterized by small, low-tech farms, but has the advantage of a large commercial dairy processing industry in Guadalajara. Hence, farmers there are struggling to remain competitive as those dairies demand that they organize, enhance their efficiency, and produce "quality" milk. In the Michoacán highlands to the immediate southwest, there are none of the advantages of the previous two locales—dairy farms are small, rudimentary affairs and there is no large-scale commercial dairy processing. In Guanajuato, there are increasingly large farm operations, and during the early to mid-1990s then-Governor Vicente Fox urged farmers to organize as an antidote to global competition. And in one case with which I've worked continuously over the past 10 years, the outcome thus far has been highly successful (McDonald 1997).

In sum, the globalizing trends and their implications for small, commercial farmers that I outlined in 1994 have continued to unfold at an accelerating pace. The Mexican government does, however, seem to have realized that unbridled market forces have devastated its agricultural sector, and government has stepped back in with some new forms of support designed to help farmers transition into a new global economy. On the U.S. side, the government provides far greater support to its farming sectors than does Mexico. Yet, the loss of small farms goes unabated, though some still hold out muted optimism in the adaptive flexibility of family-run dairy operations in such hard-hit areas as the Upper Midwest (Jackson-Smith and Barham 2000). Overall, however, as Mexican tariff barriers fall in 2003 for most agricultural products per the NAFTA accord, small-scale dairy farmers on both sides of the U.S.-Mexico border will find little reason to rejoice.

ACKNOWLEDGMENTS

Earlier versions of this essay were presented at the Michigan Sociological Association Meetings, November 14, 1992, Mount Pleasant, MI, and at the International Congress of Anthropological and Ethnological Sciences, July 29–August 4, 1993, Mexico, D.F., in a session titled, "Points of Contact Between Mexico and the United States." I am indebted to Barry Isaac, George Lord, and Diego Vigil for their contributions toward the final version of this essay. I would also like to thank Melisa Santimo and William Godby for their help preparing this manuscript.

NOTES

1. In the community of La Perla de Chipilo, Guanajuato, where I conducted part of the research included in this essay, there was an average increase of 350 percent in the major costs of production (e.g., electricity, diesel, oil, machinery and parts, and livestock feed and medicine) between the summers of 1987 and 1988. During the same period, the wholesale price of their main product, milk, rose only 210 percent (McDonald 1988:157). During my subsequent visits to the area in 1990–91 and again in 1993, farmers complained that, although inflation had been curbed somewhat by government policy, milk was still subject to government price controls aimed at delivering low-priced milk to poorly paid urban wage laborers. Additionally, the government no longer provided a major source of credit for agriculture, further hampering farm viability while new sources of credit had failed to emerge. (The Mexican government had hoped that foreign investors would provide this much-needed source of funds.)
2. Stanford (n.d.) notes that Mexican packing houses in Apatzingán keep records in terms of "crates" rather than weight. A crate holds 12–23 cantaloupes.
3. Even if tropical fruit export increases to previous levels, Calva (1991) points out that this sector already accounts for 70 percent of the U.S. import market and is unlikely to further increase its market share. Thus, it is questionable whether this sector will expand significantly beyond its present size. Additionally, Mexico must compete with other international producers of tropical products such as coffee, sugarcane, bananas, and chocolate. The creation of higher tariffs by the U.S. on imports from Brazil, Colombia, or Peru in order to protect Mexico would be in violation of the General Agreement on Tariffs and Trade (GATT).
4. Also refer to Barkin 1987, Barkin et al. 1990, Appendini 1992, Hewitt de Alcántara 1992 among others for a discussion of the relationship between the international market and the price of Mexican maize.
5. On the surface it might appear illogical to invest in dairy processing when demand in Mexico has dropped so dramatically. To the contrary, the demand for dairy products has been consistently rising over the past 30 years (McDonald 1991:34), and the current downturn is best seen as a short-term phenomenon that will reverse itself once the general economy becomes healthier and markets again expand (cf. Estrada-Berg 1981).
6. Investment of foreign capital has moved increasingly toward the high-profit Mexican food-processing sector. According to Shwedel and Haley (1992), many small- to medium-sized U.S. food corporations are considering exporting processed foods into Mexico, and if successful, they might consider opening plants in Mexico for the domestic market. Recent large-scale buy-outs of Mexican processing plants have also taken place. Pepsico, for example, recently purchased the Mexican cookie and pasta giant, Gamesa; Nestlé purchased the Carnation dairy processing facilities; Unilever purchased a *CONASUPO* (the Mexican national food marketing agency) oilseed processing facility in Mexico City.
7. The term "dry bean" is used to refer to numerous bean varieties including navy, red, pinto, black, and garbanzo beans. Most of the U.S. dry bean production is centered in the upper midwest and northern plains states, and Michigan was the second-largest domestic producer behind North Dakota in 1992 (*Farmline* 1992).
8. Most of these sources are quick to caution, however, that most of the increased exports to Mexico (estimated between 200 and 250 million dollars over the next 15 years) will be diverted from surplus production now purchased by the government (cf. USDA 1993:28). As a consequence, analysts do not foresee increased investment or expansion of the U.S. dairy industry as a result of NAFTA, but also importantly, *none* of them perceive NAFTA as a threat to U.S. dairy farmers.
9. This figure is a bit misleading, because these cows are given a protein-rich diet that increases production but also significantly decreases the productive life of the cow.

REFERENCES

AFB [American Farm Bureau] (1992) *NAFTA: Effects on Agriculture*. Washington, DC: American Farm Bureau Foundation.

Appendini, Kirsten (1992) *De la milpa a los tortibonos: La restructuración de la politica alimentaria en México*. México, DF: El Colegio de México.

——— (n.d.) "Los campesinos maiceros frente la politica de abastos: Una contradicción permanente." Paper presented before the International Congress of Latin American Studies Association, Washington, DC, 1991.

BANAMEX [Banco Nacional de México] (1991) *Review of the Economic Situation in Mexico*. Volume LXVII, Number 791, October. Mexico, DF: Banco Nacional de México.

Banco de México (1990) *Indicadores económicos*. Mexico, DF: Banmex.

Barkin, David (1987) "The End to Food Self-Sufficiency in Mexico." *Latin American Perspectives* 14(3):271–297.

——— (1990) *Distorted Development: Mexico in the World Economy*. Boulder, CO: Westview Press.

Barkin, David, Rosemary L. Batt, and Billie R. DeWalt (1990) *Food Crops vs. Feed Crops: Global Substitution of Grains in Production*. Boulder, CO: Lynne Reinner Publishers.

Borton, Larry R., Larry J. Connor, Larry G. Hamm, Bernard F. Stanton, Jerome W. Hammond, Myron Bennett, William T. McSweeney, John E. Kadlec, and Richard M. Klemme (1990) *Summary of the 1988 Northern U.S. Dairy Farm Survey*. East Lansing, MI: Michigan State University Agricultural Extension Station, Research Report 509.

Browne, William P., Jerry R. Skees, Louis E. Swanson, Paul B. Thompson, and Laurian J. Unnevehr (1992) *Sacred Cows and Hot Potatoes: Agrarian Myths in Agricultural Policy*. Boulder, CO: Westview Press.

Calva, José Luis (1991) "El eventual tratado de libre commercio y sus posibles impactos en el campo Mexicano." *México* 22(87):27–32.

Christy, Ralph D., and Lonnie R. Vandeveer (1989) "Credit Availability and the Structure of U.S. Agriculture." Pp. 285–300 in Christina Gladwin and Kathleen Truman (eds.) *Food and Farm: Current Debates and Policies*. Lanham, MD: University Press of America.

Collier, George A. (1990) *Seeking Food and Seeking Money: Changing Relations in a Highland Mexican Community*. Geneva: United Nations Research Institute for Social Development.

——— (1994) "Reforms of Mexico's Agrarian Code: Impacts on the Peasantry." *Research in Economic Anthropology* 15:105–127.

CBO [Congressional Budget Office] (1993) *Agriculture in the North American Free Trade Agreement*. Washington, DC: Congressional Budget Office Papers, May.

Darling, Juanita (1992) "Fearing a Bitter Harvest: Free-Trade Pact Would Jolt Lives of Many Farmers." *Los Angeles Times*, March 16:D1.

Durrenberger, E. Paul, and Kendall M. Thu, eds. (1998) *Pigs, Profits, and Rural Communities*. Albany, NY: State University of New York Press.

El Financiero (1993) "Campesinos maiceros exigen 15 años de protección." [August 12:24].

Estrada-Berg, Sergio (1981) "Processed Foods Reflect a Changing Lifestyle." Pp. 227–232 in John H. Christman (ed.) *Business Mexico*. Mexico, DF: American Chamber of Commerce of Mexico.

Farmline (1992) "U.S. Exports of Dry Beans Increased during Fiscal 1991." [October:9–10].

Finan, Timothy J., Mark W. Langworthy, and Roger W. Fox (1990) "Institutional Change and Smallholder Innovation: An Example from the Portugese Dairy Sector." *Economic Development and Culture Change* 38(4):699–712.

Fitchen, Janet (1991) *Endangered Spaces, Enduring Places: Change, Identity, and Survival in Rural America*. Boulder, CO: Westview Press.

Flint Journal (1992) "Sugar, Dairy Producers Hit Proposed Free-Trade Pact." [Flint, MI, September 5:A5].

Foren, John (1992) "Trade Pact Has Michigan Farmers Jittery." *Flint Journal*, September 22:D6.

García Hernández, Luis, Estela Martínez Borrego, Hernán Salas Quintanal, and Aysen Tanyeri-Abur (2000) "Transformation of Dairy Activity in Mexico in the Context of Current Globalization and Regionalization." *Agriculture and Human Values* 17:157–167.

Goldschmidt, Walter R. (1947) *As You Sow*. New York: Harcourt, Brace.

Hassebrook, Chuck (1993) "Deja Vu All Over Again." *Center for Rural Affairs Newsletter*, January:1.

Hewitt de Alcántara, Cynthia, ed. (1992) *Reestructuración Económica y Subsistencia Rural: El Maíz y la Crisis de los Ochenta*. Mexico, DF: El Colegio de México.

Jackson-Smith, Douglas, and Bradford Barham (2000) "Dynamics of Dairy Industry Restructuring in Wisconsin." Pp. 115–139 in Harry K. Schwarzweller and Andrew P. Davidson (eds.) *Dairy Industry Restructuring*. New York: JAI Press.

Jaramillo, Javier (1991) "La Ganadería en Morelos Está Abandonado: Teodoro Montesinos. *Excélsior*, November 15:1,14.

Luiselli, Cassio (1989) "Agricultural Dilemmas of Mexico: Reflections of a Policy Maker." Pp. 85–98 in Christina Gladwin and Kathleen Truman (eds.) *Food and Farm: Current Debates and Policies*. Lanham, MD: University Press of America.

Manchester, Alden C. (1983) *The Public Role in the Dairy Economy: Why and How Governments Intervene in the Milk Business*. Boulder, CO: Westview Press.

MASS [Michigan Agricultural Statistics Service] (1992) *Michigan Agricultural Statistics*. Lansing, MI: Michigan Agricultural Statistics Service.

McDonald, James H. (1988) "Household Cycles and Capital: Small-Scale Farm. Development among Italian Immigrants in Central Mexico." *International Journal of the Sociology of the Family* 18(2):129–162.

——— (1991) *The Emergence of Inequality among Capitalizing Family Farmers in Mexico*. Ph.D. dissertation, Arizona State University.

371

—— (1993a) "Corporate Capitalism and the Family Farm in the U.S. and Mexico." *Culture & Agriculture* 45/46:25–28.

—— (1993b) "Whose History? Whose Voice?: Myth and Resistance in the Rise of the New Left in Mexico." *Cultural Anthropology* 8(1):96–116.

—— (1997) "Privatizing the Private Family Farmer: NAFTA and the Transformation of the Mexican Dairy Sector." *Human Organization* 56(3):321–332.

—— (1999) "The Neoliberal Project and Governmentality in Rural Mexico: Emergent Farmer Organization in the Michoacán Highlands." *Human Organization* 58(3):274–284.

—— (2000) "Milk Quality and Globalization: Metaphors of Modernity in Northwestern Michoacán, Mexico." Pp. 181–209 in Harry K. Schwarzweller and Andrew P. Davidson (eds.) *Dairy Industry Restructuring*. New York: JAI Press.

—— (2001) "Reconfiguring the Countryside: Power, Control, and the (Re)Organization of Farmers in West Mexico." *Human Organization* 60(3):247–258.

Notimex [Noticias Mexicanas] (1992) "Mexico and Canada Invest 100 Million Dollars to Begin Dairy Project." [May 26].

Pugh, Terry (1992) "Free-Trade Creates Difficulties for Canadian Family Farmers." *Culture & Agriculture* 43:4–5.

Reding, Michael (1989) "Mexico under Salinas: A Facade of Reform." *World Policy Journal* 4(4):685–730.

Saxe-Fernández, John (1991) "Millones Dejarán el Agro." *Excélsior*, November 26:7,9.

Schminkle, Sharon (1992) "Move On over Wisconsin: Upper Midwest Is Slipping as Leading Milk Producer." *Chicago Tribune*, March 22:C4.

Schwarzweller, Harry K., and Andrew P. Davidson, eds. (2000) *Dairy Industry Restructuring*. New York: JAI Press.

Scott, David C. (1992) "Farming a Shrinking Planet: Mexico's Reforms Transform the Agricultural Sector." *Christian Science Monitor*, November 12:10.

Sepúlveda Ibarra, Armando (1991) "No se embargará al ejido por deudos con bancos: Hank G." *Excélsior*, November 15:1.

Shwedel, S. Kenneth, and Kevin Haley (1992) "Foreign Investment in the Mexican Food System." *Business Mexico* 2(1):48–49.

Sosa, José Luis (1990) "Dependencia alimentaria en México." *El Cotidiano* 34:39–43.

Stanford, Lois (1991) "Peasant Resistance in the International Market: Theory and Practice in Michoacán, Mexico." *Research in Economic Anthropology* 13:67–91.

—— (n.d.) "The Current Economic Crisis in Mexico: Impact on Peasant Economic Organization." Paper presented before the Southwestern Anthropological Association Meetings, Tucson, AZ, 1991.

Strange, Marty (1989) *Family Farming: A New Economic Vision*. Lincoln, NB: University of Nebraska Press.

Suárez, Blanca (n.d.) "La modernización del campo y la alimentación." Paper presented at the International Congress of the Latin American Studies Association, Washington, DC, 1991.

USITC [United States International Trade Commission] (1993) *Potential Impact on the U.S. Economy and Selected Industries of the North American Free-Trade Agreement*. Washington, DC: U.S. International Trade Commission Publication 2596.

USDA [United States Department of Agriculture] (1993) *Effects of the North American Free Trade Agreement on U.S. Agricultural Commodities*. Washington, DC: U.S. Department of Agriculture, Office of Economics.

Young, John and Jan M. Newton (1980) *Capitalism and Human Obsolescence*. New York: Universe Press.

28

NEW AGRICULTURAL BIOTECHNOLOGIES:

THE STRUGGLE FOR DEMOCRATIC CHOICE

GERAD MIDDENDORF, MIKE SKLADANY,

ELIZABETH RANSOM, AND LAWRENCE BUSCH

In the contemporary global agrifood system, the emergence of a plethora of new agricultural biotechnologies[1] poses a series of far-reaching social, technical and ethical consequences and contradictions. These tools have radically merged questions of design at the molecular level with those of agricultural change. With more possible technological paths than ever before, the new biotechnologies have made technology choice central in the discourse over the future of agriculture. Implicit in the choice of these technologies is a redesigning of nature that could profoundly transform the agrifood system, ecosystems, and the social organization of agriculture. Indeed, global food production and consumption currently stand on the brink of a fundamental alteration in organizational form, which conceivably could surpass the redistributional outcomes of twentieth-century industrialization of farming, agriculture and the food system.

Humans have for millennia been actively modifying nature to provide their sustenance. However, never before have the tools been available to redesign nature with the precision and speed that the new agricultural biotechnologies permit. For example, recombinant DNA techniques for conferring insect resistance in crops are both more precise and much faster than conventional plant breeding techniques, which require repeated selection over many generations of plants. Similarly, DNA probes have been developed to allow for the identification of certain traits in animals, without going through the lengthy process of waiting for the offspring to be born. This will allow farmers to select out undesirable traits and add or enhance desired livestock traits with more speed and precision.

The new biotechnologies also allow the rapid movement of diverse genetic materials across previously insurmountable biological and chemical barriers to create microorganisms, plants, and animals in a manner intentionally desired and designed by humans. In essence, genetic material can now be exchanged among virtually all living organisms. This makes all of the world's genetic diversity into raw industrial material to be used in research and development. Moreover, expanded claims to intellectual property rights for genetic resources are privatizing what was once public domain.[2] Likewise, in a global agrifood system the implications of the new biotechnologies are no longer limited by geography. The ability to produce cocoa or vanilla in a laboratory using cell culture techniques, for instance, could virtually decouple the manufacture of these foods from land-based production systems, threatening the livelihoods of populations in developing countries.[3]

This compression of time and space raises problems for directing biotechnology policy. Much of the research and development in this area is being carried out in the private sector with little public input or oversight. Companies are striving to develop novel biotechnology products as quickly as possible, while simultaneously lobbying to reduce as much as possible the public regulatory processes. They hope this will get their products to market ahead of those of competitors. This greatly reduces the opportunities for those with concerns about biotechnology to have a voice in deciding which directions biotechnology should take.

Moreover, the discourse surrounding emerging biotechnologies is often inadequate, in part because of the shortcomings of current thinking concerning the separation of science and politics. It is time to move beyond these limitations by questioning the very boundaries between science and politics. First, let us review some of the current developments in agricultural biotechnology, and their social, technical and ethical consequences and contradictions.

★ NEW BIOTECHNOLOGIES IN AGRICULTURE

The biotechnology industry declares itself to be one of the "cornerstone industries of America's future economic growth,"[4] and promises new agricultural technologies that will feed the world. In contrast, some critics have warned that the primary fruits of agricultural biotechnology will be "Frankenfoods" and environmental havoc, spawned by technologies over which we will almost surely lose control.[5] Thus far the developments in the field support neither of these claims. Rather, the story is much more complex. What is clear is that agricultural biotechnology, and the debates surrounding it, will be with us for the foreseeable future.

Biological research in agriculture was traditionally in the public domain. However, most investment in biological research in agriculture is now being done by the private sector. Some analysts predict biotechnology crops will be worth $7 billion by 2005.[6] Thus, it is not surprising that industry leaders are betting heavily on agricultural biotechnology's commercial success, and industry is dominating the research agenda.

Before turning to a discussion of specific technologies and their implications there are two general issues which should be addressed. First, biotechnologies can increase market concentration. As with other products in a capitalist market, biotechnology developers rely on being the first to get their product to market so as to capture the largest market share. Thus, only countries in the forefront of biotechnology development are likely to reap the gains of investment in research and development. Also, due to the increasing scope and complexity of intellectual property rights on life forms, many companies avoid lawsuits by swapping patented material.[7] Companies that do not have many patents or are not connected into this network may be blocked from entering the market. Furthermore, the agricultural biotechnology industry is located primarily in Western industrialized countries. Only about ten developing countries have biotechnology programs. Thus, the inequalities that currently exist between developed and developing countries are further exacerbated.

Second, advocates of biotechnology focus on increasing productivity without questioning its distributional consequences. Typically, the argument that biotechnology will help feed the world is couched in humanitarian rhetoric and the (promised) results are presented as a means to legitimate the investment in research and development. However, these arguments ignore the multiple dimensions of food security. Biotechnology may address concerns such as the amount and quality of food available, but it does not deal with issues of access and distribution. Indeed, given its potential to displace large numbers of people and to deny them access to the means of subsistence, biotechnology could in some instances actually be detrimental to helping the world feed itself. Let us turn now to specific examples of plant, food, and animal biotechnologies and their implications.

Plants

The list of new plant biotechnologies on the market has grown extensively in the past few years (see Table 1 for a partial listing). In the United States alone, the area of transgenic crops planted increased from 8.1 million hectares in 1997 to 20.5 million hectares in 1998.[8] In plant biotechnology, herbicide resistant crops (HRCs) are one example of commercial developments. HRCs allow herbicide application after the crop has emerged from the soil, extending the period in which the chemical may be used. Expectations are that by 2000 the annual value of herbicide tolerant seed will be about $2.1 billion.[9] With the top four chemical companies controlling 53 percent of the market, it is not surprising that 30 to 50 percent of industry research and development spending is presently going towards HRCs.[10]

In 1997, an estimated 3 to 4 million hectares of herbicide-tolerant soybeans were planted—roughly 15 percent of the total soybean acreage in the United States.[11] This area grew substantially in 1998 worldwide, with the result that "more than one-half of the world soybean harvest and about one-third of the corn harvest now comes from plants engineered with genes for herbicide or disease resistance."[12] One brand of HRC soybeans on the market is Monsanto's Roundup Ready transgenic[13] soybean, which is resistant to the company's leading herbicide, Roundup, the largest-selling weed killer in the world. Farmers who use the seed must sign a contract requiring them to use only Roundup and allowing Monsanto to inspect their fields at any time. Roundup accounts for about 17 percent of Monsanto's total annual sales.[14] For Monsanto, HRCs like Roundup Ready soybeans represent an opportunity for the company to increase its overall share of the agricultural inputs market by introducing genetically engineered seed that is tied to the use of its herbicides.

Today, all major seed companies have been bought by or are tied to chemical companies. The consolidation of the chemical and seed industries has allowed a few companies to gain a large share of the agricultural inputs market. Concentration in the industry has generated considerable criticism of the control that agribusi-

Table 1: Commercialized Biotechnologies in The U.S.

Name of Product (Year Commercialized)—Brief Description

Herbicide Resistant:	Identity Preserved:	Insect Resistant (Bt toxin):
Plant*		
Canola (NOM)—resistant to herbicide glufosinate	Laurical (1995)—high lauric acid oil composition in canola	KnockOut (1995)—corn resistant to corn borer
Roundup Ready Canola (NOM)—resistant to herbicide glyphosate	FlavrSavr (1994)—delayed ripening tomato (*taken off market*)	NatureGuard (1995)—corn resistant to corn borer
BXN Cotton (1995)—resistant to herbicide bromoxynil	High Oleic Acid Soybeans (NOM)—higher levels of oleic acid in the oil.	Bollgard (1995)—resistant to bollworm and budworm
Roundup Ready Cotton (1996)—resistant to herbicide glyphosate	Terminator Genes (NOM)—sterilizes plant seed	NewLeaf (1995)—resistant to Colorado potato beetle
Roundup Ready Soybeans (1995)—resistant to herbicide glyphosate	**Disease Resistant:** Freedom II (1995)—squash resistant to two viruses (*taken off market*)	

Food		
Modified Flavors: High	**New Processing Techniques:**	Biosensors (1980s)—detects biological activity in food
Fructose Corn Syrup (1980s)—corn sweetener used in soft drinks, etc.	Chymogen (1990)—recombinant rennet used in cheese making	
Aspartame (1981)—high-intensity sweetener	**Rapid Detection Systems:** DNA probes (1980s)—evaluates authenticity of food ingredients	Polymerase Chain Reaction (1985)—used in early detection of bacteria and viruses in food manufacturing

Animal		
Growth Hormones: Bovine Somatotropin (1994)—growth hormone injected into cow to increase milk production	DNA probes (1982)—allows for the identification of certain traits	Dolly (NOM)—Lamb cloned using a nonreproductive cell nucleus taken from a ewe's udder
Porcine Somatotropin (NOM)—injected growth hormone to increase average daily weight gain and lean tissue, while decreasing back fat in pigs	Embryo splitting (1980s)—produces identical animals. Not cost effective in the U.S., so not widely practiced in the industry.	**Transgenic "Pharming":** Rabbits that produce an enzyme (NOM)—used to treat a rare human genetic disorder.
Reproductive Technologies: Embryo Transfers (1979)—one of first animal biotechnologies used, primarily for farm breeding	**Transgenic Animals:** Mice (1976)—first transgenic animal	Goats (NOM)—produce a drug called TPA

*For a more complete list of agricultural biotechnology refer to http://www.bio.org. For plant biotechnologies on the market refer to *The Gene Exchange*, Fall 1997.

ness is gaining over the agrifood system. The concern is that, as fewer input suppliers increasingly dominate the market, the choices that farmers have before them will actually become more restricted. A few products will be heavily pushed as the industry standard. This can promote a narrower genetic base for agriculture as well as restrict the types of farm enterprises and narrow the range of choices available to farmers.

The commercialization of HRCs raises other long-term environmental issues as well. Some researchers have shown that herbicide tolerance engineered into crop plants can spread quite easily into weedy relatives of a crop.[15] Thus, widespread use of HRCs could lead to hardier weeds. Of course, everyone shares these consequences; they are not experienced solely by direct users of the technology.

The most recent plant biotechnology to create international controversy is the "Terminator technology." Co-developed by the USDA and seed company Delta and Pine Land, the Terminator technology encodes within each seed's DNA a gene that kills its own embryos, thereby sterilizing the seed and forcing growers to return to seed companies on a yearly basis to purchase new seeds. Grassroots organizations, particularly groups in parts of the world that struggle with food security, have vehemently opposed this technology. As one foundation research director explains, "engineering seed sterility is a logical goal for the multinational seed industry because around three-quarters of the world's farmers routinely save seed from their harvest for re-planting."[16]

While users of hybrid seed have long faced this same issue (i.e., having to return to seed companies annually), the Terminator technology is different in two fundamental ways. First, hybrids have only been successful with a few crops. In principle, all crops could be modified with the Terminator gene. In fact, if the gene works as expected, it will likely be licensed widely to seed companies, making it difficult for farmers to buy seed that does not contain the gene. Thus, farmers might well find that they have no choice in the matter.

Second, hybrids are relatively easy to produce by conventional breeding, so although the market is concentrated, there are many companies in the market. The Terminator technology could eventually allow a few chemical/seed companies to control all crop seeds worldwide. The serious inherent risk is the assumption of permanently stable institutions. If used on a large scale, it will make farmers fully dependent on seed companies for seed. If the seed is unavailable due to war, civil disturbance, natural disaster, etc. then farmers will suddenly discover that they have no seed to plant. This would obviously be catastrophic.

Another group of plant biotechnologies currently in use is identity preserved (IP) crops, which have been engineered with specific altered traits, such as tomatoes with delayed ripening (e.g., Flavr Savr), or canola with high lauric acid (an ingredient in cosmetics), such as Calgene's Laurical. IP crops are a way of adding value to a crop because the altered trait commands a premium in the market. Yet, for the developers to maximize profits they must maintain ownership or control of the product from seed to market. This encourages, and is certain to promote, contract farming. Contract farming has some advantages for farmers. For instance, farmers may not have to incur a large debt to finance the crop under contract. However, farmers entering contracts also lose autonomy as they no longer are permitted to make basic production and marketing decisions. Moreover, contract farming may also continue the shift toward larger and fewer farms, because the contracting company will face increased transaction costs as the number of contracts into which it enters increases. For example, if Calgene wishes to contract out one thousand hectares of its antisense tomato, it would likely seek out a larger, more capitalized producer for the full one thousand hectares, rather than enter into ten contracts at one hundred hectares each.

Food

Many food biotechnologies have been developed with little public awareness or discussion. In part, this is due to the fact that most consumers know very little about research and development in food processing. For example, researchers have produced chymosin, an enzyme used in cheese making, from genetically engineered organisms. The first commercial product, a recombinant chymosin called Chymogen, can be found in approximately 60 percent of all hard cheeses in the United States.[17] Yet, most people in the United States have never heard of this genetically engineered enzyme.

Food biotechnology also includes the use of enzymes in fermentation, as well as in starch processing. Today, the value of the world fermentation market is estimated at between $20 and $40 billion annually, while the market for starch enzymes is approximately $200 million annually.[18] One of the first products made with starch enzymes was High Fructose Corn Syrup (HFCS). HFCS is produced by using biotechnologically produced enzymes to convert corn into a sweetener. Corn converted by this method has attained widespread use in major food products such as soft drinks. Other products not yet commercialized include vanilla and cocoa produced in vitro.[19] In principle, any commodity that is consumed in a highly processed, undifferentiated form could be produced using these techniques. The result would be large batches of the commodity that are completely aseptic and require far less processing.

If successfully commercialized, in vitro biotechnologies will have an impact well beyond merely the technical aspects of their development. These technologies permit the global displacement of markets. Market displacement has always occurred due to product substitution, but biotechnology accelerates the process and leaves developing country populations in a precarious position. For instance, when HFCS attained widespread use it captured a large share of the cane sugar market from developing countries, threatening the livelihoods of an estimated eight to ten million people in the South.[20] Presently, vanilla and cocoa are still cheaper to import than to produce in factories. But, if such factory production can be done economically, people who depend on the export of these crops for their livelihood may see a significant loss of market share.

Animals

Unlike food biotechnologies, animal biotechnologies have created significant controversy. The fact that animals are sentient beings creates very different issues for biotechnology development. The issues are further complicated because the information about animal biotechnology research and development is not readily available. Almost all research on animal biotechnologies is funded by private industry. Furthermore, due to the controversy over the use of animals, much research is undisclosed. Often, only after research is completed do the results become public knowledge. Dolly, the lamb cloned in 1997, is a prime example of both the secrecy surrounding the industry and the controversy which animal biotechnology creates.

Early animal biotechnologies involved reproduction, particularly the ability to select certain desired livestock characteristics. Recent research has shifted towards (1) increasing the milk production of cows (i.e., bovine growth hormone), (2) improving or changing meat characteristics (e.g., porcine growth hormone), and (3) using animals to produce pharmaceuticals. Pharmaceutical manufacturing, also called "transgenic pharming," is the leading area of investment in transgenic animal[21] research and development. If successful, "pharming" will allow pharmaceutical companies to use an animal much like they would a laboratory. The animal would be engineered to produce a desired compound that would then be sold to treat various ailments. The first pharmed drug, likely to arrive on the market late in 1999, is an enzyme produced in the milk of transgenic rabbits for individuals who lack this enzyme due to a rare genetic disorder, known as Pompe's disease.[22] A list of other transgenic animals that have successfully produced a desired drug or drug ingredient includes pigs that produce human hemoglobin and sheep that produce an amino acid lacking in some humans. The intention is to eventually commercialize these products.

In addition to the issues noted above, certain concerns are specific to animal biotechnologies. Is it appropriate to treat animals as mere factories for human drugs? Will such animals suffer from their own health problems? Should we treat the patenting of animals in the same manner as we treat the patenting of a drug produced in a lab? Also, how will pharming impact the current structure of agriculture? These questions have received little public discussion.

The plant, food, and animal technologies discussed above and listed in Table 1 are merely the tip of the iceberg. In 1997 one of the largest agriculture biotechnology companies had 17 million hectares of genetically modified crops planted.[23] In addition, in the past three years there has been a dramatic increase in the use of biotechnology in production and processing of foods. Today, foods that are produced or processed using biotechnology include breakfast cereals, taco shells, corn syrup, cooking oil, candy, margarine, milk, and cheeses, to name just a few. Indeed, there are many technologies still a few years from the market that will eventually reach commercialization.[24] These include transgenic fish, such as salmon, tilapia, and catfish, which are being engineered for industrial aquaculture production. Also, there are many more developments in pharming in both plants and transgenic animals. This makes it even more urgent that society begin to grapple with how and who will decide what directions biotechnology takes.

★ BIOTECHNOLOGY AS POLITICS BY OTHER MEANS

Despite the best efforts of advocates to portray biotechnology as the logical, inevitable, and unproblematic direction of agricultural research and development, it is a series of choices being made, each with associated consequences. The consequences of developing new technologies under the direction of corporations are substantial and extend throughout the global agrifood system. Thus, everyone is a participant in a global experiment with this new set of technologies that promises to create new winners and losers around the world, yet only a few have access to decision-making processes. Discussions of critical social, technical and ethical aspects of these technologies are currently suppressed by the view that science and technology are beyond the boundaries of conventional political discourse. The new biotechnologies are potentially beneficial to society, but not unless the institutional bases for technology choice are democratized. These technical and political dimensions can no longer remain separate if a socially just biotechnology is to emerge.

The rhetoric of neutrality embedded in the science of biotechnology masks a series of social contradictions. When closely examined, technical choices are simultaneously political choices not necessarily congruent with the fuller aspirations of a free, democratic society. The current developments in biotechnology reflect a decision-making process in which commercial interests override societal and environmental concerns. Moreover, while most scientists see themselves as searchers for truth, they remain largely oblivious to the *partial* character of what they "discover" or create. Similarly, corporate managers have a vested interest in promoting their own agenda even while claiming it serves merely to advance scientific knowledge. Given the increasing influence of corporate funding of and collaboration with university and government scientists, their research agendas are reshaped as well. This fundamental contradiction is at the heart of the politics of the new agricultural biotechnologies.

Biotechnology is one valid and reliable way of knowing, representing and manipulating nature. In principle, there is nothing inherently harmful about this new set of tools. However, within industrial capitalism biotechnology is tied to private profit, short-term control over nature, and neglect of short- and long-term social consequences. In part, this emerges from our society's faith in technological progress as the sole means to resolve human problems. At the same time, the institutional basis of industrial capitalism reinforces an increasingly illegitimate distinction between the political and technical. The legacy of this distinction can be traced back to the industrialization of agriculture and the industrialization of society.

In many respects, the production-oriented arguments utilized by biotechnology advocates echo sentiments exhibited in the post–Second World War era development of industrial agriculture that produced the "green revolution." The green revolution focused on rapid production gains as a singular means to solve world food problems while stemming what was perceived as the advance of communism. Indeed, the application of new technological packages, corresponding infrastructure development, and the growth of export markets are all legacies of the green revolution. This approach did lead to significant production gains. However, the contradictions arising from these developments also led to exacerbated social, political and economic inequalities within localities, nation-states and regions of the developing and developed world.[25] Moreover, the debasing of tropical agricultural resources has led to negative long-term environmental consequences resulting in profound ecosystem alteration and, in some cases, severe degradation of the ability of the land to produce food. The green revolution provides an important lesson with respect to the application of the new agricultural biotechnologies: the ideology of inevitable technological progress excludes consideration of the distributional and environmental consequences of such efforts.

Marx was ambivalent about technological choice. On the one hand, he envisioned that new technologies could help achieve human emancipation and lead to a society of abundant production and consumption. On the other hand, Marx realized that technologies could also create routine drudgery that would alienate and demean those who use them. He foresaw the social conditions of industrial capitalism, which currently relate to how the new agricultural biotechnologies have emerged and are taking shape. However, there is nothing that necessitates this outcome.

★ **NARROW OR STRONG OBJECTIVITY**

Perhaps one of the primary sources of legitimacy for biotechnology is its connection to scientific objectivity—an association frequently highlighted by advocates in an effort to immunize their endeavors politically by attempting to draw a clear distinction between the scientific and the political. It is these very sources of legitimacy that require scrutiny. Acting on behalf of a "concerned public," proponents appeal to scientific objectivity to advance arguments for the best possible outcomes regarding support for new agricultural biotechnologies. This is not to say that biotechnology is not based on valid and even well intentioned science. What is problematic, however, is that early decisions about the direction of biotechnology become invisible after research is completed and technologies are produced. When choosing problems, scientists have a range of possibilities before them. For example, they could work on developing crops that more effectively shade out weeds, or intercropping and rotation systems for better weed control, or they could genetically modify plants to be resistant to herbicides.

Yet, after the direction of research and development has already been decided, the initial alternatives tend to disappear as scientists often portray the chosen path as the only viable one.[26] The chosen path then becomes, according to scientists, the only "accepted" objective view of the world. Hence, a *narrow objectivity* prevails in which a few scientists and corporate executives make early choices (i.e., when there are a number of viable alternative choices) about the direction of research and development, and then later define the chosen path as the standard measure for objectivity. They do so even as research is supported by corporations that have an obvious vested interest. This weaker form of objectivity can only be enhanced by increasing the number of perspectives—and the legitimate representation of those perspectives in decision making—that are included in making the initial choices.

The conventional stripping away of the social context of science facilitates the mystification of biotechnology. But, science and technology are political developments, with real constituencies and real social consequences. Democratizing science and technology policy is a necessary part of the process of addressing these contradictions. This requires developing new institutional mechanisms to promote the participation of those affected by new technologies. As a first step, the very definition of science and technology needs to be broadened to include activities that go on outside the laboratory, but that are fundamental to the scientific enterprise. Public and private funding agencies, instrument manufacturers, biotechnology firms and general farm and commodity organizations, among others, must all be recognized as essential social agents in science and technology development. Only when these intertwined components of science and technology are addressed can we speak of objective, socially responsible and ethically informed decision making.

★ **THE STRUGGLE TO DEMOCRATIZE SCIENCE
AND TECHNOLOGY**

Increasing corporate control of the biotechnology research and development agenda raises a host of problems, not the least of which is a restricting of public access to decision making in this arena. While opening the technology policy process to broad participation comes up against considerable structural constraints, a democratization of science and technology should not be seen as merely a utopian illusion. We are now accustomed to considering democracy as limited to party politics. However, there have been continuing struggles to extend it to technology choice. Several countries have made notable progress in this direction. While efforts in the United States have received limited support, in Western Europe the institutional innovations toward a more inclusive technology policy process are taking place. These initiatives should by no means be considered a panacea for dealing with technology development, but they are one approach to challenging corporate and state hegemony over technology choice.

For example, for more than a decade the Danish Board of Technology (DBT) has been running consensus conferences that have provided a forum in which ordinary citizens with diverse backgrounds are involved in technology assessment.[27] The results of these dialogues between citizens and a panel of experts are widely disseminated in the media, and are often acted on by legislative bodies. The DBT has held conferences on industrial and agricultural biotechnology (1987), irradiation of food products (1989), and genetically manipulated animals (1992). It appears that this model is now being more widely adopted in Europe.

In the United States the first promising efforts at proactively involving citizens in technically complex areas of policy are beginning to appear. In 1997 the Loka Institute, along with a number of other collaborating institutions, organized a pilot citizens' panel based on the consensus conference model. This particular panel dealt with issues arising from changes in telecommunications technologies and policy. Judging from the conference reports, the panel demonstrated that lay citizens are capable of meaningful participation in complex technical and public policy issues.[28] Both this approach and the work of the Danish Board of Technology warrant further exploration.

These are just two examples of mechanisms that attempt in some way to extend democracy to technology choice. While our purpose here is not to review the full range of extant examples, it is useful to consider some of their shared principles. In these efforts, the relationship between social priorities and technology choices is made explicit. A key feature of these strategies is that society must democratically define its priorities; only then should it ask how technologies might help to achieve those goals. This challenges the common assumption in science policy of a positive, linear relationship between scientific advance and social progress.[29] Another guiding principle is that since all citizens experience the effects of science and technology, and since citizens in democratic societies ordinarily expect to have a voice in decisions that will affect the way they live their daily lives, they must be involved in deciding the direction of science and technology policy.

These approaches also begin with the assumption that science and technology policymaking is an inherently political process, and that any constructive dialogue will necessarily bring together actors with divergent goals and values that often contradict each other. In the debates over biotechnology some might argue for values such as profitability or freedom from excessive regulation, while others might argue for safety, environmental soundness, or equity. There is no one decision rule with which to rank these competing values in a simple hierarchy. Rather, decisions must be accomplished through a process of debate, negotiation and compromise in which all stakeholders have a voice.[30]

In the United States, we have typically relieved ourselves from responsibility for the consequences of technical change by attributing them to the inevitable effects of technological advance combined with market forces. In this view, if undesirable consequences should result from technical change, we can develop not only new technical fixes, but also new products and additional economic activity. Yet, as the examples above suggest, it is not necessary to actually employ new technologies in order to determine their consequences. Such an approach leads to the never-ending search for technological fixes, even as it tears at the social fabric. Indeed, many of the negative consequences could be avoided if initial science and technology choices were made with better consideration of social priorities. We currently do not have these kinds of mechanisms in place—technical change has by far outpaced institutional innovation—but we do have the capacity in universities, nongovernmental organizations, companies, and in our citizenry to direct science and technology in more democratic and socially desirable directions.

NOTES

1. Defined broadly to include techniques that use living organisms to improve plants, animals, or products, biotechnology in itself is not new. We use "new" to refer to technologies that use rDNA, cell fusion techniques, new bioprocesses, monoclonal antibodies, plant and animal cell and tissue culture, and embryo transfer, splitting and sexing.
2. Suri Sehgal, "Biotechnology Heralds a Major Restructuring of the Global Seed Industry," *Diversity* 12.3 (1996), 13–15.
3. Lawrence Busch, William B. Lacy, Jeffery Burkhardt, and Laura R. Lacy, *Plants, Power, and Profit: Social, Economic, and Ethical Consequences of the New Biotechnologies* (Cambridge, MA: Blackwell, 1991).
4. BIO (Biotechnology Industry Organization), BIO Web site, (1996). URL: http://www.bio.org/bio/ 2usbio.html (3/17/97).
5. Jeremy Rifkin, *The Biotech Century: Harnessing the Gene and Remaking the World* (New York: Jeremy P. Tarcher/Putnam, 1998).
6. Nature Biotechnology ". . . Green Is Also the Color of Money," 16.11 (1998), 985.
7. Sehgal, "Biotechnology Heralds a Major Restructuring."
8. Anne Simon Moffa, "Toting Up the Early Harvest of Transgenic Plants," *Science* 282.5397 (1998), 2176–2178.
9. Thomas F. Lee, *Gene Future: The Promise and Perils of the New Biology* (New York: Plenum Press, 1993).
10. Ibid.
11. IFIC (International Food Information Council). "Anticipating the Harvest of Food Biotechnology Crops." (1997). URL: http://www.ificinfo.health.org/insight/Sept Oct97/foodbiotech.htm (12/18/97).
12. Moffa, "Toting Up the Early Harvest."
13. A transgenic organism is formed by inserting foreign genetic material into the germ line cells of organisms.
14. Mark Arax and Jeanne Brokaw, "No Way Around Roundup," *Mother Jones* (January/February 1997), 40–41.
15. Thomas Mikkelsen, Bente Andersen, and Rikke Bagger Jørgensen, "The Risk of Crop Transgene Spread," *Nature* 380.6569 (1996), 31.
16. RAFI (Rural Advancement Foundation International). "Monsanto Terminates Terminator?" (1998). URL: http://www.rafi.org/pr/release25.html (1/29/99).
17. BIO, 1996.
18. BIO (Biotechnology Industry Organization), BIO Web site (1998). URL: http://www.bio.org/whatis/edito7. dgw (3/21/98).
19. In vitro production is an industrial process in which the cells of a multicellular organism are treated as if they were microorganisms. They are placed in a large vat where the environment (light, temperature, nutrients, etc.) is manipulated such that the cells multiply.
20. K. van den Doel and G. Junne, "Product Substitution through Biotechnology: Impact on the Third World." *Trends in Biotechnology* 4:88–90 (1986).
21. Transgenic animals are animals into which foreign DNA is implanted into the fertilized egg.
22. "Phase II for Pharming." *Business and Regulatory News Briefs in Nature Biotechnology* 16.13 (1998), 1297.
23. Jeffrey L. Fox, "Monsanto Unaffected By Merger Halt?" *Nature Biotechnology* 16.13 (1998), 1307.
24. "Despite Opposition, Biotech Foods Ready for Primetime, Experts Say," *Food & Drink Weekly* 47.4 (1998), 1.
25. Harry M. Cleaver Jr., "The Contradictions of the Green Revolution," *American Economic Review* 2.62 (1972.), 177–186; John, H. Perkins, *Geopolitics and the Green Revolution: Wheat, Genes, and the Cold War* (New York: Oxford, 1997).
26. This case has been made for the history of hybrid corn by Jack R. Kloppenburg, Jr. in *First the Seed: The Political Economy of Plant Biotechnology, 1492–2000,* (Cambridge: Cambridge University Press, 1988).
27. Danish Board of Technology, *Technology Assessment in Denmark: A Briefing* (Copenhagen: Danish Board of Technology, 1992).
28. The Loka Institute "First Time U.S. Citizens' Panel: Telecommunications and the Future of Democracy, April 2–4, 1997." A report on The Loka Institute Web site (1997), URL: http://www. loka.org/pages/results.htm (1/25/99).
29. Daniel Sarewitz, *Frontiers of Illusion: Science, Technology, and the Politics of Progress* (Philadelphia: Temple University Press, 1996).
30. Lawrence Busch and Gerad Middendorf, "Technology Policy in a Rapidly Changing World," in William Lockeretz (ed.), *Visions of American Agriculture* (Ames: Iowa State University Press, 1997), 205–217.

HUNGER IN THE UNITED STATES:

POLICY IMPLICATIONS

MARION NESTLE

29

For centuries, advocates for the poor, social reformers, and policymakers have debated ways to address inequalities in access to food and other resources. Debates have centered on the conflict between sympathy for the plight of poor people and complaints that public assistance is too expensive and might encourage recipients to become dependent on charity. Since the English Poor Laws of the 1500s, public and private assistance policies have been explicitly designed to provide minimal support—that is, just enough to prevent overt starvation, but not so much as to encourage dependency. This balance, however, is not easily achieved. In the United States, for example, hunger and welfare policies have shifted in response to political change, sometimes strengthening but sometimes weakening the "safety net" for the poor. Today, welfare policies are dominated by concerns about dependency far more than they are about the nutritional, health, or social consequences of entrenched poverty.

The results of current policies are evident in newspaper accounts. On a consistent basis, one can read of the rising gap between the income of New York City's working poor and their daily expenses; of the inadequacy of government benefits to fill that gap (Blum, 1998); and the ways in which fiscal pressures to reduce welfare rolls have forced recipients to accept minimum-wage jobs that do not bring their incomes above the poverty level (Polner, 1998). That large numbers of New York City residents, many of them working mothers of young children, require additional aid is sufficient to demonstrate inequalities in access to food in the United States. This paper examines such inequalities, and the history and present status of policies designed to redress them, from a nutritionist's perspective.

Nutritionists view inequality in food access as a factor that increases the risk of malnutrition and disease. An ideal diet provides sufficient energy and essential nutrients to meet physiological requirements, maximize growth and longevity, and prevent nutrient deficiencies as well as conditions of nutritional excess and imbalance; it should also be obtained from foods that are available, affordable, and palatable. Most of the papers in this volume focus on the cultural,social, and historic dimensions of food. In contrast, this paper focuses on issues related to the availability and affordability of food in the United States. It addresses three questions: Does America produce enough food for its population? Does hunger exist in America? And, if so, what policies might ensure more equitable access to food? Because an unusually comprehensive and substantive body of historical and modern research bears on such questions, it is possible to address them with more clarity than might be expected. As this paper will demonstrate, centuries of study and debate about food inequalities have fully identified causes as well as solutions, but the solutions rarely are politically acceptable. Thus, prevention of hunger in America remains a matter of policy and political will.

★ DOES AMERICA PRODUCE SUFFICIENT FOOD?

Since 1909, the United States Department of Agriculture (USDA) has produced annual estimates of the amounts of food, nutrients, and calories in the U.S. food supply. These figures derive from reports of the amounts of food commodities produced in the United States each year, less exports, plus imports. In 1996, the USDA estimated that the food supply provided an average of 3,800 kilocalories (kcal) per day per capita—an increase of 500 kcal per day since 1970 (Putnam and Allshouse, 1997). This level is nearly twice the amount needed to meet the energy requirements of most women, one-third more than that needed by most men, and is far higher than that needed by infants and young children (Institute of Medicine, 1989). The 3,800-kcal figure reflects food production and supply; it provides only an indirect estimate of the number of calories actually consumed. Nevertheless, it so greatly exceeds the 2,200 kcal per day benchmark for food adequacy that it is possible to conclude that the United States not only produces enough food, but that it actually overproduces food.

Overproduction greatly affects marketing and distribution practices throughout the entire food system. In 1996, the food system generated $890 billion in sales, about 1% higher than the amount generated during the previous year; this slow rate of growth has been typical of the industry for decades. It has been shown that nearly half of all food expenditures derive from meals and drinks consumed outside the home—a fact that illustrates the increasing importance of restaurants and take-out meals as sources of food for Americans (Gallo, 1998).

Preparation of food outside the home and the development of packaged food products adds value to basic food commodities. In 1995, the "farm value" of food, the amount going to food producers, earned only 20% of total food expenditures; the remaining 80% constituted added value in the form of labor, packaging, transportation, advertising, and profit. Because value-added products are far more profitable than farm commodities, the food system favors restaurant and take-out over home-cooked food. It also favors development of new products. In 1996, U.S. manufacturers introduced 13,200 new food products into the marketplace, three-fourth of them candies, condiments, breakfast cereals, beverages, bakery products, and dairy products (Gallo, 1998). The current food marketplace includes 240,000 packaged foods from U.S. manufacturers alone (U.S. Department of Agriculture, 1996). These and other foods are advertised through more than $11 billion spent annually on electronic and print media, and another $22 billion or so on coupons, games, incentives, trade shows, and discounts (Gallo, 1998). In 1997, advertising for a typical candy bar required a $25–75 million annual expenditure, and for McDonald's more than a billion dollars (Anonymous, 1998). Such figures are vastly in excess of amounts spent by the federal government on dietary advice released to the public (Nestle, 1993). Thus, the first question about food sufficiency is readily answered. The U.S. produces more than enough food to feed all of its citizens, so much so that overproduction and waste of food resources can be considered to be the system's most critical problems (Kantor et al., 1997).

★ DOES HUNGER EXIST IN AMERICA?

This question also is addressed by a large body of research. As a result of policy and economic changes in the late 1970s, and the passage of laws leading to significant reductions in welfare benefits in the early 1980s, emergency food and shelter providers began to report increasing demands for their services by the "new poor" —unskilled and unemployed youth, families with insufficient resources, and the deinstitutionalized mentally ill. As the increasing need for food assistance became more apparent, community groups, academics, and government officials began to produce reports describing the extent of "hunger" in their local communities (Nestle and Guttmacher, 1992). By 1990, the Food Research and Action Center (FRAC), a Washington, D.C.-based advocacy group, had collected nearly 250 hunger studies that had been produced by communities in 40 states and the District of Columbia. The most widely publicized of these reports was a study issued by a group of physicians in the mid-1980s. Their report defined hunger in economic terms: individuals were at risk of hunger if their income fell below the poverty line or if their food assistance benefits were inadequate. By these criteria, the report identified 12 million children and 8 million adults in the U.S. as "hungry" (Physician Task Force, 1985).

Because the purpose of the hunger studies was to document the need for increased services rather than to produce validated estimates of the extent of need, their results—no matter how consistent—were criticized as politically motivated and unreliable. These criticisms forced activists to develop precise definitions as to what they meant by hunger and to develop increasingly elaborate and sophisticated methods for estimating its prevalence.

Definitions

Hunger studies distinguish "hunger" from "food insecurity" and "malnutrition." Food insecurity is a condition of inadequate access to food or to the resources to obtain food by means that are socially acceptable. By this definition, a person who has enough food, but acquires it through stealing, prostitution, or drug-dealing, is considered food insecure. In contrast, hunger is the unpleasant sensation that results from the lack of sufficient food, and malnutrition is the long-term physiological or cognitive consequence of insufficient food intake.

Methods

Because measurement of clinical or biochemical indices of malnutrition in population surveys is difficult and expensive, few hunger studies have measured such parameters. Instead, most studies have assessed levels of food insecurity through estimates of poverty, use of food assistance programs, or unmet needs for food assistance among individuals or groups. Some studies have gone to extraordinary lengths to document these indirect measures. For example, a statewide hunger study in Texas involved twelve public hearings and four surveys that collated responses from approximately 2,000 private emergency food providers, 1,700 elderly recipients of congregate meals, 1,300 participants in one federal food assistance program, and numerous legal aid providers who worked with recipients (State of Texas, 1984).

Even more elaborate efforts went into development of a scientifically validated survey instrument—the Community Childhood Hunger Identification Project (CCHIP)—that employs sophisticated statistical methods to evaluate the extent of inadequate access to food among defined sample groups. This instrument includes eight questions that probe food insufficiency and perceptions of hunger, such as "do your children ever say they are hungry because there is not enough food in the house?" A positive answer to five of the eight questions is considered as indicating household hunger; positive answers to one to four questions suggest an increased risk of hunger (Wehler et al., 1995).

The CCHIP survey established a standard for measurement of hunger and food security and its questions have been widely used. For example, a Task Force appointed by the Governor of the State of Washington used the CCHIP questionnaire to document the extent and nature of hunger in the state and its underlying causes among families whose incomes were below 185% of the poverty level, seniors participating in congregate and home-delivered meals programs, and representatives of nearly 300 public and private agencies providing food assistance. This state survey also included the results of interviews with state-level and local service providers, provider organizations, advocates, and food assistance recipients. Using this instrument, the survey identified as food insecure 233,000 Washington State residents who reside with children (Governor's Task Force, 1988).

Prevalence

In 1995, the USDA adapted the CCHIP questions for a survey conducted in collaboration with the U.S. Census Bureau to examine a representative sample of nearly 45,000 U.S. households, excluding homeless persons and prisoners. The survey had eighteen questions that probed whether, in the past twelve months, respondents had ever as a result of lack of food or money: skipped meals; eaten less than they wanted; not eaten for a whole day; worried whether food would run out; or relied only on limited kinds of food. On the basis of responses to these questions, the USDA reported that 12 million U.S. households lacked food security; of these, 3.3 million households reported hunger, and 800,000 households reported severe hunger (Hamilton et al., 1997).

An analysis of the results indicated that households with children under age 18 were most at risk of food insecurity and hunger, especially if members were Black or Hispanic or headed by females. Food insecurity and hunger correlated strongly with income; 12.7% of households with annual incomes below $10,000 reported hunger, whereas just 6.6% of households with incomes from $10,000–20,000 did so, and only 3.3% of households with incomes from $20,000–30,000. Only half of the households reporting hunnger were receiving federal food assistance, which suggests a considerable lack of coping skills among their members.

Additional studies confirm such reports. Analysis of data from the Third National Health and Nutrition Examination Survey, which used a version of the CCHIP questionnaire, identified 4.1% of the population (or 9–12 million Americans) as living in families lacking resources sufficient to ensure adequate food intake (Alaimo et al., 1998). Thus, two major national surveys, conducted with validated instruments and statistical techniques, thoroughly confirmed the results of the hundreds of more informal hunger studies conducted since the early 1980s. Clearly, large numbers of Americans are so poor or so socially or psychologically impaired that they cannot provide sufficient food for themselves or their families.

Taken together, hunger studies have provided substantial documentation of the chronic nature of food insufficiency in the United States. They also serve to illustrate the relationship of food insufficiency to lack of resources, rather than to lack of food per se (Nestle and Guttmacher, 1992). They clearly demonstrate that incomes considerably in excess of the federally defined poverty level still could be insufficient to prevent food insecurity (Fisher, 1992), and that the welfare system fails to provide an adequate safety net. Finally, they confirm the inability of private charity to solve problems of food insufficiency (Poppendieck, 1998).

Even as inequitable access to food is troublesome on humanitarian grounds, it also has functional consequences. Food insecurity is highly correlated with deficient intake of calories and essential nutrients (Rose and Oliveira, 1997). In the United States, such deficiencies do not usually lead to clinically evident malnutrition— the kwashiorkor and marasmus seen among adult and child victims of famine in developing countries. Instead, the deficiencies are marginal and not readily measurable, but they nevertheless induce physiological and cognitive consequences that are especially pronounced in young children: fatigue, impaired immune function, attention deficits, and impaired learning (Karp, 1993).

★ HISTORICAL PERSPECTIVE: WELFARE AND FOOD ASSISTANCE POLICIES

Data indicate that numerous American households lack appropriate means to obtain food in the presence of a food system of great overabundance. At issue, therefore, is the best way to connect food insecure households with the means to obtain food (food assistance) or the means to purchase it (welfare, or cash assistance). As noted earlier, this issue has vexed scholars and politicians for centuries. Indeed, the issues that so preoccupy today's political leaders date back to the Colonial era; those related to food assistance have been debated since the Great Depression of the 1930s. If history has anything to teach us about such matters, it is that policymakers have little that is new to offer as a solution.

It must be understood that the absence of progress in developing policies to distribute food more equitably is not due to a lack of serious thinking about the matter. A perfunctory computer search of New York University's library holdings, for example, yielded more than 800 listings of titles in response to the single probe, "welfare." A great many of these titles turned out to be books of distinguished scholarship and analysis. Even the most cursory analysis of their contents indicates that

389

food and welfare policies constitute "wicked" societal problems—those with multiple, complex causes and no easy solutions.

Welfare

Welfare—the use of public tax money to support the poor—has an ancient history. Societies have always taken measures to care for those who lacked resources or the ability to care for themselves. In Western societies, welfare measures served multiple and sometimes contradictory purposes: to relieve misery, to preserve social order, and to regulate labor. Welfare provided food, shelter, and clothing for the poor, but it also kept them from rebelling, and provided a mobile labor force that could work for very low wages. In the United States, as in some other countries, welfare acquired a fourth function—the mobilization of political support. This last function has taken increasing prominence, as political leaders have exploited either sympathy for the poor or fears of inducing dependency as a means to gain electoral votes.

Welfare policies arrived in the United States with the earliest English settlers and their Poor Law traditions. The English Poor Laws derived from the realization that private charity was inadequate to meet the needs of the indigent and that the use of taxes to support the poor was a necessary public duty in a civilized society. Care took the form of food, clothing, and fuel. In return, able-bodied adults were required to work; children also had to work and could be bound out as apprentices (Abbott, 1940). The Poor Laws established workhouses and mandated imprisonment for those who did not comply with work requirements. The resulting welfare system was based on three principles: local responsibility (towns took care of their own), family responsibility (children took care of parents, and vice versa), and local residence (people had to live in the immediate area to receive benefits).

The English welfare system was based on one overriding assumption: that the poor were inherently less worthy than everyone else, and were not simply the victims of illness, bad luck, or a rapidly transforming economic system. Such assumptions were given great credence by the writings of Malthus. In his "Essay on the Principle of Population," Malthus condemned public relief on the grounds that it fostered dependency among undeserving, alcohol-abusing people:

> The labouring poor, to use a vulgar expression, seem always to live from hand to mouth. Their present wants employ their whole attention; and they seldom think of the future. Even when they have an opportunity of saving, they seldom exercise it; but all they earn beyond their present necessities goes, generally speaking, to the alehouse. The poor-laws may therefore be said to diminish both the power and the will to save among the common people; and thus to weaken one of the strongest incentives to sobriety and industry, and consequently to happiness (Malthus, 1817: 49).

Malthus recognized the deleterious consequences of the Poor Laws: the "... crowded, unhealthy, and horrible state of the workhouses," the inability of many parishes to care for the large number of needy, and the inadequate responses of voluntary charities. These factors, he said, "... may be considered not only as incontrovertible proofs of the fact that they [the Poor Laws] do not perform what they promise, but as affording the strongest presumption that they cannot do it" (p. 57). Thus, Malthus advocated what we would today consider a form of "tough love," with fair notice given to gradually eliminating assistance so as to "...teach the labouring classes to rely more upon their own exertions and resources, as the only way of really improving their condition...." (p. 245).

The early colonists brought this system, prejudices and all, to America. In 1790, the territory of Ohio passed the first American poor law based on the English tradition of local control, family responsibility, and local residence. By the 1850s, similar provisions were written into the constitutions of most states. As with the system in England, local responsibility proved inadequate and unenforceable. Communities argued about who had to bear responsibility for taking care of the poor. By the end of the colonial period, families, churches, communities, schools, businesses, fraternal orders, and local governments all were involved in helping the poor. With the industrial revolution came an increase in urbanization, the replacement of family shops with factories, and an increase in living standards, along with an ever-rising gap between the income levels of the rich and poor (Abbott, 1940; de Grazia and Gurr, 1961; Klebaner, 1976).

From the 1700s on, poor relief involved four methods: auctions to the lowest bidder, maintenance contracts to private caretakers, town-run asylums, and outdoor relief—cash, food, soup kitchens, fuel, or shelter. As was the case in England, the system was notably ineffective and subject to abuse. People receiving public assistance were deprived of the right to vote; children were removed from families and placed in orphanages, or made to work; families were separated. The auction system drove down the cost and the quality of care, and the indigent could be forcibly removed to another community. Astonishingly, such problems lasted well into the 1940s (Katz, 1986). Overall, they illustrated the generally unsatisfactory results of leaving the care of the destitute to local authorities or to private charity.

Debates about the benefits or deficiencies of this system have existed much in their present form for at least the last 175 years. In 1824, for example, the New York State legislature asked the Secretary of State to count the number of "paupers" in the State, determine the status of poor laws across the country, review existing documents relating to the problems caused by pauperism, and suggest legislation to relieve any problems—a typical hunger survey. The resulting document is remarkable for its clear delineation of the issues raised by welfare policies—issues virtually identical to those under discussion today (Yates, 1824).

The survey identified 22,000 paupers in New York, some temporarily poor but others permanently so as a result of mental or physical illness, blindness, old age, or—for more than two-thirds—the "excessive use of ardent spirits" (Yates, 1824: 941). Nearly half the paupers lived in New York City, which was viewed as acting as a magnet to attract to its "...haunts and recesses, the idle and dissolute of every description" (p. 942).

The report expressed concerns about the nearly 9,000 children identified in pauper families in New York State. These were found to be:

> ...entirely destitute of education, and equally in want of care and attention, which are so necessary to inculcate correct moral habits: it is feared that this mass of pauperism, will at no distant day form a fruitful nursery for crime, unless prevented by the watchful superintendance of the legislature. (Yates, 1824: 942)

The Secretary of State observed that the substantial cost of poor relief—an average of $35 per person per year—raised questions about whether the whole system should be abolished and its support left to private charity, even though every country of the world, even China, had adopted a code of laws for relief and maintenance of the poor, and the absence of such laws "...would be inconsistent with a humane, liberal, and enlightened policy" (p. 950). The present system, however, was none of those:

> That our poor laws are manifestly defective in principle, and mischievous in practice, and that under the imposing and charitable aspect of affording relief exclusively to the poor and infirm, they frequently invite the able bodied vagrant to partake of the same bounty, are propositions very generally admitted. [The Poor Laws]...lead to litigation of the most expensive and hurtful kind, in appeals and law suits concerning the settlement, maintenance, and removal of paupers, exhausting nearly one-ninth of the funds intended for their relief, in the payment of fees of justices, overseers, lawyers, and constables, and are at the same time productive of much cruelty in the removal of paupers, frequently at inclement seasons of the year, regardless of the claims of age, sex, or condition. (Yates, 1824: 951)

392

Such practices seemed to be "inconsistent with the spirit of a system professing to be founded on principles of pure benevolence and humanity" (p. 951). They led to cruelty, especially to children; did not provide adequate employment; led to vice, dissipation, disease, and crime; encouraged "sturdy beggers and profligate vagrants" to become dependent on public funds; promoted "street beggary;" discouraged the care of the mentally ill; and attracted immigration of paupers from other towns, counties, and countries—even from Canada (p. 952).

> Until a system...can be devised, which, with economy and humanity, will administer relief to the indigent and infirm, incapable of labor, provide employment for the idle, and impart instruction to the young and ignorant, little hope can be entertained of meliorating the condition of our poor or relieving the community from the growing evils of pauperism...To devise such a system, is confessedly a task as arduous as any that falls within the whole range of political and economical experiment; and statesmen of the most profound talents and extensive research, have lamented their inability to provide a full and competent remedy. (Yates, 1824: 955)

Despite recommendations to establish more workhouses and to fund poor relief through increased taxes on alcoholic beverages the system continued through the 1800s with only minor modifications. In the late 19th century, selected groups such as the insane, blind, deaf, and children were removed from local control and placed in special facilities where they received better care. New welfare institutions developed: labor unions, the Salvation Army in 1880, the Red Cross in 1881, and various Settlement Houses in the late 1880s. Foundations and business service clubs also became active in poor relief prior to the onset of World War I (de Grazia and Gurr, 1961).

The federal role in welfare began only in the early 1800s with the issuance of grants of money, loans, food, clothing, tents, and seeds for victims of fires, floods, earthquakes, cyclones, and volcanoes in the U.S. and abroad (Abbott, 1940). The first federal authorization to provide food relief occurred in 1874, with aid to victims of floods in Mississippi and Tennessee. Beginning in the early 20th century, states began to supplement local agencies, with funds administered through state boards.

A federal Children Bureau was established in 1912. In 1913, the income tax passed, making possible a broader federal role. The 1921 Sheppard-Towner Act provided grants to states for welfare projects until 1929, when it was repealed. These actions established a basis for the far more serious involvement of government in welfare activities that occurred during the Great Depression of the 1930s when it became clear that local and state efforts were inadequate to meet the needs of the poor. Reports that children were going to school hungry and that people were close to starvation—in the presence of abundant food that could not be sold by farmers or purchased by consumers—led to development of the welfare and food assistance programs that still exist today (Poppendieck, 1986).

Every step toward increasing federal involvement in food and welfare assistance drew protests, particularly from wealthy and influential individuals, many of them on boards of private charities. The principal arguments were that supporting the poor induced dependency and that private charity would be more effective than using tax funds for assistance. Specifically to address this point, the Census Bureau compared levels of private and federal charity during the Depression years. The results were unequivocal: 65–70% of all relief aid—before and during the Depression—came from the state or federal government. On the local level, an even higher percentage, as much as 90%, was city-funded (Abbott, 1940: 662). Indeed, the proportion of aid from federal sources increased during the years of greatest need: from 76% in 1929 to 82% in 1932 to 97% in 1934 (Miles, 1949: 18).

Even this brief history reveals several themes common to all historic—and modern—discussions of welfare policy:

Compassion for the plight of the poor versus deterrence. Since the time of the first English Poor Laws, governments have struggled to design welfare policies that provide minimal relief of hunger without inducing dependence on such assistance.

Private charity versus tax-supported welfare. History reveals a consistent inability or unwillingness of private charity to meet the needs of the poor (Poppendieck, 1998).

Local versus state versus federal authority. Throughout history, the trend has been toward increasing centralization of welfare aid from local communities to states to the federal government, as a result of the demonstrably inadequate efforts of local and state governments to provide adequate relief. As discussed below, current efforts to reverse that trend are unlikely to succeed.

Symptoms versus causes. The history of welfare is one of policies to relieve immediate needs for food, rather than to develop lengthier and more fundamental programs that might empower people to improve their education, training, and employment opportunities.

Welfare reform versus benefit levels. Advocates of "reform" typically have used this term as a euphemism for reductions in benefits.

Means-tested programs versus entitlements. More recently, welfare debates have revealed the tension between means-tested programs that protect only the poor, such as Aid to Families with Dependent Children (AFDC) or Food Stamps, and social welfare programs that offer benefits to everyone entitled to receive them, including people of middle and upper income (e.g., Social Security, Medicare). This theme reflects racial issues when "poor" is interpreted as a code word for "Black" (Wilson, 1987).

Food Assistance

The history of food assistance in the U.S. can be conveniently divided into discrete eras by decade. The 1930s constituted the era of initiation of surplus commodity distribution. At a time when widespread unemployment, soup kitchens, and bread-lines coexisted with massive destruction of surplus food and loss of income to farm-ers, Congress voted to distribute surplus food as relief, thereby achieving two simultaneous goals: support of agricultural producers and aid to the poor (Poppendieck, 1986). Congress authorized food relief in 1930, more formal oversight of farm prices and production in 1933, a food distribution program in 1935, and pilot School Lunch and Food Stamp Programs in 1936 and 1939, respectively.

The 1940s constituted an era of full employment. With the onset of World War II, both the number of destitute families and food surpluses declined, and cash assis-tance partially replaced food distribution as a form of aid (Kerr, 1988). In the years immediately following the War, hunger and poverty demanded—and received—rela-tively little public attention, a situation that continued through the relatively quies-cent 1950s.

Beginning in 1961, Congress began to expand the distribution of surplus foods and to establish pilot Food Stamp programs in selected counties with high poverty rates; it extended the Food Stamp program nationally in 1964. In 1968, teams of investigators sent to investigate reports of overt malnutrition and hunger found these conditions to be widespread among economically-depressed people in more than 250 "hunger counties" throughout 23 states (Citizens Board of Inquiry, 1968). The report of these investigations elicited demands for immediate expansion of fed-eral efforts to improve food assistance to the poor, as did a CBS television docu-mentary based on the findings. In response, the U.S. Senate in 1968 appointed a Select Committee, chaired by George McGovern, to address issues related to hunger and poverty in America (U.S. Senate, 1977). Other surveys conducted from 1968 to 1970 identified significant levels of malnutrition or inadequate food intake among low-income children and adults, and provided further evidence for the connection between poverty and nutritional risk (Anonymous, 1972). In 1969, President Nixon declared a "War on Hunger" and called for a White House Conference to propose policies to eliminate hunger and malnutrition caused by poverty.

The White House Conference, held in 1970, resulted in calls for further expan-sion of food assistance programs, especially for the most vulnerable groups—women, infants, children, and the elderly (White House Conference, 1970). During the 1970s, the Senate Select Committee introduced numerous bills to expand food assistance, and the programs grew rapidly (U.S. Senate, 1977). From 1969 to 1977, annual federal expenditures for food assistance increased from $1.2 to $8.3 billion. These expenditures proved remarkably effective; in 1977, when investigators revis-ited poverty areas, they observed far less overt malnutrition than had been evident a decade earlier (Kotz, 1979).

In contrast, the decades of the 1980s and 1990s were eras of cost containment and welfare curtailment. Beginning with legislation passed in the early 1980s, wel-fare benefits became more restrictive and increasing numbers of people began to take advantage of food entitlement programs such as Food Stamps. By the peak year of 1994, 10% of U.S. adults—25.5 million people—were receiving Food Stamp bene-fits at a cost of $25.5 million. In the mid-1990s, the USDA sponsored the 15 food assistance programs listed in Table 1. Because the cost of these programs reached

Table 1: Department of Agriculture Food Assistance Programs, 1996[1]

Program	1996 Costs, $ Millions[2]
Food Stamps	25,000
Child Nutrition	
National School Lunch	5,300
School Breakfast	1,100
Child and Adult Care	1,500
Summer Food Service	250
Special Milk	17
Supplemental Food	
WIC[3]	3,700
CSFP[4]	99
Food Donation Programs	
Food Distribution, Indian Reservations	70
Nutrition for the Elderly	146
Disaster Feeding	<1
Temporary Emergency Food Assistance[5]	45
Charitable Institutions and Summer Camps	11
Soup Kitchens and Food Banks[5]	35
1996 Total[6]	38,000

1. Sources: Oliveira, 1997; 1998b.
2. All figures rounded off.
3. Special Supplemental Feeding Program for Women, Infants, and Children.
4. Commodity Supplemental Food Program.
5. Welfare reform legislation in 1996 combined these two programs into one, as of 1997.
6. The total amount decreased in 1997 to $35.8 billion, owing to reduction in spending for the Food Stamp program.

$38 billion annually in 1996 (Oliveira, 1997), they constituted prime targets for budget reduction.

★ CURRENT WELFARE AND FOOD ASSISTANCE POLICIES

The welfare system in the United States encompasses a complex collection of programs that assist the poor with cash, medical insurance, housing, and food. Prior to enactment of welfare reform in 1996, the principal cash assistance program was Aid to Families with Dependent Children (AFDC). Over the years, the value of AFDC monthly payments had declined from a 1970 median of $792 for a family of three to $435 in 1993. Because states were able to establish their own support levels for this program, its monthly benefits varied widely, from an average of $120 in Mississippi to $680 in Connecticut in 1994 (Gunderson, 1998).

Federal decisions about benefits depend on a definition of poverty that is demonstrably outdated (Fisher, 1992). In 1998, the poverty threshold for a family of three was $17,063. By this standard, 13.3% of Americans earned below-poverty incomes, 41% of which lived in households with incomes below half the poverty threshold (*Second Harvest*, 1998). Below-poverty incomes are unequally distributed among Americans; they are characteristic of 11% of Whites, 26.5% of Blacks, and 27.1% of Hispanics. Although children comprise 25% of the total population, 40% of them live in families with poverty-level incomes (Hamilton et al., 1997).

Welfare Reform

Current welfare and food assistance policies are governed by legislation passed in 1996 when President Clinton signed the Personal Responsibility and Work Opportunity Reconciliation Act in order to "...complete the work of ending welfare as we know it, by moving people from welfare to work, demanding responsibility, and doing better by children..." (Pear, 1996: A1). Despite the well-known problems of accountability and equity in state welfare programs (U.S. General Accounting Office, 1995; Kilborn, 1996), and the lack of previous success with attempts to move welfare recipients to work (Solow, 1998), this bill transferred most responsibility for welfare from the federal government to the states, and introduced work requirements, benefit limits, and various types of eligibility restrictions. As has been typical of welfare reform efforts throughout history, the true purpose of this bill was to reduce federal spending on assistance to the poor, in this case by $55 billion per year (Pear, 1996).

396

Welfare reform produced an immediate impact on food assistance programs, most notably by restricting eligibility for Food Stamps, introducing work requirements, and reducing benefit levels (Oliveira, 1998a). By 1997—in just one year—these changes had reduced USDA food assistance spending levels by more than $2 billion by eliminating 2.7 million recipients from Food Stamp rolls (Oliveira, 1998b). As a result of political views that assistance programs cost too much, are abused by recipients, and induce dependency, Food Stamp program costs and participation rates have declined steadily since their peak in 1994 (Oliveira, 1997; 1998b).

Although the overall costs of food assistance may appear high, the benefits to any one individual or family are rather minimal. In 1996, the average monthly Food Stamp benefit was $73 and the average benefit for WIC (the Special Supplemental Feeding Program for Women, Infants, and Children) was $31 (Oliveira, 1997). Such amounts, however, can make a significant difference to families with poverty-level incomes. Food Stamps, for example, provide an average of 8% of the income assistance to poor households (Golan and Nord, 1998).

Welfare: New York City

Because the New York State constitution contains a provision that requires "...aid, care, and support of the needy," state and city agencies are required to compensate for any shortfall in benefits that might occur as a result of the new welfare legislation (Firestone, 1996: A1). In New York City, welfare costs are exceptionally high; 2.2 million of the 7.5 million inhabitants have incomes below 125% of the poverty threshold, among them 900,000 children and 200,000 elderly. More than 800,000 people—half of them children—receive Public Assistance, and 1.1 million people receive Food Stamps (Community Food Resource Center, 1998). The City's Food Bank provides emergency food to 863 agencies that serve 400,000 people each month. Three-fourths of the recipients of emergency food report annual house hold incomes below $10,000 (*Second Harvest*, 1998).

Even with cash and food assistance benefits, New York City welfare recipients have great difficulties meeting expenses (Blum, 1998; Polner, 1998). The maximum

Public Assistance benefit is $577 per month and the maximum Food Stamp benefit is $256 per month. The *average* Food Stamp benefit in New York, however, is $77 per month. Taken together, the maximum total benefit is $9,996 per year (Community Food Resource Center, 1998). In comparison, an individual working at the minimum wage rate of $5.15 per hour, 40 hours per week, 52 weeks per year, will earn a maximum of $10,712 per year. Because even this amount is unlikely to be achieved, minimum-wage jobs provide little incentive for welfare recipients to go to work.

★ WHAT POLICIES MIGHT ADDRESS FOOD INEQUALITIES?

In the current political climate, concerns about the costs of welfare greatly outweigh considerations of social equity or sympathy for the plight of the poor. Thus, the government's major new antihunger initiative is an almost Biblical "gleaning" program that requests voluntary food donations from private corporations or individuals (Clinton, 1997). Such initiatives ignore the overwhelming historical evidence for the failure of private charity to meet the needs of the poor and tend to benefit donors far more than recipients (Poppendieck, 1998).

397

Other aspects of current welfare policies also have roots in history. Corporations, for example, viewed the 1996 legislation as a business opportunity and began competing for the rights to conduct welfare operations through fixed-price contracts with states (Bernstein, 1996). As pointed out by Yates in his 1824 study, such actions raise concerns that the desire to earn profits will cause inappropriate reductions in welfare rolls. In New York City, welfare recipients moved to workfare programs frequently replace unionized employees who are paid four times as much. As a result, public agencies and private corporations have been able to increase their employee rolls yet realize considerable savings on the costs of salaries and benefits. This situation has led some welfare activists to categorize workfare programs as "a form of slavery" (Martin, 1995: B2).

Conservative views of welfare and food assistance as ultimately harmful to recipients ignore the substantial body of evidence for the effectiveness of such programs in providing a safety net for the poor (Golan and Nord, 1998). What past and current policies have not done, singly or together, is to raise incomes above the poverty line (Mayer and Jencks, 1995). To be effective, an antihunger policy must first address the reasons why people are poor and, therefore, solve problems related to the lack of employment, other sources of income, housing (Shinn et al., 1998), education, health care, transportation, child care, and family support systems, and, when needed, mental health and substance abuse care (Schmidt et al., 1998). Meeting any one of these needs, of course, represents a major financial and social challenge.

Nevertheless, the key elements of any truly functional welfare policy—one that provides adequate food security—are well established. The policy should include an adequate minimum wage, increased tax credits, subsidized housing, health care protection, and support for child care, job training programs, and treatment of substance abuse and mental health problems (Ellwood, 1988; Shapiro, 1989). Serious consideration of such comprehensive approaches to eliminating food inequities requires understanding of hunger as a chronic societal problem that cannot be addressed in isolation from other correlates of poverty.

Whether the costs of redressing income and food inequities are too high is a question of politics, not resources. With little controversy, the federal government supports substantial "welfare" for the wealthy. Current federal programs encourage the rising gap between the incomes of rich and poor through entitlements such as Social Security and Medicare, as well as tax-deferred pension plans, tax deductions for mortgage payments and business expenses, capital gains deferrals, untaxed bonds, and tax rates that favor individuals with steady employment, higher earnings, and owned homes (Zepezauer and Naiman, 1996). Clearly, the issue of who benefits from federal funding is a matter of political priority. Otherwise, it would be difficult to explain why Congress would grant $465 million to purchase unnecessary airplanes (Cottle, 1998), more than $165 billion to bail out failed savings-and-loan banks (Labaton, 1998), or $125 billion per year in federal tax relief, subsidies, or other benefits to corporations (Bartlett and Steele, 1998).

Thus, some reduction in the income gap between rich and poor is economically—if not politically—possible. Certainly, other countries with far less wealth have far more equitable social policies, designed particularly to protect children and their families (Cornia and Danziger, 1997). Some recognition of the need to redress income inequities among Americans is evident in recent reports of investigations into the unfairness of New York City welfare policies (Swarns, 1998a), in state efforts to increase enrollments in public assistance programs (Swarns, 1998b), and in adjustments to welfare reform laws that make them somewhat less onerous (Oliveira, 1998a). People concerned about food and income inequalities can take some reassurance from the knowledge that welfare policies tend to occur in cycles. Efforts to promote a more equitable cycle with greater protection against hunger and poverty are highly worthwhile and certain to benefit those most in need of assistance.

REFERENCES

Abbott, E., *Public Assistance. Vol. 1. American Principles and Policies* (Chicago: University of Chicago Press, 1940).

Alaimo, K., Briefel, R. R., Frongillo, E. A., Jr., and Olson, C. M., "Food Insufficiency Exists in the United States: Results from the Third National Health and Nutrition Examination Survey (NHANES III)," *American Journal of Public Health* 88 (March 1998): 419–426.

Anonymous, "Highlights from the Ten-State Nutrition Survey," *Nutrition Today* 7:4 (1972): 4–11.

Anonymous, "100 Leading National Advertisers: 43rd Annual Report." *Advertising Age* (September 28, 1998): s3–s50.

Bartlett, D. L., and Steele, J. B., "Corporate Welfare," *Time* (November 9, 1998): 36–54.

Bernstein, N., "Giant Companies Entering Race to Run State Welfare Programs: Powers Like Lockheed Explore New Profit Area," *The New York Times* (September 15, 1996): 1, 26.

Blum, David, "When the Ends Don't Meet." *The New York Times* (November 1, 1998), Section 14 (City): 1, 12.

Citizen's Board of Inquiry into Hunger and Malnutrition in the United States, *Hunger, U.S.A.* (Boston: Beacon Press, 1968).

Clinton, W. J., "Proclamation 7019 of September 12, 1997: National Week of Food Recovery, 1997," *Federal Register* 62:180 (September 17, 1997): 48,929–48,930.

Community Food Resource Center, *Who Are New York City's Hungry?* (Fact Sheet, May 1998 Update).

Cornia, G. A., and Danziger, S., *Child Poverty and Deprivation in the Industrialized Countries, 1945–1995* (Oxford: Clarendon Press, 1997).

Cottle, M., "High on the Hog," *The New York Times Magazine* (November 22, 1998): 56.

de Grazia, A., and Gurr, T., *American Welfare* (New York: New York University Press, 1961).

Ellwood, D. E., *Poor Support: Poverty in the American Family* (New York: Basic Books, 1988), pp. 231–243.

Firestone, D., "New York Costs for Its Program Seen as Surging," *The New York Times* (August 1, 1996): A1, A25.

Fisher, G. M., "The Development and History of the Poverty Thresholds," *Social Security Bulletin* 55:4 (Winter 1992): 3–14.

Gallo, A. E., *The Food Marketing System in 1996. Agriculture Information Bulletin No. 743* (Washington, D.C.: U.S. Department of Agriculture, 1998).

Golan, E., and Nord, M., "How Government Assistance Affects Income," *FoodReview* 21 (January–April 1998): 2–7.

Governor's Task Force on Hunger, *Hunger in Washington State* (Spokane, WA: October 1988).

Gunderson, C., "Economic Growth, Welfare Reform, and the Food Stamp Program," *FoodReview* (January–April 1998): 23–27.

Hamilton, W. L., Cook, J. T., Thompson, W. W., Buron, L. F., Frongillo, E. A., Jr., Olson, C. M., and Wehler, C. A., Household Food Security in the United States in 1995: *Summary Report of the Food Security Measurement Project* (Washington, D.C.: U.S. Department of Agriculture, September 1997).

Institute of Medicine. *Recommended Dietary Allowances*, 10th ed. (Washington, D.C.: National Academy Press, 1989).

Kantor, L. S., Lipton, K., Manchester, A., and Oliveira, V., "Estimating and Addressing America's Food Losses," *FoodReview* 20:1 (1997): 2–12.

Karp, R. J., ed., *Malnourished Children in the United States: Caught in the Cycle of Poverty* (New York: Springer, 1993).

Katz, M. B., *In the Shadow of the Poorhouse: a Social History of Welfare in America* (New York: Basic Books, 1986).

Kerr, N. A., "The Evolution of USDA Surplus Disposal Programs," *National Food Review* 11:3 (1988): 25–30.

Kilborn, P. T., "Welfare All Over the Map," *The New York Times* (December 8, 1996): E3.

Klebaner, B. J., *Public Poor Relief in America 1790–1860* (New York: Arno Press, 1976).

Kotz, N., *Hunger in America: The Federal Response* (New York: The Field Foundation, 1979).

Labaton, S., "The Debacle That Buried Washington: Long after the S. & L. Crisis, Courts Are Handing Taxpayers a New Bill," *The New York Times* (November 22, 1998), Section 3: 1, 12.

Malthus, T. R., "An Essay on Population," Vol. II, Book III (1817). (Reprinted in New York: E.P. Dutton & Co, 1914.)

Martin, D., "New York Workfare Expansion Fuels Debate," *The New York Times* (September 1, 1995): A1, B2.

Mayer, S., and Jencks, C., "War on Poverty: No Apologies, Please," *The New York Times* (November 9, 1995): A29.

Miles, A. P., *An Introduction to Public Welfare* (Boston: D.C. Heath & Co., 1949).

Nestle, M., "Dietary Advice for the 1990s: The Political History of the Food Guide Pyramid," *Caduceus* 9 (1993): 136–153.

Nestle, M., and Guttmacher, S., "Hunger in the United States: Rationale, Methods, and Policy Implications of State Hunger Surveys," *Journal of Nutrition Education* 24 (1992): 8s–22s.

Oliveira, V., "Food-Assistance Spending Held Steady in 1996," *FoodReview* 20 (January–April 1997): 49–56.

Oliveira, V., "Welfare Reform Affects USDA's Food-Assistance Programs," *FoodReview* 21 (January–April 1998a): 8–15.

Oliveira, V., "Spending on Food-Assistance Programs Decreased in 1997," *FoodReview* 21 (January–April 1998b): 16–22.

Pear, R., "Clinton to Sign Welfare Bill That Ends U.S. Aid Guarantee and Gives States Broad Power," *The New York Times* (August 1, 1996): A1, A22.

Physician Task Force on Hunger in America, *Hunger in America: The Growing Epidemic* (Middletown, CT: Wesleyan University Press, 1985).

Polner, R., "Work and Welfare: New Rules Aim to Reduce Number on City's Rolls," *Newsday* (November 1, 1998): 4, 5.

Poppendieck, J., *Breadlines Knee-Deep in Wheat: Food Assistance in the Great Depression* (New Brunswick, NJ: Rutgers University Press, 1986).

Poppendieck, J., *Sweet Charity? Emergency Food and the End of Entitlement* (New York: Viking, 1998).

Putnam, J. J., and Allshouse, J. E. *Food Consumption, Prices, and Expenditures, 1970–95. Statistical Bulletin No. 939* (Washington, D.C.: U.S. Department of Agriculture, 1997).

Rose, D., and Oliveira, V., "Nutrient Intakes of Individuals from Food-Insufficient Households in the United States," *American Journal of Public Health* 87 (December 1997): 1956–1961.

Schmidt, L., Weisner, C., and Wiley, J., "Substance Abuse and the Course of Welfare Dependency," *American Journal of Public Health* 88:11 (1998): 1616–1622.

Second Harvest, *Hunger 1997: The Faces and Facts* (New York: Food for Survival, 1997).

Shapiro, I., and Greenstein, R. *Making Work Pay: A New Agenda for Poverty Policies* (Washington, D.C.: Center on Budget and Policy Priorities, March 21, 1989).

Shinn, M., Weitzman, B.C., Stojanovic, D., Knickman, J. R., Jiménez, L., Duchon, L., James S., and Krantz, D. H., "Predictors of Homelessness among Families in New York City: From Shelter Request to Housing Stability," *American Journal of Public Health* 88:11 (1998): 1651–1657.

Solow, R. M., *Work and Welfare* (Princeton, NJ: Princeton University Press, 1998).

State of Texas Senate Interim Committee on Hunger and Malnutrition, *Faces of Hunger in the Shadow of Plenty: 1984 Report and Recommendations* (Austin, TX: November 30, 1984).

Swarns, R. L., "U.S. Inquiry Asks If City Deprives Poor: Fear That Welfare Policy May Limit Aid Unfairly," *The New York Times* (November 8, 1998a): L39.

Swarns, R. L., "In an Odd Turn, Officials Are Pushing Welfare," *The New York Times* (November 22, 1998b), Week Section: 4.

U.S. Department of Agriculture. *Food Marketing Review, 1994–95. Agricultural Economic Report No. 743* (Washington, D.C.: U.S. Department of Agriculture, 1996).

U.S. General Accounting Office, *Block Grants: Characteristics, Experience, and Lessons Learned, GAO/HEHS-95-74* (Washington, D.C.: U.S. Government Printing Office, February 9, 1995).

U.S. Senate Select Committee on Nutrition and Human Needs, *Final Report* (Washington, D.C.: U.S. Government Printing Office, December 1977).

Wehler, C. A., Scott, R. I., and Anderson, J. J., *Community Childhood Hunger Identification Project: A Survey of Childhood Hunger in the United States* (Washington, D.C.: Food Research and Action Center, July 1995).

White House Conference on Food, Nutrition, and Health, *Final Report* (Washington, D.C.: U.S. Government Printing Office, 1970).

Wilson, W. J., *The Truly Disadvantaged: The Inner City, the Underclass, and Public Policy* (Chicago, IL: University of Chicago Press, 1987).

Yates, John V. N., "Report of the Secretary of State in 1824 on the Relief and Settlement of the Poor," in Rothman, David J., ed. *Poverty, U.S.A.: The Historical Record. The Almshouse Experience: Collected Reports* [New York: Arno Press and *The New York Times* (1971): 939–1145.]

Zepezauer, M. and Naiman, A., *Take the Rich Off Welfare* (Tucson, AZ: Odonian Press, 1996).

GROWING FOOD, GROWING COMMUNITY:
COMMUNITY SUPPORTED
AGRICULTURE IN RURAL IOWA

30

BETTY L. WELLS, SHELLY GRADWELL,
AND RHONDA YODER

★ INTRODUCTION

Community Supported Agriculture (CSA) has taken root and is thriving on the fringes of the global, industrial food system. As the name conveys, CSA benefits agriculture and producer-growers and, by implication, community, the land, and consumer-eaters. This paper examines the emergence of CSA in a rural state in the US midwest, focusing on community building processes by which CSA brings together growers and eaters in a growing circle united by food.

The CSA partnership concept originated in the 1960s, when Japanese women, concerned with the increase in imported food and the loss of farmers and farmland, asked local farmers to grow vegetables and fruits for them. The farmers agreed, on the condition that a number of families commit themselves to supporting the farmers. "The *teikei* concept was born, which translated literally means partnership, but philosophically means 'food with the farmer's face on it'" (Van En, 1995, p. 29).

This model, first applied in the USA in the mid-1980s, became known as Community Supported Agriculture, or CSA, defined by Gradwell et al. (1996, p. 1) as:

> ... farmers and community members working together as partners to create a local food system. CSA farmers may produce fresh vegetables, fruits, meats, fiber, and related products directly for local community members. CSA differs from direct marketing in that members commit to a full-season price in the spring, sharing the risks of production. With this up-front support, farmers can concentrate on growing quality food and caring for the land. In return, members know where their food comes from and how it is grown; they share a connection to the land and the farmer.

Since then, the number of CSAs in the US has grown to an estimated 635 in 1996 (Bio-Dynamic Farming and Gardening Association, 1997).

CSA has also grown in Iowa, with approximately forty CSA farms in 1996 (ISU Extension, 1996). Of this number, three CSAs began during the 1995 growing season, nine in the 1996 season, fifteen in the 1997 season and thirteen, thus far, in 1998. Because more is known about CSA consumers and urban CSA than about CSA producers and rural CSA, we interviewed CSA producers to learn more about rural CSA. After setting the context in rural Iowa, we draw upon the interviews conducted between July 1996 and March 1997 to explore rural CSA and CSA values. We then show how these values come together in the Magic Beanstalk CSA in central Iowa, and the synergistic potential of a local food system.

★ IOWA AGRICULTURE AND RURAL COMMUNITY: THEN AND NOW

Once in Iowa, rural and agriculture were nearly synonymous; rural communities and family farms were interdependent. The globalization of agriculture, which accelerated in the 1980s, and the ensuing farm debt crisis in Iowa profoundly impacted this connection. In addition to the increased competitive pressures of a global economy, domestic power shifted from rural to urban. This shift was manifest in growing public concern for safe food, the impact of agricultural technologies and practices on the environment, and the cost of farm programs to taxpayers. Waves of economic restructuring have weakened the economies and social and physical infrastructure of rural communities.

While CSA might at first glance seem ideally suited to rural areas, most CSA thrives on urban borders where markets are available and transportation costs are low. Although often associated with agriculture, and while agriculture is indeed economically important, Iowa has become an urban state and a net importer of food. The loss of our ability to feed ourselves has been accompanied with the loss of the indigenous knowledge needed to grow, process and prepare food, and the loss of local and small-scale food processing capacity essential for extending a relatively short growing season.

Yet, even today, the health of many rural communities in Iowa still depends in large part on a healthy agriculture, and a vital farm family and family farm still depend on a healthy rural community with schools, hospitals and municipal services. CSA is one way to strengthen ties between agriculture and nonagricultural rural people, and between rural and urban people, to the benefit of all.

★ RURAL CSA PRODUCERS IN IOWA

CSA offers opportunities for small-scale farmer-growers. In addition to vegetables and fruits, many Iowa CSAs provide animal products such as meat, eggs and wool. CSA in Iowa offers a supplemental, value-added market for mid-sized producers, especially of livestock. Low start-up costs and the seasonal nature of production make CSA attractive to beginning and part-time farmers.

Over half of Iowa's CSAs serve rural areas and small towns, despite producers' initial misgiving about finding support in rural areas. Among CSA producers who began by recruiting urban members, often requiring long distance deliveries, several have found willing members among their rural neighbors. Some have all their members within a few miles of the farm. Members include conventional farm families who join because they prefer, but no longer have the time to grow, homegrown vegetables. As one CSA producer explains:

> At first I thought that this was something that won't work in the rural setting. I thought that this is something for the city people. I am finding out that there are a lot of people in the rural community that really value this. I am surprised at that, but that is what I am seeing. So many of my shareholders feel that they should have a garden, but they don't want to do the work or they can't do the work, they just really can't. In this modern age when the women are outside of the home so much, I can see that this is really going to grow a lot.

She explains the very pragmatic motivation of her shareholders:

> They understand the value of freshness, absolute freshness, lack of chemicals and the fact that they didn't have to do it themselves. And they all know what real tomatoes taste like. The rural people are the ones concerned about freshness and chemicals, more than I thought.

403

The rapid growth of CSA in Iowa is a promising sign that the CSA model may suit Iowa's rural farming communities and that a smaller-scale, people-focused, and community-based agriculture belongs here.

★ CSA VALUES

What values spark CSA? All CSA producers work with a budget and want to operate in a way that makes money. If the CSA does not generate adequate income, it will not be sustained. However, CSA producers also express several, often interrelated, nonmonetary motives in deciding to begin CSA, including education, diversity, and modeling a community-based alternative food system.

Education

Education is a value expressed by most CSA producers, who find a variety of ways to integrate education within CSA. One points to educating about what it takes to grow food.

> We often feel that there's not a good understanding about what decisions you have to make to be a farmer, and constraints you're under. It's just not a real simple thing to get involved with. It just was very nice for us to have people come out and ask us real directly, "well, how does it work?"

Others emphasize food and nutrition:

> It's really education that makes a difference, the nutrition and the cooking. Making food, something pleasant and something shared.

Many CSA producers value the time they spend with children in a practical context, passing knowledge between generations, and building friendships with the extended, nonbiological family of CSA members.

Here's the greatest thing about being in a CSA. They bring all their kids, and they come piling out of the car and they start doing stuff. Yesterday this mom gave me a present. It was a book. And she wrote, "thank you for teaching our family so much about food."

Growers share in the educational process:

I have grown and eaten quite a wide variety of stuff, but not as wide a variety as I'm growing now. Some of the stuff I'm growing I had never grown before, never eaten before. I'm educating myself as well as my customers.

This emphasis on variety also speaks to diversity, another thread running through the interviews.

Diversity

404

Diversity is expressed in several ways. As in the previous example, some point to variety in their garden:

I have over thirty varieties of flowers in my two-acre CSA vegetable garden. The flowers add diversity, beneficial insects, habitat, and beauty to my gardens. My members are excited to see them each week.

In many cases CSA influences the diversification of a conventional farm:

I think CSA is a really good opportunity for producers to diversify their farms and make some money from a completely different source....CSA is diverse not only in space, but in time and enterprise requirements. The labor requirements blend well with some grain farms, since CSA labor requirements are highest in the midsummer when grain labor is needed least.

One grower sees CSA as alternative land use in which resources are managed more intensively and with more diversity—in sharp contrast to production agriculture.

Women constitute the majority of CSA producers in Iowa, 19 of 27 in 1996 and 27 of 40 by 1998 (ISU Extension, 1996; Gradwell et al., 1998). This diversity is notable in a state where men generally dominate agriculture. Some started CSAs for the opportunity to earn additional income while staying on the farm and involving children.

I want to make a certain amount per hour, that's real important. But at the same time we also want to be around home, to be around home with Johnny. To have time to push him in the swing. For that reason we can afford to take a little less per hour. It has been a part of our discussions.

For many, CSAs constitute an independent enterprise, sometimes—but not always—as part of a larger farming operation. One self-described "conventional-farmer" who markets poultry via CSA explains that:

I've always been involved in the farm operation but always as an assistant. I've helped in the fields, and with the hogs, and with the bookwork. That's been important to the farm, but never real satisfying for me. I've always been pushing for a couple of different things. One, to be the main manager of something. To have my own enterprise is how we say it at home. The other is to do something on our farm with more of a social conscience, not strictly just dollars and cents. What appealed to me [about CSA] was that I could produce some kind of food. I had a farm. I had some resources. I had some know-how. As the CSA idea developed that has felt good to me, it's given me a much stronger position in our farming family, our farming business.

Another CSA producer operating in the context of a conventional farm notes her influence on the decisions of her farming partner to move from conventional toward more sustainable farming practices.

My husband is intrigued by this and very supportive, but he thinks that being organic is just a fad. He says that if people get hungry enough they won't care if [the food] had some chemicals on it when it was a small plant. But our situation isn't that. We are not at war and fighting off starvation. I mentioned to him that I could find some contacts if he wanted to grow some organic grain. So he's toying with this idea, saying let's check into this, it might be feasible, we might try it. And once we get organic grain then we can do organic hogs. We'll see.

She is certain that he would never have considered organic production without her participation in CSA.

The Community-Based Alternative

According to Gail Feenstra (1997, p. 28), community food systems are:

...rooted in particular places, aim to be economically viable for farmers and consumers, use ecologically sound production and distribution practices, and enhance social equity and democracy for all members of the community.

Feenstra (1997, p. 34) suggests that the best examples of local food systems are characterized by

...a broad vision of the food economy that addresses both urban and rural concerns. These concerns, from food access to farmland preservation to community health, are seen as everyone's. The creation of regional food systems links people from urban neighborhoods with people from local farms to make one community. This community provides adequate food to residents, a sustainable farming system, a safe, clean environment, and satisfying social and cultural interactions around food.

Do these producers consider themselves part of a local food system? Many note the disconnect between production and consumption and between rural and urban.

CSA produce stays in the community whereas a lot of the corn and soybeans that are grown here just go away....It doesn't make sense to live in a farming community and have this food coming from California and Florida.

One grower suggests that "our urban centers are out of touch with our rural centers, and they need to get back in touch for the survival of each group." Another CSA grower goes so far as to suggest:

We wanted to make the connection between the towns and the farms because we believe if that connection had been strong that the farm crisis of the 1980s would not have been as bad.

The CSA producers interviewed clearly recognize the systemic and sensible nature of what they are doing. They view what they are doing as a choice: "People ask me, 'How do you do this?' I tell them, 'I don't go to the mall.' It's a conscious choice."

Do they see themselves as contributing to an alternative to the dominant agribusiness, industrial food model? One producer indicates that "What's really important to me is the idea of being part of a model of another way of doing things," and another that "I'm doing it because I'm trying to make a difference." Members and producers share this sentiment:

I feel like I have the power to help change the economic picture in Iowa on top of enjoying good food. We became members because we enjoy fresh vegetables and because we really believe in the philosophies behind CSA.

406

Growers value the cooperative spirit of CSA, "cooperation with nature and cooperation with people":

Before we started working together in the CSA, we didn't know each other at all. Each of us has expertise in certain areas and we have been able to put that all together and come up with a real working group. We respect each other and know that we will help each other.

A successful local food system is also a political system engaging citizens in debate about purpose, value and power, prompting recognition of limits and raising questions of equity and the reallocation of power (Feenstra, 1997, p. 34). CSA offers a home for visionaries and a focus for action:

I tend to think in the big picture realm, drawn by a rather strong vision of where and how I'd like things to be. This perspective often conflicts with the realities I find around me. The conflict has often created some real frustration. CSA is one of the places where I translate the vision into action among the real circumstances that surround me. It keeps me grounded and balanced. Being more grounded challenges me to interpret my vision in terms of the realities I've often found limiting. I believe that helps me to hold on to my vision, yet convey and understand it in a way that is more relevant to folks around me.

CSA allows Iowans with concern a place for their energies. Many Iowans are concerned about the hog issue,[1] but I do not think they believe they can impact it politically. By choosing where their food comes from, I see them voting for this new food system.

CSA empowers people to create by their own actions an alternative economy, one in which what they do makes a difference to their immediate lives and the lives of others in their community.

An Iowa Example

The values of education, diversity, and transformation come together in CSA community-building activities such as harvest festivals, potlucks, cooking groups and field tours. The Magic Beanstalk CSA in central Iowa is typical in this regard although somewhat unique in Iowa.

In 1997, some Magic Beanstalk members started the Field to Family (FTF) Community Food Project. The stated goals of the project are to work for a local, sustainable and equitable food system, to foster more self-reliant local food production, and to help lower-income families gain access to wholesome food. The project seeks to rebuild community linkages between those working for sustainable farms and food systems, and those working for sustainable families. The latter include human and social service agencies and local churches and denominational organizations seeking long-term, systemic solutions to poverty and hunger. A key partner, the Mid Iowa Community Action Agency (MICA), strongly endorsed the project proposal. This endorsement noted a keen awareness of the need to develop a more comprehensive, sustainable and grassroots approach to the problem of hunger and poor nutrition in central Iowa, and of the need for small-scale business and economic development in rural areas. MICA has actively and successfully recruited clients to participate in the FTF project.

FTF creates contact between people who haven't been in touch before, merging low-income families into a circle of weekly CSA food distributions and cooking groups, helping to bring families who are often marginalized into a broader community, thus meeting community food and human needs. In the future, low-income individuals and families will be provided opportunities and mentoring to participate in shaping and implementing FTF initiatives.

In addition to such leadership opportunities, education on food preparation and nutrition is being incorporated into project activities. FTF may integrate the curriculum of an extension food and nutrition program with a hands-on cooking class at the site of weekly food distribution, offering the nutrition program one week and the cooking class the next.

In the 1997 growing season, Magic Beanstalk donated over 3500 pounds of fresh food to the local food bank. Plans to support wider access to low-income families to wholesome food include local food currency vouchers that may be used at the farmers market. FTF is also working to expand the capacity of local food banks to handle perishable food through the purchase of restaurant-size refrigerators.

FTF is expanding the work of the Magic Beanstalk CSA in a variety of community-building ways, creating (or in some cases redefining or reinvigorating) relationships between community organizations. Plans on the horizon include supporting microenterprise development such as catering, and processing, and sponsoring community meals. One Magic Beanstalk CSA producer, in 1998, is offering all of his land to grow food for the local food bank. In so doing, he is also mentoring a number of volunteers who are assisting him to learn and practice gardening.

With food as a focal point, common ground is being created and local food system projects are becoming part of the new and existing work of growing numbers of individuals, families and organizations. Further possibilities exist for bringing others into the network, for example civic clubs, schools, hospitals, and local restaurants. The FTF project staff are working with conference centers that serve Iowa State University to develop menus that feature locally (and sustainably) grown foods. These meals are gaining statewide recognition and are coordinated with similar efforts in other institutions in Iowa. These Iowa-grown menus are creating markets for more growers, educating eaters about the source of their food, and building statewide support for community-based food systems. FTF is moving from being a

407

project to being woven into the work, consciousness and institutional fabric of central Iowa.

★ SUMMARY AND CONCLUSIONS

Food, as a focal point linking production and consumption, has much integrative potential. CSA as a community-focused food systems model transcends the conventional boundaries between producer and consumer and rural and urban. Food knits closer family and community ties. CSA makes community visible again, community as a vital living entity not an abstract, nostalgic concept.

By incorporating CSA into daily family and food rhythms and the functions of existing community groups, CSA brings a network together into a closer relationship with food, farming, each other, and the place where food is grown and eaten. The values embodied in CSA counterbalance those of competition, homogenization, standardization, fabrication (not to mention lack of flavor) often associated with the global food system. CSA builds community capacity and the potential for local action to influence the shape and quality of daily life. CSA multiplied, as part of an extended network of local, small-scale actions, provides a sensible and viable alternative to the large-scale, global-industrial food system.

NOTE

1. Megascale hog confinement operations are an extremely contentious issue in Iowa and many other states.

REFERENCES

Bio-Dynamic Farming and Gardening Association, (1997), Telephone conversation, Kimberton, PA.

Feenstra, G., (1997), Local food systems and sustainable communities. *American Journal of Alternative Agriculture*, 12 (1), 28–36.

Gradwell, S. et al., (1996), *Community Supported Agriculture: Local Food Systems for Iowa*, ISU Extension publication Pm-1692, December, Ames, IA.

Gradwell, S., (1997), "Community supported agriculture takes root in Iowa." In S. Gilman (coordinator), *CSA Farm Network, a project of the Northeast Organic Farming Association*. (Second in a series of three publications.)

Gradwell, S. et al., (1997), *Iowa Community Supported Agriculture Resource Guide for Producers and Organizers*, ISU Extension publication Pm-1694, Ames, IA.

Gradwell, S. et al., (1998), *Iowa CSA Farms: Statewide List of Iowa CSA Farms, Producers, and Organizers*, ISU Extension publication Pm-16931, Ames, IA.

ISU Extension, (1996), *Farms and Organizers: Statewide List of Iowa CSA Farms, Producers, and Organizers 1996–97*, ISU Extension publication Pm-1693, December, Ames, IA.

Norberg-Hodge, H., (1996), "Break up the monoculture." *The Nation*, 263 (15–22 July), 20–23.

Van En, R., (1995), "Eating for your community: towards Agriculture Supported Community." *In Context*, 42 (Fall), 29–31.

CONTRIBUTORS

Warren Belasco teaches American studies at the University of Maryland Baltimore County. He is the author of *Appetite for Change: How the Counterculture Took on the Food Industry* (1993) and is currently completing a book on the future of the food system.

Amy Bentley is an assistant professor in the Department of Nutrition and Food Studies at New York University. A cultural historian by training, she is the author of *Eating for Victory: Food Rationing and the Politics of Domesticity* (1998) as well as several articles on such diverse topics as food riots, Martha Stewart and food, and the politics of southwestern cuisine. She is currently working on a cultural history of the infant food industry in the United States.

Josephine Beoku-Betts is associate professor of sociology and women's studies at Florida Atlantic University. Her research focuses on African and Caribbean women in scientific careers and on gender and cultural identity in African-American communities in the Sea Islands of Georgia and South Carolina. She is co-editor of *Women and Education in Sub-Saharan Africa* and has published papers in the *NWSA Journal, Gender and Society*, and the *Journal of Women and Minorities in Science and Engineering*. She is a co-editor of *Women's Studies International Forum* and of *Gender and Society* book reviews.

Joan Jacobs Brumberg is a Stephen H. Weiss Presidential Fellow and professor at Cornell University, where she teaches courses in history, women's studies, and human development. She is the author of *Fasting Girls: The History of Anorexia Nervosa* (1988) and *The Body Project: An Intimate History of American Girls* (1997).

Lawrence Busch is University Distinguished Professor of Sociology and director of the Institute for Food and Agricultural Standards at Michigan State University. He is author of *The Eclipse of Morality: Science, State, and Market* (2000), and he is widely published in the areas of the new biotechnologies and the political economy and globalization of food and agriculture.

Eileen Chia-Ching Fung is assistant professor of English at the University of San Francisco. She has published several articles on the construction of race, gender, and sexuality in travel and immigrant narratives in Asian-American literature and films. Her current project includes examining how the acts of eating and incorporation as well as purging and expulsion relate to the cultural and psychological formation of ethnic minority identities.

Carole M. Counihan is professor of anthropology and director of women's studies at Millersville University in Pennsylvania. She is author of *The Anthropology of Food* *and Body* (1999), and co-editor with Steven Kaplan of *Food and Gender: Identity and Power* (1998) and with Penny Van Esterik of *Food and Culture: A Reader* (1997). She is working on a book on food, gender, and family in twentieth-century Florence and is conducting ethnographic fieldwork on food, gender, and ethnic identity in the San Luis Valley of Colorado.

Deborah Fink is an independent anthropologist who lives in Ames, Iowa. Her most recent book, *Cutting into the Meatpacking Line: Workers and Change in the Rural Midwest* (1998), is about gender, ethnicity, and class in the rural U.S. workforce.

Harriet Friedmann is professor of sociology and fellow of the Centre for International Studies at the University of Toronto in Canada. She is author of articles on farm structure, including class, gender, and age relations; agricultural regions; the international politics and regulation of food and agriculture; cultural and biological diversity in relation to farming systems and cuisines; and agroecology. She is working on two books, one connecting farm structures to international food regimes and the other examining food as an aspect of environmental history, linking it to cultural, social, and political-economic history through the lens of the hamburger.

Donna Gabaccia is the Charles H. Stone Professor of American History at the University of North Carolina at Charlotte. She is the author of *We Are What Eat: Ethnic Food and the Making of Americans* (1998) and *Italy's Many Diasporas* (2000), and co-editor (with Fraser Ottanelli) of *Italy's Workers of the World* (2001) and (with Franca Iacovetta) of *Foreign, Female, and Fighting Back* (forthcoming). Her new research on the American construction industry and its workers combines in new ways her long-standing interests in material culture, gender, and transnational life.

Irene Glasser is a Research Fellow at the Center for Alcohol and Addiction Studies at Brown University and received her Ph.D. in anthropology in 1986 from the University of Connecticut. Since that time, she has been conducting research on homelessness, soup kitchens, mothers in prison, and welfare, in the United States and Canada. She is interested in developing and refining research strategies that evaluate the efficacy of outreach and intervention programs for the homeless alcohol and drug abuser. She is also interested in understanding the effects of mandated treatment that is tied to the receipt of survival assistance.

Shelly Gradwell was a founder of the Magic Beanstalk CSA, one of the first CSAs in Iowa. She is now with the Iowa State Sustainable Agriculture Extension Program and the Iowa State University Department of Sociology, where her research and extension work focus on local food system development. She also coordinates sustainable agriculture youth programs for Practical Farmers of Iowa and during the summer season works as a commerical salmon fisher in Alaska.

John L. Hess, author and commentator, once served as food editor at the *New York Times.*

Karen Hess, culinary historian, published *The Carolina Rice Kitchen: The African Connection* (1998), *The Virginia Housewife* (1984), and *Martha Washington's Booke of Cookery* (1996), among others, and is completing *Mr. Jefferson's Table: The Culinary Legacy of Monticello.*

Kate Kane was a doctoral candidate in radio/television/film at Northwestern University with interests in questions of power and popular culture when she wrote her article.

Harvey Levenstein is professor emeritus of history at McMaster University in Hamilton, Ontario, Canada. He is the author of two books on the history of labor, *Labor Organizations in the United States and Mexico* (1971) and *Communism, Anticommunism, and the CIO* (1981), and two social histories of American food, *Revolution at the Table: The Transformation of the American Diet* (1988) and *Paradox of Plenty: A Social History of Eating in Modern America* (1993). He recently published *Seductive Journey: American Tourists in France from Jefferson to the Jazz Age* (1998) and is presently working on a sequel to that, as well as various projects in food history.

James H. McDonald is associate professor of anthropology at the University of Texas–San Antonio and senior editor of the journal *Culture & Agriculture*. Among his major research interests are agricultural development, globalization, and processes of political-economic change in central and western Mexico. His work appears in a variety of edited volumes and journals, and he is editor of *The Applied Anthropology Reader* (2002).

411

Gerad Middendorf is assistant professor in the Department of Sociology, Anthropology, and Social Work at Kansas State University. He is co-author of several articles and book chapters on the new agricultural biotechnologies and democratic participation in technology choice.

Christiana E. Miewald is an outcome evaluator at the Institute for Local Government Administration and Rural Development at Ohio University. She received her Ph.D. in anthropology from the University of Kentucky. Her primary interests are in issues of rural poverty, nutrition, health, gender, development, and welfare reform. She has published on diabetes among Native Americans and urban populations. Her most recent fieldwork focused on the effect of welfare reform and economic restructuring on gender relations in Appalachian Kentucky. "National Myths, State Policy, and Community-Directed Media: Representational Politics and the Reconfiguration of Welfare," based upon this research, is forthcoming in *Urban Geography.*

Sidney Mintz is the Wm. L. Straus Jr. Professor Emeritus in the Department of Anthropology at Johns Hopkins University, and the author of *Sweetness and Power* (1985) and *Tasting Food, Tasting Freedom* (1996).

Gary Paul Nabhan is director of the Center for Sustainable Environments at Northern Arizona University, and author of the recently published *Coming Home to Eat: The Pleasures and Politics and Local Foods.*

Marion Nestle has been professor and chair of the Department of Nutrition and Food Studies at New York University since fall 1988. Her research focuses on the scientific, social, cultural, and economic factors that influence the development, implementation, and acceptance of federal dietary guidance policies. She is the author of *Food Politics: How the Food Industry Influences Nutrition and Health* (2002) and *The Politics of Food Safety and Biotechnology* (2003).

Tracey N. Poe received in 1999 her Ph.D. from Harvard University's program in the History of American Civilization. She is currently assistant professor of history and the humanities at Barat College of DePaul University. Her most recent work is on food and small business among African immigrants to Chicago in the 1990s.

Elizabeth Ransom is a Ph.D. candidate in the Department of Sociology at Michigan State University. She is the author of an article on eating disorders among female college athletes in *Interpreting Weight* (1999) and is a co-author of several articles on agricultural biotechnologies. She has just completed her dissertation field research in South Africa where she is focusing on the impact of changing standards in the red meat industry.

William Roseberry served as chair and professor of anthropology at the New School for Social Research. He is the author of *Coffee and Capitalism in the Venezuelan Andes* (1983) and *Anthropologies and Histories: Essays in Culture, History, and Political Economy* (1989).

Sharon R. Sherman is professor of English and director of the Folklore Program at the University of Oregon, where she teaches courses on folklore, film, fieldwork, video production, mythology, and popular culture. Her films and videos address the interconnection between traditional expressive behavior and the creative process. In addition to numerous articles, Sherman is the author of *Chainsaw Sculptor: The Art of J. Chester Armstrong* (1995) and *Documenting Ourselves: Film, Video, and Culture* (1998).

Janet Siskind received her Ph.D. from Columbia University and is currently a professor of anthropology at Rutgers University. Her current research includes social class in New England and upper-class consciousness in the transformation from mercantile capitalism to industrial capitalism.

Mike Skladany recently earned a Ph.D. from Michigan State University. His dissertation (2000) was titled "Science, Technology and Sociology: The Case of Transgenic Fish Research and Development." Prior to attending graduate school, he worked in rural Thailand as a fisheries/aquaculture advisor on a number of small-scale development initiatives. He is the author of several of articles on aquaculture development and is currently based in Minneapolis, Minnesota, with the Institute for Agriculture and Trade Policy as a sociologist/coordinator for an industrial fish farming campaign.

Ruth Striegel-Moore received a diploma in psychology from the Eberhard-Karls-University in Tuebingen, Germany, and a Ph.D. in clinical psychology from the University of South Carolina. She is internationally renowned for her research on eating disorders. Her current research focuses on the epidemiology of eating disorders and is funded by the Institute of Mental Health, the Institute of Diabetes, Digestive and Kidney Disease, and the Office for Research on Women's Health.

James M. Taggart is Lewis Audenreid Professor of History and Archaeology at Franklin and Marshall College. He is the author of *Nahuat Myth and Social Structure*

(1983), *Enchanted Maidens: Gender Relations in Spanish Folktales of Courtship and Marriage* (1990), *The Bear and His Sons: Masculinity in Spanish and Mexican Folktales* (1997), and with José Inez Taylor *Alex and the Hobo: A Chicano Life and Story* (2002).

Becky Wangsgaard Thompson is associate professor of sociology at Simmons College, where she teaches African-American studies, women's studies, and sociology. She is the author of *A Hunger So Wide and So Deep: A Multiracial View of Women's Eating Problems* (1994), and co-editor with Sangeeta Tyagi of *Names We Call Home: Autobiography on Racial Identity* (1996) and *Beyond a Dream Deferred: Multicultural Education and the Politics of Excellence* (1993), which won the Gustavus Myers Award for Outstanding Book on Human Rights in North America. Currently, she is completing *A Promise and a Way of Life*, a social history of white antiracist activism in the United States. She earned her B.A. at the University of California at Santa Cruz and Ph.D. in sociology at Brandeis University.

James L. Watson is Fairbank Professor of Chinese Society and professor of anthropology at Harvard University. His publications include *Golden Arches East: McDonalds in East Asia* (1997), *Between Two Cultures: Migrants and Minorities in Britian* (1977), and *Emigration and the Chinese Lineage* (1975). Currently he is organizing a joint research project with East Asian colleagues to investigate the biotech revolution in Asia with emphasis on American-produced, genetically modified soybeans. He teaches courses on globalism, food studies, and post-socialist cultures and is a specialist on southern Chinese ethnography.

Mark Weiner teaches legal history and race relations at Rutgers–Newark School of Law. He holds a Ph.D. in American studies from Yale University and a J.D. from Yale Law School. His is the author of a forthcoming book on law, anthropology, and citizenship and a forthcoming study of African-American legal history. His publications include "The Semiotics of Civil Rights in Consumer Society: Race, Law, and Food Taboo," forthcoming in *The International Journal for the Semiotics of Law*, and "We Are What We Eat; or, Democracy, Community and the Politics of Corporate Food Displays," *American Quarterly* (June 1994).

Betty L. Wells, professor of sociology at Iowa State University, is a rural community development practitioner whose work focuses on local responses to rural restructuring, especially its gendered aspects, including the development of local food systems and rural women's networks and activism. Recent research explores the relationship between gender and resource management. She is currently collaborating with the Women, Food and Agriculture Network in a participatory research project with women farmland owners in southwestern Iowa.

Rhonda Yoder has conducted research on local food systems and Old Order Amish farming systems in Iowa. After completing her master's degree in International Development Studies, with a minor in Anthropology, in 1990 at Iowa State University, she worked in rural community development programs for several years in Nepal and then in Iowa. She now lives and works in Indiana.

Rafia Zafar is director of African and Afro-American studies and associate professor of English at Washington University in St. Louis. Author of *We Wear the Mask: African*

Americans Write American Literature, 1760–1870 (1997), she has also co-edited two volumes, *Harriet Jacobs and Incidents in the Life of a Slave Girl: New Critical Essays* (1996) and *God Made Man, Man Made the Slave: The Autobiography of George Teamoh* (1992). Her essay draws on her forthcoming study, *And Called It Macaroni: Eating, Writing, Becoming American*, on the role of food in forging American literary identities.

PERMISSIONS

★★

INDEX

★★

424

432